American Government

*A*merican Government

ROOTS AND REFORM

Brief Edition
Second Edition

Karen O'Connor

Professor of Government
The American University

Larry J. Sabato

Robert Kent Gooch Professor of
Government and Foreign Affairs
University of Virginia

Allyn and Bacon

Boston ◆ London ◆ Toronto ◆ Sydney ◆ Tokyo ◆ Singapore

Senior Editor: Stephen Hull
Vice President, Publisher: Susan Badger
Marketing Manager: Karon Bowers
Production Administrator: Marjorie Payne
Editorial Assistant: Sue Hutchinson
Cover Administrator: Linda Knowles
Cover Designer: Susan Paradise
Composition/Prepress Buyer: Linda Cox
Manufacturing Buyer: Megan Cochran
Text and Art Designer: Deborah Schneck, Schneck-DePippo Graphics

Library of Congress Cataloging-in-Publication Data

O'Connor, Karen, 1952–
    American government: roots and reform / Karen O'Connor, Larry J.
Sabato. — 2nd ed., brief ed.
        p. cm.
    Includes index.
    ISBN 0-02-389018-5 (alk. paper)
    1. United States—Politics and government. I. Sabato, Larry.
II. Title.
JK274.O26 1995b
320.973—dc20   95-19268
                                                            CIP

Printed in the United States of America
10 9 8 7 6 5 4 3 2   00 99 98 97 96

To Meghan, always the trouper
Karen O'Connor

———————— ◆◆◆ ————————

*To my Government 101 students
over the years, who all know
that "politics is a good thing"*
Larry Sabato

$\mathcal{B}$RIEF CONTENTS

CONTENTS

APPENDICES

PREFACE

Teaching introductory American government presents special challenges and rewards. It is a challenge to introduce a new discipline to beginning students. It is a challenge to jump from topic to topic each week. Above all, it is a challenge to motivate large and disparate groups of students to master new material. The rewards offered by success, however, can accumulate in students who pay more attention to their government, who participate in its workings as more informed citizens, and who better understand the workings of democracy as practiced in the United States.

We have witnessed some of these rewards from the lecture podium. With this book, we hope to offer our experiences in written form. Students need perspective and motivation; they also need to be exposed to information that will withstand the test of time. Our goal with this text is to transmit just this sort of information.

This Second Edition of our popular *American Government: Roots and Reform: Brief Edition* is not simply an update of the earlier edition of this book. Some chapters have been completely revised, old features such as "People of the Past" and "Then and Now" sections have been kept, but, in many chapters they have been replaced with new examples of the role that history plays in what happens today in American politics. User and reviewer suggestions prompted us to expand our popular "Toward Reform" and to add more detailed and expanded chapter summaries keyed to major headings in each chapter. And, the Glossary has been expanded and a new Case Glossary added. Sections have also been rewritten to reflect some of the major changes that continue to occur in the wake of the Republicans' takeover of both Houses of Congress.

Approach

We believe that we cannot fully understand the actions, issues, and policy decisions facing the U.S. government, its constituent states, or "the people" unless these issues are examined from the perspective of how they have evolved over time. Consequently, the title of this book is *American Government: Roots and Reform.* In its pages we try to examine how the United States is governed today by looking not just at present behavior but also at the Framers' intentions and how they have been implemented over the years. For example, we believe that it is critical to an understanding of the role of political parties in the United States to understand the Framers' fears of factionalism, how parties evolved, and when and why realignments in party identification occurred. In turn, a comprehension of these processes will help us to understand the kinds of officials we have elected over the years.

In addition to perennial questions raised by the Framers, we explore issues that the Framers could never have envisioned, and how the basic institutions of government have responded to these new demands. For instance, no one more than two centuries ago could have forseen election campaigns in an age when nearly all American homes contained television sets, and the airwaves abounded with political discussion on "talk radio." Moreover, new demands have periodically forced governmental reforms, so understanding the dynamics of change is essential for introductory students.

Our overriding concern is that students understand their government as it exists *today*. In order to do so, they must understand how it was designed in the Constitution. They must appreciate a little of how it reached its effects. Each chapter, therefore, approaches its topic with a combination of perspectives that we believe will best facilitate this approach.

In writing this book, we chose to put the Institutions of Government (Part Two) before Political Behavior (Part Three). Both sections, however, were written independently, making them easy to switch for those who prefer to teach about the actors in government and elections *before* discussing the institutions of government. To test the book, we have each taught from it in both orders with no pedagogical problems.

Features

Philosophical Perspective. Every chapter includes a few sentences from *The Federalist Papers* (with the exception of Chapter 4, which begins with an Anti-Federalist quotation). These passages are explained in captions and then used as references at relevant points in the chapter. From them, students learn that government was born amidst burning issues of representation and power, issues that continue to smolder today.

Historical Perspective. Every chapter uses history to serve two purposes: first, to show how institutions and processes have evolved to their present states, and second, to provide some of the color that makes information memorable. A richer historical texture helps to explain the present; it also helps to free the course from the time-bound nature of newspaper headlines.

Comparative Perspective. Changes in Eastern Europe, the former Soviet Union, Latin and Central America, and Asia reminds us of the preeminence of democracy, in theory if not always in fact. As new democratic experiments spring up around the globe, it becomes increasingly important for students to understand the rudiments of presidential *versus* parliamentary government, of multiparty *versus* two-party systems, and so on. In order to put American government in perspective, therefore (while avoiding the enormous complexities of huge transnational comparisons), we have used the model of Great Britain as a comparison. Throughout our chapter discussions, comparisons are drawn to Great Britain wherever appropriate points arise. By comparing the two governments, students learn the basic differences between presidential and parliamentary democracies.

In this new edition we have added diagrams to better illustrate these points.

The Ancillary Package

The ancillary package for *American Government: Roots and Reform: Brief Edition,* Second Edition, reflects the pedagogical goals of the text: to provide information in a useful context and with colorful examples. We have tried especially hard to provide materials that are useful for instructors and interesting and helpful to students.

To further extend the application of multimedia learning enhancements to the teaching of American Government, the following supplements are available for use in conjunction with *American Government: Roots and Reform:*

CNN Video.   Through an exclusive arrangement with CNN, adopters of the book will receive a specially edited compilation of recent CNN News stories for classroom use. News footage is organized chapter by chapter, and keyed to topics in the text. Ask your Allyn & Bacon representative for details.

Video Library.   A full set of videos on every major course topic is available to adopters of the text. Again, your Allyn & Bacon representative has details.

Laserdisc.   The same specially edited CNN programming is available in a laser disc format for easy search and retrieval.

CD-ROM.   A set of brief, interactive learning modules are available for students to purchase on CD-ROM. Combining text, graphics, still photographs, and full motion video, the CD-ROM contains study modules on Congress, the presidency, and the judiciary. Also included is an extensive archive collection of historical and current texts. Ask your Allyn and Bacon representative for details.

America Online.   Connect the teaching of American Government to the world of the fastest-growing on-line service with College OnLine from Allyn & Bacon. A wealth of services and products, updated frequently, keep faculty and students in step with the latest data, pedagogy, and public opinion, all linked to American Government. Adopters of this text receive a two-months free subscription to America OnLine; students receive one free month. Ask your Allyn & Bacon representative for details.

***The Washington Post* Just-In-Time Custom Reader.**   By exclusive arrangement with *The Washington Post,* the Allyn & Bacon JIT reader in American Government allows faculty to assemble their own collection of articles to suit individual course demands. Faculty can choose from a frequently updated database of over 300 articles on topics ranging across the spectrum of American Government. Ask your Allyn & Bacon representative for details.

American Government: Readings and Cases.   This separate, full-scale reader in American Goverment by Karen O'Connor may be packaged along with the text at a reduced price to students. This reader combines classic articles, including extensive selections from *The Federalist Papers,* with some of the best current political science and a strong component of key and landmark cases. Thoughtful pedagogy includes chapter introductions and end of chapter questions to foster students' critical thinking.

Study Guide. A study guide for students is available that includes chapter synopses, outlines, key terms, multiple choice, matching and true/false questions with answers for student self-tests.

Instructor's Manual. The Instructor's Manual includes lecture ideas, discussion questions, classroom activities, and a guide to video and other resources.

Test Bank. Completely revised and expanded, the test bank provides more than 1,500 multiple-choice, true/false, and essay questions. A **Computer Test Bank** in IBM or Macintosh formats is also available.

Transparencies. A full set of over 54 color transparencies, including U. S and world maps, is available for classroom use.

Acknowledgments

Karen O'Connor thanks the thousand-plus students in her National Government courses who, over the years, have pushed her to learn more about American government and to have fun in the process. She especially thanks some of her Emory colleagues—Alan Abramowitz, Courtney Brown, and Cornell Hooten—who were always willing to share books, ideas, suggestions, and newspaper clippings. She also thanks Dean Howard Hunter of the Emory Law School for providing access to LEXIS and NEXIS, which allowed this book to be as current as possible. Thanks also to former students John R. Hermann, Sue Davis, Kaenan Hertz, Jenny Jacob and Paul Fabrizio for their research assistance at various phases of the first edition. Kimberley Beakley, now at Duke University and Bernadette Nye at Emory University helped in innumerable ways in our preparation of this second edition. And, Gregg Ivers at American University and Nancy E. McGlen at Niagara University have always been there to offer suggestions, friendship, and encouragement.

While we were writing the first edition, Laura Van Assendelft provided the assistance and fresh perspective that only a graduate student studying for her Ph.D. comprehensive exam in American Government could offer. Laura worked tirelessly on the book and even brought homemade cookies as a reward for completed chapters. Her familiarity with the book proved invaluable as later when, as an assistant professor at Mary Baldwin College, she compiled the Test Bank for this new edition.

Larry Sabato wishes to thank his University of Virginia colleagues and staff, including Clifton McCleskey, Chairman of the Department of Government and Foreign Affairs; graduate students Bruce Larson and Dan Kritenbrink; and technical assistant Nancy Rae. We also thank Jeffrey Anderson of Brown University, who helped provide comparisons between the American and British systems of government.

No project such as this can ever be completed on time without tremendous support from the publisher. First with Macmillan, and now with Allyn and Bacon, we have had the good fortune to work with many talented individuals, including (at Macmillan) Bruce Nichols, Robert Miller and David Chodoff. At Allyn and Bacon we'd like to thank our editor, Stephen Hull, Marjorie Payne, the production administrator, and Karon Bowers, our marketing manager. One constant for which we are particularly grateful is the continuing involvement of development editor Jane Tufts.

Finally, many of our peers reviewed various stages of the manuscript and earned our gratitude in the process: Martin Wiseman, Mississippi State University; Mark Silverstein, Boston University; Steve Mazurana, University of Northern Colorado; Shirley Anne Warshaw, Gettysburg College; Jon Bond, Texas A&M University; Doris Graber, University of Illinois at Chicago; Bruce Oppenheimer, Vanderbilt University; Cary Covington, University of Iowa; Marjorie Hershey, Indiana University; Ruth Bamberger, Drury College; Greg Caldeira, Ohio State University; David Cingranelli, SUNY at Binghamton; Mark Landis, Hofstra University; Charles Hadley, University of New Orleans; Danny Adkison, Oklahoma State University; Kenneth Kennedy, College of San Mateo; and Evelyn Fink, University of Nebraska.

This Second Edition greatly profited from the painstaking reviews and comments of the following people:

James Anderson	Texas A&M University	John Kincaid	University of North Texas
Judith Baer	Texas A&M University	Jonathan E. Kranz	John Jay College
Christine Barbour	Indiana University	Nancy Kucinski	University of North Texas
Stephen A. Borrelli	University of Alabama	Valerie Martinez	University of North Texas
Ann Bowman	University of South Carolina	Clifton McCleskey	University of Virginia
Steve Chan	University of Colorado	Joseph Nogee	University of Houston
Clarke E. Cochran	Texas Tech University	Mary Alice Nye	University of North Texas
Anne N. Costain	University of Colorado	Richard Pacelle	University of Missouri-St. Louis
John Domino	Sam Houston State University	Marian Lief Palley	University of Delaware
Alan S. Engel	Miami University	Leroy N. Rieselbach	Indiana University
Stacia L. Haynie	Louisiana State University	David Robertson	Public Policy Research Centers, University of Missouri-St.Louis
Marjorie Hershey	Indiana University		
Cornell Hooton	Emory University	Frank Rourke	Johns Hopkins University
Dennis Judd	University of Missouri-St.Louis	Frank J. Sorauf	University of Minnesota
Donald F. Kettl	University of Wisconsin		

American Government

American Government: Roots and Reform

WHERE DID OUR IDEAS OF GOVERNMENT COME FROM?

DEVISING A NATIONAL GOVERNMENT

WHY A CAPITALIST SYSTEM?

UNDERSTANDING OUR DEMOCRATIC SYSTEM

*I*t is not only Americans who have wrestled with the problems of creating a government to meet their needs. In 1789, cries of "Liberty, Equality, and Fraternity" rang out in France as members of the working class, inspired by the American Revolution, rose up against King Louis XVI. The king, members of his family, and many French aristocrats were executed. Civil unrest continued and mobs controlled Paris until order was restored through the creation of a provisional government.

In the early 1900s in Russia, the radical Bolshevik Party mobilized citizens who were demoralized by war and who were without jobs or food, to overthrow and ultimately execute Czar Nicholas II and his family. The Bolshevik Revolution was followed by a period of civil war, and the Union of Soviet Socialist Republics was created from the ruins of the Russian Empire. Inspired by the Bolshevik model, Chinese communists similarly established a communist government in the late 1940s after a prolonged period of civil war.

More recently, these once revolutionary communist governments have themselves been faced with revolutionary discontent. In 1989, Chinese students demonstrated for democracy in Tienanmen Square, but to little avail. The communist rulers responded with a massive and bloody show of force that left many dead or injured. These events caused little political change in China. The early 1990s, however, saw the breakup of the Soviet Union. Most of this breakup was spurred by citizen demands, particularly in Eastern Europe, for democratization. In one new Eastern European state after another, citizens have gone to the polls to elect new leaders. Some of the changes have occurred with relatively little violence; others, such as the carving out of Bosnia-Herzogovenia from the former Yugoslavia, have produced all-out war and tremendous personal tragedy.

One of the hallmarks of the American system of government, the peaceful transition of power from one administration to the next, stands in marked contrast to such power shifts under other systems. Russians and the entire world watched in horror as the Russian parliament building burned in the chaos and violence that accompanied the break-up of the Soviet Union.

> T he accumulation of all powers, legislative, executive, and judiciary, in the same hands . . . may justly be pronounced the very definition of tyranny.
>
> *James Madison*
> *Federalist No. 47*

The creation of the American system of government, as this quotation from The Federalist Papers *indicates, was motivated above all by the need to break away from the English model of government and its arbitrary concentration and use of power. The colonists wanted a representative government in which their elected officials would consider their needs and opinions when forming policies that affected their lives.*

In each of these situations, whether peaceful or not, men and women have attempted to create new political systems to resolve the classic, age-old question of politics: Who gets what, when, and how?

How governments get their powers, and what rights their citizens or subjects retain, is a major focus of this book. All governments—whether democracies, such as the United States, Great Britain, and France, or authoritarian regimes such as Iraq under Saddam Hussein—exercise some kind of authority over the daily lives of their people. To understand how the U.S. government and our political system work today, it is critical to understand the philosophies that guided the American colonists as they created a system of governance different from those then in existence. It is also necessary to know how that system evolved and changed in order to understand better how government affects you and the world around you. And, just as important, a thorough understanding of the workings of government will allow you to question and think about the system—the good parts and the bad—and decide for yourself the advantages and disadvantages of possible reforms.

The question of who exercises power, and how and why they acquired it, is important to understanding a political system. The public, political parties, interest groups, the bureaucracy, and congressional committees are just part of the answer to the question of who has power, and why and how it is used. Consider, for example, the tobacco industry in the United States. A 1991 draft report from the Environmental Protection Agency concluded that *secondhand* cigarette smoke kills 53,000 nonsmokers annually. The U.S. Surgeon General requires strong warnings on tobacco products concerning the link between tobacco use and cancer. Nevertheless, not only does the government permit smoking, but it also provides *billions* of dollars a year in subsidies to tobacco farmers. At the same time, however, the national, state, and even some local governments tax cigarettes. In 1993, the federal excise tax on cigarettes was 24 cents a pack, and state excise taxes ranged from 2.5 cents in Virginia (a major tobacco-growing state) to 51 cents in Massachusetts. But in spite of the health threat, taxes on cigarettes are lower in the United States than in virtually any other industrialized nation.

In the case of cigarettes, the powerful tobacco lobby, in conjunction with equally powerful senators and representatives from tobacco-growing states, has been instrumental in seeing that the tobacco industry is allowed to flourish. In contrast, red dye

The break-up of the Soviet Union was not met with universal support within the populace. Here, a Russian man poignantly clings to the old Soviet flag and the symbol of the Soviet communism.

number 2, used to add color to certain food products, was banned in the mid-1970s when it, like tobacco, was found to contain cancer-causing agents. Unlike tobacco, it had few supporters (lobbyists) to argue for its continued use in the food industry.

Although all governments have problems, it is important to stress the good they can do in their attempts to decide who gets what, when, and how. In the aftermath of the Great Depression in the United States, for example, the government created the Social Security program, which dramatically decreased poverty among the elderly. Our contract laws and judicial system provide an efficient framework for business, assuring people that they have a recourse in the courts should someone fail to deliver goods or services as promised. Something seemingly as mundane as our uniform bankruptcy laws help protect both a business enterprise and its creditors if the business collapses.

Just as it is important to recognize that governments serve many important purposes, it is also important to recognize that government and **politics,** the process by which policy decisions are made, are not static. They are part of a never-ending dynamic process of action and interaction. Governmental actions do not occur in isolation. The United States and its people, for example, are actors in a world order that from this nation's beginning has affected and continues to affect our laws, policies, and actions. Undoubtedly, the Framers at the Constitutional Convention in Philadelphia were reacting to what they viewed as the tyrannical rule of King George when they drafted Article II of the Constitution, creating a president of the United States. Similarly, the actions of President George Bush and the U.S. Congress in the Persian Gulf War of 1991 were the product of a series of events and reactions to them. So too were President Bill Clinton's approach to the crisis in Bosnia-Herzogovenia. The unpopular and

Spring Forward, Fall Back
◆ ◆ ◆

Daylight Saving Time was introduced during World War I as a measure to save coal, which was used to produce electricity for lighting. In order to provide more natural light at the end of the working day, clocks are advanced one hour. In the United States, Daylight Saving Time begins on the first Sunday in April (clocks are moved ahead one hour) and ends on the last Sunday in October (clocks are moved back one hour). Any state may decide to remain on Standard Time during this period, as do Arizona and Hawaii; Indiana even allows *counties* to decide whether to switch.

Source: USA Today, April 2–4, 1991: p. 1-A.

Politics The process by which policy decisions are made.

Women in combat: Operation Desert Storm. In August 1990, Iraq invaded the oil-rich country of Kuwait. In response, President Bush sent tens of thousands of U.S. troops to contain Iraq's army. For the first time in U.S. history, Americans were faced with the reality of women in the armed services. Here, a young mother displays a photo of her infant left at home as she fights in the Gulf.

unsuccessful Vietnam War, the United States need for oil, Iraq's invasion of Kuwait, reelection concerns, and probably even George Bush's desire to be viewed as a strong leader—all contributed to some extent to the final decision to deploy troops and then to commence Operation Desert Storm. Similarly, Bill Clinton's decision not to send ground troops into Eastern Europe, in spite of numerous urgings to do so, was also the product of his perception of the crisis and past events. Thus, many major national and international policy decisions have their roots in the politics and policies of the past. The lessons of history are often in the mind of policy makers as they seek to lead the nation on a sure course.

Where Did Our Ideas of Government Come From?

The current American political system did not spring into being overnight. It is the result of an intellectual tradition, as well as trial and error, and even luck. To understand how we came to have the form of government we have today, we must first understand the theories of government that influenced the Framers.

From Aristotle to the Enlightenment

Natural law A doctrine that society should be governed by certain ethical principles that are part of nature and, as such, can be understood by reason.

The Greeks were the first to articulate the notion of **natural law,** the doctrine that human affairs should be governed by certain ethical principles. Being nothing more nor less than the nature of things, these principles can be understood by reason. In the thirteenth century, the Italian priest and philosopher Thomas Aquinas (1225–1274) gave the idea of natural law a new, Christian framework, arguing that natural law and Christianity were compatible because God created the natural law that established individual rights to life and liberty. In contradiction to this view, throughout Europe, kings continued to rule as absolute monarchs by divine right from God. Thus, citizens were bound by the government under which they found themselves, regardless of whether they had a say in its workings: If government reflected God's will, who could argue with it?

In the early sixteenth century, a religious movement to reform the doctrine and institutions of Roman Catholicism began to sweep through Europe. In many cases, these efforts at reform resulted in the founding of Protestant churches separate from their Catholic source. This Reformation and the resultant growth in the Protestant faith, which promoted the belief that people could talk directly to God without the intervention of a priest, altered the nature of government as people began to believe they could also have a say in their own governance. So did the ideas of philosophers and scientists such as Isaac Newton (1642–1727) during the period called the Enlightenment. Newton and others argued that the world could be improved through the use of human reason, science, and religious toleration. He and other theorists directly challenged earlier notions that fate alone controlled an individual's destiny and that kings ruled by divine right. Together the intellectual and religious developments of the Reformation and Enlightenment periods encouraged people to seek alternatives to absolute monarchy and to ponder new methods of governing.

A Growing Idea: Popular Consent

In England, when one faction called "separatists" split from the Anglican church, they did so believing that the ability to speak directly to God gave them the power to participate directly in the governing of their own local congregations. In establishing self-governing congregations, the separatists were responsible for the first widespread appearance of self-government in the form of social compacts. The separatists who moved to the English colonies in America brought their beliefs about self-governance with them. The Mayflower Compact, written while that ship was still at sea, reflects this tradition. Although it addressed itself to secular government, the Pilgrims called it a "covenant" (its form was akin to other common religious "covenants"; note the use of this word in the reproduction of the Mayflower Compact above) adopted by Congregationalists, Presbyterians, and Baptists.[1]

Two English theorists of the seventeenth century, Thomas Hobbes (1588–1679) and John Locke (1632–1704), built on conventional notions in proposing a social contract theory of government (see "People of the Past," p. 6). In contrast to Aquinas and the theorists of God-ordained government, they argued that even before the creation of governments, all individuals were free and equal by natural right. This freedom, in turn, required that all men give their consent to be governed.[2]

Hobbes and Locke.   In his now-classic political treatise *Leviathan* (1651), Hobbes argued pessimistically that man's natural state was war. In his attempt to make sense of King Charles's restoration to the throne, he theorized that life without government was a "state of nature," where, without written, enforceable rules, people would live like animals—foraging for food, stealing, and killing when necessary. To escape the horrors of the natural state, Hobbes argued, men must, in order to protect their lives, give up to government certain rights. Without government, Hobbes warned, life would

PEOPLE OF THE PAST

Hobbes

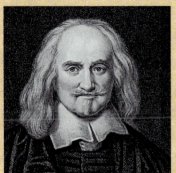

Thomas Hobbes was born in 1588 in Gloucestershire (Glouster), England and began his formal education at the age of four. By age six he was learning Latin and Greek, and by nineteen he had obtained his bachelor's degree from Oxford University. In 1608, Hobbes accepted a position as a family tutor with the Earl of Devonshire, a post he retained for the rest of his life.

Hobbes was greatly influenced by the chaos of the English Civil War of the mid-seventeenth century. Its impact is evident in his most famous work, *Leviathan* (1651), a treatise on governmental theory that states his views on Man and Citizen. *Leviathan* is commonly described as a book about politics, but it also deals with religion and moral philosophy. Hobbes characterized humans as selfishly individualistic and constantly at war with one another. Without an effective government, argued Hobbes, life would be "solitary, poor, nasty, brutish, and short." People, he claimed, surrendered themselves to rulers in exchange for protection from their neighbors.

Hobbes was quite an energetic man, and at the age of eighty-four he wrote his autobiography in Latin verse. He died at the age of ninety-one.

Locke

John Locke, born in England in 1632, was admitted to an outstanding public school at the age of fifteen. It was there that he began to question his upbringing in the Puritan faith. At twenty he went on to study at Oxford, where he became a lecturer in Aristotelian philosophy. Soon, however, he found a new interest in medicine and experimental science.

In 1666, Locke met Anthony Ashley Cooper, the first Earl of Shaftesbury, a liberal politician. It was through Cooper that Locke discovered his own talent for philosophy. In 1689, Locke published his most famous work, *Second Treatise on Civil Government,* in which he set forth a theory of natural rights. He used the concept of natural rights to support his "social contract [theory]—the view that the consent of the people is the only true basis of any sovereign's right to rule." Governments exist, he argued, because individuals agree through a contract to form one to protect their rights under natural law. They agree to abide by decisions made by majority vote in the resolution of disputes. Locke died on October 28, 1704 at the age of seventy-two.

basically be "solitary, poor, nasty, brutish, and short"—a constant struggle to survive against the evil of others. For this reason, governments had to intrude on people's rights and liberties in order to better control society and provide the proper safeguards for property.

Hobbes argued strongly for a single ruler, no matter how evil, to guarantee the rights of the weak against the strong. Leviathan, a biblical sea monster, was his characterization of an all-powerful government. Strict adherence to Leviathan's laws, however encompassing or intrusive on liberty, was but a small price to pay for living in a civilized society, or even for life itself.

The Mayflower Compact. While on the Mayflower, English colonists drew up a compact declaring their intention to form a "Civil Body Politick," or government, to preserve order and peace.

In contrast, John Locke—like many other political philosophers of the era—took the basic survival of humanity for granted and argued that government's major responsibility was the preservation of private property, an idea that ultimately found its way into the Constitution of the United States. In two of his works (*Essay Concerning Human Understanding* [1690] and *Second Treatise on Civil Government* [1689]), Locke responded to King James II's abuses of power directed at the Anglican church and Parliament. Locke denied the divine right of kings to govern. More important, he argued that men were born equal and with equal rights in nature that no king had the power to void. Under what Locke termed **social contract theory,** the consent of the people is the only true basis of any sovereign's right to rule. According to Locke, men form governments largely to preserve life, liberty, and property, and to assure justice. If governments act improperly, they break their "contract" with the people and therefore no longer enjoy the consent of the governed. Because he believed that true justice comes from laws, Locke argued that the branch of government that makes laws—as opposed to the one that enforces or interprets laws—should be the most powerful.

Locke believed that a chief executive to administer laws was important, but that he should necessarily be limited by law or by the "social contract" with the governed. Locke's writings influenced many American colonists, especially Thomas Jefferson, whose original draft of the Declaration of Independence noted the rights to "life, liberty, and property" as key reasons to split from England.[3]

Social contract theory The belief that people are free and equal by God-given right and that this in turn requires that all men give their consent to be governed; espoused by John Locke and influential in the writing of the Declaration of Independence.

Devising a National Government

Although social contract theorists agreed on the need for government, they did not necessarily agree on the form that a government should take. Thomas Hobbes argued for a single leader; John Locke and Jean-Jacques Rousseau, a French philosopher (1712–1778) saw the need for less centralized power.

As depicted in Table 1.1, the colonists rejected a system with a strong ruler, like the British **monarchy,** as soon as they had declared their independence. Most European

Monarchy A form of government in which power is vested in hereditary kings and queens.

	Table 1.1 ◆ Types of Government	
TYPES	**EXAMPLE**	**HOW MANY ARE INVOLVED IN THE GOVERNING PROCESS**
Monarchy	Eighteenth-century Great Britain	One
Oligarchy	El Salvador, 1960s Brazil, 1970s	Small number
Aristocracy	Seventeenth-century Poland Haiti, 1980s	Small number
Indirect Democracy	United States today	Many
Direct Democracy	Ancient Athens	Nearly all (free males)

monarchical systems gave hereditary rulers absolute power over all forms of activity. Many of the colonists had fled from Great Britain to avoid religious persecution and other harsh manifestations of power wielded by George II, whom they viewed as a malevolent despot. They naturally were reluctant to put themselves in the same position in their new nation.

While some colonies such as Massachusetts originally established theocracies in which religious leaders eventually ruled claiming divine guidance, they later looked to more secular forms of governance. Colonists also did not want to create an **oligarchy,** or "rule by the few," in which the right to participate is conditioned on the possession of wealth or property. Aristotle defined this form of government as a perversion of an **aristocracy,** or "rule of the highest." Again, the colonists were fearful of replicating the landed and titled system of the British aristocracy and viewed the formation of a representative form of government as far more in keeping with the ideas of social contract theorists. But the **democracy** in which we live, as settled on by the Framers, is difficult to define. Nowhere is the word mentioned in the Declaration of Independence or the U.S. Constitution. Like many of our ideas about government, however, the term comes from two Greek words: *demos* (the people) and *kratia* (power or authority). Thus, democracy can be interpreted as a form of government that gives power to the people. The question, then, is how and to which people is this power given?

Oligarchy A form of government in which the right to participate is always conditioned on the possession of wealth or property.

Aristocracy A system of government in which control is based on rule of the highest.

Democracy A system of government that gives power to the people, whether directly or through their elected representatives.

The Theory of Democratic Government

As evidenced by the early creation of the Virginia House of Burgesses in 1619, and its objections to "taxation without representation," the colonists were quick to create participatory forms of government in which most men (subject to some landowning requirements) were allowed to participate. The New England town meeting (see "Then and Now: Direct Democracy," p.11), where all citizens gather to discuss and decide issues facing the town, today stands as a surviving example of a **direct democracy**, such as was used in ancient Greece when all free, male citizens came together periodically to pass laws and "elect" leaders by lot.

Direct democracies, however, soon proved unworkable in the colonies. Although Rousseau argued that true democracy is impossible unless *all* citizens participate in

Direct democracy A system of government in which members of the polity meet to discuss all policy decisions and then agree to abide by majority rule.

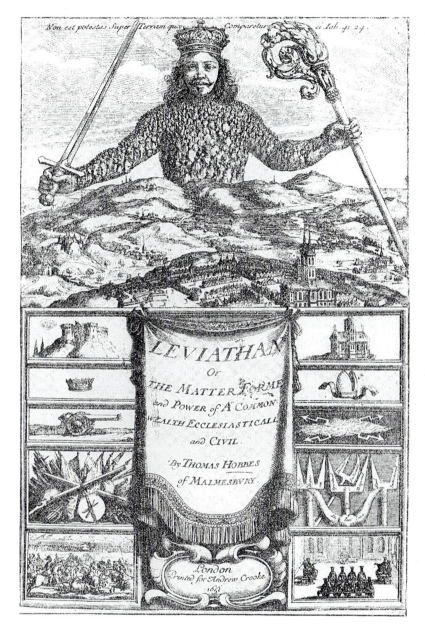

The title page from Thomas Hobbes's *Leviathan,* 1651.

governmental decision-making, as more and more settlers came to the New World, many town meetings were replaced by a system called **indirect** or **representative democracy.** Ironically, this system of government, in which representatives of the people are chosen by ballot, was considered undemocratic by ancient Greeks, who believed that all citizens must have a direct say in their governance.

Representative or indirect democracies, which call for the election of representatives to a governmental decision-making body, were formed first in the colonies and then in the new Union. Many citizens were uncomfortable with the term "democracy" and used the term **republic** to avoid any confusion between the system adopted and direct democracy. Even today, representative democracies are more commonly called

Indirect (representative) democracy A system of government that gives citizens the opportunity to vote for representatives who will work on their behalf.

Representative democracy *See* indirect (representative) democracy.

Republic A government rooted in the consent of the governed. A representative or indirect democracy.

Popular consent The idea that governments must draw their powers from the consent of the governed.

Majority rule The central premise of a direct democracy in which only policies that collectively garner the support of a majority of voters will be made into law.

Popular sovereignty The right of the majority to govern themselves.

Personal liberty A key characteristic of U.S. democracy. Initially meaning freedom from governmental interference, today it includes demands for freedom to engage in a variety of practices free from governmental discrimination.

"republics" and the words "democracy" and "republic" often are used interchangeably. Historically, the term "republic" implied a system of government in which the interests of the people were represented by more educated or wealthier citizens. In the early days of America, for example, only those who owned land could vote. But today, those barriers no longer exist.

What Are the Characteristics of American Democracy?

The United States is an indirect democracy with several distinguishing characteristics. Tremendous value is placed on the individual. All individuals are deemed rational and fair, and endowed, as Thomas Jefferson proclaimed in the Declaration of Independence "with certain unalienable rights." And the individual is deemed more important than the state.

Another key characteristic of our democracy is the American emphasis on political equality, the definition of which has varied considerably over time (as discussed in Chapter 5). The importance of political equality is another reflection of American stress on the importance of the individual. Although some individuals clearly wield more political clout than others, the adage "one man, one vote" implies a sense of political equality for all.

Popular consent, the idea that governments must draw their powers from the consent of the governed, is another distinguishing characteristic of American democracy. Derived from social contract theory, the notion of popular consent was central to the Declaration of Independence and its underlying assumption that governments *must* derive their powers from the consent of the governed. A citizen's willingness to vote is thus an essential premise of democracy.

Majority rule and the preservation of minority rights are two additional facets of American democracy. Majority rule implies that only policies supported by most of the population will be made into law. This right of the majority to govern themselves is summed up by the term **popular sovereignty.** This term, however, did not come into wide usage until pre-Civil War debates over slavery. At that time, supporters of popular sovereignty argued that the citizens of new states seeking admission to the Union should be able to decide whether or not their states would allow slavery within their borders.

Today, emphasis on majority rule also usually stresses concern with minority rights, although tension between the two concepts still exists. One example of that tension is illustrated by the issues and controversy generated over President Bill Clinton's nomination of his long-time friend and former law school classmate Lani Guinier, a University of Pennsylvania Law School professor, to head the Civil Rights Division of the U.S. Justice Department. When her position on the respective roles of the majority and the minority became public, the controversy was such that Clinton was forced to withdraw her nomination. In a 1991 *Michigan Law Review* article, Guinier attacked a "hostile permanent (white) majority" often unwilling to give minorities in legislatures their share of power. Thus Guinier proposed, among other things, a "minority veto" to allow black legislators the ability to veto measures passed by majorities in cases where minority legislators were unable to make inroads. Once he read her work, even Clinton was unwilling to accept Guinier's ideas or defend them, noting, "I cannot fight a battle . . . if I do not believe in the ground of the battle."[4]

Personal liberty is perhaps the single most important characteristic of American democracy. The Constitution itself was written to assure "life" and "liberty." Over the years, our concepts of liberty have changed. Liberty was first considered to be freedom

Lani Guinier waits on the steps of the University of Pennsylvania Law School to be interviewed on the air. Guinier told reporters that President Clinton's withdrawal of her nomination to head the Civil Rights Division in the Department of Justice was "fundamentally unfair."

THEN AND NOW

Direct Democracy

The town meeting, which is still the form of government of some municipalities in New England, is an example of direct democracy. Starting in colonial times, the men of the town would congregate at the local meeting hall to discuss issues ranging from public drunkenness to education.

Today some people suggest that electronic voting provides a means to return to direct democracy. This idea received particular attention during the 1992 presidential campaign when candidate Ross Perot called for electronic town meetings in which officials would offer three possible solutions to a public problem and viewers would electronically vote for their choice.*

Different plans—including voting by telephone, interactive TV, computer bulletin boards and on-line information services—have been proposed as possible means of conducting electronic voting. USA VOTE, a nonpartisan, nonprofit group located in Arlington, Virginia, has launched an interactive public affairs television show that consists of a 30-minute debate on a specific issue followed by an opportunity for viewers to call a toll-free number and express their opinions.

Interactive Network, Inc., a California-based company, offers another method of electronic political interaction. Consumers who purchase this firm's control units at retail stores (at a cost of $199) gain interactive access to various news programs, sports events and information services. San Franciscans had the opportunity to utilize this network after each televised presidential debate of 1992. A viewer subscribing to the service was able to vote on issues raised in the debate by pushing buttons on the control unit. Computers then compiled results and displayed them on the control unit's screen.

However, practical and philosophical problems exist with all methods. When CBS asked viewers to call in questions after George Bush's 1992 State of the Union Address, only 315,000 of 25 million calls got through. Other problems include deciding who controls the agenda, ensuring that the meetings have a representative sample of the population, providing electronic access for poor citizens, and preventing ballot-box stuffing. Political scientist Theodore Becker supports a "multilayer web of decentralized electronic meetings run by an independent, private commission and not by the White House or any government agency" to overcome some of these problems. Still, it is unlikely that a return to a pure direct democracy will occur in the near future.

*Much of this discussion is adapted from Mitch Betts, "Electronic Town Meeting, A Safe Vote?," *Computerworld* (October 26, 1992): 25; and Katherine McCarron, "Lobbying Congress from Your La-Z-Boy," *The National Journal* (November 21, 1992): 2688.

A student with an interactive TV unit

"from." Thus, Americans were to be free from governmental infringements on freedom of religion and speech, from unreasonable search and seizure, and so on (see Chapter 4). The addition to the Constitution of the Fourteenth Amendment and its emphasis on equal protection of the laws and subsequent passage of laws guaranteeing civil rights, however, expanded Americans' concept of liberty to include demands for "freedom to" be free from discrimination. Debates over how much the government should do to guarantee these rights or liberties illustrate the conflicts that continue to occur in our democratic system.

Who Makes Decisions in America?

How conflicts are resolved, and how much emphasis is placed on any of these characteristics of American democracy, is often determined by how the government is operated, and by whom. Over the years, several theorists have posited widely different points of view in their attempts to answer this important question. No one view completely explains "who gets what, when, and how," although most political scientists of today probably subscribe to some form of the pluralist view (see below).[5] Nevertheless, a knowledge of these divergent perspectives will make it possible for you to analyze political questions from more than one vantage point.

Elite theory The view that a small group of people actually makes most of the important decisions. C. Wright Mills argued that important policies were set by three loose coalitions of groups—the military, corporate leaders, and a small set of government officials. He termed these the "power elite".

Elite Theory. In *The Power Elite* (1956), American sociologist C. Wright Mills argued that important policies are set by a loose coalition of three groups with some overlap among them. According to his **elite theory,** these three major influencers of policy—corporate leaders, military leaders, and a small group of key governmental leaders—are the true "power elite" in America. (Other elite theorists have argued that the news media should be included as a fourth element in the United States.) These elite theorists believe that government has become increasingly alienated from the people and is rarely responsive to their wishes.

Bureaucratic theory The belief that all governmental and all nongovernmental institutions are, in effect, controlled by an all-powerful bureaucracy.

Bureaucratic Theory. Max Weber (1864–1920), the founder of modern sociology, argued that *all* institutions, governmental and nongovernmental, have fallen under the control of a large and ever-growing bureaucracy. This view is called **bureaucratic theory.** Because all institutions have grown more complex, Weber concluded that the expertise and competence of bureaucrats allows them to wrest power from others, especially elected officials. As we will see in Chapter 8, there is no doubt that in certain policy areas bureaucrats carry increasing amounts of power. Politicians come and go, yet most bureaucrats stay on in their positions for a good part of their working lives.

Interest group theory The belief posited by David Truman that interest groups—not elites, sets of elites, or bureaucrats—control the governmental process.

Interest Group Theory. Political scientist David B. Truman postulated what is termed the **interest group theory** of democracy in *The Governmental Process* (1951). According to Truman, interest groups—not elites, sets of elites, or bureaucrats—control the governmental process.[6]

Truman believes there are so many potential pressure points in the executive, legislative, and judicial branches of the federal government—as well as at the state level—that groups can step in on any number of competing sides, and that government becomes the equilibrium point in the system.

Pluralist theory Theory of government in which resources are scattered so widely in our diverse democracy that no single elite group can ever have a monopoly over any substantial area of policy.

Pluralist Theory. Another, more widely accepted theory about the nature of power is held by those who follow the **pluralist** school of thought. According to political scientists such as Robert Dahl, the structure of our democratic government allows only for a pluralist model of democracy. Borrowing from Truman's work, Dahl argued that resources are scattered so widely in our diverse democracy that no single elite group can ever have a monopoly over any substantial area of policy. In *Who Governs?* (1961), for example, Dahl concluded that political competition and elections coupled with the growing ethnic and socioeconomic diversity of New Haven, Connecticut, led to a situation in which a single elite could never take and hold power legally. James Madison had argued in *Federalist No. 10* that a large number of interests and "factions" clashing in the public arena serve to enhance compromise. Dahl observed this need for compromise in New Haven in the areas of public education, urban renewal, and political nomination.[7]

Adding to this debate, political scientist Theodore J. Lowi has coined the term "interest group liberalism" to describe how political decision-making occurs today. According to Lowi, participants in every political controversy get something; thus, each has some impact on how political decisions are made. Lowi also states that governments rarely say no to any well-organized interests. Thus, all interests ultimately receive some benefits or rewards. Lowi bemoans the fact that the public interest (what is good for the public at large) often tends to lose in this system.[8]

All these theories provide interesting ways to begin to view how policy decisions are made, whether at local, state, or national levels. It could be, as Dahl has argued, that no single group or interest can ever have a monopoly over any issue, let alone over larger policy programs. It also stands to reason that the patterns we discover in the United States may apply to a certain extent in other parts of the world.

Why a Capitalist System?

In addition to fashioning a democratic form of government, the colonists were also confronted with the dilemma of what kind of role the government should play in the economy. Concerns with liberty, both personal and economic, were always at the forefront of their actions and decisions in creating a new government. They were well aware of the need for a well-functioning economy, and saw that government had a key role in maintaining this. What constitutes a malfunction in the economy, however, and what steps the government should take to remedy it, were questions that dogged the Framers and continue to puzzle politicians and theorists today.

The private ownership of property and a **free market economy** are key tenets of the American system called **capitalism.** In contrast to **socialism,** in which the working class owns and controls all means of production and distribution, capitalism favors private control of business and minimal governmental regulation of private industry.

Free market economy The production and exchange of goods and services without interference from the government.
Capitalism The economic system that favors private control of business and minimal governmental regulation of private industry.
Socialism A political system in which the working class owns and controls all means of production and distribution.

Capitalism.   Capitalism is a mode of economic production characterized by private ownership by individuals or groups of land, factories, raw materials, and other instruments of production. It is the economic system found in the United States, Great Britain, and most nations of Western Europe. In capitalist systems, the laws of supply and demand in the marketplace and free trade set prices of goods and drive production.

In 1776, the same year as the signing of the Declaration of Independence, Adam Smith (1723–1790) published *An Inquiry into the Nature and Causes of the Wealth of Nations* (generally known as *The Wealth of Nations*). Smith's book marked the beginning of the modern capitalist era. He argued that free trade would result in full production and economic health. These ideas were greeted with great enthusiasm in the colonies as independence was proclaimed. Colonists no longer wanted to participate in the mercantile system of Great Britain and other Western European nations. These systems bound trade and its administration to national goals and not those of the individual. Smith and his supporters saw free trade as "the invisible hand" that produced the wealth of nations. This wealth, in turn, became the inspiration and justification for capitalism.

Under capitalism, sales occur for the profit of the individual. Capitalists believe that both national and individual production is greatest when individuals are free to do as they wish with their property and goods. The government, however, plays an indispensable role in creating and enforcing the rules of the game. One such rule is the "contract clause" in the U.S. Constitution, which prevents states from extending the time in which debtors can meet their payments or get out of contractual obligations.

Laissez-faire A French term literally meaning "to let do, to leave alone." It is a hands-off governmental policy based on the belief that governmental regulation of the economy is wrong.

From the mid- to late eighteenth century through the mid-1930s in the United States and in much of the Western world, the idea of *laissez-faire* economics (from the French, to let do) enjoyed considerable popularity. While most states regulated and intervened heavily in their economies well into the nineteenth century, the national governments routinely followed a "hands off" economic policy. By the late 1800s, however (as discussed in Chapter 8) the U.S. government felt increasing pressure to regulate some aspects of the nation's economy. This pressure often arose from the difficulties states faced in regulating large multistate industries such as the railroads, and big industry's desire to override the patchwork of regulations produced by the states. Thus, true capitalism ceased to exist.[9] The extent of this trend, however, varied by country and over time. In post–World War II Britain, for example, the extent of government economic regulation in industrial policy and social welfare was much greater than that attempted by American policy makers in the same period.

Socialism. Reaction to the overwhelming wealth of millionaire industrialists and a corresponding exploitation of workers in France, England, and ultimately the United States, led to the development of socialism, a philosophy that advocates collective ownership and control of the means of economic production. Karl Marx (1818–1883), the German socialist and founder of communism, once stated that socialism was a transitional phase between capitalism and communism.

In direct opposition to the ideas of capitalism favored by the Framers, socialists (and communists) call for governmental—rather than private—ownership of all land, property, and industry and, in turn, an equitable distribution of the income from those holdings. In Marx's words, "From each according to his ability, to each according to his needs."[10]

It is important to note that some socialists actually tolerate capitalism as long as the government maintains some kind of control over the economy. Others, including communists, reject capitalism outright and insist on the abolition of all private enterprise. Thus, all communists are socialists, but not all socialists are communists.

Over the years, socialists have been united in their view of concern for all men and women, but have not agreed about the means by which to reach a socialist ideal. Some, especially in Western Europe, have argued that socialism can evolve through democratic processes. Thus, in nations like Great Britain, certain critical industries or services such as health care or the coal industry have been *nationalized,* or taken over by the state to provide for more efficient supervision and to avoid the major concentrations of wealth that occur when individuals own key industries.

Communism. Karl Marx grew up in Germany as the socialist movement developed there and in many other parts of Western Europe. Its influence on him was profound.

Karl Marx

He came to argue that government was simply a manifestation of underlying economic forces and could be understood according to types of economic production.

According to Marx, all societies went through five stages:

(1) primitive communalism, (2) slavery, (3) feudalism, (4) capitalism, and (5) socialism. He believed that history brought with it an evolving economic and political system in which a class struggle between workers and property owners was inevitable. The clash of the interests of these two classes led to the development of the state or government. In turn, governments were used by rich capitalists, called by the French term *bourgeoisie,* to protect their property in much the same way that, according to Charles Beard, the Framers of the U.S. Constitution were motivated by their personal economic concerns when they drafted the Constitution. In *Das Kapital* (1867), Marx argued that capitalist states would inevitably be replaced by socialist states in which the working class would own the means of production and distribution and would be able to redistribute the wealth to meet its needs.

Ultimately, Marx advocated **communism,** a scheme more radical than socialism. Through communism Marx sought to abolish all class differences and to create a system of common ownership of the means of sustenance and production. In essence, Marx viewed communism as the sixth stage of history, beyond socialism. To achieve communism, Marx believed that capitalist systems would have to be overthrown, no matter how violent the means. The communism espoused by Marx, however, continues to be a theory. It was never fully implemented even in the former Soviet Union. In most countries that still profess communism, such as China, economic and political control are held by a single, frequently authoritarian political party. Moreover, economic growth and planning are overseen by some sort of central authority.

Totalitarianism. Whereas socialist and communist systems spread the wealth and control of publicly owned industries and other means of production to all members of society, in a **totalitarian** system governments retain unlimited powers for the benefit of elite rulers. In contrast to systems based on democratic beliefs, totalitarian governments have total authority over their people and their economies. George Orwell's novel *1984* is perhaps the best depiction of what a pure totalitarian regime would be like. The reign of the Ayatollah Ruhollah Khomeini in Iran from 1979 until his death, and that of President Saddam Hussein in Iraq, come close to the "total" control of forms of production, the airwaves, education, the arts, and even sports implied by totalitarianism. Some communist systems also approach totalitarianism.

Because total control by a single ruler or elite requires technological innovations and weapons of mass destruction that only modern science can provide, totalitarianism, even in partial form, did not present itself to the world until well into the 1900s.[11] Even Adolf Hitler's Germany, perhaps the most totalitarian government that has appeared so far, probably lacked the resources to assert complete control over every aspect of life for all citizens.

Understanding Our Democratic System

One key to understanding our democratic system is a recognition of the role that history and its lessons have played in the development of the American political system. The lessons of history provide a context in which to understand not only policies of the past but also policies today. Changes in ideas and public expectations about government lead to reform no less than do crisis situations.

Communism A political philosophy posited by Karl Marx in which he argued that government was simply a manifestation of underlying economic forces and could be understood according to types of economic production.

Totalitarianism A system of government in which unlimited powers are retained by elite rulers.

Understanding the "ISMs"
◆ ◆ ◆

These humorous definitions of political systems of the world appeared in an FDR-era farm journal:

Socialism: You have two cows. The government takes one and gives it to your neighbor because he doesn't have a cow.

Communism: You have two cows. The government takes both and gives you the milk.

Nazism: You have two cows. The government takes both and shoots you.

New Dealism: You have two cows. The government takes both and shoots one, milks the other and throws the milk away.

Capitalism: You have two cows. You sell one and buy a bull.

Atlanta Journal-Constitution, June 20, 1993: A2.

Hillary Rodham Clinton became only the third First Lady (the other two were Eleanor Roosevelt and Rosalyn Carter) to address a congressional committee. Rodham Clinton, in fact, appeared before five congressional committees to explain and lobby on behalf of the administration's health care plan. Health care is another example of how Americans' view of the proper role of government has changed over time, although the far-ranging solutions suggested by the Clinton administration failed to garner popular support.

Changes in Ideas and Public Expectations.   Americans' ideas about and expectations of their government have changed tremendously since colonial times. The 1994 midterm elections, for example, appeared to reflect the desire of many Americans to put a brake on big government, and they perhaps signalled a major change in what Americans expect from government at all levels.

Expectations about the "proper" role of government, however, are often tempered by an individual's (or government's) ideological approach. As discussed in Chapter 10, whether one is "liberal" (by today's definition, generally favoring social and political reform and governmental solutions) or "conservative" (favoring the existing order with less governmental intervention in business or society), may also affect expectations. Until 1994, most public opinion polls revealed that many Americans had come to expect "big government" and wanted the government—especially the national government—to tackle economic and social problems. The small percent of Americans who are libertarians, those who stress that government should not involve itself in the plight of the people or attempt to remedy any social ills, have long believed in the evils of big government, yet, of late, it has become popular to argue for downsizing government at all levels, especially the welfare system. Some people, however, still see the need for some government involvement in social welfare and health issues.

In the 1980s, for example, more than 175,000 people became infected with HIV, and 109,000 of them died. Although AIDS was first viewed as a rare disease primarily afflicting homosexual men in California and New York, its demographics have changed, and now AIDS is the most common cause of non-accidental death among large segments of the population, including, for example, men and women in certain age groups. As more people from all groups and of all ages fall victim to AIDS, pressure on the national government to find a solution to this problem increases. Victims or those in high-risk groups are fighting for federal budget increases for AIDS research in addition to antidiscrimination legislation. Others argue for better screening of the blood supply and for compulsory testing of those in the medical profession. Governmental response was urged by C. Everett Koop, U.S. Surgeon General during Ronald Reagan's presidency, who played a major role in the decision to increase the federal government's effort for AIDS education over the protest of some conservative groups. Thus, as new problems occur, the public often has looked to the government for help and solutions.

The Lessons of History.   As historians are fond of noting, history often repeats itself. Clear cycles can be seen in the evolution of our democratic system. For example, in the mid-1800s, many women's rights activists sought the right to vote on a state-by-state basis and rejected suggestions to seek a constitutional amendment. The same state-by-state approach was used later in the suffrage movement (1890–1920) by a new generation of women who sought the right to vote, but again it proved unworkable as efforts in individual states were costly and often unsuccessful. Women finally decided that an amendment to the U.S. Constitution would be the most expeditious way to secure voting rights.

In the 1980s, after a series of decisions indicated the U.S. Supreme Court's increased willingness to restrict abortion rights, pro-choice forces initially sought to fight for the right to an abortion on a state-by-state basis. But by mid-1991, the National Abortion Rights Action League (NARAL) had admitted that it had lost more than it had won with this strategy as state after state passed increasingly restrictive laws. In an effort reminiscent of that adopted by women suffragists in the 1910s, NARAL decided to throw all its efforts behind passage of the national *Freedom of Choice Act* to guarantee a woman's right to an abortion free from any state restrictions, a strategy now unlikely to work given a Republican-controlled Congress. Nevertheless, understanding the difficulty women have encountered historically helps us to understand the effectiveness, adoption, and/or abandonment of some political strategies today.

The Role of Crises and Reform.   As government at all levels continues to grow, we cannot ignore the role that crises have played. The development of the power of the national government as well as realignments in the powers of the various institutions have also been affected by crises, as will be discussed in succeeding chapters. Crises do not affect only the American state; democracies like Britain have witnessed the shaping of their politics, institutions, and conflicts by unforeseen domestic and international emergencies. The two world wars, for example, placed many new issues on the national agenda—for example, nationalization of industry, social welfare, and economic planning.

Although the U.S. Civil War and other national crises, such as the Great Depression and even the Watergate scandal (see pp. 210–211), created major turmoil, they demonstrated that our system can survive and even change in the face of enormous political, societal, and even institutional crisis. Often, these crises have produced considerable reforms. The Civil War led to the dismantling of the slavery system and to the passage of the Thirteenth, Fourteenth, and Fifteenth Amendments (see Chapter 5), which led to the seeds of recognition of African Americans as American citizens. The Great Depression led to the New Deal and the creation of a government more actively involved in economic and social regulation. More recently, the Watergate scandal resulted in stricter ethics laws that have led to the resignation or removal of many elected officials.

In this text we present you with the tools to understand the political system in which you live. We hope that you will approach the study of American politics with an open mind. When you read a daily newspaper or watch a television news program, you are actually engaged in the study of politics. Your study of the processes of government should help you become a better citizen as you become more informed about your government and its operations. We hope that you learn to ask questions. Know who gets "what, when, and how." Learn to understand why a particular law was enacted. Ask, how was it implemented? And make sure your vote counts.

Mary Fisher, the wealthy, socialite daughter of the honorary chair of the Bush/Quayle Finance Committee, addressed the Republican National Convention in 1992. The HIV-positive Fisher founded the Family Aids Network and urged Republicans to recognize that government AIDS efforts were inadequate.

Summary

To understand how our current system of government works, it is important to understand choices that were made many years ago. To that end, in this chapter we have made the following points:

1. The American political system was based on several notions that have their roots in classical Greek ideas, including natural law, the doctrine that human affairs should be governed by certain ethical principles that can be understood by reason. Also heavily influencing our ideas of how government should work were the ideas of the Reformation, the period when people began to believe that they could talk directly to God without the intermediary of a priest; the Enlightenment, the movement in Western Europe in the 1700s that espoused human reason, science, and religious toleration; and the ideas of social contract theorists John Locke and Thomas Hobbes, who held the belief that people are free and equal by God-given right. In turn, this freedom requires that all men give their consent to be governed.

2. In devising a new national government and a democratic system, the colonists opted for an indirect democracy, or republic, in which citizens may vote for representatives to work on their behalf. Key ideals of this indirect democracy are the value of the individual, political equality, popular consent, majority rule and the preservation of minority rights, and personal liberty.

   Several different theories have been offered to explain how decisions are made in an indirect democracy. They include elite theory, the idea that important policies are set by three loose coalitions of groups including the military, corporate leaders, and a small set of government officials; bureaucratic theory, the belief that all governmental and nongovernmental institutions are, in effect, controlled by an all-powerful bureaucracy; interest group theory, the belief that interest groups—not elites, sets of elites, or bureaucrats—control the govern-

mental process; and pluralist theory, in which resources are seen as so widely scattered in our diverse democracy that no single elite group can ever have a monopoly over any substantial area of policy.

3. The system set up by the Framers was capitalism, which advocates private ownership of property and a free market economy. Other nations have opted for socialism, which advocates public ownership and control of the means of economic production, or communism, in which government is seen simply as a manifestation of underlying economic forces, understood according to types of economic production.

4. Three factors are key to understanding our democratic system and its development: (1) changes in ideas and public expectations, (2) the lessons of history, and (3) the role of crisis and reform.

Key Terms

politics	indirect (representative) democracy	interest group theory
natural law	republic	pluralist theory
social contract theory	popular consent	free market economy
monarchy	majority rule	capitalism
oligarchy	popular sovereignty	socialism
aristocracy	personal liberty	*laissez-faire*
democracy	elite theory	communism
direct democracy	bureaucratic theory	totalitarian

Suggested Readings

Bentley, Arthur. *The Process of Government.* Chicago: University of Chicago Press, 1908.

Dahl, Robert. *Polyarchy: Participation and Opposition.* New Haven, CT: Yale University Press, 1971.

———*Who Governs?* New Haven, CT: Yale University Press, 1961.

Hobbes, Thomas. *Leviathan.* New York: Everyman (Library Edition), 1914.

Locke, John. *Two Treatises of Government,* ed. Peter Lasleti. New York: Mentor, 1960.

Marx, Karl. *Das Kapital.* Chicago: Regnery, 1970.

Mills, C. Wright. *The Power Elite.* New York: Oxford University Press, 1956.

Schumpeter, Joseph A. *Capitalism, Socialism, and Democracy.* New York: Harper, 1942.

Schlesinger, Arthur M. *The Age of Jackson.* Boston: Little, Brown, 1945.

Truman, David B. *The Governmental Process.* New York: Knopf, 1951.

Weber, Max. *From Max Weber: Essays in Sociology,* trans. and ed. H. H. Gerth and C. Wright Mills. London: Routledge & Kegan Paul, 1948.

The Constitution

THE ORIGINS OF A NEW NATION

THE DECLARATION OF INDEPENDENCE

THE FIRST ATTEMPT AT GOVERNMENT:
THE ARTICLES OF CONFEDERATION

THE MIRACLE AT PHILADELPHIA: WRITING A CONSTITUTION

THE U.S. CONSTITUTION

THE DRIVE FOR RATIFICATION

AMENDING THE CONSTITUTION

TOWARD REFORM

*I*n *Federalist No. 23,* James Madison walked a tight line. He fervently wanted the citizenry to adopt the proposed constitution, which conferred considerable powers on the national government at the expense of the states, yet he realized that some citizens (and states) might object. He and the Framers were nonetheless willing to confront these objections. Madison and other Federalists were convinced that a new form of government, one with a written constitution defining its scope, was key to the continued survival of the states.

In 1789, however, the Constitution was not adopted without question. Great Britain did not then have a written constitution, nor does it today. Instead, Great Britain had a king, who was guided by a House of Lords to represent the nobility, and by a House of Commons to represent all others. Moreover, England and English courts were guided by principles of **common law**, the body of law in England that arose from judge-made decisions.

Since these "laws" were not written, common law underwent many changes as it was broadened by local custom and judicial interpretation. In addition to common law, there is an unwritten British "constitution," composed of statutory law and conventions—rules of behavior that have been followed for so long that they are regarded as binding, even though they lack the force of law. This "unwritten law" was quite different from the Constitution suggested by the Framers, which carefully created three branches of government and *expressly* gave certain powers to each branch.[1]

The authors of *The Federalist Papers,* Alexander Hamilton, James Madison, and John Jay, had to convince the electorate not only that the particular wording of the

> *very view we may take of the subject, as candid inquirers after truth, will serve to convince us, that it is both unwise and dangerous to deny the federal government an unconfined authority.*
>
> James Madison
> *Federalist No. 23*

According to the Federalists, the major triumph of the new Constitution was its expansive grant of authority to the new national government over, and "unconfined" by, the states.

Constitution proposed in 1789 was the best, but also that the new nation needed a written document as well. Moreover, they had to explain why they made the choices they did, and how and why the new system would be better than the existing government. Their task was made more difficult by the fact that their proposed constitution took away from the state governments many rights that they had acquired after breaking with Great Britain in 1776. Fortunately, because all thirteen states had drafted written constitutions after independence was declared, most colonists agreed on the need for a written plan of government. Looking outside the continent, however, they saw few models to imitate.

The idea of a written code of laws can be traced to ancient times. But by the seventeenth and eighteenth centuries, most European legal and governmental systems were rooted in the notion of the common law and in systems in which a monarch ruled through divine right (see Chapter 1). Since 1215, the British monarch's power had been limited somewhat by the Magna Carta, a charter signed by King John guaranteeing the people certain liberties, including landowners' and tenants' rights, the right to trial by jury, restrictions against unreasonable punishment, and some measure of religious freedom. In contrast, most other European monarchies had no written guarantees of rights.

In the New World, however, Massachusetts Bay colonists successfully lived according to a minimal set of rules contained in the Mayflower Compact of 1620 (as discussed in Chapter 1). And later, in 1781, as discussed in this chapter, the thirteen colonies formally came together to form a union under the *written* **Articles of Confederation**, which established the basic framework for the national government that had directed the conduct of the Revolutionary War.

For the most part, the Framers charted new territory when writing the Constitution in 1789. Their achievement has survived for more than 200 years, and constitutional democracy has spread to many other countries. How did they do it? What issues did they face? What logic did they use? How can we understand their results? This chapter answers these questions by first examining the historical environment from which the Constitution emerged. We then analyze the document itself and turn to a discussion of how the Constitution has changed over time, through both formal and informal methods. We conclude with a review of proposals that have been made to change the Constitution to eliminate some problems unforeseen by the Founders.

Common law Judge-made law based on adherence to precedents; law common to the realm in the British empire.

Articles of Confederation The basic framework of the new U.S. government approved by the Second Continental Congress in 1777. Used to govern the United States during the Revolutionary War, the Articles provided for a Congress with very limited authority.

The Origins of a New Nation

Starting in the early seventeenth century, colonists came to the New World for a variety of reasons. Often it was to escape religious persecution. Others came seeking a new start on a continent where land was plentiful. The independence and diversity of the settlers in the New World made the question of how best to rule the new colonies a tricky one. Although the king ruled by decree at home, the Crown's new and distant American possessions were hard to understand, hard to reach, and hard to communicate with. More than merely an ocean separated the two; the colonists were an independent sort, and it soon became clear that the Crown could not govern the colonies with the same close rein used at home. King James I thus allowed some local participation in decision making through arrangements such as the first elected colonial assembly, the Virginia House of Burgesses, and the elected General Court that governed the Massachusetts Bay Company and that colony after 1629. Almost all the colonists agreed that the king ruled by divine right; but English monarchs allowed the colonists significant liberties in terms of self-government, religious practices, and economic organization. For 140 years, this system worked fairly well.[2]

By the early 1760s, however, a century and a half of physical separation, colonial development, and the relative self-governance of the colonies had led to weakening

 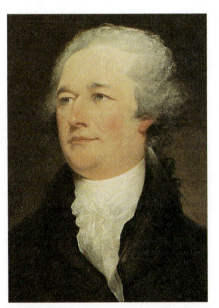 

James Madison (left), Alexander Hamilton (center), and John Jay (right) were important early Federalist leaders. Jay wrote five of *The Federalist Papers,* and Madison and Hamilton wrote the rest. Madison served in the House of Representatives (1789–1797) and as Secretary of State in the Jefferson administration (1801–1808). In 1808 he was elected fourth president of the United States and served two terms (1809–1817). Hamilton became the first Secretary of the Treasury (1789–1795) at the age of thirty-four. He was killed in 1804 in a duel with vice-president Aaron Burr, who was angered by Hamilton's negative comments about his character. Jay became the first Chief Justice of the Supreme Court (1789–1795) and negotiated the Jay Treaty with Great Britain in 1794. He then served as governor of New York from 1795 to 1801.

ties with—and loyalties to—the Crown. By this time, each of the thirteen colonies had drafted its own written constitution, which provided the fundamental rules or laws for each colony. Moreover, many of the most oppressive British traditions—feudalism, a rigid class system, and the absolute authority of church and king—were absent in the New World. Land was abundant. The restrictive guild and craft systems that severely limited entry into many skilled professions in England did not exist in the colonies. Although the role of religion was central to the lives of most colonists, there was no single state church, and the British practice of compulsory tithing (giving a fixed percentage of one's earnings to the state-sanctioned and -supported church) was nonexistent.

Trade and Taxation

Mercantilism, an economic theory based on the belief that a nation's wealth is measured by the amount of gold and silver in its treasury, justified Britain's maintenance of strict import/export controls on the colonies. After 1650, for example, Parliament passed a series of navigation acts to prevent its chief rival, Holland, from trading with the English colonies. From 1650 until well into the 1700s, England tried to regulate colonial imports and exports, believing that it was critical to export more goods than it imported as a way of increasing gold and silver in its treasury. These policies, however, were difficult to enforce, and were widely ignored by the colonists, who saw little benefit for themselves in them. Thus for years an unwritten agreement existed: The colonists relinquished to the Crown and the British Parliament the authority to regulate trade and conduct international affairs, but they retained the right to levy their own taxes.

This fragile agreement was soon put to the test. The French and Indian War, fought from 1755 to 1760 on the "western frontier" of the colonies and in Canada, was part of a global war initiated by the British. The American phase of the Seven Years' War was fought between England and France with its Indian allies. In North America its immediate cause was the rival claims of those two European nations for the lands between the Allegheny Mountains and the Mississippi River, as depicted in Figure 2-1. The Treaty of Paris (signed in 1763) signaled the end of the war. The colonists expected that with the "Indian problem" on the western frontier now "under control," westward migration and settlement could begin in earnest. They were shocked when the Crown decreed in 1763 that there was to be no further westward movement by British subjects. Parliament believed that expansion into Native American territory would lead to new expenditures for the defense of the settlers, draining the British treasury, which had yet to recover from the high cost of waging the war.

To raise money to pay for the war as well as the expenses of administering the colonies, Parliament enacted the Sugar Act in 1764, which placed taxes on sugar, wine, coffee, and other products commonly exported to the colonies. A postwar colonial depression heightened resentment of the tax. Around the colonies the political cry "No taxation without representation" was heard. Major protest, however, failed to materialize until imposition of the Stamp Act in 1765, a law passed by the British Parliament that required the purchase of stamps for all documents, including newspapers, magazines, and commercial papers. To add insult to injury, in 1765 Parliament passed the Mutiny or Quartering Act, which required the colonists to furnish barracks or provide living quarters within their own homes for British troops.

Most colonists, especially those in New England, where these acts hit hardest, were outraged. Men throughout the colonies organized the Sons of Liberty, under the lead-

FIGURE 2-1

North America Before and After the Seven Years' War

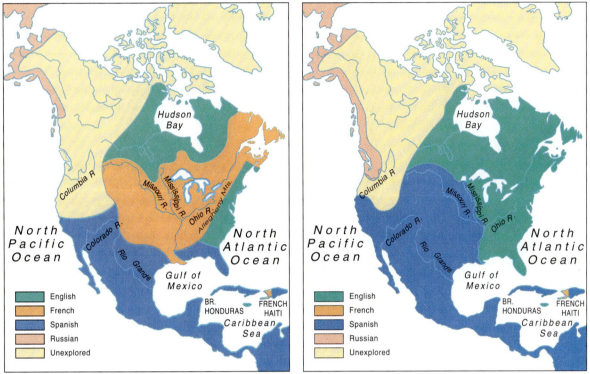

In 1754, before the Seven Years' War

After the Treaty of Paris in 1763

ership of Samuel Adams (see "People of the Past," p. 24) and Patrick Henry. Whereas the Sugar Act was a tax on trade—still viewed as being within the legitimate authority of the Crown—the Stamp Act was a direct tax on many items not traditionally under the control of the king, and protests against it were violent and loud. Riots, often led by the Sons of Liberty, broke out. They were especially violent in Boston, where the colonial governor's home was burned by an angry mob, and British stamp agents charged with collecting the tax were threatened. A boycott of goods needing the stamps as well as British imports was also organized.

First Steps Toward Independence

In 1765, the colonists called for the **Stamp Act Congress**, the first official meeting of the colonies and the first step toward a unified nation. Nine of the thirteen colonies sent representatives to a meeting in New York City, where a detailed list of Crown violations of their fundamental rights was drawn up. Attendees defined what they thought to be the proper relationship between the various colonial governments and the British Parliament; they ardently believed that Parliament had no authority to tax them without colonial representation in the British Parliament. In contrast, the British believed that direct representation of the colonists was impractical and that members of Parliament represented the best interests of all the English, including the colonists.

Stamp Act Congress Meeting of representatives of nine of the thirteen colonies held in New York City in 1765 during which representatives drafted a document to send to the king listing how their rights had been violated.

PEOPLE OF THE PAST

Samuel Adams

Although Samuel Adams (1722–1803) today is perhaps best known for the beer that bears his name, his original claim to fame was as a leader against British and Loyalist oppressors (although he did bankrupt his family's brewery business). A second cousin of President John Adams, Samuel Adams was a signer of the Declaration of Independence and a member of Massachu-

setts's constitutional convention that ratified the U.S. Constitution. He served as governor of Massachusetts from 1794 to 1797.

Adams was heavily influenced by John Locke's belief in man's natural right to be self-governing and free from taxation without representation. As a member of the Massachusetts legislature, he advocated defiance of the Stamp Act. With the passage of the Townshend Acts of 1767, he organized a letter-writing campaign urging other colonies to join in resistance. Later, in 1772, he founded the Committees of Correspondence to unite the colonies.

The Stamp Act Congress and its petitions to the Crown did little to stop the onslaught of taxing measures. Parliament did, however, repeal the Stamp Act and revise the Sugar Act in 1766, largely because of the uproar made by British merchants who were losing large sums of money as a result of the boycotts. Rather than appeasing the colonists, however, these actions emboldened them to increase their resistance. In 1767, when Parliament enacted the Townshend Acts, which imposed duties on all kinds of colonial imports, including tea, response from the Sons of Liberty was immediate. Another boycott was announced, and almost all colonists gave up their favorite drink in a united show of resistance to the tax and British authority.[3]

Tensions continued to run high, especially after the British sent 4,000 troops to Boston. On March 5, 1770, English troops opened fire on a mob that included disgruntled dock workers, whose jobs had been taken by British soldiers, and members of the Sons of Liberty who were taunting the soldiers in front of the Boston Customs House. Five colonists were killed in what became known as the "Boston Massacre." Following this confrontation, all duties except those on tea were lifted. The tea tax, however, continued to be a symbolic irritant. In 1772, at the suggestion of Samuel Adams, Boston and other towns around Massachusetts set up **Committees of Correspondence** to articulate ideas and keep communications open around the colony. By 1774, twelve colonies had formed committees to maintain a flow of information among like-minded colonists.

Committees of Correspondence Organizations originated by Samuel Adams in each of the American colonies to keep colonists abreast of developments with the British; served as powerful molders of public opinion against the British.

Meanwhile, despite dissent in England over the treatment of the colonies, Parliament passed another tea tax designed to shore up the sagging sales of the East India Company. The colonists' boycott had left that British trading house with more than 18 million pounds of tea in its warehouses. To rescue British merchants from disaster, in 1773 Parliament passed the Tea Act, granting a monopoly to the financially strapped East India Company to sell the tea imported from Britain. The company was allowed to funnel business to American merchants loyal to the Crown, thereby undercutting colonial merchants, who could sell only tea imported from other nations. The effect was to drive down the price of tea and hurt colonial merchants, who were forced to buy tea at the higher prices from other sources.

When the next shipment of tea arrived in Boston from Great Britain, the colonists responded by throwing the Boston Tea Party. In the night of December 18, 1773, after a militant town meeting presided over by Samuel Adams, about 150 colonists dressed as Indians or made up as blacks stole their way onto three British ships in Boston Harbor. As a large crowd watched from the docks, they proceeded to open and then dump nearly 350 chests of tea into the waters below. Similar "tea parties" were held in other colonies. When the news of these actions reached King George, he flew into a rage against the actions of his disloyal subjects. "The die is now cast," the king told his prime minister. "The colonies must either submit or triumph."

His first act was to persuade Parliament to pass the Coercive Acts in 1774. Known in the colonies as the Intolerable Acts, they contained a key provision calling for a total blockade of Boston Harbor until restitution was made for the tea. Another provision reinforced the Quartering Act, giving royal governors the authority to quarter in the homes of private citizens the additional 4,000 British soldiers sent to patrol Boston.

The First Continental Congress

The British could never have guessed how the cumulative impact of these actions would unite the colonists. Samuel Adams's Committees of Correspondence spread the word, and food and money were sent to the people of Boston from all over the thirteen colonies. The tax itself was no longer the key issue; now, the extent of British authority over the colonies was the far more important question. At the request of the colonial assemblies of Massachusetts and Virginia, all but one colonial assembly agreed to select a group of delegates to attend a continental congress authorized to communicate with the king on behalf of the now united colonies.

The **First Continental Congress** met in Philadelphia from September 5 to October 26, 1774. It was made up of fifty-six delegates from every colony except Georgia. The colonists had yet to think of breaking with Great Britain; at this point, they simply wanted to iron out their differences with the king. By October they had agreed upon a series of resolutions to oppose the Coercive Acts and establish a formal organization to boycott British goods. The Congress also drafted a Declaration of Rights and Resolves, portions of which later found their way into the Declaration of Independence and the U.S. Constitution.

The Declaration of Rights and Resolves called for colonial rights of petition and assembly, trial by peers, freedom from a standing army, and the selection of representative councils to levy taxes. The attendees further agreed to meet again in Philadelphia in May 1775 unless the king capitulated to their demands.

The Second Continental Congress

King George refused to yield, tensions continued to rise, and a **Second Continental Congress** was called. Before it could meet, fighting broke out early in the morning of April 19, 1775 at Lexington and Concord, Massachusetts, with what Ralph Waldo Emerson called "the shot heard round the world." Eight colonial Minutemen were killed, and 16,000 British troops besieged Boston.

First Continental Congress
Meeting held in Philadelphia from September 5 to October 26, 1774, in which fifty-six delegates (from every colony except Georgia) adopted a resolution that opposed the Coercive Acts.

Second Continental Congress
Meeting that convened in Philadelphia on May 10, 1775, in which it was decided that an army should be raised to defend the colonies; George Washington of Virginia was named commander-in-chief.

When the Second Continental Congress convened in Philadelphia on May 10, 1775, delegates were united by their increased hostility to Great Britain. The bloodshed at Lexington left no other course but war. To solidify colonial support, a Southerner was selected as the commander of the new Continental Army, since up to that date, British oppression had been felt most keenly in the Northeast. On June 15, 1775, George Washington of Virginia, who had fought in the French and Indian War, strongly hinted at his desire to head the army by being the only delegate to appear in a military uniform. He was named commander-in-chief, with the authority to enlist soldiers. The Congress sent envoys to France to ask for assistance. In a final attempt to avert conflict, the Second Continental Congress adopted the Olive Branch Petition on July 5, 1775, asking the king to end hostilities. King George rejected the petition and sent an additional 20,000 troops to quell the rebellion. The stage was set for war.

Although the colonists had not gone into the Second Continental Congress expecting to be a free and independent nation, the king's actions seemed to leave them no other choice than to declare independence. In 1774, Thomas Paine (1737–1809), whose radical political views had gotten him into considerable trouble in his native Great Britain, came to the colonies with the help of Benjamin Franklin, who saw Paine's potential use to the budding independence movement. Franklin, sensing the need for sentiment to unite the colonies, urged Paine to pen a document to fuel colonial sentiments. In January 1776, Paine issued (at first anonymously) *Common Sense,* a pamphlet forcefully arguing for independence from Great Britain. In frank, easy-to-understand language, Paine denounced the corrupt British monarchy and offered reasons for breaking with Great Britain. Concerning the English monarchy, Paine wrote,

Paul Revere's engraving of the Boston Massacre was a potent piece of political propaganda. Five men were killed, not seven, as the legend states, and the rioters in front of the State House (left) were scarcely as docile as Revere shows them.

"Ye that dare oppose not only tyranny but the tyrant, Stand forth!" Moreover, "Everything that is right," Paine argued, ". . . pleads for separation. The blood of the slain, the weeping voice of nature cries ''Tis Time to Part.'"

Common Sense, widely read throughout the colonies, was instrumental in changing minds in a very short time. In its first three months of publication, the 47-page *Common Sense* sold 120,000 copies, the equivalent of approximately 18.75 million books today (given the U.S. population in 1995). One copy of *Common Sense* was in distribution for every thirteen people in the colonies, a truly astonishing number given the low literacy rate.

After the success of *Common Sense,* Thomas Paine wrote a series of essays collectively entitled *The Crisis* to arouse colonists' support for the Revolutionary War. The first *Crisis* papers contain the famous words "These are the times that try men's souls."

The Declaration of Independence

The impact of *Common Sense* on the mood of the nation cannot be underscored too strongly. It galvanized the American public, and ridiculed all arguments for reconciliation with England. As the mood in the colonies changed, so did that of the Second Continental Congress. On May 15, 1776, Virginia became the first colony to call for independence, instructing one of its delegates to the Second Continental Congress to introduce a resolution to that effect. On June 7, 1776, Richard Henry Lee of Virginia rose to move "that these United Colonies are, and of right ought to be, free and independent States, and that all connection between them and the State of Great Britain is, and ought to be, dissolved." His three-part resolution—which called for independence, the formation of foreign alliances, and preparation of a plan of confederation—triggered hot debate. A proclamation of independence from Great Britain was treason, a crime punishable by death. Although six of the thirteen colonies had already instructed their delegates to vote for independence, the Second Continental Congress was suspended to allow its delegates to return home to their respective colonial legislatures for final instructions. Independence was not a move to be taken lightly.

At the same time, committees were set up to consider each point of Lee's proposal. A committee of five was selected to begin work on a **Declaration of Independence**. The Congress selected Benjamin Franklin, John Adams, Robert Livingston, and Roger Sherman as members. Adams lobbied hard for a Southerner to add balance. Thus, owing to his Southern origin as well as his "peculiar felicity of expression," Thomas Jefferson was selected as chair.

On July 2, twelve of the thirteen colonies (with New York abstaining) voted for independence. Two days later, the Second Continental Congress voted to adopt the Declaration of Independence penned by Thomas Jefferson. On July 9, the Declaration, now with the approval of New York, was read aloud in Philadelphia.[4]

Declaration of Independence Document drafted by Thomas Jefferson in 1776 that proclaimed the right of the American colonies to separate from Great Britain.

Social Contract Theory

In simple but eloquent language, Jefferson set out the reasons for the colonies' separation from Great Britain. Most of his stirring rhetoric drew heavily on the works of seventeenth- and eighteenth-century political philosophers, particularly the great John Locke of England (see "People of the Past," p. 6), who actually wrote South Carolina's first constitution as a colonial charter when it was formed by the king and mercantile houses in England.

The colonists agreed with Locke's argument that people have certain natural, or God-given, inalienable rights that cannot be taken away by any government.[5] They had

Landmark Events Leading to the Declaration of Independence

1620	♦	Mayflower Compact; settlement in Massachusetts
1754	♦	Colonies settled and developed
1760	♦	French and Indian War
1763	♦	Crown decrees no more westward movement
1764	♦	Sugar Act
1765	♦	Stamp Act—Sons of Liberty organized; Stamp Act Congress convened
1766	♦	Stamp Act repealed; Sugar Act revised
1767	♦	Townshend Acts—colonists boycott tea
1770	♦	Boston Massacre
1772	♦	Committees of Correspondence set up
1773	♦	Tea Act; Boston Tea Party
1774	♦	Coercive or Intolerable Acts; First Continental Congress convened
1775	♦	Fighting breaks out at Lexington and Concord; Second Continental Congress convened
1776	♦	Declaration of Independence

come to cherish, among other things, the right to property. In colonial times "property" did not mean just land; Locke's notion of property rights included life, liberty, and material possessions.

According to Locke and his adherents, government existed by the consent of the governed. Under this brand of social contract theory, individuals free and equal by natural right agree to set up a government for certain defined purposes. These individuals have the right to resist or remove rulers who deviate from those purposes. Essentially, under social contract theory, government exists for the good of its subjects and not for the benefit of those who govern. Locke argued, furthermore, that rebellion was the ultimate sanction against a government that abused its power.

It is easy to see the colonists' debt to John Locke. In ringing language the Declaration of Independence proclaims:

> We hold these truths to be self-evident, that all men are created equal, that they are endowed by their Creator with certain unalienable Rights, that among these are Life, Liberty and the pursuit of Happiness.

Jefferson and others in attendance at the Second Continental Congress wanted to have a document that would stand for all time, justifying their break with the Crown and clarifying their notions of the proper form of government. So, Jefferson continued:

That to secure these rights, Governments are instituted among Men, deriving their just powers from the consent of the governed. That whenever any Form of Government becomes destructive of these ends, it is the Right of the People to alter or abolish it, and to institute new Government, laying its foundation on such Principles and organizing its Powers in such form, as to them shall seem most likely to effect their Safety and Happiness.

After this stirring preamble, the Declaration went on to enumerate the wrongs that the colonists had suffered under British rule. All pertained to the denial of personal rights and liberties, many of which would later be guaranteed by the U.S. Constitution via the Bill of Rights.

After the Declaration was signed and transmitted to the king, the Revolutionary War was fought with a greater vengeance. At a September 1776 peace conference on Staten Island (New York), British General William Howe demanded revocation of the Declaration of Independence. The Americans refused, and the war raged on while the Congress attempted to fashion a new united government.

The First Attempt at Government: The Articles of Confederation

As noted earlier, the British had no written constitution. Now the colonists in the Second Continental Congress were attempting to codify arrangements that had never before been put into legal terminology. To make things more complicated, the delegates had to arrive at these decisions in a wartime atmosphere. Nevertheless, in late 1779 the Articles of Confederation, creating a loose "league of friendship" between the sovereign or independent states, were passed by the Congress and presented to the states for their ratification.

The Articles created a type of government called a **confederation**, in which the national government derives its powers from the states it comprises, as depicted in Figure 2-2. Although the authority of the states rested on powers derived directly from the people, the national government held only the powers that the states were willing to give it. Key provisions in the Articles included:

Confederation Type of government in which the national government derives its powers from the states; a league of independent states.

- A national government with a Congress empowered to make peace, coin money, appoint officers for an army, control the post office, and negotiate with Indian tribes.
- Each state's retention of its independence and sovereignty, or ultimate authority to govern within its territories.
- One vote in the Continental Congress for each state, regardless of size.
- The vote of nine states to pass any measure (a unanimous vote for any amendment).
- The selection and payment of delegates to the Congress by their respective state legislatures.

Thus, the Articles—finally ratified by all thirteen states in 1781—fashioned a government well reflective of the political philosophy of the times.[6] Although it had its flaws, the government under the Articles of Confederation saw the nation through the Revolutionary War. However, once the British surrendered in 1782 and the new nation found itself no longer united by the war effort, the government quickly fell into chaos.

FIGURE 2-2

The Structure of Government Under the Articles of Confederation

| Congress |
| 1 House |

| Committee of the States |
| (Committee of Representatives from each state allowed to act when Congress not in session) |

| Officers (including President) |
| (Representatives appointed to do executive work) |

| States |

Problems Under the Articles of Confederation

By 1784, just one year after the Revolutionary army was disbanded, governing the new nation under the Articles of Confederation proved unworkable.[7] Congress could rarely assemble the required quorum of nine states to conduct business. Even when it could, there was little agreement among them. To raise revenue to pay off war debts and run the government, various land, poll, and liquor taxes were proposed. But since Congress had no specific power to tax, all these proposals were rejected. At one point, Congress was even driven out of Philadelphia (then the capital) by its own unpaid army. And, although the national government could coin money, it had no resources to back up the value of its currency. Continental dollars were worth little, and trade between states became chaotic as some states began to coin their own money. Another weakness of the Articles was their failure to allow Congress to regulate commerce among the states and with foreign nations. As a result, individual states attempted to enter into agreements with other countries, and foreign nations were suspicious of trade agreements made with the United States. In 1785, for example, Massachusetts banned the export of goods in British ships, and Pennsylvania levied heavy duties on ships of nations that did not have a treaty with the U.S. government.

Fearful of a chief executive who would rule tyrannically, moreover, the draftees of the Articles had made no provision for an executive branch of government that would be responsible for executing, or implementing, laws passed by the legislative branch. Instead, the "president" was merely the presiding officer at meetings. John Hanson, a former member of the Maryland House of Delegates and of the first Continental Congress, was the first person to preside over the Congress of the Confederation, as the new government under the Articles was called. Therefore, he is often referred to as the first President of the United States.

In addition, the Articles of Confederation had no provision for a judicial system to handle the growing number of economic conflicts and boundary disputes among the individual states. Several states claimed the same lands to the west; Pennsylvania and Virginia went to war with each other; Vermont threatened to annex itself to Canada.

The Articles' greatest weakness, however, was their lack of creation of a strong central government. While states had operated independently before the war, during the war they acceded to the national government's authority to wage armed conflict. Once the war was over, however, each state resumed its sovereign status, and was unwilling to give up rights, such as the power to tax, to an untested national government. Consequently, the government was unable to force the states to abide by the provisions of the Treaty of Paris, signed in 1783, which had officially ended the war. For example, states passed laws to stay the bills of debtors who owed money to Great Britain and failed to restore property to many who had remained loyal to Britain during the war, both of which actions were in violation of the Treaty.

The crumbling economy and a series of bad harvests that failed to produce cash crops, making it difficult for farmers to get out of debt quickly, took their toll on the new nation. George Washington and Alexander Hamilton, both interested in the questions of trade and frontier expansion, soon saw the need for a stronger national government with the authority to act to solve some of these problems. They were not alone. In 1785 and 1786 some state governments began to discuss ways to strengthen the national government. Finally, several states joined together to call for a convention in Philadelphia in 1787.

Before that meeting could take place, however, new unrest broke out in America. In 1780, Massachusetts adopted a state constitution that appeared to favor the interests of the wealthy. Property-owning requirements barred the lower and middle classes from

Five Major Failures of the Articles

❖ ❖ ❖

1. No power to tax
2. No authority to regulate commerce
3. No executive to administer the government
4. No judicial system to resolve disputes among the states
5. No strong central government

With Daniel Shays in the lead, a group of farmers and Revolutionary War veterans marched on the courthouse in Springfield, Massachusetts, to prevent foreclosure on their mortgages.

voting and office holding. And, as the economy of Massachusetts worsened, banks foreclosed on farms to pay off debts to Massachusetts Continental Army veterans who were waiting for promised bonuses. The last straw came in 1786 when the Massachusetts legislature enacted a new law requiring the payment of all debts in cash. Frustration and outrage at the new law caused Daniel Shays, a former Revolutionary War army captain, and 1,500 armed, disgruntled, and angry farmers to march to Springfield. This group forcibly restrained the state court from foreclosing on mortgages on their farms.

The Congress immediately authorized the Secretary of War to call for a new national militia. A $530,000 appropriation was made for this purpose, but every state except Virginia refused the Congress's request for money. The governor of Massachusetts then tried to raise a state militia, but because of the poor economy, funds were unavailable in the state treasury. Frantic attempts at private support were made, and a militia was finally assembled. By February 4, 1787, this privately paid force put a stop to what was called **Shays's Rebellion**. The failure of the Congress to muster an army to put down the rebellion was yet another example of the weaknesses inherent in the Articles of Confederation.

The Miracle at Philadelphia: Writing a Constitution

Shays's Rebellion A rebellion led by Daniel Shays, an army veteran, during the summer of 1786 in which an army of 1,500 disgruntled and angry farmers marched to Springfield, Massachusetts and forcibly restrained the state court from foreclosing on their farms.

In the throes of economic turmoil and with domestic tranquility gone haywire, on February 21, 1787, the Congress passed an official resolution that called for a Constitutional Convention in Philadelphia for "the sole and express purpose of revising the Articles of Confederation." All states but Rhode Island sent delegates. (Rhode Island was a strong supporter of the government under the Articles and had as its state motto Thomas Paine's words "Government is best which governs least." Its absence from the

During the Revolutionary War and under the Articles of Confederation, the national government printed so much currency that its worth plummeted, giving rise to the expression "not worth a continental." Each state also coined and printed its own money, further compounding financial confusion and leading to economic chaos.

meeting led some present to suggest that its name be changed to "Rogue Island" or that it be dropped from the Union altogether.)

When twenty-nine individuals met in sweltering Philadelphia on May 14, they had much on their minds. While many of them at that initial meeting were intellectuals, others were shrewd farmers or businessmen, and others were astute politicians. All recognized that what they were doing could be considered treasonous. Revising the Articles of Confederation was one thing; to call for an entirely new government, as suggested by the Virginia delegation, was another. So they took their work quite seriously, even to the point of adopting a pledge of secrecy. George Washington, who was unanimously elected the convention's presiding officer, warned:

> Nothing spoken or written can be revealed to anyone—not even your family—until we have adjourned permanently. Gossip or misunderstanding can easily ruin all the hard work we shall have to do this summer.[8]

So concerned about leaks were those in attendance that the delegates agreed to accompany Benjamin Franklin to all of his meals, fearing that the normally gregarious gentleman might get carried away with the mood or by liquor and inadvertently let news of the proceedings slip from his tongue.

The Framers

Fifty-five out of the seventy-four delegates ultimately chosen by their state legislatures to attend the Constitutional Convention labored long and hard that hot summer behind closed doors in Philadelphia. They are often referred to as the "Founding Fathers." Most of them were quite young; many were in their twenties and thirties, and only one—Benjamin Franklin, at eighty-one—was very old. Here we generally refer to those delegates as Framers because their work provided the framework for our new government. The Framers brought with them a vast amount of political, educational, legal, and business experience. Eight had signed the Declaration of Independence, thirty-nine had attended at least one Continental Congress, and seven were former governors. One-third were college graduates, and thirty-four were lawyers. Notably absent were individuals like Patrick Henry, who had proclaimed in the Virginia House of Burgesses, "Give me liberty or give me death!" Now he stayed away because he "smelt a rat," fearing that the states could lose their powers. Also missing were Thomas Jefferson, author of the Declaration of Independence, and John Adams. Both were on ambassadorial stays in Europe. Although some scholarly debate continues concerning the motives of the Framers for shaping the new national government (see "Motives of the Framers," p. 44), it is clear that they were an exceptional lot who ultimately produced a brilliant document reflecting the best efforts of all present.

The Virginia Plan

Virginia Plan The first general plan for the Constitution whose key points were a bicameral legislature, an executive chosen by the legislature, and a judiciary also named by the legislature.

Soon after George Washington called the meeting to order, Edmund Randolph of Virginia rose to present a framework of government that James Madison had prepared prior to the meeting. The preamble of what is commonly referred to as the **Virginia Plan** proposed that "a *national* government ought to be established, consisting of a *supreme* Legislative, Executive and Judiciary" (emphasis added). Those in attendance unanimously agreed to debate that idea, and the remainder of Madison's plan was introduced for discussion.

Once the Framers had voted to consider Madison's proposals, the die was cast. The purpose of the convention was changed from revision of the Articles to the creation of an entirely new form of government.[9]

The Virginia Plan contained several key elements that shaped the new government and its final structure. It called for:

1. A national government with three separate branches of government: a legislative branch to make laws, an executive branch to enforce them, and a judicial branch to interpret them.

2. The creation of a national legislature or lawmaking body with two parts, or houses. One house was to be elected directly by the people; the other house was to be chosen from among persons nominated by the state legislatures. Total representation in the legislature would be in proportion to taxes paid to the federal or national government, corresponding to the population of free people within each state.

3. A single "national Executive" to be chosen by the national legislature for a single term.

4. A Council of Revision, consisting of the national executive and several federal judges, that would have the authority to approve or veto acts of the legislature. Vetoes could be overridden by a vote of both houses of the legislature.

5. A federal judiciary headed by a Supreme Court appointed for life by the legislature.

6. A national government with the power to override state laws. Since the government was to derive its powers from the people and the states, the plan argued that the national government should have the ability to operate on both.

During the first few weeks of the convention, discussion of this plan, which created a far stronger national government than had existed under the Articles of Confederation, dominated the proceedings. After only six days of debate, Virginia's proposal to create a new national government was voted on by the convention. By the narrowest of margins, the Virginia Plan won its first crucial test and gave momentum to those forces favoring a strong central government.

The delegates then debated other sections of the Virginia Plan. The first structural aspect of the new government that the Framers agreed on was a **bicameral legislature**, that is, one with two distinct bodies. When Thomas Jefferson returned from Paris, he asked Washington why the delegates had agreed to a two-house legislature. "Why do you pour coffee into your saucer?" asked Washington. "To cool it," responded Jefferson. "So," responded Washington, "we pour legislation into the senatorial saucer to cool it."[10]

Delegates initially appeared far from agreement over how members of each house of Congress were to be selected. Many of them appeared set against direct election of members of one house. Many who held to that view feared the idea of democracy. Their elitist views led them to believe that not "all the people" were fit to make decisions concerning the government. They feared the kinds of uprisings that Daniel Shays's actions had typified.

On the other side, Madison and other supporters of a strong central government, while still fearful of a "mobocracy," continued to insist on direct election of some representatives. They reasoned that without the confidence of the people, government could not long exist.

The Virginia Plan called for a national system with a powerful central government. It was based heavily on the European nation–state model, wherein the national government derives its powers from the people and not from the member states. In con-

Bicameral legislature A legislature divided into two houses; the U.S. Congress and every U.S. state legislature are bicameral (except Nebraska's, which is unicameral).

trast, proponents of what was *at that time* termed a federal system favored a looser confederation of states in which powers could be shared between the national and state governments. Basically comfortable with the arrangements under the Articles of Confederation, they offered another model of government, the New Jersey Plan.

The New Jersey Plan

New Jersey Plan A framework for the Constitution proposed by a group of small states. Its key features included a one-house legislature with one vote for each state, a multi-person "executive", the establishment of the acts of Congress as the "supreme law" of the land, and judiciary with limited power.

As supporters of a strong national government continued to debate various aspects of the Virginia Plan, representatives from the smaller states took advantage of a rule that allowed reconsideration of any proposal that had previously been adopted. Under the direction of William Paterson of New Jersey, the smaller states offered their own plan after about two weeks of deliberation on the Virginia Plan. The **New Jersey Plan** suggested that the Articles, instead of being replaced, only be strengthened. Its key features included:

1. A one-house legislature with one vote for each state. Representatives to the Congress were to be chosen by state legislatures. The Congress would have the power to raise revenue from duties and a post office. All other funds had to be requested from the states.
2. A multi-person "executive" to be chosen by Congress with powers similar to those in the Virginia Plan, except that the executive would not have the authority to veto acts of Congress.
3. The establishment of the acts of Congress as the "supreme law" of the land, and authorization of the federal executive to use force to compel obedience.
4. A supreme judiciary with very limited authority (although there was no provision for a system of national courts).

Not surprisingly, the New Jersey Plan was defeated, but its consideration showed that the smaller states had sufficient concerns and political clout to force some changes in the Virginia Plan.

The Great Compromise

The most serious disagreement between the Virginia and New Jersey Plans concerned representation in the two chambers of Congress. When a deadlock on this point loomed, Connecticut offered its own compromise. Each state would have an equal vote in the Senate. Again, there was a stalemate. As Benjamin Franklin put it,

> The diversity of opinions turns on two points. If a proportional representation takes place, the small states contend that their liberties will be in danger. If an equality of votes is to be put in its place, large states say that their money will be in danger.

He continued:

> When a broad table is to be made and the edges of a plank do not fit, the artist takes a little from both sides and makes a good joint. In like manner, both sides must part with some of their demands, in order that they both join in some accommodating position.[11]

A committee was appointed to see if some sort of agreement could be worked out over the Fourth of July weekend. That committee reported back what became known as the **Great Compromise**. Taking ideas from both the Virginia and New Jersey Plans, it recommended:

1. In one house of the legislature (later called the House of Representatives), there should be 56 representatives—one representative for every 40,000 inhabitants.
2. That house should have the power to originate all bills for raising and spending money.
3. In the second house of the legislature (later called the Senate), each state should have an equal vote, and representatives would be selected by the state legislatures.[12]

An additional compromise, however, was necessary before state populations could be determined. After considerable dissension, it was decided that representation in the House of Representatives was to be based on population, calculated by adding the "whole Number of Free Persons" to "three fifths of all other Persons." "All other Persons" was the delegates' "tactful" way of referring to slaves. Known as the **Three-Fifths Compromise**, this formula was based on the prevailing assumption that slaves were only three-fifths as productive as white men.[13]

Since the slave population in the Southern states was so large, these states sought to have slaves counted as part of the population for the purpose of representation. Yet they never considered the possibility of allowing these same slaves to cast ballots for representatives. In fact, throughout most of the colonies, suffrage, or the right to vote, was not universal. Instead, it was generally limited to white male property owners.

The Great Compromise ultimately met with the approval of all states in attendance. The smaller states were pleased because they got equal representation in the Senate; the larger states were satisfied with the proportional representation in the House of Representatives. The small states then would dominate the Senate while the large states, such as Virginia and New York, would control the House. But because both houses had to pass any legislation, neither body could dominate the other.

With passage of the Great Compromise, and after ten weeks of hard work, agreement was reached on most of its basic principles. On August 6, 1787, a draft of a constitution—seven pages long, with broad margins for notations—was submitted to the delegates. It contained twenty-three articles subdivided into forty-one separate sections. Still to be included, however, were provisions for an executive branch and a president.

Compromise on the Presidency

By August, the Framers had agreed on the idea of a one-person executive, but they could not settle on the length of the term of office, nor on how the chief executive should be selected. With Shays's Rebellion still fresh in their minds, the delegates feared putting too much power into the hands of the lower classes. At the same time, representatives from the smaller states feared that the selection of the chief executive by the legislature would put additional power into the hands of the large states.

Amid these fears, the Committee on Unfinished Portions, whose sole responsibility was to iron out problems and disagreements concerning the office of chief executive, conducted its work. The Committee recommended that the presidential term of office be fixed at four years instead of seven, as had earlier been proposed. By choosing not to mention a time-span within which the chief executive would be eligible for reelection, they made it possible for a president to serve more than one term. The president

Great Compromise A decision made during the Philadelphia Convention to give each state the same number of representatives in the Senate regardless of size; representation in the House was determined by population.

Three-Fifths Compromise Agreement reached at the Constitutional Convention stipulating that each slave was to be counted as three-fifths of a person for purposes of determining population for representation in the U.S. House of Representatives.

In 1787, Virginia's population was twice that of New York, four times that of New Jersey, and ten times that of Delaware.

DOONESBURY   Garry Trudeau

was to be chosen by electors. And, for the first time, the post of vice president was mentioned.

Selecting a President: The Electoral College

In setting up a system for electing the president, the Framers put in place an electoral college (see Chapter 12). The electoral college system gave individual states a key role, because each state would select electors equal to the number of representatives it had in the House *and* Senate. It was a vague compromise that removed election of the president and vice president from both the Congress and the people and put it in the hands of electors whose method of selection would be left to the states.

The delegates were quite happy with this compromise and believed that it would be acceptable to all sides. The smaller states believed they would have an equal voice should the election be forced into the House of Representatives, and the larger states believed they had a good opportunity to elect a president before this contingency would occur.

Removing a President

One more matter concerning the president remained, however. Still fearful of a leader who might turn out to resemble a British monarch, the Framers were careful to include a provision for removal of the chief executive. They proposed that both the legislative and the judicial branches be involved in the impeachment process. The House of Representatives was given the sole responsibility of investigating and charging a president or vice president with "Treason, Bribery, or other high Crimes and Misdemeanors." A majority vote would then result in the issuing of Articles of Impeachment against the president. In turn, the Senate was given sole responsibility to try the chief executive on the charges issued by the House. A two-thirds vote of the Senate was required to convict and remove the president from office. The Chief Justice of the

United States was to preside over the Senate proceedings in place of the vice president (that body's usual leader) in order to prevent any appearance of impropriety on the vice president's part.

The U.S. Constitution

After the compromise on the presidency, work proceeded quickly on the remaining resolutions of the Constitution. A committee of five members was chosen to formalize all that had been accomplished in Philadelphia. The final document was largely written by Gouverneur Morris of Pennsylvania, a friend of Washington's, and treasurer of the Continental Congress. The committee submitted its work, which included some new proposals as well as changes in matters previously accepted, to the delegates on August 6, 1787.

The Preamble to the Constitution, the last section to be drafted, contains exceptionally powerful language that formed the bedrock of American political tradition. The Preamble is directly attributable to Morris, who had a true gift for simplifying complex language. Its opening line, "We the People of the United States," boldly proclaimed that a loose confederation of independent states no longer existed; instead, there was but one American people and nation. The original version of the Preamble opened with:

> We the people of the States of New Hampshire, Massachusetts, Rhode Island and the Providence Plantations, Connecticut, New Jersey, New York, Pennsylvania, Delaware, Maryland, Virginia, North Carolina, South Carolina and Georgia, do ordain, declare and establish the following Constitution for the government of ourselves and our Posterity.

Note how different the phrases ended up under Morris's pen. The simple phrase "We the people" ended at least for the time being the question of whence the government derived its power—it came directly from the people, not from the states.

The next phrase of the Constitution explained the need for the new outline of government. "[I]n Order to form a more perfect Union" indirectly acknowledged the

A ticket for entry to the Senate's impeachment trial of Andrew Johnson, the only time in U.S. history when the full impeachment machinery created in the U.S. Constitution was used.

"Remember, gentlemen, we aren't here just to draft a constitution. We're here to draft the best damned constitution in the world."

Drawing by Steiner, © 1982 The New Yorker Magazine, Inc.

weaknesses of the Articles of Confederation in governing a growing nation. Next, the optimistic goals of the Framers for the new nation were set out: to "establish Justice, insure domestic Tranquility, provide for the common defense, promote the general Welfare, and secure the Blessings of Liberty to ourselves and our Posterity"; followed by the formal creation of a new government: "do ordain and establish this Constitution for the United States of America."

In *The Miracle at Philadelphia* (1966) Catherine Drinker Bowen wrote, "The seven verbs flowed out—to form, establish, insure, provide, promote, secure, ordain. . . . One might challenge the centuries to better these verbs."[14] These powerful words fanned the flames of a new nation. On September 17, 1787, the Constitution was finally approved by the delegates from all twelve states in attendance (Rhode Island had not sent any representatives.) While the completed document did not satisfy all the delegates, of the forty-one in attendance, thirty-nine ultimately signed. The sentiments uttered by Benjamin Franklin probably well reflected those of many others: "Thus, I consent, Sir, to this Constitution because I expect no better, and because I am not sure that it is not the best."[15]

The Basic Principles of the Constitution

The ideas of political philosophers, especially the French Baron de la Brède et de Montesquieu (1689–1755) and the English John Locke (see "People of the Past," p. 6), heavily influenced the shape and nature of the government proposed by the Framers. Montesquieu, who actually drew many of his ideas about government from the works of the Greek political philosopher Aristotle, was heavily quoted during the Constitutional Convention. Acknowledging the Framers' debt to Montesquieu, James Madison noted in *Federalist No. 47,* "if he be not the author of this invaluable precept [separation of powers] in the science of politics, he has the merit of at least displaying and recommending it most effectually to the attention of mankind."

The proposed structure of the new national government also owed much to the writings of Montesquieu, who advocated distinct functions for each branch of government, with a system of checks and balances between them. And the Constitution's concern with the distribution of power between states and the national government also reveals the heavy influence of political philosophers, as well as the colonists' experience under the Articles of Confederation.[16]

Unitary government Term applied to systems in which all power resides in the central or national government as opposed to regional (subnational) governments.

Federal system Plan of government created by the U.S. Constitution in which power is divided between the national government and the state governments and in which independent states are bound together under one national government.

Federalism. Under the Articles of Confederation, only a loose "league of friendship" existed among the states. Given the nation's experiences under the Articles, the Framers believed that a strong national government was necessary for the new nation's survival. However, they were reluctant to create a powerful government on the model of Britain, the country from which they had just won their independence. Its **unitary government**, in which all major powers resided at the national level, was not even considered by the colonists. Instead, they fashioned a system now known as **federal system,** which divides the power of government between a strong national government and the individual states. Opponents of this system feared that a strong national government would infringe on their liberty, but James Madison argued that a strong national government with distinct state governments could, if properly directed by constitutional arrangements, actually be a source of expanded liberties and national unity. The Framers viewed the division of governmental authority between the national government and the states as a means of checking power with power, and providing the people with "double security" against governmental tyranny. Later, the passage of the Tenth Amendment, which stated that powers not given to the national government were reserved by the states or the people, further clarified the federal structure (see Chapter 3).

Separation of Powers.   Madison and many of the Framers clearly feared putting too much power into the hands of any one individual or branch of government. His famous words, "Ambition must be made to counteract ambition," were widely believed at the Philadelphia convention.

   Separation of powers is simply a way of parceling out power among the three branches of government. It has three key features:

1.   Three distinct branches of government: the legislative, the executive, and the judicial.
2.   Three separately staffed branches of government to exercise these functions.
3.   Constitutional equality and independence of each branch.

   Thus, as illustrated in Figure 2-3, the Framers were careful to create a system in which lawmaking, law-enforcing, and law-interpreting functions were assigned to independent branches of government. On the national level (and in most states), only the legislature has the authority to make laws; the chief executive enforces and the judiciary interprets them. Moreover, members of the House of Representatives, members of the Senate, the President, and members of the federal courts are selected by and are therefore responsible to different constituencies. Madison believed that the scheme devised by the Framers would divide the offices of the new government and their methods of selection among many individuals, providing each office holder with the "necessary means and personal motives to resist encroachment" on his power.

   The Framers could not have foreseen the intermingling of governmental functions that has since evolved. Locke, in fact, cautioned against giving a legislature the ability to delegate its powers. In Article I of the Constitution, the legislative power is vested in the Congress, but the president is also given legislative powers via his ability to veto legislation, although his veto can be overridden by a two-thirds vote in Congress. Judicial interpretation then helps to clarify the implementation of legislation enacted through this process.

   So instead of a pure system of separation of powers, a symbiotic, or interdependent, relationship among the three branches of government has existed from the beginning. Or as one scholar has explained, there are "separated institutions sharing powers."[17] While Congress is still entrusted with making the laws, most proposals for legislation originate with the president. And although the Supreme Court's major function is to interpret the law, its involvement in areas such as criminal procedure, abortion, and other fields has led many to charge that it has surpassed its constitutional authority and become a law-making body.

   In this regard, the blurring of the separation of powers has moved the American system a little closer to Britain's parliamentary democracy (see Figure 2-3). There, too, a symbiotic relationship between the legislature and executive exists, since the prime minister and the cabinet come from the lower house of the legislature. Members of the executive branch in a parliamentary system usually retain their seats in the legislature, and thus wear two hats: one as a representative of the people and the other as an executive officer. And some members of the House of Lords also serve as justices.

Checks and Balances.   The principle of **checks and balances** also guided the Framers as they designed the new government.[18] As illustrated in Table 2.1, power is checked and balanced because the legislative, executive, and judicial branches of government share some authority, and no branch has exclusive domain over any activity.

Separation of powers A way of dividing power among the three branches of government in which members of the House of Representatives, members of the Senate, the president, and the federal courts are selected by and responsible to different constituencies; initially offered by the French political philosopher Montesquieu.

Checks and balances A governmental structure that gives each of the three branches of government some degree of oversight and control over the actions of the others.

F I G U R E   2 - 3

Separation of Powers: The
American and British Systems
Compared

AMERICAN SYSTEM

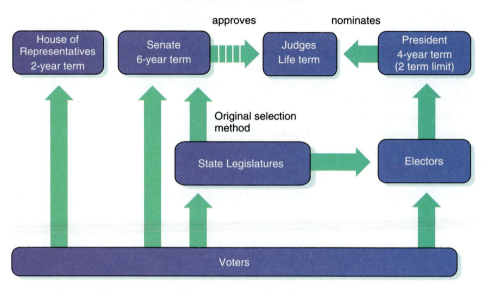

BRITISH SYSTEM

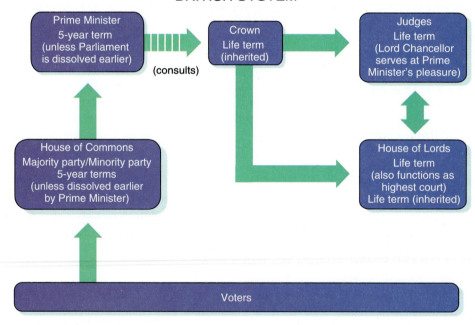

The creation of this system of checks and balances allowed the Framers to minimize
the threat of tyranny from any one branch. Thus, for almost every power granted to
one branch, an equal control was established in the other two branches. The Congress
could "check" the power of the president, the Supreme Court, and so on, carefully creating "balance" among the three branches.

Table 2.1 ◆ **Separation of Powers and Checks and Balances Outlined**

POWERS OF CONGRESS

Passes all federal laws

Establishes lower federal courts and the number of judges

Can impeach the president

Can override the president's veto by a two-thirds vote

Passes the federal budget, which finances the executive branch

Approves treaties and presidential appointments, including those to the federal courts

CHECKS ON CONGRESSIONAL POWERS

President can veto legislation

Supreme Court can rule laws unconstitutional

Both houses of Congress must vote to enact a law, thereby checking power within the legislature

POWERS OF THE CHIEF EXECUTIVE

Can approve or veto acts of Congress

Is responsible for carrying out the laws passed by Congress

Can call Congress into special session

Can submit legislation to Congress

Makes foreign treaties

Nominates Supreme Court justices and federal judges

Can pardon people convicted in federal court

Is responsible for execution of court orders

Is commander-in-chief of armed forces

CHECKS ON EXECUTIVE POWERS

Congress can override vetoes of legislation by a two-thirds vote

Senate can refuse to confirm nominees or ratify treaties

Congress can impeach and remove president (with Chief Justice of the Supreme Court presiding)

Congress can declare war

Supreme Court can declare presidential acts unconstitutional

POWERS OF THE JUDICIARY

Can invalidate, on grounds of unconstitutionality, laws passed by Congress

Can invalidate executive branch orders or actions on grounds of unconstitutionality or absence of authorizing legislation

CHECKS ON JUDICIAL POWERS

Congress can change jurisdiction (authority to hear cases) of the Supreme Court

Congress can impeach and remove federal judges

President appoints federal judges (who must be confirmed by the Senate)

Congress can propose amendments to override Supreme Court decisions

The Articles of the Constitution

The document finally signed by the Framers condensed numerous resolutions into a Preamble and seven separate articles. The first three articles established the three branches of government, defined their internal operations, and clarified their relationships with one another. All branches of government were technically considered equal, yet some initially appeared more "equal" than others. It is likely that the order in which the articles appear, and especially the relative amount of detail in the first three articles, reflects the Framers' concern that the branches of the government might abuse their powers. The four remaining articles define the relationships among the states, declare national law to be supreme, and set out methods of amending the Constitution.

Article I: The Legislative Branch. Article I vests all legislative powers in the Congress and establishes a bicameral legislature, the Senate and the House of Representatives. It also sets out the qualifications for holding office in each house, the terms of office, methods of selection of representatives and senators, and the system of apportionment among the states to determine membership in the House of Representatives. Operating procedures and the officers for each house are also outlined and described.

Enumerated powers Seventeen specific powers granted to Congress under Article I, Section 8 of the U.S. Constitution; these powers include taxation, coinage of money, regulation of commerce, and the authority to provide for a national defense.

Perhaps the most important section of Article I is Section 8. It carefully lists the powers the Framers wished the new Congress to possess. These **enumerated**—or specified—**powers** contain many key provisions that had been denied to the Continental Congress under the Articles of Confederation. For example, one of the major weaknesses of the Articles was Congress's lack of authority to deal with trade wars. The Constitution remedied this problem by authorizing Congress to "regulate Commerce with foreign Nations, and among the several States."

After careful enumeration of seventeen powers of Congress, a key clause authorizing Congress to "make all Laws which shall be necessary and proper for carrying into Execution the foregoing Powers" was added to Article I. Often referred to as the **elastic clause**, the "necessary and proper" clause has been the source of tremendous congressional activity never anticipated by the Framers, as definitions of "necessary" and "proper" have been stretched to accommodate changing needs and times. The Supreme Court, for example, has coupled Congress's authority to regulate commerce with the "necessary and proper" clause to allow Congress to ban prostitution (where travel across state lines is involved), regulate trains and planes, establish uniform federal minimum wage and maximum hour laws, and mandate drug testing for certain workers (see Chapter 6).

Elastic clause A name given to the "necessary and proper clause" found in the final paragraph of Article I, Section 8 of the U.S. Constitution. It gives Congress the authority to pass all laws "necessary and proper" to carry out the enumerated powers specified in the Constitution.

Article II: The Executive Branch. Article II vests the executive power, that is, the authority to execute the laws of the nation, in a president of the United States. Section 1 sets the president's term of office at four years and explains the electoral college. It also states qualifications for office and describes a mechanism to replace the president in case of death, disability, or removal.

The powers and duties of the president are set out in Section 3. Among the most important of these are the president's role as commander-in-chief of the armed forces, the authority to make treaties with the consent of the Senate, and the authority to "appoint Ambassadors, other public Ministers and Consuls, the Judges of the supreme Court, and all other Officers of the United States." Other sections of Article II instruct the president to report directly to Congress "from time to time," in what has come to be known as the "State of the Union Address," and to "take Care that the Laws be faithfully executed." Section 4 provides the mechanism for removal of the president, vice president, and other officers of the United States for "Treason, Bribery, or other high Crimes and Misdemeanors" (see Chapter 7).

Article III: The Judicial Branch. Article III establishes a Supreme Court and defines its jurisdiction. During the Philadelphia meeting, the small and large states differed significantly as to the desirability of an independent judiciary, and on the role of state courts in the national court system. The smaller states feared that a strong unelected judiciary would trample on their liberties. In compromise, Congress was permitted, but not required, to establish lower national courts. Thus, state courts and the national court system would exist side by side with distinct areas of authority. Federal courts were given authority to decide cases arising under federal law. The Supreme Court was also given the power to settle disputes between states, or between a state and the national government.

Although some delegates to the convention had urged that the president be allowed to remove federal judges, ultimately judges were given appointments for life, presuming "good behavior." And, like the president's, their salaries cannot be lowered while they hold office. This provision was adopted to ensure that the legislature did not attempt to punish the Supreme Court or any other judges for unpopular decisions.

Perhaps the most important power of the Supreme Court is that of **judicial review** (the authority of a court to determine the constitutional validity of acts of the legislature), although it is not mentioned in the Constitution. That power would later be assumed by the Court after Chief Justice John Marshall, writing for a unanimous Supreme Court in *Marbury* v. *Madison* (1803), concluded that the power was "implied" in the Constitution (see Chapter 9).

Articles IV through VII. Article IV deals with relations between the state and national governments, and includes the mechanisms for admitting new states to the Union. Article V specifies how amendments can be added to the Constitution. Article VI emphatically announces that the Constitution "shall be the supreme Law of the Land" and requires that all state and national members of the legislature, chief executives, and judicial officers shall swear an oath to support the Constitution. Mindful of the potential problems that could occur if church and state were too enmeshed, this article specifies that no religious test shall be required for holding any office. The seventh and final article of the Constitution concerns the procedures for ratification of the new Constitution: Nine of the thirteen states would have to agree to, or ratify, its new provisions.

President Clinton giving his second State of the Union Address on January 24, 1995. While the Constitution requires only that the president report to Congress from time to time on the state of the union, over the years an annual State of the Union message has become a regular event, attended with much pomp and circumstance. Clinton's first address to Congress in January 1993 was not technically a "State of the Union" address because he had only recently assumed office.

The Drive for Ratification

While delegates to the Constitutional Convention labored in Philadelphia, the Second Continental Congress continued to govern the former colonies under the Articles of Confederation. The day after the Constitution was signed, William Jackson, the secretary of the Constitutional Convention, left for New York City, then the nation's capital, to deliver the official copy of the document to the Congress. He also took with him a resolution of the delegates calling upon each of the states to vote on the new Constitution. Anticipating resistance from the representatives in the state legislatures, however, the Framers required the states to call special ratifying conventions to consider the proposed Constitution.

Judicial review The authority of a court to review the acts of the legislature, the executive, or states to determine their constitutionality; enunciated by Chief Justice John Marshall in *Marbury* v. *Madison* (1803).

The Motives of the Framers

♦ ♦ ♦

Debate about the Framers' motives filled the air during the ratification struggle and has provided grist for the mill of historians and political scientists over the years. Anti-Federalists, who opposed the new Constitution, charged that Federalist supporters of the Constitution were a self-serving, landed, and propertied elite with a vested interest in the capitalistic system that had evolved in the colonies. Federalists countered that they were simply trying to preserve the nation.

In his *Economic Interpretation of the Constitution of the United States* (1913), the highly respected political scientist and historian Charles A. Beard argued that the 1780s were a "critical period" (as the time under governance by the Articles of Confederation had come to be known) not for the nation as a whole, but rather for businessmen. These men feared that a weak, decentralized government could harm their economic interests. Beard argued that the merchants wanted a strong national government to promote industry and trade, protect private property, and most importantly, ensure payment of the public debt—much of which was owed to them. Therefore, according to Beard, the Constitution represents "an economic document drawn with su-

perb skill by men whose property interests were immediately at stake."*

By the 1950s this view had fallen into disfavor when other historians were unable to find direct links between wealth and the Framers' motives for establishing the Constitution. In the 1960s, however, another group of historians began to argue that social and economic factors were, in fact, important motives for supporting the Constitution. In *The Anti-Federalists* (1961), Jackson Turner Main posited that while the Constitution's supporters might not have been the united group of creditors suggested by Beard, they were wealthier, came from high social strata, and had greater concern for maintaining the prevailing social order than the general public.

In 1969, Gordon Wood's *The Creation of the American Republic* resurrected this debate. Wood deemphasized economics to argue that major social divisions explained different groups' support for (or opposition to) the new Constitution. He concluded that the Framers were representatives of a class that favored order and stability over some of the more radical ideas that had inspired the Revolution.

* Quoted in Richard N. Current, et al., *American History: A Survey*, 6th ed. (N.Y.: Knopf, 1983), p. 170.

Jackson carried a letter from General George Washington with the proposed Constitution. In a few eloquent words, Washington summed up the sentiments of the Framers and the spirit of compromise that had permeated the long weeks in Philadelphia:

> That it will meet the full and entire approbation of every state is not perhaps to be expected, but each [state] will doubtless consider, that had her interest alone been consulted, the consequences might have been particularly disagreeable or injurious to others; that it is liable to as few exceptions as could reasonably have been expected, we hope and believe; that it may promote lasting welfare of that country so dear to us all, and secure her freedom and happiness is our ardent wish.[19]

The Second Continental Congress immediately accepted the work of the convention and forwarded the proposed constitution to the states for their vote. It was by no means certain, however, that the new constitution would be adopted.

From the fall of 1787 to the summer of 1788, the proposed constitution was debated hotly around the nation. State politicians understandably feared a strong central government. Farmers and other working class people were fearful of a distant national government. And those who had accrued substantial debts during the economic chaos following the Revolutionary War feared that a new government with a new financial policy would plunge them into even greater debt. The public in general was very leery of taxes—these were the same people who had revolted against the king's taxes. At the heart of many of their concerns was an underlying fear of the massive changes that would be brought about by a new system.

Favoring the Constitution were wealthy merchants, lawyers, bankers, and those who believed that the new nation could not continue to exist under the Articles of Confederation. For them, it all boiled down to one simple question offered by Madison: "Whether or not the Union shall or shall not be continued."

Federalists Versus Anti-Federalists

Almost as soon as the ink was dry on the last signature to the Constitution, those who favored the new strong national government chose to call themselves **Federalists**. They were well aware that many still generally opposed the notion of a strong national government. Thus they did not want to risk being labeled "nationalists," so they tried to get the upper hand in the debate by nicknaming their opponents **Anti-Federalists**. Those put in the latter category insisted that they were instead "Federal Republicans" who believed in a federal system. As noted in Table 2.2, Anti-Federalists argued that they simply wanted to protect state governments from the tyranny of a too powerful national government.[20]

Federalists Those who favored a stronger national government and supported the proposed U.S. Constitution; later became the first U.S. political party.

Anti-Federalists Those who favored strong state governments and a weak national government; opposed the ratification of the U.S. Constitution.

Table 2.2 ◆ Federalists and Anti-Federalists Compared		
	FEDERALISTS	ANTI-FEDERALISTS
Who were they?	Property owners, landed rich, merchants of Northeast and Middle Atlantic states	Small farmers, shopkeepers, laborers
Political philosophy	Elitist: saw themselves and those of their class as most fit to govern (others were to *be* governed)	Believed in decency of common man and in participatory democracy; viewed elites as corrupt; sought greater protection of individual rights
Type of government favored	Powerful central government; two-house legislature; upper house (six-year term) further removed from the people, whom they did not trust	Wanted stronger state governments (closer to the people) at the expense of the powers of the national government. Sought smaller electoral districts, frequent elections, referendum and recall, large unicameral legislature to provide for greater class and occupational representation
Alliances	Pro-British Anti-French	Anti-British Pro-French

Federalists and Anti-Federalists participated in the mass meetings that were held in state legislatures to discuss the pros and cons of the new plan. Tempers ran high at public meetings where differences between the opposing groups were highlighted. Fervent debates were published in newspapers. Indeed, newspapers played a powerful role in the adoption process. The entire Constitution, in fact, was printed in the *Pennsylvania Packet* just two days after the convention's end. Other major papers quickly followed suit. Soon, articles on both sides of the adoption issue began to appear around the nation, often written under pseudonyms such as "Caesar" or "Constant Reader," as was the custom of the day.

One name stood out from all the rest: "Publius" (Latin for "the people"). Between October 1787 and May 1788, eighty-five articles written under that pen name routinely appeared in newspapers in New York, a state where ratification was in doubt. Most were written by Alexander Hamilton and James Madison. Hamilton, a young, fiery New Yorker born in the British West Indies, wrote fifty-one, Madison wrote twenty-six, and jointly they penned another three. John Jay, also of New York, and later the first Chief Justice of the United States, wrote five of the pieces. These eighty-five essays became known as ***The Federalist Papers.***[21]

The Federalist Papers A series of eighty-five political papers written by John Jay, Alexander Hamilton, and James Madison in support of ratification of the U.S. Constitution.

Today, *The Federalist Papers* are considered masterful explanations of the Framers' intentions as they drafted the new Constitution. At the time, although they were reprinted widely, they were far too theoretical to have much impact on those who would ultimately vote on the proposed Constitution. Dry and scholarly, they lacked the fervor of much of the political rhetoric that was then in use. *The Federalist Papers* did, however, highlight the reasons for the structure of the new government and its benefits. According to *Federalist No. 10,* for example, the new Constitution was called "a republican remedy for the disease incident to republican government." Moreover, these musings of Madison, Hamilton, and Jay continue to be the best single source of the political theories and philosophies at the heart of our Constitution.

Forced on the defensive, the Anti-Federalists responded with their own series of "letters" written under the pen names of "Brutus" and "Cato," two ancient Romans famous for their intolerance of tyranny. These "letters" (actually essays) undertook a line-by-line critique of the Constitution and were designed to counteract *The Federalist Papers*.

Anti-Federalists argued that a strong central government would render the states powerless.[22] They stressed the strengths the government had been granted under the Articles, and argued that these Articles, not the proposed Constitution, created a true federal system. Moreover, they argued that the strong national government would tax heavily, that the Supreme Court would overwhelm the states by invalidating state laws, and that the president eventually would have too much power, as commander-in-chief of a large and powerful army.

In particular, the Anti-Federalists feared the power of the national government to run roughshod over the liberties of the people. They proposed that the taxing power of Congress be limited, that the executive be curbed by a council, that the military consist of state militias rather than a national force, and that the jurisdiction of the Supreme Court be limited to prevent it from reviewing and potentially overturning the decisions of state courts. But their most effective argument concerned the absence of a bill of rights in the Constitution.

James Madison answered these criticisms in *Federalists Nos. 10* and *51*. In *Federalist No. 10,* he pointed out that the voters would not always succeed in electing "enlightened statesmen" as their representatives. The greatest threat to individual liberties would therefore come from factions within the government, who might place narrow

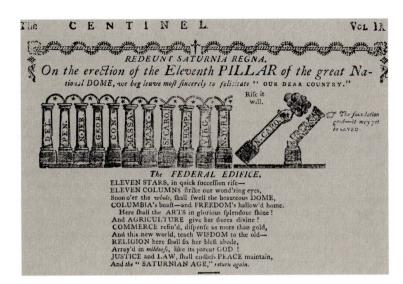

The FEDERAL EDIFICE.

With the Constitution ratified in eleven states and only North Carolina and Rhode Island still uncommitted, cartoonists celebrated certain victory.

interests above broader national interests and the rights of citizens. While recognizing that no form of government could protect the country from unscrupulous politicians, Madison argued that the organization of the new government would minimize the effects of political factions. The great advantage of a federal system, Madison maintained, was that it created the "happy combination" of a national government too large to be controlled by any single faction, and several state governments that would be smaller and more responsive to local needs. Moreover, he argued in *Federalist No. 51* that the proposed federal government's separation of powers would prohibit any one branch from either dominating the national government or violating the rights of citizens.

Debate continued in the thirteen states as votes were taken from December 1787 to June 1788, in accordance with the ratifying process laid out in Article VII of the proposed Constitution. Three states acted quickly to ratify the new Constitution. Two small states, Delaware and New Jersey, voted to ratify before the large states could rethink the notion of equal representation of the states in the Senate. Pennsylvania, where Federalists were well organized, was one of the first three states to ratify. Massachusetts assented to the new government but tempered its support by calling for an immediate addition of amendments including one protecting personal rights. New Hampshire became the crucial ninth state to ratify on June 21, 1788. This action completed the ratification process outlined in Article VII of the Constitution and marked the beginning of a new nation. But because New York and Virginia (which between them accounted for more than 40 percent of the new nation's population) had not yet ratified the Constitution, the practical future of the new nation remained in doubt.

Hamilton in New York and Madison in Virginia worked feverishly to convince delegates to their state conventions to vote for the new government. In New York, sentiment against it was high. In Albany, New York, fighting broke out over the proposed Constitution, resulting in injuries and death. While *The Federalist Papers* undoubtedly had some impact on the delegates, the support of prestigious backers such as Benjamin Franklin and George Washington also helped the ratification effort. Washington, in fact, was widely reported to say, "There is more wickedness than ignorance in Anti-Federalism." When news of Virginia's acceptance of the Constitution reached the New

York convention, Hamilton was finally able to convince a majority of those present to follow suit by a narrow margin (thirty to twenty-seven). Both states also recommended the addition of a series of structural amendments, and a bill of rights.

Two of the original states—North Carolina and Rhode Island—continued to hold out against ratification. Both had recently printed new currencies and feared that values would plummet in a federal system where the Congress was authorized to coin money. On August 2, 1788, North Carolina became the first state to reject the Constitution on the ground that no Anti-Federalist amendments were included. Soon after Congress submitted a Bill of Rights in September 1789, North Carolina ratified the Constitution by a vote of 194 to 77. Rhode Island, the only state that had not sent representatives to Philadelphia, remained out of the Union until 1790. Finally, under threats from its largest cities to secede from the state, the legislature called a convention that ratified the Constitution by a very narrow vote (34 to 32) one year after George Washington became the first president of the United States.

Amending the Constitution

Once the Constitution was ratified, elections were held. When Congress convened, it immediately sent a set of amendments to the states for their ratification. An amendment authorizing the enlargement of the House of Representatives and another to prevent members of the House from raising their own salaries failed to garner favorable votes in the necessary three-fourths of the states (see "The Twenty-Seventh [Madison] Amendment," p. 52; it was ultimately ratified more than 200 years after it was sent to the states). The remaining ten amendments, known as the **Bill of Rights**, were ratified by 1791 in accordance with the procedures set out in the Constitution (see Table 2.3). Sought by Anti-Federalists as a protection for individual liberties, they offered numerous specific limitations on the national government's ability to interfere with a wide variety of personal liberties, some of which were already guaranteed by many state constitutions (see Chapters 4 and 5).

Bill of Rights The first ten amendments to the U.S. Constitution guaranteeing specific rights and liberties; ratified in 1791.

The Bill of Rights includes numerous specific protections of personal rights. Freedom of expression, speech, press, religion, and assembly are guaranteed by the First Amendment. The Bill of Rights also contains numerous safeguards for those accused of crimes.

In addition to guaranteeing these important rights, two of the amendments of the Bill of Rights were reactions to British rule—the right to bear arms (Second Amendment) and the right not to have soldiers quartered in private homes (Third Amendment). More general rights are also included in the Bill of Rights. The Ninth Amendment notes that these enumerated rights are *not* inclusive, meaning they are not the only rights to be enjoyed by the people, and the Tenth Amendment states that powers not given to the national government are reserved by the states or the people.

Article V of the Constitution creates a two-stage amendment process: proposal and ratification.[23] The Constitution specifies two ways to accomplish each stage. As illustrated in Figure 2-4, amendments to the Constitution can be proposed by:

1. A vote of two-thirds of the members in both houses of Congress, or
2. A vote of two-thirds of the state legislatures specifically requesting Congress to call a national convention to propose amendments.

Table 2.3 ◆ The Bill of Rights*	
First Amendment	Freedom of religion, speech, press, and assembly
Second Amendment	The right to bear arms
Third Amendment	Prohibition against quartering of troops in private homes
Fourth Amendment	Prohibition against unreasonable searches and seizures
Fifth Amendment	Rights guaranteed to the accused: requirement for grand jury indictment; protections against double jeopardy, self-incrimination; guarantee due process
Sixth Amendment	Right to a speedy and public trial before an impartial jury, to cross-examine witnesses, and to have counsel
Seventh Amendment	Right to a trial by jury in civil suits
Eighth Amendment	Prohibition against excessive bail and fines, and cruel and unusual punishment
Ninth Amendment	Rights not listed in the Constitution retained by the people
Tenth Amendment	States or people reserve those powers not denied to them by the Constitution or delegated to the national government

*For full text of the Bill of Rights, see Appendix II.

The second method has never been used. Historically, it has served as a fairly effective threat, forcing Congress to consider amendments that might otherwise never have been debated. In the 1980s, for example, several states called on Congress to enact a balanced-budget amendment. To forestall the need for a special constitutional convention, Congress enacted the Gramm-Rudman-Hollings Act, which called for a balanced budget. When that Act proved ineffective, the 104th Congress took up the issue of passage of a Balanced Budget Amendment as one of its planks in what Republicans term their "Contract with America."

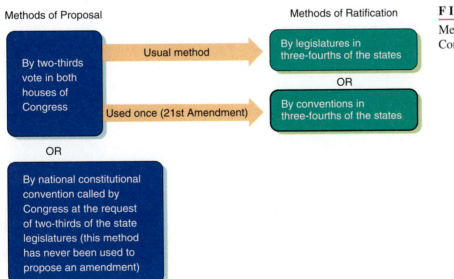

FIGURE 2-4

Methods of Amending the Constitution

Of the ten thousand-plus amendments that have been introduced on one or both floors of the Congress, only thirty-three mustered the two-thirds vote required for them to be sent to the states for debate and ratification through 1994 and only six proposed amendments sent to the states failed to be ratified.

The ratification process is fairly straightforward. When Congress votes to propose an amendment, the Constitution specifies that the ratification process must occur in one of two ways:

1. A favorable vote in three-fourths of the state legislatures, or
2. A favorable vote in specially called ratifying conventions in three-fourths of the states.

The Constitution itself, however, was to be ratified by specifically called ratifying conventions. The Framers feared that the power of special interests in state legislatures would prevent a positive vote on the new Constitution. Since ratification of the Constitution, however, only one ratifying convention has been called. The Eighteenth Amendment, which caused the "Prohibition Era" by outlawing the sale of alcoholic beverages, was ratified by the first method—a vote in state legislatures. Millions broke the law, others died from drinking homemade liquor, and others made their fortunes selling bootleg or illegal liquor. After a decade of these problems, Congress decided to act. An additional amendment—the Twenty-first—was proposed to repeal the Eighteenth Amendment. It was sent to the states for ratification, but with a call for ratifying conventions, *not* a vote in the state legislatures.[24] Members of Congress correctly predicted that the move to repeal the Eighteenth Amendment would encounter opposition in the statehouses, which were largely controlled by conservative rural interests. Thus, Congress's decision to use the convention method led to quick approval of the Twenty-first Amendment.

The intensity of efforts to amend the Constitution has varied considerably depending on the nature of the change proposed. Whereas the Twenty-First Amendment took only ten months to ratify, an equal rights amendment (ERA) was introduced in every session of Congress from 1923 until 1972, when Congress finally voted favorably on it.

Even then, years of lobbying by women's groups were insufficient to garner necessary state support. By 1982, the congressionally mandated date for ratification, only thirty-five states—three short of the number required—had voted favorably on the amendment.[25]

Amendments passed after the Bill of Rights can be organized into four categories: (1) those effecting a structural change in government, (2) those affecting public policy, (3) those expanding rights, and (4) those overruling a U.S. Supreme Court decision.

Most amendments that change the structure or mechanics of government have been ratified quite easily in response to some sort of "emergency." In the wake of President John F. Kennedy's assassination in 1963, which left the nation without a vice president when Lyndon B. Johnson became president, the Twenty-Fifth Amendment was added to the Constitution to allow the president to fill, subject to the approval of Congress, a vacancy in the office of vice president. For the most part, the public has accepted the structural changes as a natural working out of the kinks in the Constitution.

Amendments expanding rights, especially those concerned with enlarging the electorate, make up the next significant group of amendments. Generally, once these amendments secure congressional favor, state ratification follows quickly. For exam-

THEN AND NOW

The Constitution and the Right to Vote

On March 31, 1776, Abigail Adams wrote to her husband, John, in attendance at the Continental Congress, urging him to "Remember the Ladies" in any "new Code of Laws" that was to be written. She urged him and other delegates to "be more generous . . . to them than [their] ancestors." And, she warned, ultimately women would not consider themselves "bound by any Laws in which [they had] no voice, or Representation."* In spite of Abigail Adams's admonitions, neither the Articles of Confederation nor the Constitution mention women.

While the Constitution begins with the ringing words "We the People," at the time the Constitution was ratified, *no* state allowed women to vote in their state elections (Article I specifies that each state could set qualifications for voters in national elections). Nor could women hold state or national elective office. Moreover, the Constitution makes frequent use of the masculine pronouns "him" and "he."

* Quoted in H. L. Butterfield, et al., eds. *The Book of Abigail and John* (Cambridge, MA: Harvard University Press, 1975), p. 21.

It was not only women who were denied participation in ratification of the Constitution. Most states had stringent land-owning or property requirements. Thus, few poor men could vote, either.

Over the years, states eliminated most of the restrictions on voter eligibility. After the Civil War, in spite of the complaints of many women, the Fourteenth Amendment was added to the Constitution. For the first time the term *male* was specifically introduced into that document. Adding insult to injury, passage of the Fifteenth Amendment guaranteeing the right to vote to newly freed male slaves soon followed, without a provision to guarantee women the same right. Women did not secure the right to vote until the 1920 passage of the Nineteenth Amendment.

In 1971, fifty-one years after passage of the Nineteenth Amendment, the Constitution was again altered to expand the electorate. In 1971, the Twenty-Sixth Amendment, guaranteeing the right to vote to all U.S. citizens "eighteen years of age or older" was formally adopted. Today, no constitutional bans exist on voting, yet many citizens choose not to exercise this right so hard fought for by many groups.

ple, women tried for decades to secure a constitutional amendment guaranteeing their right to vote, yet once Congress voted favorably on the Nineteenth Amendment, ratification by the states took less than two years.[26]

Amendments designed to affect existing public policies form a third category of constitutional amendments. Many constitutional scholars regard these amendments as troublesome. They argue that the Constitution should be a basic outline of principles, and not a list of desired outcomes. Critics today, for example, fear that efforts to amend the Constitution to prohibit flag burning, allow prayer in schools, or ban abortions would be foolhardy and unnecessary interference with the basic nature of the Constitution. The first two are regarded as particularly risky because they would alter the First Amendment, which to this day has never been modified.

A final category of amendments consists of those enacted to overrule specific Supreme Court decisions. As discussed in greater detail in Chapter 9, the Supreme Court is the final authority on the Constitution. Once the Court construes a provision of the Constitution, only the Court itself or a constitutional amendment can change

The Twenty-Seventh (Madison) Amendment
◆ ◆ ◆

On June 8, 1789, in a speech before the House of Representatives, James Madison stated,

> [T]here is seeming impropriety in leaving any set of men without controul [sic] to put their hand into the public coffers, to take out money to put into their pockets. . . . I have gone therefore so far as to fix it, that no law, varying the compensation, shall operate until there is a change in the legislation.

When Madison spoke these words about his proposal, now known as the Twenty-Seventh Amendment, he had no way of knowing that more than two centuries would pass before it would become an official part of the Constitution. In fact, Madison deemed it worthy of addition only because the conventions of three states (Virginia, New York, and North Carolina) had demanded that it be included.

By 1791, when the Bill of Rights (see Table 2.3, p. 49) was added to the Constitution, only six states had ratified Madison's amendment, and it seemed destined to fade into obscurity. In 1982, however, Gregory Watson, a sophomore majoring in economics at the University of Texas-Austin, discovered the unratified compensation amendment while looking for a paper topic for an American government class. Intrigued, Watson wrote a paper arguing that the proposed amendment was still viable because it had no internal time limit and, therefore, should be adopted. Watson received a "C" on the paper.

Despite his grade, Watson began a ten-year, $6,000 self-financed crusade to renew interest in the compensation amendment. Watson and his allies reasoned that the amendment should be revived because of the public's growing anger with the fact that members of Con-

Gregory Watson with a document that contains the first ten amendments to the constitution, as well as the compensation amendment ("Article the second: No law varying the compensation for the services of the Senators and Representatives shall take effect until an election of Representatives shall have intervened") that was finally ratified as the Twenty-Seventh Amendment in 1992.

gress had sought to raise their salaries without going on the record as having done so. Watson's perseverance paid off, and on May 7, 1992, the amendment was ratified. On May 18, the United States Archivist certified that the amendment was part of the Constitution, a decision that was overwhelmingly confirmed by the House of Representatives on May 19 and by the Senate on May 20.

At the same time that the Senate approved the Twenty-Seventh Amendment, it also took action to ensure that a similar situation never occurred by declaring "dead" four other amendments that did not have internal deadlines.

Source: Fordham Law Review, December 1992, pp. 497–539, and Anne Marie Kilday, "Amendment Expert Agrees with Congressional Pay Ruling." *The Dallas Morning News,* February 14, 1993: p. 13A.

that interpretation. Through 1995, only two of the Supreme Court's decisions have been overruled by constitutional amendments.

Informal Methods of Amending the Constitution

The formal amendment process is not the only way that the Constitution has been changed over time. Judicial interpretation, cultural change, and technological change also have had a major impact on the way the Constitution has evolved.

Judicial Interpretation.   As early as 1803, under the brilliant leadership of Chief Justice John Marshall, the Supreme Court declared that the federal courts had the power to nullify acts of the nation's government when they were found to be in conflict with the Constitution. Over the years this check on the other branches of government and on the states has increased the authority of the Court and has significantly altered the meaning of various provisions of the Constitution, a fact that prompted Woodrow Wilson to call the Supreme Court "a constitutional convention in continuous session."

When the Framers authorized Congress to regulate commerce among the states, they could not have imagined the controversial course that interpretation of that authorizing clause would take. In *Gibbons* v. *Ogden* (1824), Chief Justice Marshall proclaimed that commerce was "any intercourse between states," including navigation. This interpretation allowed Congress to increase its regulatory activity. Later, in the 1930s, a pro-business Court interpreted the commerce clause very narrowly as it repeatedly ruled unconstitutional legislation backed by President Franklin D. Roosevelt, designed to bring the country out of the economic chaos of the Depression. It was not until 1937—in the face of strong public pressure and the threat of congressional attacks—that the Court reinterpreted the commerce clause to find constitutional justification for such sweeping congressional power. Since that time, most congressional efforts to regulate any form of business or employment practice have been held to be within the scope of Congress's power under the commerce clause.

Today, some argue that the original intent of the Framers, as evidenced in *The Federalist Papers* as well as in private notes taken by James Madison at the Constitutional Convention, should govern judicial interpretation of the Constitution.[27] Others argue that the Framers knew that a changing society needed an elastic, flexible document that could conform to the ages.[28] In all likelihood, the vagueness of the document was purposeful. Those in attendance in Philadelphia recognized that they could not agree on everything and that it was wiser to leave interpretation to those who would follow them.

Social and Cultural Change.   Even the most far-sighted of those in attendance at the constitutional convention could not have anticipated the vast changes that have occurred in the United States. For example, although many were uncomfortable with the Three-Fifths Compromise and others hoped for the abolition of slavery, none could have imagined the status of African Americans today, or that Colin Powell could serve as Chairman of the Joint Chiefs of Staff and be frequently mentioned as a viable candidate for president or vice president in 1992 and 1996. Likewise, few of the Framers could have anticipated the diverse roles that women would come to play in American society. The Constitution has often been bent to accommodate such social and cultural changes. Thus, although there is no specific amendment guaranteeing women equal protection of the law, the federal courts have interpreted the Constitution to prohibit many forms of gender discrimination, thereby recognizing cultural and societal change.

Technological Change.   Technological innovation has also contributed to a changing Constitution. The Framers could not have envisioned the need for an air traffic control system or for regulation of the airwaves. In 1995, for example, instantaneous forms of communication allowed many Americans to watch in horror as the federal building in Oklahoma City, Oklahoma, continued to burn after it was destroyed by a terrorist bomb two years after the compound in Waco, Texas, was enveloped in flames, killing at least eighty-five cult members. Moreover, as computers and other technological advances

The bombing in Oklahoma City not only revealed the stark horror of domestic terrorism, it immediately led to calls for changes in many laws affecting gun control and civil liberties.

The Contract with America and Constitutional Amendments

◆ ◆ ◆

The Republicans' Contract with America contains several provisions that most scholars agree will require several amendments to the Constitution. At no other period in American history since the adoption of the first ten Bill of Rights has Congress so seriously been debating so many new amendments, a fact that disturbs some who believe that the Constitution should be amended only after both Congress and the states have had the opportunity to carefully deliberate each proposed amendment and its pos-

sible effects. Although it is unlikely that all of these will soon result in constitutional amendments, among some key planks in the Contract with America initially appearing to require constitutional amendments are:

1. A Balanced Budget Amendment
2. The Line Item Veto
3. Congressional Term Limits
4. A Prayer in School Amendment (although not part of the Contract, the Speaker has also spoken of his desire to add an amendment of this nature to the Constitution).

have allowed the government and, in particular, the bureaucracy (see Chapter 8) to grow, our expectations of the role of government have also changed. It is unlikely that the Framers could have envisioned a Social Security system that has the capacity to mail more than 35 million checks per month to retirees and the disabled.

Advances in technology have required new interpretations of the Bill of Rights. Wiretapping and other forms of electronic surveillance, for example, are now regulated by the First and Fourth Amendments. Similarly, HIV testing and drug screening, which involve scientifically advanced tests, must be juxtaposed against constitutional protections.

Toward Reform

When asked in a May 1987 CBS News/New York Times poll, "Do you think it is too easy or too hard to amend the Constitution, or is the process about right?" 11 percent of those polled responded, "Too easy"; 20 percent responded, "Too hard"; and 60 percent responded, "About right." A Gallup poll conducted the same year found that 72 percent of those questioned believed that a modern constitutional convention might make things worse, but 44 percent expressed their belief that the "Constitution needs basic changes." (Some of these respondents may have been ardent supporters of the ERA or a Right to Life Amendment, who continue to believe that the Constitution should be amended.)

When the Framers met in Philadelphia in 1787, they sought to fashion a constitution that would provide the basic framework for running the nation in 1787 and also well into the future. Since ratification of the Bill of Rights in 1791 through 1994, only seventeen amendments have been added, and only fifteen continue to be functional (the Twenty-First Amendment repealed the Eighteenth Amendment). The basic framework of government, although "reformed" considerably over time through informal means, remains vital today. Emotionally charged calls for change often have occurred in the wake of highly unpopular Supreme Court decisions such as *Texas* v. *Johnson* (1989), in which the justices ruled that flag burning was a form of political speech protected by the First Amendment. Politicians, veterans' groups, and members of the general public all immediately clamored for passage of a constitutional amendment to limit the reach of the First Amendment and expressly to prohibit flag burning. But, as time passed, cooler heads prevailed, and this move to amend the Constitution failed to make headway, although some members of Congress plan to reintroduce the proposed amendment.

As early as 1889, James Bryce argued that the Constitution had two major defects—too much power was divided between the president and Congress to allow for prompt and effective action, and the system of checks and balances caused excessive friction between these two branches.[29] Many of these problems continue to the present day. The Committee on the Constitutional System (CCS), an influential non-partisan group of more than 200 former members of Congress, former Cabinet officials, and political scientists, has made several serious proposals to stop this "gridlock."[30] Political scientist and CCS member James L. Sundquist, for example, has written extensively about the negative effects of "divided government;" that is, the situation that results when Congress and the President come from different political parties.[31] Since the Framers did not envision the role of political parties in the system, the separation of powers and checks and balances schemes that unify the national government can become gridlocked when different political parties control the legislative and executive branches of government. Although he admits that it would be politically and practically infeasible, Sundquist has suggested altering the electoral system to prohibit split ticket voting (i.e., voting for a Democrat for Congress and a Republican for President in national elections).

Prohibitions against split ticket voting could take several forms, such as allowing voters to select from political "teams" of candidates composed of a single party's candidates for president, vice president, Senate and House,[32] or requiring a party's congressional candidates to be its candidates for electors in the electoral college. Other proposed reforms include making the American system operate more like the British: whenever divided government became gridlocked, either the president or the majority of both Houses of Congress could dissolve the government and call for new elections.[33]

While these suggestions for reform provide food for thought, the CCS admits that these ideas would not be greeted with open arms in the Congress, where under normal constitutional amendment procedures, such changes would have to be initiated. While these proposals aren't particularly "hot" topics among most legislators today, others are. Thus, in view of cries for dramatic governmental reform (see p. 54) several important amendments are being debated that could have wide-ranging consequences on how government works, as well as on some personal liberties.

Summary

The U.S. Constitution has proven to be a remarkably enduring document. In explaining how and why the Constitution came into being, this chapter has covered the following points:

1. While settlers came to the New World for a variety of reasons, most remained loyal to Great Britain and con-

sidered themselves subjects of the king. Over the years, those ties weakened as new generations of Americans were born on colonial soil. A series of taxes levied by the Crown ultimately led the colonists to convene a Continental Congress and to declare their independence.

2. The Declaration of Independence (1776), which drew heavily on the writings of John Locke, carefully enu-

merated the wrongs of the Crown and galvanized public resentment and willingness to take up arms against Great Britain in the Revolutionary War (1775–1782).

3. The Articles of Confederation (1781) created a loose league of friendship between the new national government and the states. Numerous weaknesses in the new government became apparent by 1784. Among the major flaws were Congress's inability to tax or regulate commerce, the absence of an executive to administer the government, and a weak central government.

4. When the weaknesses under the Articles of Confederation became apparent, the states called for a meeting to reform them. The Constitutional Convention (1787) quickly threw out the Articles of Confederation and fashioned a new, more workable form of government. The Constitution was the result of a series of compromises, including those over representation questions involving large and small states, and over how to determine population. Compromises were also made about how members of each branch of government were to be selected. The electoral college was created to give states a key role in the selection of the president.

5. The proposed U.S. Constitution created a federal system that drew heavily on Montesquieu's ideas about separation of powers; that is, a way of parcelling out power among the three branches of government, and checks and balances to prevent any one branch from having too much power.

6. The drive for ratification became a fierce fight between Federalists and Anti-Federalists. Federalists lobbied for the strong national government created by the Constitution; Anti-Federalists favored greater state power.

7. The Framers created a formal two-stage amendment process to include the Congress and the states. Amendments could be proposed by a two-thirds vote in Congress or of state legislatures, requesting that Congress call a national convention to propose amendments. Amendments could be ratified by a positive vote of three-fourths of the state legislatures or specially called state ratifying conventions. Judicial interpretation and cultural and technological changes have also caused constitutional change.

Key Terms

common law

Articles of Confederation

Stamp Act Congress

Committees of Correspondence

First Continental Congress

Second Continental Congress

Declaration of Independence

confederation

Shays's Rebellion

Virginia Plan

bicameral legislature

New Jersey Plan

Great Compromise

Three-Fifths Compromise

unitary government

federal system

separation of powers

checks and balances

enumerated powers

elastic clause

judicial review

Federalists

Anti-Federalists

The Federalist Papers

Bill of Rights

Suggested Readings

Bailyn, Bernard. *The Ideological Origins of the American Revolution.* Cambridge, MA: Harvard University Press, 1967.

Beard, Charles. *An Economic Interpretation of the Constitution of the United States.* New York: Macmillan, 1913.

Bernstein, Richard B. and Jerome Agel. Amending America. New York: Random House, 1992.

Bowen, Catherine Drinker. *Miracle at Philadelphia.* Boston: Little-Brown, 1966.

Hamilton, Alexander, James Madison, and John Jay. *The Federalist Papers,* ed. Isaac Kramnick. New York: Penguin, 1987 (first published in 1788).

Ketchman, Ralph. *The Anti-Federalist Papers and the Constitutional Convention Debated.* New York: New American Library, 1986.

Levy, Leonard W., ed. *Essays on the Making of the Constitution.* New York: Oxford University Press, 1969.

McDonald, Forest. *The Formation of the American Republic.* New York: Penguin, 1967.

Main, Jackson Turner. *The Social Structure of Revolutionary America.* Princeton, NJ: Princeton University Press, 1965.

Rossiter, Clinton. *1787: Grand Convention.* New York: Macmillan, 1966.

Wood, Gordon S. *The Creation of the American Republic.* Chapel Hill: University of North Carolina Press, 1969.

Federalism

THE ROOTS OF THE FEDERAL SYSTEM

THE EVOLUTION AND DEVELOPMENT OF FEDERALISM

THE NEW DEAL AND A RAPIDLY CHANGING BALANCE OF POWER

THE CHANGING NATURE OF FEDERALISM

THE INTERGOVERNMENTAL LOBBY

FEDERALISM AND THE SUPREME COURT

TOWARD REFORM

From its very beginning, the challenge for the United States of America was to preserve the traditional independence and rights of the states while establishing an effective national government. In *Federalist No. 51*, James Madison highlighted the unique structure of governmental powers created by the Framers.

Although most of the delegates to the Constitutional Convention favored a strong federal government, they knew that some compromise about the distribution of powers would be necessary. Some of the Framers wanted to continue with the confederate form of government defined in the Articles of Confederation; others wanted a more centralized system like that of Great Britain. Their solution was to create the world's first **federal system**, in which the thirteen sovereign or independent states were bound together under one national government. The result was a system of government that was "neither wholly *national* nor wholly *federal*," as Madison explained in *The Federalist Papers*.

The nature of the federal relationship between the national government and the states, including their respective duties, obligations, and powers, is outlined in the U.S. Constitution, although the word *federal* does not appear in that document. Throughout history, however, this system and the rules that guide it have been continually stretched, reshaped and reinterpreted by crises, historical evolution, public expectations, and judicial interpretation. All these forces have had tremendous influence on who makes policy decisions and how these decisions get made.

Issues involving the distribution of power between the national government and the states affect you on a daily basis. You do not, for example, need a passport to go from Texas to Oklahoma. There is one national currency and a national minimum wage. But

> The power surrendered by the people is first divided between two distinct governments, and then . . . subdivided among distinct and separate departments. Hence, a double security arises to the rights of the people.
>
> *James Madison*
> *FEDERALIST NO. 51*

The Framers, fearing tyranny, divided powers between the state and the national governments. At each level, moreover, powers were divided among executive, legislative, and judicial branches.

many differences exist among the laws of the various states. The age at which you may marry is a state issue, as are laws governing divorce, child custody, and the purchase of guns. Even before congressional passage of the Brady Bill requiring a five-day waiting period for the purchase of handguns, one-half of the states already required some sort of waiting period.

While some policies or programs are under the authority of the state or local government, others, such as air traffic regulation, are solely within the province of the national government.[1] In many areas, however, the national and state governments work together cooperatively. For example, you may receive national as well as state loans, grants, or other forms of assistance to finance your education. Similarly, many of the poor receive help from the national, state, and local governments. At times the national government cooperates or supports programs only if the states meet certain conditions. In order to receive federal funds for the construction and maintenance of highways, for example, states must follow federal rules about the kinds of roads they build.

In this chapter, we look at the nature of the government created by the Framers, and at their attempt to divide the power and the functions of government between one national and several state governments. We also explore the reasons why a federal system was adopted, and analyze how the relationship and allocation of powers between the national and state governments have changed over time. Crises, public expectations, political ideology, and decisions of the Supreme Court have played especially important roles in the development of what political scientists today mean by federalism. As you read this chapter, keep in mind the arguments made by the Framers in support of the system they created. Are the changes advocated in the 104th Congress designed to make the federal system more or less like the system the Framers intended to fashion?

Federal system Plan of government created by the U.S. Constitution in which power is divided between the national government and the state governments and in which independent states are bound together under one national government.

The Roots of the Federal System

The Framers worked to create a form of government familiar to Americans, but one that would remedy many of the problems experienced under the Articles of Confederation. The relationship between and the intertwined powers of the national and state governments are the heart of **federalism**, which has its origins in the Latin *foedus*, or "covenant." Thus, federalism can be envisioned as the philosophy that defines the allocation of power between the national government and the states. Ironically, as discussed in Chapter 2, those who supported the government under the Articles of Confederation argued for what *they* called a federal system. But the fear of being labeled "nationalists" prompted supporters of the new Constitution to call themselves "Federalists," thus co-opting this popular term of the day. Like other Federalist supporters of the new Constitution, Alexander Hamilton articulated three major arguments for federalism: (1) the prevention of tyranny; (2) the provision for increased participation in politics; and (3) the use of the states as testing grounds or "laboratories" for new policies and programs.

The national government created by the Framers draws its powers directly from the people, so that both national *and* state governments are ultimately directly accountable to the public. Each government also has the ability to tax, and has its own set of public officials. The Framers envisioned each government to be supreme in some spheres, as depicted in Figure 3-1. In *Federalist No. 51,* James Madison explained what he perceived to be the beauty of this system: The shifting support of the electorate between the two governments would serve to keep each in balance.

In fashioning the new federal system of government, the Framers recognized that they could not define precisely how all the relations between the national government and the individual states would work. But the Constitution makes it clear that separate spheres of government were to be at the very core of the federal system, with some allowances made for concurrent powers.

The Powers of Government in the Federal System

The distribution of powers in the federal system is often described as two overlapping circles, as illustrated in Figure 3-1. On the left are powers specifically granted to Congress in Article I. Chief among the exclusive powers delegated to the national government are the authorities to coin money, conduct foreign relations, provide for an army and navy, declare war, and establish a national court system. All of these powers set out in Article I, Section 8 of the Constitution are called **enumerated powers**.

Article I, Section 8 also contains the **necessary and proper clause**, giving Congress the authority to enact any laws "necessary and proper" for carrying out any of its enumerated powers. Thus, for example, Congress's power to charter a national bank (see pp. 63–64) has been held to be an **implied power** derived from its enumerated power to tax and spend.[2]

The Constitution does not specifically delegate or enumerate many specific powers to the states. Because states had all the power at the time the Constitution was written, the Framers felt no need, as they did for the new national government, to list and restate the powers of the states. Article I, however, allows states to set the "Times, Places and Manner, for holding elections for senators and representatives," and Article II requires that each state appoint electors to vote for president. States were also given the power to ratify amendments to the U.S. Constitution. Nevertheless, the enumeration of so many specific powers to the national government and so few to the states is a clear indication of the Federalist leanings of the Framers. It was not until the addition of the Bill of Rights and the Tenth Amendment that the states' powers were better described: "The powers not delegated to the United States by the Constitution, nor prohibited by it to the States, are reserved to the States respectively, or to the people." These powers,

Federalism The philosophy that describes the governmental system created by the Framers. *See also* federal system.

Enumerated powers Seventeen specific powers granted to Congress under Article I, Section 8 of the U.S. Constitution; these powers include taxation, coinage of money, regulation of commerce, and the authority to provide for a national defense.

Necessary and proper (elastic) clause A name given to the "necessary and proper clause" found in the final paragraph of Article I, Section 8 of the U.S. Constitution. It gives Congress the authority to pass all laws "necessary and proper" to carry out the enumerated powers specified in the Constitution.

Implied power A power derived from an enumerated power and the necessary and proper clause. These powers are not stated specifically but are considered to be reasonably implied through the exercise of delegated powers.

FIGURE 3-1

The Distribution of Governmental Power in the Federal System

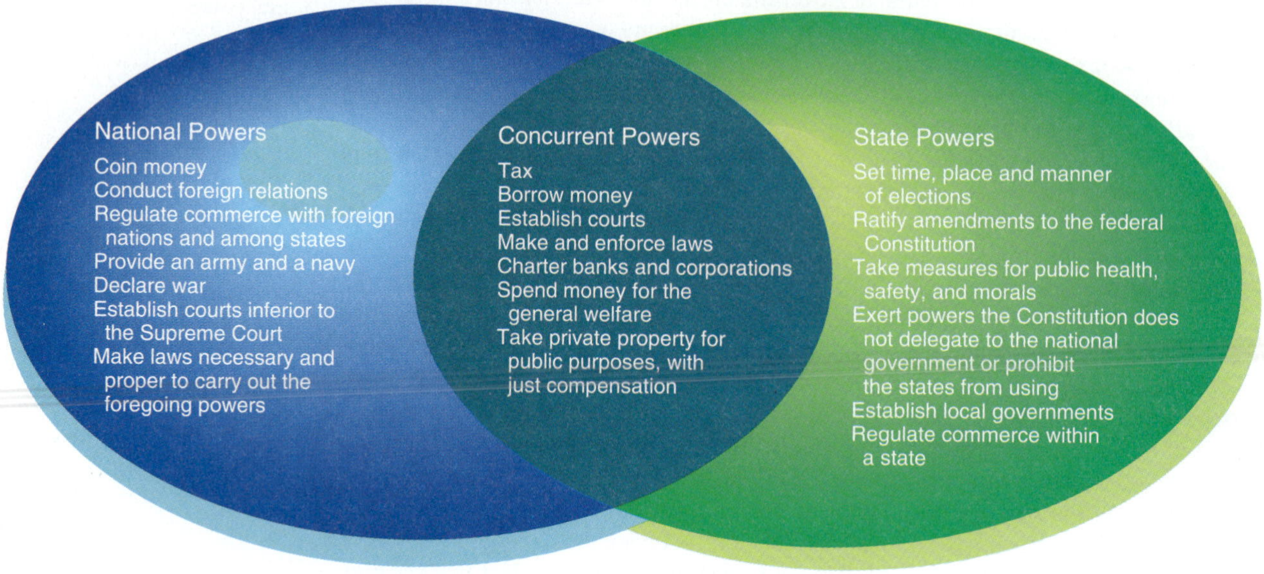

National Powers

Coin money
Conduct foreign relations
Regulate commerce with foreign
  nations and among states
Provide an army and a navy
Declare war
Establish courts inferior to
  the Supreme Court
Make laws necessary and
  proper to carry out the
  foregoing powers

Concurrent Powers

Tax
Borrow money
Establish courts
Make and enforce laws
Charter banks and corporations
Spend money for the
  general welfare
Take private property for
  public purposes, with
  just compensation

State Powers

Set time, place and manner
  of elections
Ratify amendments to the federal
  Constitution
Take measures for public health,
  safety, and morals
Exert powers the Constitution does
  not delegate to the national
  government or prohibit
  the states from using
Establish local governments
Regulate commerce within
  a state

Source: *USA Today*, November 26-28, 1993, p. A1.

often called the states' reserve or police powers, include the ability to legislate for the public health, safety and morals of their citizens.

As revealed in Figure 3-1, national and state powers also overlap. The area where the circles overlap represents **concurrent powers**—powers shared by the national and state governments. States already had the power to tax; the Constitution extended this power to the national government as well. Other important concurrent powers include the right to borrow money, establish courts, and enact and enforce laws necessary to carry out these powers.

Concurrent powers Powers shared by the national and state governments.

Denied Powers. Article I also *denies* certain powers to the national and state governments. In keeping with the Framers' desire to forge a national economy, states are prohibited from entering treaties, coining money, or impairing obligation of contracts.

States are also prohibited from entering into "compacts" with other states without express congressional approval. In a similar vein, Congress is barred from favoring one state over another in regulating commerce, nor can it lay duties on items exported from any state.

Both the national and state governments are denied the authority to take arbitrary actions affecting constitutional rights and liberties. Neither national nor state governments may pass a **bill of attainder**, a law declaring an act illegal without a judicial trial. The Constitution also bars either from passing **ex post facto** laws, laws that make an act punishable as a crime if the action was legal at the time it was committed.

Bill of attainder A law declaring an act illegal without a judicial trial.

Ex post facto law Law passed after the fact, thereby making previously legal activity illegal and subject to current penalty; prohibited by the U.S. Constitution.

Guarantees to the States. In return for giving up some of their powers, the states received several guarantees in the Constitution. Among them:

- Article I guarantees each state two members in the U.S. Senate and guarantees that Congress would not limit slavery before 1808.
- Article IV guarantees the citizens of each state the privileges and immunities of citizens of all other states, guarantees each state a "Republican Form of Government," meaning one that represents the citizens of the state, and guarantees that the national government will protect the states against foreign attacks and domestic rebellion.

Relations Among the States.   The Constitution was designed to improve relations among the squabbling states. To that end, it provides that disputes between states are to be settled directly by the U.S. Supreme Court under its original jurisdiction to avoid any sense of favoritism (see Chapter 9). Moreover, Article IV requires that each state give "Full Faith and Credit . . . to the public Acts, Records and judicial Proceedings of every other State." This clause ensures that judicial decrees and contracts made in one state will be binding and enforceable in another, thereby facilitating trade and other commercial relationships.

In a similar vein, the Constitution requires states to extradite, or return, criminals to states where they have been convicted or are to stand trial. Moreover, Article IV, Section 2 specifies that escaped slaves must be returned to their owners.[3] For example, Willis Lago, a free black man living in Ohio, was accused of helping a female slave from Kentucky escape to Ohio, a free state. In 1861, the Supreme Court ruled that although the governor of Ohio had a *legal* obligation to return Lago to Kentucky for prosecution for his crime, the federal government lacked the power to force the governor to comply, in spite of Article IV.[4] In 1987, however, the Supreme Court ruled that this decision under Article IV must be interpreted in light of the fact that it was made during the Civil War, when the federal government's power over the states was at its lowest ebb. Thus, when the governor of Iowa refused to honor Puerto Rico's request to extradite a man charged with first degree murder, the Court ruled that the extradition clause is binding on the states and is *not* discretionary. Iowa's governor had argued that the charges against the accused were unreasonable, and because the defendant was white, he would be unlikely to receive a fair trial in Puerto Rico.[5] Nevertheless, because the federal government today has the authority to enforce the extradition law, the Court found that Iowa was bound by the Constitution.

National Supremacy.   Even during the Constitutional Convention, the Framers were aware that conflict and friction between the national government and the states was inevitable. Article VI, Section 2 was added to the Constitution to provide a way to resolve these conflicts. It declares that the U.S. Constitution, the Laws of the United States, and its treaties are to be "the supreme Law of the Land; and the Judges in every State shall be bound thereby . . ."

In spite of this explicit language, the meaning of what is called the "**supremacy clause**" has been subject to continuous judicial interpretation and reinterpretation. In *Missouri* v. *Holland* (1920),[6] for example, Missouri sought to prevent a U.S. game warden from enforcing the Migratory Bird Treaty Act of 1918, which prohibited the killing or capturing of many species of birds as they made their annual migration across the international border from Canada to parts of the United States. Missouri argued that the Tenth Amendment, which reserved a state's powers to legislate for the general welfare of its citizens, allowed Missouri to regulate hunting. But the Court ruled that since the treaty was legal, it was the supreme law of the land. Thus, when national law and state law come into conflict, national law (including treaties) is supreme. (See also *McCulloch* v. *Maryland* [1819], pp. 63–64.)

The Port Authority jointly operated by New York and New Jersey is just one example of cooperative ventures of the states approved by Congress. States are encouraged to enter into these kinds of compacts by the nature of our federal system. Before adoption of the U.S. Constitution, the states were not encouraged to share their powers and commerce often suffered.

Supremacy clause Portion of Article IV of the U.S. Constitution that mandates that national law is supreme to (i.e., supersedes) all other laws passed by the states or by any other subdivision of government.

Landmark Periods in the Evolution of the Federal System

1789–1834 ♦ **Nationalization:** The Marshall Court broadly interprets the Constitution to expand and consolidate national power.

1835–1860 ♦ **Dual Federalism:** Phase 1—Power of national government limited to enumerated powers; states consider themselves sovereign; governments in state of tension over scope of their respective authorities.

1861–1933 ♦ **Dual Federalism:** Phase 2—Dual characteristics continue, but national government gains power; land-grant era.

1934–1960 ♦ **Cooperative Federalism:** Dramatic increase in grants-in-aid; federal, state, and local sharing of responsibilities; increased regulation by national government.

1960–1968 ♦ **Creative Federalism:** Hallmark of Johnson era; increased grants to state and local governments and direct aid to individuals.

1968–1993 ♦ **New Federalism:** Emphasis on the return of power to the states; later characterized by the significant reduction in federal aid to the states.

1995 ♦ **"Contract with America" or the "New Covenant":** Possible major restructuring of the federal system.

The Evolution and Development of Federalism

The victory of the Federalists—those who supported a strong national government—had long-lasting consequences on the future of the nation. Over the course of our nation's history, the nature of federalism and its allocation of power between the national government and the states have changed dramatically. And because the distribution of power between the national and state governments is not clearly delineated in the Constitution, over the years the U.S. Supreme Court has played a major role in defining the nature of the federal system.

The Supreme Court

From the beginning, the courts were involved in developing the structure and mechanics of the federal system. At the head of the federal judiciary sat John Marshall (1801–1835), an ardent Federalist. In a series of important decisions, Chief Justice Marshall and the Supreme Court reaffirmed the Federalists' beliefs in a strong national government. Federalist sentiments could be seen especially clearly in the Court's broad interpretations of the Constitution's supremacy clause and the commerce clause, both of which were used to expand and consolidate the power of the national government.

It is important to remember, however, that during the period the Marshall Court was nationalizing the federal system, the national government itself was small, with limited activities and minimal spending. In contrast, the state governments' role in everyday life was far more pervasive than it is today. States exercised tremendous powers over the electoral process (including who voted and how congressional districts were drawn) and were the center of party organizations. States also controlled labor conditions, race relations, education, property rights, criminal and family law, and, in the South, slavery.

***McCulloch* v. *Maryland* (1819).**   *McCulloch* was the first major decision of the Marshall Court to define the relationship between the national and state governments. In 1816 Congress chartered the Second Bank of the United States. (The charter of the First Bank had been allowed to expire.) The Second Bank was never popular and had detractors on several fronts. As was true since the time of Daniel Shays's march on the courthouse in Massachusetts, farmers and the poor had a strong suspicion and hatred of banks. So did many Jeffersonian Democratic-Republicans (see Chapter 11) who believed that the national government lacked the authority to establish a bank. They believed that because the power to issue corporate charters was not granted to Congress by the Constitution, the Bank of the United States was unconstitutional. States also disliked the national bank; it was the largest corporation in the United States and provided stiff competition for state-chartered banks.

In 1818, the Democratic-Republican–controlled Maryland assembly levied a tax requiring all banks not chartered by Maryland (that is, the Second Bank of the United States) to (1) buy stamped paper from the state on which the Second Bank's notes were to be issued, (2) pay the state $15,000 a year, or (3) go out of business. Maryland was not the only state to attempt to tax the U.S. bank out of business. Tennessee, Georgia, Ohio, and North Carolina, for example, enacted laws requiring each branch of the national bank to pay $50,000 to their respective state treasuries to stay in business. Illinois and Indiana, which had no branches of the national bank, passed laws prohibiting their establishment.

James McCulloch, the head cashier of the Baltimore branch of the Bank of the United States, refused to pay the tax, and Maryland brought suit against him. After losing in a Maryland court, McCulloch appealed his conviction to the U.S. Supreme Court by order of the U.S. Secretary of the Treasury. Arguing on behalf of the federal government and for the constitutionality of the Bank was Daniel Webster, a former Federalist member of Congress and one of the best lawyers in the nation. Maryland was represented by Luther Martin, who had been an active opponent of the new Constitution at the Philadelphia Convention. There he had railed against the chains being forged for "his country"—Maryland—and its subjugation to new national power.[7]

Although Chief Justice John Marshall still presided over the Court, only he and one other Federalist justice remained. The other five justices were Democratic-Republicans appointed by Presidents Jefferson and Madison. Nevertheless, in a unanimous opinion, the Court answered the two central questions that had been put to it: First, did Congress have the authority to charter a bank, and, second, if it did, could a state tax it?

As to the first question—whether Congress had the right to establish a bank or another type of corporation, given that the Constitution does not explicitly mention such a power—Chief Justice Marshall's answer continues to stand as the classic exposition of the doctrine of implied powers, and as a reaffirmation of the propriety of a strong national government. Therefore, although the word *bank* cannot be found in the Constitution, the Constitution enumerates powers that give Congress the authority to levy and collect taxes, issue a currency, and borrow funds. From these enumerated powers, Marshall found, it was reasonable to imply that Congress had the power to charter a bank, which could be considered "necessary and proper" to the exercise of its enumerated powers.

In some of the most famous language from the case, Marshall carefully set out an expansive interpretation of the necessary and proper clause of Article I, Section 8, and the possible scope of implied powers, proclaiming:

> Let the end be legitimate, let it be within the scope of the Constitution, and all means which are appropriate, which are plainly adapted to that end, which are not prohibited, but consistent with the letter and spirit of the Constitution, are constitutional.[8]

Marshall next addressed the question of whether a federal bank could be taxed by any state government. To Marshall, this was not a difficult question. The national government was dependent on the people, not the states, for its powers. In addition, Marshall noted, the Constitution specifically calls for the national law to be supreme. Thus, the national government and its "instrumentalities" such as the Bank had to be immune from state interference. "The power to tax involves the power to destroy," wrote Marshall. Thus, the state tax violated the supremacy clause, since states cannot interfere with the operations of the national government, whose laws are supreme.

Gibbons v. Ogden (1824). Shortly after *McCulloch*, the Marshall Court had another opportunity to rule in favor of a broad interpretation of the scope of national power. *Gibbons* involved a dispute that arose after the New York state legislature granted to Robert Fulton the exclusive right to operate steamboats on the Hudson River. Simultaneously, Congress licensed a ship to sail on the same waters. By the time the case reached the Supreme Court, it was complicated both factually and procedurally. Suffice it to say that both New York and New Jersey wanted to control shipping on the lower Hudson River. But, *Gibbons* actually addressed one simple, very important question: What was the scope of Congress's authority under the commerce clause? The states argued that "commerce," as mentioned in Article I, should be interpreted narrowly to include only direct dealings in products. Thus, regulation of shipping on

The *Gibbons* v. *Ogden* decision opened the waters to free competition; this is the New York waterfront in 1839.
New York Public Library, Stokes Collection.

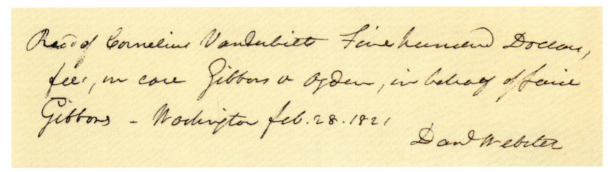

Daniel Webster's 1821 handwritten note to Cornelius Vanderbilt acknowledging receipt of a $500 retainer to represent Thomas Gibbons in the case of *Gibbons* v. *Ogden*.

inland waterways would be beyond the scope of Congress's authority to regulate. In *Gibbons*, however, Chief Justice Marshall ruled that Congress's power to regulate interstate commerce included the power to regulate commercial activity as well, and that the commerce power had no limits *except* those specifically found in the Constitution. Thus, New York had no constitutional authority to grant a monopoly to a single steamboat operator, thereby interfering with interstate commerce.[9]

The Taney Court.   In spite of the nationalist Marshall Court decisions, strong debate continued in the United States over national versus state power. It was under the leadership of Chief Justice Marshall's successor, Roger B. Taney (1835–1863), that the Supreme Court articulated the notions of concurrent power, the belief that separate and equally powerful levels of government is the best arrangement, and **dual federalism,** which holds that the national government should not exceed its enumerated powers expressly set out in the Constitution.

In a series of cases involving the scope of Congress's power under the commerce clause, the Taney Court further developed doctrines first enunciated by Marshall, but put greater stress on a concurrent national/state relationship that allowed state involvement in commerce, so long as it did not interfere with federal law. The Taney Court attempted to allow new businesses to flourish, broadened the sphere of *laissez-faire*, and allowed the states greater involvement in corporate affairs. In spite of Taney's major contributions defining the economic and commercial roles of the national and state governments in the federal system, his Court is best remembered for its unfortunate handling of the slavery issue, which threatened the federal system itself.

Dual federalism The belief that having separate and equally powerful levels of government is the best arrangement.

Federalism and Slavery.   During the Taney era, the comfortable role of the Court as the arbiter of competing national and state interests became troublesome when the Court found itself called upon to deal with the highly political issue of slavery. In cases such as *Dred Scott* v. *Sandford* (1857) and others, the Court tried to manage the slavery issue by resolving questions of ownership, the status of fugitive slaves, and slavery in the new territories.[10] These cases generally were settled in favor of slavery and states' rights within the framework of dual federalism. In its treatment of slavery (see "People of the Past: Dred Scott," p. 66), the Taney Court erred grievously and thereby contributed to the coming of the Civil War, since its decision seemed to rule out any political (legislative) solution by the national government.

While the Court was carving out the appropriate role of each level of government in the federal system, the political debate over states' rights (especially where slavery

PEOPLE OF THE PAST

Dred Scott

Dred Scott was born into slavery in Virginia around 1795. In 1833 he was sold by his original owners, the Blow family, to an army surgeon named Dr. Emerson, who lived in St. Louis. In 1834 he was taken by the doctor to Illinois and later to the Wisconsin Territory, returning to St. Louis in 1838.

When Emerson died in 1843, Scott tried to buy his freedom. Before he could, however, he was transferred to Emerson's widow, who moved to New York state, leaving Scott in the custody of his first owners, the Blows. Some of the Blows (Henry Blow later founded the anti-slavery Free Soil Party) and other abolitionists gave money to support a test case seeking Scott's freedom on the ground that since he had resided in Illinois and in the Wisconsin Territory, both of which prohib-

ited slavery, he became free by virtue of his residence there. His return to a slave state could not invalidate this change in his condition, and even in Missouri, he was a free man.

After many delays, in 1857 the U.S. Supreme Court ruled seven to two that Scott was not a citizen and that slaves "were never thought of or spoken of except as property."

At the urging of President James Buchanan, Justice Roger B. Taney tried to fashion a broad ruling that would settle the slavery question. He ruled that the Congress of the United States lacked the constitutional authority to bar slavery in the territories, thus narrowing the scope of national power while enhancing that of the states. Moreover, for the first time since *Marbury* v. *Madison* (1803), the Court found an act of Congress—the Missouri Compromise—unconstitutional.

Source: Excerpts from *Quarrels That Have Shaped the Constitution*, by John A. Garraty (ed). Copyright © 1963 by Harper & Row Publishers, Inc. Reprinted by permission of HarperCollins Publishers.

Nullification doctrine The claimed right of a state to nullify, or reject, a federal law.

was concerned) continued to swirl in large part over the **nullification doctrine**, the purported right of a state to nullify a federal law. As early as 1798, Congress approved the very unpopular Alien and Sedition Acts to prevent criticism of the national government (see Chapter 4). Men like Thomas Jefferson and James Madison who opposed the Acts suggested that the states had the right to nullify any federal law that *in the opinion of the states* violated the Constitution.

The question of nullification came up again in 1828 when the national government enacted a tariff act, commonly referred to as the "Tariff of Abominations," which raised duties on raw materials (iron, hemp, and flax) and reduced protections against imported woolen goods. John C. Calhoun, who served as vice president from 1825 to 1832 under President Andrew Jackson, broke with Jackson over the tariff act because it badly affected his home state of South Carolina. Not only did South Carolinians have to pay more for raw materials because of the new tariff law; it was also becoming more and more difficult for them to sell their dwindling crops abroad for a profit. Calhoun thus used the nullification doctrine to justify South Carolina's refusal to abide by the federal tariff law. Later, he used the same doctrine to justify the Southern states' resistance to national actions to limit slavery.

Calhoun theorized that the federal government was but the agent of the states (the people and the individual state governments) and that the Constitution was simply a compact that provided instructions about how the agent was to act. Calhoun thus reasoned that the U.S. Supreme Court was not competent to pass on the constitutional validity of acts of Congress. Like Congress, the Court was only a branch of a government created by and answerable to the states. Calhoun posited that if the people of any individual state did not like an act of Congress, they could hold a convention to declare that act null and void. In the state contesting the act, the law would have no force until three-fourths of all of the states ratified an amendment expressly giving Congress that power. If the nullifying state still did not wish to be bound by the new provision, it could secede (withdraw) from the Union. In their fight (begun in the 1850s) to keep slavery, the Southern states relied heavily on Calhoun's theories to justify their secession from the Union, ultimately leading to the Civil War.

The Transformation of Dual Federalism

The Civil War forever changed the nature of federalism, but the Supreme Court continued to adhere to its belief in the concept of dual federalism. Thus, the importance and powers of the states were not diminished in spite of the addition of the Thirteenth, Fourteenth, and Fifteenth Amendments to the Constitution (see Chapter 5), or by Abraham Lincoln's appointment of the first Republican Chief Justice, Salmon Chase (1864–1873). In *The Slaughterhouse Cases* (1873), for example, the Court interpreted the Civil War Amendments very narrowly.[11] Other cases also indicated the Court's reluctance to allow Congress to expand its authority further, whether by amendment or by statute.

Between 1865 (the end of the Civil War) and 1933 (when the next major change in the federal system occurred) the Court generally continued to support dual federalism along several lines. State courts, for example, were considered to have the final say on the construction of laws affecting local affairs.[12] Generally, the Court upheld any laws passed under the states' police powers, which allow states to pass laws to protect the general welfare of their citizens. These laws included those affecting commerce, labor relations, and manufacturing. After the Court's decision in *Plessy* v. *Ferguson* (1896)[13] (see pp. 129–130), in which the Court ruled that state maintenance of "separate but equal" facilities for blacks and whites was constitutional, most civil rights and voting cases also became state matters, in spite of the Civil War Amendments.

The Court also developed legal doctrine in a series of cases that reinforced the national government's ability to regulate commerce. By the 1930s, these two somewhat contradictory approaches led to confusion: states, for example, could not tax gasoline used by federal vehicles,[14] and the national government could not tax the sale of motorcycles to the city police department.[15] In this period the Court did recognize the need for national control over new technological developments, such as the telegraph.[16] And beginning in the 1880s, the Court allowed Congress to regulate many aspects of economic relationships such as outlawing monopolies, a type of regulation or power formerly thought to be in the exclusive realm of the states. Passage of laws such as the Interstate Commerce Act in 1887 and the Sherman Anti-Trust Act in 1890 allowed Congress to establish itself as an important player in the growing national economy.

Despite finding that most of these laws were constitutional, the Supreme Court did not consistently enlarge the scope of national power. In 1895, for example, the United States filed suit against four sugar refiners, alleging that their sale would give their buyer control of 98 percent of the U.S. sugar-refining business. The Supreme Court ruled that con-

This famous cartoon by noted political cartoonist Thomas Nast pokes fun at the myriad trusts that led to congressional passage of the Sherman Anti-Trust Act.

gressional efforts to control monopolies (through passage of the Sherman Anti-Trust Act) did not give Congress the authority to prevent the sale of these sugar-refining businesses, because manufacturing was not commerce. Therefore, the companies and their actions were beyond the scope of Congress's authority to regulate.

The New Deal and a Rapidly Changing Balance of Power

The era of dual federalism came to an abrupt end in the 1930s. Its demise began in a series of economic events that ended in the cataclysm of the Great Depression:

- In 1921, the nation experienced a severe slump in agricultural prices.
- In 1926, the construction industry went into decline.
- In the summer of 1929, inventories of consumer goods and automobiles were at an all-time high.
- Throughout the 1920s, bank failures had become common.
- On October 29, 1929, stock prices, which had risen steadily since 1926, crashed, taking with them the entire national economy.

Rampant unemployment (historians estimate it was as high as 40 to 50 percent) was the hallmark of the Great Depression. To combat this unemployment and a host of other problems facing the nation, newly elected President Franklin D. Roosevelt (FDR) proposed in 1933 a variety of innovative programs under the rubric "the New Deal." Just as historical circumstances propelled the writings of Hobbes and Locke discussed in Chapter 1, the economic chaos of the period inspired the New Deal and ushered in a new era in American politics. FDR used the full power of the office of president as well as his highly effective communication skills to sell the American public and Congress on a whole new ideology of government. Not only were the scope and role of national government remarkably altered, but so was the relationship between each state and the national government. (See "Landmark Periods," p. 62.)

The New Deal period (1933 to 1939) was characterized by intense government activity on the national level. It was clear to most politicians that to find national solutions to the Depression, which was affecting the citizens of every state in the Union, the national government would have to exercise tremendous authority.

In the first few weeks of the legislative session after FDR's inauguration, Congress and the president acted quickly to bolster confidence in the national government. Soon after, Congress passed a series of acts creating programs proposed by the president. These new agencies, often known by their initials, created what many termed an "alphabetocracy." Among the more significant programs were the Federal Housing Administration (FHA), which provided federal financing for new home construction; the Civilian Conservation Corps (CCC), a work relief program for farmers and homeowners; and the Agricultural Adjustment Administration (AAA) and the National Recovery Administration (NRA), which imposed restrictions on production in agriculture and many industries.

These programs tremendously enlarged the scope of the national government. Those who feared this unprecedented use of national power quickly challenged the constitutionality of New Deal programs in court.[17] And at least initially, the Supreme Court often agreed with them.

Through the mid-1930s, the Supreme Court continued to rule that certain aspects of the New Deal went beyond the authority of Congress to regulate commerce. In fact, many believe that the Court considered the Depression to be no more than the sum of the economic woes of the individual states and that it was a problem most appropriately handled by the states. The Court's *laissez-faire* or "hands-off" attitude toward the economy was reflected in a series of decisions ruling various aspects of New Deal programs unconstitutional.

FDR and the Congress were outraged. FDR's frustration with the *laissez-faire* attitude of the Court prompted him to suggest what was ultimately nicknamed his "Court-packing plan." Knowing that there was little he could do to change the minds of those already on the Court, FDR suggested enlarging its size from nine to thirteen justices, which would have given him the opportunity to "pack" the Court with a majority predisposed to the constitutional validity of the New Deal.

Even though Roosevelt was popular, the Court-packing plan was not. Congress and the public were outraged that he even suggested tampering with an institution of government. Nevertheless, the Court appeared to respond to this threat. In 1937, it reversed its series of anti-New Deal decisions, concluding that Congress (and therefore the national government) had the authority to legislate in areas that only *affected* commerce. Congress then used this newly recognized power to legislate in a wide array of areas, including maximum hour and minimum wage laws, and regulation of child labor. Moreover, the Court also upheld the constitutionality of the bulk of the massive New Deal relief programs, such as the National Labor Relations Act of 1935, which authorized collective bargaining between unions and employees,[18] the Fair Labor Standards Act of 1938, which prohibited the interstate shipment of goods made by employees earning less than the federally mandated minimum wage,[19] and the Agriculture Adjustment Act of 1938, which provided crop subsidies to farmers.[20]

The New Deal programs forced all levels of government to work cooperatively with one another. Indeed, local governments—mainly big cities—became a third partner in the federal system, as FDR relied on big city Democratic political machines to turn out voters to support his programs. For the first time in U.S. history, in essence, cities were embraced as equal partners in an intergovernmental system and became players in the national political arena.

The Changing Nature of Federalism

Prior to the Depression and the New Deal, most political scientists likened the federal system to a layer cake; each level or layer of government—national, state and local—had clearly defined powers and responsibilities. After the New Deal, however, the nature of the federal system changed:

> The federal system is not accurately symbolized by a neat layer cake of three distinct and separate planes. A far more realistic symbol is that of the marble cake. Wherever you slice through it you reveal an inseparable mixture of differently colored ingredients.... Vertical and diagonal lines almost obliterate the horizontal ones, and in some places there are unexpected whirls and an imperceptible merging of colors, so that it is difficult to tell where one ends and the other begins. So it is with federal, state, and local responsibilities in the chaotic marble cake of American government.[21]

Cooperative federalism A term
used to characterize the relationship
between the national and state
governments that began with the
New Deal.

This kind of "marble cake" federalism is often called **cooperative federalism**, a term used to characterize the relationship between the national and state governments that began with the New Deal. The New Deal created a stronger, more influential national government, and federalism again experienced a change. States began to take a secondary, albeit important, "cooperative" role in the scheme of governance. Nowhere is this shift in power more clear than in the growth of federal grant programs that began in earnest during the New Deal. The tremendous growth in these programs and in federal government spending in general, as illustrated in Table 3.1, changed the nature and discussion of federalism from "How much power should the national government have?" to "How much say in the policies of the states can the national government buy?"

Federal Grants

As early as 1790, Congress appropriated funds for the states to pay debts incurred during the Revolutionary War. But it wasn't until the Civil War that Congress enacted its first true federal grant program, in which federal funds were allocated to the states for a specific purpose.

Most view the start of this redistribution of funds with the Morrill Land Grant Act of 1862, which gave each state 30,000 acres of public land for each representative in Congress. Income from the sale of these lands was to be earmarked for the establishment and support of agricultural and mechanical arts colleges. Sixty-nine land-grant colleges—including Texas A&M University, Purdue University, and Michigan State

Table 3.1 ◆ Federal Grants-in-Aid, 1950–1996

Year	Total (in billions of dollars)	GRANTS-IN-AID AS A PERCENTAGE OF	
		Federal outlays	State and local outlays
1950	$ 2.3	5.3	—
1955	3.2	4.7	—
1960	7.0	7.6	15.0
1965	10.9	9.2	16.0
1970	24.1	12.3	20.0
1975	49.8	15.0	24.0
1980	91.5	15.5	28.0
1985	105.9	11.2	23.0
1990	135.4	10.8	20.0
1992	178.1	12.8	22.0
1996 *est.*	262.8	16.2	23.0

Source: 1950–1991: Office of Management and Budget, *Budget Baselines, Historical Data, and Alternatives for the Future* (Washington, DC: U.S. Government Printing Office, 1993), p. 428; *Budget of the United States Government, Fiscal Year 1994* (Washington, DC: U.S. Government Printing Office, 1993), pp. 6, 22, 77, 79.

HEN AND NOW

The Sheppard–Towner Maternity Act of 1923

The Sheppard–Towner Maternity Act (STMA) was enacted by Congress at the urging of women's rights groups who were still flushed with the success of their efforts to win the right to vote. The Act called for Congress to make money available to the states for pre- and postnatal care for mothers and infants. The program was passed largely due to findings that the United States had the highest infant mortality rate in the Western world. Those who had opposed suffrage challenged this first grant-in-aid program in court, arguing that Congress had surpassed its authority under the commerce clause. In *Frothingham* v. *Mellon* (1923), the Supreme Court ruled that federal taxpayers lacked standing to challenge the constitutional validity of these kinds of programs, because their interest in the program *as taxpayers* was too remote to give them a sufficient stake in the outcome of the case. Thus, to this day, most congressionally enacted aid programs remain out of the reach of taxpayer challenge. Congress allowed the Act to expire in 1929.

University—were founded, making this grant program the single most important piece of education legislation passed in the United States up to that time.

Franklin Roosevelt's New Deal program included massive federal dollars for a variety of programs such as road construction and other public works. These grants made the imposition of national goals on the states easier, and as the federal grant idea began to flourish, it often appeared that there would be no stopping it.

In the boom times of World War II, new programs were introduced, and by the 1950s and 1960s, federal grant-in-aid programs were well entrenched. They often defined federal/state relationships and made the national government a major player in domestic policy.

Until the 1960s, most federal grants programs were constructed in cooperation with the states and were designed to assist the states in furthering their traditional responsibilities to protect the health, welfare, and safety of their citizens. Most of these programs were **categorical grants**, ones for which Congress appropriates funds for a specific purpose. Funds are allocated by a precise formula and are subject to detailed conditions imposed by the national government, often on a matching basis; that is, states must contribute money to match federal funds, although the national government may pay as much as 90 percent of the total.

By the early 1960s, however, as concern about the poor and minorities rose, and as states (especially in the South) were blamed for perpetuating discrimination,[22] those in power in the national government saw grants as a way to force states to behave in ways desired by the national government: if the states would not cooperate with the national government to further its goals, it would withhold funds.

In 1964, the Democratic administration of President Lyndon B. Johnson (1963–1969) launched its renowned War on Poverty, a broad attempt to combat poverty and discrimination. In a frenzy of activity in Washington not seen since the New Deal, federal funds were channeled to states, to local governments, and even directly to citizen action groups in an effort to alleviate social ills that the states had been unable or un-

Categorical grants Grants for which Congress appropriates funds for a specific purpose.

willing to remedy. The move to fund local groups directly was made by the most liberal members of Congress in order to bypass not only conservative state legislatures but also conservative mayors and councils in cities like Chicago.

These new grants altered the fragile federal/state balance of power that had been at the core of most older federal grant programs. During the Johnson administration, the national government began to use federal grants as a way to further what federal (and not state) officials perceived to be national needs. Thus, grants based on what states wanted or believed they needed began to decline, while grants based on what the national government wanted states to do in order to foster national goals increased dramatically. Soon, states routinely asked Washington for help: "pollution, transportation, recreation, economic development, law enforcement and even rat control evoked the same response from politicians: create a federal grant."[23] As shown in Table 3.1, by 1970 federal aid accounted for 20 percent of all state and local government spending; this amount of money made the states ever more dependent on the national government.

As Congress increased the number of programs for which cities were eligible, many critics argued that the federal grants system was out of hand. By 1971, there were more than 500 different types of grants available, in contrast to only 51 in 1964.[24] Each program had its own complicated set of rules and formulas for matching and distributing the money, and had bureaucracies and recipients with a vested interest in enlarging the program.

Between 1965 and 1980, federal aid to cities and states tripled. One political scientist ventured that in the world of bake-shop metaphors, a "new special" was in the offing: "fruitcake federalism." Not only was it formless, but it also offered (political) plums to all.[25]

Negative reaction to this far-reaching federalism was not long in coming. States simply wanted more control. Many believed that the grant situation had produced ridiculous consequences as states and local governments found themselves applying for federal money they did not particularly need. These "federal-aid junkies," as one commentator called them, could not resist the lure of federal funds, no matter what the nature of the grant.[26] As states and localities tailored their budgets to maximize their share of federal dollars, they often neglected basic services. Said New York City Mayor Edward I. Koch,

> Left unnoticed in the cities' rush to reallocate their budgets so as to draw down maximum . . . aid were the basic service-delivery programs. . . . New roads, bridges, and subway routes were an exciting commitment to the future, but they were launched at the expense of routine maintenance to the unglamorous, but essential, infrastructure of the existing systems.[27]

Revenue Sharing.   In 1964, the Chair of President Johnson's Council of Economic Advisors proposed a new program, a form of revenue sharing that would channel federal dollars back to the states without the strings that went with categorical grants. Johnson rejected the proposal and favored continued federal control of grant programs. President Richard M. Nixon, however, found the idea attractive. He believed that states and local governments needed federal assistance but should have greater freedom to spend it. Under his **revenue-sharing** program, money was given to state and local governments to spend where they believed the money was most needed, with no "strings attached."

Revenue sharing Method of redistributing federal monies back to the states with "no strings attached"; favored by President Richard M. Nixon.

Revenue sharing was popular with states, which in 1972 were in fiscal crisis. But during the second Reagan administration, when the budget deficit soared, there were few funds to share. Thus, Congress terminated the program over which it had little control. By 1987 it had been phased out completely.

The growth of government spending revealed in Table 3.1 (p. 70) was one reason that Jimmy Carter, a former governor of Georgia, was able to run successfully for president in 1976 as an "outsider" opposed to big government and federal grants mandating state policies. The reforms Carter introduced were insufficient to override the rest of his political woes, however, and in 1980 Ronald Reagan was elected, in part by pledging a "New Federalism."

New Federalism and Beyond

President Reagan's New Federalism had many facets. The "Reagan Revolution" had at its heart strong views about the role of states in the federal system. Shortly after taking office, he proposed massive cuts in domestic programs and drastic income tax cuts. The Reagan administration's budget and its policies dramatically altered the relationships among the federal, state, and local governments. For the first time in thirty years, federal aid to state and local governments declined.[28]

President Reagan, picking up on Richard M. Nixon's revenue-sharing plan, persuaded Congress to consolidate many categorical grants (for specific programs that often require matching funds) into far fewer, less restrictive **block grants**. Block grants are broad grants to states for specified activities such as secondary education or health services, with few strings attached. Eventually, Congress consolidated fifty-seven categorical grants covering a range of broad programs—including health care, child welfare, and crime prevention—into seven block grants in 1981. Initially, the states were happy with this action—until they learned that the administration also proposed to cut back on the financing of these programs by 25 percent. These cuts fell heaviest on cities. In 1980, federal funds made up 26 percent of state expenditures and 17.7 percent of city and county budgets. By 1990, however, federal dollars were 18 percent of state and 6.4 percent of city and county budgets, respectively. Moreover, the proportion of federal income security aid to individuals in the forms of assistance programs such as Medicaid, Social Security, and Aid to Families with Dependent Children (AFDC) rose significantly at the same time that the proportion of moneys to the state and local governments for general purposes fell by half.

Many programs cut by the Reagan and then Bush administrations involved those that aided the "have nots" of society, and the poor and working poor were hard hit. Though even more people were poorer and technically qualified for benefits, the rate of spending growth for programs declined. Although by 1995 most block grants fell into one of four categories—(1) health, (2) income security, (3) education, or (4) transportation, many politicians, including most state governors, were urging the consolidation of even more programs into block grants. Calls to reform the welfare system, in particular, to allow more latitude to the states in an effort to get back to the Hamiltonian notion of states as laboratories of experiment, seem especially popular.

Controlling the States Through Preemption and Mandates

In *Federalist No. 17,* Alexander Hamilton noted that "it will always be far more easy for the State government to encroach upon the national authorities than for the national

Block grants Broad grants with few strings given to states by the federal government for specified activities, such as secondary education or health services.

Types of Grants-in-Aid
❖❖❖

Categorical Grants: U.S. government gives money for more specific purposes and has more control. There are two types:

a. Formula Grants: Generally designated to apply to certain geographical areas within states; local governments must compete for dollars.

b. Project Grants: Government units and agencies apply for projects that federal agencies have announced. Generally reflect agency agendas; very competitive.

Block Grants: U.S. government gives money to the states for a general purpose, such as education. No strings attached. Preferred by states.

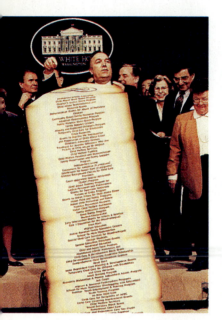

Michigan Governor John Engler unfurls a scroll of nearly 3,000 federal anti-poverty programs that several Republican governors want dismantled in favor of lump-sum block grants that would allow the states to decide where federal dollars in the states are best spent.

Preemption A concept derived from the Constitution's supremacy clause that allows the national government to override or preempt state or local actions in certain areas.

Mandates National laws that direct states or local governments to comply with federal rules or regulations (such as clean air or water standards) under threat of civil or criminal penalties or as a condition of receipt of any federal grants.

government to encroach upon the State authorities." How wrong he was. Some argue that the federal/state relationship has moved from "cooperation to coercion,"[29] a fact that has led many state governors to rebel openly against this growth of national power, especially in view of the fact that the actual value of grants-in-aid to the states declined in the 1980s (when controlled for inflation). Nevertheless, the national government continued to "direct" state policy through statutes preempting traditional state functions and federal mandates.

Preemption.[30] One method through which the federal government has cut into the authority of the states to set their own policy preferences derives from the Constitution's supremacy clause. This practice, known as **preemption**, allows the national government to override, or preempt, state or local actions in certain areas. As discussed earlier, the Tenth Amendment expressly reserved to the states and the people all powers not delegated to the national government. The phenomenal growth of preemption statutes, laws that Congress has passed to allow the federal government to assume partial and/or full responsibility for traditional state and local governmental functions, began in 1965 during the Johnson administration. Since then, Congress has routinely used its authority under the commerce clause to preempt state laws. The Clean Air Act Amendments of 1990, the Hazardous and Solid Waste Amendments of 1984, the Safe Drinking Water Act Amendments of 1986, and the Water Quality Act of 1987 are examples of federal preemption at work. These statutes not only take authority away from states, they often impose significant costs on them in the form of mandates.

Mandates. From the beginning, most categorical grants were matching grants that came with a variety of strings attached. As categorical grants have declined, the national government continued to exercise a significant role in state policy priorities through **mandates**—laws that direct states or local governments to comply with federal rules or regulations (such as clean air or water standards) under threat of civil or criminal penalties, or as a condition of receipt of any federal grants (a city might not get federal transportation funds, for example, unless the disabled have access to particular means of transportation).

Until passage in 1995 of what is called the unfunded mandates bill, the federal government required the states to shoulder the financial burden of programs it did not fund. Through 1994, unfunded mandates made up as much as 30 percent of a local government's annual operating budget. Between 1983 and 1990, it is estimated that the cumulative cost of unfunded mandates to the states and local governments was between 8.9 and 12.7 billion dollars.[31]

As shown in Figure 3-2, the enactment of federal regulations requiring state and local spending has increased tremendously. During the 1980s, twenty-seven new programs requiring state spending were added, in addition to many expensive unfunded provisions that were attached to existing grant-in-aid programs. For example, costly new requirements were tacked on to the Medicaid program, workfare conditions were added to the Aid to Families with Dependent Children program as a welfare reform measure, and local contributions to mandated federal water projects were added.[32] Columbus, Ohio, for example, with 633,000 residents, faced a one-billion dollar bill to comply with the federal Clean Water Act and the Safe Drinking Water Act at an estimated cost of $685 a year per household. Likewise, New York City faced a $1.3 billion bill with no federal financial support to refit elevators in subways to accommodate the disabled.[33] Altogether, for example, state compliance with the Americans with Disabilities Act cost $355.7 million in 1993. And since most states, unlike the national

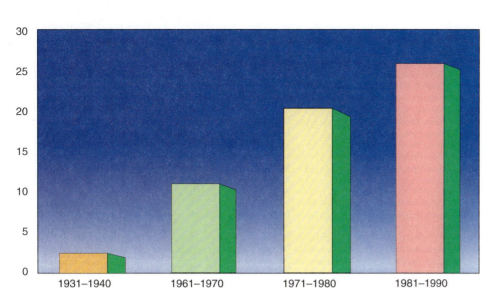

FIGURE 3-2

The Growth of Regulatory Federalism: Enactments Added per Decade, 1931–1990 (includes new programs and major amendments)

Source: ACIR, *Regulatory Federalism,* Appendix Table 1. Reprinted in Timothy J. Conlan and David R. Beam, "Federal Mandates: The Record of Reform and Future Prospects," *Intergovernmental Perspective* (Fall 1992): 9.

government, are required to have balanced budgets, mandates increasingly mean more taxes and more trouble for state and local legislators.

In 1993, costs like these led Alabama and South Dakota to pass laws summoning their senators and representatives home to explain to their state legislatures why laws are passed imposing costly regulations on states without providing funds to implement them.[34] Such pressures prompted the 104th Congress to ban unfunded mandates and to begin to prune laws that require costly state expenditures. Speaker Newt Gingrich has promised a monthly "Corrections Day" to "correct" existing laws and regulations to ease the financial burdens on states.

Rethinking Federalism

Federal grants-in-aid and unfunded mandates clearly forced the states to rethink their position in the federal system, and most are unhappy with it, especially since in 1995 Republican governors controlled thirty of the fifty state houses. Many Republicans, who generally favor a more limited role for the national government, attack many grants-in-aid programs as ways for the national government to exercise powers reserved to the states under the Tenth Amendment.

Some argue that the original reason for federal grants—perceived overrepresentation of rural interests in state legislatures, for example—has been removed as the Supreme Court has ordered redistricting to ensure better representation of urban and suburban interests. Moreover, state legislatures have become more professional, state and local bureaucracies more responsive, and the delivery of services better. In fact, the greatest growth in government hiring has been in the state and local sectors. Poll after poll, moreover, reveals that Americans believe that the national government creates more problems than it solves (76 percent) and that they trust their states (51 percent) and local governments (61 percent) more than the national government (42 percent) to carry out the functions of government.

When thousands of city officials met in Orlando, Florida, in late 1993, one of the most popular accessories was this "Stop Unfunded Mandates" button, which was distributed by the National League of Cities. Unfunded mandates soon became a rallying point for conservatives who decried federal power over the states.

Forcing a National Policy:
The Twenty-One-Year-Old Drinking Age
◆ ◆ ◆

In 1984, only sixteen U.S. senators voted "Nay" on an amendment to the Surface Transportation Act of 1982, a provision designed to withhold 5 percent of federal highway funds from states that allowed those under the age of twenty-one to buy alcoholic beverages. Because the national government did not have the power to regulate the drinking age, it resorted to the "carrot and stick," whereby the national government dangles money in front of the states but places conditions on its use. Unless a state raised its drinking age to twenty-one by 1988, Congress would withhold 10 percent of all federal highway grants to the recalcitrant states. In other words, no raised drinking age, no federal dollars. Even most conservative Republican senators—those most attached to the notion of states' rights—supported the provision in spite of the fact that it imposed a national ideal on the states. And after congressional action, the bill was signed into law by Ronald Reagan, another conservative long concerned with the national government's trampling on state power. States still retain the power to define intoxication, however. The presumptive blood alcohol content required for determining legal intoxication varies from a low of less than .05% in Colorado to a high of .10% in several states.

While many argue that grants-in-aid are an effective way to raise the level of services provided to the poor, others attack them as imposing national priorities on the states. Policy decisions are largely made at the national level, and the states, always in search of funds, are forced to follow the priorities of the national government. States find it very hard to resist the lure of grants, even though many are contingent upon some sort of state investment of matching or proportional funds.

When Republican governors met in Williamsburg, Virginia, in late 1994, they had one message for the new Republican Congress: Get Off Our Backs. Governors Pete Wilson and George W. Bush made it clear that their support of a Balanced Budget Amendment was conditional on its not shifting costs from the national government back to the states.

Clinton's New Federalism

As a former governor, President Clinton is keenly aware of the impact of the national government's actions on the states. Many of his ideas build on those of former President Reagan and in his 1995 State of the Union Message his proposed "New Covenant" sounded a lot like Reagan's new federalism to many—with a twist. Clinton wants to redirect responsibilities to the states to avoid costly duplication of programs, but also to accompany those shifts with more funding from the national government. He also wants to reduce the burden that federal requirements impose on some state and local programs. Vice President Gore, for example, has described the "hodgepodge of categorical mandates that are uncoordinated, costly, and cumbersome" and also advocates the "transfer of the power and authority to the grass roots level."[35]

The Intergovernmental Lobby

Increasing federal regulations, mandates, and conditions of aid have all contributed to the need for state and local governments to hire lobbyists to advance their interests in Washington. School districts, school systems, cities, states, police chiefs, hospital administrators, and many more groups form part of the **intergovernmental lobby**. Many of these groups have either banded with others or set up individual offices in Washington to lobby for funds. Others hire full-time or part-time lobbyists to work solely on their behalf to keep abreast of funding opportunities, or to lobby for programs. Today, searches for scarcer federal dollars can be nearly as futile as Ponce de León's search for the Fountain of Youth. (See Figure 3-3, p. 78.)

Intergovernmental lobby The pressure group or groups that are created when state and local governments hire lobbyists to lobby the national government.

Literally thousands of governments exist in the United States, and most have a Washington presence. Table 3.2 reveals that, in 1987, there were over 83,000 governmental units in the United States. Many of these units—even within a single state—find themselves in competition with one another as the "New Federalism" has changed the nature of state politics. Caught by revenue shortfalls caused by the recession of the early 1990s, legal requirements mandating balanced budgets, and growing demands for new social services and the replacement of some formerly provided by the federal government, many governors around the nation found themselves in trouble as they slashed services and asked for tax increases. "A governor with over a 50 percent approval is more the exception than the rule now, and that just wasn't true three or four years ago," noted one pollster in 1991.[36]

The public's blaming of governors for the effects of New Federalism first became evident in the fall of 1990 when an unprecedented ten incumbent governors chose not to seek reelection, and an additional six were defeated. In contrast, only one incumbent senator was ousted. In 1993, in New Jersey, Governor James Florio was ousted by voters who were angered by tax increases. Similarly, incumbent mayors and county executives were turned out of office by voters angered by property tax increases which were often required to fund federally mandated programs.

Ironically, the fiscal policies of Reagan/Bush New Federalism left many states in weakened positions. In 1991, legislators in forty-six states nearly missed deadlines for their new budget authorizations because of rising costs. Nevertheless, in 1994 no Republican governor who sought reelection lost, but some popular Democratic governors such as Ann Richards of Texas lost. By 1995, thirty statehouses were controlled by Republican governors, including Christine Todd Whitman and William Weld of Mass-

Table 3.2 ◆ Number of Governments in the U.S. in 1987

U.S. government	1
State governments	50
Local governments	
County	3,042
Municipal (city)	19,200
Township and town	16,691
School district	14,721
Special district	29,532
TOTAL	83,237

Source: U.S. Bureau of the Census, *Statistical Abstract of the U.S.: 1990,* 110th ed. (Washington, DC: 1990).

FIGURE 3-3

How Well Did Your State Do in the Scramble for Federal Dollars?

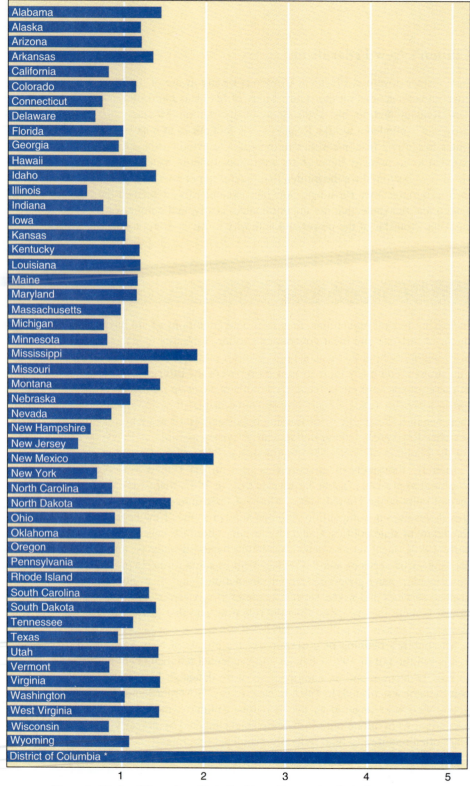

Percent of Federal Taxes from State Residents Returned to State Governments

* Figures for the District of Columbia are so high because it is not a state and therefore depends heavily on Congress for support.

Source: From Harold W. Stanley and Richard G. Niemi, *Vital Statistics on American Politics,* 4E CQ Press, 1994, Table 10-4, pp.321–322. Reprinted by permission.

achusetts, fiscal conservatives with relatively liberal social positions, especially on issues such as abortion.

Federalism and the Supreme Court

Funds from the national government have not been the only factor that has altered the nature of the federal system. The Supreme Court also has played an important role in the configuration of power between the national government and the states. From the days of Marshall's Federalist opinions to *laissez-faire* to the New Deal, the Supreme Court has periodically interjected itself into areas (most notably education and the electoral process) that the Framers intended to leave within the authority of the states.

Education.   Through grants-in-aid programs like the Morrill Land Grant Act of 1862, through the 1950s, Congress has long tried to encourage the states to develop their university and educational systems. Still, education was usually considered a function of the states under their police powers, which allow them to provide for public health and welfare. That tradition was shattered when the Supreme Court ruled in *Brown* v. *Board of Education of Topeka* (1954) that state-mandated segregation has no place in the public schools (see Chapter 5). *Brown* forced states to dismantle their segregated school systems and ultimately led the federal courts to play an important role in monitoring the efforts of state and local governments to tear down the vestiges of segregation.

The Electoral Process.   A decade after *Brown*, the Supreme Court again involved itself in one of the most sacred areas of state regulation in the federal system—the conduct of elections. Convention attendees in Philadelphia had, as a trade-off for giving the national government more powers, allowed the states control over voter qualifications in national elections, as well as over how elections were to be conducted. But in 1964, the Court began to limit the states' ability to control the process of congressional redistricting. In 1966, for example, the Supreme Court invalidated the poll tax, a state-imposed tax of from one to five dollars imposed on those who wished to vote. The poll tax was widely used in the Southern states as an effective barrier to the poor, who often were black.[37] Most Southern legislators assailed the Court's decision, viewing it as illegal interference with their powers to regulate elections under the Constitution, and as a violation of state sovereignty.

On other fronts, however, states' power has been upheld by the U.S. Supreme Court. In 1991, for example, Missouri's policy of mandatory retirement at age seventy was ruled constitutional, because a state's power to determine qualifications of its key governmental officials lies "at the heart of representative government." According to the U.S. Supreme Court, the federal Age Discrimination Act could not be applied to state court judges. If a state wants to impose a mandatory retirement age on its state court judges, it can.[38]

The Performance of State Functions.   In 1974, Congress extended the provisions of the Fair Labor Standards Act (FLSA), which regulated minimum wages and maximum hours for most workers, to cover state and local employees. The National League of Cities, a clearinghouse association of the National Governors' Conference, and several

In New Jersey, Christine Todd Whitman defeated incumbent Democratic Governor James Florio in 1993, promising to reduce taxes and government spending. Today, after reducing taxes by 30 percent she is considered to be a rising star in the Republican Party. In a highly unusual move meant to underscore the Republicans' commitment to transferring power back to the states, Whitman was chosen to deliver the Republican Party's rebuttal to President Clinton's 1995 State of the Union Address.

individual states and cities challenged the new measures, arguing that Congress had no authority to regulate the wages of state employees. In *National League of Cities* v. *Usery* (1976), a closely divided Court (five to four), decided that Congress had overstepped its authority. In 1941, the Supreme Court had upheld the constitutionality of the FLSA and of Congress's authority to set minimum wages for employees in the private sector. The 1974 amendment (which covered state and local employees), said the Court, had gone too far: "Congress has sought to wield its power in a fashion that would impair the States' ability to function effectively in a federal system,"[39] concluded the majority. The case was viewed as especially important because it was the first major instance of the Court's establishing any limits on national authority over the states since before the New Deal era. States' rights advocates believed that this brake on federalism was long overdue. Conservatives hailed the decision as the dawn of a "New Federalism."

Ironically, *National League of Cities* was reversed by an equally divided Court just nine years later in *Garcia* v. *San Antonio Metropolitan Transit Authority* (1985).[40] This case also involved the constitutionality of applying federally imposed minimum wage and maximum hour provisions to state governments. In *Garcia*, the Court ruled that Congress has broad power to impose its will on state and local governments, even in areas that traditionally have been left to their discretion. The Court ruled that the "political process ensures that laws that unduly burden the states will not be promulgated" and that it should not be up to an "unelected" judiciary to preserve state powers. Furthermore, the majority of the Court concluded that the Tenth Amendment, which ensured that any powers not given to the national government be reserved for the states, was, at least for the time being, essentially meaningless! But by 1995, there were indications that the Court believes that Congress has gone too far in interfering with functions best left to the states. In a 1995 case involving the conviction of a student charged with carrying a concealed handgun onto school property, a five-person majority of the Court ruled that Congress lacked constitutional authority under the commerce clause to regulate guns in a local school zone.[41] The majority concluded that local gun control in the schools was a state, not a federal, matter.

Federalism and the Reagan–Bush Court.   When Ronald Reagan left Washington to return to California at the end of his second term of office in January 1989, he left a lasting legacy. While president, he had the opportunity to appoint not only the Chief Justice, William Rehnquist, but also Associate Justices Sandra Day O'Connor, Antonin Scalia, and Anthony Kennedy. All were staunch conservatives, but O'Connor in particular, as a former state legislator and then state court judge, held a strong belief that the national government had intruded far too many times on the powers of the states. The Bush appointments of David Souter, a former state attorney general and state court judge, and Clarence Thomas, a leading African-American conservative, solidified the new, conservative, states'-rights–oriented majority.

Mario M. Cuomo, the former liberal Democratic New York governor, has referred to the decisions of the Reagan–Bush Court as creating "a kind of new judicial federalism." According to Cuomo, this new federalism can be characterized by the Court's withdrawal of "rights and emphases previously thought to be national."[42] Perhaps most illustrative of this trend were the Supreme Court's decisions in *Webster* v. *Reproductive Health Services* (1989)[43] and *Casey* v. *Planned Parenthood of Southeastern Pennsylvania* (1992).[44] In *Webster*, the Court first gave new latitude—and even encouragement—to the states to fashion more restrictive abortion laws. Since *Webster*, as illustrated in Figure 3-4, numerous states have enacted or are considering new restrictions. In 1991 alone, more than 200 bills restricting abortion were introduced in forty-five state legislatures.[45] Moreover, the Court has consistently upheld the authority of the individual states to limit a minor's access to abortion through imposition of parental consent or notification laws. And it has consistently declined to review other restrictions, including twenty-four–hour waiting requirements.

For the most part, decisions of the Reagan–Bush Court support Cuomo's characterization of the role of the national government in the newest federalism. But in spite of its conservative, pro-states' rights leanings, the Court has surprised observers. Even before Justice Souter was added to the Court, for example, it upheld the authority of a federal district court judge who had imposed a local tax increase to finance a school desegregation order.[46] National authority also received a boost when the Court ruled

FIGURE 3-4

State-by-State Abortion Restrictions

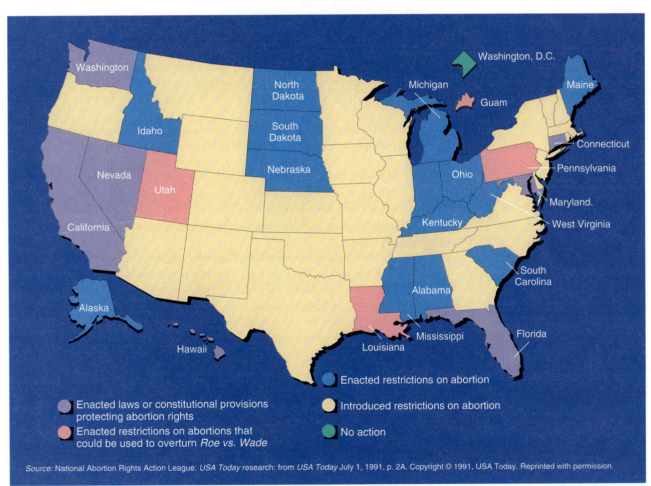

Source: National Abortion Rights Action League; *USA Today* research; from *USA Today* July 1, 1991, p. 2A. Copyright © 1991, USA Today. Reprinted with permission.

that a federal law limiting the authority of state governors to withhold consent for state National Guards' active duty does not violate the militia clauses of the U.S. Constitution. Several governors had argued that the Constitution reserved to the states the power to train militia.[47]

Toward Reform

As the power of the national government has risen at the expense of the states, a variety of calls for reform of the federal system have been made by politicians and political scientists. Moreover, inconsistent Court decisions—on the one hand returning costly national programs to the states while on the other hand continuing to order expensive educational and penal programs—prompted fifteen state legislatures to approve resolutions calling for an amendment to the Constitution giving the states more authority in relation to the federal government. With the strong support of the Bush administration, those states proposed two avenues of change, largely in response to recent Court decisions. One sought to allow the states to initiate amendments without calling a constitutional convention. The other would change the Tenth Amendment to direct the state courts to determine whether the Supreme Court had overstepped its boundaries with respect to the states. Neither proposal stands much chance of success, especially in light of the 1994 elections and the Republican-controlled Congress's resolve to return national power back to the states and also to free states to spend federal monies with fewer strings attached in the form of fewer specific programs and more block grants.

The Republicans in 1995 were not the first to make these calls for reform. In 1993, the Progressive Policy Institute, a project of the Democratic Leadership Council (see Chapter 11), called on the Clinton administration to "transform the federal government's entire approach to state and local grant programs."[48] Among its recommendations were establishing a commission eliminating several categorical grants and consolidating others into more general block grants, increasing the number of waivers to federal regulations given to states and local governments, and appointing a Cabinet level "federalism" czar.

In the wake of the resolve of the 104th Congress, however, more changes may be coming in the federal system and in the relationship of the national government to the states than in any period since the New Deal. The Speaker of the House, Newt Gingrich, and his fellow Republicans, along with Republican governors who control the majority of the state houses, are committed to dramatic overhaul of the federal system and a return of substantial power to the states. Some of these changes require state ratification of constitutional amendments; others require acts of Congress. And others, such as major changes in the welfare system, require cooperative action and reform by both the national governments and the states. The nation's governors have even formed a Conference of the States where the fifty governors and bipartisan delegates from each state will meet biannually to suggest structural proposals for constitutional changes in the federal system aimed at "redressing the balance" between the national government and the states.[49] Political scientist David B. Walker argues that this is an especially auspicious time for reform given the rampant distrust of government that permeates all levels of government.[50]

Summary

The inadequacies of the confederate form of government created by the Articles of Confederation led the Framers to create an entirely new, federal system of government. From the summer of 1776 until today, the tension between the national and state governments has been at the core of our federal system. In describing the origins of that tension and its results, we have made the following points:

1. The Framers created a federal system to replace the confederate form of government that had existed under the Articles of Confederation. The national government has both enumerated and implied powers, and also exercises concurrent powers with the states. Certain powers are denied to both the state and national governments. Certain guarantees concerning representation in Congress and protection against foreign attacks and domestic rebellion were made to the states in return for giving up some of their powers in the new federal system. Despite limitations, the national government is ultimately supreme.

2. Over the years, the powers of the national government have increased tremendously at the expense of the states. The Supreme Court, in particular, has played a key role in defining the relationship and powers of the national government through its broad interpretations of the supremacy and commerce clauses. For many years, however, it adhered to the notion of dual federalism, which tended to limit the national government's authority in areas such as slavery and, after the Civil War, civil rights. This notion of a limited role for the national government in some spheres ultimately fell by the wayside after the Great Depression.

3. The rapid creation of New Deal programs to alleviate many problems caused by the Depression led to a tremendous expansion of the federal government through the growth of federal services and grants-in-aid programs. This growth escalated during the Johnson administration and in the mid- to late 1970s. After his election in 1980, Ronald Reagan, upset by the growth of federal services, tried to reverse the tide through what he termed "New Federalism." He built on earlier efforts by Richard Nixon to consolidate categorical grants into fewer block grant programs, and to give state and local governments greater control over programs. In spite of these efforts, however, mandates and national preemption of state laws continue to influence state policies and budgets.

4. The intergovernmental lobby exists to help states and local governments resist federal mandates, learn more about conditions of aid, and advance their interests in Washington.

5. The Supreme Court has been a major player in recent trends in the federal–state relationship. Its decisions in the areas of education, civil rights, voting rights, and the performance of state functions have given the federal government a wider role in the day-to-day functioning of the states, and have limited the scope of the states' police powers. During the Reagan–Bush era, however, the Supreme Court, especially in the area of abortion, was willing to return some powers to the states.

Key Terms

federal system	bill of attainder	categorical grants
federalism	ex post facto	revenue sharing
enumerated powers	supremacy clause	block grants
necessary and proper clause	dual federalism	preemption
implied power	nullification doctrine	mandates
concurrent powers	cooperative federalism	intergovernmental lobby

Suggested Readings

Bowman, Ann O'M., and Richard Kearney. *The Resurgence of the States*. Englewood Cliffs, NJ: Prentice Hall, 1986.

Derthick, Martha. *The Influence of Federal Grants*. Cambridge, MA: Harvard University Press, 1970.

Elazar, Daniel. *American Federalism: A View from the States*. New York: Harper & Row, 1984.

Gillespie, Ed, and Bob Schellhas, eds. *Contract with America*. New York: Times Books, 1994.

Grodzins, Morton. *The American System*. Chicago: Rand McNally, 1966.

Hamilton, Christopher, and Donald T. Wells. *Federalism, Power, and Political Economy: A New Theory of Federalism's Impact on American Life*. Englewood Cliffs, NJ: Prentice Hall, 1990.

Daphne A. Kenyon and John Kincaid, eds. *Competition among States and Local Governments*. Washington, DC: The Urban Institute Press, 1991.

Phillips, Kevin. *The Politics of Rich and Poor: Wealth and the American Electorate in the Reagan Aftermath*. New York: HarperCollins, 1990.

Riker, William H. *Federalism: Origin, Operation, Significance*. Boston: Little, Brown, 1964.

Rivlin, Alice M. *Reviving the American Dream: The Economy, the States, and the Federal Government*. Washington, DC: The Brookings Institution, 1993.

Walker, David B. *The Rebirth of Federalism*. Chatham, NJ: Chatham House, 1994.

Zimmerman, Joseph F. *Contemporary American Federalism: The Growth of National Power*. New York: Praeger, 1992.

Civil Liberties

THE FIRST CONSTITUTIONAL AMENDMENTS: THE BILL OF RIGHTS

FIRST AMENDMENT GUARANTEES: FREEDOM OF RELIGION

FIRST AMENDMENT GUARANTEES: FREEDOM OF SPEECH AND PRESS

THE RIGHTS OF CRIMINAL DEFENDANTS

THE RIGHT TO PRIVACY

TOWARD REFORM

When Samuel Bryan penned the words opening this chapter on October 5, 1787, he voiced the fears not only of other Anti-Federalists but also of some supporters of the proposed Constitution. Although the Federalists—Alexander Hamilton and James Madison in particular—argued that the checks and balances proposed in the Constitution prevented the national government from usurping the civil liberties of Americans, many others were not so certain. In 1787, most state constitutions explicitly protected a variety of personal liberties: speech, religion, freedom from unreasonable searches and seizures, trial by jury, and more. It was clear that the new Constitution would redistribute power in the new federal system between the national government and the states. Without the guarantee of specific civil liberties, could the national government be trusted to uphold the freedoms already granted to citizens by their states?

Recognition of the increased power that would be held by the new national government led Anti-Federalists to stress the need for a bill of rights. Note that the Bill of Rights—as drafted by the Framers—applies only to the national government. It was not until much later that the Supreme Court interpreted the Bill of Rights as applying to the states (see pp. 96–99). In 1790, however, it was the power of the national government, not that of the states, that the people feared. Anti-Federalists and many others were confident that they could control the actions of their own state legislators, and most state constitutions already included bills of rights guaranteeing various civil liberties.

Although the debate over the Bill of Rights and its ratification may seem far removed from or even irrelevant to your life today, the liberties contained in it are central to many of today's most controversial issues. Can prayer be a part of a public high school graduation? Can a student be expelled from college for shouting racial slurs at other students? Can a state prohibit a physician from performing an abortion not nec-

> **T**he constitution of this commonwealth . . . provides *that people have a right to FREEDOM OF SPEECH. . . .* How long those rights will appertain to you, you yourselves are called upon to say. . . .
>
> *Samuel Bryan*
> *"CENTINEL" NO. 1*

The Constitution of Pennsylvania included guarantees of free speech. Bryan, an Anti-Federalist, warned Philadelphians against ratifying the U.S. Constitution, saying that since it did not include such guarantees, they risked losing those hard-won freedoms.

essary to save the life of the mother? Why aren't hand guns banned by the national government? Why is there a death penalty in some states and not in others? Many of these questions involve issues never envisioned by the authors of the Bill of Rights. Nevertheless, each of these issues has found its way into the courts where the Constitution, the Bill of Rights, and the civil liberties it contains have been subject to interpretation and reinterpretation over the course of our nation's history.

Civil liberties are the personal rights and freedoms that the federal government cannot abridge, either by law, constitution, or judicial interpretation. Civil liberties place limitations on the power of the government to restrain or dictate how individuals act. Thus, when we discuss civil liberties such as those found in the Bill of Rights, we are concerned with limits on what governments can and cannot do. In contrast, when we discuss **civil rights,** the subject of Chapter 5, we are concerned with political and social rights—to be free from governmental discrimination based on race or gender, for example—that the government must provide its citizens. As discussed in Chapter 5,

Civil liberties The personal rights and freedoms that the federal government cannot abridge by law, constitution, or judicial interpretation.

Civil rights The political and social right to be free from arbitrary infringement by the government or any individual.

In spite of the First Amendment's general ban on state entanglement with religion, prayer is still common at many public ceremonies. Here, the President of the United States is shown praying at the 1993 graduation at West Point, a public institution.

the term *civil rights* implies that the government is expected to play a positive role in ensuring all citizens equal protection under the laws and equal opportunity to participate in all aspects of national life. Clearly, the concepts of liberty and equality often overlap and interact.

In this chapter, we trace the origins of the Bill of Rights and then examine many of its key guarantees in detail. Just as the meaning of the U.S. Constitution has been altered over time by judicial interpretation and by cultural and technological change, so has our concept of civil liberties and the proper role of the government in protecting them. Each guarantee in the Bill of Rights could be (and indeed is) the subject of several books. Here we hope to give you a greater appreciation of the historical development of the liberties Americans enjoy today, an understanding of the conflicts and crises these liberties often cause, and the key role the Supreme Court has played in this debate.

The First Constitutional Amendments: The Bill of Rights

As we saw in Chapter 2, most of the Framers originally opposed even the idea of a bill of rights. When George Mason of Virginia proposed that such a bill be added to the preface of the proposed constitution, for example, his resolution was defeated unanimously.[1] In the subsequent ratification debates, Federalists advanced three main arguments in opposition to the Bill of Rights:

1. A bill of rights was unnecessary. Most state constitutions already contained bills of rights. Alexander Hamilton asked, "Why declare that things shall not be done which there is no power to do?"[2]
2. A bill of rights would be dangerous.
3. A national bill of rights would be impractical. Enforcement would depend largely on public opinion and the spirit of the people and government.

Some Federalists, however, supported the idea. After the Philadelphia Convention, for example, James Madison conducted a lively correspondence about the need for a national bill of rights with Thomas Jefferson. Jefferson was far quicker to support such guarantees than was Madison, who continued to doubt their utility. Politics soon intervened, however, when Madison found himself in a close race against James Monroe for a seat in the House of Representatives in the First Congress. The district was largely Anti-Federalist. So to garner support, Madison, in an act of political expediency, issued a series of public letters vowing support for a bill of rights.

Once elected, he made good on that promise. He became the prime mover and author of the Bill of Rights, although he considered the Congress to have far more important matters to handle and viewed his labors on the Bill of Rights "a nauseous project."[3] The insistence of Anti-Federalists on a bill of rights, the fact that some states conditioned their ratification of the Constitution on addition of these guarantees, and the disagreement among Federalists about such a bill led to prompt congressional action to put an end to further controversy, since this was a time when national stability and support for the new government were particularly needed. In 1789, the proposed Bill of Rights was sent to the states by Congress for ratification; this was finally achieved in 1791.

The separation of church and state advocated by Thomas Jefferson has not always been clearly defined. In *Lynch* v. *Donnelly* (1984) the Supreme Court upheld the constitutionality of a city-sponsored nativity scene as part of a larger Christmas display in a park. In response to this decision, many municipalities began to erect nativity scenes that were not part of a larger seasonal display. For example, in 1987 the city of Chicago erected, removed, and then re-erected a creche when faced with lawsuits from various groups protesting what they viewed as an unconstitutional intermingling of church and state. At first the city asked local churches to raise a $100,000 bond for protection against litigation. The money was not forthcoming, and the city dismantled the scene. A federal judge then ruled that the city had not violated the First Amendment, and the scene returned.

The Bill of Rights contains numerous specific guarantees, including those of free speech, press, and religion (see Appendix II for the full text). The Ninth and Tenth Amendments, moreover, highlight Anti-Federalist fears of too powerful a national government. The Ninth Amendment makes it clear that this special listing of rights does not mean that others don't exist. And the Tenth Amendment simply reiterated that powers not delegated to the national government are reserved to the states or the people.

First Amendment Guarantees: Freedom of Religion

A democracy depends on a free exchange of ideas, and the First Amendment shows that the Framers were well aware of this. Despite the fact that many colonists had fled Europe primarily to escape religious persecution, most colonies actively persecuted those who did not belong to their predominant religious groups. Pennsylvania, for example, was a "Quaker" colony. The Congregationalist Church of Massachusetts, a "Puritan" colony, taxed and harassed those who held other religious beliefs. Nevertheless, the colonists were uniformly outraged in 1774 when the British Parliament passed a law establishing Anglicanism and Roman Catholicism as official religions in the colonies. The First Continental Congress immediately sent a letter of protest announcing its "astonishment that a British Parliament should ever consent to establish . . . a religion [Catholicism] that has deluged [England] in blood and dispersed bigotry, persecution, murder and rebellion through every part of the world."[4]

This distaste for a national church or religion was reflected in the Constitution. Article VI of the Constitution, for example, provides that "no religious Test shall ever be required as a Qualification to any Office or Public Trust under the United States." This simple sentiment, however, did not reassure those who feared the new Constitution would curtail individual liberty. Thus, the First Amendment to the Constitution was ultimately ratified to lay those fears to rest.

The First Amendment to the Constitution begins, "Congress shall make no law respecting an establishment of religion, or prohibiting the free exercise thereof." This statement sets the boundaries of governmental action. The **establishment clause** ("Congress shall make no law respecting an establishment of religion") directs the national government not to involve itself in religion. It creates, in Thomas Jefferson's immortal words, a "wall of separation" between church and state. The **free exercise clause** ("or prohibiting the free exercise thereof") guarantees citizens that the national government will not interfere with their practice of religion. These guarantees, however, are not absolute. In *Cantwell* v. *Connecticut* (1940), the Supreme Court observed that the First Amendment "embraces two concepts—freedom to believe and freedom to act. The first is absolute, but in the nature of things, the second cannot be. Conduct remains subject to regulation of society."[5] In the mid-1800s, for example, Mormons traditionally practiced and preached polygamy, the taking of multiple wives. In 1879, when it was first called on to interpret the free exercise clause, the Supreme Court upheld the conviction of a Mormon under a federal law barring polygamy. The Court reasoned that to do otherwise would provide constitutional protections to a full range of religious beliefs, including those as extreme as human sacrifice. "Laws are made for the government of actions," noted the Court, "and while they cannot interfere with mere religious belief and opinions, they may with practices."[6]

Establishment clause The first clause in the First Amendment that prohibits the national government from establishing a national religion.

Free exercise clause The second clause of the First Amendment. It prohibits the U.S. government from interfering with a citizen's right to practice his or her religion.

The Establishment Clause

Over the years, the Court has been divided over how to interpret the establishment clause. Does this clause erect a total wall between church and state, or is some governmental accommodation of religion allowed?

In 1947, for example, the Court split five to four in upholding the constitutionality of a New Jersey town's practice of reimbursing parents for the costs of transporting their children to Roman Catholic schools. In *Everson* v. *Board of Education of Ewing Township* (1947),[7] the majority made it clear that the monies were not spent in furtherance of a religion, but were a subsidy to parents, not to churches. Writing for the narrow majority, Justice Hugo L. Black suggested, moreover, that a strict separation of church and state required only that a state be neutral in its relationships with religious groups and nonbelievers.

Over the years, state subsidies that could be considered to aid children or certain other identifiable recipients have been held not to violate the Constitution. This analysis has allowed the Court to permit "dismissed time" (allowing public school children to leave school early to attend religious instruction off public school grounds),[8] federal aid for the construction of buildings on religiously affiliated college campuses,[9] state-loaned textbooks for parochial school children,[10] and state laws giving parents tax deductions for parochial school tuitions.[11] And, again in a five-to-four decision, the Rehnquist Court ruled in 1993 that public funding to provide sign language interpreters for deaf students in religious schools did not violate the constitutionally required separation of church and state.[12]

While it has upheld the constitutionality of these kinds of church/state entanglements, the Court has held fast to the rule of strict separation between church and state when issues of prayer in school are involved. In *Engel* v. *Vitale* (1962),[13] the Court ruled that the recitation in public school classrooms of a twenty-two-word nondenominational prayer drafted by the New Hyde Park, New York, school board was unconstitutional.

The Court has gone back and forth in its effort to come up with a workable way to deal with church/state questions. In *Lemon* v. *Kurtzman* (1971),[14] the Court heard a case that challenged direct state aid to parochial schools, including the use of state funds to pay salaries of teachers at these schools. In its decision, the Court tried—as it often does—to carve out a new "test" by which to measure the constitutionality of these types of laws. To be constitutional, a challenged law or practice must:

1. Have a secular purpose;
2. Have a primary effect that neither advances nor inhibits religion; and
3. Not foster an excessive government entanglement with religion.

State funding of parochial school teachers' salaries was found to fail this test and was therefore prohibited by the Constitution, said the Court in *Lemon*.[15] In 1980, the *Lemon* test was interpreted to invalidate a Kentucky law that required the posting of the Ten Commandments in public school classrooms. The Court ruled the posting had no secular purpose.[16] And later, in *Wallace* v. *Jaffree* (1985),[17] an Alabama law requiring a daily minute of silence for meditation or voluntary prayer was also ruled unconstitutional.

Even the more conservative Rehnquist Court has been for the most part unwilling to lower the wall of separation when it comes to religious influences in the public schools. In *Edwards* v. *Aguillard* (1987),[18] for example, the Court found that a Louisiana statute requiring that creationism be taught as a balance to evolution also violated the establishment clause. And in *Lee* v. *Weisman* (1992),[19] the Court continued its unwillingness to allow prayer in public schools by finding unconstitutional the saying of prayer at a middle school graduation.

After 1980, however, the Court has appeared more willing to ignore the *Lemon* test and lower the wall between church and state so long as school prayer is not involved. In 1981, for example, the Court ruled unconstitutional a Missouri law prohibiting the use of state university buildings and grounds for "purposes of religious worship," that had been used to ban religious groups from using school facilities. With only one dissent, the Court ruled that "University students are . . . less impressionable than younger students and should be able to appreciate that the university's policy is one of neutrality towards religion."[20]

This decision was taken by many members of Congress as a sign that this principle could be extended to secondary and even primary schools. In 1984, Congress passed the Equal Access Act, which bars public schools from discriminating against groups of students on the basis of "religious, political, philosophical or other content of the speech at such meetings." The constitutionality of this law was upheld in *Board of Education* v. *Mergens* (1990),[21] when the Court ruled that a school board's refusal to allow a Christian Bible club to meet in a public high school classroom during a twice weekly "activity period" violated the Act. According to Justice Sandra Day O'Connor, writing for the majority, the primary effect of the Act was neither to advance religion nor to excessively entangle government and religion—in spite of the fact that religious meetings would be held on school grounds with a faculty sponsor. The important factor seemed to be that the students had complete choice in their selection of activities with numerous non-religious options. In 1993, the Court also ruled that religious groups must be allowed to use public schools after hours if that access is also given to

Although banned by law, snake-handling practices as part of religious services continue today in many parts of the South.

other community groups.[22] The 1993 replacement of Justice White by Ruth Bader Ginsburg, a former attorney for the American Civil Liberties Union (see "The American Civil Liberties Union," p. 102) could halt this trend toward lowering the wall between church and state.

The Free Exercise Clause

The free exercise clause of the First Amendment proclaims that "Congress shall make no law . . . prohibiting the free exercise [of religion]." As in the case of the establishment clause, the Supreme Court has been continually forced to interpret this clause, often trying to balance the sometimes conflicting implications of the two clauses. Is it, for example, permissible for a state to ban the use of snakes during religious services, although some fundamentalist Christians view snake handling as an important part of their religious services? Is it reasonable to force some men into combat if their religious beliefs ban them from participating? In the latter example, if exemptions (called "conscientious objector deferments") are given to some men and not to others, is the government favoring one religion over another?

Although the free exercise clause of the First Amendment guarantees individuals the right to be free from governmental interference in the exercise of their religion, this guarantee, like other First Amendment freedoms, is not absolute. When secular law comes into conflict with religious law, the right to exercise one's religious beliefs is often denied—especially if the religious beliefs in question are held by a minority, or by an unpopular or "suspicious" religious group. State statutes barring the use of certain illegal drugs, snake handling, and polygamy—all practices of particular religious sects—have been upheld as constitutional. Similarly, states can require some businesses to close on Sundays although some major religious groups observe Saturday as their day of worship. Nonetheless, the Court has made it clear that the free exercise clause requires that a state or the national government remain neutral toward religion.

Many critics of rigid enforcement of such neutrality argue that the government should do what it can to accommodate the religious diversity in our nation. In the early 1960s, for example, a South Carolina textile mill shifted to a six-day work week, requiring that all employees work on Saturday. When an employee, a Seventh-Day Adventist whose Sabbath was Saturday, said she could not work on Saturdays, she was fired. She sought to receive unemployment compensation and her claim was denied. She then sued to obtain her benefits. The Supreme Court ordered South Carolina to extend benefits to the woman in spite of its law that *required* an employee to be available for work on all days but Sundays. The Court ruled that the state law was an unconstitutional violation of the free exercise clause because it failed to accommodate the worker's religious beliefs.[23]

This accommodationist approach was further advanced in *Wisconsin* v. *Yoder* (1972),[24] a challenge to the constitutionality of a Wisconsin law requiring all students to stay in school through the age of sixteen. Yoder and several other members of the Old Order Amish religion were convicted of violating the Wisconsin law when they refused to send their children to school after they had completed the eighth grade. The Amish believed that high school attendance would expose their children to secular influences and "worldly views," thus endangering their way of life. Citing the long, peaceful history of the Amish and their traditional ways, the Court concluded that the statute violated the free exercise clause and interfered with the Amish's practice of their religion. In another case, however, the Court did rule that it was permissible for Minnesota to compel the Amish to comply with highway safety laws.[25]

The ways of the Amish often stand in sharp contrast to those of their neighbors. Often, they coexist with no problems. In *Wisconsin* v. *Yoder* the Supreme Court ruled that Amish children did not have to attend public school past the eighth grade although state law required all other children to attend school until age 16. The Amish, however, have been required to have lanterns on their buggies at night as a public safety measure, First Amendment considerations notwithstanding.

In the same vein, the Court has interpreted the Constitution to mean that governmental interests can outweigh free exercise rights: in 1986, for example, it ruled that it was reasonable for the military to ban the wearing of yarmulkes by Orthodox Jewish officers.[26] In 1988, the Court upheld the U.S. Forest Service's right to permit road construction and tree harvesting in areas of the national forest traditionally used for religious purposes by American Indian tribes.[27] Later, in *Oregon* v. *Smith* (1990), the Supreme Court ruled that the free exercise clause allowed Oregon to ban the use of sacramental peyote (an illegal hallucinogenic drug) in some American Indian tribes' traditional religious services. The Court upheld the state's right to deny unemployment compensation to two workers who had been fired by a private drug rehabilitation clinic because they had ingested an illegal substance.[28] (In 1994 the Religious Freedom Restoration Act was passed and signed into law to overturn this decision.) In contrast, in 1993 the Supreme Court ruled that members of the Santería Church, an Afro-Cuban religion, had the right to sacrifice animals during religious services. In upholding that practice, the Court ruled that a city ordinance banning such practices was unconstitutionally aimed at the group, thereby denying its members the right to free exercise of their religion.[29]

Although conflicts between religious beliefs and the government are often difficult to settle, the Court has attempted to walk the fine line between the free exercise and establishment clauses. Moreover, in the area of free exercise, the Court often has had to confront questions of "What is a god?" and "What is a religious faith?"—questions that theologians have grappled with for centuries. In *U.S.* v. *Seeger* (1965),[30] for example, a case involving three men who had been denied conscientious objector deferments during the Vietnam War because they did not subscribe to "traditional" organized religions, the Court ruled unanimously that the men were entitled to the deferments because their belief in a supreme being placed their views parallel to those who practiced traditional religions. In contrast, despite the Court's having ruled that Catholic, Protestant, Jewish, and Buddhist prison inmates must be allowed to hold religious services,[31] in 1987 it held that Islamic prisoners could be denied the same right for security reasons.[32]

First Amendment Guarantees: Freedom of Speech and Press

Historically, one of the most volatile areas of constitutional interpretation has been in the interpretation of the First Amendment's mandate that "Congress shall make no law . . . abridging the freedom of speech, or of the press." Like the establishment and free exercise clauses of the First Amendment, the speech and press clauses have not been interpreted as absolute bans against government regulation. In fact, over the years the Court has used a hierarchical approach, with some items getting greater protection than others. Generally, thoughts have received the greatest protection, and actions or deeds the least. Words have come somewhere in the middle, depending on their content and purpose.

In the United States, with few exceptions, thoughts are considered beyond the scope of governmental regulation. Although people may experience a negative reaction for revealing their thoughts, the government has no legal right to punish or sanction Americans for what they think. Words, or speech, which stand between thoughts and deeds, are subject to some forms of restraint. Speech that is obscene, libelous (false, or caus-

Freedom of Speech and the Common-Law Tradition

♦ ♦ ♦

In Great Britain, government censorship of the press and speech had its origins in a 1275 pronouncement from the Crown. Later, in the sixteenth and seventeenth centuries, the King's Council, which sat in what was fearfully called the "Star Chamber" by British subjects, harshly meted out cruel sentences for seditious libel, that is, language tending to incite rebellion against the state. In one of the Star Chamber's most infamous cases, the Trial of William Prynn (1632), Prynn was sentenced to life imprisonment, branded on the forehead, had his nose split, his ears cut off, and was fined £10,000 for publishing a book that criticized actors and actresses. The book was viewed as seditious libel against the queen, because she had recently appeared in a play!

The Star Chamber was abolished in 1641, but its precedents were often relied upon by common-law courts. Criminal liability for slander (unlawful, untrue speech) remained a question of law, not of fact, to be decided by juries. Moreover, partisan publications were discouraged by law. In sum, the British experience concerning speech laws focused largely on issues of prior restraint and not on the protection of speech per se.

Source: From *Constitutional Law and Politics, Volume Two. Civil Rights and Civil Liberties,* by David M. O'Brien, by permission of the author and W. W. Norton & Company, Inc. Copyright © 1991 by David M. O'Brien.

ing someone disrepute), or seditious (advocating violent overthrow of the government), or that amounts to "fighting words" that could incite or cause injury to those to whom they are addressed, has been interpreted as not protected by the First Amendment. Often, however, these exceptions to constitutional protection have troubled the Court. What is considered obscene in rural Mississippi, for example, may not offend someone in another part of the nation.

Actions, or deeds, are given the least constitutional protection. Thus, actions are subject to the most governmental restrictions. You may have a right to shoot a pistol in your back yard, but you can't do it on a city street. Over the years these competing rights have been balanced by the now classic observation that your "right to swing your arm ends at the tip of my nose."[33]

When the First Amendment was ratified in 1791, it was considered to protect only against **prior restraint**; that is, the government could not prohibit speech or publication before the fact. As was the case in Great Britain concerning free speech, the First Amendment was not considered to provide absolute immunity from governmental sanction for what speakers or publishers might say or print. Thus, over the years, the meaning of this amendment's mandate has been subject to thousands of cases seeking judicial interpretation of its meaning.

Prior restraint Judicial doctrine stating that the government cannot prohibit speech or publication before the fact.

The Alien and Sedition Acts

Soon after passage of the Bill of Rights, a constitutional crisis arose in 1798 when the Federalist Congress enacted the Alien and Sedition Acts. Designed to ban any political criticism by the growing numbers of Jeffersonian Democratic-Republicans, these Acts made publication of "any false, scandalous writing against the government of the United States" a criminal offense. Overtly partisan Federalist judges imposed fines and even jail terms on at least ten Democratic-Republican newspaper editors for allegedly violating the Acts. The Acts became a major issue in the 1800 presidential election campaign, which led to the election of Thomas Jefferson, a vocal opponent of the Acts. He quickly pardoned all who had been convicted under their provisions, and the new Democratic-Republican Congress allowed the Acts to expire before the Supreme Court had an opportunity to rule on the constitutionality of these serious infringements of the First Amendment.

Slavery, the Civil War, and Rights Curtailments

After the public outcry over the Alien and Sedition Acts, the national government largely got out of the business of regulating speech, but in its place the states began to prosecute those who published articles critical of governmental policies. In the 1830s, at the urgings of abolitionists, the publication or dissemination of any positive information about slavery became a punishable offense in the North. In the opposite vein, in the South, supporters of the "peculiar institution" of slavery enacted laws to prohibit publication of any anti-slavery sentiments. Southern postmasters refused to deliver Northern abolitionist papers throughout the South, which amounted to censorship of the mails.

During the Civil War, President Abraham Lincoln effectively suspended the free press provision of the First Amendment (as well as many other sections of the Constitution) and even went so far as to order the arrest of the editors of two New York papers that were critical of him. Far from protesting against these blatant violations of the First Amendment, Congress acceded to them. Right after the war, for example, Congress actually prevented the Supreme Court from issuing a judgment on a case, *Ex parte McCardle* (1869),[34] because members feared its decision would be critical of the powers Lincoln had taken on during the war. William McCardle, a Mississippi newspaper editor, had sought to arouse sentiment against Lincoln and the Union occupation. Even though he was a civilian, McCardle was jailed by a military court without having any charges brought against him. He appealed to the U.S. Supreme Court, arguing that he was being held unlawfully. Congress, fearing that a victory for McCardle would prompt other Confederate newspaper editors to follow his lead, enacted a law barring the Supreme Court from hearing appeals of cases involving convictions for publishing statements critical of the Union. Because Article III of the Constitution gives Congress the power to determine the jurisdiction of the Court, the Court was forced to conclude that it had no authority to rule in the matter.

After the Civil War, states also began to prosecute individuals for seditious speech when they uttered or printed statements critical of the government. Between 1890 and 1900, for example, there were more than 100 state prosecutions for sedition in state courts.[35] Moreover, by the dawn of the twentieth century, public opinion in the United States had become exceedingly hostile to the preachings of such groups as socialists and communists (see "People of the Past: Eugene V. Debs," p. 97) who attempted to appeal to the thousands of new and disheartened immigrants. Groups espousing socialism and communism became the targets of state laws curtailing speech and the written word. By the end of World War I, over thirty states had passed laws (often known as criminal syndicalism statutes) to punish seditious speech, and more than 1,900 individuals and over 100 newspapers were prosecuted for violations.[36]

New Restrictions/New Tests

The first major federal law restricting freedom of speech and the press since the Alien and Sedition Acts was the Espionage Act of 1917. Nearly 2,000 Americans were convicted of violating its various provisions, especially those making it illegal to urge resistance to the draft, and prohibiting the distribution of anti-war leaflets.

In 1919, the Supreme Court decided several important cases calling for interpretation of the First Amendment. Charles T. Schenck, a secretary of the Socialist Party, was tried and convicted for printing, distributing, and mailing anti-war leaflets to men eligible for the draft. In *Schenck* v. *United States* (1919),[37] his conviction for urging others to resist military induction was upheld in an opinion written by Justice Oliver Wendell Holmes. The Court interpreted the First Amendment to allow Congress to restrict speech that was "of such a nature as to create a clear and present danger that will bring about the substantive evils that Congress has a right to prevent." Holmes relied on the **bad tendency test**, which had been used in earlier cases. He reasoned that in times of war, Schenck's leaflets could obstruct recruitment into the military because their "tendency" and "intent" were the same. During the same term, in another case involving the bad tendencies of anti-war speech, Holmes concluded for a unanimous Court that the leaflets in question constituted a danger. He explained that even the U.S. Constitution does not protect an individual from "falsely shouting fire in a theater and causing a panic."[38]

Under the **clear and present danger test**, which allowed Congress to ban speech that could cause a clear and present danger to society, the circumstances surrounding the incident counts, according to the Court. Whereas the leaflets might have been permissible in peacetime, they posed too much of a danger in wartime to be allowed. The clear and present danger test used by the Court attempted to draw a line between protected and unprotected speech in this new area of constitutional interpretation. Holmes appeared to use the clear and present danger and bad tendency tests interchangeably. For example, in *Debs* v. *United States* (1919), Holmes concluded for the Court that Eugene Debs's anti-war speeches "had as their natural tendency and reasonably probable effect to obstruct the recruitment" of men into the armed services, and that his conviction was thus constitutional.[39]

In that same year, however, division among the members of the Court concerning the clear and present danger test became apparent. In *Abrams* v. *United States* (1919),[40] a majority of the Court upheld Abrams's conviction for distributing leaflets critical of President Wilson's decision to send American soldiers to Russia. In dissent, however, Holmes rejected the majority's reliance on the clear and present danger test. He concluded that the activities of six anarchists who had been convicted for writing a "silly leaflet by an unknown man" protesting the U.S. government's attempts to overthrow Russia's newly formed Bolshevik government posed no imminent danger to the United States. The majority, however, remained unconvinced by Holmes's arguments. From 1919 to 1927, the convictions of defendants in five other cases brought under the Espionage Act were upheld by the Court.

For decades, the Supreme Court continued to wrestle with what constituted a "danger." Finally, fifty years after the Abrams decision, in *Brandenburg* v. *Ohio* (1969),[41] the Court fashioned a new test: the **direct incitement test**. Now the government could punish the advocacy of illegal action only if "such advocacy is directed to inciting or producing imminent lawless action and is likely to incite or produce such action." Brandenburg was convicted under an Ohio law after he advocated racial strife during a televised KKK hearing. A trial court concluded that his speech, in context, produced

Bad tendency test Engaging in speech that has a tendency to induce illegal behavior or to create a danger; speech that is not protected by the First Amendment.

Clear and present danger test Used by the Supreme Court in an attempt to draw a line between protected and unprotected speech. As the test is applied, the Court looks to see if there is an imminent danger that illegal action would occur in response to the contested speech.

Direct incitement test The advocacy of illegal action is protected by the First Amendment unless imminent action is intended and likely to occur.

no imminent danger. Thus, the statute, in its interpretation, and his conviction were unconstitutional. The requirement of "imminent harm" makes it more difficult for the government to punish speech and is consistent with the Framer's notion of the special role played by speech in a democratic society.

The First Amendment Applied to the States: The Incorporation Doctrine

As discussed in Chapter 2, the Bill of Rights was intended to limit the powers of the *national* government to infringe upon the rights and liberties of the citizenry. And in *Barron* v. *Baltimore* (1833),[42] the Supreme Court ruled that the federal Bill of Rights limited only the U.S. government and *not* the states. In 1868, however, the Fourteenth Amendment was added to the U.S. Constitution. Its language suggested the possibility that some or even all of the protections guaranteed in the Bill of Rights might be interpreted to prevent *state* infringement of those rights. Section 1 of the Fourteenth Amendment reads: "No State shall . . . deprive any person of life, liberty, or property, without due process of law."

Until 1925, the Supreme Court steadfastly rejected numerous arguments urging it to interpret the **due process clause** as making various provisions contained in the Bill of Rights applicable to the states. As a consequence, states were free throughout this period to pass sedition laws, knowing that the Supreme Court would uphold their constitutional validity. Then, in 1925, all of this changed dramatically. Benjamin Gitlow, a member of the Left Wing Section of the Socialist Party, was convicted of violating a New York law which, in language very similar to that of the federal Espionage Act, prohibited the advocacy of the violent overthrow of the government. Gitlow had printed 16,000 copies of a manifesto in which he urged workers to rise up to overthrow the U.S. government. Although Gitlow's conviction was upheld, in *Gitlow* v. *New York* (1925) the Supreme Court noted that the states were not completely free to limit forms of political expression:

> For present purposes we may and do assume that freedom of speech and of the press—which are protected by the First Amendment from abridgement by Congress—are among the *fundamental personal rights and "liberties"* protected by the due process clause of the Fourteenth Amendment from impairment by the states (emphasis added).[43]

Gitlow, with its finding that states could not abridge free speech protections, was the first step in the slow process of the judicial development of the **incorporation doctrine**. After *Gitlow*, it took the Court six more years to "incorporate" another First Amendment freedom—that of the press. *Near* v. *Minnesota* (1931)[44] was the first case in which the Supreme Court found that a state law violated freedom of the press as protected by the First Amendment. Jay Near, the publisher of a weekly Minneapolis newspaper, regularly attacked a variety of groups—blacks, Catholics, Jews, and labor union leaders. Few escaped his hatred. Near's paper was closed under the authority of a state criminal libel law banning "malicious, scandalous, or defamatory" publications. Near appealed the closing of his paper, and the Supreme Court ruled that "The fact that the liberty of the press may be abused by miscreant purveyors of scandal does not make any the less necessary the immunity of the press from previous restraint."[45]

As revealed in "Landmark Dates in the Selective Incorporation of the Bill of Rights" (p. 99), not all the guarantees in the Bill of Rights have been made applicable to the

Due process clause Clause contained in the Fifth and Fourteenth Amendments. Over the years, it has been construed to guarantee to individuals a variety of rights ranging from economic liberty to criminal procedural rights to protection from arbitrary governmental action.

Incorporation doctrine Principle in which the Supreme Court has held that most, but not all, of the specific guarantees in the Bill of Rights limit states and local governments by making those guarantees applicable to the states through the due process clause of the Fourteenth Amendment.

Until *Gitlow* v. *New York* (1925) involving Benjamin Gitlow, the Executive Secretary of the Socialist Party, it was generally thought that the Fourteenth Amendment did not apply the protections of the Bill of Rights to the states. Here Gitlow is shown testifying before the Dees Committee, which was investigating un-American activities.

*P*EOPLE OF THE PAST

Eugene V. Debs

Eugene Victor Debs was a prominent American socialist and a central figure in challenging the free speech restrictions of the Espionage Act of 1917. He was born in Terre Haute, Indiana in 1855. Debs went to work on the railroads in 1870, and in 1875 he helped form a lodge of the Brotherhood of Locomotive Firemen, an early union, and later served as its national secretary and treasurer, and editor of its magazine. In 1893 he helped form the American Railway Union and was made its president.

As part of the Cleveland administration's attempts to crush the 1894 Pullman strike in Chicago, Debs was held in contempt of court for violating a federal injunction against striking and was sentenced to six months in jail. While in jail, he read widely on the philosophy of socialism, and in 1897 he transformed the remains of the American Railway Union into the Social Democratic Party of America, later called the Socialist Party of America.

Debs ran for president of the United States on the Socialist ticket in 1900, 1904, 1908, and 1912. In 1918, as one of the most visible critics of Woodrow Wilson's decision to enter World War I, he again found himself in court, this time charged with violating the Espionage Act of 1917.

Debs was tried and sentenced to ten years in prison for a speech he delivered in Canton, Ohio at a socialist anti-war rally. In his speech, Debs praised other imprisoned leaders of his party who had been jailed for aiding draft resistors. He accused the U.S. government of using false testimony to convict another anti-war activist and labeled the war a plot by "the predator capitalists in the United States" against the working class "who furnish the corpses. . . . You need to know," he told his listeners, that "you are fit for something better than slavery and cannon fodder."

By the time the appeal of his conviction reached the Supreme Court, a post-war "red scare" had spread through the country. Without even a reference to the "clear and present danger" test enunciated just a week earlier in *Schenck* v. *United States*, a unanimous Court affirmed his conviction. Although in *Debs* v. *United States* (1919) Justice Oliver Wendell Holmes conceded that "the main theme" of Debs's speech was the growth and eventual triumph of socialism, he argued that "if a part of the manifest intent of the more general utterance was to encourage those present to obstruct recruiting . . . the immunity of the general theme may not be enough to protect the speech."

Although he was in prison, Debs again ran for president in 1920 and received more than 900,000 votes. President Wilson, still bitter about Debs's opposition to the war, refused to pardon him. Wilson's successor, Warren G. Harding, showed more compassion and pardoned him in 1921. Debs devoted much of his remaining life to campaigning for improved prison conditions. He died in 1926.

---

states through the due process clause of the Fourteenth Amendment. Instead, the Court has selectively chosen to limit the rights of states by protecting the rights it considers most fundamental. This process is referred to as selective incorporation.

Selective Incorporation and Fundamental Freedoms. The rationale for **selective incorporation**, the judicial application to the states of only some of the rights enumerated by the Bill of Rights, was set out in *Palko* v. *Connecticut* (1937).[46] Frank

Selective incorporation A judicial doctrine whereby most but not all of the protections found in the Bill of Rights are made applicable to the states via the Fourteenth Amendment.

Palko was charged with first-degree murder for killing two police officers, found guilty of a lesser charge of second-degree murder, and sentenced to life imprisonment. Connecticut appealed, Palko was retried, found guilty of first-degree murder, and re-sentenced to death.

Palko then appealed his second conviction on the grounds that it violated the Fifth Amendment's prohibition against double jeopardy, because the Fifth Amendment had been made applicable to the states by the due process clause of the Fourteenth Amendment.

The Supreme Court upheld Palko's second conviction and the death sentence, thereby choosing not to bind states to the Fifth Amendment's double jeopardy clause. Writing for the majority, Justice Benjamin Cardozo set forth principles that were to guide the Court's interpretation of the incorporation doctrine for the next several decades. Some protections found in the Bill of Rights were absorbed into the concept of due process only because they are so fundamental to our notions of liberty and justice that they cannot be denied by the states. "Neither liberty nor justice would exist if [fundamental rights] are sacrificed," wrote Cardozo. Because the Court concluded that the protection against double jeopardy was not a fundamental right, Palko died in Connecticut's gas chamber one year later. Cardozo's argument that those rights were necessary to a "fair and enlightened system of justice" was nonetheless gradually expanded by the Court in later years to include most guarantees contained in the Bill of Rights and were especially critical in the development of criminal law (see "Landmark Dates in the Selective Incorporation of the Bill of Rights," p. 99).

Symbolic Speech

Symbolic speech Symbols, signs, and other methods of expression generally also considered to be protected by the First Amendment.

In addition to the general protection accorded pure speech, the Supreme Court has extended the reach of the First Amendment to other means of expression often called **symbolic speech**—symbols, signs, and the like—as well as to activities like picketing, sit-ins, and demonstrations. In the words of Justice John Marshall Harlan, these kinds of "speech" are part of the "free trade in ideas."[47]

The Supreme Court first acknowledged that symbolic speech was entitled to First Amendment protection in *Stromberg* v. *California* (1931).[48] There, the Court overturned the conviction of the director of a communist youth camp under a state statute prohibiting the display of a red flag, a symbol of opposition to the U.S. government. Later, in 1943, the Supreme Court struck down a state law requiring students to salute the American flag, thus reaffirming the notion that nonverbal expressions are also entitled to First Amendment protection.[49] In a similar vein, the right of high school students to wear black armbands to protest the Vietnam War was upheld in *Tinker* v. *Des Moines Independent Community School District* (1969).[50]

Burning the American flag has also been held to be a form of protected symbolic speech. In 1989, a sharply divided Supreme Court (five to four) reversed the conviction of Gregory Johnson, who had been found guilty of setting fire to an American flag during the 1984 Republican national convention in Dallas.[51] A major public outcry against the Court went up, and President George Bush and numerous members of Congress called for a constitutional amendment to ban flag burning. Others, including Justice William J. Brennan, Jr., noted that if it had not been for acts like that of Johnson, the United States would never have been created, nor would a First Amendment guaranteeing a right to political protest exist.

Landmark Dates in the Selective Incorporation of the Bill of Rights

Date	Amendment	Right	Case
1925 ♦	I.	Speech	*Gitlow* v. *New York*
1931 ♦		Press	*Near* v. *Minnesota*
1937 ♦		Assembly	*DeJonge* v. *Oregon*
1940 ♦		Religion	*Cantwell* v. *Connecticut*
	II.	Right to bear arms	*not incorporated* (Generally, the Supreme Court has upheld reasonable regulations of the right of private citizens to bear arms. Should a tough gun-control law be adopted by a state or local government and a challenge to it be made, a test of incorporation might be presented to the Court in the future.)
	III.	No quartering of soldiers	*not incorporated* (The quartering problem has not recurred since colonial times.)
	IV.	Unreasonable searches and seizures	
1949 ♦			*Wolf* v. *Colorado*
1961 ♦		The exclusionary rule	*Mapp* v. *Ohio*
1897 ♦	V.	Just compensation	*Chicago, B&O RR. Co.* v. *Chicago*
1964 ♦		Self-incrimination	*Malloy* v. *Hogan*
1969 ♦		Double jeopardy	*Benton* v. *Maryland*
		Grand jury indictment	*not incorporated* (The trend in state criminal cases is away from grand juries and toward reliance upon the sworn written accusation of the prosecuting attorney.)
1948 ♦	VI.	Public trial	*In re Oliver*
1963 ♦		Right to counsel	*Gideon* v. *Wainwright*
1965 ♦		Confrontation of witnesses	*Pointer* v. *Texas*
1966 ♦		Impartial trial	*Parker* v. *Gladden*
1967 ♦		Speedy trial	*Klopfer* v. *North Carolina*
1967 ♦		Compulsory process	*Washington* v. *Texas*
1968 ♦		Jury trial	*Duncan* v. *Louisiana*
	VII.	Right to jury trial in civil cases	*not incorporated* (While Warren Burger was Chief Justice he conducted a campaign to abolish jury trials in civil cases to save time and money, and for other reasons.)
	VIII.	Freedom from cruel and unusual punishment	
1962 ♦			*Robinson* v. *California*
		Freedom from excessive fines or bail	*not incorporated*

THEN AND NOW

The Second Amendment and the Right of the People to Keep and Bear Arms

During colonial times, the English tradition of distrust of standing armies was evident: all white men in whole sections of the colonies were deputized to defend their settlements against Indians and other European powers. Most colonies required all white men to keep and bear arms. These local militias were viewed as the best way to keep order and liberty.

The Second Amendment was added to the Constitution to ensure that Congress could not pass laws to disarm state militias. It also appeased Anti-Federalists who feared that the new Constitution would cause them to lose the right to keep and bear arms. And it recognized an unstated right—the right to revolt against governmental tyranny.

Through the 1930s, few state statutes regulating firearms were passed (generally these few laws dated from the pre-Civil War era and dealt with the possession of firearms by slaves). And the Supreme Court's decision in *Barron* v. *Baltimore* (1833), limiting the application of the Bill of Rights to actions of Congress alone, prevented federal review of those state laws. Moreover, in *Dred Scott* v. *Sanford* (1857; see Chapter 3), Chief Justice Taney listed the right to own and carry arms as a basic right of citizenship.

In 1934, Congress passed the National Firearms Act in response to the increase in organized crime that occurred in the 1920s and 1930s. The Act imposed taxes on automatic weapons (such as machine guns) and sawed-off shotguns. In *United States* v. *Miller* (1939) a unanimous Court upheld the constitutionality of the Act by finding that the Second Amendment was intended to protect a citizen's right to own ordinary militia weapons, and not unregistered sawed-off shotguns, which were at issue in the *Miller* case. *Miller* was the last time the Supreme Court directly addressed the Second Amendment. In *Quilici* v. *Village of Morton Grove* (1983), the Supreme Court refused to review a lower court's ruling that had upheld the constitutionality of a local ordinance banning handguns.

In the 1980s through the 1990s, as crime and violence increased, the issue of gun control became and remains a particularly hot topic in American politics.

In the aftermath of the assassination attempt on President Ronald Reagan in 1981, many lawmakers called for passage of gun control legislation. At the forefront of that effort was Sarah Brady, the wife of James Brady, the presidential press secretary who was badly wounded and left partially disabled by John Hinkley, Jr. Her efforts led to passage of the "Brady Bill" in 1993, which imposed a federal five-day waiting period on the purchase of handguns.

In 1994, in spite of extensive lobbying by the National Rifle Association, Congress passed the Violent Crime Control and Law Enforcement Act. In addition to providing money to the states for additional police officers and prisons, the Act banned the manufacture, transport, sale, or possession of nineteen semi-automatic assault weapons. In 1995 Congress revamped the crime bill further by requiring convicted criminals to make restitution to their victims. Congress even weakened the reach of the Fourth Amendment by allowing federal prosecutors to use information seized in an illegal search without a warrant so long as they believed that they possessed the authority.

James and Sarah Brady being applauded for their efforts to win congressional approval of the Brady Bill after it was signed into law by President Clinton.

Instead of a constitutional amendment, Congress passed the Federal Flag Protection Act of 1989, which authorized federal prosecution of anyone who intentionally desecrated a national flag. Those who originally had been arrested burned another flag and were convicted; their conviction was again overturned by the Supreme Court. As they had in *Johnson*, the justices divided five to four in holding that this federal law "suffered from the same fundamental flaw" as had the earlier state law that was declared in violation of the First Amendment.[52] After that decision by the Court, additional efforts were made to pass a constitutional amendment so that congressional attempts to ban flag burning would not be subject to "interpretation." Those efforts, however, initially fell short of passage in both houses of Congress, but many legislators continue to press for a flag desecration amendment.

Prior Restraint

In *Near* v. *Minnesota* (1931), the Court made it clear that individuals could be punished by the state *after the fact* for libelous statements. But, with only a few exceptions, the Court made it clear that it would not tolerate **prior restraint** of speech or expression; that is, prohibition of speech or publication before the fact. Later, for example, in *New York Times Co.* v. *United States* (1971)[53] (also called the "Pentagon Papers" case), the Supreme Court ruled that the U.S. government could not block the publication of secret Defense Department documents illegally furnished to the *Times* by anti-war activists. In *Nebraska Press Association* v. *Stuart* (1976), the Supreme Court went even further, noting that any attempt by the government to prevent expression carried "a 'heavy presumption' against its constitutionality."[54] In *Nebraska*, a trial court had issued a "gag order" barring the press from reporting the lurid details of a crime. In balancing the defendant's constitutional right to a fair trial against the press's right to cover a story, the trial judge concluded that the defendant's right carried greater weight. The Supreme Court disagreed, holding the press's right to cover the trial paramount.

> **Prior Restraint** Judicial doctrine stating that the government cannot prohibit speech or publication before the fact.

"Politically Correct" Speech

A particularly thorny First Amendment area has emerged as universities have attempted to ban what they view as offensive speech. Since 1989, more than 200 colleges and universities have banned racial slurs directed at minority groups. The University of Connecticut, for example, banned "inappropriately directed laughter" and "conspicuous exclusion of students from conversations."

While easy to poke fun at, the "PC movement," as it is known, has a serious side. At Dartmouth, a student was expelled for shouting anti-Semitic, anti-black, and anti-homosexual obscenities at students in their dorm rooms at 2:00 A.M. At the University of Michigan in 1990, a student was accused of violating the university's regulation banning speech that stigmatizes individuals for their sexual orientation, when he said during a classroom discussion that he considered homosexuality to be a disease treatable with therapy. The university's code was challenged by the American Civil Liberties Union and found unconstitutional by a federal district court.

In 1993 some began to question if the PC Movement had gone too far. In January 1993, Eden Jacobowitz, an Israeli student at the University of Pennsylvania, was charged with violating the school's speech policy and threatened with expulsion when he called five African-American women "water buffaloes." The black students were noisily participating in a sorority rite below the Israeli student's dorm room late at night. Frustrated by his inability to study, Jacobowitz yelled, "Shut up, you water

The Pledge of Allegiance
♦♦♦

The flag and even the Pledge of Allegiance have long inspired controversy. The Pledge of Allegiance was written in 1892 as a way for schoolchildren to celebrate the new national holiday, Columbus Day. The pledge was officially recognized by Congress in 1945, although in 1945 the Supreme Court ruled that no person could be required to recite it. In 1954, when the Cold War spread fear of communism and "godlessness," President Eisenhower signed a law to add "under God" after "one nation" to its text.

The American Civil Liberties Union

◆ ◆ ◆

The American Civil Liberties Union (ACLU) was created in 1920 by a group that had defended the civil liberties of conscientious objectors to World War I. As the nation's oldest, largest, and premier nonpartisan civil liberties organization, the ACLU works in three major areas of the law: freedom of speech and religion, due process, and equality before the law. The ACLU lobbies for legislation affecting these areas and conducts extensive public education campaigns to familiarize Americans with the guarantees granted in the Bill of Rights. Its main energies historically have been devoted to litigation to maintain these rights and liberties.

The ACLU has been involved in most speech and religion cases heard by the U.S. Supreme Court. In its own words, it "has been a zealous advocate of the First Amendment and has steadfastly opposed government efforts to regulate either free speech or free thought, no matter how well-intentioned those efforts might be."[*] It also has specialized projects. The National Prison Project, for example, monitors prison conditions to ensure that prisoner rights are not violated. Its Women's Rights Project, originally headed by Ruth Bader Ginsburg, has been at the fore of advancing women's rights through litigation. Similarly, its Reproductive Freedom Project is one of the most active litigators on behalf of pro-choice activists. It regularly sponsors challenges to restrictive state abortion laws and files "friend of the court" briefs in cases in which it is not lead counsel. Among the major cases in which the ACLU has participated are:

First Amendment Rights:

The *Scopes Case* (1945): challenged a Tennessee law making the teaching of evolution a crime

Tinker v. *Des Moines Independent School Board* (1969): upheld the right of students to wear black armbands in protest of the Vietnam War

Lynch v. *Donnelly* (1984): in a defeat for the ACLU, the court held that a city's inclusion of a creche in its annual Christmas display in a private park did not violate the establishment clause

Criminal Defendants' Rights:

Mapp v. *Ohio* (1961): established that illegally obtained evidence cannot be used at trial

Gideon v. *Wainwright* (1963): granted indigents the right to counsel

Miranda v. *Arizona* (1966): guaranteed all suspects a right to counsel

Privacy Rights:

Roe v. *Wade* and *Doe* v. *Bolton* (1973): established a woman's right to an abortion

Bowers v. *Hardwick* (1986): unsuccessfully challenged Georgia's sodomy law

Planned Parenthood v. *Casey* (1992): unsuccessfully challenged Pennsylvania's restrictive abortion regulations

Although the positions taken by the ACLU on these cases generally have been extremely popular with its members, an outcry arose in 1977 when it decided to represent members of the National Socialist Party who had been denied a parade permit to march in Nazi uniforms through Skokie, Illinois, home to many Nazi concentration camp survivors. The ACLU lost more than 60,000 members who protested its involvement in the case, but it stayed true to its purpose—upholding the First Amendment, no matter how offensive the speech or actions in question. Its 1993 membership was approximately 300,000.

Recognition of the growing conservative nature of the Supreme Court has caused the ACLU to rethink its litigation strategies. In fact, from 1987 to 1993 the ACLU's policy was to stay as far away from the Supreme Court as possible, a major shift in tactics. Previously, the ACLU had appeared before the Court more than any organization except the Justice Department. "We're going to be looking for appropriate ways to bring cases in state courts and to insulate them from Supreme Court review,"[**] said one ACLU official in 1987. Recognizing also that "Civil liberties are not something people intuitively grasp,"[†] the ACLU is undertaking a campaign to gain more attention for its cause. But, with its former legal counsel, Ruth Bader Ginsburg, now on the Supreme Court and with a Democrat in the White House, it may rethink its strategies.

---

[*] Brief Amicus Curiae, *Wisconsin* v. *Mitchell,* October Term, 1992, LEXIS.

[**] Quoted in Tony Mauro, *"Supreme Court* v. *Civil Liberties;* the ACLU's New Strategy of Avoidance," *Legal Times* (June 1, 1987): 13.

[†] Ibid.

buffaloes. If you're looking for a party there's a zoo a mile from here."[55] A national debate ensued, and much was made of the fact that the Israeli student maintained that "water buffalo" was a loose translation of a mild Hebrew epithet referring to a rude person. The African-American students ultimately dropped their racial harassment charge, but the ACLU, which had represented Jacobowitz, vowed to continue seeking the repeal of the university's speech code, which it argues violates the First Amendment.

Libel and Slander

False or libelous statements are not restrained by the courts, yet the Supreme Court has consistently ruled that individuals or the press can be sued after the fact for untrue or libelous statements. **Libel** is a written statement that defames the character of a person. If the statement is spoken, it is **slander.** In many nations—such as Great Britain, for example—it is relatively easy to sue someone for libel. In the United States, however, the standards of proof are much more difficult. A person who believes that he or she has been a victim of libel, for example, must show that the statements made were untrue. Truth is an absolute defense against the charge of libel, no matter how painful or embarrassing the revelations.

It is often more difficult for individuals the Supreme Court considers to be "public persons or public officials" to sue for libel or slander. *New York Times Co.* v. *Sullivan* (1964),[56] was the first major libel case considered by the Supreme Court. An Alabama state court had found the *Times* guilty of libel for printing a full-page advertisement accusing Alabama officials of physically abusing blacks during various civil rights protests (the ad was paid for by civil rights activists, including former First Lady Eleanor Roosevelt). The Supreme Court ruled that a finding of libel against a public official could stand only if there were a showing of "actual malice." Proof that the statements were false or negligent was not sufficient to prove "actual malice."

The concept of actual malice can be difficult and confusing. In 1991, the Court directed lower courts to use the phrases "knowledge of falsity" and "reckless disregard of the truth" when giving instructions to juries in libel cases.[57] Given the high degree of proof required, few public officials or public persons have been able to win libel cases.

Libel False statements or statements tending to call someone's reputation into disrepute.

Slander Untrue spoken statements that defame the character of a person.

Obscenity and Pornography[*]

Although the Supreme Court has allowed few governmental bans on most types of speech, some forms of expression are not protected. In *Chaplinsky* v. *New Hampshire* (1942), the Supreme Court set out the rationale by which it would distinguish between protected and unprotected speech. According to the Court, obscenity, lewdness, libel, and fighting words are not protected by the First Amendment because "such expressions are no essential part of any exposition of ideas, and are of such slight social value as a step to truth that any benefit that may be derived from them is clearly outweighed by the social interest in order and morality."[58]

---

[*] Technically, obscenity refers to those things considered "disgusting, foul or morally unhealthy." Pornography, in contrast, is often broader in meaning and generally refers to "depictions of sexual lewdness or erotic behavior." While distasteful to many, pornography is not necessarily obscene. See Donald Downs, "Obscenity and Pornography," in Kermit Hall, ed. *The Oxford Companion to the Supreme Court of the United States* (New York: Oxford University Press, 1992), pp. 602–604.

U.S. courts have often based their decisions of what was obscene on an English common-law test that had been set out in *Regina* v. *Hicklin* (1868): "whether the tendency of the matter charged as obscenity is to deprive and corrupt those whose minds are open to such immoral influences and into whose hands a publication of this sort might fall."[59] Under a test this broad, many materials—especially those that could fall into the hands of children—could be considered obscene. The Supreme Court's use of this test prompted Justice Felix Frankfurter to note, "The incidence of this standard is to reduce the adult population of [the United States] to reading what is fit for children."[60]

The Court did not abandon use of the *Hicklin* test until 1957. In *Roth* v. *United States* (1957), the Court held that to be considered obscene, the material in question must be "utterly without redeeming social importance," and articulated a new test for obscenity: "whether to the average person, applying contemporary community standards, the dominant theme of the material taken as a whole appeals to the prurient interests."[61] In many ways, the *Roth* test brought with it as many problems as it attempted to solve. Throughout the 1950s and 1960s, "prurient" remained hard to define, as the Court struggled to find a standard by which to judge actions or words. In general, only "hardcore" pornography was found obscene by the liberal Warren Court, prompting some to argue that the Court fostered the increase in the number of sexually oriented publications designed to appeal to those living amidst what many called the "sexual revolution." Nevertheless, in 1968, the Court upheld the conviction of Ralph Ginzburg for "pandering" by selectively mailing his magazine *Eros* from such cities as Middlesex, New Jersey; Blue Balls, Montana; and Intercourse, Pennsylvania. Ginzburg's sense of humor was clearly lost on the Court, which decided that he had chosen to exploit the sexual nature of his publication by selective use of provocative postmarks.[62]

Richard M. Nixon made the growth in pornography a major issue when he ran for president in 1968, and he pledged to appoint to federal judgeships only those who would uphold "law and order." Once elected president, Nixon made several appointments to the Court including Chief Justice Warren Burger, and Associate Justices Harry A. Blackmun, William H. Rehnquist, and Lewis F. Powell, Jr. In *Miller* v. *California* (1973),[63] the Burger Court began to formulate rules designed to return to communities a greater role in determining what is obscene, based on local standards.

In *Miller* v. *California* the Court set out a test that redefined obscenity. To determine whether or not material in question was obscene, the Justices instructed that a court must ask "whether the work depicts or describes, in a patently offensive way, sexual conduct specifically defined by state law." Moreover, courts were to determine "whether the work, taken as a whole, lacks serious literary, artistic, political or scientific value." And in place of the contemporary community standards gauge used in earlier cases, the Court defined community standards to mean local, and not national, standards under the rationale that what is acceptable in Times Square in New York City might not be tolerated in Peoria, Illinois.

Until recently, however, community standards could not be the sole criterion of obscenity. In 1974, for example, the Court overturned a decision of a Georgia state court that found *Carnal Knowledge* (a movie starring Jack Nicholson, Ann-Margret, and Art Garfunkel, that included scenes of a partially nude woman) obscene. The Court concluded that the scenes were neither "patently offensive" nor designed to appeal to "prurient interest."[64] As Justice Potter Stewart had once announced, he couldn't define obscenity, but "I know it when I see it."[65] He did not see it in *Carnal Knowledge*.

Time and contexts clearly have altered the Court's and indeed, much of America's perceptions of what is obscene. *Carnal Knowledge* is now often shown on television on Saturday afternoons with only minor editing. But through the early 1990s, the

Rehnquist Court (William H. Rehnquist became Chief Justice in 1986; see Chapter 9) allowed communities greater leeway in drafting statutes to deal with obscenity, and even more important, forms of non-obscene expression. In 1991, for example, the Supreme Court voted five to four to allow Indiana to ban totally nude erotic dancing, concluding that its statute did not violate the First Amendment's guarantee of freedom of expression.[66] Justice Antonin Scalia, concurring in the opinion, went so far as to state that the law should be upheld on the ground that moral opposition to nudity is a sufficient reason for the state to ban it altogether.

The Rights of Criminal Defendants

The Fourth, Fifth, Sixth, and Eighth Amendments provide a variety of procedural guarantees (often called **due process rights**) for those accused of crimes. Particular amendments, as well as other portions of the Constitution, specifically provide procedural guarantees to protect individuals accused of crimes at all stages of the criminal justice process. And as is the case with the First Amendment, many of these rights have been interpreted by the Supreme Court to apply to the states.

Due process rights Procedural guarantees provided by the Fourth, Fifth, Sixth, and Eighth Amendments for those accused of crimes.

In interpreting the amendments dealing with what are frequently termed "criminal rights," the courts have to grapple not only with the meaning of the amendments, but also with how their protections are to be implemented. The Eighth Amendment, for example, prohibits "cruel and unusual punishments." The question of what is cruel and unusual, however, has vexed the Supreme Court for years. In 1972, for example, the Supreme Court interpreted the Eighth Amendment to mean that the death penalty was cruel and unusual. But as crime increased and public opinion toward the death penalty changed, so did the Court's interpretation of the Eighth Amendment.

Today the Court routinely allows executions to be carried out. Perhaps even more than in the area of First Amendment guarantees, prevailing thoughts about the rights of criminal defendants are changing quickly and dramatically as the Supreme Court moves away from what some view as the "excesses" of the Warren Court (1953–1969).

Over the years, many individuals have criticized the liberal Warren Court's rulings, arguing that they gave criminals more "rights" than their victims. The Warren Court made several provisions of the Bill of Rights dealing with the rights of criminal defendants applicable to the states through the Fourteenth Amendment. It is important to remember that most procedural guarantees apply to individuals charged with crimes, that is, *before* they have been tried. These rights were designed to protect those wrongfully accused, although, of course, they often have helped the guilty. But as Justice William O. Douglas once noted, "respecting the dignity even of the least worthy citizen . . . raises the stature of all of us."[67] Many continue to argue, however, that only the guilty are helped by the American system and that criminals should not go unpunished because of simple police error. The dilemma of balancing the rights of the individual against those of society permeates the entire debate, and often even judicial interpretations of the rights of criminal defendants.

The Fourth Amendment and Searches and Seizures

The Fourth Amendment to the Constitution declares:

> The right of the people to be secure in their persons, houses, papers, and effects, against unreasonable searches and seizures, shall not be violated, and no Warrants

Surveillance can include indoor as well as outdoor activities. This photo was taken after state and federal narcotics agents raided this sophisticated indoor marijuana farming operation in east Texas.

shall issue, but upon probable cause, supported by Oath or affirmation, and particularly describing the place to be searched, and the persons or things to be seized.

This amendment's purpose was to deny the national government the authority to make general searches. The English Parliament had often issued general "writs of assistance" that allowed such searches. These general warrants were also used against religious and political dissenters, a practice the Framers wanted banned in the new nation. But still, the language that they chose left numerous questions to be answered, including, what is an "unreasonable" search? Over the years, in a number of decisions, the Supreme Court has interpreted the Fourth Amendment to allow the police to search:

1. The person arrested;
2. Things in plain view of the accused person; and,
3. Places or things that the arrested person could touch or reach or are otherwise in the arrestee's "immediate control."

Warrantless searches often occur "incident to an arrest," meaning simultaneously with it. In such cases, the police may generally seize only potential evidence in "plain view" or in the "immediate control" of the person detained. In 1993, the Court unanimously ruled that police could seize contraband discovered through what it termed a "plain feel" based on an officer's sense of touch.[68] Police may also search if they are in "hot pursuit" of a suspect, or if they believe evidence will be destroyed.

If police suspect that someone is committing or is about to commit a crime, they may "stop and frisk" the individual under suspicion. Whereas the liberal Warren Court limited those searches to "outer clothing . . . in an attempt to discover weapons which might be used to assault [a police officer],"[69] the Burger and Rehnquist Courts have expanded that limitation. In 1989, the Court upheld a drug-enforcement officer's search of a suspected drug courier at an airport. Chief Justice Rehnquist ruled that there need be only a "reasonable suspicion" for stopping a suspect—a much lower standard than "probable cause."[70]

Searches can also be made without a warrant if consent is obtained, and the Court has ruled that consent can be given by a variety of persons. It has ruled, for example, that police can search a bedroom occupied by two persons as long as they have the consent of one of them.[71]

In situations where no arrest occurs, police must obtain search warrants from a "neutral and detached magistrate" prior to conducting more extensive searches of houses, cars, offices, or any other place where an individual would reasonably have some expectation of privacy.[72] Police can't get search warrants, for example, to require you to undergo surgery to remove a bullet that might be used to incriminate you since your expectation of bodily privacy outweighs the need for evidence.[73] But courts don't require search warrants in possible drunk driving situations. Thus, the police can require you to take a Breathalyzer test to determine whether you have been drinking in excess of legal limits.[74]

Homes, too, are presumed to be private. Firefighters can enter your home to fight a fire without a warrant. But if they decide to investigate the cause of the fire, they must obtain a warrant before their reentry.[75] In contrast, under the "open fields doctrine" first articulated by the Supreme Court in 1924,[76] if you own a field, and even if you post "No Trespassing" signs, the police can search your field without a warrant to see if you are illegally growing marijuana, because you cannot reasonably expect privacy in an open field.[77] In a series of five-to-four decisions, the Rehnquist Court expanded the open fields doctrine to allow other kinds of warrantless searches, including aerial observations of a fenced-in back yard by police looking for marijuana,[78] aerial photography of a Dow Chemical site to inspect for pollution violations,[79] and a nighttime search of a barn in a field.[80]

Cars have proven problematic for police and the courts because of their mobile nature. As noted by Chief Justice William Howard Taft as early as 1925, "the vehicle can quickly be moved out of the locality or jurisdiction in which the warrant must be sought."[81] Over the years the Court has become increasingly lenient about the scope of automobile searches. In 1991, for example, the Court upheld a warrantless search of a container found in a car, even though the police lacked probable cause to search the car itself.[82]

Kimberly Bergalis, who claimed that she contracted HIV from her dentist, appears before a House subcommittee to advocate mandated HIV testing of all health care workers.

Testing for Drugs and HIV.   Testing for drugs and HIV has become an especially thorny search-and-seizure issue. If the government can require you to take a Breathalyzer test, can it require you to be tested for drugs? For HIV? In the wake of growing public concern over drug use, in 1986 President Ronald Reagan signed an executive order requiring many federal employees to undergo drug tests. While many private employers and professional athletic organizations routinely require drug tests upon application or as a condition of employment, *governmental* requirements present constitutional questions of the scope of permissible searches and seizures. Initially, the federal courts adopted the view that mandatory testing of those in certain occupations such as the police and firefighting forces was unconstitutional unless there was suspicion that the employee had been using drugs. In 1989, however, the Supreme Court ruled that mandatory drug and alcohol testing of employees involved in accidents was constitutional.[83] And in 1995, the Court upheld the constitutionality of random drug testing of public high school athletes in a 5 to 4 decision.[84]

Testing for the human immunodeficiency virus (HIV), which causes AIDS, has also produced questions of unreasonable searches and seizures, especially since those with the virus generally experience discrimination in many walks of life. In July 1991, the Centers for Disease Control (CDC) recommended that all health-care professionals who perform surgery undergo voluntary testing to determine if they are infected with HIV. If they are, the CDC suggested that they disclose the condition to patients and refrain from practicing unless they are cleared to do so by a local medical review panel. In the absence of federal legislation, however, many medical organizations have refused to comply with the CDC's recommendations.

The Fifth Amendment and Self-Incrimination

The Fifth Amendment provides that "No person shall be . . . compelled in any criminal case to be a witness against himself." The Supreme Court has interpreted this guarantee to be "as broad as the mischief against which it seeks to guard,"[85] finding that criminal defendants do not have to take the stand at trial to answer questions, nor can a judge make mention of their failure to do so as evidence of guilt. Moreover, lawyers cannot imply that a defendant who refuses to take the stand must be guilty or have something to hide. This right not to testify extends to defendants in grand jury proceedings and legislative investigations, and even to witnesses in judicial proceedings, if the information they give could result in their own prosecution. "Taking the Fifth" is shorthand for exercising one's constitutional right not to self-incriminate.

Even though Ernesto Miranda's confession was not admitted as evidence at his retrial, his ex-girlfriend's testimony and that of the victim were enough to convince the jury of his guilt. He served nine years in prison before he was released on parole. After his release, he routinely sold autographed cards inscribed with the Miranda rights now read to all suspects. In 1976, four years after his release, Miranda was stabbed to death in Phoenix in a bar fight during a card game. Two Miranda cards were found on his body, and the person who killed him was read his Miranda rights upon his arrest.

Miranda rights Statements that must be made by the police informing a suspect of his or her constitutional rights protected by the Fifth Amendment, including the right to an attorney provided by the court if the suspect cannot afford one.

Exclusionary rule Judicially created rule that prohibits police from using illegally seized evidence at trial.

This right also means that prosecutors cannot use as evidence in a trial any of a defendant's statements or confessions that were not "voluntary." As is the case in many areas of the law, however, judicial interpretation of the term *voluntary* has changed over time. Police often used to beat defendants to obtain their confessions. In 1936, however, the Supreme Court ruled convictions for murder based solely on confessions given after physical beatings unconstitutional.[86] Police then began to resort to other measures to force confessions. Defendants, for example, were "given the third degree"— questioned for hours on end with no sleep or food, or threatened with physical violence until they were mentally "beaten" into a confession. In other situations family members were threatened. In one case a young mother was told that her welfare benefits would be terminated and her children taken away from her if she failed to talk.[87]

Miranda v. *Arizona* (1966) was the Supreme Court's response to these creative efforts to obtain confessions that were not truly voluntary.[88] On March 3, 1963, an eighteen-year-old girl was kidnapped and raped on the outskirts of Phoenix, Arizona. Ten days later, police arrested Ernesto Miranda, a poor, mentally disturbed man with a ninth-grade education. In a police-station lineup, the victim identified Miranda as her attacker. Police then took Miranda to a separate room and questioned him for two hours. At first he denied guilt. Eventually, however, he confessed to the crime and wrote and signed a brief statement describing the crime and admitting his guilt. At no time was he told that he did not have to answer any questions or that he could be represented by an attorney.

After Miranda's conviction, his case was appealed on the grounds that his Fifth Amendment right not to incriminate himself had been violated, because his confession had been coerced. Writing for the Court, Chief Justice Earl Warren, himself a former district attorney and California State Attorney General, noted that because police have a tremendous advantage in any interrogation situation, criminal suspects must be given greater protection. A confession obtained in the manner of Miranda's was not truly voluntary; thus, it was inadmissible at trial.

To provide guidelines for police to implement *Miranda*, the Court mandated that:

> Prior to any questioning, the person must be warned that he has a right to remain silent, that any statements he does make may be used as evidence against him, and that he has a right to the presence of an attorney, either retained or appointed.

In response, police routinely began to read suspects their **Miranda rights**, a practice you undoubtedly have seen repeated over and over in movies or on TV police dramas.

Although the Burger Court did not enforce the reading of Miranda rights as vehemently as had the Warren Court, Chief Justice Burger, Warren's successor, acknowledged that they had become an integral part of established police procedures.[89] The Rehnquist Court, however, has been more tolerant of the use of coerced confessions and has employed a much more flexible standard to alow their admissibility. In 1991, for example, it ruled that the use of a coerced confession in a criminal trial does not automatically invalidate a conviction.[90]

The Exclusionary Rule

In *Weeks* v. *United States* (1914),[91] the U.S. Supreme Court adopted the **exclusionary rule**, barring the use of illegally seized evidence at trial. Thus, although the Fourth and Fifth Amendments do not bar the use of evidence obtained in violation of their provisions, the exclusionary rule is a judicially created remedy to deter constitutional violations. In *Weeks*, for example, the Court reasoned that allowing police and prosecutors to use the "fruits of a poisonous tree" (a tainted search) would only encourage that activity. Later, in *Mapp* v. *Ohio* (1961),[92] where a questionable search of a house was at issue, the Court ruled that the exclusionary rule applied to the states via the Fourteenth Amendment.

The Warren Court resolved the dilemma of balancing the goal of deterring police misconduct against the likelihood that a guilty individual would go free in favor of deterrence. In contrast, the Burger and Rehnquist Courts and more recently, Congress, have gradually chipped away at the exclusionary rule. In 1976 the Burger Court dramatically reduced the opportunities for defendants to appeal their convictions based on tainted evidence in violation of the Fourth Amendment.[93] If objections to the evidence have already been raised in state court, convicted defendants cannot seek a rehearing of the issue in federal court. The Court noted that the exclusionary rule "deflects the truth-finding process and often frees the guilty." Since then, the Court has carved out a variety of "good faith exceptions" to the exclusionary rule, allowing the use of "tainted" evidence in a variety of situations, especially when police thought they were acting within the Fourth Amendment's mandates, or what Congress terms "good faith."

The Sixth Amendment and the Right to Counsel

The Sixth Amendment guarantees to an accused person "the Assistance of Counsel in his defense." In the past, this provision meant only that an individual could hire an attorney to represent him or her in court. Since most criminal defendants are impoverished, this provision was of little assistance to many who found themselves on trial. Recognizing this, Congress required federal courts to provide an attorney for defendants too poor to afford one. This was first required in capital cases (where the death penalty is a possibility); eventually attorneys were provided to the poor in all federal criminal cases.[94] In 1932, the Supreme Court directed states to furnish lawyers to defendants in capital cases.[95] It also began to expand the right to counsel to other state offenses, but did so in a piecemeal fashion that gave the states little direction. Given the high cost of providing legal counsel, this ambiguity often made it cost-effective for the states not to provide counsel at all.

These ambiguities came to an end with the Court's decision in *Gideon* v. *Wainwright* (1963).[96] As depicted in Anthony Lewis's book *Gideon's Trumpet* and in the made-for-television movie of the same name, Clarence Earl Gideon, a fifty-one–year-old drifter, was charged with breaking into a Panama City, Florida, pool hall and stealing beer, wine, and some change from a vending machine. At his trial he asked the judge to appoint a lawyer for him because he was too poor to hire one himself. The judge refused, and Gideon was convicted and given a five-year prison term for petty larceny. The case against Gideon had not been strong, but as a layperson unfamiliar with the law and with trial practice and procedure, he was unable to point out its weaknesses.

The apparent inequities in the system that had resulted in Gideon's conviction continued to bother him. Eventually he borrowed some paper from a prison guard and, after consulting the prison library, drafted and mailed to the U.S. Supreme Court a petition asking it to overrule his conviction.

In a unanimous decision, the U.S. Supreme Court agreed with Gideon and his court-appointed lawyer, Abe Fortas, a future associate justice of the Supreme Court. Writing for the Court, Justice Hugo Black explained that "lawyers in criminal courts are necessities, not luxuries." Therefore, the Court concluded, the state *must* provide an attorney to poor defendants in felony cases. Underscoring the Court's point, Gideon was acquitted when he was retried with a lawyer to argue his case.

When Clarence Earl Gideon wrote out his petition for a writ of *certiorari* to the Supreme Court (asking the Court, in its discretion, to hear his case) he had no way of knowing that his case would lead to the landmark ruling on the right to counsel, *Gideon* v. *Wainwright*. Nor did he know that Chief Justice Earl Warren had actually instructed his law clerks to be on the look-out for a *habeas corpus* petition (literally "you have the body," which argues that the person in jail is there in violation of some statutory or constitutional right) that could be used to guarantee the assistance of counsel for defendants in criminal cases.

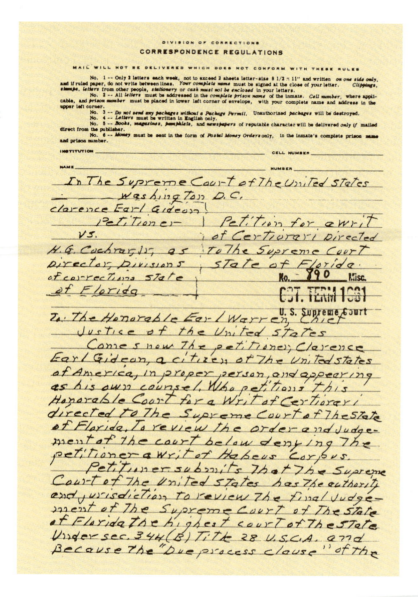

In 1972, the Burger Court expanded the *Gideon* rule, holding that "even in prosecutions for offenses less serious than felonies, a fair trial may require the presence of a lawyer."[97] Seven years later, the Court clarified its decision by holding that defendants charged with offenses where imprisonment is authorized but not actually imposed do not have a Sixth Amendment right to counsel.[98]

The Sixth Amendment and Jury Trials

The Sixth Amendment (and to a lesser extent, Article III of the Constitution) provides that a person accused of a crime shall enjoy the right to a speedy and public trial by an impartial jury—that is, a trial in which a group of the accused's peers act as a fact-finding, deliberative body to determine guilt or innocence. The Supreme Court has held that jury trials must be available if a prison sentence of six or more months is possible.

"Impartiality" is a requirement of jury trials that has undergone significant change, with the method of selecting jurors being the most frequently challenged part of the process. For example, whereas potential individual jurors who have prejudged a case are not eligible to serve, no groups can be systematically excluded from serving. In 1880, for example, the Supreme Court ruled that African Americans could not be excluded from state jury pools (lists of those eligible to serve).[99] And in 1975, the Court ruled that to bar women from jury service violated the mandate that juries be a "fair cross section" of the community.[100]

In the 1980s, the Court expanded the requirement that juries reflect the community by invalidating various indirect means of excluding African Americans. For example, when James Batson, a black man, was tried for second-degree burglary, the state prosecutor used all his peremptory challenges to the jury to eliminate all four potential black jurors, leaving an all-white jury.[101] The state court judge overruled the contention of Batson's lawyer that the exclusion of African Americans violated Batson's constitutional rights, and Batson was found guilty. The Supreme Court, however, overturned his conviction. While noting that lawyers historically used peremptory challenges to select juries they believed most favorable to the outcome they desired, the Court held that the use of peremptory challenges specifically to exclude African-American jurors violated the equal protection clause of the Fourteenth Amendment.[102]

In 1994, the Supreme Court answered the major remaining unanswered question about jury selection—can lawyers exclude women from juries through their use of peremptory challenges? This question came up frequently because in rape trials and sex discrimination cases, one side or another often finds it advantageous to select jurors on the basis of their sex. At issue in *J.E.B.* v. *Alabama* ex rel *T.B.* (1994)[103] was Alabama's use of peremptory challenge to exclude nine men from a group of potential jurors in a case brought by the state to establish that James Bowman, Sr. had fathered a child and was responsible for child support payments. Bowman was declared to be the father by a jury of twelve women. The Supreme Court ruled that the equal protection clause prohibits discrimination in jury selection on the basis of gender. Thus, striking all potential male jurors based on the belief that males might be more sympathetic to the arguments of a man charged in a paternity suit, is unconstitutional.

The Eighth Amendment and Cruel and Unusual Punishment

The Eighth Amendment prohibits "cruel and unusual punishments," a concept rooted in the English common-law tradition. In the 1500s, religious heretics and those critical of the Crown were subjected to torture to extract confessions, and then were condemned to an equally hideous death by the rack, disembowelment, or other barbarous means. The English Bill of Rights and its safeguard against "cruel and unusual punishments" was a result of public outrage against those practices. The same language found its way into the U.S. Bill of Rights. Prior to the 1960s, however, little judicial attention was paid to the meaning of that phrase, especially in the context of the death penalty.

The death penalty was in use in all the colonies at the time the Constitution was adopted, and its constitutionality went unquestioned. In fact, in two separate cases in the late 1800s, the Supreme Court ruled that deaths by public shooting[104] and electrocution were not "cruel and unusual" forms of punishment in the same category as "punishments which inflict torture, such as the rack, the thumbscrew, the iron boot, the stretching of limbs and the like. . . ."[105]

In the 1960s, the National Association for the Advancement of Colored People (NAACP) Legal Defense Fund, believing that the death penalty was applied more fre-

"Cruel and unusual punishment" has meant different things to different societies. In colonial America, the dunking stool was a common form of punishment that few would advocate today.

quently to African Americans than to members of other groups, orchestrated a carefully designed legal attack on its constitutionality.[106]

Public opinion polls revealed that in 1971, on the eve of the NAACP's first major death sentence case to reach the Supreme Court, support for the death penalty had fallen to below 50 percent of the American public. With the timing just right, in *Furman* v. *Georgia* (1972), the Supreme Court upheld the NAACP's position and effectively put an end to capital punishment, at least in the short run.[107] The Court ruled that because the death penalty was often imposed in an arbitrary manner, it constituted cruel and unusual punishment in violation of the Eighth and Fourteenth Amendments.

Following *Furman*, several state legislatures enacted new laws designed to meet the Court's objections to the arbitrary nature of the sentence. In *Gregg* v. *Georgia* (1976), Georgia's rewritten death penalty statute was ruled constitutional by the Supreme Court in a seven-to-two decision.[108] Troy Gregg had murdered two hitchhikers and was awaiting execution on Georgia's death row. Although his lawyers argued that to put him to death would constitute cruel and unusual punishment, the Court concluded that the death penalty "is an expression of society's outrage at particularly offensive conduct. . . . [I]t is an extreme action, suitable to the most extreme of crimes." Before he could be executed, however, Gregg escaped from death row using a hand-crafted hacksaw and a homemade prison guard uniform. He and three other inmates escaped to North Carolina, where Gregg was beaten to death before he could be recaptured by authorities.

Unless minors are involved, the Supreme Court is currently unwilling to intervene to overrule state courts' imposition of the death penalty. In *McCleskey* v. *Kemp* (1987),[109] a five-to-four Court ruled that imposition of the death penalty—even when it appeared to discriminate against blacks—did not violate the equal protection clause. Despite the testimony of social scientists and evidence that the state was eleven times more likely to seek the death penalty against a black defendant, the Court upheld Warren McCleskey's death sentence. It noted that even if statistics clearly show discrimination, "racial bias is an inevitable part of our criminal justice system." Within hours of that defeat, McCleskey's lawyers filed a new appeal, arguing that the informant who gave the only testimony against McCleskey at trial had been placed in McCleskey's cell illegally. Four years later, McCleskey's death sentence challenge again produced an equally, if not more important ruling on the death penalty and criminal procedure from the U.S. Supreme Court. In the second *McCleskey* case, *McCleskey* v. *Zant* (1991), the Court found that the issue of the informant should have been raised during the first appeal, in spite of the fact that McCleskey's lawyers were initially told by the state that the witness was *not* an informer. *McCleskey* v. *Zant* produced new standards designed to make it much more difficult for death-row inmates to file repeated appeals, a practice frequently decried by many of the justices.[110] Ironically, the informant against McCleskey was freed the night before McCleskey was electrocuted.

The Right to Privacy

There is no mention of a right to privacy in either the main body of the Constitution or the Bill of Rights. Nevertheless, as Justice William O. Douglas noted in 1965, the notion of privacy is "older than the Bill of Rights." It is questionable, however, whether the Framers would ever have considered birth control, surrogate motherhood, or *in vitro* fertilization, all defended under "right to privacy" claims, proper subjects of constitutional protection.

Although the Constitution is silent about the right to privacy, the Bill of Rights contains many indications that the Framers expected that some areas of life were "off limits" to governmental regulation. The right to freedom of religion guaranteed in the First Amendment implies the right to exercise private, personal beliefs. The guarantee against unreasonable searches and seizures contained in the Fourth Amendment similarly implies that persons are to be secure in their homes and should not fear that police will show up at their doorsteps without cause. As early as 1928, Justice Louis Brandeis hailed **privacy** as "the right to be left alone—the most comprehensive of rights and the right most valued by civilized men."[111] It was not until 1965, however, that the Court attempted to explain the origins of this right.

Birth Control

Griswold v. *Connecticut* (1965)[112] involved a challenge to the constitutionality of an 1879 Connecticut law prohibiting the dissemination of information about and/or the sale of contraceptives. In 1943 and again in 1961, groups seeking legislative repeal of the law had challenged its constitutionality. In 1961, the Supreme Court, however, with four justices dissenting, refused to address the merits of the case. The majority concluded that a doctor who had not been charged with violating the statute had no standing (legal right) to bring the lawsuit.[113] But because the majority opinion had stressed the fact that the law had long gone unenforced, Planned Parenthood officials decided that they would need to create a test case. So Estelle Griswold, the executive director of Planned Parenthood League of Connecticut, and Dr. C. Lee Buxton opened a birth-control clinic, and were arrested ten days later. Now Planned Parenthood had parties actually charged with violating the law, a prerequisite to a challenge of its constitutionality. After Griswold and Buxton's conviction in the state courts, they appealed to the U.S. Supreme Court. In *Griswold*, seven justices decided that various portions of the Bill of Rights, including the First, Third, Fourth, Fifth, and Fourteenth Amendments, cast "penumbras" (unstated liberties on the fringes or in the shadow of more explicitly stated rights), thereby creating zones of privacy, including a married couple's right to plan a family. Thus, the Connecticut statute was ruled unconstitu-

In order to challenge the constitutionality of a Connecticut law that barred physicians and clinics from prescribing contraceptives, Estelle Griswold, the director of Planned Parenthood, opened a clinic for the express purpose of being arrested. Her appeal of her conviction resulted in the Supreme Court ruling that the state law was unconstitutional in *Griswold* v. *Connecticut* (1965).

Privacy The right to be let alone; a judicially created doctrine encompassing an individual's decision to use birth control or secure an abortion.

Operation Rescue staged large-scale protests in Buffalo, New York in front of several abortion clinics in 1992. Protesters were welcomed to the city by the pro-life mayor, an act that angered pro-choice activists who viewed the clinic blockades as illegal and costly (in terms of overtime pay for police officers, etc.).

In 1994, in response to these kinds of demonstrations and violence, Congress passed an abortion clinic access act providing prison terms and fines for those convicted of blocking access to clinics or threatening patients or employees of clinics.

tional as a violation of marital privacy, a right the Court concluded could be read into the U.S. Constitution.

Later, the Court expanded the right of privacy to include the right of unmarried individuals to have access to contraceptives. "If the right of privacy means anything," wrote Justice William J. Brennan, "it is the right of the individual, married or single, to be free from unwarranted governmental intrusion into matters so fundamentally affecting a person as the decision to bear or beget a child."[114]

Abortion

In the early 1960s, a worldwide panic arose after the birth of babies with congenital defects to pregnant women who had been given the drug thalidomide, and a nationwide measles epidemic resulting in the birth of more babies with other severe problems. Simultaneously, the increasing medical safety of abortions, and the growing women's rights movement combined with these tragedies to put pressure on the legal and medical establishments to institute laws that would guarantee a woman's access to a safe and legal abortion. By the late 1960s, fourteen states had voted to liberalize their abortion policies, and four states decriminalized abortion in the early stages of pregnancy. But many women's rights activists wanted more. They argued that the decision to carry a pregnancy to term was a woman's fundamental constitutional right. In 1973, in one of the most controversial decisions ever handed down, seven members of the Court agreed with this position.

The woman whose case became the catalyst for pro-choice and anti-abortion groups was an itinerant circus worker. Norma McCorvey was the mother of one toddler she was unable to care for; she could not leave another child in her mother's care. So she decided to terminate her second pregnancy. Unable to secure a legal abortion and frightened by the conditions she found when she sought an illegal, back-alley abortion, McCorvey turned to two young Texas lawyers who were looking for a plaintiff to bring a lawsuit to challenge Texas's restrictive statute, which allowed abortions only when they were necessary to save the life of the mother. Although McCorvey was unable to obtain a legal abortion and later gave birth and put the baby up for adoption, she allowed her lawyers to proceed with the case using her, under the pseudonym Jane Roe, to challenge the Texas law as enforced by Henry Wade, the district attorney for Dallas County, Texas.

When the case finally came before the Supreme Court, Justice Harry A. Blackmun, a former lawyer at the Mayo Clinic, relied heavily on medical evidence to rule that the Texas law violated a woman's constitutionally guaranteed right to privacy, which he argued included her decision to terminate a pregnancy. Writing for the majority in *Roe* v. *Wade*, Blackmun divided pregnancy into three stages. In the first trimester, a woman's right to privacy gave her an absolute right (in consultation with her physician), free from state interference, to terminate her pregnancy. In the second trimester, the state's interest in the health of the mother gave it the right to regulate abortions—but only to protect the woman's health. Only in the third trimester—when the fetus became potentially viable—did the Court find that the state's interest in potential life outweighed the woman's privacy interests. Even in the third trimester, however, abortions to save the life or health of the mother were to be legal.[115]

Roe v. *Wade* unleashed a torrent of political controversy. Anti-abortion groups, caught off guard, scrambled to recoup their losses in Congress. Representative Henry Hyde (R.-Ill.) persuaded Congress to ban the use of Medicaid funds for abortions for poor women, and the constitutionality of the Hyde Amendment was upheld by the Supreme Court in 1977 and again in 1980.[116]

From the 1970s through the present, the right to an abortion and its constitutional underpinnings in the right to privacy have been under attack by well-organized anti-abortion groups. The Reagan and Bush administrations were strong advocates of the anti-abortion position, regularly urging the Court to overrule *Roe*. They came close to victory in *Webster* v. *Reproductive Health Services* (1989).[117] In *Webster*, the Court upheld state-required fetal viability tests in the second trimester, even though these tests would increase the cost of an abortion considerably. The Court also upheld Missouri's refusal to allow abortions to be performed in state-supported hospitals or by state-funded doctors or nurses. Perhaps most noteworthy, however, were the facts that four justices seemed willing to overrule *Roe* v. *Wade*, and that Justice Antonin Scalia publicly rebuked his colleague Sandra Day O'Connor, then the only woman on the Court, for failing to provide the critical fifth vote to overrule *Roe*.

After *Webster*, states began to enact more restrictive legislation (see map on p. 81). In the most important abortion case since *Roe*, *Planned Parenthood of Southeastern Pennsylvania* v. *Casey* (1992), Justice O'Connor, in an opinion supported by Justices Kennedy and Souter, wrote that Pennsylvania could limit abortions as long as its regulations did not pose "an undue burden" on pregnant women.[118]

The narrowly supported decision, which upheld a twenty-four-hour waiting period and parental consent requirements, did not overrule *Roe*, but clearly limited its scope by abolishing its trimester approach and substituting the "undue burden" standard. Since *Casey*, the Court has, for example, refused to find unconstitutional Mississippi's mandatory twenty-four-hour waiting period before an abortion. Mississippi has only three abortion clinics—all in Jackson. With this required waiting period, many women have to take time off work to drive over 100 miles, and then pay for a hotel. The number of abortions dropped 40 percent, and the clinics unsuccessfully argued that the waiting period posed an "undue burden." The U.S. Supreme Court refused to hear the appeal.[119] Moreover, in 1993, the Court ruled that judges cannot use federal civil rights laws to stop those who block access to abortion clinics, narrowing federal protections for women seeking abortions.[120]

Given these decisions, pro-choice activists concluded that the Supreme Court was not the place to seek protection of what they see as basic privacy rights. In the wake of the 1992 elections, they decided to press Congress to pass a Freedom of Choice Act and looked to President Clinton, who ran on a pro-choice platform, for support. On the twentieth anniversary of *Roe*, Clinton ended bans on fetal tissue research, abortions at military hospitals, and federal financing for overseas population control programs, and lifted the "gag" rule, a federal regulation barring public health clinics receiving federal dollars from discussing abortion, which had been upheld by the Supreme Court in *Rust* v. *Sullivan* (1991).[121] He also lifted the ban on testing of RU-486, the French abortion pill. President Clinton used the occasion of his first appointment to the U.S. Supreme Court to select a longtime supporter of abortion rights to the Supreme Court, Ruth Bader Ginsburg, to replace Justice Byron White, one of the original dissenters in *Roe*. Most commentators believe that this was an important first step in shifting the Court away from any further curtailment of abortion rights as was the later appointment of Justice Stephen Breyer in 1994.

Homosexuality

Although the Supreme Court has ruled that the right to privacy includes the right to decide whether "to bear or beget a child," it has declined to interpret the right of privacy to include the right to engage in homosexual acts. In 1985, the Court, in a four-to-four decision (Justice Lewis F. Powell was ill), upheld a lower court decision that found

In April 1993, gay rights activists and their supporters staged one of the largest marches ever to take place in Washington, D.C. to draw attention to their numbers and discriminatory laws and treatment.

unconstitutional an Oklahoma law allowing the dismissal of teachers who advocate homosexual relations.[122] So the next year, when another case involving homosexual rights, *Bowers* v. *Hardwick* (1986),[123] was argued before the Court, Lawrence Tribe, the lawyer representing Michael Hardwick, pitched his arguments toward Justice Powell, who he believed would be the crucial swing vote in this controversial area. Tribe, a professor at the Harvard Law School, argued against the constitutionality of a Georgia law prohibiting consensual heterosexual and homosexual oral or anal sex.

In August 1982, in Atlanta, Georgia, Michael Hardwick was arrested in his bedroom by a police officer who was there to serve an arrest warrant on Hardwick for his failure to appear in court on another charge. One of his roommates let the officer in and directed him to Hardwick's room. After Hardwick's arrest on a sodomy charge, the local prosecutor decided not to prosecute. Nonetheless, Hardwick, a local gay activist, joined forces with the American Civil Liberties Union to challenge the constitutionality of the law under which he had been arrested. In a five-to-four decision, the Supreme Court upheld the law. At conference, Justice Powell reportedly seemed torn by the case. He believed that the twenty-year sentence that came with conviction was excessive but was troubled by the fact that Hardwick hadn't actually been tried and convicted. Although he originally voted with the majority to overturn the law, he was bothered by the broadness of Justice Blackmun's original draft of the majority opinion. Thus, he changed his mind and voted with the minority view to uphold the law, making it the new majority.[124]

The Court's refusal to expand the right to privacy to invalidate state laws criminalizing some aspects of homosexual behavior is not that surprising. As discussed in Chapter 5, the controversy over allowing gays to join or remain in the military revealed how distasteful the gay lifestyle is to many, including, as *Bowers* indicated, several members of the Court.

Toward Reform

The addition of the Bill of Rights to the Constitution was one of the first acts of the First Congress. Since that time, no amendments have been added to the Constitution to alter the basic liberties guaranteed by the Bill of Rights. In the aftermath of the flag-burning controversy in the 1980s, many called for the enactment of an amendment to ban flag burning. But reluctance to alter the First Amendment's far-reaching protections in any way ultimately led to the defeat of such proposals. Opponents argued fervently that this nation was built upon political protest and that free expression should be constitutionally protected at all costs, no matter how repugnant to the majority.

Congress has occasionally acted to restrict various guarantees contained in the Bill of Rights but the Court has often ruled those acts unconstitutional, as was the case with the flag desecration statute. In 1993, in the wake of stepped-up violence against abortion clinics and providers, a new drive was launched to make it a federal crime to threaten, commit violence, or to blockade clinics, and to give the U.S. Justice Department the power to obtain court orders to break up the blockaders. The need for this kind of law was lessened, however, after the U.S. Supreme Court ruled that the Pro-Life Action Network and groups such as Operation Rescue could be prosecuted under a federal criminal law for engaging in a national conspiracy to shut down abortion clinics "through threatened or actual force, violence or fear." Pro-life activists claimed that the ruling violated their First Amendment rights, arguing that it interfered with their rights to freedom of speech and assembly.[125] In spite of that ruling, however, in 1994 Congress passed legislation making it a crime to block access to women's reproductive health clinics or to threaten patients or employees of those clinics.

Congress has also concerned itself with civil liberties and criminal rights of late. Shortly after his election, Speaker of the House Newt Gingrich called for the passage of a constitutional amendment to restore school prayer. He also has been a major leader of the move to pass laws to limit the scope of the search-and-seizure clause of the Fourth Amendment. He and many other conservatives believe that liberal interpretations of that amendment only straightjacket the police while protecting criminals.

Summary

The Bill of Rights is a fundamental part of the American tradition. Within its provisions are the heart of Americans' protections from the excesses of government the Framers sought to avoid. Disputes over the scope of its provisions are common, and over the years all three branches of government—especially the legislative and the judicial—have played key roles in defining them.

In this chapter, we have made the following points:

1. Most of the Framers originally opposed the Bill of Rights. Anti-Federalists, however, continued to stress the need for a Bill of Rights during the drive for ratification of the Constitution, and some states tried to make their ratification contingent on the addition of a Bill of Rights. Thus, during its first session, Congress sent the first ten amendments to the Constitution, the Bill of Rights, to the states for their ratification.

2. The First Amendment guarantees freedom of religion. The establishment clause, which prohibits the national government from establishing a religion, does not, according to Supreme Court interpretation, create an absolute wall between church and state. While the national and state governments may generally not give direct aid to religious groups, many forms of aid, especially many that benefit children, have been held to be constitutionally permissible. In contrast, the Court has generally barred prayer in public schools. Moreover, the Court generally has adopted an accommodationist approach when interpreting the free exercise clause by allowing some governmental regulation of religious practices.

3. The First Amendment also guarantees freedom of speech and of the press. The Alien and Sedition Acts in 1798 were the first national effort to curtail free speech, but they were never reviewed by the U.S. Supreme Court.

Some forms of speech were punished during the Civil War, and the Supreme Court refused to address their constitutionality directly. By the twentieth century, several states, and later the national government, passed laws restricting freedoms of speech and of the press. These curtailments were upheld by the Court, using the clear and present danger test. Later, the Court used the more liberal, direct incitement test, which required a stronger showing of imminent danger before speech could be restricted.

The First Amendment and most others were made applicable to the states by the Fourteenth Amendment and the incorporation doctrine.

Symbolic speech has been afforded the same protection as other forms of speech. Historically, the Supreme Court has disfavored any attempts at prior restraint of speech or press; thus, "politically correct speech" requirements have come under constitutional challenge.

Libel, slander and obscenity (as well as some forms of pornography) are not protected by the First Amendment.

4. The Fourth, Fifth, Sixth, and Eighth Amendments provide a variety of procedural guarantees to persons accused of crimes. In particular, the Fourth Amendment prohibits unreasonable searches and seizures, and the Court has generally refused to allow evidence seized in violation of this safeguard to be used at trial.

Among other rights, the Fifth Amendment guarantees that "no person shall be compelled to be a witness against himself." The Supreme Court has interpreted this provision to require that the government inform the accused of his or her right to remain silent. This provision has also been interpreted to require that illegally obtained confessions must be excluded at trial.

The Sixth Amendment's guarantee of "assistance of counsel" has been interpreted by the Supreme Court to require that the government provide counsel to defendants unable to pay for it in cases where prison sentences may be imposed. The Sixth Amendment also requires an "impartial" jury, although the meaning of "impartial" continues to evolve through judicial interpretation.

The Eighth Amendment's ban against "cruel and unusual punishments" has been held not to bar imposition of the death penalty.

5. The right to privacy is a judicially created right carved from several amendments including the First, Third, Fourth, Fifth, and Fourteenth Amendments. Statutes limiting access to birth control and abortion rights have been ruled unconstitutional violations of the right to privacy. In contrast, the Supreme Court has not expanded the right to privacy to invalidate state statutes criminalizing homosexual acts.

6. Few efforts have been made to alter the basic guarantees contained in the Bill of Rights. Periodically, however, Congress has enacted legislation to "clarify" certain provisions or to restrict rights in times of emergency.

Key Terms

civil liberties	clear and present danger test	libel
civil rights	direct incitement test	slander
establishment clause	due process clause	due process rights
free exercise clause	incorporation doctrine	Miranda rights
prior restraint	selective incorporation	exclusionary rule
bad tendency test	symbolic speech	privacy

Suggested Readings

Chaffe, Zachariah, Jr. *Free Speech in the United States*. Cambridge, MA: Harvard University Press, 1948.

Clor, Harry M. *Obscenity and Public Morality*. Chicago: University of Chicago Press, 1967.

Craig, Barbara Hinkson, and David M. O'Brien. *Abortion and American Politics*. Chatham, NJ: Chatham House Publishers, 1993.

Friendly, Fred. W. *Minnesota Rag: The Dramatic Story of the Landmark Case That Gave New Meaning to Freedom of the Press*. New York: Random House, 1981.

Ivers, Gregg. *Redefining the First Freedom: The Supreme Court and the Consolidation of State Power*. New Brunswick, NJ: Transaction Press, 1993.

Leonard, Levy, et al. *The First Amendment*. New York: Macmillan, 1986.

Lewis, Anthony. *Make No Law: The Sullivan Case and the First Amendment*. New York: Random House, 1991.

Manwaring, David R. *Render unto Caesar: The Flag Salute Controversy*. Chicago: University of Chicago Press, 1962.

O'Brien, David M. *Constitutional Law and Politics, Vol. 2: Civil Rights and Civil Liberties*. New York: Norton and Co., 1991.

Weddington, Sarah. *A Question of Choice*. New York: Grosset/Putnam, 1993.

Civil Rights

SLAVERY, ABOLITION, AND WINNING THE RIGHT TO VOTE, 1800–1890

THE PUSH FOR EQUALITY, 1889–1954

THE CIVIL RIGHTS MOVEMENT

OTHER GROUPS MOBILIZE FOR RIGHTS

THE POLITICS OF CIVIL RIGHTS

TOWARD REFORM

*W*hile the Declaration of Independence boldly proclaims, "We hold these truths to be self-evident, that all men are created equal, that they are endowed by their Creator with certain inalienable rights," the Constitution is silent on the concept of equality. And only through constitutional amendment and Supreme Court definition and redefinition of the rights contained in that document have Americans come close to attaining equal rights.

Those at the Constitutional Convention—in spite of pleas such as those of Abigail Adams to her husband, John, to "remember the ladies" in the new code of laws—generally gave little thought to what we call today **civil rights**—the powers or privileges guaranteed to individuals and protected by law from arbitrary infringement by the government or any individual. Today, gay and lesbian rights activists press for many rights, especially the right to serve in the military. Similarly, individuals with disabilities lobby for the enforcement of existing legislation, such as the Americans with Disabilities Act of 1990, and for greater constitutional protections against abridgements of their civil rights. But in the late 1700s, the Framers were more concerned with rights we take for granted, such as the Sixth Amendment's guarantee of the right to a trial by jury. In the 1990s, when we think of civil rights, we usually think of those policies that explicitly and specifically extend basic rights to women and minority groups including African Americans, Hispanic Americans, the elderly, and other groups whose members have historically faced discrimination and differential treatment. One could say that civil liberties place limitations on the power of the state to restrain or dictate how individuals act; civil rights concern rights that the government must provide to its citizens.

Some civil rights issues were considered by the Framers, but, as James Madison's reflections in *Federalist No. 42* indicate, slaves were treated in the new Constitution more like property than like persons. Whereas earlier the Declaration of Independence

119

> It were doubtless to be wished that the power of Prohibiting the transportation of slaves had not been postponed. . . . It ought to be considered as a great point gained in favor of humanity . . . that [it] may terminate forever.
>
> *James Madison*
> *Federalist No. 42*

Madison considered slavery a blight on the nation and wanted the importation of slaves to be banned altogether. Yet it would take some of the country's most tumultuous times—including the Civil War and the civil rights movement of the 1960s—to begin to rectify the evils of slavery and its legacy.

Civil rights The political and social right to be free from arbitrary infringement by the government or any individual.

had so eloquently proclaimed that "all men are created equal," the delegates to the Constitutional Convention put political expediency before the immorality of slavery. In fact, the Constitution specifically stated that the importation of slaves could not be prohibited for twenty years. Through the Three-Fifths Compromise, slaves were considered three-fifths of a person for the purpose of calculating state populations upon which representation in the House of Representatives was to be based (see p. 35). Why three-fifths? A committee of twelve members, one representing each state at the Constitutional Convention, concluded that a slave was, on average, "three-fifths" as productive as a white man. Thus, slaves could not vote, but they counted, at least fractionally.

There was never any question that white women would be considered full citizens for purposes of determining state population. But voting qualifications were left to the states and none allowed women to vote at the time the Constitution was ratified.

Immediately after the Revolutionary War, women had voted in some parts of Virginia and New Jersey, but those rights were terminated by the adoption of state constitutions limiting suffrage to white, property-owning males.

In general, the idea of voting rights or any other civil rights did not concern the Framers. Since the 1700s, however, concepts of civil rights have changed dramatically. The addition of the Fourteenth Amendment, one of three amendments passed after the Civil War, introduced the notion of equality into the Constitution by specifying that states could not deny their citizens "equal protection of the laws."

Since its addition to the Constitution, the Fourteenth Amendment has generated more litigation to determine and specify its meaning than any other provision of the Constitution. Within a few years of its ratification, women—and later, African Americans and other minorities and disadvantaged groups—took to the courts to seek expanded civil rights in all walks of life. But the struggle to augment rights was not limited to the courts. Public protest, civil disobedience, legislative lobbying, and appeals to public opinion have all been part of the arsenal of those seeking equality.

Equal protection clause Section of the Fourteenth Amendment that guarantees that all citizens receive "equal protection under the laws"; has been used to bar discrimination against African Americans, women, and other groups.

As we will see, the Constitution has been interpreted to protect African Americans and women from discrimination or any other unequal treatment that violates their civil rights. The Supreme Court, however, has chosen not to interpret the **equal protection clause** of the Fourteenth Amendment to prohibit discrimination against a variety of other groups, including the poor, the disabled, the elderly, and people with HIV/AIDS. Congress, however, *has* acted to extend rights to many of those groups by passage of various anti-discrimination laws.

Confederate President Jefferson Davis's slaves are shown here anxiously awaiting announcement of their fate in a photograph taken after the fall of Vicksburg, which ended the Civil War.

Since passage of the Civil War Amendments (1865–1870), there has been a fairly consistent pattern of the expansion of civil rights to more and more groups. To better understand how notions of equality and civil rights have changed in this country, we examine the evolution of African-American rights and women's rights in tandem. Until recently, African-Americans' struggle for rights and women's efforts to achieve greater rights have been closely intertwined. To appreciate how each group has drawn ideas, support, and success from the other, we discuss their parallel developments. In addition, as African Americans and women have gained fuller equality, their actions have become the model for other groups that consider themselves disadvantaged in the political system—Native Americans, Hispanics, homosexuals, and the disabled, for example.

Full equality still remains a dream for many groups, but major improvements and progress have been made. As was the case in the development of civil liberties, the Supreme Court has played a major role in the development and even our conception of civil rights through its interpretation of the U.S. Constitution and federal civil rights laws. A Democratic administration and the addition of new, more liberal justices to replace conservatives who retire from the Court are likely to change this direction. How far the tide will turn is yet to be seen.

Slavery, Abolition, and Winning the Right to Vote, 1800–1890

The period from 1800 to 1890 was one of tremendous change and upheaval in America. The Civil War was fought and slaves were freed, yet the promise of equality guaranteed to African Americans by the Civil War Amendments failed to become a reality. And, while women's rights activists also began to make claims for equality, often using the arguments enunciated for the abolition of slavery, they too fell far short of their

Landmark Events in the Quest for Civil Rights: From the Nineteenth Century to *Brown* v. *Board of Education of Topeka*

1833	◆	American Anti-Slavery Society founded by William Lloyd Garrison
1840	◆	International Anti-Slavery Society meeting in London
1848	◆	Seneca Falls Convention
1851	◆	*Uncle Tom's Cabin* published
1857	◆	*Dred Scott* v. *Sandford*
1861–1865	◆	Civil War
1863	◆	Emancipation Proclamation
1865	◆	Thirteenth Amendment ratified Lincoln assassinated
1865–1876	◆	Reconstruction
1868	◆	Fourteenth Amendment ratified
1869	◆	American Woman Suffrage Association created National Woman Suffrage Association created
1870	◆	Fifteenth Amendment ratified
1873	◆	Women's Christian Temperance Union founded *Bradwell* v. *Illinois*
1875	◆	*Minor* v. *Happersett*
1889–1920	◆	The Progressive Era
1890	◆	National American Woman Suffrage Association founded
1896	◆	*Plessy* v. *Ferguson*
1908	◆	*Muller* v. *Oregon*
1909	◆	NAACP founded
1914–1918	◆	World War I
1920	◆	Nineteenth Amendment ratified
1939	◆	Legal Defense and Educational Fund of the NAACP created
1941–1945	◆	World War II
1947	◆	Commission on Civil Rights created by Harry S Truman
1954	◆	*Brown* v. *Board of Education of Topeka*

PEOPLE OF THE PAST

Frederick Douglass

Frederick Douglass (1817–1895), a leading advocate of civil rights for both blacks and women, was the son of a slave and an unidentified white man. Although born into slavery, Douglass learned how to read and write. Once he escaped to the North (where 250,000 free blacks lived), he became a well-known orator and journalist. He spoke to abolitionist groups about his experiences as a slave and included these experiences in his autobiography, *Narrative of the Life of Frederick Douglass*. His life was also romanticized in song.

In 1847 he started a newspaper, *The North Star*, in Rochester, New York, and it quickly became a powerful voice against slavery. Douglass was a strong abolitionist, who urged President Abraham Lincoln to emancipate the slaves and helped recruit black soldiers for the Union forces in the Civil War. His home in Rochester, New York, was a station along the Underground Railroad. Douglass was also a firm believer in women's suffrage, and he attended the Seneca Falls Convention in 1848. He was a close friend of John Brown, whose raid at Harpers Ferry was a pivotal moment in the anti-slavery movement. Douglass was appointed to several minor federal posts, including that of minister to Haiti from 1889 to 1891. He was considered the greatest black leader of his time. When he died in 1895, five states adopted resolutions of regret, and two U.S. senators and one Supreme Court justice were among his honorary pallbearers.

Source: New York Public Library.

ing the arguments enunciated for the abolition of slavery, they too fell far short of their goals.

Slavery and Congress

Congress banned slave trade in 1808 (after the expiration of the twenty-year period specified by the Constitution). In 1820, blacks made up 25 percent of the population. By 1840, that figure had fallen to 20 percent. As the South became even more dependent on agriculture after the invention of the cotton gin (a machine invented in 1793 that separated seeds from cotton very quickly), technological advances turned the Northern states into an increasingly industrialized region. The growing industrialization of the North intensified the cultural and political differences and animosity between the two regions.

Slavery presented the national government with a divisive political issue. Conflicts between Northern and Southern states over the admission of new states to the Union with "free" or "slave" status emerged as the nation grew westward. The first major sectional crisis occurred in 1820, when the territory of Missouri applied for admission to the Union as a "slave state"—that is, one in which slavery would be legal. Missouri's admission would have weighted the Senate in favor of slavery and was therefore opposed by Northern senators. The resultant Missouri Compromise of 1820 allowed the admission of Missouri as a slave state, along with the admission of Maine (formed out of the territory of Massachusetts with the permission of Congress and Massachusetts) as a free state. Other compromises concerning slavery were eventually necessitated as the nation continued to grow and new states were added to the Union.

The Abolitionist Movement: The First Civil Rights Movement

The controversy that occurred over the Compromise of 1820, while solidifying the South in its determination to keep slavery legal, fueled the fervor of those who opposed slavery. In the early 1800s, some private charities purchased slaves and transported them to the west coast of Africa, where, in the 1820s, eighty-eight former slaves formed the independent nation of Liberia.[1] But this solution to the slavery problem was not all that practical. Few owners were willing to free their slaves, and the trip to Africa and conditions there were dangerous. The abolitionist movement might have fizzled had it not been for William Lloyd Garrison, a white New Englander who became active in the movement in the early 1830s. Garrison founded the American Anti-Slavery Society in 1833; by 1838 it had more than 250,000 members. To put this number in perspective, that would be equivalent to the National Association for the Advancement of Colored People's (NAACP) having 3.8 million members in the United States today. (In 1994, it actually had 500,000 members.)

The Women's Rights Tie-in.   Slavery was not the only inequality that people began to question in the decades following adoption of the Constitution. In 1840, for example, Garrison and even Frederick Douglass (see "People of the Past," p. 123) parted from the Anti-Slavery Society when it refused to accept their demand that women be allowed to participate equally in all its activities. At that time, custom dictated that women not speak out in public, and most laws made women second-class citizens. In most states, for example, women could not divorce their husbands or keep their own wages and inheritances. And, of course, they could not vote.

Also in 1840, Elizabeth Cady Stanton and Lucretia Mott, two women who were to found the woman's movement, attended the 1840 meeting of the International Anti-Slavery Society in London with their husbands. They were not allowed to participate because they were women. As they sat in the balcony apart from the male delegates, they paused to compare their status to that of the slaves they sought to free. Believing that women were not much better off than slaves, they resolved to call a meeting to address these issues. In 1848 they sent out a call for the first women's rights convention. Three hundred women and men, including Frederick Douglass, traveled to the sleepy little town of Seneca Falls, New York, to attend the first meeting for women's rights.

The Seneca Falls Convention (1848).   The Seneca Falls Convention attracted women and men from all over New York State who believed that all men and women should be able to enjoy all rights of citizenship. At that meeting, resolutions calling for the abolition of legal, economic, and social discrimination against women were passed. All the documents reflected the attendees' dissatisfaction with contemporary moral codes, divorce and criminal laws, and the limited opportunities for women in education, the church, and careers in medicine, law, and politics. Only the call for an expanded franchise—the legal right of women to vote—failed to win unanimous approval. Most who attended the Seneca Falls meeting continued to press for women's rights along with the abolition of slavery.

The 1850s: The Calm Before the Storm.   By 1850, much was changing in America—the Gold Rush had spurred westward migration, cities grew as people were lured from their farms, railroads and the telegraph increased mobility and communication, and immigrants flooded into the United States. Reformers called for change, the women's movement gained momentum, and slavery continued to tear the nation apart. Harriet Beecher Stowe's *Uncle Tom's Cabin*, which showed the evils of slavery by depicting a slave family torn apart, further inflamed the country. *Uncle Tom's Cabin* sold more than 300,000 copies in a single year, 1852.

The tremendous national reaction to Stowe's work, which later prompted Abraham Lincoln to call Stowe "the little woman who started the big war," had not yet faded when a new controversy over the 1820 Missouri Compromise became the lightning rod of the first major civil rights case to be addressed by the U.S. Supreme Court. As discussed in Chapter 3, in *Dred Scott* v. *Sandford* (1857),[2] the Supreme Court bluntly ruled unconstitutional the 1820 Missouri Compromise, which prohibited slavery north of the 36° 30′ line. Furthermore, the Court found that slaves were not U.S. citizens and therefore could not bring suits in federal court. Moreover, the justices concluded that "the Negro might justly and lawfully be reduced to slavery for his benefit." Ironically, after the case was decided, Scott's owner freed him.

The Civil War and Its Aftermath: Civil Rights Laws and Constitutional Amendments

The Civil War had many causes, including (1) the political conflict between the North and the South over the doctrines of nullification and secession, (2) the Northern states' increasing political strength in Congress, (3) Southern agrarianism versus Northern industrialization, and (4) the clash of conservative Southern culture with more progressive Northern ideas. Slavery, however, was clearly the key issue.

During the war (1861–1865), abolitionists kept their activities alive and were rewarded in 1863 when President Abraham Lincoln issued the Emancipation Proclamation, which provided that all slaves in states still in active rebellion against the United States would automatically be freed on January 1, 1863. Designed as a measure to gain favor for the war in the North, the Emancipation Proclamation did not free all slaves—it freed only those who lived in the Confederacy. Complete abolition of slavery did not occur until congressional passage and ultimate ratification of the Thirteenth Amendment.

The Civil War Amendments.   Enacted in 1865, the **Thirteenth Amendment** was the first of the three so-called Civil War Amendments. It banned all forms of "slavery [and] involuntary servitude." Although Southern states were required to ratify the Thirteenth Amendment as a condition of their readmission to the Union after the war, most quickly passed laws that were designed to restrict opportunities for newly freed slaves dramatically. These **Black Codes** prohibited African Americans from voting, sitting on juries, or even appearing in public places. Although Black Codes differed from state to state, all empowered local law-enforcement officials to arrest unemployed blacks, fine them for vagrancy, and hire them out to employers to satisfy their fines. Some state codes went so far as to require African Americans to work on plantations or to be domestics. The Black Codes laid the groundwork for Jim Crow laws, which would later institute segregation in all walks of life (see "Who Was Jim Crow?" p. 129).

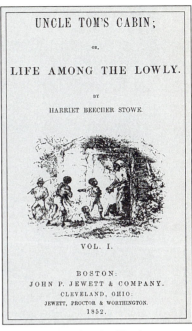

Uncle Tom's Cabin, by Harriet Beecher Stowe.

Thirteenth Amendment First of the three Civil War Amendments; specifically banned slavery in the United States.

Black Codes Laws passed by Southern states following the Civil War to deny most legal rights to newly freed slaves.

Students who took their school district to court to challenge compulsory "volunteerism."

"The Thirteenth Amendment Revisited"

❖ ❖ ❖

Since the 1860s, the Thirteenth Amendment, which bans "slavery or involuntary servitude," has not been an issue in American courts. But in the 1990s, as more and more school districts made community service work a requirement for high school graduation, some students have questioned the legality of those programs in federal court. "People should volunteer because they want to, not because of a government threat," says Lynn Steirer, one of 175 seniors who may not graduate because they failed to perform the sixty hours of public service required by their high school. She and another student, with the help of the Institute for Justice, a Washington, D.C.-based libertarian group, took their school district to court arguing that the policy violates the Thirteenth Amendment's ban against slavery. Two lower courts upheld the requirements.*

And, in 1993, the United States Supreme Court refused to review the case, thus letting the decision of the lower courts stand.

* *Steirer* v. *Bethlehem Area School District*, 987 F. 2nd 989 (1992).

Fourteenth Amendment Second of the three Civil War Amendments; guaranteed equal protection and due process of laws to all U.S. citizens.

Cartoonist Thomas Nast drew this rendition of a "carpetbagger" headed South with a bag on his back.

The outraged Reconstructionist Congress enacted the Civil Rights Act of 1866 to invalidate some of the Black Codes. President Andrew Johnson vetoed the legislation, but for the first time in history Congress overrode a presidential veto. The Civil Rights Act formally made African Americans citizens of the United States and gave the Congress and the courts the power to intervene when states attempted to restrict male, African-American citizenship rights in matters such as voting. Congress reasoned that African Americans were unlikely to fare well if they had to file discrimination complaints in state courts where judges were elected. Passage of a federal law allowed African Americans to challenge discriminatory state practices in the federal courts, where judges were appointed.

Because controversy remained over the constitutionality of the Act (since the Constitution gives states the right to determine qualifications of voters), the **Fourteenth Amendment** was proposed simultaneously with the Civil Rights Act to guarantee, among other things, citizenship to all freed slaves. Other key provisions of the Fourteenth Amendment barred states from abridging "the privileges and immunities of citizenship" or depriving "any person of life, liberty, or property without due process of law."

Unlike the Thirteenth Amendment, which had near-unanimous support in the North, the Fourteenth Amendment was opposed by many women. During the Civil War, women's rights activists, including Elizabeth Cady Stanton and Susan B. Anthony, put aside their claims for expanded rights for women, most notably the right to vote, and threw their energies into the war effort. They were convinced that once slaves were freed and blacks were given the right to vote, women similarly would be rewarded with the franchise. They were wrong.

After ratification of the Fourteenth Amendment (which specifically added the word "male" to the Constitution for the first time), women's rights activists met in Washington, D.C. in early 1869 for the first National Woman's Suffrage Association convention. There, activists argued against passage of any new amendment that would extend suffrage to black males and not to women. The convention resolved that "a *man's* government is worse than a *white* man's government, because, in proportion as you increase the tyrants, you make the condition of the disenfranchised class more hopeless and degraded."

In spite of these arguments, the **Fifteenth Amendment** was passed by Congress in February, 1869. It guaranteed the "right of citizens" to vote regardless of their "race, color or previous condition of servitude."

Women's rights activists were shocked when Congress failed to include a provision to enfranchise females. Abolitionists' continued support of the Fifteenth Amendment prompted many women's rights supporters to leave that movement to work solely for the cause of women's rights. Twice burned, Anthony and Stanton decided to form their own National Woman Suffrage Association (NWSA) to achieve that goal.[3] In spite of the NWSA's opposition, however, the Fifteenth Amendment was ratified by the states in 1870.

Fifteenth Amendment Last of the three Civil War Amendments; prohibited states from discriminating against potential voters because of race or previous condition of servitude.

Civil Rights and the Supreme Court

While the Congress was clear in its wishes that the rights of African Americans be expanded and that the Black Codes be rendered illegal, the Supreme Court was not nearly so protective of those rights under the Civil War Amendments. In the first two tests of the scope of the Fourteenth Amendment, the Supreme Court ruled that the citizenship rights guaranteed by the amendment applied only to rights of national citizenship and not to state citizenship. Ironically, neither case involved African Americans. In *The Slaughterhouse Cases* (1873),[4] the Court upheld Louisiana's right to create a monopoly in the operation of slaughterhouses, despite the Butcher's Benevolent Association's claim that this action deprived its members of their livelihood and thus the privileges and immunities of citizenship guaranteed by the Amendment. Similarly, in *Bradwell* v. *Illinois* (1873),[5] when Myra Bradwell asked the U.S. Supreme Court to find that Illinois's refusal to allow her to practice law (although she had passed the bar examination) violated her citizenship rights guaranteed by the privileges and immunities clause of the Fourteenth Amendment, her arguments fell on deaf ears. In *Bradwell*, the Court went even further than it had in *The Slaughterhouse Cases*, ruling that it was reasonable for the state to bar women from the practice of law because "the natural and proper timidity and delicacy which belongs to the female sex evidently unfits it for many of the occupations of civil life." The combined message of these two cases was that state and national citizenship were separate and distinct. In essence, the Supreme Court ruled that neither African Americans nor any others could be protected from discriminatory state action, because the Fourteenth Amendment did not enlarge the limited rights guaranteed by U.S. citizenship.

Claims for expanded rights, and requests for a clear definition of U.S. citizenship rights continued to fall on deaf ears in the halls of the Supreme Court. In 1875, for example, the Court heard *Minor* v. *Happersett*,[6] the culmination of a series of test cases launched by women's rights activists.[7] Virginia Minor, after planning with Anthony and other NWSA members, attempted to register to vote in her hometown of St. Louis, Missouri. When the registrar refused to record her name on the list of eligible voters, Minor sued, arguing that the state's refusal to let her vote violated the privileges and immunities clause of the Fourteenth Amendment. Rejecting her claim, the justices ruled unanimously that voting was not a privilege of citizenship.

In the same year, Southern resistance to African-American equality led Congress to pass the Civil Rights Act of 1875, designed to grant equal access to public accommodations such as theaters, restaurants, and transportation. The Act also prohibited the exclusion of African Americans from jury service. After 1877, however, as Reconstruction was dismantled, national interest in the legal condition of African Americans waned. Most white Southerners had never believed in equality for "freedmen," as former slaves were called. Any rights freedmen received had been contingent upon federal enforcement. Once federal troops were no longer available to guard polls and prevent whites from excluding black voters, Southern states moved to limit African Americans' access to the ballot. Other forms of discrimination were also allowed by judicial decisions upholding **Jim Crow laws**, which required segregation in public schools and facilities including railroads, restaurants, and theaters. Many also barred interracial marriage. All these laws, at first glance, appeared to conflict with the Civil Rights Act of 1875. In 1883, however, a series of cases decided by the Supreme Court severely damaged the vitality of the 1875 Act. In the **Civil Rights Cases** (1883)[8] (five separate cases involving the convictions of private individuals found to have violated the Civil Rights Act by refusing to extend accommodations to African Americans in theaters, a hotel, and a railroad), the Supreme Court ruled that Congress could prohibit only state or governmental action, and not private acts of discrimination. The Court thus seriously limited the scope of the Fourteenth Amendment by concluding that Congress had no authority to prohibit private discrimination in public accommodations.

The Court's opinion in the *Civil Rights Cases* provided a moral reinforcement for the Jim Crow system. Southern states viewed the Court's ruling as an invitation to gut the Thirteenth, Fourteenth, and Fifteenth Amendments.

In devising ways to make certain that African Americans did not vote, Southerners had to avoid the *intent* of the Fifteenth Amendment. This amendment did not guarantee suffrage; it simply said that states could not deny anyone the right to vote on account of race or color. So to exclude African Americans in a seemingly racially neutral way, Southern states used two devices before the 1890s: (1) poll taxes (small taxes on

Jim Crow laws Laws enacted by Southern states that discriminated against blacks by requiring segregation in public schools and public facilities, including railroads, restaurants, and theaters.

Civil Rights Cases Five separate cases involving the convictions of private individuals found to have violated the Civil Rights Act of 1875. The Supreme Court ruled that Congress lacked the authority to prohibit private discrimination in public accommodations.

Throughout the South, examples of Jim Crow laws abounded. One such law required separate public drinking fountains, shown here. Notice the obvious difference in quality.

the right to vote that often came due when poor African-American sharecroppers had the least amount of money on hand) or some form of property-owning qualifications, and (2) "literacy" or "understanding" tests, which allowed local registrars to administer difficult reading-comprehension tests to potential voters whom they did not know.

These voting restrictions had an immediate impact. By the late 1890s, black voting fell by 62 percent from the Reconstruction period, while white voting fell by only 26 percent. To make certain that these laws didn't further reduce the numbers of poor or uneducated white voters, many Southern states added **grandfather clauses** to their voting qualification provisions, granting voting privileges to those who failed to pass a wealth or literacy test only if their grandfathers had voted before Reconstruction. Grandfather clauses effectively denied the descendants of slaves the right to vote.

While African Americans continued to face wide-ranging racism on all fronts, women, too, confronted discrimination. During this period, married women, by law, could not be recognized as legal entities. Women often were treated in the same category as juveniles and "imbeciles," and in many states were not entitled to wages, inheritances, or custody of their children.

The Push for Equality, 1889–1954

The Progressive Era (1889–1920) was characterized by a concerted effort to reform political, economic, and social affairs. Evils like child labor, the concentration of economic power in the hands of a few industrialists, limited suffrage, political corruption, business monopolies, and prejudice against African Americans were all targets of progressive reform efforts. Distress over the legal inferiority of African Americans was aggravated by the U.S. Supreme Court's decision in *Plessy* v. *Ferguson* (1896), a case that some commentators point to as the Court's darkest hour.

Plessy v. *Ferguson:* **"Separate But Equal."**   In 1892, a group of African Americans in Louisiana decided to test the constitutionality of a Louisiana law mandating racial segregation on all public trains. They found an "ideal" individual to test the law. Homer Adolph Plessy, with blond hair and blue eyes, was widely known in the community to have had an African-American great-grandmother. His coloring made him an excellent subject for a potential test case of the Louisiana law. Plessy boarded a train in New Orleans and proceeded to the "whites only" car. He was arrested when he refused to leave his seat and take one in the car reserved for African Americans. Plessy sued the railroad company, arguing that segregation was illegal under the provisions of the Fourteenth Amendment.[9]

The Supreme Court disagreed. After analyzing the history of African Americans in the United States, the majority concluded that the Louisiana law was constitutional. The justices based the decision on their belief that separate facilities for blacks and whites provided equal protection of the laws. After all, they reasoned, African Americans were not prevented from riding the train; the Louisiana statute required only that the races travel separately. Justice John Marshall Harlan (1877–1911), the lone dissenter on the Court, criticized the majority and argued that it was senseless to hold constitutional a law "which, practically, puts the badge of servitude and degradation upon a large class of our fellow citizens."

Not surprisingly, the separate-but-equal doctrine enunciated in *Plessy* v. *Ferguson* soon came to mean only "separate," as new legal avenues for states to discriminate against African Americans opened up. The Jim Crow system soon became a way of

Grandfather clauses Statutes that allowed only those whose grandfathers had voted before Reconstruction to vote unless they passed a wealth or literacy test.

Who Was Jim Crow?
❖ ❖ ❖

The term "Jim Crow" symbolized the continued discrimination of African Americans in the South through state-enacted "separate but equal" laws following *Plessy* v. *Ferguson* (1896). The name "Jim Crow" came from a song-and-dance routine first performed in the 1830s, wherein whites made fun of black songs and speech. Jim Crow was "a comic, jumping, stupid rag doll of a man." The term "Jim Crow" quickly became a synonym for "Negro."

The Jim Crow laws created separate facilities for African Americans in public places including railroad cars, restaurants, and schools. The last was perhaps the most damaging, because black schools were not given the same funding or teachers of the same quality as white schools. It was not until 1954, in *Brown* v. *Board of Education of Topeka*, that racial segregation was ruled unconstitutional.

life in the American South. In 1898, the Court upheld the constitutionality of literacy tests[10] and indicated its apparent willingness to allow the Southern states to define their own suffrage standards, whether or not they disproportionately affected African Americans. One year later, the Supreme Court chose to ignore the fact that educational opportunities for African-American children were far inferior to those of whites. In *Cumming* v. *County Board of Education* (1899),[11] black parents who were also taxpayers challenged their tax assessments because the money was used to support a "whites only" high school. The Board of Education had originally supported a black public high school, but when funds got tight, it was closed to free up funds for the black elementary school. The Supreme Court unanimously upheld the constitutionality of this disparate treatment. The justices appeared concerned that the relief requested could have impaired the functioning of the white high school or required that it be closed altogether.

By 1900, then, equality for African Americans was far from the promise first offered by the passage of the Civil War Amendments. Again and again the Supreme Court nullified the intent of the amendments and sanctioned racial segregation while the states avidly followed its lead. While discrimination was widely practiced in many parts of the North, Southern states passed laws legally imposing segregation in education, housing, public accommodations, employment, and most other spheres of life. Miscegenation laws, for example, prohibited blacks and whites from marrying.

Laws alone were not the only practices designed to keep African Americans in a secondary position. Jim Crow established a way of life with strong social as well as legal codes. Journalist Juan Williams notes in *Eyes on the Prize*:

> There were Jim Crow schools, Jim Crow restaurants, Jim Crow water fountains, and Jim Crow customs—blacks were expected to tip their hats when they walked past whites, but whites did not have to remove their hats even when they entered a black family's home. Whites were to be called "sir" and "ma'am" by blacks, who in turn were called by their first names by whites. People with white skin were to be given a wide berth on the sidewalk; blacks were expected to step aside meekly.[12]

Notwithstanding these degrading practices, by the early 1900s, a small cadre of African Americans (largely from the North) had been able to attain some formal education and were ready to push for additional rights. They found some progressive citizens and politicians amenable to their cause.

The Founding of the National Association for the Advancement of Colored People

In 1909, a handful of individuals active in a variety of progressive causes—including women's suffrage and better working conditions for women and children—met to discuss the idea of a group devoted to the problems of "the Negro." Major race riots had recently occurred in several American cities, and progressive reformers who sought change in political, economic, and social relations were concerned about these outbreaks of violence and the possibility of others. Oswald Garrison Villard, the influential publisher of the New York *Evening Post*—and grandson of William Lloyd Garrison—called a conference to discuss the problem. This group soon evolved into the National Association for the Advancement of Colored People (NAACP). Among its first leaders were Villard; Jane Addams of Hull House, vice president of the National American Woman Suffrage Association; Moorfield Storey, a past president of

William E. DuBois (second from the right in the second row, facing left) is pictured with the original leaders of the Niagara Movement in this 1905 photo taken on the Canadian side of Niagara Falls.

the American Bar Association; and W.E.B. DuBois, a founder of the Niagara Movement, a group of educated African Americans who took their name from their first meeting place, Niagara Falls, in Ontario, Canada. (The Niagara reformers met in Canada because no hotel on the American side of the Falls would accommodate them.)

Key Women's Groups

The NAACP was not the only group getting off the ground. The struggle for women's rights was revitalized by the formation of the National American Woman Suffrage Association (NAWSA) in 1890, when the National and American Woman Suffrage Associations merged, with Susan B. Anthony as its president. Unlike the National Woman Suffrage Association, which had sought a wide variety of expanded rights for women, this new association was devoted largely to securing women's suffrage. Its task was greatly facilitated by the proliferation of women's groups that emerged during the Progressive Era. In addition to the rapidly growing temperance movement, which sought to ban the sale of alcohol, which many women blamed for many social ills, women's groups were created to seek protective legislation in the form of maximum hour or minimum wage laws for women and to work for improved sanitation, public morals, education, and the like. Other organizations that were part of what was called the "club movement" were created to provide increased cultural and literary experiences for middle-class women. With increased industrialization, some women found for the first time that they had the opportunity to pursue activities other than those centered on the home.

One of the most active groups lobbying on behalf of women during this period was the National Consumers' League (NCL). After it successfully lobbied for Oregon legislation limiting women to ten hours of work a day, it insisted that its legislative effort be properly defended before the U.S. Supreme Court when its constitutionality was

Suffragettes demonstrating for the franchise. Parades like this one took place in cities all over the United States.

In 1908, the U.S. Supreme Court ruled that Oregon's law barring women from working more than 10 hours a day in laundries was constitutional. Thus, the conviction of Curt Muller (with arms folded) for violating the statute was upheld.

challenged. Curt Muller had been convicted of employing women more than ten hours a day in his small laundry. When the U.S. Supreme Court agreed to hear his appeal, the NCL sought permission from the state to conduct the defense of the statute.

At the urging of NCL attorney and future U.S. Supreme Court Justice Louis Brandeis, NCL members amassed an impressive array of sociological and medical data that were incorporated into what became known as "The Brandeis brief." This contained only three pages of legal argument, while more than 100 were devoted to nonlegal data. Sociological and other data were used to convince the Court that Oregon's statute was constitutional—a position not supported by other legal precedents. And, in finding the law constitutional in *Muller* v. *Oregon* (1908),[13] the Court relied heavily on these data to document women's unique status as mothers to justify their differential treatment.

Women seeking the vote used reasoning reflecting the Court's opinion in *Muller*. Discarding earlier notions of full equality, NAWSA based its claim to the right to vote largely on the fact that women, as mothers, should be enfranchised. Furthermore, although many members of the suffrage movement were NAACP members, the new women's movement—called the **suffrage movement** because of its focus on the vote alone and not on broader issues of women's rights—took on racist overtones as women argued that if undereducated African Americans could vote, why couldn't women? Some NAWSA members even argued that "the enfranchisement of women would ensure immediate and durable white supremacy."[14]

Diverse attitudes were clearly present in the growing suffrage movement, which often tried to be all things to all people. Its roots in the Progressive Era gave it an exceptionally broad base that transformed NAWSA from a small organization of just over 10,000 members in the early 1890s to a true social movement of more than 2 million members in 1917. By 1920, this coalition was able to secure ratification of the Nineteenth, or Susan B. Anthony, Amendment to the Constitution. And, unlike the provision first passed in Great Britain in 1918 that gave only women over the age of thirty the right to vote, this Amendment guaranteed *all* women the right to vote, albeit fifty-five years after African-American males had been enfranchised by the Fifteenth Amendment.[15]

Suffrage movement Term used to refer to the drive for womens right to vote that took place in the United States from 1890 to 1920.

After passage of the suffrage amendment in 1920, the fragile alliance of diverse women's groups that had come together to fight for the vote quickly disintegrated. Women returned to their "home" groups, such as the NCL, the Women's Christian Temperance Union, or a book club, to pursue their goals of protective legislation, prohibition of alcohol, or self-improvement. In fact, after the tumult of the suffrage movement, widespread, organized activity on behalf of women's rights did not reemerge until the 1960s. In the meantime, however, the NAACP continued to fight racism. In fact, its activities and those of others in the civil rights movement would later give impetus to a new women's movement.

Litigating for Equality

During the 1930s, leaders of the NAACP began to sense that the time was right to launch a full-scale challenge in the federal courts to the constitutionality of *Plessy*'s separate-but-equal doctrine. The NAACP mapped out a long-range strategy that would first target segregation in professional and graduate education. Clearly, the separate-but-equal doctrine and the proliferation of Jim Crow laws were a bar to any hope of full equality for African Americans. Traditional legislative channels were unlikely to work, given blacks' limited or nonexistent political power. Thus, the federal courts and a long-range litigation strategy were the NAACP's only hope. And it often relied on Brandeis-type briefs, so-called because they relied heavily on sociological data. In fact, the NAACP eventually hired a statistician to help its lawyers amass data to help present evidence of discrimination to the courts.

Test Cases.   The NAACP opted first to challenge the constitutionality of Jim Crow law schools. In 1935, all Southern states maintained fully segregated elementary and secondary schools. Colleges and universities were also segregated, but most states did not provide for postgraduate education for African Americans. NAACP lawyers chose to target law schools because they were institutions that judges could well understand, and integration there could prove less threatening to most whites.

Lloyd Gaines, a graduate of Missouri's all-black Lincoln University, sought admission to the all-white University of Missouri Law School in 1936. He was immediately rejected, but the state offered to build a law school at Lincoln (although no funds were allocated for the project) or, if he didn't want to wait, to pay his tuition at an out-of-state law school. Gaines lost his appeal of this rejection in the lower court, and the case was appealed to the U.S. Supreme Court.[16]

Gaines's case was filed at an auspicious time. As you may recall from Chapter 3, a "constitutional revolution" occurred in 1937. Prior to 1937, the Court was most receptive to and interested in the protection of economic liberties. In 1937, however, the Court reversed itself in a series of cases and began to place individual freedoms and personal liberties on a more protected footing. Thus, in 1938, it was to a far more sympathetic Supreme Court that Gaines's lawyers finally pleaded his appeal. NAACP attorneys argued that the creation of a separate law school of any less caliber than that of the University of Missouri would not and could not afford Gaines an *equal* education. The justices agreed with the NAACP's contention and ruled that Missouri had failed to meet the separate-but-equal requirements of *Plessy*, and the Court ordered Missouri to admit Gaines to the school.

Recognizing the importance of the Court's ruling, in 1939 the NAACP created a separate, tax-exempt, legal defense fund to devise a strategy to build on *Gaines* to bring about equal educational opportunities for all African-American children. The

The *Muller* Opinion
♦ ♦ ♦

According to the Court in *Muller* (1908):

That woman's physical structure and the performance of maternal functions place her at a disadvantage in the struggle for subsistence is obvious. . . . As healthy mothers are essential to vigorous offspring, the physical well-being of women becomes an object of public interest and care in order to preserve the strength and vigor of the race. . . . As minors though not to the same extent, she has been looked upon in the courts as needing especial care that her rights may be preserved.

Lloyd Gaines was the subject of the major test case, *Missouri* ex rel. *Gaines* v. *Canada,* which contested the principle of segregated schools. Gaines chose to attend the University of Michigan, from which he strangely disappeared, never to be heard from again.

first head of the NAACP Legal Defense and Educational Fund (LDF), as it was called, was Thurgood Marshall, who later became the first African American to serve on the U.S. Supreme Court (1967–1991). Sensing that the Court would be more amenable to the NAACP's broader goals if it was first forced to address a variety of less threatening claims to educational opportunity, Marshall and the LDF brought a series of carefully crafted test cases to the Court.

The first case involved a forty-six-year-old African-American mail carrier, Herman Sweatt, who in 1946 applied for admission to the all-white University of Texas Law School. Rejected on racial grounds, Sweatt sued and the judge gave the state six months to establish a law school or to admit him to the University of Texas. The university then rented a few rooms in downtown Houston and hired two local African-American attorneys to be part-time faculty members. (At that time there was only one full-time African-American law school professor in the United States.) The state legislature, seeing the handwriting on the wall, authorized $3 million for the creation of the Texas State University for Negroes. One hundred thousand dollars of that money was to be for a new law school in Austin across the street from the state capitol. It consisted of three small basement rooms, a library of more than 10,000 books and access to the state law library, and three part-time first-year instructors as the "faculty." Sweatt declined the opportunity to obtain an education there and instead chose to continue his legal challenge.

While working on *Sweatt*, the NAACP LDF and Marshall also decided to pursue another case. Thurgood Marshall chose to use the case of George W. McLaurin, a retired university professor who had been denied admission to the doctoral education program at the University of Oklahoma. Marshall reasoned that McLaurin, at sixty-eight years of age, would be immune from the charges that African Americans wanted integration in order to intermarry. After a lower court ordered McLaurin's admission, the university reserved a dingy alcove in the cafeteria for him to eat in during off hours, and he was given his own table in the library behind a shelf of newspapers. And, in what surely "was Oklahoma's most inventive contribution to legalized bigotry since the adoption of the 'grandfather clause,'"[17] McLaurin was forced to sit outside classrooms while lectures were given and seminars were held.

The Supreme Court handled these two cases—*Sweatt* v. *Painter*[18] and *McLaurin* v. *Oklahoma State Regents for Higher Education*[19]—as companion cases. The eleven Southern states filed an *amicus curiae* (friend of the court) brief, in which they argued that *Plessy* should govern both cases. The NAACP LDF received assistance, however, from an unexpected source—the U.S. government. In a dramatic departure from the past, the administration of Harry S Truman filed a friend of the court brief urging the Court to overrule *Plessy*. Since the late 1870s, the U.S. government had never sided against the Southern states in a civil rights matter and had never submitted an *amicus* brief supporting the rights of African-American citizens. President Truman believed that because many African Americans had fought and died for their country in World War II, this kind of executive action was proper. The Court traditionally gives great weight to briefs from the U.S. government. The Court, however, again did not overrule *Plessy*, but the justices found that the measures taken by the states in each case failed to live up to the strictures of the separate-but-equal doctrine. The Court unanimously ruled that the "remedies" to each situation were inadequate to afford a sound education. In the *Sweatt* case, for example, the Court declared that the "qualities which are incapable of objective measurement but which make for greatness in a law school . . . includ(ing) the reputation of the faculty, experience of the administration, position and influence of the alumni, standing in the community, traditions and prestige" made it impossible for the state to provide an equal education in a segregated setting.

After these decisions were handed down in 1950, the NAACP LDF concluded that the time had come to launch a full-scale attack on the separate-but-equal doctrine. The decisions of the Court were encouraging, and the position of the U.S. government and the population in general appeared to be more receptive to an outright overruling of *Plessy*.

Brown v. Board of Education of Topeka, Kansas (1954).[20] As discussed in "Why It's Called *Brown* v. *Board of Education of Topeka*" (see p. 136), *Brown* was actually four cases brought from different areas of the South, the border states, and others involving public elementary or high school systems that mandated separate schools for blacks and whites.

In *Brown*, NAACP lawyers, again headed by Thurgood Marshall, argued that *Plessy*'s separate-but-equal doctrine was unconstitutional under the equal protection clause of the Fourteenth Amendment, and that if the Court was still reluctant to overrule *Plessy*, the only way to equalize the schools was to integrate them. A major component of the NAACP's strategy was to prove that the intellectual, psychological, and financial damage that befell African Americans as a result of segregation precluded any court from finding that equality was served by the separate-but-equal policy.

In *Brown*, the NAACP LDF presented the Supreme Court with evidence of the harmful consequences of state-imposed racial discrimination. To buttress its claims the NAACP introduced the now-famous "doll study," conducted by Kenneth Clark, a prominent African-American sociologist who had long studied the negative effects of segregation on African-American children. His research revealed that black children not only preferred white dolls when shown black and white dolls, but that most liked the white doll better, many adding that the black doll looked "bad." This information was used to illustrate the negative impact of racial segregation and bias on an African-American child's self-image.

The NAACP's legal briefs were supported by important *amicus curiae* briefs submitted by the U.S. government and major civil rights groups, labor unions, and religious groups decrying racial segregation. On May 17, 1954, Chief Justice Earl Warren

Brown v. Board of Education of Topeka, Kansas Supreme Court case that overturned the separate-but-equal doctrine as unconstitutional under the equal protection clause of the Fourteenth Amendment.

Why It's Called *Brown v. Board of Education of Topeka*

❖ ❖ ❖

Seven-year–old Linda Brown of Topeka, Kansas, lived close to a good public school, but it was reserved for whites. So every day she had to cross railroad tracks to catch a run-down school bus that took her across town to a school for black students. Her father, Oliver Brown, concerned for her safety and the quality of her education, became increasingly frustrated with his daughter's having to travel far from home to get an education.

"The issue came up, and it was decided that Reverend Brown's daughter would be the goat, so to speak," recalled a member of the Topeka NAACP. "He put forth his daughter to test the validity of the [law], and we had to raise the money."*

The NAACP continued to gather plaintiffs and test cases from around the nation. The Supreme Court first agreed to hear *Brown* and *Briggs* v. *Elliott* (South Carolina) in 1952. Two days before they were to be heard, the Court issued a postponement and added *Davis* v. *Prince Edward County* (Virginia) to its docket. A few weeks later, the Court added *Bolling* v. *Sharpe* (District of Columbia) and

Ten years after the Court's decision in *Brown* v. *Board of Education,* Linda Brown Smith stood in front of the school whose refusal to admit her ultimately led to the Court's 1954 ruling, *Brown* v. *Board of Education,* named after her. The decision came too late for her, but her two younger sisters were able to attend integrated schools.

Gebhart v. *Belton* (Delaware). According to U.S. Supreme Court Justice Tom Clark of Texas, the Court "consolidated them and made *Brown* the first so that the whole question would not smack of being purely a Southern one."** Thus, the case became known as *Brown* v. *Board of Education of Topeka.*

* Quoted in Juan Williams, *Eyes on the Prize: America's Civil Rights Years, 1954–1965* (New York: Penguin, 1987), p. 21.

** Ibid., p. 31.

delivered the fourth opinion of the day, *Brown* v. *Board of Education of Topeka.* Writing for the Court, Warren stated:

> To separate [some school children] from others . . . solely because of their race generates a feeling of inferiority as to their status in the community that may affect their hearts and minds in a way very unlikely ever to be undone.

We conclude, unanimously, that in the field of public education the doctrine of "separate but equal" has no place.[21]

There can be no doubt that *Brown* was the most important civil rights case decided in the twentieth century. It immediately evoked an uproar that shook the nation. Some called the day the decision was handed down "Black Monday." The governor of South Carolina decried the decision, saying, "Ending segregation would mark the beginning of the end of civilization in the South as we know it."[22] The NAACP LDF lawyers who had argued these cases and those leading to *Brown,* however, were jubilant.

Since 1890, remarkable changes had occurred in the civil rights of Americans. Women had won the right to vote, and after a long and arduous trail of litigation in the federal courts, the Supreme Court had finally overturned the most racist case of the era, *Plessy* v. *Ferguson.* The Court boldly proclaimed that separate but equal (at least in education) would no longer pass constitutional muster. The question then became how *Brown* would be interpreted and implemented. Could it be used to invalidate other Jim Crow laws and practices? Would African Americans be truly equal under law?

The Civil Rights Movement

Since 1954, profound changes have occurred in our notion of civil rights. First African Americans and then women have built upon existing organizations to forge successful movements for increased rights. *Brown* served as a catalyst for change, sparking the development of the modern civil rights movement. Women's work in that movement and the student protest movement that arose in reaction to the U.S. government's involvement in Vietnam gave women the experience needed to form their own organizations to press for full equality.[23] As African Americans and women became more and more successful, they served as the model for others who sought equality—Native Americans, Hispanic Americans, homosexuals, the disabled, and others.

School Desegregation After *Brown*

One year after *Brown I,* in what is referred to as *Brown II,*[24] the Court ruled that racially segregated systems must be dismantled "with all deliberate speed." To facilitate implementation, the Court placed enforcement of *Brown* in the hands of nonelected federal district court judges, who were considered more immune to local political pressures than were regularly elected state court judges.

The NAACP and its Legal Defense Fund continued to resort to the courts to see that *Brown* was implemented, while the South entered into a near-conspiracy to avoid the mandates of *Brown II.* In Arkansas, for example, Governor Orval Faubus, facing a re-election bid, announced that he would not "be a party to any attempt to force acceptance of change to which people are overwhelmingly opposed."[25] The day before school was to begin, Faubus announced that he would surround Little Rock's Central High School with National Guardsmen to prevent African-American students from entering. While the federal courts in Arkansas continued to order the admission of African-American children, the governor remained adamant. Finally, President Dwight D. Eisenhower sent federal troops to Little Rock to protect the rights of the nine students who had attempted to attend Central High.

In reaction to the governor's outrageous conduct, in *Cooper* v. *Aaron* (1958),[26] each justice individually signed the unanimous opinion, underscoring each one's personal support of the statement that "no state legislator or executive or judicial officer can war against the Constitution without violating his undertaking to support it." (Unanimous opinions are usually written and signed by a single justice.) The state's actions, thus, were ruled unconstitutional and its "evasive schemes" illegal.

The saga of Little Rock is telling and illustrative of the massive resistance to *Brown* and the NAACP throughout the South. It is hard to imagine these kinds of confrontations occurring today—a governor calling a press conference to announce that he would defy a federal order, a president sending in federal troops to protect the rights of African-American citizens against the state militia, and legislation requiring the NAACP to identify its members. All of this, including the violence that greeted the new students, was duly recorded in the press and on television in vivid detail. And it added fuel to the fire of opponents of racism throughout the South and elsewhere.

A New Move for African-American Rights

In 1955, soon after *Brown II*, in Montgomery, Alabama, the local NAACP's Youth Council advisor, Rosa Parks, wanted to challenge the constitutionality of the segregated bus system. So Parks and other NAACP officials began to raise money for litigation and made speeches around town to garner public support. On December 1, 1955, Rosa Parks made history when she refused to leave her seat on a bus to move to the back and make room for a white male passenger. Parks was arrested for violating an Alabama law banning integration of public facilities, including buses. After being freed on bond, Parks and the NAACP decided to enlist city clergy to help her cause. At the same time, 35,000 handbills calling for African Americans to boycott the Montgomery bus system on the day of Parks's trial were distributed. Black ministers used Sunday services to urge their members to support the boycott. That Monday, African Americans walked, carpooled, or used black-owned taxicabs. That night, local ministers decided that the boycott should be continued. A twenty-six-year-old minister, Martin Luther King, Jr., was selected to lead the newly formed "Montgomery Improvement Association." King was new to town, and church leaders had been looking for a way to get him more involved in civil rights work.

As the boycott dragged on, Montgomery officials and local business owners began to harass the city's African-American citizens. But King urged Montgomery's African-American citizens to continue their protest. The residents held out, despite suffering personal hardship for their actions, ranging from harassment to bankruptcy to job loss. In 1956, a federal court ruled that the segregated bus system violated the equal protection clause of the Fourteenth Amendment.[27] After a year of walking, African Americans ended their protest as the buses were ordered to integrate. The first effort at nonviolent protest had been successful.

After a ruling from the U.S. Supreme Court that banned segregation on public buses operated by the city of Montgomery, Alabama, Rosa Parks, whose refusal to give up her seat on the bus sparked the Montgomery Bus Boycott, takes a seat on an integrated bus.

Formation of New Groups. The recognition and respect that King earned within the African-American community helped him to launch the Southern Christian Leadership Conference (SCLC) in 1957, soon after the end of the Montgomery bus boycott. Unlike the NAACP, which had Northern origins and had come to rely largely on litigation as a means of achieving expanded equality, the SCLC had a Southern base and was rooted more closely in black religious culture. The SCLC's philosophy was reflective of King's growing belief in the importance of nonviolent protest.

On February 1, 1960, students at the all-black North Carolina Agricultural and Technical College participated in the first "sit-in." Angered by their inability to be served at local lunch counters and heartened by the success of the Montgomery bus boycott, African-American students marched to the local Woolworth's and ordered a cup of coffee. They were refused service. So they sat at the counter until police came and carted them off to jail. Soon thereafter, African-American college students around the South joined together to challenge the Jim Crow laws in the region. These mass actions immediately brought extensive attention from the national news media.

With the assistance of an $800 grant from the SCLC, over spring break 1960, 200 student delegates—black *and* white—met at Shaw University in North Carolina to consider recent sit-in actions and to plan for the future. Later that year, two more meetings were held in Atlanta, Georgia, and the Student Nonviolent Coordinating Committee (SNCC) was formed.

Among SNCC's first leaders were Marion Barry, who was to serve as mayor of Washington, D.C. (1978–1990, 1995–); John Lewis, who at this writing is a member of Congress serving as the Deputy House Majority Whip; and Marian Wright Edelman (a close friend of Bill and Hillary Rodham Clinton), who became first an NAACP lawyer and later the founder and head of the Children's Defense Fund. While the SCLC generally worked with church leaders in a community, SNCC was much more of a grassroots organization. Always perceived as more radical than the SCLC, SNCC tended to focus its organizing activities on the young, both black and white.

In addition to joining the sit-in bandwagon, SNCC also came to lead what were called "freedom rides," designed to focus attention on segregated public accommodations. Bands of college students and other civil rights activists traveled throughout the South by bus in an effort to force bus stations to desegregate. These protesters were frequently met with brutal violence as local police chose not to defend protesters' basic constitutional rights to free speech and peaceful assembly against angry mobs of segregationists. Not only African Americans participated in these freedom rides;

A prime objective of the protesters in Birmingham was to focus national attention on their cause. For the first time in American history, a majority of the public owned television sets and could see the horrors of police brutality. But the print media continued to be a powerful tool. This picture was reprinted over and over again and even frequently mentioned on the floor of Congress during debates on the Civil Rights Act of 1964.

At this historic gathering in March, 1963, on the Mall in Washington D.C., Martin Luther King, Jr. delivered his famous "I Have a Dream" speech.

increasingly, white college students from the North began to play an important role in SNCC.

While SNCC continued to sponsor sit-ins and freedom rides, in 1963 Martin Luther King, Jr. launched a series of massive nonviolent demonstrations in Birmingham, Alabama, long considered a major stronghold of segregation. Thousands of blacks and whites marched to Birmingham in a show of solidarity. Peaceful marchers were met there by Birmingham Police Commissioner Eugene "Bull" Conner, who ordered his officers to use dogs, clubs, fire hoses, and other tactics on the marchers, whose ranks included small children. All the marchers, including the children, suffered at the hands of local police. Americans across the nation watched in horror as they witnessed the brutality and abuse heaped on the protestors. As the marchers hoped, these shocking scenes helped convince President John F. Kennedy to propose important civil rights legislation.

The Civil Rights Act of 1964

The older faction of the civil rights movement, as represented by the SCLC, and the younger branch, represented by SNCC, both sought a similar goal: implementation of Supreme Court decisions and an end to racial segregation and discrimination. The cumulative effect of collective actions such as sit-ins, boycotts, marches, and freedom rides—as well as the tragic bombings and deaths inflicted in retaliation—led to congressional passage of the first major piece of civil rights legislation since the post-Civil War era.

In 1963, President Kennedy requested that Congress pass a law banning discrimination in public accommodations. Seizing the moment and recognizing the potency of a show of massive support, Martin Luther King, Jr. called for a monumental march on Washington, D.C., to demonstrate widespread support for legislation to ban discrimination in *all* aspects of life, not just public accommodations. Held only four months after the Birmingham demonstrations, the "March on Washington for Jobs and Freedom" was attended by more than 250,000 people, who heard King's immortal "I Have a Dream" speech, delivered from the Lincoln Memorial. Before Congress had the opportunity to vote on any legislation, however, Kennedy was assassinated in Dallas, Texas.

It was clear that national laws outlawing discrimination were the only answer, because Southern legislators would never vote to repeal Jim Crow laws. It was much more feasible for African Americans to seek national laws and then their implementation from the federal judiciary. But through the 1960s, African Americans lacked sufficient political power or the force of public opinion to sway enough congressional leaders. Their task was further stymied by loud and strong opposition from Southern members of Congress, many of whom, because of the Democratic Party's total control of the South, had been in office far longer than most, and therefore held powerful committee chairmanships that were awarded on seniority. The Senate Judiciary Committee was controlled by a coalition of Southern Democrats and conservative Republicans, and the House Rules Committee was chaired by a Virginian who was opposed to any civil rights legislation and who, by virtue of his position, could block such legislation in committee.

When Vice President Lyndon B. Johnson, a Southern-born former Senate majority leader, succeeded John F. Kennedy as president, he put civil rights reform at the top of his legislative priority list, and civil rights activists gained a critical ally. Thus, through the 1960s, the movement subtly changed in focus from peaceful protest and litigation to legislative lobbying. Now its focus had broadened from integration of school and public facilities and voting rights to issues of housing, jobs, and equal opportunity.

The push for civil rights legislation in the halls of Congress was also helped by changes in public opinion. Between 1959 and 1965, Southern attitudes toward integrated schools had changed enormously as the proportion of Southerners who responded that they would not mind their child's attendance at a half-black school doubled.

In spite of strong presidential support and the sway of public opinion, however, the Civil Rights Act of 1964 did not sail through Congress easily. Southern senators, led by South Carolina's Strom Thurmond, a Democrat who later switched to the Republican Party, conducted the longest filibuster in the history of the Senate. For eight weeks they held up voting on the bill until cloture (see Chapter 6) was invoked and the filibuster was brought to an end. Once passed, the **Civil Rights Act of 1964:**

> **Civil Rights Act of 1964** Legislation passed by Congress to outlaw segregation in public facilities and racial discrimination in employment, education, and voting; created the Equal Employment Opportunity Commission.

- Barred discrimination based on race, color, religion, or national origin in the "full and equal enjoyment" of goods and services in any public accommodation.
- Authorized the Attorney General to initiate lawsuits to force desegregation of public schools on behalf of private individuals.
- Made illegal the use of literacy tests or other administrative devices or tests designed to impede minority voting.
- Barred discrimination in any program or activity receiving federal assistance.
- Prohibited discrimination in employment on grounds of race, color, religion, national origin, or sex.
- Created the Equal Employment Opportunity Commission (EEOC) to monitor and enforce the bans on employment discrimination.

While these changes were occurring in the law, other changes were sweeping the nation. Violence began to rock the country as ghetto riots broke out in the Northeast. Although Northern African Americans were not subject to Jim Crow laws, many lived in poverty and faced pervasive daily discrimination and its resultant frustration. Some, including Malcolm X, even argued that to survive, African Americans must separate themselves in every way from white culture. Thus, given a growing "black power" movement and increased racial tensions, it is not surprising that from 1964 to 1968, many Northern African Americans took to the streets, burning and looting to vent their rage.

Violence also marred the continued activities of civil rights workers in the South. During the summer of 1964 three civil rights workers—one black, two white—were killed in Neshoba County, Mississippi. In 1965, King again led his supporters on a massive march, this time from Selma to the Alabama state capital in Montgomery, in support of additional voting rights protections. Again, Southern officials unleashed a reign of terror in Selma as they used whips, dogs, cattle prods, clubs, and tear gas to deter the protestors. One marcher was killed. Again, Americans watched in horror as they witnessed this brutality on their television screens. This march and the public's reaction to it led to quick passage of the Voting Rights Act of 1965, which suspended the use of literacy tests and authorized the federal government to monitor all elections

Controversial Black Muslim leader, Malcolm X.

in areas where discrimination was found to be practiced or where less than 50 percent of the voting-age public was registered to vote in the 1964 election. (For more on the effect of the Voting Rights Act, see Chapter 12).

The Effect of the Civil Rights Act of 1964

Many Southerners were adamant in their belief that the 1964 and 1965 Acts were unconstitutional because they went beyond the scope of Congress's authority to legislate under the Constitution.

Public Accommodations. The Supreme Court heard the first challenge to the Civil Rights Act of 1964 on an expedited review (which bypasses the intermediate courts). In *Heart of Atlanta Motel* v. *United States* (1964),[28] the operator of a hotel that refused African-American guests asked the Court to rule Section 2 of the Act, barring discrimination in public accommodations, unconstitutional. Hotel attorneys argued that the Act exceeded congressional authority granted by the commerce clause to "regulate interstate commerce." The Court disagreed and found that Congress was acting within the scope of its authority when it acted to prohibit discrimination in any commercial enterprises engaged in interstate commerce.

Education. One of the key provisions of the Civil Rights Act of 1964, Title VI, authorized the U.S. Justice Department to bring actions against school districts that had not complied with *Brown* v. *Board of Education*. In 1964, a full decade after *Brown*, fewer than 1 percent of African-American children in the South attended integrated schools.[29]

In *Swann* v. *Charlotte-Mecklenburg School District* (1971),[30] the Supreme Court ruled that lower federal courts could order busing as an appropriate remedy to end dual, segregated school systems. After *Brown*, the school board assigned students to schools closest to their homes without regard to race, leaving over half of African-American students attending schools at least 99 percent black. In interpreting Title VI's provisions, the Court ruled that because the school district formerly had engaged in intentional, statutory discrimination (*de jure*, or *by law*, **discrimination**), the continued presence of so many all black or white schools created a legal presumption that the school board intended to discriminate.

The Supreme Court ruled that busing was an appropriate remedy only when the discrimination was a result of *de jure* discrimination. In *Swann*, the Court was careful to distinguish *de jure* from **de facto discrimination**, unintentional discrimination often attributable to housing patterns and/or private acts. The Court was careful to note its approval of busing as a remedy for intentional, governmental-imposed or -sanctioned discrimination. The Court did not, however, address the question of where busing was an appropriate remedy if it was the result of *de facto* discrimination.

Busing, however, soon became a highly emotional issue. Few parents want to see their child bused, and most Americans argue that it is better for children to attend schools close to their homes. In fact, the relative quality of local school districts is often the reason why many families move to particular neighborhoods or localities. When busing was ordered in urban school districts, many whites fled to the suburbs. And the Supreme Court found that federal courts lacked the authority to impose inter-

De jure discrimination Racial discrimination that is a direct result of law or official policy.

De facto discrimination Racial discrimination that results from practice (such as housing patterns or other social factors) rather than law.

district remedies for school segregation without a showing of an interdistrict violation of the law.[31]

Over the years, forced, judicially imposed busing has found less and less favor with the Supreme Court, even in situations where *de jure* discrimination had earlier been proven. In 1992, the U.S. Supreme Court even ruled that in situations where all-black schools still existed after having been under a court order since 1969 to dismantle the *de jure* system, a showing that the persistent segregation was not a result of the board's actions was sufficient to remove the district from court supervision.[32]

Employment. Title VII of the Civil Rights Act of 1964 prohibits employers from discriminating against employees for a variety of reasons, including race, sex, age, and national origin. (In 1978 the Act was amended to prohibit discrimination based on pregnancy.)

In one of the first major cases decided under the Act, the Supreme Court found that employers could be found liable for discrimination if the *effect* of their employment practices was to exclude African Americans from certain positions. So in *Griggs* v. *Duke Power Company* (1971),[33] African-American employees were allowed to use statistical evidence to show that they had been excluded from all but one department of Duke Power Company. Blacks were effectively kept out of all but low-paying, manual labor positions because the company instituted a high-school education requirement, or passing of a special test in order to be eligible for promotion. Many of the African-American applicants had been deeply affected by the inferior education provided by North Carolina segregated school systems and either had no high school diploma or scored badly on the test.

The Supreme Court ruled that although the tests did not *appear* to discriminate against African Americans, their effects—that there were no African-American employees in any other departments—were sufficient to shift the burden of proving lack of discrimination on the employer. Thus, the Duke Power Company would have to prove that the tests were "a business necessity" that had a "demonstrable relationship to successful performance" (of a particular job).

The notion of "business necessity" as set out in the Civil Rights Act of 1964 and interpreted by the federal courts was especially important for women. For years, women had been kept out of many occupations as employers argued that their customers preferred to deal with male personnel. Conversely, males were barred from flight-attendant positions because the airlines believed that passengers preferred to be served by women. The airlines justified their "females only" employment policy by noting that flyers often became nervous, and many male passengers would feel uneasy if they had to seek comfort from another male. Similarly, many large factories, manufacturing establishments, and police and fire departments refused outright to hire women by using arbitrary height and weight requirements. These height and weight requirements also often disproportionately affected Hispanics. Like the tests in *Griggs*, these requirements often could not be shown to be related to job performance and were eventually ruled illegal by the federal courts.

As noted earlier, one of the key provisions of the Civil Rights Act allowed the Justice Department and/or the **Equal Employment Opportunity Commission (EEOC)** to enforce key provisions of the Act. Employment discrimination litigation is very expensive and beyond the means of most salaried workers. Thus, if the EEOC chooses to enforce the law vigorously and bring cases on behalf of individuals, an employee's chances of proving discrimination increase tremendously, especially since the courts

Equal Employment Opportunity Commission Federal agency created to enforce provisions of the Civil Rights Act of 1964.

generally look with favor on claims brought by the U.S. government. In fact, the failure of the EEOC to investigate claims of sex discrimination contributed to the rise of the modern women's rights movement.

The Women's Rights Movement.   Just as women had been involved in the abolitionist movement in the 1800s, women from all walks of life also participated in the civil rights movement. Women were important members of both SNCC and more traditional groups like the NAACP and the SCLC.[34] Yet they often found themselves treated as second-class citizens. At one point, Stokely Carmichael, chair of SNCC, openly proclaimed: "The only position for women in SNCC is prone."[35] Statements and attitudes like these led some women to found early women's liberation groups that were generally quite radical, small in membership, and not intended to use more conventional political tactics.

As discussed earlier, initial efforts to convince the Supreme Court to declare women enfranchised under the Fourteenth Amendment were uniformly unsuccessful. The paternalistic attitude of the Supreme Court, and perhaps society as well, continued well into the 1970s. As late as 1961, Florida required women who wished to serve on juries to travel to the county courthouse and register for that duty. In contrast, all men who were registered voters were automatically eligible to serve. When Gwendolyn Hoyt was convicted of bludgeoning her adulterous husband to death with a baseball bat, she appealed her conviction, claiming that the exclusion of women from juries prejudiced her case. She believed that female jurors—her peers—would have been more sympathetic to her and the emotional turmoil that led to her attack on her husband and her claim of "temporary insanity." She therefore argued that her trial by an all-male jury violated her rights as guaranteed by the Fourteenth Amendment. In rejecting her contention, Justice John Harlan (the grandson of the lone dissenting justice in *Plessy*) wrote in *Hoyt* v. *Florida* (1961):

Despite the enlightened emancipation of women from the restrictions and protections of bygone years, and their entry into many parts of community life formerly considered to be reserved to men, a woman is still regarded as the center of home and family life.[36]

These kinds of attitudes and decisions were not sufficient to forge a new movement for women's rights. Shortly after *Hoyt*, however, three events occurred to move women to action. In 1961, soon after his election, President John Kennedy had created a President's Commission on the Status of Women. The Commission's report, *American Women*, released in 1963, documented pervasive discrimination against women in all walks of life. In addition, the civil rights movement and publication of Betty Friedan's *The Feminine Mystique* (1963),[37] which led some women to question their lives and status in society, added to their dawning recognition that something was wrong. Soon after, the Civil Rights Act of 1964 prohibited discrimination based not only on race, but also on sex. Ironically, that provision had been added to Title VII of the Civil Rights Act by Southern Democrats. These senators saw a prohibition against sex discrimination in employment as a joke, and viewed its addition as a means to discredit the entire Act and ensure its defeat. Thus it was added at the last minute, and female members of Congress seized the opportunity to garner support for the measure.

In 1966, after the Equal Employment Opportunity Commission failed to enforce Title VII as it applied to sex discrimination, women activists formed the National Organization for Women (NOW). From its inception, NOW was closely modeled on the NAACP. Women in NOW were quite similar to the founders of the NAACP; they wanted to work within the system to prevent discrimination. Initially, most of this activity was geared toward two goals: achievement of equality through passage of an equal rights amendment to the Constitution, or by judicial decision. But because the Supreme Court failed to extend constitutional protections to women, the only recourse that remained was an amendment.

The Equal Rights Amendment (ERA).   Not all women agreed with the notion of full equality for women. Members of the National Consumers' League, for example, feared that an ERA would invalidate protective legislation of the kind specifically ruled constitutional in *Muller* v. *Oregon* (1908). Nevertheless, from 1923 to 1972, a proposal for an equal rights amendment was made in every session of every Congress. Every president since Harry S Truman backed it, and by 1972, public opinion favored its ratification.

Finally, in 1972, in response to NOW, the National Women's Political Caucus, and a wide variety of other women's groups, Congress passed the Equal Rights Amendment by overwhelming majorities (84–8 in the Senate; 354–24 in the House).

The amendment provided that:

- Equality of rights under the law shall not be denied or abridged by the United States or by any state on account of sex.
- The Congress shall have the power to enforce, by appropriate legislation, the provisions of this article.

Within a year, twenty-two states had ratified the amendment, most by overwhelming margins. In *Roe* v. *Wade* (1973),[38] however, the Supreme Court decided that women had a constitutionally protected right to privacy that included the right to terminate a pregnancy. Almost overnight *Roe* gave the ERA's opponents political fuel. Although privacy rights and the ERA have nothing to do with each other, opponents effectively persuaded many persons in states that had yet to ratify the Amendment that the two were linked. If abortion was legal, why not marriages between and adoptions by homosexuals? They also claimed that the ERA would force women out of their homes and into the work-force, as husbands would no longer be responsible for their wives' support.[39]

These arguments and the amendment's potential to make women eligible for the military draft brought the ratification effort to a near standstill. In 1974–1975, the amendment only squeaked through the Montana and North Dakota legislatures, and two states—Nebraska and Tennessee—voted to rescind their earlier ratifications.[40]

By 1978, one year before the deadline for ratification was to expire, thirty-five states—three short of the three-fourths necessary for ratification—had voted for the Amendment. Efforts in key states such as Illinois and Florida failed as opposition to the Amendment intensified.

Faced with the prospect of defeat, ERA supporters heavily lobbied Congress to extend the deadline. Congress extended the time period for ratification by three years, but to no avail. No additional states ratified the Amendment, but three more rescinded their votes.[41]

Thus, what began as a simple correction to the Constitution turned into a highly controversial proposed change. In spite of the fact that large numbers of the public favored the ERA, opponents needed to stall ratification in only thirteen states while supporters had to convince legislators in thirty-eight. Hurting the effort was the success that women's rights activists were having in the courts. When women first sought the ERA in the late 1960s, the Supreme Court had yet to rule that women were protected by the Fourteenth Amendment from any kind of discrimination, thus clearly showing the need for an amendment. But as the Court widened its interpretation of the Constitution to protect women from some sorts of discrimination, in the eyes of many the need for a new amendment became less urgent.

Litigation for Equal Rights.   While several women's groups worked toward passage of the ERA, NOW and several other groups, including the Women's Rights Project of the American Civil Liberties Union (ACLU), formed litigating arms to pressure the courts. An immediate roadblock that women faced was the Supreme Court's interpretation of the equal protection clause of the Fourteenth Amendment.

The Equal Protection Clause and Constitutional Standards of Review

The Fourteenth Amendment protects all U.S. citizens from state action that violates equal protection of the laws. But early on, the Supreme Court decided that certain rights were entitled to a heightened standard of review. As early as 1937,[42] the Supreme Court recognized that certain rights were so fundamental that a very heavy burden would be placed on any government that sought to restrict those rights. When fundamental rights such as First Amendment freedoms or **suspect classifications** such as race are involved, the Court uses a heightened standard of review called **strict scrutiny** to determine the constitutional validity of the challenged practices, as detailed in Table 5.1. Beginning with *Brown* v. *Board of Education* (1954), the Supreme Court viewed race-based distinctions with strict scrutiny. In legal terms, this means that if a statute or governmental practice makes a classification based on race, the statute is presumed to be unconstitutional unless the state can provide "compelling affirmative justifications"—that is, unless the state can prove the law in question is nec-

Suspect classifications Categories or classes such as race that trigger the highest standard of scrutiny from the Supreme Court.

Strict scrutiny A heightened standard of review used by the Supreme Court to determine the constitutional validity of a challenged practice.

Table 5.1 ♦ **The Equal Protection Clause and Standards of Review Used by the Supreme Court to Determine Whether It Has Been Violated**

TYPES OF CLASSIFICATION	STANDARD OF REVIEW	TEST	EXAMPLE
What kind of statutory classification is an issue?	What standard of review will be used?	What does the court ask?	How does the court apply the test?
Fundamental freedoms: Religion, assembly, press, privacy, "suspect" classifications (including race)	Strict scrutiny or heightened standard	Is classification *necessary* to the accomplishment of a permissible state goal?	*Brown* v. *Board of Education* (1954) Racial segregation not necessary to accomplish the state goal of educating its students
Gender	Intermediate standard	Does it serve an important governmental objective, and is it substantially related to those ends?	*Craig* v. *Boren* (1976) Keeping drunk drivers off the roads may be an important governmental objective, but allowing eighteen- to twenty-one-year-old women to drink alcoholic beverages while prohibiting men of the same age from drinking is not substantially related to that goal.
Others (including age, wealth, and sexual preference)	Minimum rationality standard	Is there any rational foundation for the discrimination?	*Bowers* v. *Hardwick* (1986) It is rational for Georgia to prohibit consensual sodomy because of traditional taboos against homosexual behavior.

---

essary to accomplish a permissible goal. During the 1960s and into the 1970s, the Court routinely struck down as unconstitutional practices and statutes that discriminated on the basis of race. "Whites only" public parks and recreational facilities, tax-exempt status for private schools that discriminated, and statutes prohibiting racial intermarriage were declared unconstitutional. In contrast, the Court refused even to consider the fact that the equal protection clause might apply to discrimination against women. Finally, in a case brought in 1971 by Ruth Bader Ginsburg as Director of the Women's Rights Project of the ACLU (see "The American Civil Liberties Union," p. 102), the Supreme Court ruled that an Idaho law granting male parents automatic preference over female parents as the administrator of their deceased children's estates violated the equal protection clause of the Fourteenth Amendment.

Reed v. *Reed* (1971),[43] the Idaho case, turned the tide in terms of constitutional litigation. While the Court did not rule that sex was a suspect classification, it concluded that the equal protection clause of the Fourteenth Amendment prohibited unreasonable classifications based on sex. And in 1976, the Court ruled that sex-discrimination complaints would be judged by a new, judicially created intermediate standard of review a step below strict scrutiny. In *Craig* v. *Boren* (1976),[44] the owner of the Honk 'n' Holler Restaurant in Stillwater, Oklahoma, and Craig, a male under twenty-one, challenged the constitutionality of a state law prohibiting the sale of 3.2 percent beer to males under the age of twenty-one and to females under the age of eighteen. The state introduced a considerable amount of evidence in support of the statute, including:

- Eighteen- to twenty-year-old males were more likely to be arrested for driving under the influence than were females of the same age.
- Youths aged seventeen to twenty-one were the group most likely to be injured or to die in alcohol-related traffic accidents, with males exceeding females.
- Young men were more inclined to drink and drive than females.

The Supreme Court found that this information was "too tenuous" to support the legislation. In coming to this conclusion, the Court carved out a new "test" to be used in examining claims of sex discrimination. According to the Court, "[T]o withstand constitutional challenge, . . . classifications by gender must serve important governmental objectives and must be substantially related to achievement of those objectives." As *Craig* demonstrates, men, too, can use the Fourteenth Amendment to fight gender-based discrimination. Since 1976, the Court has applied that intermediate standard to most claims that it has heard involving gender. Thus, the following kinds of practices have been found to violate the Fourteenth Amendment:

- Single-sex public nursing schools.
- Laws that consider males adults at twenty-one years but females at eighteen years.
- Laws that allow women but not men to receive alimony.
- State prosecutors' use of pre-emptory challenges to reject men or women to create more sympathetic juries.

In contrast, the Court has upheld the following governmental practices and laws:

- Draft registration provisions for males only.
- Statutory rape laws that apply only to female victims.

The level of review used by the Court is crucial. Clearly, a statute excluding African Americans from draft registration would be unconstitutional. But, because gender is not subject to the same higher standard of review that is used in racial discrimination cases, the exclusion of women from the requirements of the Military Selective Service Act was ruled permissible because the government policy was considered to serve "important governmental objectives."[45]

This history has perhaps clarified why women's rights activists continue to argue that until the passage of an equal rights amendment, women will never enjoy the same rights as men. An amendment would automatically raise the level of scrutiny that the Court applies to gender-based claims.

Statutory Remedies for Sex Discrimination.   In part because of the limits of the intermediate standard of review and the fact that the equal protection clause applies only to *governmental* discrimination, women's rights activists began to bombard the courts with sex-discrimination cases. These cases have been filed under Title VII of the Civil Rights Act, which prohibits discrimination by private (and, after 1972, public) employers, or Title IX of the Education Amendments of 1972, which bars educational institutions receiving federal funds from discriminating against female students. Key victories under Title VII include:

- Consideration of sexual harassment as discrimination.
- Inclusion of law firms, which many argued were *private* partnerships, in the coverage of the Act.

- A broad definition of what can be considered sexual harassment.
- Allowance of voluntary affirmative action programs to redress historical discrimination against women.

Title IX, which parallels Title VII, has also greatly expanded the opportunities for women in elementary, secondary, and post-secondary institutions. Since women's groups, like the NAACP before them, saw eradication of educational discrimination as key to improving other facets of women's lives, they lobbied for it heavily.[46] Most of today's college students did not go through school being excluded from home economics or shop classes on account of their sex. Nor, probably, did many attend schools that had no team sports for females. Yet, this was commonly the case in the United States prior to passage of Title IX.

Other Groups Mobilize for Rights

African Americans and women are not the only groups that have suffered unequal treatment under the law. Denial of civil rights has led many other disadvantaged groups to mobilize to achieve greater civil rights. And their efforts to achieve those rights have many parallels to the efforts made by African Americans and women. In the wake of the successes of those two groups in achieving greater rights, and sometimes even before, other traditionally disenfranchised groups have organized to gain fuller equality. Many of them have also recognized that litigation and the use of test-case strategies would be key to further civil rights gains. The Ford Foundation, which had heavily funded the NAACP LDF and some women's rights litigation, also helped interested Mexican-Americans to found the Mexican American Legal Defense and Education Fund (MALDEF). Established in 1968, and modeled after the NAACP LDF, MALDEF has played and continues to play a major role in expanding civil rights for Hispanics. The Ford Foundation also facilitated the 1970 creation of the Native American Rights Fund to litigate for Indian rights.

Native Americans

Native Americans are the first "true" Americans, and their status under U.S. law is unique. Under the U.S. Constitution, "Indian tribes" are considered distinct governments, which has affected Native Americans' treatment by the Supreme Court in contrast to other groups of ethnic minorities. And "minority" is truly a term that accurately describes American Indians. It is estimated that there were as many as 10 million Indians in the New World at the time it was discovered with 3 to 4 million living in what is today the United States. By 1900, the number in the continental United States had plummeted to less than 2 million.

Many commentators would agree that for years the Congress and the courts manipulated Indian law to promote the westward expansion of the United States. The Northwest Ordinance of 1787, passed by the Continental Congress, specified that "the good faith should always be observed toward the Indians; their lands and property shall never be taken from them without their consent, and their property rights, and liberty, they shall never be invaded or disturbed, unless in just and lawful wars authorized by Congress" . . .[47] This is not what happened. Instead, over the years "American Indian policy has been described as 'genocide-at-law' promoting both land acquisition and cultural extermination."[48] At first, during the eighteenth and nineteenth centuries, the U.S. government isolated Indians on reservations as it confiscated their lands and denied them basic political rights. Indian reservations were administered by the federal government and Native Americans often lived in squalid conditions.

With passage of the Dawes Act in 1887, however, the government switched policies to promote assimilation over separation. Each Indian family was given land within the reservation; the rest was sold to whites, thus reducing Indian lands from about 140 million acres to about 47 million. Moreover, to encourage Native Americans' "assimilation," Indian children were sent to boarding schools off the reservation, and native languages and rituals were banned. In 1924, Native Americans were made U.S. citizens and given the right to vote.

At least in part because tribes were small and scattered (and the number of Indians declining), no protest movement was formed in reaction to these drastic policy changes. It was not until the 1960s, at the same time that women were beginning to mobilize for greater civil rights, that Indians too began to mobilize to act. And, like the civil rights and women's rights movements, it had a radical as well as a more traditional branch. In the late 1960s, for example, a small band of Indians occupied Alcatraz Island, claiming it as part of their ancestral lands. In 1972, several hundred Indians marched to Washington, D.C. to "sit in" at the Bureau of Indian Affairs to draw attention to government mistreatment. And in 1973, national attention was drawn to the plight of Indians when members of the radical American Indian Movement took over Wounded Knee, South Dakota, the site of the massacre of 150 Indians by the U.S. government army in 1890. Just two years before the protest, the treatment of Indians had been highlighted in the best-selling *Bury My Heart at Wounded Knee*,[49] which in many ways served to mobilize public opinion against the oppression of Native Americans the same way *Uncle Tom's Cabin* had against slavery.

Native Americans in Washington, D.C. protest the name of the Washington Redskins football team. Similar demonstrations took place in other cities with team names offensive to Native Americans and at least one newspaper has refused to refer to offending teams by any name other than their city.

THEN AND NOW

Native Americans and Land Rights

When Americans first began colonizing what is now the United States, Indians populated the land from Maine to Florida, and from the Carolinas to the west coast. Of the nearly 2 billion acres controlled by Indians 500 years ago, by 1900 they had but 140 million acres. Today, less than 50 million acres are controlled by Indian tribes as tribe after tribe was forced off its lands. "Land is the basis of all things Indian," concluded a Citizens Advisory Report in 1969. Moreover, an integral part of many tribes' beliefs is that most land is sacred. The relationship of a tribe to its land defines the tribe. In 1993, only 287 federal Indian reservations existed in the United States. It is not surprising, then, that since the 1970s, Native Americans have been litigating against the United States over two major questions in the land area: (1) In the eastern states, are the treaties ceding lands to white settlers valid? and (2) In the west, where most Indians were forced to live on reservations, were the treaties violated, and if so, how should tribes be compensated? This litigation has produced some strange allies and some surprising victories.

One of the largest Indian land claims lawsuits was filed in 1972 on behalf of the Passamaquoddie and the Penobscot tribes, who were seeking return of 12.5 million acres in Maine—about two-thirds of the entire state—and 25 billion dollars in damages. The suit was filed by the Native American Rights Fund and the Indian Service Unit of a legal services office that was funded by the U.S. Office of Economic Opportunity. It took intervention from the White House before a settlement was reached in 1980, giving each tribe over 40 million dollars.

Native Americans are also litigating to gain access to their sacred places. All over the nation they have filed lawsuits to stop the building of roads and new construction on ancient burial grounds or other sacred spots. "We are in a battle for the survival of our very way of life," said one tribal leader. "The land is gone. All we've got left is our religion."*

* Hugh Dellios, "Rites by Law: Indians Seek Sacred Lands," *Chicago Tribune* (July 4, 1993): C-1.

At the same time, just as the growing number of women in the legal profession contributed to the push to secure greater rights for women through litigation, Indians, many attracted by the American Indian Law Center at the University of New Mexico, began to file hundreds of test cases in the federal courts involving tribal fishing rights, tribal land claims, and the taxation of tribal profits. Soon, the Native American Rights Fund (NARF), founded in 1970, became the NAACP LDF of the Indian rights movement as the "courts became the forum of choice for Indian tribes and their members."[50]

Native Americans have won some very important victories concerning hunting, fishing, and land rights as discussed above. Native American tribes all over America have begun to sue to reclaim lands they say were stolen from them by the U.S., often more than 200 years ago. Communities all over the U.S. have been entering into agreements to settle these suits, which cloud the titles to all properties in issue.

Native Americans have not fared nearly so well in areas such as religious freedom, especially where tribal practices come into conflict with state law. As noted in

Chapter 4, the Supreme Court has limited their use of peyote in religious ceremonies and their access to religious sites during timber harvesting, but Congress has acted to restore some of those rights.

Given the uncertain and uneven treatment of Indians by the U.S Supreme Court, in the 1990s Congress has replaced the courts as the preferred forum of Native Americans. The 1992 election of Ben Nighthorse Campbell (R-Colo.) as the only Native American in the U.S. Senate should heighten legislative sensitivity to these issues. Campbell, for example, introduced a bill to prevent the U.S. government from transferring property to facilitate building a new football stadium for the Washington Redskins unless the team's owner changes the name, which Campbell considers derogatory to Native Americans.

Hispanic Americans

Like women's efforts to garner expanded political rights, Hispanic Americans, too, can date their first real push for equal rights to 1965–1975. This civil rights movement included many tactics drawn from the African-American civil rights movement, including sit-ins, boycotts, marches, and other activities designed to attract publicity to their cause.[51] Like blacks, women, and Native Americans, Hispanic Americans have some radical militant groups, but have been dominated by more conventional organizations. The more conventional groups have pressed for Chicano and Latino studies programs and have built up ties with existing, powerful mainstream associations, including unions and the Roman Catholic church.

They have also relied heavily on litigation to secure greater rights. Key groups are the Mexican American Legal Defense and Educational Fund (MALDEF) and the Puerto Rican Legal Defense and Educational Fund.

MALDEF was founded in 1968 after members of the League of United Latin American Citizens (LULAC), the nation's largest and oldest Hispanic organization, met with NAACP LDF leaders and, with their assistance, secured a $2.2 million start-up grant from the Ford Foundation. Not only was MALDEF helped into being by the NAACP LDF, but like women's groups that were beginning to litigate for expanded civil rights, it was modeled after the older organization. It was created to bring test cases to force school districts to allocate more funds to schools with predominantly low-income minority populations, to implement bilingual education programs, to force employers to hire Chicanos, and to challenge election rules and apportionment plans that undercount or dilute Hispanic voting power.[52] Just as Native American and women's rights groups had depended on the legal expertise of their own constituents, MALDEF quickly drew on the talent of Hispanic attorneys to staff offices in San Antonio and Los Angeles. It also started a scholarship fund to train more Hispanic attorneys, and established a New Mexico branch office in conjunction with the New Mexico Law School.

MALDEF lawyers quickly moved to bring major test cases to the U.S. Supreme Court, both to enhance the visibility of their cause and to win cases. MALDEF has been quite successful in its efforts to expand voting rights and opportunities to Hispanic-Americans. In 1973, for example, it won a major victory when the Supreme Court ruled that multi-member electoral districts (in which more than one person represents a single district) in Texas discriminated against African Americans and Hispanic Americans.[53] In multi-member systems, legislatures generally add members to larger districts instead of drawing smaller districts in which a minority candidate could get a majority of the votes necessary to win.

MALDEF, LULAC, and other civil rights groups have successfully challenged election plans that make it more difficult for Hispanics to win elective office. LULAC has played a key role in legislative redistricting and has joined with MALDEF when court action is necessary. In 1990, for example, a U.S. Court of Appeals ruled that Los Angeles County's governing body intentionally diluted Hispanic voting strength (Hispanics made up one-third of the county's population) when it redrew county election districts after the 1980 census. Nine candidates—eight of them Hispanic—ran in the new district the county was forced to create.

While enjoying greater access to elective office (see Chapter 12), Hispanics still suffer discrimination. Language barriers and substandard educational opportunities continue to plague their progress. In 1973, for example, the U.S. Supreme Court refused to find that a Texas law under which the state appropriated a set dollar amount to each school district per pupil, while allowing wealthier districts to enrich educational programs from other funds, violated the equal protection clause of the Fourteenth Amendment.[54] The lower courts had found that wealth was a suspect classification (see Table 5.1) entitled to strict scrutiny. Using that test, the court had found the Texas plan discriminatory. In contrast, a divided Supreme Court concluded that education was not a fundamental right (see Chapter 4), and that a charge of discrimination based on wealth would be examined only under a minimal standard of review (the rational basis test).

Throughout the 1970s and 1980s, inter-school-district inequalities continued, and often had their greatest impact on poor Hispanic children, who often had inferior educational opportunities. Recognizing that the increasingly conservative federal courts (see Chapter 9) offered no recourse, in 1984 MALDEF filed suit in *state* court alleging that the Texas school finance policy violated the Texas constitution. In 1989, it won a case in which a state district judge elected by the voters of only a single county declared the state's entire method of financing public schools to be unconstitutional under the state constitution.[55]

School boards have been taken to court to compel them to provide education to the children of illegal aliens.

Homosexuals

Homosexuals have had an even harder time than African Americans, women, Native Americans, or Hispanics in achieving fuller rights. Gays do, however, have on average far higher household incomes and educational levels than do these other groups. And they are beginning to convert these advantages into political clout at the ballot box. As discussed in Chapter 4 (pp. 115–116), the cause of gay and lesbian rights, like that of African Americans and women early in their quest for greater civil rights, did not fare well in the Supreme Court. In the late 1970s, the Lambda Legal Defense and Education Fund, the Lesbian Rights Project, and Gay and Lesbian Advocates and Defenders were founded by gay and lesbian activists dedicated to ending legal restrictions on the civil rights of homosexuals. Although these groups have won important legal victories concerning HIV/AIDS discrimination, insurance policy survivor benefits, and even some employment issues, they generally have not been as successful as other disadvantaged groups.

In *Bowers* v. *Hardwick* (1986),[56] for example, the Supreme Court ruled that a Georgia law that made private acts of consensual sodomy illegal (whether practiced by homosexuals or by heterosexual married adults) was constitutional. Gay and lesbian rights groups had argued that a constitutional right to privacy included the right to engage in consensual sex within one's home, but the Court disagreed. Although privacy rights may attach to relations of "family, marriage, or procreation," those rights did not extend to homosexuals, wrote Justice Byron White for the Court. In a concurring opinion—his last written on the Court—Chief Justice Warren Burger called sodomy "the infamous crime against nature."

The public's and Congress's discomfort with gay and lesbian rights can be seen most clearly in the controversy that occurred after Bill Clinton attempted to lift the ban on gays in the armed services. Clinton tried to get an absolute ban on discrimination against homosexuals, who were subject to immediate discharge if their sexual orientation was discovered. Military leaders and Senator Sam Nunn (D-Ga.), head of the Senate Armed Services Committee, led the effort against Clinton's proposal. Eventually, Clinton and the Senate leaders compromised on what was called the "don't ask, don't tell" policy. It stipulated that gays and lesbians would no longer be asked if they were homosexual, but barred them from revealing their sexual orientation (under threat of discharge from the service). But when the Senate finally voted on the "compromise," its version of the new policy labelled homosexuality "an unacceptable risk" to morale. In spite of gay and lesbian groups' labeling the new policy "lie and hide," the Clinton administration chose to back off on the issue, correctly sensing only minimal support in Congress.[57]

The Supreme Court's unwillingness to expand privacy rights or special constitutional protections to homosexuals, and Congress's failure to end discrimination in the military, has led many gay and lesbian rights groups to other, potentially more responsive, political forums: state and local governments. Around the nation, such groups have lobbied for anti-discrimination legislation with mixed success. In 1992 in Colorado, for example, voters passed a state constitutional amendment that rescinded several local gay and lesbian rights ordinances and prevents the adoption of any such measures. (It was, however, declared unconstitutional the following year by a federal district court.) Generally, gay and lesbian groups have been most successful in gaining anti-discrimination ordinances in cities like San Francisco and Atlanta, which have large gay populations although many city ordinances have faced constitutional challenge.

In May 1993 members of ADAPT (Americans Disabled for Access to Public Transportation) protested and marched in Washington, D.C. to draw attention to the need for full implementation of the Americans with Disabilities Act.

Disabled Americans

Disabled Americans also have lobbied hard for anti-discrimination legislation. In the aftermath of World War II, many veterans returned to a nation unequipped to handle their disabilities. The Korean and especially the Vietnam Wars made the problems of disabled veterans all the more clear. These disabled veterans saw the successes of African Americans, women, and other minorities, and they too began to lobby for greater protection against discrimination. In 1990, in coalition with other disabled persons, veterans were finally able to convince Congress to pass the Americans with Disabilities Act. The statute defines a disabled person as someone with a physical or mental impairment that limits one or more "life activities," or who has a record of such impairment. It thus extends the protections of the Civil Rights Act of 1964 to all of those with physical or mental disabilities, including persons with AIDS. It guarantees access to public facilities, employment, and communication services. It also requires employers to acquire or modify work equipment, adjust work schedules, and make existing facilities accessible. Thus, buildings must be accessible to those in wheelchairs, and telecommunications devices provided for deaf employees, for example.

Changing laws alone, however, while often important first steps in achieving civil rights, is not the end of the process. Attitudes must also change. And, as history has shown, that can be a very long process. Stereotypes often are hard to eliminate.

In 1994, long-time civil rights attorney David Tatel became the first federal judge who was blind at the start of his tenure in office. He was nominated by President Clinton to fill the seat on the U.S. Court of Appeals for the District of Columbia left vacant by Ruth Bader Ginsburg. Tatel helped found the Lawyers' Committee for Civil Rights Under Law and served as a civil rights enforcement official in the Carter administration.

The Politics of Civil Rights

The Civil Rights Act of 1964 was passed by a Democratic Congress at the urgings of a Democratic president, Lyndon B. Johnson. The Republican Nixon and Ford administrations were not avid supporters of some of the more sweeping provisions of the Act—especially those that were disfavored by employers, who often supported the Republican Party. A particularly troublesome area of civil rights law is the concept of affirmative action.

Affirmative Action

The civil rights debate has often centered on the question of equality of opportunity versus equality of results. Most civil rights and women's rights organizations argue that the lingering and pervasive burdens of racism and sexism can be overcome only by taking race or gender into account in fashioning remedies for discrimination. They argue that the Constitution is not and should not be color- or sex-blind. Therefore, busing should be used to integrate schools, and women should be given child-care assistance to allow them to compete equally in the marketplace.

The counter-argument holds that if it was once wrong to use labels to discriminate against a group, it should be wrong to use those same labels to help a group. Laws should be neutral or color-blind. According to this view, quotas and other forms of **affirmative action**, policies designed to give special attention or compensatory treatment to members of a previously disadvantaged group, should be illegal. As early as 1871, Frederick Douglass ridiculed the idea of racial quotas, arguing that they would

Affirmative action Policies designed to give special attention or compensatory treatment to members of a previously disadvantaged group.

Alan Bakke, whose initial rejection from medical school led to an important Supreme Court ruling on affirmative action, was ultimately admitted to the medical school he sued. Here, he is shown at his 1982 medical school graduation. He did well enough in medical school to be selected to intern at the prestigious Mayo Clinic.

promote "an image of blacks as privileged wards of the state." They were "absurd as a matter of practice" because some could use them to argue that blacks "should constitute one-eighth of the poets, statesmen, scholars, authors and philosophers."

The debate over affirmative action and equality of opportunity became particularly intense during the Reagan years in the wake of two court cases that were generally decided in favor of affirmative action shortly before Reagan's election.

In 1978, the Supreme Court for the first time fully addressed the issue of affirmative action. Alan Bakke, a thirty-one-year-old paramedic, sought admission to several medical schools and was rejected because of his age. The next year, he applied to the University of California at Davis and was placed on its waiting list. The Davis Medical School maintained two separate admissions committees—one for white students and another for minority students. Bakke was not admitted to the school, although his grades and standardized test scores were higher than those of all of the African-American students admitted to the school. In *Regents of the University of California* v. *Bakke* (1978),[58] a sharply divided Court concluded that Bakke's rejection had been illegal because the use of strict quotas was inappropriate. The medical school, however, was free to "take race into account."

Bakke was quickly followed in 1979 by another case in which the Court ruled that a factory and a union could voluntarily adopt a quota system in selecting black workers over more senior white workers for a training program.[59]

For a while, the Court continued to uphold affirmative action plans, especially when there was clear-cut evidence of prior discrimination, although it was by five-to-four votes. And in 1987, in *Johnson* v. *Transportation Agency, Santa Clara County* (1987),[60] the Court for the first time ruled that a public employer could use a voluntary plan to promote women even if there was no judicial finding of prior discrimination.

In all these cases, the Reagan administration strongly urged the Court to invalidate the plans in question, but to no avail. With changes on the Court, however, including the 1986 elevation to Chief Justice of William Rehnquist, a strong opponent of affirmative action, the continued efforts of the Reagan administration finally began to pay off as the Court heard a new series of cases signaling an end to the advances in civil rights law. In a three-month period in 1989, the Supreme Court handed down five civil rights decisions limiting affirmative action programs and making it harder to prove employment discrimination.

The Legislative Response

In February 1990, congressional and civil rights leaders unveiled legislation designed to make it easier for minorities and women to fight job bias through the courts. In introducing the legislation, Senator Edward M. Kennedy (D-Mass.) noted that the act was necessary to overrule the Court's rulings, which "were an abrupt and unfortunate departure from its historic vigilance in protecting"[61] the rights of minorities. The bill sought to blunt the effort of recent Court rulings by:

- Barring harassment or firing of employees based on racial bias. (The Court had ruled that the 1866 Civil Rights Act, used by a North Carolina credit union worker to press her racial-bias claim, barred only hiring discrimination, not on-the-job harassment.)
- Forcing employers to show that any practice with proven discriminatory impact was prompted by business necessity. (The Court had ruled that the burden of proof belongs with workers who allege they are the victims of discrimination.)

- Making it clear that it is always illegal to use race, ethnicity, gender, or religion as the criterion for employment decisions. (The Court had ruled that the burden of proof belongs to employers if accused of discriminating illegally in personnel decisions; however, the ruling was vague enough to confuse lower courts.)
- Making permanent the court-approved affirmative action plans designed to remedy discrimination. (The Court had made it easier for white men to challenge such plans years after they were put into effect.)
- Easing the deadlines for workers who sue over allegedly biased seniority systems. (The Court had ruled that the time frame for filing such lawsuits is determined by when a seniority plan is adopted, not when an individual worker is affected.)
- Assuring victims of intentional discrimination the right to sue for monetary damages.

The bill passed both houses of Congress but was vetoed by President Reagan's successor, George Bush, and Congress failed to override the veto. In late 1991, however, Congress and the White House reached a compromise on a weaker version of the civil rights bill, which was passed by overwhelming majorities in both the House (381–31) and Senate (93–5). The Civil Rights Act of 1991 overruled the Supreme Court rulings noted above, but specifically prohibited the use of quotas. And in the wake of the Clarence Thomas hearings and their focus on sexual harassment, victims of sexual harassment were given the explicit right to sue for intentional discrimination. The new Act also made it easier for victims of discrimination to recover damages, which should encourage more victims of discrimination to sue.

Toward Reform

In March 1990, civil rights activists met in Selma, Alabama, to recreate the famous march from Selma to Birmingham on its twenty-fifth anniversary. Clearly, tremendous progress has been made in the years since so much blood was shed in Alabama. All around the nation, individuals who played major roles in the civil rights movement are in important positions of power. A new generation of African-American and female leaders is emerging as additional barriers continue to fall.

Women, too, are reaping the rewards of legislation and judicial interpretation. They are being elected or appointed to policy-making positions where they can be expected to continue to urge civil rights reform.

The civil rights movement has had international effects as well. In the late 1960s and 1970s, the leaders of racial minority communities in Britain consciously patterned their organizations on American models. Moreover, the urban riots that rocked Liverpool, Birmingham, and London during the 1980s evoked the image of those in the United States during the hot summers of the 1960s. The emerging British feminist movement also looked to the United States for both positive and negative lessons.

In this country, the political environment for minorities is changing as some begin to be assimilated, and more groups press for rights. The 1980s was not a good decade for most who advocated expanded civil rights. Presidents Reagan and Bush were not particularly receptive to the expansion of civil rights. Both men appointed conservatives to fill vacancies on the U.S. Supreme Court. George Bush's replacement for Thurgood Marshall, Clarence Thomas, the African-American former head of the EEOC, publicly stated his opposition to affirmative action and quotas prior to his appointment.

Not surprisingly, President Clinton's election in 1992 was met with elation by most civil rights activists. Clinton quickly moved to appoint more women and minorities to

Race and Politics

♦ ♦ ♦

In 1994, a *Times Mirror* poll revealed that Americans were less concerned about race and racial issues than in any poll since 1987. Fifty-one percent of all whites surveyed believed that the United States had gone "too far" in pushing equal rights as opposed to only 26 percent of black respondents. Moreover, only 25 percent of white respondents agreed that "every possible effort" should be made to help minorities. And since 59 percent responded that blacks can't get ahead because it's "their own fault," it becomes easier to understand the hostility of many Americans toward affirmative action programs.*

*Julie Stacey, "Poll: Less Concern about Racial Issues," *USA Today* (February 11, 1994): 8A.

high-level positions than had any other president in history. He also appointed a long-time advocate of women's rights, Ruth Bader Ginsburg, to the Supreme Court.

But his withdrawal of Lani Guinier's nomination to head the Civil Rights Division in the Justice Department angered many as did the fact that it took him nearly two years to fill that position and to appoint someone to chair the Equal Employment Opportunity Commission. And in spite of his campaign promise to end the ban on gays in the military, he ultimately backed down, to the dismay of many of his supporters.

At this point in history, while some legislation to ensure fuller rights is still necessary for some groups (Native Americans and gays, in particular), enforcement is key. President Clinton and his Attorney General pledged to enforce civil rights laws to the fullest extent of the law. Republican congressional leaders, however, argue that many of those laws, especially those involving affirmative action, should be repealed. And even President Clinton has ordered an examination of all federal affirmative action programs.

Thus, for groups like gays, for whom there are few statutory or constitutional protections, the achievement of full civil rights may be more difficult, given the backlash against President Clinton's attempts to end discrimination against gays in the military. Even where gays have won some advances toward reform at the local level, conservative Christian groups are mobilizing to run local candidates who actively oppose any expansion of homosexual rights. In 1992, for example, the liberal People for the American Way estimated that conservative fundamentalist Christians ran in about 500 local races and won 40 percent of those offices. Thus, reform could become more difficult for civil rights activists to achieve in the wake of growing local and national conservative opposition, often fueled by conservative radio talk show hosts, despite a generally sympathetic Democratic national administration.

At the same time, there is growing opposition to the goals of some civil rights groups. African Americans and women in particular may be hampered by their very successes. Leaders have found it increasingly difficult to mobilize followers, since the most blatant discriminatory practices have ended, and disagreement exists on how to achieve remaining goals. For example, although African Americans still agree on the need for improved educational opportunities, they disagree on how best to achieve that goal. At a time when 40 percent of the African-American men in the United States are functionally illiterate and many cities are overwhelmingly African American, busing is no longer as major an issue as it was in the past. For some, the trend in the 1990s should be toward reinstating all-black schools with a focus on black pride. In 1990 and 1991, several big cities, including Detroit and Milwaukee, set up all-male black elementary and high schools designed to provide young African-American males from female-headed households with positive black male role models and a better education. The constitutionality of these schools, however, was challenged in court by women's rights groups who argue that gender-segregated schools—black, white, or racially mixed—are unconstitutional.

To some extent, the civil rights movement has come full circle. Opportunities for African Americans and women have improved, lessening (in the eyes of some) the need for further reform. Equality of opportunity enjoys more support than equality of results. Much of the American public no longer believes that African Americans, women, or other minorities need additional help from the government, especially in the form of affirmative action programs, and most believe that the quality of life for African Americans has improved.

Summary

While the Framers and other Americans basked in the glory of the newly adopted Constitution and Bill of Rights, their protections did not extend to all Americans. In this chapter we have shown how rights have been expanded to ever-increasing segments of the population. To that end, we have made the following points:

1. When the Framers tried to "compromise" on the issue of slavery, they only postponed dealing with a volatile question that was later to rip the nation apart. Ultimately, the Civil War was fought to end slavery. Among its results were the triumph of the abolitionist position and adoption of the Thirteenth, Fourteenth, and Fifteenth Amendments. During this period, women also sought expanded rights, especially the right to vote, but to no avail.

2. Although the Civil War Amendments were added to the Constitution, the Supreme Court limited their application. As Jim Crow laws were passed around the South, the NAACP was founded in the early 1900s to press for equal rights for African Americans. Women's groups were also active during this period as they successfully lobbied for passage of the Nineteenth Amendment assuring them the right to vote.

   First, women's groups such as the National Consumers' League, and then others, including the NAACP, began to view litigation as a means to their ends. The NCL was forced to court to argue for the constitutionality of legislation protecting women workers; in contrast, the NAACP sought the Court's help in securing equality under the Constitution.

3. In 1954, the U.S. Supreme Court ruled in *Brown* v. *Board of Education* that state segregated school systems were unconstitutional. This victory empowered African Americans as they sought an end to other forms of pervasive discrimination. Bus boycotts and sit-ins were common tactics.

   As new groups were formed, freedom rides, pressure for voting rights, and massive non-violent demonstrations became common "lobbying" tactics. This activity culminated in passage of the Civil Rights Act of 1964 and the Voting Rights Act of 1965. These acts gave African-American and women's rights groups two potential weapons in their legal arsenals: They could attack private discrimination under the Civil Rights Act, or state-sanctioned discrimination under the Equal Protection Clause of the Fourteenth Amendment. And over the years, the Supreme Court developed different tests to determine the constitutionality of various forms of discrimination. In general, strict scrutiny, the most stringent standard, was applied to race-based claims. An intermediate standard of review was developed to assess the constitutionality of sex discrimination claims.

4. Building on the successes of African Americans and women, other groups, including Native Americans, Hispanic Americans, homosexuals, and the disabled have organized to litigate for expanded civil rights as well as to lobby for anti-discrimination laws.

5. Although 1960s civil rights legislation was at first widely acclaimed in most sections of the country, lax enforcement soon plagued many of its provisions. Affirmative action programs came under particular attack from the Reagan administration. Soon, a conservative Supreme Court overruled earlier liberal interpretations of anti-discrimination laws, forcing Congress to enact new civil rights legislation in 1986 and 1991 to reverse these decisions.

Key Terms

civil rights

equal protection clause

Thirteenth Amendment

Black Codes

Fourteenth Amendment

Fifteenth Amendment

Jim Crow laws

Civil Rights Cases

grandfather clauses

suffrage movement

Brown v. *Board of Education of Topeka*

Civil Rights Act of 1964

de jure discrimination

de facto discrimination

Equal Employment Opportunity Commission

suspect classifications

strict scrutiny

affirmative action

Suggested Readings

Browning, Rufus P., Dale Rogers Marshall, and David H. Tabb. *Protest Is Not Enough*. Berkeley: University of California Press, 1984.

Bullock, Charles III, and Charles Lamb, eds. *Implementation of Civil Rights Policy*. Monterey, CA: Brooks/Cole, 1984.

Flexner, Eleanor. *Century of Struggle*. New York: Atheneum, 1971.

Freeman, Jo. *The Politics of Women's Liberation*. New York: Longman, 1975.

King, Mary. *Freedom Song*. New York: Morrow, 1987.

Kluger, Richard. *Simple Justice*. New York: Vintage, 1975.

McGlen, Nancy E., and Karen O'Connor. *Women, Politics and American Society*. Englewood Cliffs, NJ: Prentice Hall, 1995.

Mansbridge, Jane J. *Why We Lost the ERA*. Chicago: University of Chicago Press, 1986.

Sindler, Alan P. *Bakke, DeFunis, and Minority Admissions*. New York: Longman, 1978.

Verba, Sidney, and Gary R. Orren. *Equality in America: The View from the Top*. Cambridge, MA: Harvard University Press, 1985.

Vose, Clement E. *Constitutional Change: Amendment Politics and Supreme Court Litigation Since 1900*. Lexington, MA: Heath, 1972.

Williams, Juan. *Eyes on the Prize: America's Civil Rights Years, 1954–1965*. New York: Penguin, 1987.

Woodward, C. Vann. *The Strange Career of Jim Crow*. New York: Oxford University Press, 1957.

Congress

As indicated by James Madison in *Federalist No. 51*, the Framers quickly opted for a two-house legislature, as was the practice in England. But the nature of the powers vested in Congress as a whole and in each house individually caused a considerable amount of debate at the Philadelphia convention. Moreover, the Framers also had to consider whose interests were to be represented in each legislative body. Was it to be "We the People," or the states, or special interests? In the centuries since the writing of the Constitution and the creation of the Congress, Congress has evolved in size, shape, and power. And despite the difficulties that sometimes seem to occur in the legislative process, there is no doubt that Congress has overwhelming powers *and* that most Americans believe that it should—to an extent.

The relationship between Americans and the Congress is full of contradictions. For example, in 1993, in the wake of hearings on Clarence Thomas's nomination to the U.S. Supreme Court and the House check-cashing scandal, only 12 percent of the American people had confidence in Congress, and criticism of it, its members, and its rules and procedures abounded.[1] Before the 1994 midterm elections, public confidence in Congress fell to 8 percent. This general disapproval of Congress as a whole stands in stark contrast to the public's generally high level of support for their *individual* representatives. One 1994 poll, for example, found that 59 percent of those polled believed that their *own* representatives deserved another term.[2] Part of this seeming public schizophrenia may stem from the dual roles that Congress plays—its members must combine representation functions with law- and policy-making functions—a combination that often produces role conflicts for individual legislators.

> I n republican government, the legislative authority naturally predominates. The remedy for this inconvenience is to divide the legislature into different branches. . . .
>
> *James Madison*
> *Federalist No. 51*

The Framers believed that a legislature would dominate the national government. By dividing Congress into two houses—the Senate and the House of Representatives—they thought they could diffuse its power to prevent legislative tyranny over the other two branches of government.

In the sections that follow, we analyze the powers of Congress and the competing roles members of Congress play as they represent the interests of their constituents, make laws, and oversee the actions of the other two branches of government. We also see that as these functions have changed throughout U.S. history, so has Congress itself.

The Roots of the Legislative Branch

As discussed in Chapter 2, Congress's powers evolved from Americans' experiences in the colonies and under the Articles of Confederation. When the colonists came to the New World, their general approval of Britain's parliamentary system led them to adopt similar two-house legislative bodies in the individual colonies. One house was directly elected by the people; the other was a Crown-appointed council that worked under the authority of the colonial government.

While originally established as advisory bodies to the royal governors appointed by the king, the colonial assemblies gradually assumed more power and authority in each colony, particularly over taxation and spending. The assemblies also legislated on religious issues and established quality standards for such colonial goods as flour, rice, tobacco, and rum. Prior to the American Revolution, colonists turned to their colonial legislatures (the only bodies elected directly by the "people") to represent and defend their interests against British infringement.

The first truly national legislature in the colonies, the First Continental Congress, met in Philadelphia in 1774 to develop a common colonial response to the Coercive Acts. All the colonies except Georgia sent a representative. Even though this Congress had no power to force compliance, it advised each colony to establish a militia and organized an economic boycott of British goods, among other things (see Chapter 2).

By the time the Second Continental Congress met in Philadelphia in May 1775, fighting had broken out at Lexington and Concord. The Congress quickly helped the now-united colonies gear up for war, raise an army, and officially adopt the Declaration of Independence. During the next five years, the Congress directed the war effort and administered a central government. But it did so with little money or stability as the Revolutionary War necessitated that it move from city to city.

Although the Articles of Confederation were drafted and adopted by the Second Continental Congress in 1777, the states did not ratify them until 1781. Still, through-

Rep. Marjorie Margolies-Mezvinsky here defends her vote in support of the Clinton budget plan at an angry town meeting in her district. She, like many other first-term Democrats, lost her 1994 reelection bid. Public disapproval of Congress and the Democratic Party's long-time control of it led to disastrous results for congressional Democrats in the 1994 midterm elections

out the Revolutionary War, the Congress exercised the authorities the Articles granted it: to declare war, raise an army, make treaties with foreign nations, and coin money. As described in Chapter 2, however, the Congress had no independent sources of income; it had to depend on the states for money and supplies. After the war, the states began acting once again as if they were separate nations rather than parts of one nation, despite the national government created under the Articles of Confederation. The "national" government, moreover, was insufficient to establish the new nation securely and to serve its needs. Discontent with the Articles grew and led eventually to the Constitutional Convention in Philadelphia in 1787.

The Constitution and the Legislative Branch of Government

Article I of the Constitution created the legislative branch of government we know today. Any two-house legislature, such as the one created by the Framers, is called a bicameral legislature. All states except Nebraska, which has a one-house or unicameral legislature, follow this model. As discussed in Chapter 2, the Great Compromise resulted in the creation of an upper house, the Senate, and a lower house, the House of Representatives. Each state is represented in the Senate by two senators, regardless of the state's population. The number of representatives each state sends to the House of Representatives, in contrast, is determined by that state's population.

Members of each body were to be elected differently and would thus represent different interests and constituencies. Senators were to be elected to six-year terms by state legislatures, and one-third of them would be up for reelection every two years. Senators were to be closely tied to their state legislatures and were expected to represent those interests in the Senate. State legislators lost this influence with ratification of the Seventeenth Amendment in 1913, which provides for the direct election of senators by the voters.

In contrast to senators' six-year terms, members of the House of Representatives were to be elected to two-year terms by a vote of the eligible voters in each congressional district. It was expected that the House would be the more "democratic" branch of government because its members would be more responsible to the people. Not only were they directly elected by the people, but they also were up for reelection every two years.

Apportionment and Redistricting

The U.S. Constitution requires that a census, which entails the counting of all Americans, be conducted every ten years. Until the first census could be taken, the Constitution fixed the number of representatives at sixty-five. In 1790, then, one member represented 37,000 people. As the population of the new nation grew and states were added to the Union, the House became larger and larger. In 1910 it expanded to 435 members, and in 1929 its size was fixed at that number by statute.

Because the Constitution requires that representation in the House be based on state population, congressional districts must be redrawn by state legislatures to reflect population shifts so that each member in Congress will represent approximately the same number of residents. When shifts occur in the national population, states gain or lose congressional seats. For example, in the 1990 census (as in most censuses since 1960), many Northeastern states showed a population decline and lost congressional seats, whereas states in the South, Southwest, and West (the sunbelt) showed great population growth and gained seats. New York lost five congressional seats after the 1980 census and an additional three in 1990. Conversely, Florida picked up four seats after the 1980 census and an additional four after the 1990 census. And, California picked up seven seats in 1990 for a total of fifty-two seats. In contrast, Alaska, Delaware, Montana, North Dakota, South Dakota, Vermont, and Wyoming, the least populous states, have only one representative each.

Redistricting The redrawing of congressional districts to reflect increases or decreases in seats allotted to the states as well as population shifts within a state.

Gerrymandering The legislative process through which the majority party in each statehouse tries to assure that the maximum number of representatives from its political party can be elected to Congress through the redrawing of legislative districts.

Apportionment The determination and assignment of representation in a legislature based on population.

Through the process of **redistricting**, or the redrawing of congressional districts to reflect increases or decreases in seats allotted to the states as well as population shifts within a state, the majority party in each statehouse tries to assure that the maximum number of representatives from its political party can be elected to Congress. This redistricting process, which has gone on since the first census in 1790, is often called **gerrymandering**. The term was first coined in 1812, when the powerful Republican governor of Massachusetts, Elbridge Gerry, persuaded the state legislature to create the oddly shaped district reproduced in Figure 6-1 in order to favor the election of a fellow Republican. The story goes that upon seeing how the district was drawn, one critic observed, "Why, that looks like a salamander!" to which another retorted, "That's not a salamander, that's a gerrymander."

Creative redistricting and the actions of state legislators have often created problems that have ended up in litigation. The Supreme Court faced the question of **apportionment**—the determination and assignment of representation in a legislature—in *Baker v. Carr* (1962).[3] The Court found that the Tennessee legislature's apportionment plan,

FIGURE 6-1

Gerrymandering

The Original "Gerrymander" Cartoon, 1812

Contested 1990 North Carolina Gerrymander

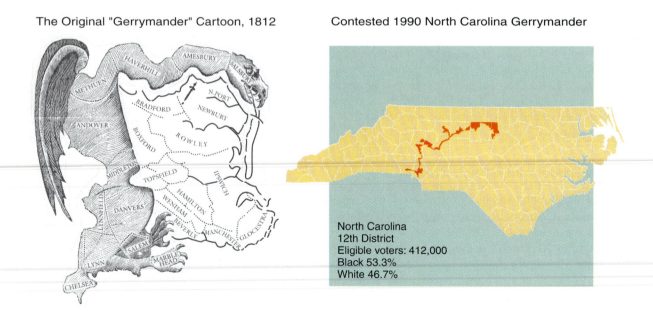

North Carolina
12th District
Eligible voters: 412,000
Black 53.3%
White 46.7%

Source: From David Van Biema, "Snakes or Ladders?" *Time*, July 12, 1993, p. 30. Copyright 1993 Time, Inc. Reprinted by permission.

which failed to alter district lines despite large shifts in population, was unconstitutional because it violated the constitutional principle of equal protection of the law. Furthermore, the Court ruled that the equitable apportionment of voters among districts was a legal question of constitutional rights and *not a political question*, thereby allowing the courts to direct states to correct malapportionment. Two years later, in *Reynolds* v. *Sims* (1964),[4] the Supreme Court ruled that congressional as well as state legislative districts must have "substantially equal" populations and enunciated the principle of "one man, one vote."

In 1986, the Supreme Court ruled that any gerrymandering of a congressional district that purposely dilutes minority strength—a common reason for gerrymandering in the past—was illegal under the 1965 Voting Rights Act.[5] Most observers interpreted the ruling to mean that the drawing of districts to enhance party strength was permissible, but redistricting to dilute African-American or Hispanic political clout was not. Just how far a state can go to "create" congressional districts to facilitate the election of minority representatives continues to be questioned.

After the 1990 census, for example, North Carolina proposed to create one African-American majority congressional district; the Bush administration Justice Department demanded two districts to more accurately reflect the racial composition of the state. (African Americans made up 22 percent of North Carolina's population; the state had twelve congressional districts.) To create the second district, the Democratic majority in the statehouse created the serpentine district shown in Figure 6-1 on page 164. It basically connected small black population centers by winding down I-85 like a 160-mile-long ribbon. In finding this kind of gerrymander in violation of the Voting Rights Act of 1965, Justice Sandra Day O'Connor called the district "bizarre" and even quoted one legislator's joke about the district: "If you drove down the interstate with both car doors open, you'd kill most of the people in the district." This kind of redrawing of districts for obvious racial purposes was unconstitutional, concluded a majority of the Court, because it denies the constitutional rights of white citizens.[6]

After that decision, state legislators and the U.S. Justice Department were left in a quandary about how future congressional districts were to be drawn. In 1995, in a 5 to 4 decision, the Court gave further guidance in setting aside all of the majority Black districts that were created in the South. In ordering these districts redrawn, the Court left the fate of the majority of Black elected House members in peril.

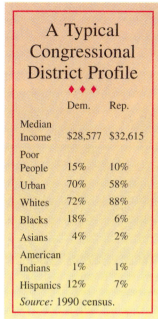

A Typical Congressional District Profile

❖ ❖ ❖

	Dem.	Rep.
Median Income	$28,577	$32,615
Poor People	15%	10%
Urban	70%	58%
Whites	72%	88%
Blacks	18%	6%
Asians	4%	2%
American Indians	1%	1%
Hispanics	12%	7%

Source: 1990 census.

Constitutional Powers of Congress

The Constitution specifically gives to Congress its most important power—the authority to make laws. This law-making power is shared by both houses. No bill (proposed law) can become a law without the consent of both houses. Examples of other powers shared by both houses include the power to declare war, raise an army and navy, coin money, regulate commerce, establish the federal courts and their jurisdiction, establish rules of immigration and naturalization, and to "make all Laws which shall be necessary and proper for carrying into Execution the foregoing Powers."

The powers of Congress provide it with far-reaching authority to make not only individual laws but also broader public policy. As interpreted by the Supreme Court, the necessary and proper clause, when coupled with one or more of the specific powers enumerated in Article I, section 8, has allowed Congress to increase the scope of its authority, often at the expense of the states and into areas not necessarily envisioned by the Framers.

Rep. Alcee Hastings is shown here before his impeachment from the federal bench, which inspired him to run for Congress.

Impeachment The power delegated to the House of Representatives in the Constitution to charge the president, vice president, or other "civil officers", including federal judges, with "Treason, Bribery, or other high Crimes and Misdemeanors". This is the first step in the constitutional process of removing such government officials from office.

Reflecting the different constituencies and size of each house of Congress (as well as the Framer's intentions), Article I also gives special, exclusive powers to each house. As noted in Table 6.1, for example, the Constitution specifies that all revenue bills must originate in the House of Representatives. Over the years, however, this mandate has been blurred, and it is not unusual to see budget bills being considered simultaneously in both houses, especially since each must approve all bills in the end, whether or not they involve revenues. In 1993, for example, President Clinton submitted a budget deficit-reduction plan to Congress, and both houses deliberated his and similar proposals simultaneously.

The House also has the power of **impeachment**, the authority to charge the president, vice president, or other "civil officers," including federal judges, with "Treason, Bribery or other high Crimes and Misdemeanors." Only the Senate is authorized to conduct trials of impeachment, and a two-thirds vote is necessary before a federal official can be removed from office.

Only one president, Andrew Johnson, has been impeached by the House, but he was acquitted by the full Senate by a one-vote margin. More recently, as we discuss in greater detail in Chapter 7, President Richard M. Nixon resigned from office in 1974 after the House Judiciary Committee voted to impeach him for his role in the Watergate scandal. In 1986, for the first time in fifty years, the House voted to impeach a federal judge. Judge Harry R. Claiborne was impeached after he had been convicted in federal court of income-tax evasion but had refused to resign from the bench. Following a trial in the Senate, he was removed from the bench after being convicted on three of the four articles of impeachment that the House had brought against him.

In 1988, in the most unusual case to date, the process was repeated: Florida's first black federal judge, Alcee Hastings, was impeached and removed from the bench even though he had been acquitted of bribery charges in a U.S. federal district court. In 1992, twelve years after the original charges were filed, Hastings was elected to the House of Representatives, the body that had originally initiated the impeachment proceedings against him.

While the House and Senate share in the impeachment process, the Senate has the sole authority to approve major presidential appointments, including those of federal judges, ambassadors, and Cabinet and sub-Cabinet-level positions. The Senate, too, must approve by a two-thirds vote all treaties entered into by the president. Failure by the president to court the Senate can be costly. For example, at the end of World War I, President Woodrow Wilson worked long and hard to convince other nations to accept the Treaty of Versailles, which contained the charter of the proposed League of Nations. He overestimated his support in the Senate, which refused to ratify the treaty, dealing Wilson and his international stature a severe setback.

The Members of Congress

For most, being a member of Congress is a glamorous and exciting job. House Speaker Newt Gingrich (R-Ga.) once gleefully remarked, "There are very few games as fun as being a congressman."[7] It is also a difficult job that requires one continually to seek re-election, expend enormous sums of money, and work very long hours, often for much less pay than could be earned in the private sector. According to one study, the average member of the House of Representatives spends 11.18 hours a day working on congressional-related activities. Hedrick Smith, a Pulitzer Prize-winning reporter for the *New York Times*, notes that:

Table 6.1 ◆	**Key Differences Between the House and Senate**

CONSTITUTIONAL DIFFERENCES

House	Senate
Initiates all revenue bills	Offers "advice and consent" on many major presidential appointments.
Initiates impeachment procedures and passes articles of impeachment	Tries impeached officials
Two-year terms*	Six-year terms ($^1/_3$ up for reelection every two years)*
Comprises 435 members (apportioned by population)	Comprises 100 members (2 from each state)
	Approves treaties

DIFFERENCES IN OPERATION

House	Senate
More centralized, more formal; stronger leadership	Less centralized, less formal; weaker leadership
Rules Committee fairly powerful in controlling time and rules of debate (in conjunction with the majority leader)	No Rules Committee; limits on debate come through unanimous consent or cloture of filibuster
More impersonal	More personal
Power less evenly distributed	Power more evenly distributed
Members are highly specialized	Members are generalists
Emphasizes tax and revenue policy	Emphasizes foreign policy

CHANGES IN THE INSTITUTION

House	Senate
Power centralized in the leadership and in the Speaker's inner circle of advisors	Senate workload increasing and informality breaking down; filibusters more frequent
House procedures are becoming more efficient	Members are becoming more specialized
Turnover is relatively high**	Turnover is moderate

*By 1994, 25 states passed some kind of term-limit provision. Because the constitutionality of these limits is in question at this writing, one key point of the Contract with America was congressional passage of a term-limit amendment to the Constitution.
**In 1995, 60 percent of House Republicans had been elected in the last four years.

Days are a kaleidoscopic jumble: breakfast with reporters, morning staff meetings, simultaneous committee hearings to juggle, back-to-back sessions with lobbyists and constituents, phone calls, briefings, constant buzzers interrupting office work to make quorum calls and votes on the run, afternoon speeches, evening meetings, receptions, fund-raisers, all crammed into four days so they can race home for a weekend gauntlet of campaigning. It's a rat race. . . .[8]

In spite of the long hours and hard work, thousands of people aspire to the job every year. Yet a total of only 535 men and women get to vote in the U.S. Congress. (The District of Columbia's members are not allowed to vote.)

As House Minority Whip in the 103rd Congress, Newt Gingrich was the second most powerful Republican in the House and a continual thorn in the side of House leaders. And he wasn't too popular back home—at least with the Democratic majority that controlled the Georgia legislature. As a result of the 1990 census, Georgia was given an additional congressional district. An outraged Gingrich complained that Democratic state legislators had carved his congressional district into four pieces "in an effort to destroy me." His home was then thrown into the overwhelmingly Democratic district of John Lewis, the House Deputy Whip, which forced Gingrich to run in a new district in 1992. Although he won that election by less than 1,000 votes, he handily won reelection in 1994 and was elected Speaker of the House when his party trounced Democrats in the 1994 midterm elections.

Formal Requirements

The U.S. Constitution sets out the legal requirements for membership in the House and Senate. House members must be at least twenty-five years old; Senators, thirty. Members of the House must have resided in the United States for at least seven years; those elected to the Senate, nine. In addition to being U.S. citizens, representatives and senators must be legal residents of the states from which they are elected.

Informal Requirements

These formal requirements, however, are only part of the picture. There also are several informal requirements. For example, membership in one of the two major political parties is almost always the norm. Election laws in various states often discriminate against independents (those without party affiliation) and minor-party candidates.

Money is another informal requirement. As discussed in Chapter 13, money is the mother's milk of politics. And often key to any member's victory is his or her ability to raise money.

Incumbency is another informal factor. Being in office helps you stay in office. This "incumbency factor" usually weighs against non-incumbents in a variety of ways, including fund raising. As illustrated in Figure 6-2 (p. 169), which compares the way poll respondents feel about Congress overall to the way they feel about their own representatives, most Americans approve of their own members of Congress. Thus, while people may criticize the Congress as a whole, they rarely reject their own incumbent representatives at the polls (see Figure 6-3, p. 169). From 1980 to 1990, in fact, an average of 95 percent of those who ran actually won their primary and general election races.[9] One study concluded that unless a member of Congress was involved in a serious scandal, his or her chances of defeat were minimal.[10] The incumbency factor facilitated the growth in what some termed "congressional careerists," that is, individuals who made a career for themselves in the nation's capital.

The advantages of the incumbency factor diminished in 1992, when fifty-two House members and eight Senators chose not to seek reelection and thirteen other House incumbents opted to run for other political offices.[11] Their decisions not to run were based on several factors, including redistricting, an unpopular series of congressional pay raises, the savings and loan scandal, mismanagement of the House Post Office and House "bank," Congress's seeming inability to solve the budget crisis, and a loophole in federal election law that allowed members of Congress leaving by 1992 to keep any leftover campaign monies for their personal use.

For many House members, the decision not to seek reelection was a wise move. In the 1992 primaries, more House members lost their primary bids than at any other time since World War II.[12] Political scientist Marjorie Randon Hershey concludes that most of those who lost were involved in the House bank scandal; "the biggest overdrafters were themselves bounced."[13] Nonetheless, in the 1992 November general elections, after the scandal had faded somewhat, nearly 90 percent of the incumbents who sought reelection were returned to office, as shown in Figure 6-3 (p. 169).

Similarly, during the 1994 congressional elections, the decision of many incumbents not to run left a sizable number of seats open. These open seats, coupled with a public that was fueled by an anti-incumbency, anti-Washington, anti-Clinton mood led to what one political scientist called "a revolution that happened without any bullets." Although in the 1994 midterm elections incumbency showed no ill effects on Republi-

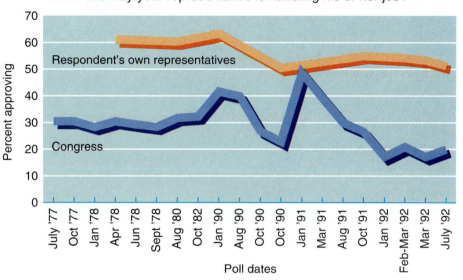

FIGURE 6-2
Approval of Congress

Questions: "Do you approve or disapprove of the way Congress is handling its job? How about the representative in Congress from your district? Do you approve or disapprove of the way your representative is handling his or her job?"

Source: Marjorie Randon Hershey, "Congressional Elections," in *The Election of 1992* by Gerald M. Pomper et al. (1993) Reprinted by permission of Chatham House Publishers.

cans—all Republican Senators, Representatives, and even governors who sought re-election won—for Democrats, incumbency proved to be a decided negative even if they had only recently been elected. In fact, the fifteen Democrats elected in 1992 who lost in 1994 made up nearly one-half of all of the thirty-five incumbents who lost their House races. Women elected for the first time in 1992 when an unprecedented 24 new

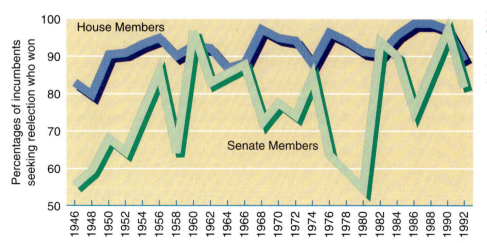

FIGURE 6-3
The Percentage of Incumbents in the House and Senate Successfully Seeking Reelection, 1946–1992

Source: Marjorie Randon Hershey, "Congressional Elections," in *The Election of 1992* by Gerald M. Pomper et al. (1993) Reprinted by permission of Chatham House Publishers.

House Minority Whip Newt Gingrich of Georgia addresses Republican congressional candidates on Capitol Hill Tuesday, Sept. 27, 1994 during a rally in which they pledged a "Contract with America."

women were added to the U.S. House of Representatives fared especially badly; seven of them, or 30 percent, lost in their effort to seek a second term.

Voters were clearly turned off by the 103rd Congress. As revealed in Figure 6–2 (p. 169), during the 103rd Congress it rarely enjoyed better than a 20 percent approval rating. Mindful of these numbers and seeking to take advantage of voter frustration, House Minority Whip Newt Gingrich persuaded 350 Republican candidates to come to Washington D.C., to sign what he called a "*Contract with America.*" By signing this contract, Republican candidates pledged to vote in favor of a balanced budget amendment, a line item veto, congressional term limits, and to pass meaningful welfare reform, cut taxes, raise national defense spending, roll back government regulations, and to reform the legal system to prevent excessive claims. If Republicans cannot make good on these pledges as the party in power, incumbency may serve no better purpose than it did the Democrats in 1994.

Contract with America Republican 10-point plan to reform government.

What Does Congress Look Like?

When Bill Clinton was elected president in 1992, he said that he wanted to appoint an administration that "looked like America." Historically, Congress has never looked like America—it is richer, older, better educated, more white, and more male. Most members of Congress are well-off if not wealthy (the Senate has often been called the "Millionaires' Club"). In the 104th Congress (1995–1997) nearly half the senators are millionaires and many have a net worth of more than $2 million. Many, in fact, criticized the millions spent—much of it personal wealth—in Senate races as Republicans and Democrats alike called for campaign finance reform. In the House, which has historically had a more "common man" orientation than the Senate, fewer than 10 percent of the members are multi-millionaires.

The Congress, especially the Senate, still has the "look" of a private club, although, since the 1992 election, both bodies are more diverse than ever before. In the 104th Congress, the average age of senators is 58 years, 57 percent are lawyers, and 89 percent are white males (see Table 6.2, p. 171).

Table 6.2 ◆	**Some Characteristics of the 104th Congress**	

	HOUSE	SENATE
Total Membership	435	100
Party affiliation		
Democrats	203	47
Republicans	231	53
Independents	1	0
New Members	87	11
Gender		
Women	49	8
Race		
African American	39	1
Hispanic	18	0
Asian American	6	2
Native American	0	1
% With law degree	35	57
Average age	51	58
Baby boomers	41	14
Generation X	2	0
Average length of service	8 yrs	11 yrs

Change is occurring, however. Over the years, more and more women and minorities have been running for office and winning (see Figure 6-4, p. 172). In the 103rd Congress, for example, twenty-nine new women were elected, and a record fifty-five women served; the number of women in the Senate rose from two to seven—a 350 percent increase! Both senators elected from California were women.

The 103rd Congress also saw the election of the largest class of new African-American legislators since Reconstruction (see Figure 6-4) and the election of the first African-American woman, Carol Moseley-Braun (D-Ill.), to the Senate (she is also the only African American in the Senate).

The 1992 elections were also a banner year for other minority groups. The number of Hispanic Americans in the House rose from thirteen to seventeen (see Figure 6-4). Moreover, the first Korean American was elected to the House of Representatives (Jay Kim, R-Cal.), and Ben Nighthorse Campbell (R-Col.) became the first Native American to serve in the U.S. Senate in more than sixty years.

The 1994 midterm elections were disappointing for women and minorities. After their record gains in 1992, 1994 was more of a holding action. Women gained only one new seat in the House in spite of the fact that a record number of women sought seats. Only one additional woman was added to the Senate, former House member Olympia Snowe (R-Me.). Similarly, although 23 Republican African-Americans sought election to the House, only two won, bringing the total number of African-Americans in both houses to forty. Other minority groups also posted only small gains as illustrated in Figure 6-4 (p. 172).

FIGURE 6-4

Numbers of Women and Minorities in Congress

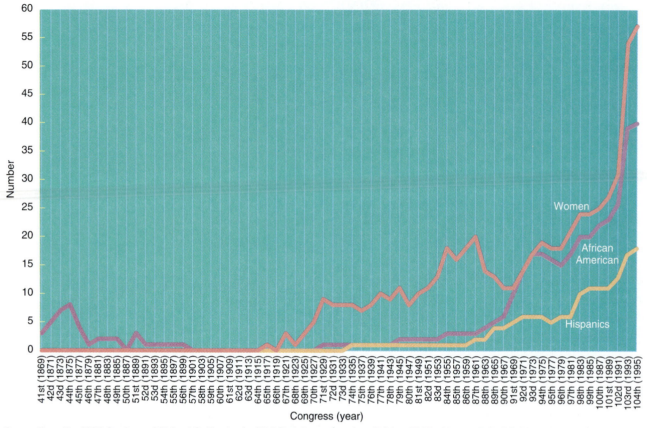

Source: From Harold W. Stanley and Richard G. Niemi, eds. *Vital Statistics on American Politics,* 4E, Washington, D.C.: CQ Press, 1994, p. 203.

Six female House members attempted to gain entrance to a meeting of Senate Democrats in 1991 to demand that allegations of sexual harassment receive a full hearing before the Senate vote to confirm Clarence Thomas to the Supreme Court.

The Representational Function of Members of Congress

Does it make a difference if members of Congress actually come from or are members of a particular group? The answer to this question may depend on your view of the representative function of legislators.

In Great Britain, although members of Parliament are elected from specific districts, they are expected to represent the *entire* nation. This is called virtual representation. Because members are the "virtual" or actual representatives of all English people, in colonial times it followed that they could legislate for all British subjects—even those living in America. Colonists, in contrast, argued for a system of "actual representation," in which members represent only those voters who elect them.

Questions of who should be represented and how this representation should be achieved are critical in a republic. Over the years, political theorists have enunciated various ideas about how constituents' interests are best represented in any legislative body. One famous political theorist, Edmund Burke (1729–1797), who also served as a member of the British House of Commons in the late 1700s, argued that once elected, a representative need not vote the way his constituents would expect him to. According to Burke, representatives should be "trustees" who listen to the opinions of their constituents and then use their own best judgment to make final decisions.

A second theory of representation holds that representatives are "delegates." A delegate representative votes according to constituents' opinions regardless of whether those opinions coincide with those of the representative.

Members of Congress and other legislative bodies generally don't fall neatly into either category. It is often unclear how constituents feel about a particular issue, or conflicting opinions may abound within a single constituency. With these difficulties in mind, a third theory of representation holds that "politicos" alternately don the hats of trustee or delegate, depending on the issue. On an issue of great concern to voters in their districts, representatives will most likely vote as delegates; on other issues, perhaps on issues that are less visible, representatives will act as trustees and use their own best judgment as they cast their votes.

How a representative views his or her role—as a trustee, delegate, or politico—may still not answer the question of whether it makes a difference if a representative or senator is male or female; African American, Hispanic, Native American, or white; young or old; gay or straight. Can a man, for example, represent the interests of women as well as a woman? Can a rich woman represent the interests of the poor? The combinations are endless.

Senator Edward M. Kennedy (D-Mass.), for example, is one of the wealthiest members of the Senate, yet he has been an effective champion of the poor, of women, and of other minorities throughout his six terms in the Senate. But during the Clarence Thomas hearings (see p. 480) many commentators noted that Kennedy's well-chronicled problems in his personal life precluded him from effectively questioning Thomas and contributed to his uncharacteristic silence during those hearings. Female representatives in the House were outraged by the glaring absence of any women on the Senate Judiciary Committee that grilled Anita Hill concerning her charges that Thomas had sexually harassed her while he was her supervisor at the Equal Employment Opportunity Commission. Presumably in response to this complaint, Diane Feinstein (D-Cal.) and Carol Moseley-Braun (D-Ill.) were added to the Committee in 1993.

Female representatives historically have played prominent roles in efforts to expand women's rights. It was Representative Martha Griffiths (D-Mich.) who successfully added "sex" to the list of discriminatory qualifications prohibited by the Civil Rights Act of 1964 and Representative Bella Abzug (D-N.Y.) who led the fight for congressional passage of the Equal Rights Amendment.

Studies reveal that female legislators are more likely than their male counterparts to sponsor legislation of concern to women.[14] In the 101st Congress, for example, two bills supported by most women in Congress were passed: an extension of Medicare to cover mammograms for women over sixty-five and the establishment of a $30-million screening program for breast and cervical cancer for poor women, who die of these diseases at higher rates than does the rest of the population. Representative Mary Rose Oakar (D-Ohio), who co-sponsored these bills, noted that she made progress by seeking help from male representatives whose wives had breast cancer. "There are at least ten of them, and when it hits you in the family, boy, do attitudes change."[15] Without a push from women, however, it is unlikely that even those male representatives would have acted.

Actions of the one Native American and one African American in the Senate underscore the representative function that can be played in Congress. Ben Nighthorse Campbell (R-Col.), for example, sits on the Senate Committee on Indian Affairs. As a member of the House, he led the fight to change the name of Custer Battlefield Monument in Montana to Little Bighorn Battlefield National Monument to honor the Indians who died

In 1994, 83 percent of the women in Congress, including 66 percent of the Republican women, supported the crime bill. Since only 46 percent of the men supported it, women's votes made the difference in its passage.

Ben Nighthorse Campbell (R-Col.). Campbell was elected as a Democrat in 1992 but changed political parties in 1995.

in battle. He also fought successfully for legislation to establish the National Museum of the American Indian within the Smithsonian Institution. But his biggest fight on behalf on Native Americans has been to block congressional approval of a $200-million stadium for the Washington Redskins unless the football team changes its name. Campbell told a House panel that the word "redskin" is a racial slur. In February 1995 Campbell surprised his state and party leadership by switching party affiliation, becoming the second Republican convert following the 1994 midterm election.

How Congress Is Organized

Every two years, a new Congress is seated. After determining qualifications of new members, the Congress organizes its business for the coming session: it elects leaders, chooses committee assignments for the two-year period, and sets its agenda. Each year, members of Congress introduce up to 10,000 bills and pass between 700 and 2,000 into law. Having rules and organization is, therefore, critical to congressional operation. Figure 6-5 illustrates the leadership structure of each house. The Republicans were the majority party in both houses during the 104th Congress. Figure 6-6 shows the physical layout of the two houses in the Capitol building.

The House of Representatives

Even in the First Congress in 1789, the House of Representatives was almost three times larger than the Senate. It is not surprising, then, that from the beginning, the House has been more tightly organized, more elaborately structured, and governed by stricter rules. Traditionally, loyalty to the party leadership and voting along party lines have been more common in the House than in the Senate. House leaders also play a key role in moving along the business of the House.

Speaker of the House The only officer of the House of Representatives specifically mentioned in the Constitution; elected at the beginning of each new Congress by the entire House; traditionally a member of the majority party.

The Speaker of the House.   The **Speaker of the House** is the only officer of the House of Representatives specifically mentioned in the Constitution, and the office is the House's most powerful position. The Speaker is elected at the beginning of each new Congress by the entire House and is traditionally a member of the majority party, as are all committee chairs. While typically not the member with the longest service, the Speaker generally has served in the House for a long time and in other House leadership positions as a sort of apprenticeship. Generally, a Speaker is reelected until he chooses to retire.

The Speaker presides over the House, oversees House business, is the official spokesperson for the House of Representatives, and is second in the line of presidential succession. Moreover, he is the House liaison with the president and generally has great political influence within the chamber. Through his parliamentary and political skills he is expected to smooth the passage of party-backed legislation through the House.

The first "powerful" Speaker was Henry Clay, elected to the position in 1810 (see "People of the Past," p. 177). Clay dominated the Democratic-Republican Party in the House and kept party members in line by the use of his power to appoint committee

Party caucus A formal gathering of all party members.

members and committee chairs. Clay used not only the **party caucus** (a formal gathering of all party members), which he controlled, to decide which issues were to be addressed on the House floor, but also his power as Speaker to appoint his "hawk" allies

FIGURE 6-5

Organizational Structure of the House of Representatives and the Senate during the 104th Congress (1995–1997)

House of Representatives

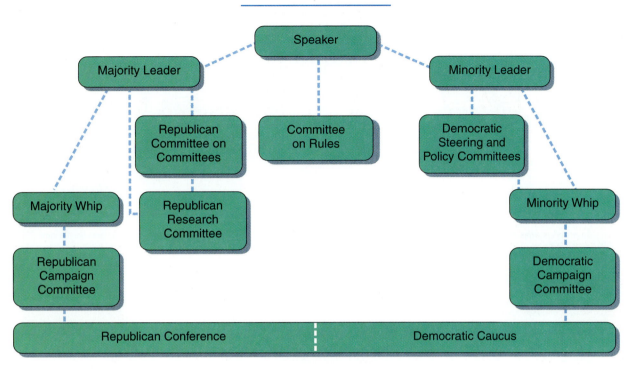

Senate

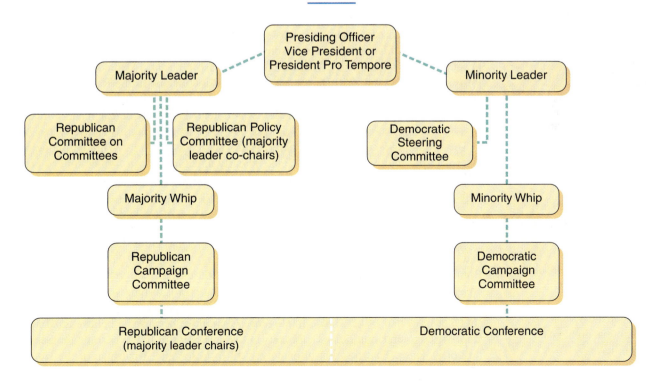

FIGURE 6-6

Floor Plan of the Capitol Building

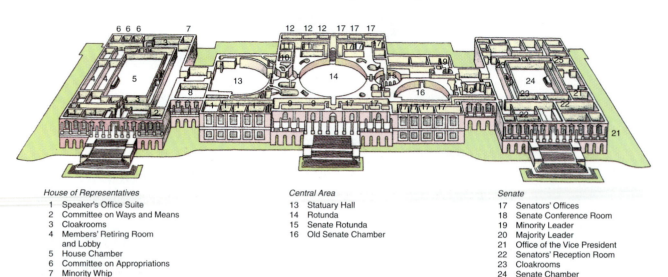

House of Representatives
1 Speaker's Office Suite
2 Committee on Ways and Means
3 Cloakrooms
4 Members' Retiring Room
   and Lobby
5 House Chamber
6 Committee on Appropriations
7 Minority Whip
8 House Reception Room
9 House Conference Room
10 Committee Meeting Room
11 Representatives' Offices
12 Minority Leader

Central Area
13 Statuary Hall
14 Rotunda
15 Senate Rotunda
16 Old Senate Chamber

Senate
17 Senators' Offices
18 Senate Conference Room
19 Minority Leader
20 Majority Leader
21 Office of the Vice President
22 Senators' Reception Room
23 Cloakrooms
24 Senate Chamber
25 President's Room

Speaker's Powers Grow

◆ ◆ ◆

Many of the reforms made in the 104th Congress have served to make the Speaker more powerful—a step long advocated to make the Speaker more effective. While even many in Congress agreed that power needed to be centralized, they feared that concentrating power in one person for too long a time could lead to abuse. Thus, House members voted to cap the Speaker's tenure at eight years—four terms.

to key positions on the Military and Foreign Affairs Committees in anticipation of the War of 1812.

Modern Speakers (until the election of Newt Gingrich) did not enjoy the formal powers of their predecessors who served before 1910. Nevertheless, they had substantial powers based largely on their personal ability to persuade. The 103rd Congress was presided over by a Democrat, Thomas Foley (D-Wash.), because Democrats held a majority of House seats—256 Democrats and 178 Republicans. In the Republican landslide midterm elections of 1994, however, not only did Republicans take control of the House (and Senate, too), Speaker Foley was defeated. Foley's defeat made him the first Speaker since Abraham Lincoln's time not to be reelected to his House seat.

The fiftieth Speaker, Newt Gingrich (R-Ga.), served as Minority Whip before being elected to preside over the House. Since an early age, Gingrich, a former college professor, had aspired to become House Speaker. As minority party whip he took every opportunity to bolster other Republican's electoral successes. His well-publicized Contract with America solidified Republicans and also gave him a blueprint for action when the 104th Congress met.

As illustrated in Table 6.3, (p. 178), the Speaker of the House enjoys both formal and informal powers. Unlike the new Speaker, Speaker Foley used those powers rarely. But, in 1993 he chose to take advantage of new House rules that gave the Speaker increased power over committee chairs, including the power to remove them from Senate-House Conference Committees. He removed Representative Dave McCurdy (D-Okla.) as Chair of the House Intelligence Committee because he believed that McCurdy tried to undercut other Democrats in his unsuccessful bid to become the Secretary of Defense. That position ultimately went to Les Aspin, Chairman of the House Armed Services Committee (Aspin resigned from that position in late 1993 to become Secretary of Defense). McCurdy was a vocal critic of Foley during the House banking

PEOPLE OF THE PAST

Henry Clay

Henry Clay (1777–1852) was a congressional giant of his time, playing an active role in national politics for more than forty years. He served as Speaker of the House as a Democratic-Republican for six terms (longer than anyone else in the nineteenth century) and later was a leader of the new Whig Party. He was five times an unsuccessful presidental candidate, and he served as Secretary of State under John Quincy Adams.

Clay's personality and skill in oratory won him authority in Washington. As Speaker of the House of Representatives, in 1812 Clay became the leader of the "War Hawks," urging President James Madison to declare war on Great Britain in order to prevent British control of the seas, which Madison did on June 1, 1812.

As a presidential candidate, Clay developed his "American System," calling for national defense, construction of roads and canals using federal aid, protection of home industry through duties on foreign imports, and establishment of a second Bank of the United States. Clay wanted federal land in the West to be sold rather than given away to homesteaders so that the proceeds could be used to build schools and roads. The American System became the major plank in the platform of Clay's Whig Party.

Clay is remembered as the Great Compromiser. As a Southerner and a slaveholder on the one hand, and a friend to Northern industry on the other, Clay mediated between North and South over the question of slavery. Clay played a major role in three landmark compromises: the Missouri Compromise of 1820, the Tariff Compromise of 1850, and the Compromise of 1850. Clay hoped that the last of these compromises would prevent a civil war.

Although Clay's actions were not able to prevent the Civil War and his Whig Party disappeared shortly after his death, many features of his American System were later put into operation by the Republican Party.

---

scandal; he frequently accused Foley of inadequate leadership and even suggested publicly that Foley be replaced. Instead, Foley opted to replace McCurdy.

Other House Leaders.   After the Speaker, the most powerful people in the House are the majority and minority leaders, who are elected in their individual party caucuses. The majority leader is the second most important person in the House; his counterpart on the other side of the aisle (the House is organized so that Democrats sit on the left side and Republicans on the right side of the center aisle) is the minority leader. The majority and minority leaders work closely with Speaker Newt Gingrich, and the majority leader helps the Speaker schedule proposed legislation for debate on the House floor.

The Speaker and majority and minority leaders are assisted in their leadership efforts by the majority and minority whips. The concept of whips originated in the

Table 6.3 ◆ Formal and Informal Powers of the Speaker of the House	
FORMAL	INFORMAL
Presides over House when in session	Tries to build support for the president's programs when they are from the same party
Plays a major role in committee assignments	Acts as national party leader when president is from different party
Appoints or plays a major role in the selection of other party leaders	Sets the public agenda through ability to attract media attention
Exercises considerable control over assignment of bills to particular committees	Helps other members with fund raising by making appearances at events in their districts, etc.

British House of Commons, where they were named after the "whipper in," the rider who keeps the hounds together in a fox hunt. Party whips, who were first designated in the House in 1899 and in the Senate in 1913, do, as their name suggests, try to "whip" fellow Democrats or Republicans into line on partisan issues. They try to maintain close contact with all party members on important votes, prepare summaries of content and implications of bills, get "nose counts" during debates and votes, and in general get members to toe the party line. For example, when John Conyers, Jr. (D-Mich.), became upset that no one consulted him in drafting the crime bill in 1993, he voted against the budget package out of irritation. "House Democratic whips swarmed over him like bees to honey," and he soon fell in line after being told he would become a major player.[16]

Whips and deputy whips are elected by party members in caucuses. When Republicans took control of both houses of Congress in 1994, Newt Gingrich, the House Republican whip, became the Speaker, and new majority and minority whips as well as deputy whips were elected by the party caucuses. (The Republican minority leader did not seek re-election in 1994.)

The Senate

The Constitution specifies that the presiding officer of the Senate is the president of the Senate (see Figure 6-5, p. 175). The vice president of the United States fills this job. Because he is not a member of the Senate, he votes only in the case of a tie. Vice President Al Gore Jr., for example, cast the tie-breaking vote in the Senate on the Budget Deficit Reduction bill in 1993.

The official chair of the Senate is the president pro tempore, who is selected by the majority party and presides over the Senate in the absence of the vice president. The position of president pro tempore is today primarily an honorary office that generally goes to the most senior senator of the majority party. Once elected, the pro tem, as he is called, stays in that office until there is a change in the majority party in the Senate. Because presiding over the Senate is a rather dull duty, neither the vice president nor the president pro tempore performs the task often. Instead, the duty of presiding over the Senate rotates among junior members of the chamber.

Majority leader The elected leader of the party controlling the most seats in the U.S. House of Representatives or the Senate; is second in authority to the Speaker of the House and in the Senate is regarded as its most powerful member.

The true leader of the Senate is the **majority leader,** elected by senators of the majority party. Although not as powerful as the Speaker of the House, as the leader of the majority party, he sets the Senate agenda, refers legislation to committees, and assigns members to committees. George Mitchell (D-Me.), served in this position from 1988 to 1994, when he resigned from the Senate. When Republicans won control of the

THEN AND NOW

Life on the Floor and in the Halls of Congress

Throughout Congress's first several decades, partisan, sectional, and state tensions of the day often found their way onto the floors of the U.S. House and Senate. Many members were armed, and during one House debate thirty members brandished their weapons. In 1826, for example, Senator John Randolph of Virginia insulted Secretary of State Henry Clay from the floor of the Senate, referring to Clay as "this being, so brilliant yet so corrupt, which, like a rotten mackerel by moonlight, shined and stunk." Clay immediately challenged Randolph to a duel on the Virginia side of the Potomac River. Both missed, although Randolph's coat fell victim to a bullet hole. Reacting to public opinion, however, in 1839 Congress passed a law prohibiting dueling in the District of Columbia.

Nevertheless, dueling continued. A debate in 1851 between representatives from Alabama and North Carolina ended in a duel, but no one was hurt. In 1856, Representative Preston Brooks of South Carolina, defending the honor of his region and family, assaulted Senator Charles Sumner of Massachusetts on the floor of the Senate. Sumner was disabled and unable to resume his Congressional duties for several years. Guns and knives were abundantly evident on the floor of both House and Senate, along with a wide variety of alcoholic beverages.

Today the House and the Senate are usually much more sedate. In 1984, however, a group of newly elected Republican representatives began taking over the House floor every day after the end of normal hours to berate their Democratic colleagues. The chamber was usually empty but, like all other action on the floor, those speeches were broadcast live on C-SPAN and often used by the members for distribution to local television stations back home. During a particularly strong attack on several Democrats' views on Central America, Representative Newt Gingrich (R-Ga.) paused suggestively in mid-speech, as though waiting for an objection or daring the Democrats to respond. No other House members were on the floor at the time, but since C-SPAN cameras focused only on the speaker, viewers were unaware of that fact.

Speaker Thomas P. O'Neill angrily reacted by ordering C-SPAN cameras to span the empty chamber to expose the tactics of Gingrich and other Republicans, but he failed to inform the Republicans of the change. O'Neill later apologized to the House Minority Leader, Robert Michel (R-Ill.), but what Republicans labeled "CAMSCAM" ignited a firestorm on the floor. Incensed by remarks made by Gingrich, O'Neill dropped his gavel, left his spot on the dais, and took to the floor, roaring at Gingrich, "You challenged their [House Democrats'] patriotism, and it is the lowest thing that I have ever seen in my thirty-two years in Congress!" Trent Lott (R-Miss.) then demanded that the Speaker be "taken down," the House term to call someone to order for violating House rules prohibiting personal attacks. The House Parliamentarian looked in the dictionary to see if the word "lowest" was a slur. As a hush fell on the House, the presiding officer told O'Neill that he had violated House rules. Bristled O'Neill, "I was expressing my views very mildly because I think much worse than I said."

O'Neill's penalty? The rarely invoked enforced silence for the remainder of the day's debate. So uncomfortable with that action was the House Minority Leader that he asked Lott to make a motion exempting O'Neill from the penalty, to which Lott agreed. No other House Speaker has ever been so reprimanded.*

* Alexander Stanley, "Tip Topped: O'Neill Tangles with Some Republican Turks over Camera Angles," *Nation* (May 28, 1984): 36.

Senate in the 1994 midterm elections, the Senate Republican minority leader, Robert Dole (R.-Kans.), became the majority leader. (Dole served as the majority leader during the Republicans' control of the Senate from 1981 to 1987.) The majority and minority whips round out the leadership positions in the Senate; they perform functions similar to those of their House counterparts.

The organization of both houses of Congress is closely tied to political parties. The parties also play a key role in the committee system, an organizational feature of Congress that facilitates its law-making and oversight functions.

The Role of Political Parties in Congress

When the first Congress met in 1789 in New York City, the nation's temporary capital, it consisted of only twenty-six senators and sixty-five representatives. These men faced the enormous task of creating much of the machinery of government as well as drafting a bill of rights, for which the Anti-Federalists had argued so vehemently. During their debates, the political differences that had divided Americans during the early years of the union were renewed. When Alexander Hamilton, the first Secretary of the Treasury and a staunch Federalist, proposed to fund the national debt and create a national bank, for example, he aroused the ire of those who feared vesting the national government with too much power. This conflict led Hamilton's opponents to create the Democratic-Republican Party to counter the Federalists, creating a two-party system in Congress. Control of the political parties quickly gave Congress many more powers. The Democratic-Republican Party caucus nominated Thomas Jefferson (1804), James Madison (1808 and 1812), and James Monroe (1816) for president, all of whom were elected.

At the beginning of each new Congress—the 104th Congress sits in two sessions, one in 1995 and one in 1996—the members of each party gather in caucus or conference. Historically, these caucuses have enjoyed varied powers, but today the party caucuses—called "caucus" by House Democrats and "conference" by House and Senate Republicans and Senate Democrats—are used by party members to select leaders and make decisions on pending issues.

Majority party The political party in each house of Congress with the most members.

The **majority party** in each house is the party with the greatest number of members. Being in the majority party allows members of that party to choose the major officers of Congress and thereby control debate on the floor, hold all committee chairmanships, and have a majority on all committees. In parliamentary systems like Britain's, the majority party in the House of Commons is entitled to form the government.

Both parties are organized by conferences or caucuses, and each has specialized committees that fulfill certain tasks. House Democrats, for example, in addition to their Caucus, have a Steering Committee that makes committee assignments. The Republicans have a Committee on Committees that performs this function. Each party also has a Congressional Campaign Committee to assist members in their reelection bids. In the Senate, the twenty-five-person Democratic Steering Committee makes Democratic committee assignments. Republican assignments are made by its smaller, five-member Committee on Committees.

Loyalty to party is an important concept in both houses. Senate and House leaders and whips try to keep members of their respective parties in line, although this is often a very difficult task. During the 1993 vote on the North American Free Trade Agreement (NAFTA), for example, the House Democratic Majority Leader and a deputy whip opposed NAFTA, while the Speaker of the House and the House Minority Whip supported it. In general, however, party loyalty is more common in the House. There, members rely more on the party for reelection help.

The Committee System

"Congress in session is Congress on exhibition, whilst Congress in its committee rooms is Congress at work."[17] This statement is even more true today than when Woodrow Wilson wrote it in 1883. A quick look at the floor of the House or the Senate would lead most observers to conclude that not much goes on up on "the Hill" (as the Capitol is often called). Unless a vote is in progress, few members are on the floor. Instead, they are attending committee or subcommittee meetings. It is in these "little legislatures" that the most important legislative action takes place: Bills are drafted and discussed, and substantive and technical amendments are debated.[18] In essence, committees are the first and last places that all bills go. (When different versions of a bill are passed in the House and Senate, a conference committee with members of both houses meets to iron out the differences.) And it is usually committee members who play key roles in floor debate in the full House or Senate about the merits of the proposed bill.

Committees allow members of Congress to specialize and become experts in a small number of areas instead of attempting to be "jacks-of-all-trades, masters of none." The establishment of subcommittees further subdivides issues and allows for even greater specialization. In addition, some committee assignments allow members to act on behalf of the specific interests of their constituents. Midwestern representatives, for example, often favor an assignment to the Agriculture Committee because of that committee's jurisdiction over farm matters. And in the Senate, committee assignments and chairs often determine the policy orientation of the committee, and thus the kind of proposed legislation that comes out of the committee.

Committees are not mentioned in the Constitution. Originally, they were created on an ad hoc (as necessary) basis, but they had historical precedents in the British Parliament and in the colonial legislatures. These ad hoc committees were dissolved as soon as their specific tasks were accomplished. By the Second Congress, 350 such committees had been formed, and soon the increasing scope of congressional activities made the establishment, dissolution, and reestablishment of ad hoc committees increasingly time-consuming and inconvenient.

Over the years, as issues became more complex, some specialization became an absolute necessity. An institutionalized committee system was created in 1816, and, until recently when several committees were abolished in the 104th Congress, committees have been added over time. Committees are especially important in the House because its size makes organization and specialization especially key.

Types of Committees.   There are four types of congressional committees: (1) standing, (2) ad hoc, special, or select, (3) joint, and (4) conference.

1. *Standing committees* are the committees to which proposed bills are referred for consideration. Fewer than 10 percent of the more than 10,000 measures sent to them are ever reported out of the standing committees. These committees are called "standing" because they continue from one Congress to the next; therefore, they are generally viewed as the permanent workshops of congressional lawmaking.
2. *Ad hoc, special,* or *select committees* are temporary committees appointed for specific purposes with fairly limited mandates, generally to conduct special investigations or studies and to report back to the chamber that established them. Unlike standing committees, select committees do not ordinarily draft and report legislation.
3. *Joint committees* are formed with members from both houses of Congress, generally to coordinate investigations or special studies. In practice, they are set up to expedite

business between the houses and to help focus public attention on major matters such as the economy, taxation, or scandals. A joint committee, for example, was formed to investigate the Iran-Contra scandal.

4. *Conference committees* are a special kind of joint committee with the explicit function of reconciling differences in bills passed by the House and Senate. The conference committee is made up of members from the House and Senate committees that originally considered the bill. Because the Constitution mandates that all bills pass both houses in the same form, compromises are often needed on the versions that pass each house of Congress. Once the committee comes up with a satisfactory compromise bill, it is presented to both houses of Congress for their approval. At this point, they can only accept or decline the compromise legislation; they cannot change or amend it in any way.

Standing committees The committees to which proposed bills are referred for consideration.

The House and Senate **standing committees** listed in Table 6.3 (p. 183) were created by statute. The House has 19 standing committees (and a total of 84 subcommittees). The standing committees collectively act as the eyes, ears, and hands of the House. They consider issues roughly parallel to those of the departments represented in the president's cabinet. For example, in the House of Representatives there are committees on agriculture, the judiciary, veterans' affairs, transportation, and commerce.

Standing committees have tremendous power. They can defeat bills, delay them, amend them so that they are radically changed, or hurry them through the process. A committee reports out to the full House or Senate only a small fraction of the bills first assigned to it. Bills can be "forced" out of a House committee by a **discharge petition** signed by a majority (218) of the House membership, but legislators are reluctant to take this drastic measure. Discharge petitions were begun in 1924 to give a majority in the House the ability to bring a matter to the floor in the face of committee inaction. Since World War II, fewer than five bills have been enacted into law through this procedure. In 1971, for example, a discharge petition was used to force the proposed equal rights amendment out of the Judiciary Committee, where it had been stalled by the committee's powerful chair, Emanuel Celler (D-N.Y.). It later went on to be passed by the full House on a vote of 350 to 15.

Discharge petitions Petitions that give a majority of the House of Representatives the authority to bring an issue to the floor in the face of committee inaction.

Discharge petitions, in spite of a House rule that keeps the names of the signees secret, are under attack in the House. In late 1993, the system was targeted by House Republicans; they charged that the secrecy surrounding discharge petitions allows some members to claim that they support legislation bottled up in committee even though they have done nothing to advance it (such as sign a discharge petition to allow a vote). The secrecy rule assures that there is no way for constituents to learn if their legislators have tried to force a stalled bill out of committee. A proposed bill would force a change in the sixty-three-year-old House tradition and make public the names of those signing a discharge petition.

The Senate has seventeen standing committees that range in size from sixteen to twenty-nine members. It also has 68 subcommittees, allowing many senators the opportunity to chair one. As illustrated in Table 6.4 (p. 183), the Senate Judiciary Committee, for example, has six subcommittees. The plethora of subcommittees in the Senate, in fact, has been the subject of much debate in the Senate, and numerous calls have been made to reduce that number.

In contrast to the House, whose members hold few committee assignments (an average of two standing and four subcommittees), senators are spread more thinly, with each serving on an average of three committees and five subcommittees. Whereas the committee system allows House members to become policy or issue specialists, Senate members are often generalists (see Table 6.1, p. 167). Senator Nancy Kassebaum

Table 6.4 ◆	**Committees of the House and Senate (with a Subcommittee Example)**

STANDING COMMITTEES

House

Agriculture
Appropriations
Banking and Financial Services
Budget
Commerce
Economic and Educational Opportunities
Government Reform and Oversight
House Oversight
International Relations
Judiciary
National Security
Resources
Rules
Science
Small Business
Standards of Official Conduct (Ethics)
Transportation and Infrastructure
Veterans' Affairs
Ways and Means

Senate

Agriculture, Nutrition, and Forestry
Appropriations
Armed Services
Banking, Housing, and Urban Affairs
Budget
Commerce, Science and Transportation
Energy and Natural Resources
Environment and Public Works
Finance
Foreign Relations
Governmental Affairs
Indian Affairs
Judiciary   *Judiciary Subcommittees:*
                  Administrative Oversight and
                    the Courts
                  Antitrust, Business Rights
                    and Competition
                  Constitution, Federalism, and
                    Property Rights
                  Immigration
                  Terrorism, Technology, and
                    Government Information
                  Youth Violence
Labor and Human Resources
Rules and Administration
Small Business
Veterans' Affairs

SELECT AND SPECIAL COMMITTEES

House

Select Intelligence

Senate

Special Aging
Select Ethics
Select Intelligence

JOINT COMMITTEES

Joint Committee on the Library
Joint Committee on Printing
Joint Committee on Taxation
Joint Economic Committee

Pork barrel Legislation that allows representatives to "bring home the bacon" to their districts in the form of public works programs, military bases, or other programs designed to benefit their districts directly.

Minority party Party with the second most members in either house of Congress.

(R-Kans.) is typical; she chairs the Committee on Labor and Human Resources and sits on the Foreign Relations and Indian Affairs standing committees. She also sits on five subcommittees of those committees. Similarly, Charles Robb (D-Va.) sits on the Senate Armed Services and Foreign Relations Committees, six subcommittees, and the Senate Select Committee on Intelligence, as well as the Joint Economic Committee.

Senate committees enjoy the same power over framing legislation as do House committees, but the Senate is more likely to force bills out of committee by the use of discharge petitions. During the 1960s, in particular, the Senate was regularly forced to use discharge petitions to bypass the Judiciary Committee in order to get full consideration of civil rights laws. The Judiciary Committee as chaired by Senator James Eastland (D-Miss.) became known as the "graveyard of civil rights legislation." (From 1953 to 1963 only 1 of 121 civil rights bills emerged from Eastland's fiefdom.)

Committee Membership.   To gain a seat on a committee, one must be associated with either of the two major political parties. This becomes important on the rare occasions when an independent or third-party candidate is elected to one of the chambers. In 1990, for example, when Socialist Bernard Sanders of Vermont was elected to the House of Representatives, he had to choose a party affiliation for the purposes of committee placement. (He chose the Democratic Party.)

Representatives often seek committee assignments that have access to what is known as the **pork barrel**. Pork barrel legislation allows representatives to "bring home the bacon" to their districts in the form of public works programs, military bases, or other programs designed to benefit their districts directly. Until the recent end of the Cold War, a seat on the Armed Services Committee, for example, was particularly attractive. It could allow members to bring lucrative defense contracts back to their districts, encourage the building of bases, or discourage their closing within their districts or states, thus pleasing constituents.

In both the House and the Senate, committee membership generally reflects the party distribution within that chamber. For example, if the Democrats are the majority party and hold two-thirds of the seats, they control the chairmanship and usually hold two-thirds of the seats on a committee, with the Republicans making up the other one-third. This distribution is based on tradition, not rules. Moreover, some committees have traditions of either partisanship or bipartisanship. For instance, the House Armed Services Committee has a tradition of strong bipartisanship and therefore has a large number of **minority party** members. In contrast, the House Rules Committee has tended to be more partisan and thus has a higher number of majority party members. In the 104th Congress, for example, it had nine Republicans and only four Democrats.

Although most committees in one house parallel those in the other, one committee unique to the House of Representatives plays a key role in the lawmaking process: the House Rules Committee. This committee reviews most bills after they come from a committee and before they go to the full chamber for consideration. Performing a "traffic cop" function, the House Rules Committee gives each bill what is called a rule, which contains the date the bill will come up for debate, the amount of time that will be allotted for discussion, and often even specifications concerning what kinds of amendments can be offered. Majority party members of this committee are directly appointed by the Speaker.

The Power of Committee Chairs.   The position of committee chair is one of tremendous power and prestige. When House speakers were strong, they personally selected all committee chairs on the basis of friendships and loyalty. After what is termed the "revolution of 1910," when members revolted against the powerful Speaker

Joseph Cannon, committee chairs were chosen by **seniority**—the person of the majority party with the longest continuous service on that committee was automatically made chair.

In 1971 and again in 1973, moderate and liberal Democrats pushed through a series of changes in the House designed to break the hold that conservative committee chairs from the South had long enjoyed because of the seniority system. In 1971, House Democrats voted to elect committee chairs by secret ballot in the party caucus at the beginning of the session, and seniority was no longer the sole criterion for becoming a House chair. (In the Senate there was little change, because seniority is not nearly so important there; however, if one-fifth of the party conference requests it, a secret ballot may be used to elect committee chairs.)

In 1995, Speaker Gingrich, operating under new rules enhancing his power, ignored the seniority system and selected committee chairs whom he trusted to move his reforms through the House. Carlos Moorhead (R-Cal.), for example, was in line to chair either the Commerce or Judiciary Committees, but Gingrich selected others to head those key committees.

Although their power was reduced by these reforms and a recentering of power in the office of the Speaker, committee chairs still establish the agenda for the committee in conjunction with the ranking minority member and may sit as nonvoting members on all subcommittees. They also now select all subcommittee chairs. Moreover, committee chairs call meetings, strategize, recommend majority members to sit on conference committees, and direct the committee staff. The chair may choose not to schedule a hearing on a bill so that the bill can die, may convene meetings when opponents are absent, and may adjourn meetings when things are going badly. Personal skill, influence, and expertise are a chair's best allies.

The long-term power of committee chairs, however, was dramatically limited in 1995. New House rules prevent chairs from serving more than six years—three consecutive Congresses.[19]

Subcommittees.   Another reform that occurred in the early 1970s was the adoption of "the subcommittee bill of rights," which decentralized committee power enormously. It took the power to select subcommittee chairs away from the committee chairs of the House standing committees and gave the 127 subcommittee chairs the power to control their own budgets and staffs. Previously, subcommittee chairs were appointed by committee chairs. Republicans in the 104th Congress not only cut the number of subcommittees in the House from 127 to 84, they also reinstated the power of committee chairs to appoint subcommittee chairs, abandoning the Democratic practice of allowing members to bid for those posts.

Committee chairs are barred from heading their own subcommittees. Multiple subcommittee chairships are also prohibited and each member is allowed to chair only one. This practice has allowed so many House members to become subcommittee chairs and to have their own base of power that former Representative Morris K. Udall (D-Ariz.) once joked that if he passed a young colleague in the hall and didn't remember his name, he'd simply greet him with "good morning, Mr. Chairman," knowing he'd be right about half the time.[20] Of course, with the reduction in subcommittees, the number of chair positions has declined considerably.

As the workload of Congress has increased, so has the importance of subcommittees, leading to the rise of what some term "subcommittee government." On some committees it has become the norm for committee members simply to defer to the judgment of the subcommittee and its specialists in order to speed up the legislative process.

Seniority The method by which the person of the majority party with the longest continuous service on a particular committee was automatically made chair.

The Lawmaking Function of Congress

Chief among the responsibilities of Congress is its lawmaking function, which is greatly facilitated by the committee system. Proposals for legislation can come from the president, executive agencies, committee staffs, interest groups, or even private individuals, but only members of the House or Senate can formally submit a bill for congressional consideration. Once a bill is proposed, it usually reaches a dead end. Of the more than 6,000 bills introduced each year in Congress, fewer than 25 percent are enacted, or made into law.

It is probably useful to think of Congress as a system of multiple vetoes, which was what the Framers desired. They wanted to disperse power, and as Congress has evolved it has come closer and closer to the Framers' intentions. As a bill goes through Congress, a dispersion of power occurs as roadblocks to passage must be surmounted at numerous steps in the process. In addition to realistic roadblocks, caution signs and other opportunities for delay abound. A member who sponsors a bill must get through *every* obstacle; in contrast, successful opposition means "winning" at only one of many stages, including (1) the House subcommittee, (2) the House full committee, (3) the House Rules Committee, (4) the House, (5) the Senate subcommittee, (6) the full Senate committee, (7) the Senate, (8) floor leaders in both Houses, (9) the House–Senate Conference Committee, and (10) the president.

In Britain, the daily rhythm of parliamentary activity contrasts sharply with that in the U.S. Congress. The emphasis in Parliament is overwhelmingly on formal debate, in which government and opposition teams clash regularly and in an animated fashion. For an individual Member of Parliament (MP), the fastest route to prestige and influence is to shine in debate and thus come to the attention of the party leadership. Consequently, there are few incentives for members to spend a lot of time in committee, since committee work takes the MP off the debate floor and encourages cross-party cooperation. The combination of strong parliamentary parties and a neglected committee system leads to a situation where Parliament, though a spirited forum, is a relatively weak institution in the overall governmental scheme. Virtually all bills emanate from the executive (Prime Minister), and the scope for an individual MP's influence on the legislative process is minimal. The British parliament is, to employ the conventional distinction, a debating parliament, not a working parliament (like the U.S. Congress or the German Bundestag).

How a Bill Becomes a Law

A bill must survive three stages before it becomes a law. Because it may be killed during any of these stages, it is much easier to defeat a bill than it is to get one passed. The House and Senate have parallel processes, and often the same bill is introduced in each chamber at the same time.

Although a bill must be introduced by a member of Congress, it is often sponsored by a whole list of other members in an early effort to show support for it. Once introduced, the bill is sent to the clerk of the chamber, who gives it a number (for example, HR 1, or S 1—indicating House or Senate bill number one for the session). The bill is then printed, distributed, and sent to the appropriate committee for consideration.

The first stage of action takes place within the committee. The committee usually refers the bill to one of its subcommittees, which researches the bill and decides whether to hold hearings on it. The subcommittee hearings provide the opportunity for people on both sides of the issue to voice their opinions. Most of these hearings are now open to the public because of 1970s "sunshine" laws, which require open sessions. After the hearings, the bill is revised, and the subcommittee votes to approve or defeat the bill. If the subcommittee votes in favor of the bill, it is returned to the full committee, which then either rejects the bill or sends it to the House or Senate floor (see Figure 6-7).

The second stage of action takes place on the House or Senate floor. Before the bill may be debated on the floor, in the House, however, it must be sent to the Rules Committee to be given a rule to be placed on the calendar, or schedule. The rule given to the bill determines the limits on the floor debate and specifies what types of amendments, if any, may be attached. (House budget bills [and all Senate bills] do not go to the Rules Committee.) Once the House Rules Committee considers the bill, it is put on the calendar.

FIGURE 6-7
How a Bill Becomes a Law

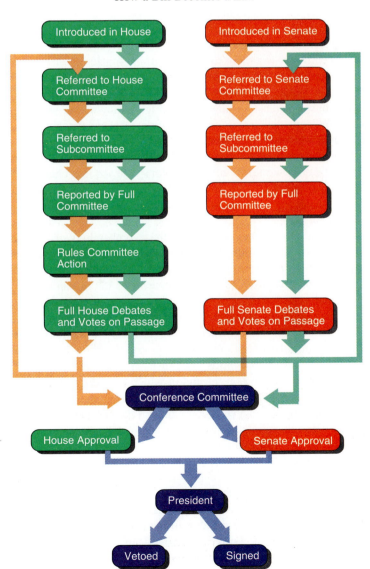

When the day arrives for floor debate, the House may choose to form a "Committee of the Whole," which allows the House to deliberate with the presence of only one hundred members, to expedite consideration of the bill. On the House floor, the bill is debated, amendments are offered, and a vote is taken by the full House. If the bill survives, it is sent to the other chamber of Congress for consideration if it has not been considered there simultaneously.

Unlike the House, where debate is necessarily limited given the size of the body, in the Senate bills may be held up by **holds** or **filibusters**. A hold is a tactic by which a senator asks to be informed before a particular bill is brought to the floor. This request signals the Senate leadership and the sponsors of the bill that a colleague may have objections to the bill and should be consulted before any further action is taken.

The hold system has recently come under attack by some Senate members. "It's gotten out of control," says Senator Bennett Johnston (D-La.).[21] In the first session of the 102nd Congress, for example, holds were placed on more than two-thirds of the 250 bills reported out of committee in the Senate. In the 103rd Congress, holds were used to delay several presidential appointments.

Filibusters, which allow for unlimited debate on a bill, grew out of the absence of rules to limit speech in the Senate and are often used to "talk a bill to death." In contrast to a hold, a filibuster is a more formal way of halting action on a bill by means of long speeches or unlimited debate in the Senate. The filibuster became an increasingly common feature of Senate life during the slavery debates. In 1917, after eleven senators waged a filibuster against an important foreign policy matter supported by President Woodrow Wilson, the Senate adopted a rule to avoid the potential disaster of tying the president's hands during World War I. To end a filibuster, cloture must be invoked. To cut off debate, sixteen senators must first sign a motion for cloture. Then, a roll-call vote is taken. Two-thirds of the senators—subsequent changes now require only sixty instead of sixty-six—must vote to end the filibuster. Each member of the Senate can then speak for one hour before debate is closed and the legislation on the floor is brought to a vote.

The third stage of action takes place when the two chambers of Congress approve different versions of the same bill. When this happens, a conference committee is established to iron out the differences. The conference committee, whose members are from the original House and Senate committees, revises the bill and returns it to each chamber for a final vote. No changes or amendments are allowed at this stage. If the bill is passed, it is sent to the president, who either signs it or vetoes it.

The president has ten days to consider the bill, and has four options. (1) He can sign the bill, at which point it becomes law. (2) He can veto the bill. Congress may override the president's veto with a two-thirds vote in each chamber, a very difficult task. (3) He can wait the full ten days, at the end of which time the bill becomes law without his signature if Congress is still in session. (4) If the Congress adjourns before the ten days are up, the president can choose not to sign the bill, and it is thus "pocket vetoed." A **pocket veto** allows bills figuratively stashed in the president's pocket to die. The only way for the bill to become law is for it to be reintroduced in the next session and go through the process again. Because Congress sets its own date of adjournment, technically the session could be continued the few extra days necessary to prevent a pocket veto. Extensions are unlikely, however, as sessions are often scheduled to adjourn close to the November elections or the Christmas holidays.

Any kind of legislation is more difficult to pass when the president and Congress are of different political parties. For years, Republican presidents blamed the Democrats, who controlled the Congress, for gridlock, as fewer and fewer important pieces of

Holds Tactics by which a senator asks to be informed before a particular bill is brought to the floor.

Filibusters A formal way of halting action on a bill by means of long speeches or unlimited debate in the Senate.

Pocket veto If Congress adjourns during the ten days the president has to consider a bill passed by both Houses of Congress without the president's signature, it is considered vetoed.

legislation could be agreed on by both parties. If Reagan or Bush wanted passage of certain legislation, the Democratic Congress often rejected their proposals. Conversely, if Congress passed a particular bill, President Bush, in particular, often vetoed it and the Democrats repeatedly failed to muster enough votes to override his veto.

In 1993, however, for the first time since 1968, both Houses of Congress and the presidency were controlled by the same political party. Most major presidential programs were passed, and several bills previously passed by Congress but vetoed by George Bush became law. "Gridlock is gone," declared House Majority Leader Richard Gephardt (D-Mo.) after the end of the first session of the 103rd Congress, which was one of the most productive sessions in recent years. In 1993 Bill Clinton enjoyed an exceptionally high success rate as Congress supported 86.4 percent of legislation he supported including the budget bill, NAFTA, the Family and Medical Leave Act, and the Brady Bill. In 1995, however, once Republicans took over control of both Houses, many commentators expected gridlock to return. And it may well occur. Yet, through June, 1995, President Clinton did not veto a single piece of legislation passed by the Republican Congress.

How Members Make Decisions

As a bill wends its way through the labyrinth of the lawmaking process described above, members are confronted with this question: How should I vote? Although most legislation pertains to fairly mundane matters, members nonetheless fear that they will "miss" something in a bill and vote the "wrong" way, alienating voters at home. Unless a bill is controversial, this could be easy to do. In the 102nd Congress, for example, 9,601 bills were introduced and 603 were passed. Yet, these 603 bills amounted to more than 7,000 pages of new laws.

Of course, members often listen to their own personal beliefs on the matter. But those views can often be moderated by other considerations. In an effort to avoid making any voting mistakes, members look to a variety of sources for "cues." Major cue givers include political parties, colleagues, caucuses, interest groups, staff members, the president, and, of course, constituents. And frequently, how a member ultimately decides or votes on any particular measure will vary according to the issues involved and in the context in which they are presented.[22]

Political Parties

Not all issues voted on in Congress divide members along party lines. In fact, only one-third to one-half of the votes in Congress are considered to be party votes (that is, when a majority in one party opposes a majority in the other). However, on these party votes members vote with their party between 70 and 80 percent of the time. In the first session of the 103rd Congress, that figure was even higher. Democrats voted with other Democrats 90 percent of the time. For Republicans, the figure was 88 percent. Interestingly, freshman Democrats of both parties supported their party even more frequently—93 percent for Democrats and 90 percent for Republicans. Political parties clearly have an interest in increasing their representation in Congress and in maintaining party unity on votes in Congress. Toward that end, party officials have several sources of influence.

Members of Congress elected on a partisan ticket feel a degree of obligation to their party and also to the president if he is of the same party. Although the national political parties have little say in who gets a party's nomination for the U.S. Senate or the House, once a candidate has emerged successfully from a primary contest (see Chapter 12), both houses have committees that provide campaign assistance since it is to each party's advantage to win as many seats as possible in each house. Once a member is elected, especially if he or she was the recipient of financial support or campaign visits from popular members, party leaders expect some degree of loyalty in return.

In Britain, virtually all votes (called *divisions*) taken in the House of Commons divide Members of Parliament along party lines; indeed, in this sense we speak of British parliamentary parties as "disciplined," as they are able to marshal the support of their members on questions before the legislature.

Colleagues and Caucuses

Special-interest caucuses Groups that allow congressional members from either party to cross party lines to band together with their colleagues who have a common interest.

Special-interest caucuses, including such disparate groups as farmers, footwear manufacturers, and first-term members of Congress, allow members from either party to cross party lines in order to band together with their colleagues who have a common interest. In 1994, there were 140 special interest caucuses, including the Black Caucus, the Congressional Caucus for Women's Issues, and caucuses formed to promote certain industries, such as textiles, tourism, wine, coal, steel, mushrooms, and cranberries; or to advance particular views or interests. Twenty-eight of these were legislative service organizations (LSOs), which qualified them for office space, access to House equipment, and funding. From 1984 to 1994, over $35 million dollars were spent by LSOs.

African-American legislators formed their own caucus—an LSO—in 1971, and lobbyists from major women's rights groups urged the women in Congress to do likewise. But senior female House members were opposed to the idea, and other members feared being associated with the liberal agenda of Bella Abzug (D-N.Y.). Thus, the Congresswoman's Caucus was not formed until 1977, with fifteen of the eighteen women in the House joining. The Caucus soon changed its name to the Congressional Women's Caucus, but it was hurt by the refusal of several Republican women to join after their election in 1980.

The Caucus reorganized in 1981, changed its name to the Congressional Caucus for Women's Issues, and opened its doors to men. Now, one of the largest caucuses in the House, it has more than 150 members, most of whom are men. (It is more formal than many caucuses; women pay $1,500 a year, men $650, to support its staff.) This Caucus has been instrumental in garnering support for increased research on women's health issues and for the Family and Medical Leave Act, among other items. In 1991, it outlined the Women's Health Equity Act, a package of twenty-two bills designed to improve women's health through new initiatives in research, services, and prevention. In 1993, the Caucus, bolstered by the addition of 24 new women, had its most successful year ever. "Issues of concern to women and families truly came of age . . . and, largely, it was the congresswomen who set the agenda," said Representative Patricia Schroeder (D-Colo.), co-chair of the Caucus.[23] She claimed that Congress passed more legislation of importance to U.S. women in 1993 than in any other year since the Caucus began keeping track a decade ago. Among its victories: the Family and Medical Leave Act, several laws increasing federal research on women's health issues, and the Violence Against Women Act.

In 1995, as part of the Republican effort to reform Congress and reduce the costs of the institution itself, LSOs were abolished in an effort to save the $5 million that they cost yearly. Most of the LSOs, including the Arts Caucus, the Automotive Caucus, the Rural Caucus, Space Caucus, and Women's Caucus, have announced plans to become Congressional Member Organizations, or CMOs. As CMOs, these groups cannot receive any congressional funding or support from outside groups, but members can use personal funds to help support them.[24] These "new" caucuses can't have separate staffs, but caucus members can pool their respective office allowances to fund an aide to work on caucus affairs.[25] In this new form, a CMO must register with the House Oversight Committee, report its purpose, and list any member's personal staffers who work on CMO issues. Other caucuses are debating whether to reorganize as foundations.

Members also strongly identify by their class—that is, the year in which they were elected. For example, until 1993, the largest "new" class in years was the class of 1974, when the Watergate scandal and the resignation of President Richard M. Nixon resulted in a Democratic landslide that produced seventy-five new House Democrats. In 1978, thirty-six new Republicans arrived in the House, followed by fifty-two more in 1980. Members of the same class share information with one another and form networks that often solidify as the members' tenure in the House increases.

State and regional caucuses are two other important sources of information exchange among members and across party lines. Large state delegations, such as those of California, New York, and Texas, often work together, regardless of party lines, to bring the bacon home to their states. Some state caucuses hold weekly meetings to assure that their interests are adequately represented on important committees and to keep abreast of pending legislation that might affect their states.

Regional caucuses cut across not only state lines but both houses of Congress as well. In the early years of the nation, members of Congress even roomed in boarding houses organized around the regions from which they came. These "boarding-house networks" enforced discipline through the threat of social ostracism. While these kinds of strictures no longer exist, informal frostbelt and sunbelt caucuses advance sectional interests.[26]

Because members, especially those in the House, tend to specialize, they often look to certain of their colleagues for what Donald R. Matthews and James A. Stimson call "cues."[27] Each member has a different set of cue givers, depending on the issue involved. A cue giver may be a respected member of a particular caucus, the state delegation, or a committee chair or subcommittee chair whom a member particularly admires or who has a reputation for exceptional expertise. Other cue-givers can be friends who tend to think the same way as the representative does.

Members also trade votes with friends or even foes in a practice called logrolling. For example, vote trading often takes place on specialized bills designed to bring home the bacon to certain areas. A yea vote by an unaffected member often is given in exchange for the promise of a future yea vote on a similar piece of legislation affecting his or her district.

Staff

Because of the amount of work members have, they tend to rely heavily on members of their staff for information on pending legislation. Generally, staff members prepare summaries of bills and brief the representative or senator based on their research. If the bill is non-ideological or one on which the member has no real position, staff members can be very influential. Staff members also do research on and even draft bills that a member wishes to introduce.

Staff aides are especially crucial in the Senate. Because senators have so many committee assignments and are often spread quite thin, they frequently rely heavily on aides. The next time you see a televised Senate hearing, notice how each senator has at least one aide sitting behind him or her, ready with information and often even with questions for the senator to ask. Some critics believe that staff members have become too important, too powerful, and that their bosses are too dependent on them. Said Senator Lloyd Bentsen (D-Tx.) (who resigned to become Secretary of the Treasury), "I get so damned tired of members who can't go any place without staff. They don't know the issues themselves."[28]

Support Agencies.   Congress has developed four support agencies—the Congressional Research Service, the General Accounting Office, the Office of Technology Assessment, and the Congressional Budget Office—in order to provide the specialized knowledge necessary for members of Congress to make informed decisions on complex issues.

Congressional Research Service (CRS).   Created in 1914 as the Legislative Research Service (LRS), the CRS is administered by the Library of Congress and responds to more than a quarter of a million congressional requests for information each year. The CRS is staffed with almost 900 employees, many of whom have advanced academic training. The service provides nonpartisan studies of public issues, compiling facts on many sides of each issue, and conducts major research projects for committees at the request of members. The CRS also prepares summaries of all bills introduced and tracks the progress of major bills. All this information is available via computer terminals in Senate and House offices.

General Accounting Office (GAO).   The GAO was established in 1921 as an independent regulatory agency for the purpose of auditing the financial expenditures of the executive branch and federal agencies. Today, staffed with more than 5,000 employees, the GAO has expanded to perform four additional functions: It sets government standards for accounting, provides a variety of legal opinions, settles claims against the government, and conducts studies on congressional request. Through its investigation of the efficiency and effectiveness of agencies, the GAO has acted as a watchdog of military funds in particular, often making headlines by reporting when products are bought at prices far above market value.

Office of Technology Assessment (OTA).   The OTA, an agency of about two hundred employees, was created in 1972 to study and evaluate the long-range effects of new and existing technology. The OTA has dealt with such issues as the impact of computers on privacy rights and the effect of the chemical Agent Orange on Vietnam veterans and their children.

Congressional Budget Office (CBO).   The CBO was created in 1974 in order to evaluate the economic effect of different spending programs and to provide information on the cost of proposed policies. The CBO employs more than 200 people on its staff and is responsible for analyzing the president's budget and economic projections, thereby providing Congress and individual members with a valuable second opinion for use in budget debates.

Interest Groups

The primary function of most interest-group lobbyists is to provide information to supportive or potentially supportive legislators and their staffs. It's likely, for example, that a representative knows the position of the National Rifle Association (NRA) on gun control legislation. What the legislator needs to get from the NRA are information and substantial research on the feasibility and impact of such legislation. How could the states implement such legislation? Is it constitutional? Will it really have an impact on violent crime or crime in schools? It is in presenting this kind of information that an interest group can solidify a member's support or influence a member leaning in its direction. Pressure groups often urge their members in a particular state or district to call or write their senator or representative. Lobbyists can't vote, but voters back home can. Thus, an interest group can attempt to influence how a member votes by drawing his or her attention to the issue, providing information, and urging voters to contact their representatives.

As technology has improved, so has the force of interest groups. When Congress proposed to reduce the deductibility of business meals from 80 to 50 percent, the National Restaurant Association fought back. It launched a well-done television ad featuring a waitress discussing how she might lose her job and her ability to support her three sons. The punch line? "Call 1–800–999–8945 now, and you'll be connected to your Senator."[29] Banks of operators were on hand to patch irate constituents through to their representatives' offices. (Ultimately, however, the 50-percent deduction was passed.) These kinds of measures are designed to alert legislators as quickly as possible to concerns back home.

Constituents

Constituents—the people who live and vote in a member's district or state—are always in mind when a member casts a vote. It is rare for a legislator to vote against the wishes of his or her constituency regularly, particularly on issues of welfare rights or domestic policy or on other highly salient issues such as affirmative action, abortion, or war. Most constituents often have strong convictions on one or more of these issues. For example, during the 1960s, representatives from Southern states could not hope to keep their seats for long if they voted in favor of proposed civil rights legislation. But gauging how voters feel about any particular issue is often not easy. Because it is virtually impossible to know how the folks back home feel on all issues, a representative's perception of their preferences is important.

Political scientist Richard F. Fenno Jr. concludes that members perceive their constituencies to consist of four groups, as illustrated in Figure 6-8. Members initially describe their "geographical constituency"—the location and size of the district—and its internal makeup, or socioeconomic and political characteristics, and the proportion of people who are "blue collar," Jewish, Democratic, or elderly, for example. Within the geographical constituency, members define a second group, the "reelection constituency," consisting of the people who the member thinks vote for him or her. This is the member's perceived political base; to disagree with the reelection constituency could cost the member his or her seat. Within the reelection constituency is a third, smaller group consisting of the member's strongest supporters, the "primary constituency." These loyalists vote for the member and provide campaign assistance and financial support. The fourth and final constituency is made up of the people closest to the member—his or her "personal constituency"—including friends and advisers.

FIGURE 6-8

How Members View Their Districts

Source: From *Homestyle: House Members in Their Districts* by Richard Fenno. Reprinted by permission of HarperCollins College Publishers.

Thus, a member of Congress may perceive his district in a variety of ways, and sometimes the four constituencies may be in conflict. The typical voter in the district may have quite different views from those of the member's strongest supporters. Although most of the member's constituency will usually be unaware of the member's voting decisions, it would be foolish for a representative or senator to ignore an overwhelming majority of his or her constituents' views on an issue of salience.

Congress and the President

Over the years, especially since the presidency of Franklin D. Roosevelt, Congress has allowed the president to play an ever-growing role in the legislative process. Today, for example, Congress often finds itself responding to executive branch proposals, as it did in the case of the Clean Air Act Amendments of 1990 discussed earlier in this chapter. Critics of Congress point to its slow, unwieldy process and the complexity of national problems as reasons why Congress often seems not to act on its own.

Individual members, especially if the president is popular with voters, often find themselves voting in favor of legislation supported by the White House. Legislators "on the fence" often are targeted by the White House or inundated with invitations to state dinners. Lyndon B. Johnson was a master of this strategy. One widely recounted story tells how Lyndon Johnson called Senator Harry Byrd (D-Va.) over to the White House because he was resisting passage of the civil rights bill. According to Senator Dale Bumpers (D-Ark.), Johnson said, " 'You know, Harry, [Defense Secretary Robert] McNamara says we got to close that Norfolk naval base down there, and I don't much want to do it.' And Harry Byrd couldn't wait to get back over to the Senate to vote for the civil rights bill."[30]

President Clinton's initial efforts at "persuasion" were hailed by some people. During his efforts to convince Congress to pass his budget deficit-reduction plan and NAFTA, he courted and cajoled numerous legislators and punished those who didn't go along. After Senator Richard Shelly (D-Ala.) criticized Clinton's tax plan, the White House retaliated by moving ninety federal jobs out of the Marshall Space Flight Center in Alabama and even denied Shelly an extra ticket to a White House South Lawn ceremony honoring his alma mater's championship football team.[31] It doesn't take many episodes like these to convince some legislators how to vote.

Although the president, especially a popular one, undoubtedly can have an impact on how a member votes, political scientist John W. Kingdon found that overall, colleagues and constituents have the greatest impact of the many factors discussed here.[32]

Over the years, the balance of power between Congress and the executive branch has seesawed. The post–Civil War Congress attempted to regain control of the vast executive powers that President Abraham Lincoln, recently slain, had taken from them. Angered at the refusal of Lincoln's successor, Andrew Johnson, to go along with its radical "reforms" of the South, Congress passed the Tenure of Office Act, which prevented the president, under the threat of civil penalty, from removing any cabinet-level appointments of the previous administration. Johnson accepted the challenge and suspended Lincoln's Secretary of War, Edwin M. Stanton, who many believed guilty of heinous war crimes. The House voted to impeach Johnson, but only the desertion of a handful of Republican senators prevented him from being removed from office. (The impeachment effort fell short by one vote.) Nonetheless, the president's power had been greatly weakened, and the Congress again became the center of power and authority in the federal government.

Beginning in the early 1900s, however, a series of strong presidents acted at the expense of congressional power. Theodore Roosevelt, Franklin D. Roosevelt, and Lyndon B. Johnson, especially, all viewed the presidency as carrying with it enormous powers. Although these presidents facilitated an expansion of the role of the federal government, over time the perception grew that presidents were abusing their power, particularly after the events of the Vietnam War and Watergate. By the 1970s, then, scholars were discussing the "imperial presidency,"[33] and Congress made efforts to reassert itself by exercising its oversight function zealously.

Oversight of the Executive Branch

According to political scientist Joel D. Aberbach, since 1961 there has been a substantial increase in the oversight activity of Congress.[34] Key to Congress's performance of its oversight function is its ability to question members of the administration and the bureaucracy to see if they are enforcing and interpreting the laws passed by Congress as its members intended. Oversight occurs on both the domestic and foreign policy fronts.

Domestic Oversight. The greatest increases in domestic oversight occurred in the 1970s, when mushrooming budget deficits, fiscal shortfalls, and public suspicion about any forms of new (or old, for that matter) spending discouraged lawmakers from supporting expensive new programs.[35] In 1974, Congress passed the Budget and Impoundment Control Act in response to President Nixon's refusal to spend money on certain programs authorized by Congress. The act also created budget committees in the House and in the Senate and the Congressional Budget Office (CBO) to analyze budget proposals and their potential impact on the economy. The 1974 Act requires Congress to consider and thoroughly study the president's fiscal policy goals and to set specific spending, tax, and deficit limits for each fiscal year. Prior to 1974, the Office of Management and Budget (OMB) in the executive branch controlled the budget process, and Congress had no way of systematically evaluating budgets or their impact. "The creation of the CBO began to redress the balance of power," said Stuart Eisenstadt, the Carter White House domestic policy chief.[36] It ended the president's monopoly on information and gave Congress a powerful weapon to oversee the budget process.

Believing it could not trust the executive branch to provide it with accurate information, Congress also expanded the staffs of members and committees in both houses. It also added to the research service of the Library of Congress, and other support services were expanded.

All these developments have helped Congress improve its oversight of the executive branch. Hearings and investigations are common ways for members of Congress to make sure that laws are routinely and properly administered by the executive branch. Authorizations and frequent reviews of agency performance and appropriations are probably the most effective types of oversight. Since money is the lifeblood of any agency, threatening funding can often assure compliance with congressional wishes.

Legislative vetoes, a procedure by which one or both houses of Congress could disallow an act of an executive agency by a simple majority vote, also help Congress perform its oversight function. Provisions for so-called legislative vetoes were first added

President Bill Clinton reached out to Speaker Gingrich at a Washington dinner by humorously suggesting that, together, they could cut government waste by replacing spoons and forks with the cheaper "sporks."

to statutes in 1932 but were not used frequently until the 1970s. They were usually included in laws that delegated congressional powers to the executive branch while retaining the power of Congress to restrict their use. By 1981, more than 200 statutes contained legislative veto provisions.

In *Immigration and Naturalization Service* v. *Chadha* (1983), however, the U.S. Supreme Court ruled that the legislative veto as used in many circumstances was unconstitutional.[37] The Court concluded that although the Constitution gave Congress the power to make laws, the Framers were clear in their intent that Congress should separate itself from executing or enforcing the laws. In spite of *Chadha*, however, the legislative veto continues to play an important role in executive–legislative relations.

Foreign Affairs Oversight.   The Constitution divides foreign policy powers between the executive and the legislative branches. The president has the power to wage war and negotiate treaties, whereas the Congress has the power to declare war and the Senate has the power to ratify treaties. Throughout the twentieth century, the executive branch has become preeminent in foreign affairs despite the constitutional division of powers. This is partly due to the series of crises and the development of nuclear weapons in this century; both have necessitated quick decision making and secrecy, which are much easier to manage in the executive branch. Congress, with its 535 members, has a more difficult time reaching a consensus and keeping secrets.

After years of playing second fiddle to a series of presidents from Theodore Roosevelt to Richard M. Nixon, a "snoozing Congress" was "aroused"[38] and seized for itself the authority and expertise necessary to go head-to-head with the chief executive. In a delayed response to Lyndon B. Johnson's 1964–1969 conduct of the Vietnam War, Congress passed in 1973 the **War Powers Act** over President Nixon's veto. This Act requires any president to obtain congressional approval before committing U.S. forces to a combat zone and to notify Congress within forty-eight hours of committing troops to foreign soil. In addition, the president must withdraw troops within sixty days unless Congress votes to declare war. The president is also required to consult with Congress, if at all possible, prior to committing troops.

The War Powers Act has been of limited effectiveness in claiming a larger congressional role in international crisis situations. Presidents Ford, Carter, and Reagan never consulted Congress in advance of committing troops, citing the need for secrecy and swift movement, although each president did notify Congress shortly after the incidents. They contended that the War Powers Act was probably unconstitutional—although it has been upheld by the Supreme Court—because it limits presidential prerogatives as commander-in-chief.

War Powers Act Passed by Congress in 1973, the president was limited in his deployment of troops overseas to a sixty-day period in peacetime (which could be extended for an extra thirty days to permit withdrawal) unless Congress explicitly gave its approval for a longer period.

Confirmation of Presidential Appointments

The Senate's ability to confirm key members of the executive branch as well as presidential appointments to the federal courts gives it a special oversight function. As discussed in Chapters 8 and 9, although the Senate confirms most presidential nominees, it does not always do so. And a wise president will consider senatorial reaction before nominating potentially controversial individuals to his administration or the federal courts. Furthermore, thanks to a policy called **senatorial courtesy**, presidents often defer to senators of their own party to suggest nominees for district court vacancies in the senators' states, giving them considerable influence over the nomination of district court judges.

Senatorial courtesy A practice by which senators can have near veto power over laws or appointments that affect their state in a specific way.

Toward Reform

In the aftermath of the 1992 congressional elections, in which questions about perks, campaign finances, the honesty of individual members, and the integrity and usefulness of the Congress itself seemed to be at issue, Speaker of the House Thomas Foley opened the 103rd Congress heralding a "year of reform." The public was angry, and Foley and the rest of the members of Congress knew it. Still, little change or "reform" was apparent, and many credit the abscence of reform as a reason for the Republican's recapture of both Houses.

Reform from Within

Rep. Newt Gingrich seized on the country's mood; before the 1994 congressional elections, he gathered more than 300 Republicans running for national office together to sign what he termed the Republican Party's Contract with America. Its key provisions bound any Republican elected that November to voting for major reforms in government, including within Congress itself. Although the Republican majority in both houses is one of the slimmest party majorities in several decades, under the leadership of the new Speaker, many reforms were quickly made as the Republicans claimed a clear mandate for change.

Chief among the internal reforms that took place in Congress were:

1. Elimination of proxy voting. To improve deliberations in Congress and in its committees, House rules were changed; members now must be present for votes in committee.
2. Cuts in committees and their staffs to streamline the legislative process and cut costs. In the House, three committees and twenty-five subcommittees were abolished as a step toward reform of the committee system suggested by the Joint Committee on the Reorganization of Congress. House committees were also renamed to reflect Republican priorities. The Government Operations Committee, for example, became the Government Reform and Oversight Committee.
3. Hearings were opened to the public and the media to promote accountability.
4. Limits on the terms of committee chairs and the Speaker of the House. Having served under many Democrats, several of whom had chaired committees as their own personal fiefdoms for decades, Republicans resolved to limit the time that committee chairs served. This limit, along with the eight-year limit for the Speaker, was seen as a first step in limiting congressional terms. The Speaker's term limit was also part of a reform suggested by scholars as a consolidation of power in that office to counterbalance the president. Most members went along with increased power for the Speaker so long as there were limits on the time he or she could serve.
5. Abolition of Legislative Service Organizations (LSOs), which accounted for twenty-eight of the most powerful caucuses in the Congress. This was designed to cut costs and to lessen factionalization and the influence of special interests in Congress. Most caucuses, however, still exist with scaled-down operations.
6. Passage of Congressional Accountability Act. As signed into law by President Clinton, this legislation made Congress subject to many laws that apply to the public sector, including the Fair Labor Standards Act, the Civil Rights Act of 1964, the Americans with Disabilities Act, and the Family and Medical Leave Act. Republicans argued that Congress would be less likely to pass legislation unfavorable to business if it was also subject to its provisions; many Democrats saw it as an expansion of worker protections.

Other reforms suggested by the Joint Committee on the Organization of Congress were not implemented. Three committees were abolished in the House, but more consolidation had been suggested. The Joint Committee had also called for revamping the committee and subcommittee systems to end jurisdictional problems. More than ninety committees and subcommittees, for example, have jurisdiction over the Environmental Protection Agency. But the Speaker realized that it would be difficult to get committee chairs to accept these changes. He thus opted to wait until Congress streamlines the bureaucracy and combines or eliminates some departments or agencies before pushing the House to streamline its committee system.

Term Limits.   Frustrated by apparent inaction, gridlock, and ethics problems in Congress, in the late 1980s a term-limits movement began sweeping the nation as citizens and citizens groups lobbied their statehouses for laws to limit the number of elected terms of not only their state representatives but also members of Congress. Given the power of incumbency, proponents of term limits argued that election to Congress, in essence, equaled life tenure. The concept of term limits is a simple one that has appealed to many people who oppose the notion of career representatives. As it generally applies to Congress, it allows members of the Houses to serve three two-year terms; senators can serve two six-year terms. By 1995, twenty-five states had enacted some form of term-limit laws and action was pending in several more.

The idea of term limits isn't new. In 1787, the Framers considered, but rejected, the Virginia Plan, which restricted members of the House to one term. Moreover, many of the Founders believed in the regular rotation of offices among worthy citizens, and for the most part this was the practice in the early years of the republic. There is also a precedent for term limitation in the office of governor. From the very first, Americans were suspicious of executive power and have preferred to restrict their governors to a fixed number of terms in the statehouse, and even today, the two-term limit (with each term four years in length) is the gubernatorial norm. And, of course, the president of the United States has been limited to two full four-year terms since the Twenty-second Amendment was ratified after the death of four-term President Franklin D. Roosevelt.

The Contract with America promised that a Republican Congress would bring a term-limit amendment to a vote in Congress. Gaining control of Congress from the Democrats, however, appears to have changed some Republicans' perspective on the desirability of term limits. Before the 1994 elections, many Republicans argued that incumbents had too many advantages in running for office and that limits would build in competition and ensure turnover. They argued that many good people, hesitant to start a lengthy second career in politics, would be willing to serve for a short time, as the Founders envisioned. Before the Republicans won control of both Houses, they saw term limits as a way of increasing Republican representation in Congress. They believed that term limits would force many Democrats out of office, making it easier for Republicans to win these open seats.

Term-limit opponents have a different view of this reform. They note that the people already have the power to limit terms—and to do so more severely than the reformers' proposals advocate. If the electorate so desires it could replace the entire U.S. House of Representatives every two years. Term limits, opponents say, deny these constituents their right to retain a good member of Congress in office if they so desire; under term limitation, good and bad legislators are ousted equally and without distinction.

Term-limit opponents also note that the loss of senior, experienced legislators means the diminishing of an important check on other actors in the legislative process who

STILL THE BEST CONGRESSIONAL TERM-LIMITING DEVICE.

would *not* be limited by term, such as lobbyists, legislative staff, and executive department bureaucrats. Few Americans are any more fond of these groups than they are of legislators. This last problem with term limits is an example of the *unintended consequences* of reform. The U.S. system of government is so complex that each new action can produce somewhat unpredictable reactions, and wise reformers must be alert to the "ripple effects" of their proposals.

In 1994, the U.S. Supreme Court heard a challenge to an Arkansas term-limit provision. While upholding portions of the state law that set term limits for state legislators, the Arkansas Supreme Court had ruled that state-imposed term limits for members of the U.S. House and Senate were unconstitutional.

In 1995, recognizing that a constitutional amendment to limit the terms of members of Congress had little chance of passage, the Speaker began to explore other ways to advance term limits. One alternative would allow states to set their own term limits. The Contract with America only promised a vote on term limits; it did not guarantee a constitutional amendment.

Summary

The size, scope, and demands on Congress have increased tremendously over the years. In presenting the important role that Congress plays in U.S. politics, we have made the following points:

1. The experiences of Great Britain, colonial assemblies, and the Articles of Confederation all contributed in a variety of ways to the powers granted to the new Congress.

2. The Constitution created a bicameral legislature, with members of each body to be elected, and thus to represent, different constituencies. The Constitution also requires that seats in the House of Representatives be apportioned by population. Thus, after every census, district lines must be redrawn to reflect population shifts. The Constitution also provides a vast array of enumerated and implied powers to Congress. Some, such as lawmaking and oversight, are shared by both houses of Congress; others are not.

3. Members of Congress must meet formal, constitutional requirements before they can take office. They also must generally conform to several informal re-

quirements, including membership in a major political party, and must have the ability to attract campaign contributions. Most members are wealthy, well educated, middle-aged, and male. This shared perspective may have important consequences on how members vote, or on how they view their representational function.

4. Each house of Congress has a hierarchical leadership structure in which political party and the seniority system play major roles, especially in the committee system, which facilitates the workings and organization of Congress. Because committees and subcommittees are where most of the work of Congress gets done, committee chairs are very powerful actors in the legislative process.

5. The chief power of Congress is making laws. Numerous formal rules exist to facilitate the passage of legislation. Yet in spite of these formal guideposts, most bills do not pass in a "textbook" fashion.

6. To help them make up their minds on how to vote, members of Congress rely on a variety of sources. These sources include political parties, colleagues, informal caucuses, staff (including support agencies), interest groups, and constituents. The president, if he is of the same political party, can also be a factor.

7. The president and the Congress enjoy a peculiar, symbiotic relationship. Today, the president plays an increasingly important role in the legislative process, yet without congressional approval, he can do little. To reassert itself in the legislative process, Congress has stepped up its oversight role in both domestic and foreign affairs arenas. And the Senate has always played a significant oversight function through its ability to ratify treaties and confirm presidential appointments.

Key Terms

redistricting	majority leader	hold
gerrymandering	majority party	filibuster
apportionment	standing committees	pocket veto
impeachment	discharge petition	special-interest caucuses
Contract with America	pork barrel	War Powers Act
Speaker of the House	minority party	senatorial courtesy
party caucus	seniority	

Suggested Readings

Aberbach, Joel D. *Keeping a Watchful Eye: The Politics of Congressional Oversight*. Washington, DC: The Brookings Institution, 1990.

Cain, Bruce, John Ferejohn, and Morris P. Fiorina. *The Personal Vote*. Cambridge, MA: Harvard University Press, 1987.

Dodd, Lawrence C., and Bruce I. Oppenheimer. *Congress Reconsidered*, 5th ed. Washington, DC: CQ Press, 1993.

Fenno, Richard F., Jr. *Congressmen in Committees*. Boston: Little, Brown, 1973.

———*Home Style: House Members in Their Districts*. Boston: Little, Brown, 1978.

Fox, Harrison W., and Susan Webb Hammond. *Congressional Staffs: The Invisible Force in American Lawmaking*. New York: Free Press, 1977.

Hinckley, Barbara. *Coalitions and Politics*. San Diego: Harcourt Brace Jovanovich, 1981.

Jones, Rochelle, and Peter Woll. *The Private World of Congress*. New York: Free Press, 1979.

Loomis, Burdett A. *The American Politician*. New York: Basic Books, 1988.

Mayhew, David R. *Congress: The Electoral Connection*. New Haven, CT: Yale University Press, 1974.

Sabato, Larry J. *PAC Power*. New York: Norton, 1984.

Sinclair, Barbara, *The Transformation of the U.S. Senate*. Baltimore: Johns Hopkins University Press, 1989.

Smith, Hedrick. *The Power Game*. New York: Ballantine Books, 1989.

CHAPTER 7

The Presidency

THE ROOTS OF THE OFFICE OF PRESIDENT OF THE UNITED STATES

THE FRAMERS AND THE CREATION OF THE PRESIDENCY

THE CONSTITUTIONAL POWERS OF THE PRESIDENT

THE DEVELOPMENT OF PRESIDENTIAL POWER

THE PRESIDENTIAL ESTABLISHMENT

TOWARD REFORM

*I*n 1787, when Alexander Hamilton penned *Federalist No. 70,* he was expressing the views of the majority of the Framers who saw a need for a chief executive, but feared putting significant powers into the hands of any one individual. Under the Articles of Confederation, there had been no executive branch of government, and the eighteen men who served as the "president" of the Continental Congress of the United States of America were president in name only—they had no actual authority or power in the new nation. Yet, since the Framers were sure that George Washington, who had led the new nation as its general during the Revolutionary War, would become the first president of the new nation, many of their deepest fears were calmed. They agreed upon the necessity of having one individual speak on behalf of the new nation, and they all agreed that that one individual should be George Washington.

Though the Framers agreed nearly unanimously about the need for a strong central government and a greatly empowered Congress, they did not agree about the proper role of the president or the sweep of his authority. In contrast to Article I's laundry list of provisions for authority of the legislative branch, Article II details few presidential powers. Distrust of a powerful chief executive led to the Constitution's intentionally vague prescriptions for the presidency.

It is highly unlikely that the Framers—even Alexander Hamilton, probably the greatest supporter of a strong chief executive—ever envisioned the growth in executive power that has occurred over the years. Just think of the differences in governance faced by two Georges—Washington and Bush. George Washington supervised the nation from a temporary headquarters with a staff of but one aide—his nephew, paid out of Washington's own funds—and only four Cabinet members. In contrast, when George Bush left office in 1993, he had presided over a White House staff of 461, a Cabinet of fourteen members, and an executive branch of government that employed

201

> I t were doubtless to be wished that the power of Prohibiting the transportation of slaves had not been postponed. . . . Energy in the Executive is a leading character in the definition of good government. It is essential to the protection of the community against foreign attacks; it is not less essential to the steady administration of the laws.
>
> *Alexander Hamilton*
> *Federalist No. 70*

Hamilton and other Federalists believed that a chief executive was critical to the proper functioning of a strong national government. While aware of the excesses of those who "aspired to tyranny," Hamilton argued that the Constitution protected against excess while recognizing the importance of a vigorous president.

more than 3 million people. Both presidents faced staggering federal budget deficits, but what was considered staggering in Washington's day pales in comparison with the national deficit of nearly $3 trillion the year George Bush left office.

The changes in the size of government and in public expectations about government, especially about the role of the president in our political system, were not foreseen by the Framers. In fact, as the president has been brought closer to the people through democratization, expansion of the electorate, and technological change—from Franklin D. Roosevelt's "Fireside Chats" to Bill Clinton's unprecedented use of Town Hall meetings to bring his programs (and himself) directly to the public—the president's formal powers have often been inadequate to allow him to deliver on his promises.

The tension between public expectations and formal powers of the president permeate our discussion of how the presidency has evolved from its humble origins in Article II of the Constitution to its current stature. In particular, we focus on the "modern presidency," which began with the election of Franklin D. Roosevelt in 1932. The term "modern presidency" refers not only to the change in expectations about the role of the president in national affairs, but also to the growth of what some term the presidential establishment. This includes a large staff, Cabinet positions, and an executive bureaucracy that has grown to help the president meet expectations about his role in the policy process.

The Roots of the Office of President of the United States

The earliest form of executive power in the colonies was the position of royal governor. A royal governor was appointed by the king of England to govern a colony and was normally entrusted with the "powers of appointment, military command, expenditure, and—within limitations—pardon, as well as with large powers in connection with the powers of law making."[1] Royal governors often found themselves at odds with the colonists and especially with the elected colonial legislatures. As representa-

Presidents Clinton, Bush, Reagan, Carter and Ford stand with their wives in order of their presidencies at the grave side ceremony of Richard Nixon in 1994.

tives of the Crown, the governors were distrusted and disdained by the people, many of whom had fled from Great Britain to escape royal domination, and others who, after generations removed from England, no longer felt strong ties to the King.

When the colonists declared their independence from England in 1776, their distrust of a strong chief executive remained. Most state constitutions reduced the office of governor to a symbolic post, whose holder was elected annually by the legislature. Governors were stripped of most rights we assume essential today, including the rights to call the legislature into session and to veto its acts. The constitution adopted by Virginia in 1776 illustrates prevailing colonial sentiment. It cautioned that "the executive powers of government" were to be exercised "according to the laws" of the state, and that no powers could be claimed by the governor on the basis of "any law, statute, or custom of England."[2]

Although most of the states opted for a more "symbolic" governor, some states did entrust wider powers to their chief executives. The governor of New York, for example, was elected directly by the people. And, perhaps *because* he was directly accountable to the people, he was given the power to pardon, the duty to execute the law faithfully to the best of his ability, and to act as commander-in-chief of the state militia.

The Framers and the Creation of the Presidency

As we saw in Chapter 2, the delegates to the Philadelphia Convention quickly decided to dispense with the Articles of Confederation and fashion a new government composed of three branches—the legislative (to make the laws), the executive (to execute, or implement, the laws), and the judicial (to interpret the laws).

The Framers had little difficulty in agreeing that executive authority should be vested in one person, although some delegates suggested multiple executives to diffuse the power of the executive branch. The Framers also had no problem in agreeing

At the 1968 Democratic National Convention, Julian Bond of Georgia's name was placed in nomination for the vice presidency. Bond was forced to decline the honor because he was only twenty-eight; the Constitution requires that the vice president be at least thirty-five years of age.

on a title for the new office. Borrowing from the constitutions of Pennsylvania, Delaware, New Jersey, and New Hampshire, the Framers called the new chief executive the "president." How and by whom the president was to be chosen was a major stumbling block. The Virginia delegation proposed a "Virginia Plan" which called for a single national executive, elected by the national legislature, who would be ineligible for a second term. Reflecting the limited powers given to the Virginia governor by the state constitution, Virginia's delegates proposed an executive strictly accountable to the legislature.

In contrast, James Wilson of Philadelphia suggested a single, more powerful president who would be elected by the people and would be "independent of the legislature." Wilson also suggested giving the executive an absolute veto over the acts of Congress. "Without such a defense," he wrote, "the legislature can at any moment sink it [the executive] into non-existence."[3]

The manner of the president's election haunted the Framers, and their solution to the dilemma is described in detail in Chapter 12. We leave that issue aside for now and turn instead to details of the issues the Framers resolved quickly.

Qualifications for Office

The Constitution requires that the president (and the vice president, whose major function is to succeed the president in the event of his death or disability) be a natural-born citizen of the United States, at least thirty-five years old, and a resident of the United States for at least fourteen years. In the 1700s it was not uncommon for those engaged in international diplomacy to be out of the country for substantial periods of time. Thus, the Framers wanted to make sure that prospective presidents spent some time in this country before running for its highest elective office.

Term of Office

Initially, the length of the executive's term of office was the subject of considerable controversy. Not surprisingly, the issue of term length quickly became associated with eligibility to seek reelection. From the beginning, it was clear that if the delegates agreed to allow the *state* legislatures to choose the president, then shorter terms with the possibility of reelection would be favored. If they agreed to allow the national legislature to select the president, there would be no possibility for reelection. After the Framers of the Constitution reached agreement on the selection process (see Chapter 12), the delegates in favor of a reelection option prevailed, and a four-year term with eligibility for reelection was added to the proposed Article II of the Constitution.

The first president, George Washington (1789–1797), sought reelection only once, and a two-term limit for presidents became traditional. Although Ulysses S. Grant unsuccessfully sought a third term, the two terms established by Washington remained the standard for 150 years, avoiding the Framers' much-feared "constitutional monarch," a perpetually reelected tyrant. In the 1930s and 1940s, however, Franklin D. Roosevelt ran successfully in four elections as Americans fought first the Great Depression and then World War II. Despite Roosevelt's popularity, negative reaction to his long tenure in office ultimately led to passage (and ratification in 1951) of the Twenty-Second Amendment, which limits presidents to two four-year terms or a total of ten years in office, should a vice president assume a portion of a president's remaining term.

Removal

During the Constitutional Convention, Benjamin Franklin, a staunch supporter of impeachment, a process for removing an official from office, noted that "historically, the lack of power to impeach had necessitated recourse to assassination."[4] Not surprisingly, he urged the rest of the delegates to formulate a legal mechanism for removing the president and vice president.

Just as the presidential veto power was a check on Congress, the impeachment provision ultimately included in Article II was adopted as a check on the power of the president (as well as the judiciary). Each house of Congress was given a role to play to assure that the chief executive could be removed only for "Treason, Bribery, or other high Crimes and Misdemeanors."

The Constitution gives the House of Representatives the power to conduct a thorough investigation to determine (in a manner similar to a grand jury proceeding) whether the president had engaged in any impeachable offenses (see Chapter 4). If the finding is affirmative, the House is empowered to vote to impeach the president by a simple majority. The precise charges against the president are called **articles of impeachment**, which are similar to a grand jury indictment. The Senate then acts as a court of law and tries the president for the charged offenses. The Chief Justice of the United States Supreme Court presides over the vote on the articles and the Senate hearing. A two-thirds majority vote in the Senate on any count contained in the articles of impeachment is necessary to remove the president from office. As noted in Chapter 6, only one president, Andrew Johnson in 1868, has ever been impeached, but the Senate vote fell one vote short of forcing his removal.

Articles of impeachment Precise charges against a president, vice president, or other "civil officers" that are approved by the House of Representatives as a first step to that individual's removal from office.

Succession

Through 1994, eight presidents have died in office, through illness or assassination. William Henry Harrison was the first president to die in office—he caught a cold at his inauguration in 1841 and died one month later. John Tyler thus became the first vice president to succeed to the presidency. In 1865, Abraham Lincoln became the first president to be assassinated. And in 1974, Richard M. Nixon, facing impeachment and likely conviction, became the first president to resign from office.

Whether the president has died or resigned, the vice president has always taken over the reins of office. The Constitution directs Congress to select a successor if the office of vice president is vacant. To clarify this provision, Congress passed the Presidential Succession Act of 1947, which lists in order those in line (after the vice president) to succeed the president:

1. Speaker of the House of Representatives
2. President pro tempore of the Senate
3. Secretaries of State, Treasury, and Defense, and other Cabinet heads in order of the creation of their department (see p. 232).

The Succession Act has never been used because there has always been a vice president to take over. The Twenty-Fifth Amendment, in fact, was added to the Constitution in 1967 to assure that this will continue to be the case. Should a vacancy occur in the office of vice president, the Twenty-Fifth Amendment directs the president to appoint a new vice president, subject to the approval (by a simple majority) of both houses of Congress. (See also "What Happens If a President Can't Do His Job?," p. 207.)

Watergate Term used to describe the events and scandal resulting from a break-in at the Democratic National Committee headquarters in 1972 (at the Watergate office complex in Washington, DC) and the subsequent cover-up of White House involvement, which led to the eventual resignation of President Richard M. Nixon under the threat of impeachment.

The Twenty-Fifth Amendment has been used twice in its relatively short history. In 1973, President Richard M. Nixon selected the House Minority Leader, Gerald R. Ford, to replace Vice President Spiro T. Agnew, after Agnew resigned in the wake of charges that he had accepted bribes while a local public official in Maryland and while vice president. Less than a year later, when Vice President Ford became the thirty-eighth president after Nixon's resignation after the **Watergate** scandal (see "Watergate and Its Effect on the Presidency," pp. 210–211), he appointed (and the Senate approved) former four-term New York State Governor Nelson A. Rockefeller to the vice presidency. This set up, for the first time in U.S. history, a situation in which neither the president nor the vice president had been elected to those positions.

Formal procedures for succession, removal, and impeachment have no parallels in the British parliamentary system. When the prime minister resigns, dies in office, or loses the confidence of the majority party in Parliament, one of two things can happen: (1) either a new prime minister is named out of the sitting Parliament, again from the majority party, or (2) Parliament is "dissolved" and new elections are held, with a new prime minister emerging from the new Parliament.

The Vice President

The Framers gave little attention to the office of vice president beyond the need to have an immediate official "stand in" for the president. Initially, the vice president's only function was to assume the office of president in the case of the death of the president or some other emergency. After further debate, the delegates made the vice president the presiding officer of the Senate (except in cases of presidential impeachment). They feared that if the Senate's presiding officer were chosen from the Senate itself, one state would be short a representative. The vice president was given the authority to vote only in the event of a tie, however.

With so little authority, the office of vice president was considered until recently a sure place for a public official to disappear into obscurity. When John Adams wrote to his wife, Abigail, about his position as America's first vice president, he said it was "the most insignificant office that was the invention of man . . . or his imagination conceived."[5]

Power and fame generally come only to those vice presidents who become president. Just "one heartbeat away" from the presidency, the vice president serves as a constant reminder of the president's mortality. In part, this situation has given rise to a trend of uneasy relationships between presidents and vice presidents, beginning as early as Adams and Jefferson. As historian Arthur M. Schlesinger, Jr., once noted, "The Vice President has only one serious thing to do: that is, to wait around for the President to die. This is hardly the basis for a cordial and enduring friendship."[6]

In the past, presidents chose their vice presidents largely to "balance"—politically, geographically, or otherwise—the presidential ticket, with little thought given to the possibility of the vice president becoming president. Franklin D. Roosevelt, for example, a liberal New Yorker, selected Garner, a conservative Texan, to be his running mate in 1932. After serving two terms, Garner—who openly disagreed with Roosevelt over many policies, including Roosevelt's Court-packing plan (see Chapter 9) and his decision to seek a third term—unsuccessfully sought the 1940 presidential nomination himself.

In general, presidential candidates since Eisenhower have selected running mates of such a caliber that they might eventually take over the reins of the nation's highest office. Since Jimmy Carter, recent presidents have given their vice presidents more and

President Jimmy Carter confers with Walter F. Mondale, his vice president.

What Happens If a President Can't Do His Job?

♦ ♦ ♦

When the twentieth president, James A. Garfield, was wounded by an assassin's bullet in July 1881, he lingered until mid-September. In 1919, President Woodrow Wilson had what many believed to be a nervous collapse in the summer and a debilitating stroke in the fall that incapacitated him for several months. His wife, Edith Bolling Galt Wilson, refused to admit his advisers to his sickroom, and rumors flew about "the First Lady President," as many suspected it was his wife and not Wilson who was issuing written orders.

A section of the Twenty-Fifth Amendment allows the vice president and a majority of the Cabinet (or some other body determined by Congress) to deem a president unable to fulfill his duties. It sets up a procedure to allow the vice president to become "acting president" if the president is incapacitated. The president can also

Woodrow Wilson with his wife Edith

voluntarily relinquish his power. Following the spirit of the amendment, before he underwent surgery for cancer of the colon in 1985, President Ronald Reagan sent his vice president, George Bush, a letter that made him acting president for eight hours.

more responsibility as well as access to information vital to the country's national security. Thus, the office of vice president has begun to come into its own after years of ridicule and insignificance. Today, it is viewed as a jumping-off point for higher office, and not as a dead-end position, as more and more vice presidents have become president.

How much power a vice president has, however, depends upon how much the president is willing to give him. Although Jimmy Carter, a Southerner, chose Walter F. Mondale, a Northerner, as his running mate in 1976 to balance the ticket, he was also the first president to give his vice president more than ceremonial duties. Mondale—a former senator from Minnesota with Washington connections—became an important adviser to President Carter, who had run for office as a Washington "outsider." Whereas previous vice presidents had tried to make numerous trivial tasks appear significant, Mondale did his best to carve out a new role as an adviser to the president, an activity encouraged by Carter. The "Mondale model" of an active vice president set the expectations for what the influence, powers, and limitations of modern vice presidents should be.

President Clinton has expanded on the "Mondale model." Gore and Clinton forged a close working (and apparently personal) relationship when they traveled the country

Gore's Top Ten ❖❖❖

In an appearance on David Letterman's show in September, 1993, Vice President Al Gore Jr. listed the top ten best things about being vice president:

10. Police escort gets you to the movies faster.
9. You know that game tetherball? I played tetherball with the inventor of tetherball.
8. After they sign a bill, there's lots of free pens.
7. If you close your left eye, the seal on the podium reads "President of the United States."
6. I get intellectual property rights to my speeches.
5. Dan Quayle and Gerald Ford are pretty easy to beat during Vice-President's Week on Jeopardy!
4. You don't have to be funny to get invited on the Letterman show.

3. You get to eat all the french fries the president can't get to.
2. You don't have to be a good speller to get the job.
1. Secret Service code name "Buttafuoco."

The usually formal Vice President Gore really loosened up with David Letterman, going so far as to introduce his own "Top Ten" list.

Source: World Wide Pants, Incorporated.

In keeping with and even expanding upon the "Mondale model," President Clinton has attempted to involve Vice President Al Gore Jr. in all aspects of decision making. Gore was at Clinton's side in Little Rock, Arkansas, as Cabinet selections were made and is playing a key role in policy making, especially concerning the environment and bureaucratic waste.

campaigning by bus in 1992. With many more personal characteristics in common than many president/vice president teams (they are both Southerners, young, religious, fathers of teenage girls, and married to strong, independent women, for example), Clinton made sure Gore was at his side when key appointments were made, and the two consult on a daily basis.

The Constitutional Powers of the President

Despite the Framers' faith in George Washington as their intended first president, it took considerable compromise to overcome their continued fear of a king. The specific powers of the executive branch that the Framers agreed upon are enumerated in Article II of the Constitution. Perhaps the most important section of Article II is its first sentence. It provides that "The executive Power shall be vested in a President of the United States of America." Just what the Framers meant by "executive power" was left intentionally vague.

Over the years, the expected limits of these constitutional powers have changed as individual presidents asserted themselves in the political process. Some presidents are powerful and effective; others just limp along in office. Much of the president's authority stems from his position as the symbolic leader of the nation and his ability to wield power. When the president speaks—especially in the area of foreign affairs—he speaks for the whole nation. But the base of all presidential authority is Article II, which outlines only a limited policy-making role for the president. Thus, as administrative head of the executive branch, the president is charged with taking "Care that the

Laws be faithfully executed," but he has no actual power to make Congress enact legislation he supports.

The Appointment Power

To help him enforce the laws passed by Congress, the Constitution authorizes the president to appoint, with the advice and consent of the Senate,

> Ambassadors, other public Ministers and Consuls, judges of the supreme Court, and all other Officers of the United States, whose Appointments are not herein otherwise provided for, and which shall be established by Law. . . .

Joycelyn Elders' appointment as U.S. Surgeon General was controversial from the start. Eventually, continual public outcries over her often controversial positions caused the president to request her resignation.

Today, with the growth of the Executive Office of the President—as well as of the Cabinet, executive agencies, and commissions discussed in Chapter 8—the president has accumulated the authority to make more than 3,000 appointments to his administration (technically more than 75,000, if military officers are included). Although only about half of these appointments are to policy-making positions, this power gives a president considerable influence over policy making. In the context of his ability to make appointments to the federal courts, especially, his influence can be felt far past his term of office. The British prime minister enjoys a similarly broad power of appointment; however, the prime minister does not have to seek the approval of either chamber of the legislature for executive and bureaucratic appointments. This ability to select an executive team without the formal participation of Parliament is one of the many sources of the prime minister's power.

Selecting the "right" people is often one of a president's most important tasks. Presidents must look for a blend of loyalty, competence and integrity. Identifying these qualities in people is a major challenge that every new president faces. And, as every president has learned, appointees who lack any of those characteristics endanger the success of their administration, and many presidents have paid dearly for appointment mistakes.

Once a president sends appointments to the Senate, they are traditionally given great respect—especially those for the Cabinet. It is rare for the Senate to reject a presidential appointment. President Dwight D. Eisenhower's nomination of Lewis L. Strauss to be Secretary of Commerce was rejected by a forty-nine to forty-six vote because of a combination of policy differences and lingering questions about Strauss's integrity. After Eisenhower, it was thirty years before the next Cabinet nominee was rejected. In fact, the Senate's rejection of President Bush's nominee for Secretary of Defense, former Senator John G. Tower (R-Tex.), marked only the eighth time in history that a president's choice for a Cabinet post has been rejected. Tower's nomination was rejected on a vote of fifty-three to forty-seven, because of charges of a potential conflict of interest with defense contractors (for whom he had worked since retiring from the Senate), excessive drinking, and womanizing.

Certain kinds of nominees receive more congressional scrutiny than others. Regulatory commission members, discussed in detail in Chapter 8, are located in the world of politics somewhere between the legislative and executive branches, yet they are appointed by the president. Supreme Court appointees also lie outside the executive branch of government and are increasingly subject to greater senatorial review and public, televised grilling.

Senatorial courtesy, the tradition requiring that a president consult members of the Senate about nominees from their home states, often grants senators of the president's

Watergate and Its Effect on the Presidency
❖ ❖ ❖

Richard M. Nixon, in a recorded conversation from the Oval Office:

> I don't give a —— what happens, I want you to stonewall it, let them plead the Fifth Amendment, cover up or anything else, if it'll save the plan.

Nixon's plan was to get reelected to the presidency by any means necessary. What Nixon did not anticipate was getting caught. On June 17, 1972, five men were arrested during a break-in at the Democratic National Committee's (DNC) headquarters in the Watergate office complex in Washington, D.C. The men were caught with burglary tools, bugging devices, and a stack of $100 bills; their mission was to install listening devices in the phones of the DNC to learn of campaign strategies and information that could be used against the Democratic presidential nominee, who was to be selected the next month at the 1972 Democratic National Convention. Among the burglars was James W. McCord Jr., the security director of the Committee to Re-Elect the President (CREEP). Later, two former White House aides also working on the re-election campaign were arrested for their role in planning the break-in. Immediately after the arrests, the White House and CREEP shredded all documents in their possession that might link the burglars to the White House. Meanwhile, Nixon assured the press that there was no connection between him or his staffers and the burglary.

In 1973, after pleading guilty, McCord wrote to Judge John J. Sirica, who had accepted his plea of guilty, explaining that he and the other Watergate defendants had been pressured to remain silent and that other highly placed public officials were involved, including John N. Mitchell, a close friend of Richard Nixon's, who had resigned from his position as U.S. Attorney General to head CREEP.

Soon thereafter, the director of the FBI resigned after admitting he had destroyed evidence connected to the Watergate case. Ten days later Attorney General Richard Kleindienst and two top presidential aides resigned, and Nixon fired the presidential counselor, John Dean.

In June, Dean testified before the specially impaneled Senate Watergate Committee that Nixon had participated in an attempt to cover up the Watergate affair, that the break-in was part of a larger program of political espionage, and that the president was a party to an attempt to cover that up too. In July, a former White House aide disclosed that the president had secretly tape-recorded all conversations that took place in the Oval Office. The Committee immediately demanded the tapes, but the president refused to turn them over, citing "executive privilege," and continuing to maintain his innocence. The Committee then obtained subpoenas for several of the taped conversations. The White House special prosecutor, Archibald Cox, who had been appointed by Nixon to "investigate" the break-in, also requested the tapes, and refused to accept a White House compromise that would have provided him with a "synopsis" of their content. When Cox refused to back down, the president ordered that he be fired. Both the Attorney General and his deputy refused to carry out the president's order. Cox was finally fired by Solicitor General Robert H. Bork.

Three days later, the House Judiciary Committee announced that it would begin hearing impeachment charges against Nixon. Finally, on October 30, Nixon reluctantly turned over the requested tapes, but two were "missing." Moreover, one contained a "mysterious" 18 1/2-minute gap that the White House claimed was erased accidentally by Nixon's secretary, Rose Mary Woods. (Later analysis of the tape determined that the erasure had been deliberate.) By January 1974, Nixon was still refusing to surrender the additional 500 tapes and documents subpoenaed by the Senate Watergate Committee. As Nixon steadfastly refused to turn over the tapes, the Supreme Court, acknowledging the gravity of the matter, agreed to hear the case immediately.

On July 24, 1974, a unanimous Court ruled in *United States* v. *Nixon* that there was no absolute "executive privilege" that could justify Nixon's refusal to comply with a court order to produce information. Nixon was ordered to turn over the tapes, and within hours the White House agreed to comply. One of the three tapes released revealed that the president had ordered not only a halt to the FBI's investigation of the

Continued

Watergate break-in, but also a subsequent coverup to prevent the discovery that his campaign was involved. This was the "smoking gun" for which congressional investigators had been looking. On July 27, 1974, the House Judiciary Committee approved the first of three articles of impeachment against Nixon. On August 9, Nixon resigned.

One month later, President Gerald R. Ford pardoned Nixon, arguing that this action was necessary to prevent the spectacle of a former president on trial, and that it was time for the nation to turn its attention elsewhere.

Rosemary Woods, Richard Nixon's secretary, in her office.

Watergate made a lasting impact on the presidency. It proved that the system created by the Framers worked: Under threat of certain impeachment and conviction, a president was succeeded in an orderly, nonviolent fashion. Watergate also facilitated the 1976 election of Jimmy Carter, who ran as an "outsider" in opposition to the corrupting influences of Washington. It also spurred many reforms. Ethics laws were tightened up, stricter campaign finance laws were enacted, and a special prosecutor law, allowing for independent investigation of the executive branch, was enacted.

party a virtual veto over appointments to posts in their states. Although this limits the president's discretion in filling state-specific jobs, especially federal district court vacancies, "national" positions provide the opportunity for the president to shape the direction and image of his administration. There are, of course, some traditions—such as the nomination of a Westerner to be Secretary of the Interior—but these are not requirements. The Constitution is silent on the president's authority to remove those subject to senatorial appointment, but the Supreme Court has interpreted the Constitution to allow the president to remove most appointees at will.

The Power to Convene Congress

The Constitution requires the president to inform the Congress periodically on "the State of the Union," and authorizes the president to convene either or both houses of Congress on "extraordinary Occasions." In *Federalist No. 77,* Hamilton justified the latter by noting that because the Senate and the chief executive enjoy concurrent powers to make treaties, "it might often be necessary to call it together with a view to this object, when it would be unnecessary and improper to convene the House of Representatives."

Because Thomas Jefferson spoke with a lisp, he sent a written message to Congress, establishing a tradition that lasted 113 years, until 1913, when Woodrow Wilson became the first president since John Adams to deliver his State of the Union message to Congress in person.

President Clinton meeting with his national security team to discuss the situation in Bosnia.

The British prime minister possesses one power relative to the legislature that the President does not: the power to dissolve Parliament and call new elections. While a Parliament has a maximum life of five years, technically speaking, the prime minister can call an election at any time, which gives the party in power a significant advantage in terms of picking the optimal time—politically and economically—to go to the people. This power contributes to an executive branch that is ascendant over its legislature.

The Power to Make Treaties

The president's power to make treaties with foreign nations is checked by the Constitution's stipulation that all treaties must be approved by at least two-thirds of the members of the Senate. The chief executive can also "receive ambassadors," wording that has been interpreted to allow the president to recognize the very existence of other nations.

Historically, the Senate ratifies about 70 percent of the treaties submitted to it by the president.[7] Only sixteen that have been put to a vote have been rejected, often under highly partisan circumstances. Perhaps the most notable example of the Senate's refusal to ratify a treaty was its defeat of the Treaty of Versailles submitted by President Woodrow Wilson. The Treaty was an agreement among the major nations to end World War I, and it called for, at Wilson's insistence, the creation of a League of Nations—a precursor of the United Nations—to foster continued peace and international disarmament. In struggling to gain international acceptance for the League, Wilson had taken American support for granted. This was a dramatic miscalculation. Isolationists, led by Senator William Jennings Bryan (D-Neb.), opposed U.S. participation in the League on the grounds that the League would place the United States in the center of every major international conflict. Proponents countered that, League or no League, the United States had emerged from World War I as a world power, and that membership in the League would enhance its new role. The vote for ratification was very close, but the isolationists prevailed—the United States stayed out of the League, and Wilson was devastated.

The Senate may also require substantial amendment of a treaty prior to granting its consent. When President Carter proposed the controversial Panama Canal Treaties in 1977, for example, the Senate required that several conditions be ironed out between the Carter and Torrijos administrations before its approval was forthcoming.

Presidents often try to get around the "advise and consent" requirement of treaties by entering into an **executive agreement**, which allows the president to enter into secret and highly sensitive arrangements with foreign nations without congressional approval. Presidents have used these agreements since the days of George Washington, and their use has been upheld by the courts. Although executive agreements are not binding on subsequent administrations, since 1900 they have been used far more frequently than treaties, further cementing the role of the president in foreign affairs.

Executive agreement A secret and highly sensitive arrangement with a foreign nation entered into by the president that does not require the "advise and consent" of Congress.

Veto Power

Another way presidents can affect the policy process is through **veto** power, the authority to reject any congressional legislation. Although Article II gives the president the authority to veto any act of Congress (with the exception of joint resolutions that propose constitutional amendments), Congress was given the authority to override an executive veto by a two-thirds vote in each House. The veto is a powerful policy tool because Congress cannot usually muster enough votes to override it. Thus, in over 200 years there have been approximately 2,500 presidential vetoes and only 100-odd have been overridden (see Figure 7-1).

President Bush was never reluctant to use his veto power and only one of his vetoes was overridden. In contrast, during Bill Clinton's first year in office, he became the first president since James A. Garfield (1881) not to veto any act of Congress.

Veto A constitutional power of the president to send a bill back to Congress with reasons for rejecting it. A two-thirds vote in each house can override a presidential veto.

Commander-in-Chief of the Military

One of the most important executive powers is the president's authority over the military. Article II states that the president is "Commander-in-Chief of the Army and Navy of the United States." The Framers saw this power as consistent with state practices, and since the eighteenth century it has proven to be wide-ranging. While the Constitution specifically grants Congress the authority to declare war, presidents since Abraham Lincoln have used the commander-in-chief clause in conjunction with the chief executive's duty to "take Care that the Laws be faithfully executed" to wage war (and to broaden various powers).

Modern presidents continually clash with Congress over who has the power to commence hostilities. The Vietnam War, in which 58,000 American soldiers were killed and 300,000 wounded, was conducted (at a cost of $150 billion) without a congressional declaration of war. In fact, acknowledging President Johnson's claim to war-making authority, in 1964 Congress passed, with only two dissenting votes, the Gulf of Tonkin Resolution which authorized a massive commitment of U.S. forces in South Vietnam.

George Washington enjoyed dressing in full military regalia as commander-in-chief.

FIGURE 7-1

Presidential Vetoes,
1789–1994

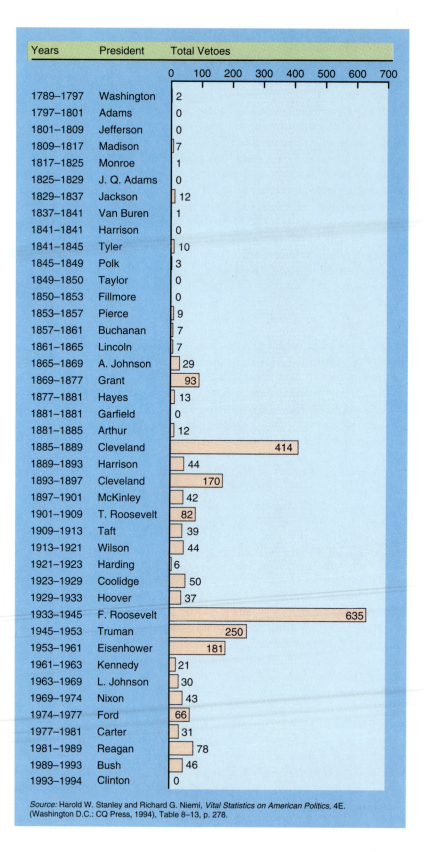

Years	President	Total Vetoes
1789–1797	Washington	2
1797–1801	Adams	0
1801–1809	Jefferson	0
1809–1817	Madison	7
1817–1825	Monroe	1
1825–1829	J. Q. Adams	0
1829–1837	Jackson	12
1837–1841	Van Buren	1
1841–1841	Harrison	0
1841–1845	Tyler	10
1845–1849	Polk	3
1849–1850	Taylor	0
1850–1853	Fillmore	0
1853–1857	Pierce	9
1857–1861	Buchanan	7
1861–1865	Lincoln	7
1865–1869	A. Johnson	29
1869–1877	Grant	93
1877–1881	Hayes	13
1881–1881	Garfield	0
1881–1885	Arthur	12
1885–1889	Cleveland	414
1889–1893	Harrison	44
1893–1897	Cleveland	170
1897–1901	McKinley	42
1901–1909	T. Roosevelt	82
1909–1913	Taft	39
1913–1921	Wilson	44
1921–1923	Harding	6
1923–1929	Coolidge	50
1929–1933	Hoover	37
1933–1945	F. Roosevelt	635
1945–1953	Truman	250
1953–1961	Eisenhower	181
1961–1963	Kennedy	21
1963–1969	L. Johnson	30
1969–1974	Nixon	43
1974–1977	Ford	66
1977–1981	Carter	31
1981–1989	Reagan	78
1989–1993	Bush	46
1993–1994	Clinton	0

Source: Harold W. Stanley and Richard G. Niemi, *Vital Statistics on American Politics,* 4E. (Washington D.C.: CQ Press, 1994), Table 8–13, p. 278.

During that highly controversial war, Presidents Johnson and Nixon routinely assured members of Congress that victory was near. In 1971, however, publication of the Pentagon Papers revealed what many had suspected all along—Lyndon Johnson had systematically altered casualty figures and distorted key facts to place the conduct of the war in a more positive light. In 1973, Congress passed the War Powers Act, limiting the president's authority to introduce American troops into foreign nations without congressional approval (as noted in Chapter 6). President Nixon's veto of the Act was overridden by a two-thirds majority in both houses of Congress.

President Bill Clinton, already the object of derision from many members of the military because of the questions surrounding his failure to fight in the Vietnam War, faced a strong test of his commander-in-chief abilities when he proposed that discrimination against gays in the military be ended.

The Pardoning Power

Presidents can exercise a check on judicial power through their constitutional authority to grant reprieves or pardons. A **pardon,** which restores all rights and privileges of citizenship, is usually granted to a specific individual convicted of a crime. In 1974, President Gerald R. Ford granted the most famous presidential pardon, to former President Richard M. Nixon, who had not been formally charged with any crime, "for any offenses against the United States, which he, Richard M. Nixon, has committed or may have committed while in office." (See "Watergate and Its Effects on the Presidency," pp. 210–211.) This unilateral pardon unleashed a torrent of public criticism that many blame for Ford's ultimate defeat in his 1976 bid for the presidency.

Pardon The restoration of all rights and privileges of citizenship to a specific individual convicted of a crime.

In the waning days of his term, George Bush was showered with a torrent of criticism when he pardoned former Secretary of Defense Caspar Weinberger and five other administration officials on Christmas Eve, 1993 for their conduct related to the Iran–Contra affair. Bush tried to place his pardons in the context of the historic use of the pardoning power to "put bitterness behind us and to look to the future." Said Bush:

> This healing tradition reaches at least from James Madison's pardon of Lafitte's pirates after the War of 1812, to Andrew Johnson's pardon of soldiers who had fought for the Confederacy, to Harry Truman's and Jimmy Carter's pardons of those who violated the Selective Service laws in World War II and Vietnam.[8]

Even though pardons are usually directed toward specific individuals, presidents historically have used their pardoning power to offer general amnesties. Presidents Washington, John Adams, Madison, Lincoln, Andrew Johnson, Theodore Roosevelt, and Carter all used general pardons to grant amnesty to large groups of individuals for illegal acts. Carter, for example, incurred the wrath of many veterans' groups when he made an offer of unconditional amnesty to approximately 10,000 men who had fled the United States or gone into hiding to avoid being drafted to serve in the Vietnam War.

The Development of Presidential Power

Each of the forty-one men who has served as president of the United States has brought with him some expectation of presidential authority.

Commander-in-chief: President Bush
and his wife Barbara with troops in the
Persian Gulf.

Chief law enforcer: National Guard troops
sent by President Eisenhower enforce
federal court decisions ordering the integration of public schools in Little Rock,
Arkansas.

Leader of the party: Presidential
candidate Bill Clinton accepts the
Democratic Party's nomination for
president at the party's 1992
convention.

The President's Many Hats

Shaper of domestic policy: President
Lyndon B. Johnson conferring with the
Reverend Martin Luther King, Jr. and
other black leaders about Johnson's War
on Poverty.

Key player in the legislative process:
Clinton confers with Republican leaders
to promote bipartisanship.

Chief of State: President Kennedy and
his wife, Jacqueline, are greeted by the
President of France and his wife during
the Kennedys' widely publicized 1961
trip to that nation.

Said John F. Kennedy in his Inaugural Address:

The President . . . is rightly described as a man of extraordinary powers, yet it is also true that he must wield these powers under extraordinary limitations. . . . Every president must endure a gap between what he would like and what is possible.[9]

Less optimistically, after serving two terms, Harry S Truman mused about what surprises awaited his successor, Dwight D. Eisenhower, a former general: "He'll sit here and he'll say, 'Do this! Do that!' *And nothing will happen.* Poor Ike—it won't be a bit like the army. He'll find it very frustrating."[10] Like Truman, political scientist Richard E. Neustadt notes that presidents have been limited in their ability to turn the formal powers of the presidency into effective policy making. The tension that limitation produces puts them in a position that Neustadt likens to that of "a cat on a hot tin roof."

A president's personal expectation of authority (and the public's expectations of him) are limited by the formal powers bestowed on the president by the Constitution and by the Supreme Court's interpretation of those constitutional provisions. These formal checks on presidential power are also affected by the times in which the president serves, and by the president's personality. The postwar era of good feelings and economic prosperity presided over in the 1950s by the grandfatherly war hero Dwight Eisenhower, for instance, called for a very different kind of leader from that needed by the Civil War-torn nation governed by Abraham Lincoln.

The presidency that we see today is quite different from the office assumed by George Washington in 1789. According to Benjamin I. Page and Mark P. Petracca, two main trends are responsible for the office's evolution:[11]

1. Democratization of the office, which has brought the president closer to the people. As the presidency has been brought closer to the people, however, people have expected more of their presidents, so presidential actions often fall short of public expectations. These expectations have contributed to the second trend, namely:
2. The phenomenal growth in presidential responsibilities and the need for the president to delegate authority. And, because modern presidents often realize how difficult it is to deliver on their promises, many have responded by trying to centralize authority and responsibility in the White House, where their control is greatest.[12]

The First Three Presidents

Each of the first three presidents—George Washington, John Adams, and Thomas Jefferson—contributed significantly to the development of the office of chief executive, although in different ways. When George Washington was sworn in as the first president of the United States, he took over an office and government that were really yet to be created. Eventually a few hundred postal workers were hired, and Washington appointed a small group of Cabinet advisers and clerks. During Washington's two terms, the entire federal budget was only about $40 million, or approximately $10 for every citizen. In contrast, in fiscal 1995 the federal budget was about $1.5 trillion, or about $6,000 for every man, woman, and child.

As the first president, Washington set several important precedents for future presidents:

- He took every opportunity to establish the primacy of the national government. For example, when John Hancock, the governor of Massachusetts, came to New York City, Washington insisted that Hancock call upon *him* rather than the other way around. For two days, Washington played an uncomfortable waiting game, but his patience and insistence paid off when the governor finally came to pay his respects. In 1794, Washington's use of the militia of four states to put down the Whiskey Rebellion, an uprising of 3,000 Western Pennsylvania farmers opposed to the payment of federal excise tax on liquor, also helped establish the idea of federal supremacy and the authority of the executive branch to collect the taxes levied by Congress.

- Washington began the practice of regular meetings with his advisers (called the Cabinet), thus establishing the Cabinet system, the popular name for the meeting of the executive departments.

- He asserted the prominence of the role of the chief executive in the conduct of foreign affairs. He sent envoys to negotiate the Jay Treaty with Great Britain. Then, over senatorial objection, he continued to assert his authority to negotiate treaties first, and then simply submit them to the Senate for its approval. Washington made it clear that the Senate's function was limited to approval of treaties and did *not* include negotiation with foreign powers.

Inherent power Power of the president that can be derived from inferences in the Constitution.

- He claimed the **inherent power** of the presidency as the basis for proclaiming a policy of strict neutrality when the British and French were at war. Although the Constitution

PEOPLE OF THE PAST

George Washington

On April 30, 1789, thirteen guns sounded in New York City to signal the inaugural day of the first president of the United States, George Washington. Around noon, a delegation from Congress arrived to escort Washington, who greeted them in powdered hair, a brown suit, and silk stockings. They went in a carriage drawn by four horses amidst a cheering crowd to the steps of Federal Hall in New York City. After his swearing in, Washington went to church to offer up a prayer, and then went home for dinner.

George Washington's heritage is a part of our daily lives. His name is that of the nation's capital and its forty-second state, and his portrait appears on the nation's basic unit of currency, the dollar bill.

Unlike some presidents to follow him, Washington reveled in the dignity of the office. He rode in a carriage drawn by six cream-colored horses, or alone on a white steed with a saddle trimmed in gold. His house had fourteen white servants and seven slaves to help with elaborate dinners. And his birthday was a day of celebration in many towns across the new nation as it had been since the Revolutionary War. "Even Cincinnatus received no adulations of this kind," the *National*

Gazette observed. "Surely the office [the President] enjoys is a sufficient testimony of the people's favor, without worshipping him likewise."

Washington's appreciation of regality was also evident in his tours through the new nation. From October to November 1789, he traveled through New England in a hired coach, accompanied by his aide, his private secretary, six servants, nine horses, and a luggage wagon.

During Washington's administration, a string of measures was pushed through Congress to make the new nation stronger. A national currency was instituted, the Bank of the United States was established, manufacturing and trade were fostered by tariffs and bounties, and inventions were protected by patent and copyright laws. While the United States reorganized the armed forces and built new fortifications in the East and West, national security was preserved by a neutrality proclamation in regard to an ever-widening European war between France and Great Britain. In fact, in his Farewell Address, Washington warned against any entangling alliances, noting that it should be "our true policy to steer clear of permanent alliances with any portion of the foreign world."

is silent about a president's authority to declare neutrality, Washington's supporters argued that the Constitution granted the president inherent powers, that is, powers that can be derived or inferred from what is formally described in the Constitution. Thus, they argued that the president's power to conduct diplomatic relations could be inferred from the Constitution. And since neither Congress nor the Supreme Court disagreed, this power was added to the list of presidential powers that other presidents consider to be theirs.

The next two presidents, John Adams and Thomas Jefferson, also acted in ways critical to the development of the office of the chief executive, especially the president's role in the political system. Adams's poor leadership skills, for example, heightened the divisions between Federalists and Anti-Federalists, and probably quickened the development of political parties (see Chapter 11). Soon thereafter, Jefferson used the party system to cement strong ties with the Congress and thereby expand the role of the president in the legislative process.

Congressional Triumph: 1804–1933

The first three presidents made enormous contributions to the office of the chief executive and established important precedents to guide the conduct of those who came after them. But the very nature of the way government had to function in its formative years caused the balance of power to be heavily weighted in favor of a strong Congress. Americans routinely had intimate contacts with their representatives in Congress, while to most, the president seemed a remote figure.

By the end of Jefferson's first term, it seemed clear that the Framers' initial fear of an all-powerful, monarchical president was unfounded. The strong Congress and the

Andrew Jackson, widely hailed as the "People's President," threw open the White House to celebrate his inauguration. In 1993, the Clintons followed his lead.

relatively weak presidents who came after Jefferson allowed Congress quickly to assert itself as the most powerful branch of government. In fact, with but two exceptions—Andrew Jackson and Abraham Lincoln—most presidents from Jefferson to Franklin D. Roosevelt failed to exercise the powers of the presidency in any significant manner.

Exception to the Rule, No. 1: Jackson. Andrew Jackson was the first president truly to act as a strong *national* leader. By the time Jackson ran for president in 1828, eleven new states had been added to the Union, and the number of white males eligible to vote had increased dramatically as property requirements for voting were removed by nearly all states. When Jackson, a Tennessean, was elected the seventh president, it signalled the end of an era; he was the first president not to be either a Virginian or an Adams. His election launched "Jacksonian democracy," a label that embodied the Western, frontier, egalitarian spirit personified by Jackson, the first "common man" to be elected president. The masses loved him, and legends were built around his down-to-earth image. Jackson, for example, once was asked to give a postmastership to a soldier who had lost his leg on the battlefield and needed the job to support his family. Although he was also told that the man hadn't voted for him, Jackson responded: "If he lost his leg fighting for his country, that is vote enough for me."[13]

Jackson used his image and personal power to buttress the developing party system. For example, he rewarded loyal followers of his Democratic Party with presidential appointments. And, frequently finding himself at odds with Congress, Jackson also made extensive use of the veto power. His vetoes of twelve bills surpassed the combined total of nine vetoes used by his six predecessors. Jackson also reasserted the supremacy of the national government (and the presidency) by facing down South Carolina's nullification of a federal tariff law.

Exception to the Rule, No. 2: Lincoln. Abraham Lincoln's approach to the presidency was similar to Jackson's. Moreover, the unprecedented emergency of the Civil War allowed Lincoln to assume powers that no president before him had claimed. Lincoln believed that he needed to move quickly for the very survival of the Union. Thus, he frequently acted without first obtaining the approval of Congress. Among many of Lincoln's "questionable" acts were:

- The suspension of the writ of *habeas corpus* (which allows those in prison to petition to be released), citing the need to jail persons even suspected of disloyal practices (see Chapter 4).
- The expansion of the size of the U.S. army above congressionally mandated ceilings.
- The institution of a blockade of Southern ports, in effect initiating a war without the approval of Congress.
- Closing the mails to treasonable correspondence.

Lincoln argued that the inherent powers of his office allowed him to circumvent the Constitution in a time of war or national crisis. Since the Constitution conferred upon the president the duty to make sure that the laws of the United States are faithfully executed, reasoned Lincoln, the acts enumerated above were constitutional. He simply refused to allow the nation to crumble because of what he viewed as technical requirements of the Constitution. Noting the secession of the Southern states and their threat to the sanctity of the Union, Lincoln queried, "Are all of the laws *but one* to go unexecuted, and the Government itself go to pieces lest that one be violated?"[14]

Few presidents other than Jackson and Lincoln subscribed to a broad and expansive interpretation of executive power prior to the administration of Franklin D. Roosevelt (1933–1945). Neither Jackson nor Lincoln was succeeded by strong presidents; the nation was possibly just not ready to submit to a series of powerful leaders.

The Growth of the Modern Presidency

Before the days of instantaneous communication, the nation could afford to allow the relatively slow deliberative processes of Congress to make most decisions. And it was Congress, not the president, that was closest to the people. But as times and especially technology have changed, the public now personalizes the presidency and has high expectations of anyone who holds that office. Moreover, as the times have changed, and national and international events are reported with breakneck speed by the electronic media such as the Cable News Network (CNN), the need for one individual to act quickly and decisively on behalf of the entire nation seems clear. Congress is often just too slow to respond to the fast-changing pace of events—especially in foreign affairs.

The need to act quickly appears especially vital in times of crisis, which long have played a key role in the development of presidential authority. Lincoln, for example, one of the most powerful presidents, and as noted in "The Best and the Worst Presidents" (p. 227), generally ranked as the "best" president, governed during the peculiar circumstances of a national civil war. Times of danger to the union required that a strong leader take up the reins of government. In the twentieth century, especially, presidential—as opposed to congressional—decision making has become more and more important. And much of this growth can be traced to the four-term presidency of Franklin D. Roosevelt (FDR), which included several crises, including World War II.

FDR and the Modern Presidency.   FDR took office in 1933 in the midst of a major crisis, the Great Depression. Noting the sorry state of the national economy in his inaugural address, he concluded, "This nation asks for action and action now." To jumpstart the American economy, FDR asked Congress for "broad executive powers to wage a war against the emergency, as great as the power that would be given to me if we were in fact invaded by a foreign foe."[15]

Just as Lincoln had taken bold steps upon his inauguration, Roosevelt also acted quickly. He immediately fashioned a plan for national recovery called the "New Deal." The New Deal was a package of bold and controversial programs designed to invigorate the failing American economy. As part of that plan, Roosevelt

Chicago Historical Society

- Declared a bank holiday to end public runs on the depleted resources of many banks.
- Persuaded Congress to pass broad pieces of legislation providing for emergency relief, public works jobs, regulation of farm production, and improved terms and conditions of work for thousands of workers in a variety of industries.
- Regularized the practice of sending legislative programs from the executive branch to Congress for its approval, instead of merely reacting to congressional proposals.
- Increased the size of the federal bureaucracy from fewer than 600,000 to more than 1 million workers.

Throughout Roosevelt's unprecedented twelve years in office (he was elected to four terms but died shortly after beginning the last one), which saw the nation go from the economic "war" of the Great Depression to the real international conflict of World War II, the institution of the presidency changed profoundly and permanently. All kinds of federal agencies were created to implement New Deal programs, and the executive branch became more and more involved in a wide variety of programs.

Not only did FDR create a new bureaucracy by which to implement his pet programs, he also established a new relationship between the presidency and the people. In his radio addresses—or "fireside chats," as he liked to call them—he spoke directly to the public in a relaxed and informal manner, yet he discussed serious issues. He opened his radio addresses with "My friends . . . ," making it seem as though he were speaking directly to each listener. In response to these chats, Roosevelt began to receive about 4,000 letters per day, in contrast to the 40 per day received by his predecessor, Herbert Hoover. The head of the White House correspondence section remembered that "the mail started coming in by the truckload. They couldn't even get the envelopes open."[16] One letter that found its way to the White House was simply addressed "My Friend, Washington, D.C." Roosevelt "personalized" the presidency—his style was successful, and his innovations became the routine and the expected. To his successors FDR left the "modern presidency," including a burgeoning (many would say bloated) federal bureaucracy (see Chapter 8), an active and usually leading role in foreign policy, and a nationalized executive office, as technology—first radio and then television—brought the president closer to the public than ever before.

The rhetorical and personalized styles of post-FDR presidents are very different from those of their predecessors. George Washington believed that the purpose of public appearances was to "see and be seen," not to discuss policy issues. Today, presidents use every opportunity to sell their programs. Whereas the rhetoric of early presidents was written, formal, and addressed principally to Congress, today oral speeches addressed to the public at large are the norm. Abraham Lincoln was applauded for refusing to speak about the impending Civil War. In contrast, Ronald Reagan was hailed as "the Great Communicator." And Bill Clinton has truly taken the personalized presidency to new levels. Beginning during his campaign, Clinton often appeared on "Larry King LIVE ON CNN." Even after becoming president, Clinton continued to take his case directly to the people. He launched his health care reform proposals, for example, on a prime time edition of Nightline hosted by Ted Koppel.

Clinton is keenly aware of the importance of maintaining his connection with the public. At a black-tie dinner honoring radio and television correspondents, Clinton responded to criticisms levied against him for not holding traditional press conferences by pointing out how clever he was to ignore the traditional press. "You know why I can stiff you on the press conferences? Because Larry King liberated me from you by giving me to the American people directly," quipped Clinton.[17]

The Role of the President in the Legislative Process

When FDR sent his first legislative package to Congress, he broke the traditional model of law making. Said FDR of this new relationship, "It is the duty of the President to propose and it is the privilege of the Congress to dispose."[18] Since FDR, the public has generally looked to the president to formulate concrete legislative plans to propose to Congress.

Although the public looks to the president to set the agenda, "merely placing a program before Congress is not enough," declared President Lyndon B. Johnson. "Without constant attention from the administration, most legislation moves through the congressional process at the speed of a glacier."[19] The president's most important power (and often the source of his greatest frustration) is his ability to construct coalitions to work for passage of his legislation. Frequently, presidents must "deal" with legislators and have "goodies" to trade for votes. Ronald Reagan's first budget director, David Stockman, once stated that "the last 10 or 20 percent of the votes needed for a majority of both houses [on the 1981 tax cut bill] had to be bought, period." Concessions took the form of real estate tax shelters, special breaks for oil lease holders, and loopholes in the corporate income tax. "The hogs were really feeding," said Stockman. "The greed level, the level of opportunism, just got out of control."[20] When asked by the administration if his vote could be bought, one representative from Louisiana retorted, "No, but it can be rented." With votes bought and rented, Reagan ultimately was able to get what he wanted from Congress.

FDR and Lyndon B. Johnson (LBJ) were among the best presidents at "working" Congress, but they were helped by Democratic majorities in both houses of Congress. On the whole, presidents, especially when they preside over what is called a "divided government" (when the presidency and Congress are controlled by different political parties), have a hard time getting Congress to pass their programs.[21] Throughout their terms presidents experience declining support for policies they favor. That's why it is so important for a president to propose key plans early in his administration.

Presidential Involvement in the Budgetary Process. The Framers gave Congress the power of the purse, and through 1930 Congress had primary responsibility for the budget process (see Chapters 6 and 17). The economic disaster set off by the stock market crash of 1929, however, gave FDR the opportunity to assert himself in the congressional budgetary process. In 1939, the Bureau of the Budget, which had been created in 1921 to help the president tell Congress how much money it would take to run the executive branch of government, was made part of the newly created Executive Office of the President. In 1970, President Nixon changed its name to the Office of Management and Budget (OMB) to underline its function in the executive branch.

The OMB works exclusively for the president and employs hundreds of budget and policy experts. OMB reports allow the president to attach price tags to his legislative proposals, and to defend the presidential budget. The OMB budget is a huge document and even those who prepare it have a hard time deciphering all its provisions. While even OMB directors may not know all the details and intricacies of the federal budget, their reputed expertise often gives them an advantage over members of Congress. As a single actor, the president may be able to do more to harness the deficit and impose order on the federal budget and its myriad programs than can the 535 members of Congress, who are torn by several different loyalties.

Winning Support. According to political scientist Thomas E. Cronin, a president has three ways to improve his role as a legislative lobbyist to get his favored programs passed. He can use **patronage** (jobs, grants, or other special favors given to friends and political allies as rewards for support) and personal rewards to win supporters. Invitations to the White House and campaign visits to members of Congress running for office are two such ways to curry favor with legislators. Inattention to key members can prove deadly to a president's legislative program. House Speaker Thomas P. ("Tip") O'Neill reportedly was quite irritated when the Carter team refused his request for extra tickets to Carter's inaugural, getting the president off to a poor start with the powerful Speaker.

A second way a president can bolster support for his legislative package is to call on his party. As the informal leader of his political party, he should be able to use that po-

Patronage Jobs, grants, or other special favors that are given as rewards to friends and political allies for their support.

sition to his advantage in Congress, where party loyalty is very important. This strategy works best when the president has carried members of his party into office on his coattails, as was the case in the Johnson and Reagan landslides of 1964 and 1984.

Party support for the executive's proposals in the legislature is much less problematic in parliamentary systems. For example, since the British prime minister holds office precisely because he or she enjoys the support of the majority party in Parliament, many of the roadblocks that plague legislative–executive relations in the United States do not exist in Britain. But if the president is unpopular, even members of his own party may not jump to his support. After all, if you are a member of the House seeking re-election, the last visitor you want coming to your district is an unpopular president. Thus, a president popular with the folks back home is most likely to get support from a member of Congress, regardless of party affiliation.

The third way a president can influence Congress is through close contact with the American people. By going directly to the public on a particular issue, the president can bring constituent pressures on key members of Congress. This is just what Bill Clinton did to gain support of his health care reform program, for example. The quality and effectiveness of a president's success in the policy making process are often dependent on what is termed "**presidential style**."

Presidential Style

Presidential style A president's ability to get things done; determined by factors such as his character and approach to office, the perception of others of his ability to lead, and his ability to mobilize public opinion to support his actions.

A president's ability to get things done depends on many factors, including his character, his approach to the office, others' perceptions of his ability to lead, and his ability to mobilize public opinion to support his actions. The forty-one men who have held the nation's highest office are a diverse lot. (Bill Clinton is considered the forty-second president because Grover Cleveland served as the twenty-second and twenty-fourth presidents, having been elected to nonconsecutive terms in 1884 and 1892.) Some have been quite unassuming in their approach to the office. James Madison, for example, wore out-of-date knee breeches, silk stockings, and a sword. He met visitors in ink-spotted clothing and worn-down shoes, often looking more like an unkempt clerk than president of the United States.[22] Jimmy Carter also adopted an unassuming approach to the presidency. During the energy crunch of the 1970s he ordered White House thermostats set to a chill 65 degrees and suggested that his advisers wear sweaters to work. Carter often appeared before the nation in cardigan sweaters instead of suits. He tried to build his "common man" image by carrying his own luggage and prohibiting the Marine band from playing the traditional fanfare "Hail to the Chief" to signify his arrival on official occasions.

In contrast, other presidents have been much more attuned to the trappings of office. Many believe that the Kennedys did it best. During their thousand days in the White House, it became a royal palace—"Camelot." John F. Kennedy (JFK) and his family had looks, youth, and wealth, and JFK was a gifted speaker.

Presidential character According to political scientist James David Barber, the patterns of behavior exhibited by presidents based on their energy level and the degree of enjoyment they find in their job.

Presidential Character.   How one approaches the job of president often reflects long-held behaviors. Political scientist James David Barber has suggested that patterns of behavior, many ingrained during childhood, can help explain presidential behavior.[23] Barber believes that there are four **presidential character** types, based on (1) energy level (whether the president is active or passive), and (2) the degree of enjoyment a president finds in his job (whether the president has a positive or negative attitude about what he does). Barber believes that active and positive presidents are more successful than passive and negative presidents. Active-positive presidents generally enjoyed warm and supportive childhood environments and are basically happy individuals open to new life experiences. They approach the presidency with a zest for life and have a drive to lead and succeed. In contrast, passive presidents find themselves reacting to circumstances, and are likely to take direction from others, thus failing to make full use of the enormous resources of the executive office. Table 7.1 classifies presidents from Taft through Bush according to Barber's categories. Where would you place Bill Clinton?

Although Barber's typology can be an amusing way to discuss the men who have served as president, some disagree with his approach and its ability to predict presidential success. Journalist Garry Wills, for example, describes Barber's work as an example of the "games academics play."[24]

The Power to Persuade.   A president is many things to many people: a symbol of the nation, a political organizer, a moral teacher. But to do his job, according to George E. Reedy, a president must be able to accomplish two things: first, resolve policy questions that will not yield to quantitative, empirical analyses; and second, persuade enough of the country that his actions are right that he can carry them out without national strife.[25] Exercising the constitutional powers of the chief executive is not enough; a president's personality and ability to persuade others are key to amassing greater power and authority.

Frequently, the difference between great and mediocre presidents centers on their ability to grasp this fact of political life. Truly "great" presidents, such as Lincoln and Franklin D. Roosevelt, understood that the White House was a seat of power from which decisions could flow to shape the national destiny. They recognized that their day-to-day activities should be designed to bolster support for their policies, and to secure backing that could translate their intuitive judgment into meaningful action. Mediocre presidents, on the other hand, have tended to regard the White House as "a stage for the presentation of performances to the public" or a fitting honor to cap a career.[26]

Younger than any recent president since John F. Kennedy, President Clinton is often kidded about being a "fast food junkie" whose work schedule allows little time for rest. His taste for McDonald's, however, enhanced his image of being in touch with the public.

Table 7.1 ♦	Barber's Presidential Personalities	
	ACTIVE	PASSIVE
Positive	F. D. Roosevelt Truman Kennedy Ford Carter* Bush	Taft Harding Reagan
Negative	Wilson Hoover L. B. Johnson Nixon	Coolidge Eisenhower

*Some scholars think that Carter better fits the active-negative typology.

A president risks his prestige, power, and ability to persuade when he tackles issues that he may not be able to settle. Thus, when President Clinton unsuccessfully attempted to settle the baseball strike in early 1995, some people argued that his personal prestige and the prestige of the office were diminished.

Presidential character and political skills often determine how effectively a president can exercise the broad powers of the modern presidency. Political scientist Richard E. Neustadt has developed a theory of how presidents win, lose, or maintain their personal power and influence. According to Neustadt, "Presidential power is the *power to persuade*,"[27] and the power to persuade comes largely from an individual's ability to bargain. And, according to Neustadt, persuasion is key because constitutional powers alone do not provide modern presidents with the authority to meet rising public expectations.

Truly effective presidents have the ability and power to persuade not only what Neustadt calls "Washingtonians"[28]—members of Congress, interest-group leaders, and media moguls—but also the general public.

FDR and LBJ both had excellent reputations among lawmakers for being able to get their legislative packages through Congress. Presidents Kennedy and Carter had more mixed successes, whereas Richard M. Nixon believed (wrongly) that the power of his office was enough to get recalcitrant legislators to support his programs. He failed to grasp the importance of the need to persuade members of Congress personally of the soundness of legislation he sought.

Public Opinion and the President.   Recognition of the need to persuade the public and the ability to do so are also key elements of a successful presidency. Even before the days of FDR's personal presidency, others reached out to gain public support for their programs. Theodore Roosevelt (1901–1909) referred to the presidency as a "bully pulpit" that he used to try to garner support for progressive programs. Woodrow Wilson took a whistle-stop train tour around the country to try (in vain) to build support for the League of Nations. Not until the development of commercial air travel and television were presidents able to communicate directly with large numbers of people.

Harry S Truman was the first president to address the nation on television, although neither he nor Eisenhower, his successor, used that medium very often. By the 1960s, television and jet transportation were no longer novel. John F. Kennedy, the first real "media darling," made even his press conferences media events as he used his good

President Bush, one of the most physically active presidents in recent history, was an avid fisherman who tired even his younger Secret Service detail with his frenetic schedule.

looks and quick sense of humor to his advantage to drum up public support for his programs.

Political scientist Sam Kernell refers to these kinds of direct, presidential appeals to the electorate as "going public."[29] Going public, in essence, means that a president goes over the heads of members of Congress to gain support from the people, who, in turn, can place pressure on their elected officials in Washington.

Most presidents do all they can to woo public opinion because of its impact on their ability to govern. Nevertheless, "cycles" of popularity have occurred since 1938, when pollsters first began to track presidential popularity. As revealed in Figure 7-2 (p. 228), with the exception of George Bush, the general trend has been toward increasingly lower rates of support for presidents. Many credit this trend to events such as Vietnam, Watergate, the Iran hostage crisis, and the Iran–Contra scandal, which have made the public increasingly skeptical of presidential performance. Even Bush's popularity, however, plummeted as the good feelings from the Gulf war faded and Americans began to feel the pinch of recession.

Bill Clinton used the "town hall meeting" format as an effective tool during his campaign and later as president to mobilize

The Best and the Worst Presidents
♦ ♦ ♦

Who was the best president and who was the worst? Many surveys of scholars have been taken over the years to answer this question, and virtually all have ranked Abraham Lincoln the best and Warren G. Harding the worst. A 1982 Chicago Tribune poll,* for example, came up with these results:

TEN BEST PRESIDENTS	TEN WORST PRESIDENTS
1. Lincoln (best)	1. Harding (worst)
2. Washington	2. Nixon
3. F. Roosevelt	3. Buchanan
4. T. Roosevelt	4. Pierce
5. Jefferson	5. Grant
6. Wilson	6. Fillmore
7. Jackson	7. A. Johnson
8. Truman	8. Coolidge
9. Eisenhower	9. Tyler
10. Polk (10th best)	10. Carter (10th worst)

Lincoln broke all kinds of laws and violated the

*From "Evaluating the Presidents of the United States," by Arthur Murphy, *Presidential Studies Quarterly* 14 (1984): 117–126. Permission granted by the Center for the Study of the Presidency, publisher of *Presidential Studies Quarterly.*

Constitution to keep the nation together in its darkest hour—the Civil War. Had he not succeeded he would undoubtedly be ranked with Harding at the bottom of the heap.

And just who was Harding? In 1923, he said, "This is a hell of a job! I have no trouble with my enemies. I can take care of my enemies all right. But my damn friends, my God-damned friends . . .! [T]hey're the ones who keep me walking the floor nights." Indeed, it *was* Harding's friends who got him into trouble. He was elected in a landslide victory in 1920 not so much because of his popularity, but because of public backlash against World War I and Woodrow Wilson's League of Nations fiasco. When he came to Washington, he brought with him "friends" bent more on enriching themselves than on public service. They found abundant opportunities for corruption, including the sale of property owned by aliens in the aftermath of World War I, the sale of U.S. ships, the enforcement of Prohibition after 1921, outlays for the care of veterans, and the management of oil-rich lands. Eventually, numerous scandals surfaced during Harding's administration. The head of the Veterans' Bureau was forced to resign and was ultimately jailed for corruption. Other scandals were emerging when Harding suddenly died in office in 1923.

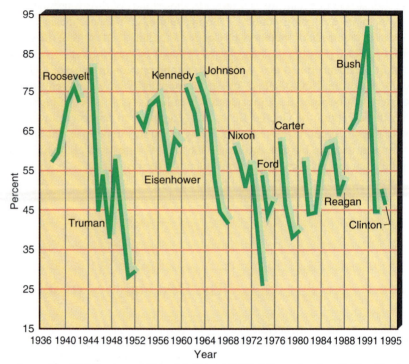

FIGURE 7-2

Presidential Approval Since 1938

Source: Harold W. Stanley and Richard G. Niemi, *Vital Statistics on American Politics*, 4th ed. (Washington D.C.: CQ Press, 1994), Figure 8–1, p. 279, from Gallup Poll data, 1938–1991. 1991–September 1994 data based on USA Today/CNN/Gallup Poll data.

Presidential popularity generally follows a cyclical pattern. Typically, presidents enjoy their highest level of popularity at the beginning of their terms. Presidents try to take advantage of this "honeymoon" period and work hard to get their programs passed by Congress as soon as possible. Each action a president takes, however, is divisive—some people will approve, and others will disapprove. And disapproval tends to have a cumulative effect. Inevitably the honeymoon ends about midway through the term.

Although surges caused by major international events do occur, they generally don't last long. As revealed in Table 7.2, each of the last ten presidents prior to President Clinton experienced at least one "rallying" point based on a foreign event. Rallies lasted an average of ten weeks, with the longest being seven months.[30]

Two presidencies A theory postulated by Aaron Wildavsky that there are two presidencies; in one, a president is a strong leader in foreign affairs, and in the other he is a weak one in the realm of domestic affairs.

Two Presidencies. Even when George Bush enjoyed phenomenally high popularity ratings, most Americans were unhappy with his domestic policies. So was the Democrat-controlled Congress. Presidents generally enjoy far more congressional support for their conduct of foreign affairs than for their handling of domestic and economic matters. Political scientist Aaron B. Wildavsky concluded that America really has **two presidencies**—a strong leader in foreign affairs, and a weak one on the domestic side.[31] For example, even though the congressional vote authorizing President Bush to use force in the Persian Gulf was close and along partisan lines, once the president was given authorization, the often partisan Congress was united in its support of the president. The two presidencies phenomenon observed by Wildavsky may, however, be more the consequence of divided government and its resultant gridlock than of anything inherent in the presidency itself. Republican presidents (such as Eisenhower, Nixon, Reagan, and Bush), who are traditionally more conservative than the Democrats usually in control of Congress, have disagreed with the Congress concerning domestic policies, thus making it difficult for a Republican president to shine in the domestic sphere.

Table 7.2 ◆ Temporary Rises in Presidential Popularity

Gallup poll measurements of the size and duration of the largest increase in each president's approval rating before and after dramatic international events.

PRESIDENT/EVENT	PERCENTAGE POINT INCREASE IN PUBLIC APPROVAL	DURATION OF THE INCREASE IN WEEKS
Franklin D. Roosevelt		
Pearl Harbor	12	30
Harry S Truman		
Truman Doctrine	12	N.A.[a]
South Korea invaded	9	10
Dwight D. Eisenhower		
Bermuda Conference/Atoms for Peace speech	10	20
John F. Kennedy		
Cuban Missile Crisis	13	31
Lyndon B. Johnson		
Speech halting bombing of North Vietnam and withdrawing from 1968 campaign	14	19
Richard M. Nixon		
Vietnam peace agreement	16	15
Gerald R. Ford		
Mayaquez incident	11	25
Jimmy Carter		
Hostages seized in Iran	19	30
Ronald Reagan		
Beirut bombing/Grenada invasion	8	N.A.[b]
First summit with Gorbachev	7	4
George Bush		
Iraqi invasion of Kuwait	14	9
Gulf War begins	18	30

[a] No polls conducted
[b] Overlapping events

Source: The Gallup Poll Monthly, #309 (June 1991), pp. 15–27; *The New York Times* (May 22, 1991): p. A-10. Copyright © 1991 by The New York Times Company. Reprinted by permission.

The Presidential Establishment

As the responsibilities and scope of presidential authority have grown over the years, so has the executive branch of government and the number of people working directly for the president in the White House itself. No longer does the executive branch consist of the small group of men who gathered around George Washington's dining room table to discuss affairs of state. Today a president is surrounded by policy advisers of all types—from the Attorney General, who advises him on legal issues, to the Surgeon General, who advises him on health matters. His personal staff, the vice president, and the Cabinet all help him fulfill his duties as chief executive.

The Cabinet

Although the Framers had discussed the idea of some form of national executive council, they did not include a provision for one in the Constitution. They did, however, recognize the need for departments of government and departmental heads. Consequently, although there is no provision for a cabinet in the Constitution per se, Article II, Section 2, notes that the president "may require the Opinion, in writing, of the Principal Officer in each of the executive Departments, upon any Subject relating to the Duties of their respective Offices. . . ."

Just prior to and immediately after Washington's inauguration on April 30, 1789, he consulted with Hamilton, Madison, and others concerning their views of the powers and duties of the president. Collectively they adopted the position that department heads should be assistants to the president, rather than to Congress. These sentiments led Washington to ask Congress to create three executive departments—one for foreign affairs (State), one for military affairs (War, which was incorporated into the Defense Department in 1947), and one for fiscal matters (Treasury). These three departments closely reflected what these men saw as the major role of the new national government—the conduct of foreign affairs and regulation of a national economy. Washington viewed his advisers as a council of sorts, and frequently called them together. He also established the tradition that Cabinet members' loyalties must be to

The British Cabinet
♦ ♦ ♦

Although it bears the same name, the British Cabinet is quite distinct from its American counterpart. There are some similarities: for example, Cabinet officials in both countries are appointed by their respective chief executives and provide political guidance to the bureaucracy. However, British Cabinet ministers hail exclusively from the legislature (indeed, they retain their seats in Parliament while they serve as executive officers), and they participate in a collective executive decision-making body—the Cabinet—for which there is no counterpart in the United States. As a result, although the prime minister is clearly "first among equals" in the Cabinet, the decisions of the British government are issued formally in the name of the Cabinet, not the prime minister.

THEN AND NOW

First Ladies

From Martha Washington to Hillary Rodham Clinton, First Ladies (a term coined during the Civil War) have made significant contributions to American society. Until recently, the only formal national recognition given to that role was an exhibit of inaugural ball gowns at the Smithsonian Institution. Not any more. Heightened interest—doubtless at least partially attributable to the highly visible role Hillary Rodham Clinton plays in the Clinton administration—has led the Smithsonian to launch an exhibit highlighting the personal accomplishments of First Ladies since Martha Washington. The new exhibit is built around three themes: the political role of the First Ladies, including how they have been portrayed in the media and perceived by the public; their contributions to society, especially their personal causes; and, of course, a display of their gowns.

Although every action and even haircut of Hillary Rodham Clinton is chronicled by the media, she is not the first First Lady to work for or with her husband. Martha Washington followed George to his winter camps. At Valley Forge she helped feed the troops and nursed the wounded.

Abigail Adams was a constant sounding board for her husband, and an early feminist. As early as 1776 she cautioned him to "Remember the Ladies" in any new code of laws.

Edith Bolling Galt Wilson was probably the most powerful First Lady. When Woodrow Wilson collapsed and was left partly paralyzed in 1919, Mrs. Wilson be-came his surrogate as she decided whom and what the stricken president saw. Her detractors dubbed her "Acting First Man."

Eleanor Roosevelt, too, played a powerful and much criticized role in national affairs. Not only did she write a nationally syndicated daily newspaper column, she also traveled and lectured widely. She worked tirelessly on thankless Democratic Party chores while raising six children. After FDR's death she shone in her own right as U.S. delegate to the United Nations, where she headed the commission that drafted the covenant on human rights. Later she headed John F. Kennedy's Commission on the Status of Women until her death.

Rosalyn Carter also took an activist role. Not only did she help with Cabinet chores, she also attended Cabinet meetings (as did Helen Taft).

When Hillary Rodham Clinton is viewed in the light of some strong First Ladies who came before her, her prominent role in the administration is not that surprising. Her role is not so much a radical break with tradition as a logical evolution in a society where women's role is no longer simply that of homemaker. As a former law professor and nationally prominent lawyer and activist, she is continuing much of the work she did as First Lady of Arkansas. Yet, in light of the failure of her national health care plan and continued criticism of her activism, in 1995 she appeared to begin to take on the persona of a more "conventional" First Lady.

the president. After his Secretary of State publicly disagreed with Washington's support of the Jay Treaty, for example, he fired him.

Over the years, the Cabinet has grown as departments have been added to accommodate new pressures on the president to act in more and more areas not initially considered within the national government's scope of concern. As interest groups, in particular, pressured Congress and the president to recognize their demands for services and governmental action, they often were rewarded with the creation of an executive department. And since each was headed by a secretary who automatically became a member of the president's Cabinet, powerful groups including farmers (Agriculture), business persons (Commerce), workers (Labor), and teachers (Education) saw creation of a department as increasing their access to the president. The departments and their responsibilities are detailed in Table 7.3.

From the beginning, Cabinet secretaries have found themselves in the uncomfortable position of having two masters. They serve the president, but must also report to Congress on the activities of their respective departments. The inevitable clash between these two roles first surfaced in 1833. Disliking the National Bank, Andrew Jackson ordered his Secretary of the Treasury to transfer federal funds to another bank. The secretary believed the National Bank to be sound, and Congress had recently voiced its support of the bank in a resolution to that effect. When the secretary refused to comply with Jackson's direct order, he was fired.

Table 7.3 ♦ The U.S. Cabinet

DEPARTMENT	DATE OF CREATION	RESPONSIBILITIES
Department of State	1789	Responsible for making foreign policy, including treaty negotiation
Department of the Treasury	1789	Responsible for government funding and regulation of alcohol, firearms and tobacco
Department of Defense	1789; 1947	Responsible for national defense; created by consolidating the former departments of War, the Army, the Navy, and the Air Force
Department of Justice	1870 (Attorney General's position created in 1789)	Represents U.S. government in all federal courts, investigates and prosecutes violations of federal law
Department of the Interior	1849	Manages the nation's natural resources, including wildlife and public lands
Department of Agriculture	Created in 1862; elevated to Cabinet status in 1889	Assists nation's farmers, oversees food quality programs, administers food stamp and school lunch programs
Department of Commerce	1903	Aids businesses and conducts the U.S. census (originally the Department of Commerce and Labor)
Department of Labor	1913	Runs manpower programs, keeps labor statistics, aids labor through enforcement of laws
Department of Health and Human Services	1953	Runs health, welfare, and Social Security programs; created as the Department of Health, Education, and Welfare (lost its education function in 1979)
Department of Housing and Urban Development	1965	Responsible for urban and housing programs
Department of Transportation	1966	Responsible for mass transportation and highway programs
Department of Energy	1977	Responsible for energy policy and research, including atomic energy
Department of Education	1979	Responsible for the federal government's education programs
Department of Veterans' Affairs	1989	Responsible for programs aiding veterans

The Executive Office of the President

The **Executive Office of the President** (EOP) is actually several offices, a "mini-bureaucracy" located in the ornate Executive Office Building next to the White House on Pennsylvania Avenue. FDR established the EOP in 1939 because he needed someone to oversee his New Deal programs. The EOP has expanded over time to include eight advisory and policy-making agencies responsible to the executive branch. These expert staff units play key roles in advancing the president's policy preferences. Three of the most important agencies are the National Security Council, the Council of Economic Advisors, and the Office of Management and Budget.

The National Security Council (NSC) was established in 1947 to advise the president on American military and foreign policies. The NSC is composed of the president, the vice president, and the Secretaries of State and Defense. The president's national security adviser runs the staff of the NSC, coordinates information and options, and advises the president (see Chapter 19).

The Council of Economic Advisors (CEA) consists of three economic experts appointed by the president, subject to Senate confirmation, plus a small staff evenly divided between support personnel and professional economists. The CEA prepares the *Annual Report of the Council of Economic Advisors* and advises the president on economic policy. Through constant analysis of the economy and economic trends, the CEA attempts to anticipate rather than react to economic events.

As we mentioned earlier, the Office of Management and Budget (OMB) was created in 1970 as a replacement for the Bureau of the Budget (created in 1921). While the CEA's major concern is with controlling the business cycle and achieving national economic growth, the OMB's major focus is on preparing the president's annual budget proposal, designing the president's program, and reviewing the progress, budget, and program proposals of the executive department agencies. It also supplies economic forecasts to the president and conducts detailed analyses of proposed bills and agency rules.

Although the president appoints the members of these bodies, they must still perform their tasks in accordance with congressional legislation. Thus, like the Cabinet, depending on who serves in key positions, these mini-agencies may not be truly responsible to the president.

White House Staff

George Washington's closest confidants were Alexander Hamilton and Thomas Jefferson—both Cabinet secretaries—but this has often not been the case with modern presidents. As the size and complexity of the government grew, Cabinet secretaries had to preside over their own ever-burgeoning staffs, and presidents increasingly looked to a different inner circle of informal advisers. By the 1830s, Andrew Jackson had chosen to rely on his own inner circle, nicknamed his "Kitchen Cabinet," instead of his department heads, to advise him. So too, FDR surrounded himself with New York political operatives and his more intellectual "brain trust;" Jimmy Carter brought several Georgians to the White House with him; and Ronald Reagan initially surrounded himself with fellow Californians—Edwin Meese III, William French Smith (the Attorney General), and Michael Deaver. Bill Clinton initially followed suit by appointing two of his best friends—Thomas "Mack" McLarty and Vincent Foster[32]—to important White House positions. Several other White House advisers, including George Stephanopoulos, played key roles in Clinton's campaign.

President Clinton's first Secretary of Housing and Urban Development Henry Cisneros inspects damage done by the Los Angeles earthquake.

Executive Office of the President
Establishment created in 1939 to help the president oversee the bureaucracy.

Loyalty is often the strong suit of presidential aides. Richard M. Nixon's first chief of staff, H.R. Haldeman, for example, believed it was his role to "take the heat" for any presidential gaffes. According to him, "Every president needs a son of a bitch and I'm Nixon's. I get what he wants done and I take the heat instead of him."[33] This loyalty led President Nixon to consider Haldeman his alter ego.

Although each president organizes his staff in different ways, presidents typically have a chief of staff. Other key White House aides include those who help plan domestic policy, maintain relations with Congress and interest groups, deal with the media, provide economic expertise, and execute political strategies. Presidents also typically have a national security adviser (who runs the NSC) who provides them with daily briefings on international affairs. During the Persian Gulf war, for example, National Security Adviser Brent Scowcroft played an important role in advising President Bush. Too many advisers, however, can lead to confusion over policies. When several American soldiers, for example, were killed in Somalia in late 1993, initial press reports noted that the Secretaries of State and Defense, and National Security Adviser Anthony Lake all appeared unclear about who was running the show.

As presidents have tried to consolidate power in the White House and as demands on the president have grown, so has the size of the White House staff—from 51 in 1943, to 247 in 1953, to a high of 583 in 1972. Since that time, staffs have been trimmed, generally running in the 400-person range. During his campaign for the presidency, Bill Clinton promised to cut the size of the White House staff and the Executive Office. As revealed in Table 7.4, he reduced the size of his staff by approximately 25 percent.

White House office space is limited, so many staffers are relegated to the old Executive Office Building next door. In spite of small offices, most prefer to be located in the White House (see Figure 7-3, p. 236). In Washington, the size of the office is not the measure of power it often is in corporations. Instead, power in the White House goes to those who have the president's ear and the offices closest to the Oval Office.

Toward Reform

The presidency is a peculiar institution. Only forty-one men have held the position, and each has been different in style and temperament. Some have been brilliant; others have not. Some have appeared to thrive in office; others have labored under the strain. Several have broken laws for different reasons and to very different fates: Lincoln earned a place in history as one of the greats; Richard M. Nixon resigned to avoid impeachment.

Over the years, various reforms have been proposed to "improve" the presidency, but the consensus appears to be that as an institution it works fairly well. Most serious calls for reform have not been concerned with the Framers' chief fear—a too-powerful president. Instead they have centered on giving the president greater power.

The Two-Term Limitation

Ever since passage of the Twenty-Second Amendment, some have argued against the two-term limit, believing it, too, to be "undemocratic." After all, if a president is enjoying the support of the people and doing a good job, why shouldn't he be allowed to

Table 7.4 ◆ Comparisons of Bush and Clinton Staffs		
	BUSH STAFF	CLINTON STAFF
Office of the President	461	419
Executive Residence	95	89
Office of the Vice President	49	35
National Security Council	179	147
Policy Development	58	*
National Economic Council	*	28
Domestic Policy	*	21
Office of National Drug Control Policy	146	25
CEQ**/Environmental Policy	31	10
Science, Technology and Space Policy	95	46
Council of Economic Advisors	42	35
National Critical Material Council	2	0
Office of Administration	236	189
TOTAL	1,394	1,044

*Reflects Clinton's restructuring of Policy Development Office
**Council on Environmental Quality

Source: The White House, Office of Personnel Management.

Bill Clinton hugs his childhood friend, Thomas "Mack" McLarty, at a Little Rock, Arkansas news conference announcing McLarty as his first White House Chief of Staff.

seek a third or fourth term? Early in the second terms of Richard Nixon and Ronald Reagan, some of their supporters launched trial balloons concerning third terms, but to little avail.

Although it is likely that calls for change in the office, election procedures, and term of office will continue, change is highly unlikely as long as the system continues to work with some degree of effectiveness.

The Line-Item Veto

As early as 1873 in his State of the Union message, President Ulysses S. Grant proposed a constitutional amendment to give the president a **line-item veto**, the power enjoyed by many governors to veto individual items within a spending bill without invalidating the bill in its entirety. Since then, over 150 resolutions calling for a line-item veto have been introduced in Congress, and FDR, Eisenhower, Ford, Carter, Reagan, Bush, and Clinton have supported the concept.

George Bush was a particularly vocal proponent of the line-item veto although only one of his vetoes was overridden. Said Bush during his 1992 State of the Union message, "the press has a field day making fun of outrageous examples [of pork barrel appropriations]: A Lawrence Welk museum, research grants for Belgian endive. . . . Maybe you need someone to help you say no. I know how to say it, and I know what I need to make it stick. Give me the same thing 43 governors have: the line-item veto."[34] Many agree with Bush that the line-item veto could result in considerable sav-

Line-item veto The power to veto specific provisions of a bill without vetoing the bill in its entirety.

FIGURE 7-3

Office Space at the White House, 1994

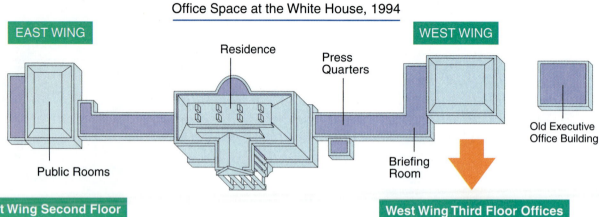

West Wing Second Floor

This floor includes the offices of First Lady Hillary Rodham Clinton; the president's domestic policy adviser; legal counsel; senior economic policy adviser; political director; public liaison director; Cabinet secretary; and congressional lobbyist.

West Wing Basement

This floor houses the top-secret "Situation Room," where national security officials monitor foreign crises; the White House lunchroom reserved for senior officials; administrative offices; official photographers; and the copying room.

West Wing Third Floor Offices

- Roosevelt Room Conference Hall
- Presidential Study
- Private Dining Room
- Senior Adviser to the President
- Appointments Secretary
- Secretaries
- Deputy Chief of Staff
- Chief of Staff
- Vice President's Staff
- Vice President
- Staff Assistants to Chief of Staff
- National Security Adviser
- Secretaries
- Deputy National Security Adviser
- Lobby / Receptionist
- Press Secretary
- Deputy Director of Communications
- Director of Communications
- Cabinet Room
- Secretaries
- The President's Main Office (Oval Office)

Old Executive Office Building

The Old Executive Office Building houses some other members of the president's staff, which totals more than 1,800. Among those next door at the Old EOB are the budget director; chairman of the Council of Economic Advisers; director of the Office of National Service; many of Hillary Rodham Clinton's aides and the staff of the health care task force, and Vice President Gore's second office suite.

ings, since it would allow a president to do away with more outrageous examples of "pork," or what a president might see as needless fat in the budget.

On Ronald Reagan's birthday in 1995, the House of Representatives voted to give the president the line-item veto as part of the conservative plan to rein in the federal deficit. Senator Robert C. Byrd (D-W.Va.), often called the King of Pork and a true wizard of Senate rules, quickly used his expertise as former chair of the Rules committee to block the Senate from taking up the bill. In June 1994, when the Senate first began hearings of the line-item veto, the Justice Department concluded that a constitutional amendment would be necessary before a president could have this kind of power, which would allow him to kill many legislators' pet projects. Thus, if the line-item veto passes the Senate, it is likely to be sent to the states for their ratification as a constitutional amendment.

Summary

Because the Framers feared a tyrannical monarch, they gave considerable thought to the office of the chief executive. Since ratification of the Constitution, the office has changed considerably—more through practice and need than from changes in the Constitution. In chronicling these changes, we have made the following points:

1. Distrust of a too-powerful leader led the Framers to create an executive office with limited powers. They mandated that a president be thirty-five years old and opted not to limit the president's term of office. To further guard against tyranny, they also made provisions for the removal of the president and created an office of vice president to provide for an orderly transfer of power.

2. The Framers gave the president a variety of specific constitutional powers in Article II, including the powers to make appointments, to convene Congress, to make treaties, and to veto. The president also derives considerable power from being Commander-in-Chief of the military. The Constitution also grants the president the power to grant pardons.

3. The development of presidential power has been highly dependent on the force of those who have held the office. George Washington, in particular, took several actions to establish the primacy of the president in national affairs and as true chief executive of a strong national government. But, with the exceptions of Andrew Jackson and Abraham Lincoln, subsequent presidents often let Congress dominate in national affairs. The election of FDR, however, forever changed all that as a new era of the modern presidency began. A hallmark of the modern presidency is the close relationship between the American people and their chief executive.

4. Since FDR, the public has looked to the president to propose legislation to Congress. The modern president also plays a major role in the budgetary process. To gain support of his programs or proposed budget, the president can use patronage, personal rewards, and party connections, and can go directly to the public. How the president goes about winning support is reflected in his style, affected by his character and his ability to persuade, and, in general, his ability to maintain high ratings in public opinion polls.

5. As the responsibilities of and expectations about the president have grown, so has the executive branch of government. The Cabinet has expanded, and FDR established the Executive Office of the President to help him govern. Perhaps the most key policy advisers are those closest to the president—the White House staff.

6. Ending term limits and the line-item veto are often discussed as possible ways to reform the presidency.

Key Terms

articles of impeachment	pardon	presidential character
Watergate	inherent power	two presidencies
executive agreement	patronage	Executive Office of the President
veto	presidential style	line-item veto

Suggested Readings

Campbell, Colin, S.J., and Bert A. Rockman. *The Bush Presidency: First Appraisals*. Chatham, NJ: Chatham House, 1991.

Corwin, Edwin S. *The Presidential Office and Powers*, 1787–1957, 4th ed. New York: New York University Press, 1957.

Cronin, Thomas E. *The State of the Presidency,* 2nd ed. Boston: Little, Brown, 1980.

Edwards, George C., III. *At the Margins*. New Haven, CT: Yale University Press, 1989.

Edwards, George, C. III. et al., eds. *Researching the Presidency: Vital Questions, New Approaches*. Pittsburgh: University of Pittsburgh Press, 1993.

George, Alexander L. *Presidential Decisionmaking in Foreign Policy*. Boulder, CO: Westview Press, 1980.

Kellerman, Barbara. *The Political Presidency*. New York: Oxford University Press, 1984.

Neustadt, Richard E. *Presidential Power: The Politics of Power from FDR to Carter*. New York: Wiley, 1980.

Reedy, George E. *The Twilight of the Presidency*. New York: New American Library, 1970.

Skowrorek, Stephen. *The Politics Presidents Make: Leadership from John Adams to George Bush*. Cambridge: Harvard University Press, 1993.

Tulis, Jeffrey K. *The Rhetorical Presidency*. Princeton, NJ: Princeton University Press, 1987.

Watson, Richard A., and Norman C. Thomas. *The Politics of the Presidency*, 2nd ed. Washington, DC: CQ Press, 1988.

The Bureaucracy

THE DEVELOPMENT OF THE FEDERAL BUREAUCRACY

THE MODERN BUREAUCRACY

POLICY MAKING

MAKING AGENCIES ACCOUNTABLE

PROBLEMS WITH THE MODERN BUREAUCRACY

TOWARD REFORM

*A*lexander Hamilton could not have envisioned that the power of the president to appoint "a good administration" would ultimately result in an executive branch that numbered over 2.9 million civilian non-postal federal employees in 1993. This federal **bureaucracy**, a set of complex hierarchical departments, agencies, commissions, and their staffs, exists to help the president carry out his constitutionally mandated charge to enforce the laws of the nation. As the bureaucracy has grown to help the president, it has become so large that it is often called the "fourth branch" of government. Without the bureaucracy, government as we know it would come to a grinding halt. The military could not function, social service programs would cease, and all air traffic would be grounded.

Harold D. Lasswell once defined political science as the "study of who gets what, when, and how."[1] It is by studying the bureaucracy that those questions can perhaps best be answered.

The term *bureaucracy* is used to refer to any large, complex organization in which employees have specified responsibilities and work within a hierarchy of authority. Corporations, companies, states, and the federal government have bureaucracies. Without them, these organizations could not function.

The employees who work in bureaucracies are called **bureaucrats**. While the term is often used derisively today, the term *bureau* originally referred to the cloth covering of desks and writing tables used by seventeenth-century French government officials. In the eighteenth century, the word was coupled with the suffix *-cracy*, signifying rule of government (as in *aristocracy*, *democracy*, and *theocracy*).[2]

The American bureaucracy is distinctive in many ways. For example, political authority over the bureaucracy is not in a single set of hands, but is shared by many institutions. Although the president can remove officials from their positions in the executive branch, it has never been clear exactly how much authority the chief execu-

> T he true test of a good government is its aptitude and tendency to produce a good administration. . . . It is not easy to conceive a plan better calculated than this to produce a judicious choice of men for filling the offices of the Union.
>
> *Alexander Hamilton*
> *Federalist No. 76*

Hamilton believed that the separation of powers to appoint and confirm key members of the bureaucracy (appointment by the president, confirmation by the Senate) would assure the appointment of only those well qualified for the job.

Bureaucracy A set of complex hierarchical departments, agencies, commissions, and their staffs, that exist to help the president carry out his constitutionally mandated charge to enforce the laws of the nation.

Bureaucrats Career government employees who work for federal, state, or local governments.

tive actually exercises in this regard. Because of the system of checks and balances created by the Framers of the Constitution, Congress can authorize the creation of departments, fund them, and pass the laws that the agencies are expected to implement. Therefore, it is often unclear to whom bureaucratic loyalty lies.

The bureaucracy can be thought of as that part of the government that links together the three branches of the national government and the federal system. Although Congress makes the laws, it must rely on the executive branch and the bureaucracy to enforce those laws. Commissions such as the Equal Employment Opportunity Commission (EEOC) have the power not only to make rules but also to settle disputes between parties concerning the enforcement and implementation of those rules. Often, however, many agency determinations end up being challenged in the courts. And, because most administrative agencies that make up part of the bureaucracy enjoy reputations for special expertise in clearly defined policy areas, the federal judiciary routinely defers to administrative decision makers.

We study the federal bureaucracy because of the key role it plays in the democratic process and in facilitating interactions within the federal system. Although many bureaucratic agencies interact directly with the public—the Internal Revenue Service collects your taxes, and the Postal Service delivers your mail—other bureaucratic agencies routinely interact with only state and local governments, and act as key players in the continuing definition and redefinition of federalism.

Even though the bureaucracy performs many valuable tasks we have come to take for granted, attacking the bureaucracy often appears to be a national pastime. Americans dislike the bureaucracy for a variety of reasons. Conservatives charge that it is too liberal and that its functions constitute unnecessary government meddling in our lives. They argue that the bureaucracy is too large, too powerful, and too unaccountable to the people or to elected officials. In contrast, liberals view it as too slow, too unimaginative to solve America's problems, and too zealous a guardian of the status quo. Whether conservative, liberal, or moderate, most Americans think that the bureaucracy works poorly and is wasteful. Tales of bureaucratic agency payments for $640 toilet seats and $7,622 coffee makers (no matter how these costs are justified) do not help the public's image of the bureaucracy.

THEN AND NOW

The Equal Employment Opportunity Commission and Sex Discrimination

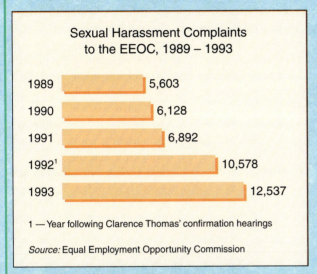

Sexual Harassment Complaints to the EEOC, 1989 – 1993

Year	Complaints
1989	5,603
1990	6,128
1991	6,892
1992[1]	10,578
1993	12,537

1 — Year following Clarence Thomas' confirmation hearings

Source: Equal Employment Opportunity Commission

Sexual Harassment Complaints Before and After the Thomas Hearings

The EEOC was created in 1965 to implement the anti-discrimination provisions of the Civil Rights Act of 1964. It prohibited discrimination by private employers on the basis of race, creed, color, religion, national origin, or sex. In spite of that broad mandate, the EEOC initially failed to investigate complaints of sex discrimination. In fact, the National Organization for Women was founded by women who saw the need to create an advocacy group to pressure the EEOC to treat claims of sex discrimination seriously and to enforce the law.[*]

Ironically, when Clarence Thomas was nominated by George Bush to be the 106th Justice of the U.S. Supreme Court, sexual harassment quickly became the major issue when a former employee of Thomas's charged he had harassed her while he headed the EEOC. In the wake of nationally televised hearings into the allegations, public awareness of the problem increased. In the year following Thomas's appointment, complaints of sexual harassment in the workplace were up 35 percent. Then, in late 1993, a unanimous U.S. Supreme Court ruled that a woman did not have to show severe psychological damage to prove that illegal sexual harassment occurred.[**] This decision was expected to open the flood gates to the filing of more complaints with the agency.

[*] Jo Freeman, *The Politics of Women's Liberation* (New York: Longman, 1975).

[**] *Harris* v. *Forklift Systems*, 1993 LEXIS 7155.

Candidates for public office, presidents, and Congress constantly criticize the bureaucracy and speak about it as though it were a foreign power to be conquered. Members of Congress joke that there is a game called "Bureaucracy" in which "There is only one rule. The first one to move loses." Even *Roget's Thesaurus* equates the term "bureaucracy" with officialism and red tape.

In spite of the criticisms, the bureaucracy is here to stay. This chapter traces the growth of the bureaucracy and examines how it is organized, how it interacts with the three branches of government, how it implements policy, and what role it plays in our national system of government.

As you read the pages that follow, you will see why many people, including presidents, have criticized the bureaucracy. We hope, however, that you will also see that the bureaucracy has in many respects expanded to meet the needs of a growing nation and the rising expectations and demands of the American public.

The Development of the Federal Bureaucracy

Just as the legislative, executive, and judicial branches started out modestly, so did the bureaucracy (or federal service, as some preferred to call it). The presidency of George Washington was quite uncomplicated, and so was the administration that he hired to assist him. As noted in "Landmark Events" below, in 1789, Washington's executive branch consisted of only three departments, which had existed under the Articles of Confederation: State (called Foreign Affairs under the Articles), War, and Treasury. The head of each department was called its *secretary*. Since the president often needed legal advice, the Congress created the office of Attorney General. The original status of the Attorney General, however, was unclear; i.e., was he a member of the judicial or executive branch? That confusion was remedied in 1870 with the creation of the Justice Department as part of the executive branch, with the Attorney General as its head. From the beginning, individuals appointed as Cabinet secretaries (as well as the Attorney General) were subject to approval by the U.S. Senate, but were "removable by the president" alone. Even the first Congress realized how important it was for a president to be surrounded by those in whom he had complete confidence and trust.

From 1816 to 1861, the size of the federal bureaucracy grew as increased demands were made on existing departments and new departments were added. For example, the Post Office, which Congress was constitutionally authorized to create in Article I,

Landmark Events in the Development of the Bureaucracy

1789	◆ First three departments created
1861–1865	◆ Civil War
1883	◆ Civil Service Reform Act (Pendleton Act)
1887	◆ Interstate Commerce Commission created
1903	◆ Department of Commerce and Labor established
1921	◆ General Accounting Office and Bureau of Budget created
1933–1937	◆ New Deal "alphabetocracy" established
1939	◆ Hatch Act
1964–1966	◆ New social welfare agencies created; EEOC, Departments of Housing and Urban Development and Transportation created
1978	◆ Civil Service Reform Act
1993	◆ Federal Employees Political Activities Act

was forced to expand to meet the needs of a growing and westward-expanding population. In 1892, the Post Office was removed from the jurisdiction of the Treasury Department by Andrew Jackson. Recognizing the tremendous potential increases in demands on the Post Office, Jackson promoted the Postmaster General to Cabinet rank, thereby giving him greater control over the office and its immense number of employees.

The Civil War and Big Government

The Civil War (1861–1865) permanently changed the nature of the federal bureaucracy. As the nation geared up for war, thousands of additional employees were added to existing departments. The Civil War also spawned the need for new government agencies. A series of poor harvests and marketing problems led President Abraham Lincoln (who understood that one needs food in order to conduct a war) to create the Department of Agriculture in 1862, although it was not given full Cabinet-level status until 1889.

After the Civil War, the need for big government continued unabated. In 1866, the Pension Office was established to pay benefits to the thousands of northern veterans who had fought in the war (more than 127,000 veterans were initially eligible for benefits). Justice was made a department in 1870 and other departments were added through 1900. Agriculture became a full-fledged department and began to play an important role in informing farmers about the latest developments in soil conservation, livestock breeding, and planting techniques. The increase in the types and nature of government services resulted in a parallel rise in the number of federal jobs, as illustrated in Figure 8-1. Many of the new jobs were used by the president or leaders of the president's political party for **patronage**; that is, jobs, grants, or other special favors given as rewards to friends and political allies for their support.

Becoming a Bureaucrat: From Spoils to Merit

In 1831, describing a "rotation in office" policy for bureaucrats supported by President Andrew Jackson, Senator William Learned Marcy of New York commented, "To the victor belong the spoils." From his statement derives the phrase **spoils system** to describe the firing of public-office holders of the defeated political party and their replacement with loyalists of the new administration. Jackson, in particular, faced severe criticism for populating the federal government with his political cronies. But many presidents, including Jackson, argued that in order to implement their policies, they had to be able to appoint those who subscribed to their political views.

By the time James A. Garfield, a former distinguished Civil War officer, was elected president in 1880, many reformers were calling publicly for changes in the **civil service system**, by which appointments to the federal bureaucracy are made. Upon his election to office, Garfield, like many presidents before him, was besieged by office seekers. Washington, D.C., had not seen such a demand for political jobs since the election of Abraham Lincoln as the first president of the Republican Party. Garfield's immediate predecessor, Rutherford B. Hayes, had favored the idea of the replacement of the spoils system with a merit system based on test scores and ability. Congress, however, failed to pass the legislation he proposed. Possibly because potential job seekers wanted to secure positions before Congress had the opportunity to act on an overhauled civil service system, thousands pressed Garfield for positions. This siege

More than two hundred years after its founding, the Post Office employs more civilians than any other segment of the federal government.

Patronage Jobs, grants, or other special favors that are given as rewards to friends and political allies for their support.

Spoils system The firing of public-office holders of a defeated political party and their replacement with loyalists of the newly elected party.

Civil service system The system created by civil service laws by which many appointments to the federal bureaucracy are made.

FIGURE 8-1

Number of Federal Employees, 1792–2000

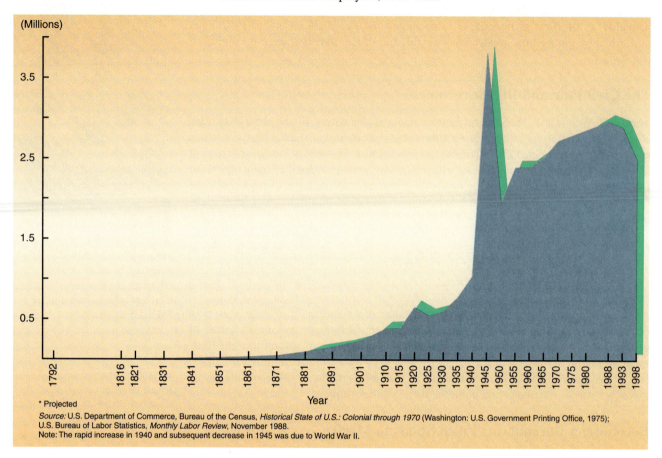

* Projected

Source: U.S. Department of Commerce, Bureau of the Census, *Historical State of U.S.: Colonial through 1970* (Washington: U.S. Government Printing Office, 1975); U.S. Bureau of Labor Statistics, *Monthly Labor Review*, November 1988.
Note: The rapid increase in 1940 and subsequent decrease in 1945 was due to World War II.

Pendleton Act Reform measure that created the Civil Service Commission to administer a partial merit system. It classified the federal service by grades to which appointments were made based on the results of a competitive examination. It made it illegal for political appointees to be required to contribute to a particular political party.

Merit system The system by which federal civil service jobs are classified into grades or levels to which appointments are made on the basis of performance on competitive examinations.

prompted Garfield to record in his diary: "My day is frittered away with the personal seeking of people when it ought to be given to the great problems which concern the whole country."[3] And although he resolved to reform the civil service, Garfield's life was cut short by the bullets of an assassin who, ironically, was a frustrated job seeker.

Public reaction to Garfield's death prompted Congress to pass the Civil Service Reform Act in 1883, more commonly known as the **Pendleton Act**, to reduce patronage. It created a bipartisan three-member Civil Service Commission, which operated until 1978. Under the Act's provisions, about 15 percent of the positions in the federal civil service were classified into grades or levels to which appointments would be made on the basis of performance on competitive examinations. This was called the **merit system**. The Pendleton Act also made it illegal to fire a civil servant for failure to contribute to a political party or campaign.

National Efforts to Regulate the Economy

Soon after passage of the Pendleton Act, Congress took other actions that served to spur the growth of the bureaucracy. In the wake of the tremendous growth of big busi-

An artist's representation of President Garfield's assassination. He was killed by an unhappy office seeker.

ness (especially railroads), widespread price fixing, and other unfair business practices, in 1887 Congress created the Interstate Commerce Commission (ICC), the first independent **regulatory commission.** The creation of the ICC also marked a shift in the focus of the bureaucracy from service to regulation. In the case of the ICC, Congress was reacting to public outcries over the exorbitant rates charged by railroad companies for hauling freight. Independent regulatory commissions such as the ICC are created by Congress to be independent of direct presidential authority. Commission members, although appointed by the president, hold their jobs for fixed terms and are not removable by the president unless they fail to uphold their oaths of office.

Regulatory commission An agency created by Congress that is generally concerned with a specific aspect of the economy.

The 1900 election of Theodore Roosevelt, a progressive Republican, strengthened the movement toward regulation and further increased the size of the bureaucracy when Roosevelt asked Congress to establish a Department of Commerce and Labor in 1903 to oversee employer/employee relations. Roosevelt was motivated by the existence of intolerable labor practices, including low wages, long hours, substandard working conditions, the refusal of employers to recognize the rights of workers to join a union, and the fact that many businesses had grown so large and powerful that they could force workers to accept substandard conditions.

In 1913, President Woodrow Wilson created a separate Department of Labor when it became clear that one agency could not well represent the interests of both employers and employees, factions with greatly differing perspectives. The creation of this department reflected the economic and societal changes that occurred as immigration increased and the economy became increasingly industrialized. One year later, in 1914, Congress created the Federal Trade Commission (FTC). Its function was to protect small businesses and the public from unfair competition, especially from big business.

Also affecting the size of government and the possibilities for growth was the ratification of the Sixteenth Amendment to the Constitution in 1913. It gave Congress the authority to implement a federal income tax to supplement the national treasury, which provided an infusion of funds to support new federal agencies, services, and governmental programs.

PEOPLE OF THE PAST

William Henry Harrison and Office Seekers

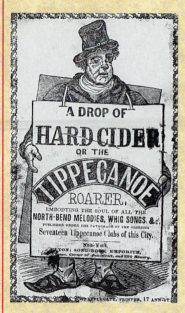

Nominated by the Whig Party in 1839, William Henry Harrison was the "log cabin, hard cider" candidate in the presidential campaign of 1840. Although Harrison was the son of a wealthy Virginia planter, the Whig Party developed an image of Harrison as one who had risen to distinction through his own efforts while retaining the tastes of the ordinary citizen. Harrison went to college and then enlisted in the army, where he was promoted to major general. Harrison was a hero in the Battle of Tippecanoe, thus earning the nickname "Tippecanoe," which led to the catchy campaign slogan "Tippecanoe and Tyler too" when Harrison selected his running mate, John Tyler.

Harrison ran his campaign without a platform. The advice given to him by Whig leaders was to say nothing about principles or creed. Many silly campaign songs were composed and noisy conventions and rallies were held everywhere, but no campaign promises were made.

At his inaugural address on March 4, Harrison droned on for close to two hours, producing the longest inaugural speech on record. He paid dearly for it. It was a cold and wintry day and Harrison did not wear gloves or an overcoat. Not surprisingly, he developed pneumonia later that month and died on April 4, serving the shortest term of any president.

Repeatedly dunned by supporters seeking patronage jobs, Harrison's last words were: "I can't stand it. . . . Don't trouble me. . . . These applications, will they never cease . . . ?" Even on Harrison's deathbed, the problems of a growing bureaucracy continued to hound him.

Laissez-Faire **Attitudes.**   During the early 1900s, while Progressives raised the public cry for regulation of business, many Americans, especially members of the business community, continued to resist such moves. They believed that any federal government regulation was wrong. Instead they favored governmental facilitation of the national economy through a commitment to *laissez-faire*, a French term literally meaning *to allow to do*; *to leave alone*. In America, the term was used to describe a governmental hands-off policy concerning the economy. And the courts, especially the U.S. Supreme Court, were at the forefront of the philosophical debate over how much power the national government had to regulate the private sector. In a series of key decisions made through 1937, the Supreme Court repeatedly invalidated key provisions in congressional legislation designed to regulate various aspects of the economy. The Court and others who subscribed to *laissez-faire* principles of a free enterprise system argued that natural economic laws at work in the marketplace control the buying and selling of goods. Thus, it was believed, the government had no right to regulate business in any way.

The New Deal and Bigger Government. In the wake of the high unemployment and weak financial markets of the Great Depression, Franklin Roosevelt's plan to revitalize the economy included the creation of hundreds of new government agencies to regulate business practices and various aspects of the economy. Although the *laissez-faire*-minded Supreme Court stood adamantly opposed to increased regulation and bureaucratization, Roosevelt proposed and the Congress enacted far-ranging economic legislation. The desperate mood of the nation supported these moves as most Americans began to change their ideas about the proper role of government and the provision of governmental services. Formerly, Americans had believed in a hands-off approach; they now considered it the government's job to get the economy going and get Americans back to work.

Within the first 100 days of Roosevelt's administration, Congress approved every new regulatory measure proposed by the president. Among others, Congress approved the National Industrial Recovery Act (NIRA), an unprecedented attempt to regulate industry; and the Agricultural Adjustment Act (AAA), to provide government support for farm prices and to regulate farm production to ensure market-competitive prices. Congress also created the Federal Deposit Insurance Corporation (FDIC) to insure bank deposits and passed the Federal Securities Act, which gave the Federal Trade Commission the authority to supervise and regulate the issuance, buying, and selling of stocks and bonds.

Until 1937, however, the Supreme Court refused to allow Congress or the president to delegate to the executive branch or the bureaucracy such far-ranging authority to regulate the economy. *Laissez-faire* was alive and well at the Court, and attempts to end the economic slump through greater governmental involvement were repeatedly stymied by the justices. In 1937, however, FDR, frustrated by the Court, proposed his famous Court-packing plea (see Chapter 9), which would have allowed him to add his own appointees to the Court. In the wake of that institution-threatening proposal, the Court quickly fell into sync with public opinion. In a series of cases discussed in Chapter 9, the Supreme Court reversed a number of its earlier decisions and upheld what some have termed the "alphabetocracy" (see Chapter 3). For example, the Court upheld the constitutionality of the National Labor Relations Act of 1935 (NLRA), which allowed recognition of unions and established formal arbitration procedures for employers and employees.[4] Subsequent decisions upheld the validity of the Fair Labor Standards Act (FLSA) and the Agricultural Adjustment Act (AAA).[5]

Once these new programs were declared constitutional, the bureaucracy needed to expand yet again in order to monitor the numerous programs created by the new laws. And with the growth in the bureaucracy came more calls for reform of the system.

The Hatch Act. As an increasing proportion of the American workforce came to work for the U.S. government as a result of the New Deal recovery programs, many began to fear that the members of the civil service would play major roles not only in implementing public policy but also in electing members of Congress and even the president. Consequently, in 1939, Congress enacted what is commonly known as the **Hatch Act**, which was designed to prohibit the use of federal employees to affect elections. In effect, the Hatch Act was intended to neutralize the civil service politically by prohibiting civil servants from taking activist roles in partisan campaigns; under its provisions, federal employees could not run for public office, campaign for or against candidates, make speeches, raise funds for candidates, organize political rallies, circulate petitions, or participate in registration drives that seek voters for one party only.

President Franklin D. Roosevelt urges the Court to work with the executive and legislative branches in a cooperative effort to end the Great Depression.

Hatch Act Enacted by Congress in 1939 to prohibit civil servants from taking activist roles in partisan campaigns. This act prohibited federal employees from making political contributions, working for a particular party, or campaigning for a particular candidate.

Poor working conditions in the early 1900s: a sweatshop in New York.

The Liberalized Hatch Act

◆ ◆ ◆

Here are some examples of permissible and prohibited activities for federal employees under the Hatch Act, as modified by the Federal Employees Political Activities Act of 1993.

- **May** be candidates for public office in nonpartisan elections
- **May** assist in voter registration drives
- **May** express opinions about candidates and issues
- **May** contribute money to political organizations
- **May** attend political fundraising functions
- **May** attend and be active at political rallies and meetings
- **May** join and be an active member of a political party or club
- **May** sign nominating petitions
- **May** campaign for or against referendum questions, constitutional amendments, municipal ordinances
- **May** campaign for or against candidates in partisan elections
- **May** make campaign speeches for candidates in partisan elections
- **May** distribute campaign literature in partisan elections
- **May** hold office in political clubs or parties

- **May not** use their official authority or influence to interfere with an election
- **May not** collect political contributions unless both individuals are members of the same federal labor organization or employee organization and the one solicited is not a subordinate employee
- **May not** knowingly solicit or discourage the political activity of any person who has business before the agency
- **May not** engage in political activity while on duty
- **May not** engage in political activity in any government office
- **May not** engage in political activity while wearing an official uniform
- **May not** engage in political activity while using a government vehicle
- **May not** solicit political contributions from the general public
- **May not** be candidates for public office in partisan elections

Source: U.S. Special Counsel's Office.

Although presidents as far back as Thomas Jefferson had advocated efforts to limit the opportunities for federal civil servants to influence the votes of others, many criticized the Hatch Act as too extreme. Critics argued that it denied millions of federal employees the First Amendment guarantees of freedom of speech and association, and discouraged political participation among a group of people who might otherwise be strong political activists. Critics also argued that civil servants *should* become more involved in campaigns, particularly at the state and local level, in order to understand better the needs of the citizens they serve.

The Federal Employees Political Activities Act. In response to these criticisms and at the urgings of President Bill Clinton, Congress enacted the **Federal Employees Political Activities Act**. This liberalization of the Hatch Act allows employees to run for public office in non-partisan elections, contribute money to political organizations, and campaign for or against candidates in partisan elections. During the signing ceremony, Clinton said the law will "mean more responsive, more satisfied, happier, and more productive federal employees."[6]

Federal Employees Political Activities Act 1993 liberalization of Hatch Act. Federal employees are now allowed to run for office in nonpartisan elections and to contribute money to campaigns in partisan elections.

The Modern Bureaucracy

One of the most difficult tasks facing those who study the bureaucracy is determining to whom bureaucracies are responsible. Is it the president? Congress? the citizenry? We often think of bureaucrats as "them." But they are actually quite like "us." To understand the modern bureaucracy, it is essential to understand who bureaucrats are, how the bureaucracy is organized, and how it works.

Who Are Bureaucrats?

Federal bureaucrats are career government employees who work in the executive branch, in the fourteen Cabinet-level departments and the more than 60 independent agencies that comprise more than 2,000 bureaus, divisions, branches, offices, services, and other sub-units of the federal government. There are approximately 2.9 million federal bureaucrats (in contrast to only 800,000 in Great Britain) who come from all walks of life—they vary in race, religion, ethnicity, level of education, and income. Because the representation of women and minorities at higher levels is still low (see Figure 8-2 below), Congress has ordered federal agencies to make special efforts in their recruitment of minority and other disadvantaged workers. And overall, women and minorities are better represented as a proportion of the workforce in the bureaucracy than in the nation as a whole.

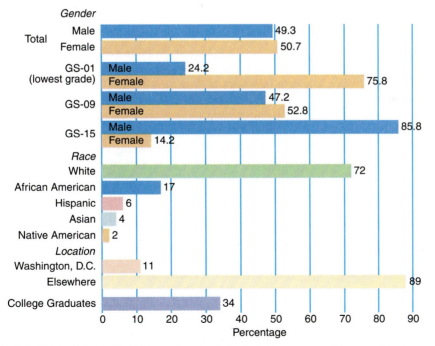

FIGURE 8-2

Characteristics and Rank Distributions of Federal Civilian Employees, 1991

Sources: Statistical Abstract of the United States, 1990 (Washington: U.S. Government Printing Office, 1990), pp. 323–326. Office of Personnel Management, Federal Civilian Workforce Statistics, Employment and Trends as of November 1988 (Washington: U.S. Government Printing Office, 1989), pp. 70. Harold W. Stanley and Richard G. Niemi, Vital Statistics on American Politics, 4E. (Washington, D.C.: Congressional Quarterly Press, 1994), p. 406.

As a result of reforms made during the Truman administration, most civilian federal governmental employees are selected by merit standards, which include tests (such as civil service or foreign service exams) and educational criteria. Merit systems protect federal employees from being fired for political reasons. Positions in the politically neutral civil service in Britain are also filled on the basis of competitive examinations; nevertheless, most entrants continue to come from either Oxford University or Cambridge University, which has given the English bureaucracy, unlike its American counterpart, an elitist image.

While the stereotypical image of a bureaucrat is that of the "paper pusher," more than 15,000 job skills are represented in the federal government, and its workers are perhaps the best trained and most skilled and efficient in the world. Working for the government are forest rangers, FBI agents, foreign service officers, computer programmers, security guards, librarians, administrators, engineers, plumbers, lawyers, doctors, postal carriers, and zoologists, among others. And the diversity of government jobs mirrors the diversity of jobs in the private sector.

Another myth is the perception that most bureaucrats work in Washington. In reality, only about 11 percent of the nearly 3 million federal bureaucrats work in the nation's capital; the rest are located in regional, state, and local offices scattered throughout the country. The decentralization of the bureaucracy facilitates accessibility. The Social Security Administration, for example, has numerous offices so that its clients may have a place nearby to take their paperwork, questions, and problems. Decentralization also helps distribute jobs and incomes across the country. Although the Centers for Disease Control and Prevention might easily have been situated in Washington, the CDC is instead located in Atlanta, Georgia.

Many Americans also believe that the federal bureaucracy is growing bigger each year. Although it is true that the number of federal government employees has been increasing until lately, most growth has taken place at the state and local levels, as revealed in Figure 8-3 (p. 251).

The stability of a federal agency and the expansion or reduction in the number of its employees are the responsibility of Congress; legislators have the power to abolish existing agencies or to create new ones as they see fit. Moreover, as each president has entered office, most have pledged to eliminate an agency or two or, at the very least, combine some. But as President Ronald Reagan soon learned after he campaigned in part on a pledge to eliminate the Department of Education, abolishing an agency is easier said than done. (Reagan, in fact, ended up elevating the Veterans Administration to the Department of Veterans' Affairs by an act of Congress in 1988.)

Formal Organization

While even experts can't agree on the exact number of separate agencies that make up the bureaucracy,[7] there are probably more than 400. A distinctive feature of the bureaucracy is its division into areas of specialization: One agency handles occupational safety, for example, another specializes in education, another in foreign affairs, another in employment discrimination, another in the environment, and so on. Because each concentrates on a particular issue area, no two agencies are identical, but they do fall into four general types: (1) departments, (2) government corporations, (3) independent agencies, and (4) regulatory commissions.

Departments. As depicted in Figure 8-4 (p. 252), the largest units of the federal bureaucracy are the fourteen executive branch departments headed by Cabinet mem-

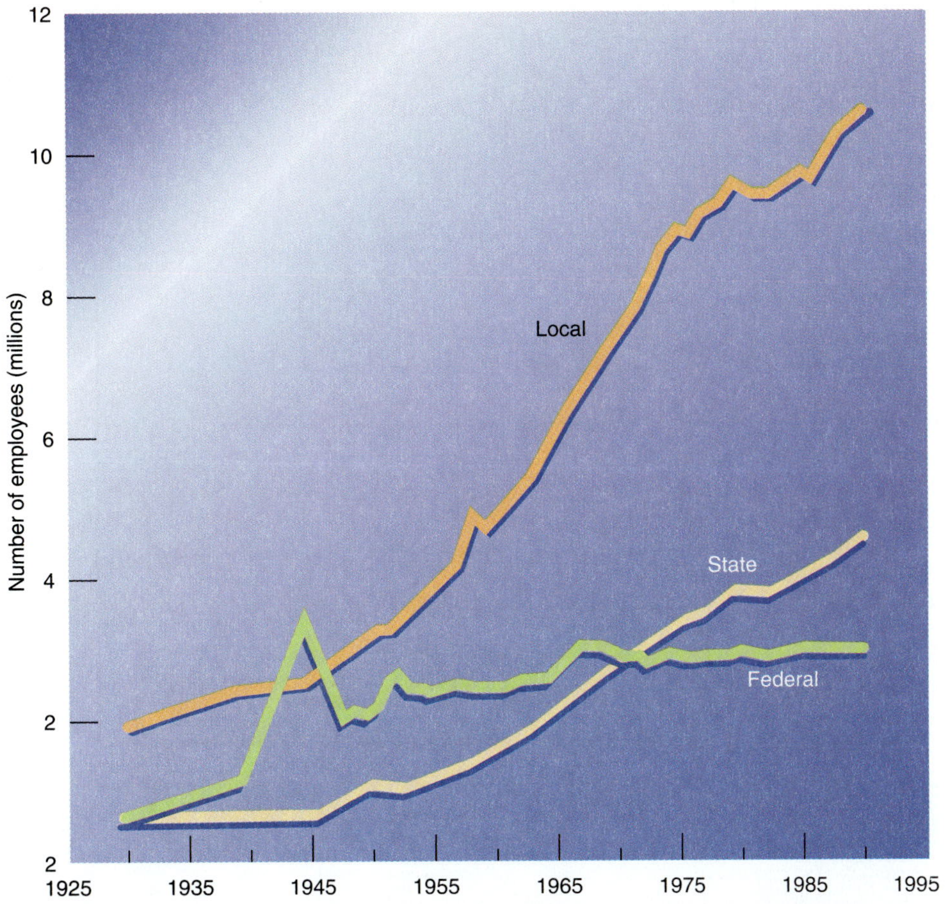

FIGURE 8-3

Number of Federal, State, and Local Government Employees, 1929–1991

Source: Harold W. Stanley and Richard G. Niemi, *Vital Statistics on American Politics,* 4th ed. (Washington: CQ Press, 1994), p. 315. 1929–1944, 1949, 1954, 1959, 1964, 1969–1988: U.S. Advisory Commission on Intergovernmental Relations, *Significant Features of Fiscal Federalism, 1990,* vol. 2 (Washington: U.S. Advisory Commission on Intergovernmental Relations, 1990), p. 177; other years: Bureau of the Census, *Historical Statistics of the United States,* Series Y189–198 (Washington: U.S. Government Printing Office, 1975), p. 1100.

bers called secretaries (except the Justice Department, which is headed by the Attorney General). The secretaries are responsible for establishing their department's general policy and overseeing its operations. As discussed in Chapter 7, Cabinet secretaries are directly responsible to the president, although they are often viewed as having two masters—the president and those affected by their department. Cabinet secretaries are also tied to Congress, from which they get their appropriations and discretion to implement legislation and make rules.

Although departments vary considerably in size, prestige, and power, they share certain features. Each department covers a broad area of responsibility generally reflected by its name. Each secretary is assisted by a deputy or undersecretary to take part of the administrative burden off the secretary's shoulders, as well as by several assistant secretaries, who direct major programs within the department. In addition, each secretary, like the president, has numerous assistants who help with planning, budgeting, personnel, legal services, public relations, and other key staff functions. All departments are subdivided into smaller agencies, bureaus, offices, and services, and it is at this level

FIGURE 8-4
Departments of the Executive Branch

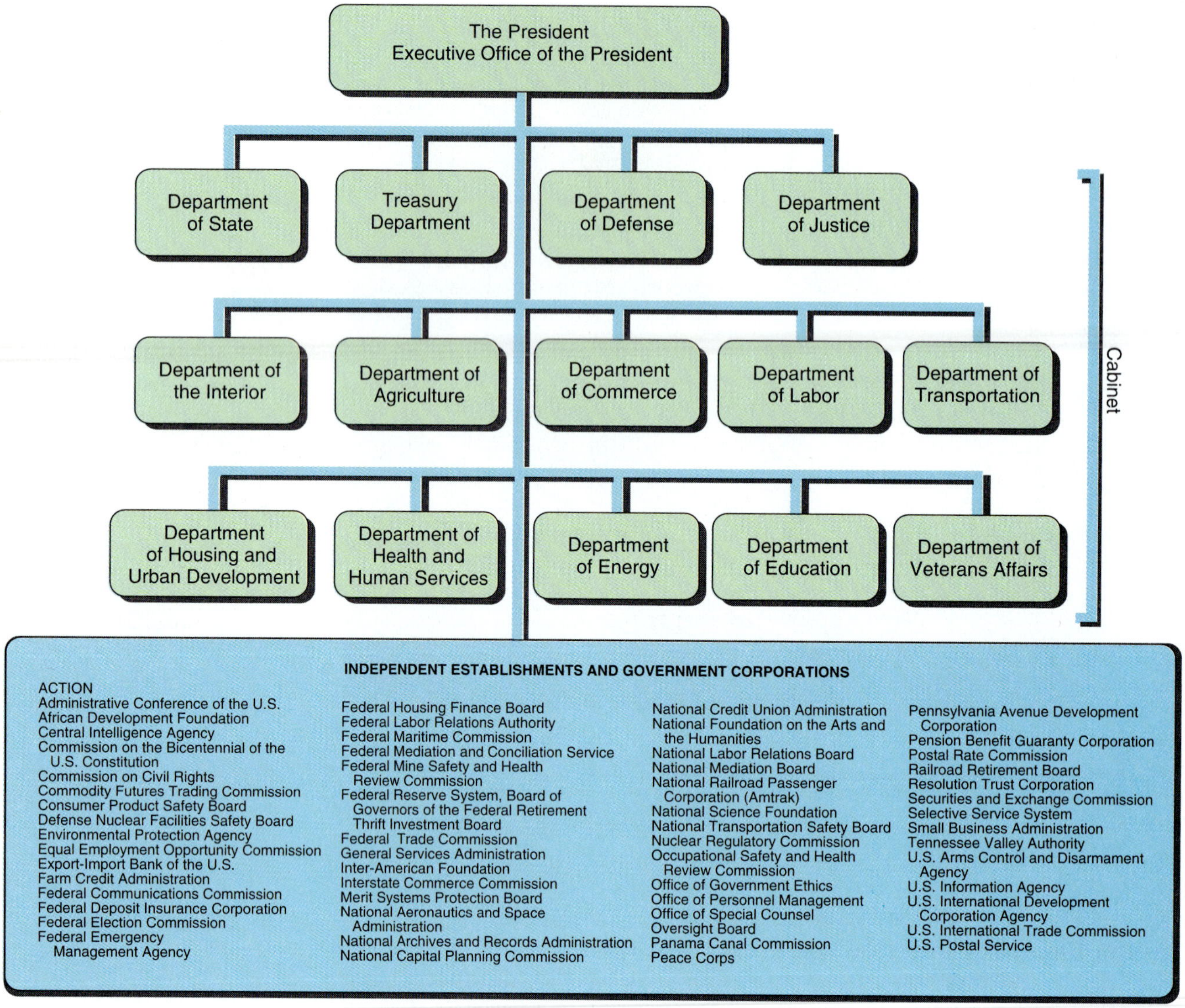

The President
Executive Office of the President

Department of State | Treasury Department | Department of Defense | Department of Justice

Department of the Interior | Department of Agriculture | Department of Commerce | Department of Labor | Department of Transportation

Department of Housing and Urban Development | Department of Health and Human Services | Department of Energy | Department of Education | Department of Veterans Affairs

Cabinet

INDEPENDENT ESTABLISHMENTS AND GOVERNMENT CORPORATIONS

ACTION
Administrative Conference of the U.S.
African Development Foundation
Central Intelligence Agency
Commission on the Bicentennial of the
   U.S. Constitution
Commission on Civil Rights
Commodity Futures Trading Commission
Consumer Product Safety Board
Defense Nuclear Facilities Safety Board
Environmental Protection Agency
Equal Employment Opportunity Commission
Export-Import Bank of the U.S.
Farm Credit Administration
Federal Communications Commission
Federal Deposit Insurance Corporation
Federal Election Commission
Federal Emergency
   Management Agency

Federal Housing Finance Board
Federal Labor Relations Authority
Federal Maritime Commission
Federal Mediation and Conciliation Service
Federal Mine Safety and Health
   Review Commission
Federal Reserve System, Board of
   Governors of the Federal Retirement
   Thrift Investment Board
Federal Trade Commission
General Services Administration
Inter-American Foundation
Interstate Commerce Commission
Merit Systems Protection Board
National Aeronautics and Space
   Administration
National Archives and Records Administration
National Capital Planning Commission

National Credit Union Administration
National Foundation on the Arts and
   the Humanities
National Labor Relations Board
National Mediation Board
National Railroad Passenger
   Corporation (Amtrak)
National Science Foundation
National Transportation Safety Board
Nuclear Regulatory Commission
Occupational Safety and Health
   Review Commission
Office of Government Ethics
Office of Personnel Management
Office of Special Counsel
Oversight Board
Panama Canal Commission
Peace Corps

Pennsylvania Avenue Development
   Corporation
Pension Benefit Guaranty Corporation
Postal Rate Commission
Railroad Retirement Board
Resolution Trust Corporation
Securities and Exchange Commission
Selective Service System
Small Business Administration
Tennessee Valley Authority
U.S. Arms Control and Disarmament
   Agency
U.S. Information Agency
U.S. International Development
   Corporation Agency
U.S. International Trade Commission
U.S. Postal Service

Source: United States Government Manual 1990–91 (Washington: Government Printing Office).

that the real work of each agency is done. Most departments are subdivided along function lines, but the basis for division may be geography, work processes (for example, the Economic Research Service in the Department of Agriculture), or clientele (such as the Bureau of Indian Affairs in the Department of Interior). In addition to national offices in Washington, D.C., or its immediate suburbs, each executive department has regional offices to serve all parts of the United States.

Some departments are directed by law to foster and promote the interests of a given clientele—that is, a specific segment or group in the U.S. population. Such departments are called **clientele agencies**.

Because many of these agencies were created at the urgings of well organized interests to advance their particular objectives, it is not surprising that clientele groups are powerful lobbies with their respective agencies in Washington. The clientele agencies and groups are also active at the regional level, where the agencies devote a substantial part of their resources to program implementation. One of the most obvious examples of regional "outreach" is the Extension Service of the Department of Agriculture. Agricultural extension agents are scattered throughout the farm belt and routinely work with farmers on farm productivity and other problems. Career bureaucrats in the Agriculture Department know that farm interests will be dependable allies year in and year out. Congress and/or the president are not nearly so reliable because they must balance the interests of farmers with those of other segments of society.

Government Corporations. **Government corporations** are businesses set up and created by Congress to perform functions that could be provided by private businesses. Figure 8-5 lists some of the better-known government corporations. Unlike other governmental agencies, government corporations charge for their services. For example, the largest government corporation, the U.S. Postal Service—whose functions could be handled by a private corporation, such as Federal Express or the United Parcel Service (UPS)—exists today to ensure delivery of mail throughout the United States at cheaper rates than those a private business might charge. Similarly, the Tennessee Valley Authority (TVA) provides electricity at reduced rates to millions of Americans in the Appalachian region of the Southeast, a generally low-income area that had failed to attract private utility companies to provide service there.

In cases like that of the TVA where the financial incentives for private industry to provide services are minimal, Congress often believes that it must act. In other cases, it steps in to salvage valuable public assets. For example, when passenger rail service in the United States no longer remained profitable, Congress stepped in to create Amtrak and thus nationalized the passenger-train industry to keep passenger trains running.

Independent Agencies. **Independent agencies** closely resemble Cabinet departments, but have narrower areas of responsibility. Generally speaking, all agencies that are not corporations or do not fall under the departments are called independent agencies (see Figure 8-5, p. 254). Many of these agencies are tied to the president and Congress as closely as executive departments. Heads of these agencies are appointed by the president and serve, like Cabinet secretaries, at his pleasure.

Independent agencies most frequently exist apart from executive departments for practical or symbolic reasons. The National Aeronautics and Space Administration (NASA), for example, could have been placed within the Department of Defense. That kind of placement, however, could have conjured up thoughts of a space program dedicated solely to military purposes, rather than for civilian satellite communication or scientific exploration.

Regulatory Boards or Commissions. Another type of independent agency is the independent regulatory board or commission, such as the National Labor Relations

---

Clientele agencies Executive departments that are directed by law to foster and promote the interests of a specific segment or group in the U.S. population (such as the Department of Education).

Clientele Agencies
❖ ❖ ❖

- Department of Agriculture
- Department of Commerce
- Department of Education
- Department of Energy
- Department of the Interior
- Department of Labor
- Department of Veterans Affairs

Government corporations Businesses set up and created by Congress that perform functions that could be provided by private businesses (such as the U.S. Postal Service).

Independent agencies Governmental units that closely resemble Cabinet departments but have narrower areas of responsibility (such as the Central Intelligence Agency).

FIGURE 8-5

Corporations, Independent
Agencies, and Regulatory
Commissions

Some Government Corporations

Amtrak
Federal Deposit Insurance Corporation
Tennessee Valley Authority

Some Independent Agencies

Central Intelligence Agency
Federal Emergency Management Agency
General Services Administration

Some Regulatory Agencies or Commissions

Consumer Product Safety Commission
Federal Communications Commission
Federal Election Commission
National Labor Relations Board

Board, the Federal Reserve Board, and the Securities and Exchange Commission (SEC) (see Figure 8-5).[8] Congress started setting up regulatory commissions as early as 1887, recognizing the need for close and continuous guardianship of particular economic activities. Once the Supreme Court decided to allow Congress to begin regulating aspects of the economy, the number of independent regulatory agencies—now over sixty—grew. Older boards and commissions, such as the Interstate Commerce Commission (ICC), the Securities and Exchange Commission, and the Federal Reserve Board, are generally charged with overseeing a certain industry. Regulatory agencies created since the 1960s are more concerned with how the business sector relates to public health and safety. The Occupational Safety and Health Administration (OSHA), for example, promotes job safety, and the Environmental Protection Agency (EPA) regulates industrial pollution. (In 1994, the Senate voted to elevate the EPA to Cabinet-level status, but action was stalled in the House.)

Most of the older independent agencies were specifically created to be relatively free from immediate (partisan) political pressure. They are headed by a board composed of several members (always an odd number to avoid ties) who are selected by the president and confirmed by Congress. (Commissioners are appointed for fixed, staggered terms to increase the chances of a bipartisan board.) Unlike executive department heads, they cannot be easily removed by the president. In 1935, the U.S. Supreme Court ruled that in creating independent commissions, the Congress had intended that they be independent panels of experts as far removed as possible from immediate political pressures.[9]

Newer regulatory boards lack this kind of autonomy and freedom from political pressures; they are generally headed by a single administrator who can be removed by the president. These boards and commissions, such as the EEOC, are therefore far more susceptible to political pressure and political wishes.

Policy Making

When Congress creates any kind of department, agency, or commission, it is actually delegating some of its powers listed in Article I, Section 8, of the U.S. Constitution. Therefore, the laws creating agencies carefully describe their purpose and give them the authority to make numerous policy decisions, which have the effect of law. Congress recognizes that it does not have the time, expertise, or ability to involve itself in every detail of every program; therefore, it sets general guidelines for agency action and leaves it to the agency to work out the details. How agencies execute congressional wishes is called **implementation**, the process by which a law or policy is put into operation. Essentially, bureaucrats make as well as implement policy. They take the laws and policies made by Congress, the president, and the courts, and develop rules and procedures for making sure they are carried out. Most implementation involves what is called **administrative discretion**, the ability to make choices concerning the best way to implement congressional intentions. If Congress does not like an agency's actions, it can pass laws that invalidate specific rules or procedures. Members of Congress, however, are not always able to agree on how policies are to be implemented. More often than not, then, when Congress is unable to decide upon clear-cut guidelines, it passes the political hot potato to an agency for resolution.

A good example of how Congress often passes the buck is the Occupational Safety and Health Act of 1970. It provided only a rough expression of the desired end results of ensuring a safe and healthy workplace for every man and woman in the nation. The legislation, however, was silent on how two competing interests were to be balanced: the rights of workers injured, killed, or exposed to hazards on the job and the interests of employers who, in order to minimize risks, would have to expend large sums of money to comply with the Act's mandates. Congress left it to the Occupational Safety and Health Administration (OSHA) to determine how to implement the Act.

Policy making takes place on informal and formal levels. Practically, many decisions are left to individual government employees on a day-to-day basis. Justice Department lawyers, for example, make daily decisions about whether or not to prosecute someone. Similarly, Internal Revenue Service agents make many decisions during personal audits. Other forms of bureaucratic policy making are more formal.

Rule Making

Administrative discretion is also exercised through two formal administrative procedures: rule making and adjudication. **Rule making** is the administrative process that results in regulations. **Regulations** are the rules that govern the operation of all government programs and have the force of law. In essence, then, bureaucratic rule makers often act as lawmakers as well as law enforcers when they make rules or draft regulations to implement various congressional statutes. Thus, rule making is called a quasi-legislative process. (See Figure 8.6, p. 256.)

Implementation The process by which a law or policy is put into operation by the bureaucracy.

Administrative discretion The ability of the bureaucracy to make choices concerning the best way to implement congressional intentions.

Rule making The administrative process that results in rules and regulations.

Regulations Rules that govern the operation of all government programs and have the force of law.

FIGURE 8-6

How a Regulation Is Made

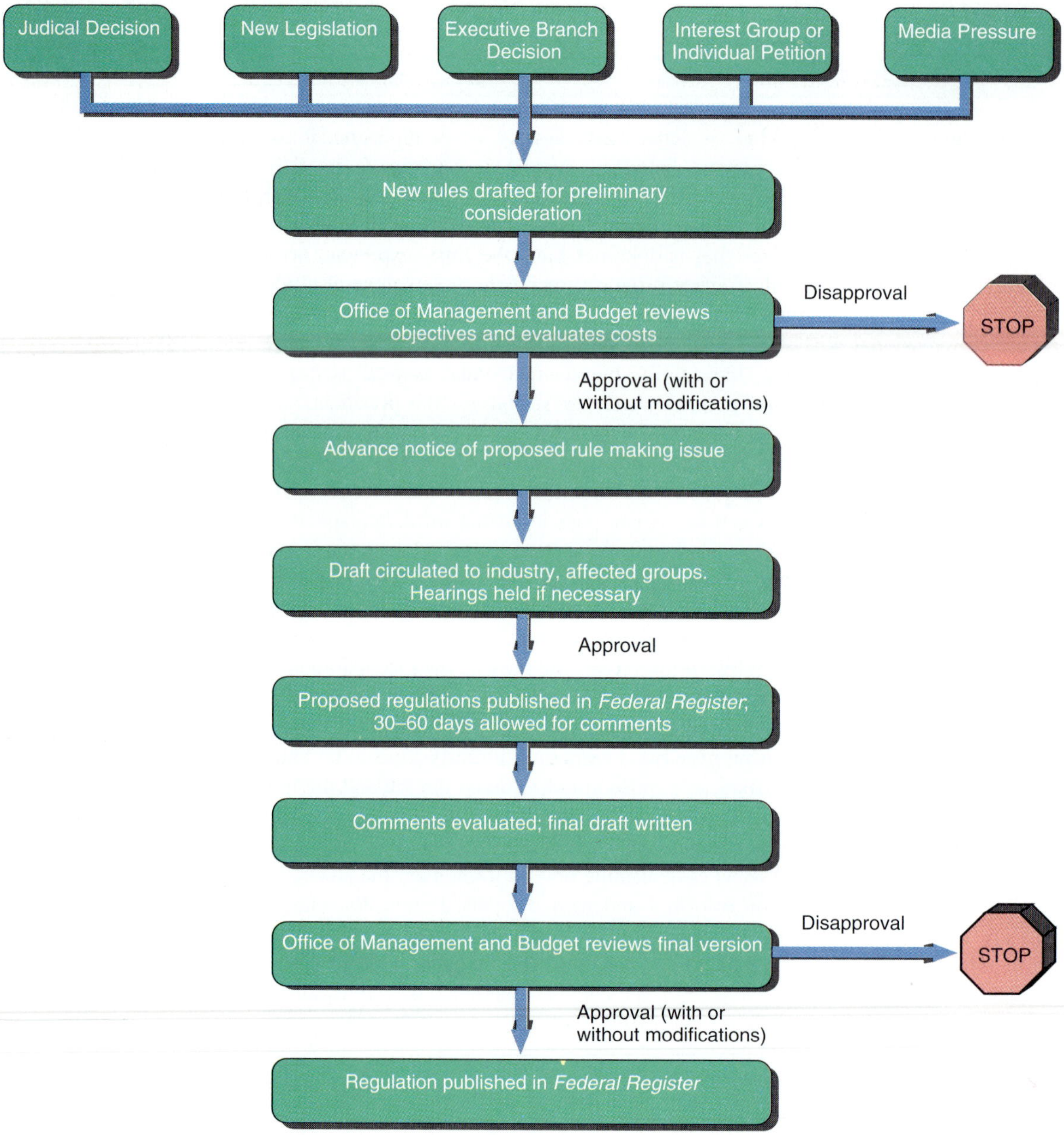

```
┌──────────────┐  ┌──────────────┐  ┌──────────────┐  ┌──────────────────┐  ┌──────────────┐
│Judical Decision│ │New Legislation│ │Executive Branch│ │Interest Group or │ │Media Pressure│
│              │  │              │  │   Decision    │  │Individual Petition│ │              │
└──────┬───────┘  └──────┬───────┘  └──────┬───────┘  └────────┬─────────┘  └──────┬───────┘
```

New rules drafted for preliminary consideration

Office of Management and Budget reviews objectives and evaluates costs → Disapproval → STOP

Approval (with or without modifications)

Advance notice of proposed rule making issue

Draft circulated to industry, affected groups. Hearings held if necessary

Approval

Proposed regulations published in *Federal Register*; 30–60 days allowed for comments

Comments evaluated; final draft written

Office of Management and Budget reviews final version → Disapproval → STOP

Approval (with or without modifications)

Regulation published in *Federal Register*

As we discuss both rule making and administrative adjudication below, it is important to remember that a great deal of bureaucratic policy making occurs through informal channels, rather than through these formal processes. How bureaucrats interpret or apply (or choose not to apply) various policies are equally important parts of the policy-making process. Thus, what is sometimes called administrative discretion allows decision makers (whether they are in a Cabinet-level position or at the lowest GS levels) a tremendous amount of leeway.

Because regulations often involve political conflict, the 1946 Administrative Procedure Act established rule-making procedures to give everyone the chance to participate in the process. The Act requires that (1) public notice of the time, place, and nature of the rule-making proceedings be provided in the *Federal Register*, (2) interested parties be given the opportunity to submit written arguments and facts relevant to the rule, and (3) the statutory purpose and basis of the rule be stated. Once rules have been written, thirty days must elapse before they take effect.

Sometimes an agency is required by law to conduct a formal hearing before issuing rules. Evidence is gathered, and witnesses testify and are cross-examined by opposing interests. The process can take weeks, months, or even years, at the end of which agency administrators must review the entire record and then justify the rules. Although cumbersome, the process has reduced criticism of the rules and bolstered the deference given by the courts to agency decisions.

Administrative Adjudication

Administrative adjudication is a quasi-judicial process in which a bureaucratic agency settles disputes between two parties in a manner similar to the way courts resolve disputes. Administrative adjudication, like rule making, is referred to as "quasi" (meaning "almost") judicial, because law making by any body other than Congress, or adjudication by any body other than the judiciary would be a violation of the constitutional principle of separation of powers.

Agencies regularly find that persons or businesses are not in compliance with the federal laws the agencies are charged with enforcing, or that they are in violation of an agency rule or regulation. To force compliance, some agencies resort to administrative adjudication, which is generally less formal than a trial. Several agencies and boards employ administrative law judges to conduct the hearings. Although these judges are employed by the agency, they are strictly independent and cannot be removed except for gross misconduct.

David McIntosh was Director of Vice-President Dan Quayle's Council on Competitiveness. After the Council was abolished, McIntosh won election to Congress from Indiana's second district. In the 104th Congress he quickly emerged as the leader of the House's effort to reduce federal regulations.

Administrative adjudication A quasi-judicial process in which a bureaucratic agency settles disputes between two parties in a manner similar to the way courts resolve disputes.

Making Agencies Accountable

The question of to whom bureaucrats should be responsible is one that continually comes up in any debate about governmental accountability. Should the bureaucracy be answerable to itself? to organized interest groups? to its clientele? to the president? to Congress? or to some combination of all of these? While many would argue that bureaucrats should be responsive to the public interest, the public interest is difficult to define. As it turns out, several factors work to control the power of the bureaucracy and, to some degree, the same kinds of checks and balances that operate among the three branches of government serve to check the bureaucracy (see "Making Agencies Accountable," p. 258).

Many argue that the president should be in charge of the bureaucracy because it is up to him to see that popular ideas and expectations are translated into adminis-

A worker from the Environmental Protection Agency disposing of toxic waste.

Making Agencies Accountable

◆ ◆ ◆

The president has the authority to:

- Appoint and remove agency heads and a few additional top bureaucrats.
- Reorganize the bureaucracy (with congressional approval).
- Make changes in an agency's annual budget proposals.
- Ignore legislative initiatives originating within the bureaucracy.
- Initiate or adjust policies that would, if enacted by Congress, alter the bureaucracy's activities.
- Issue executive orders.

Congress has the authority to:

- Reduce an agency's annual budget.
- Pass legislation that alters the bureaucracy's activities.

- Abolish existing programs.
- Investigate bureaucratic activities and force bureaucrats to testify about them.
- Influence presidential appointments of agency heads and other top bureaucratic officials.
- Write legislation to limit the bureaucracy's discretion.

The courts have the authority to:

- Rule on whether bureaucrats have acted within the law and require policy changes to comply with the law.
- Force the bureaucracy to respect the rights of individuals through hearings and other proceedings.

trative action. But under our constitutional system, the president is not the only actor in the policy process. Congress creates the agencies, funds them, and establishes the broad rules of their operation. Moreover, Congress continually reviews the various agencies through oversight committee investigations, hearings, and its power of the purse.

The question of bureaucratic accountability is even more acute in Britain. The oversight function provided by Parliament, though improved in the 1980s, has generally been inadequate. Because political appointees constitute no more than the top two or three layers of Britain's bureaucracy, the vast majority of civil servants are shielded from national election results and therefore, some would argue, from executive control. The perception is of a small set of relatively inexperienced ministers set against a large, permanent, expert civil service. It is no wonder, critics argue, that elections produce so little change in Britain's governmental policies. Although often exaggerated, these concerns have sparked numerous attempts to reform the British civil service.

Executive Control

As the size and scope of the American national government in general, and of the executive branch and the bureaucracy in particular, have grown, presidents have delegated more and more power to bureaucrats. Recognizing this, each chief executive tries to appoint the best possible persons to carry out his wishes and policy preferences. Presidents may make thousands of appointments to the executive branch; in doing so, they have the opportunity to appoint individuals who share their views on a range of policies. And although presidential appointments make up less than 1 percent of all federal jobs, presidents usually fill most top policy-making positions.

Many presidents have expressed dismay over their inability to oversee the day-to-day workings of the bureaucracy. John F. Kennedy claimed that to give anyone at the State Department an instruction was comparable to putting it in a dead-letter box.[10] George Bush faced similar problems. In December 1990, for example, the Assistant Secretary for Civil Rights in the Department of Education announced that it was illegal for colleges and universities supported by federal monies to give scholarships designated solely for minority students. Although the White House strongly opposed quotas, the ruling deeply embarrassed Bush, who learned of it only after it was reported in the press. Still smarting from the wide criticisms he received over his vetoing of a civil rights bill, Bush ordered his aides to come up with a way to reverse the policy.[11]

Presidents can issue **executive orders** to provide direction to bureaucrats. Executive orders are presidential directives to an agency that provide the basis for carrying out laws or for establishing new policies. Even before Congress acted to protect women from discrimination by the federal government, for example, the National Organization for Women convinced President Lyndon B. Johnson to sign Executive Order 11375 in 1967. This amended an earlier order prohibiting the federal government from discriminating on the basis of race, color, religion, or national origin in the awarding of federal contracts, by adding to it the category of "gender." Nevertheless, although the president signed the Order, the Office of Federal Contract Compliance, the executive agency charged with implementing the Order, failed to draft appropriate guidelines for implementation of the Order until several years later.[12] A president can direct an agency to act, but it may take some time for his orders to be carried out. Given the many "jobs" of any president, few can ensure that all their orders will be carried out, or, as was the case with minority scholarships, that they will like all the rules that are made.

Historically, presidents have tried to control the bureaucracy by reorganizing it, but in general these efforts have not been particularly successful.[13] All recent presidents have tried to streamline the bureaucracy, a persistent goal of government reform, to make it more accountable. President Nixon, for example, proposed a plan to combine fifty domestic agencies and seven different departments into four large "super departments."

Because sweeping changes are seldom adopted, most presidents try only to tinker with the bureaucracy. Minor changes, however, don't appear to be of much real consequence, and the same problems of control generally reemerge elsewhere.[14] According to political scientists Benjamin I. Page and Mark P. Petracca, "In any case, reorganization is only an ultimate weapon—of last resort—in a continuing widespread struggle between presidents and the bureaucracy."[15]

Congressional Control

Congress, too, plays an important role in checking the power of the bureaucracy. Congress exercises considerable oversight over the bureaucracy in three main areas: its investigatory powers, its "powers of the purse," and its law-making power.

1. Investigatory powers. It is not at all unusual for a congressional committee or subcommittee to hold hearings on a particular problem, and then to direct the relevant

Executive orders Presidential directives to an agency that provide the basis for carrying out laws or for establishing new policies.

Who to Call?
♦ ♦ ♦

As part of the Clinton administration's efforts to assert executive control of "waste, fraud, and abuse," Vice President Al Gore Jr. was put in charge of a program to make government "less expensive and more efficient." In announcing the program, the President released toll-free telephone numbers for twenty-one federal agencies, and invited all Americans to call them with complaints, or to write to him or the vice president at 1600 Pennsylvania Avenue, Washington, D.C. 20006.

Here are the numbers:

- Commerce
  1-800-424-5197
- Commission on Civil Rights
  1-800-552-6843
- Defense
  1-800-424-9098
- Education
  1-800-647-8733
- Energy
  1-800-541-1625
- Environmental Protection Agency
  1-800-424-4000
- Health and Human Services
  1-800-368-5779
- Housing and Urban Development
  1-800-347-3735
- Justice
  1-800-869-4499
- Labor
  1-800-347-3756
- Nuclear Regulatory Commission
  1-800-233-3497
- Treasury
  1-800-359-3898
- Veterans Affairs
  1-800-488-8244

In 1993 President Clinton made history when he appointed Dade County, Florida, prosecutor Janet Reno as the first female U.S. Attorney General.

agency to study the problem or find ways to remedy it. Representatives of the agencies also appear before these committees on a regular basis to inform members about agency activities, ongoing investigations, and so on.

2. Power of the purse. To control the bureaucracy, Congress dangles its ability to fund or not fund an agency's activities like the sword of Damocles over the heads of various agency officials.[16] The House Appropriations Committee routinely holds hearings to allow agency heads to justify their budget requests. Authorization legislation originates in the various legislative committees that oversee particular agencies (such as Agriculture, Veterans' Affairs, Education, and Labor) and sets the maximum amounts that agencies can spend on particular programs. While some authorizations, such as Social Security, are permanent, others, including the State Department and Defense Department procurements, are watched closely and are subject to annual authorizations.

Once funds are authorized, they must be appropriated before they can be spent. Appropriations originate with the House Appropriations Committee, not the specialized legislative committees. Often, the Appropriations Committee allocates sums smaller than those authorized by the legislative committee. Thus, the Appropriations Committee, a budget cutter, has an additional oversight function.

3. Law Making. Congress can also pass new legislation to clarify policies or overturn regulations or rules. If Congress, for example, does not approve of agency regulations written to enforce existing statutes, it can redraft legislation to make its wishes clearer.

Congress's oversight of the bureaucracy is difficult, has few political rewards unless the problems addressed are of interest to a member's district or otherwise worthy of publicity, and requires professional accounting expertise. Recognizing that the bureaucracy's financial affairs were big and important enough to be professionally handled, in 1921 Congress created the General Accounting Office (GAO; see p. 192) at the same time that the Office of the Budget was created in the executive branch. And with the establishment of the GAO, the Congressional Research Service, and later, the Congressional Budget Office, Congress essentially created its own bureaucracy to keep an eye on what the executive branch and its bureaucracy were doing.

Today the GAO not only tracks how money is spent in the bureaucracy, but also monitors how policies are implemented. The Congressional Budget Office also conducts oversight studies. If it or the GAO uncovers problems with an agency's work, Congress is notified immediately.

Judicial Control

The judiciary's oversight function is less direct than that of the other two branches of government. Although injured parties can bring suit against agencies for their failure to enforce the law, or even challenge agency interpretations of the law, in general the courts give great weight to the opinions of bureaucrats and usually defer to their expertise.

The courts have, however, ruled that agencies must give all affected individuals their due process rights guaranteed by the U.S. Constitution. A Social Security recipient's checks cannot be stopped, for example, unless that individual is provided with reasonable notice and an opportunity for a hearing.

Problems with the Modern Bureaucracy

As the modern bureaucracy has grown, so have its problems. Not only do the executive branch and Congress have difficulty in overseeing the actions of the numerous bureaus, agencies, and commissions, but often the right hand of any agency does not know what its left hand is doing. This confusion is complicated by the presence of interagency committees, which have been established to coordinate the implementation of various public policies that require interdepartmental cooperation. Other factors that contribute to problems with the bureaucracy include red tape, waste, conflict, and duplication.

Iron Triangles and Issue Networks

While Congress and the president continually criticize the bureaucracy and, indeed, often take steps to control it, the strong ties that agencies enjoy with interest groups on the one hand and congressional committees and subcommittees on the other help to explain the uphill battle to "control" the bureaucracy.

Iron Triangles.   For many years, political scientists observed the relatively stable relationships and patterns of interaction that occur among an agency, interest groups, and congressional committees or subcommittees, and dubbed these relationships **iron triangles**, or subgovernments.

Policy-making subgovernments are "iron" because they are virtually impenetrable to outsiders and are largely autonomous. Even presidents have difficulty piercing the workings of these subgovernments, which have endured over time. Examples of iron triangles abound. Senior citizens' groups (especially the American Association of Retired Persons), the Social Security Administration, and the House Subcommittee on

Iron triangles The relatively stable relationships and patterns of interaction that occur among an agency, interest groups, and congressional committees or subcommittees.

President Clinton and Vice President Gore stand in front of a forklift loaded with tons of government regulations to dramatize their plan to cut and reshape government in an effort to trim over $100 billion from the national budget.

The Head Start program identifies deserving preschool
children and provides much
needed education, nutrition, and
socializing.

Aging all are likely to agree on the need for increased Social Security benefits. Similarly, the Department of Veterans' Affairs, the House Committee on Veterans' Affairs,
and the American Legion and Veterans of Foreign Wars—the two largest organizations
representing veterans—are usually in agreement on the need for expanded programs
for veterans.

The policy decisions made within these iron triangles often foster the interests of a
clientele group and have little to do with the advancement of national policy goals. In
part, subgovernmental decisions often conflict with other governmental policies and
tend to tie the hands of larger institutions such as Congress and the president. The
White House is often too busy dealing with international affairs or crises to deal with
smaller issues like veterans' benefits. Likewise, Congress defers to its committees and
subcommittees. Thus, these subgovernments decentralize policy making and make it
more difficult to control.[17]

Issue Networks.   Today, iron triangles no longer dominate most policy processes for
three main reasons: an increasingly complex society, issues that cut across several policy areas, and the phenomenal increase in number of Washington, D.C.-based interest
groups. As these three changes have occurred, many iron triangles have become rusty,
and new terms have been coined to describe the policy-making process and the bureaucracy's role in it. Hugh Heclo argues that this system of separate subgovernments
is overlaid with an amorphous system of **issue networks**;[18] that is, the fuzzy set of relationships among a large number of actors in broad policy areas. In general, like iron
triangles, issue networks are made up of agency officials, members of Congress (and
committee staffers), and interest-group lobbyists. But they also often include lawyers,
consultants, academics, public relations specialists, and sometimes even the courts.[19]
Unlike iron triangles, issue networks are constantly changing as members with technical expertise become involved in various issues.

Issue networks A term used to
describe the loose and informal set
of relationships that exist among a
large number of actors who work in
broad policy areas.

Issue networks reflect the complexity of the issues that lawmakers and policy makers face. As an example, let's look at the plight of many American children. Lawmakers routinely call for new programs to make children's lives better, and the Clinton administration is sympathetic. First Lady Hillary Rodham Clinton, in fact, at one time chaired the board of the Children's Defense Fund, a national child advocacy group. But the plight of children isn't an easy problem to solve. All kinds of complex and interrelated issues are involved. It is, for example, a health issue, because many children don't have access to medical care; an education issue because many can't read, go to poor schools, or are dropouts; a labor issue because many have no job skills; and a drug and crime issue because many of these children live in drug-infested neighborhoods and often ultimately turn to crime, ending up in jail as a result. But given the segmented nature of policy making, how can the nation expect one coherent and encompassing policy to better the lives of American children from the Departments of Health and Human Services, Education, Labor, and Justice—*plus* all their associated House and Senate subcommittees, interest groups, and experts? And most of these agencies have to make do in the face of growing budget cutbacks.

Accountability

Accountability, that is, holding members of the bureaucracy responsible for how they implement laws and presidential directives, is one of the greatest issues in bureaucratic politics. Because the way bureaucracies are designed affects the way they operate, most presidents have tried to change the structure and design of many agencies to make them function better and to facilitate oversight. This would make bureaucrats more accountable to both the president and Congress for their decisions. Making bureaucrats more accountable is problematic for two main reasons: the sheer size of the bureaucracy and shortcomings inherent in the bureaucratic system itself.

Size Problems.   The bureaucracy's size has led to a system that encourages some bureaucrats to believe that they, and not elected officials, actually make laws and policy:

1. Red Tape. As rules and regulations established by the huge bureaucracy become increasingly complex, policy goals are often lost in a mass of red tape, complex rules, and procedures that must be followed before anything can get done. The paperwork and maze of regulations that one must get through, to obtain, say, Social Security disability benefits or veteran's benefits are so overwhelming that many people are discouraged from ever applying for what is rightfully theirs.

2. Waste. Duplication of services and faulty coordination are also problems in most bureaucracies. Within the executive branch, for example, economic policy is split among the Office of Management and Budget, the Departments of Treasury and Commerce, the Council of Economic Advisors, and the Federal Reserve Board. Lack of coordination among these bodies helps explain the problems inherent in economic policy.

System Problems.   While red tape and waste result from the size of the bureaucracy, other problems arise from the way the bureaucratic system is set up.

1. Inadequate Mechanisms for Evaluation. Often, the success of a program may be difficult to gauge, because there are no precise standards of evaluation. EPA air cleanup targets in the 1970s, for example, were not based on scientific analysis. And if information concerning success is not available or cannot be measured with any precision, it becomes difficult for policy makers to know what to do with the program. Should it be continued, changed, or eliminated?

2. Decentralized Authority. The basic structure of a central agency in Washington, D.C. and regional offices makes coordination difficult, as does the structure of the federal system itself. While an agency in Washington, D.C., may have clear ideas concerning how a particular program should work, state and local officials may have very different ideas and different ways of implementing them.

3. Vague Objectives. Vague instructions are yet another problem that haunts bureaucrats. Congress often states only broad policy goals in its legislation and leaves the specifics of how to achieve these goals up to bureaucrats. In this way Congress cannot be blamed for any particularly unpopular interpretations.

One particularly controversial policy was at the heart of Title IX of the Education Amendments of 1972, which mandated that

> No person in the United States shall, on the basis of sex, be excluded from participation in, be denied the benefits of, or be subjected to discrimination under any education program or activity receiving federal financial assistance.

The law further instructed the Secretary of Health, Education, and Welfare (it now applies to the Secretary of Education) to "prepare and publish proposed regulations . . . which shall include with respect to intercollegiate athletic activities reasonable provisions considering the nature of particular sports" to implement the amendments. Supporters of women's athletics in colleges and universities went around and around with HEW officials over the intent of Congress. Supporters of women's sports argued that discrimination against women in all sports was prohibited. Others said that revenue-producing sports such as basketball and football were exempt.

Finally, in December, 1978—six years after passage of the amendments—the Office for Civil Rights in HEW released a "policy interpretation" of the law dealing largely with the section that concerned intercollegiate athletics.[20] More than thirty pages of text were devoted to dealing with 100 or so words from the statute. Football was recognized as unique, so it could be inferred that male-dominated football programs could continue to outspend women's athletic programs. The more than sixty women's groups that had lobbied for equality of spending were outraged, and turned their efforts toward seeking more favorable rulings on the construction of the statute from the courts.

4. Insufficient Funding. Congress often fails to fund some programs fully, making their success unlikely. Head Start and the Food Stamps program, for example, are never sufficiently funded to allow all who are eligible to receive the benefits of those programs. Domestic social welfare programs are perennially the target of presidential and congressional budget cutters who seek political gains from attacking the "bloated bureaucracy" while seriously attempting to get the national deficit in check.

Title IX Enforcement Leads Way for a Dramatic Increase in Women and Sports

❖ ❖ ❖

Since passage of Title IX in 1972, there has been a dramatic increase in the number of high school and college women competing in school sports.

YEAR	COLLE-GIATE	HIGH SCHOOL
1972	32,000	817,000
1976	64,000	1,645,000
1994	158,000	2,125,000*

*Source: Data only from *Atlanta Journal and Constitution* (February 1, 1995): C-1.

Toward Reform

Historically, politicians and presidents have called for reform of the bureaucracy. Thomas Jefferson was the first. He attempted to cut the waste and bring about a "wise and frugal government." But it wasn't until the Progressive Era (1890–1920) that calls for reform began to be taken seriously. Later, Calvin Coolidge urged spending cuts and other reforms. His Two Percent Club was created to cut staff, as its name implies, by 2 percent each year; his Correspondence Club was designed to reduce bureaucratic letter writing by thirty percent.[21] And as the box below illustrates, all recent presidents have had a plan to streamline government. Some plans, like those of Presidents Johnson and Carter, have involved budget systems; others, like Nixon's, have been more programmatic. As discussed earlier in this chapter, Nixon suggested that all executive departments be combined into four "super" departments organized by function. But according to his former aide John Erlichman, this plan to "disrupt iron triangles" was dead on arrival. "Why? Because such a reorganization would have broken up the hoary

Re-Re-Re-Re-Re-Reinventing Government
◆ ◆ ◆

U.S. leaders before Bill Clinton and Al Gore Jr. have had high hopes for domestic *perestroika*

President	Name of Plan	Comment
Johnson	Programming, Planning, and Budgeting Systems	"[This is] a very revolutionary system . . . so that through the tools of modern management the full promise of a finer life can be brought to every American at the lowest possible cost."
Nixon	Management By Objectives	"The time has come . . . to organize the government by conscious, comprehensive design to meet the new needs of a new era."
Carter	Zero-Based Budgeting	"It's simple and it works . . . It will make sure that the money that is allocated . . . goes further."
Reagan	President's Private Sector Survey On Cost Control (Grace Commission)	"[The commission] will work like tireless bloodhounds, leaving no stone unturned in their search to root out inefficiency and waste of taxpayer dollars."
Bush	Right-Sizing Government	"I honestly believe that this is the only way to get the size and spending of government under control."
Clinton/Gore	Reinventing Government (National Performance Review)	"It's about whether we can restore the trust of the American people in their government."

Source: From: "Re-Re-Re-Re-Re-Reinventing Government, *Time,* September 13, 1993. Copyright ©1993 Time, Inc. Reprinted by permission. Clinton/Gore information provided by authors.

congressional committee organization that corresponded to the existing departments and agencies." More specifically,

> A subcommittee chairman with oversight of the Agriculture Department would lose power, perks and status if we were authorized to fold Agriculture into a new Department of Natural Resources. The powerful farm lobbies were equally hostile to the idea.[22]

President Bill Clinton also offered a reform plan. As part of his "reinventing government campaign" Clinton signed executive orders early in 1993 to:

- cut the size of the federal work force by 252,000 people within five years.
- cut in half the growing number of federal regulations within three years.
- set customer service standards to direct agencies to put the people they serve first.

Author Karen Berger holds a silicone gel breast implant at a press conference in November, 1991. Berger testified at a Food and Drug Administration hearing considering banning the implants due to health fears. In 1992, the FDA took those implants off the market. Manufacturers failed to prove the implants were safe.

Heading the President's Task Force on Reinventing Government is Vice President Gore. His task force report, the 200-page *National Performance Review*, made over 800 recommendations, citing problems and offering solutions. Most of the solutions were geared toward making the bureaucracy more accountable and cost-effective. While some of these reforms may be fairly easy to implement, if we are to learn anything from the lessons of history, major change is unlikely.

But in 1995, both President Clinton and the Congress began to call for dramatic reforms not seen in American politics since the New Deal. Still, during the New Deal era, both the president and the Congress were from the same political party. Today, however, although the president and the Congress both see a need for major changes in government, the differences in their basic approach to government and the role of bureaucracy are likely to get in the way of major change. Yet, calls for downsizing government are coming from both sides of the aisle in Congress, and President Clinton appears to agree with the Republican majority on the need for some reforms.

The President, for example, has called for abolishing the Interstate Commerce Commission. In Congress, Republicans have called for eliminating the Department of Education, downsizing the Department of Housing and Urban Development and the Environmental Protection Agency, slashing funds to or eliminating the Corporation for Public Broadcasting, the National Endowment for the Arts, the Federal Trade Commission, and the Consumer Product Safety Commission, and also for privatizing the U.S. Post Office.

Sunshine laws After passage by Congress in 1976, sunshine laws require that about 50 multi-headed federal agencies hold their meetings in sessions open to the public.

Sunshine Laws.   To date, one of the most successful first steps in reforming the bureaucracy and making it more accountable was congressional passage in 1976 of the Government in the Sunshine Act. For the first time, it required that about fifty multi-headed federal agencies hold their meetings in sessions open to the public. The Act defined *meetings* very broadly. Included in the open meetings requirement were almost any formal or informal meeting of agency members—including conference calls. The Act exempted some meetings, including those dealing with personnel matters or judicial proceedings, but it went a long way toward opening up the process. Many states also require that their agency meetings be held in the open.

Sunset Laws. Of the bureaucracy, President Gerald R. Ford once wrote,

> One of the enduring truths of the nation's capital is that bureaucrats survive. Agencies don't fold their tents and quietly fade away after their work is done. They find Something New to Do. Invariably, that Something New involves more people with more power and more paperwork—all involving more expenditures.[23]

One proposal to limit the size and scope of government and the problems noted by Ford are **sunset laws**, which provide that agencies or programs be abolished automatically after a fixed period of years unless Congress extends their life. The theory behind this reform is that new agencies or programs will not have the opportunity to be "captured" by special interests and will perform their duties more free of outside influences and more in accord with the public interest.

Sunset laws Laws that provide that agencies or programs are automatically abolished after a fixed period of years unless Congress extends their life.

Summary

The bureaucracy plays a major role in America as a shaper of public policy, earning it the nickname the "fourth branch" of government. To explain the evolution and scope of bureaucratic power, in this chapter we have made the following points:

1. The federal bureaucracy started off quite small. George Washington, for example, presided over an executive branch that had only three departments—State, War, and Treasury. It was not until the Civil War that significant gains occurred in the size of the federal bureaucracy as the government geared up to conduct a war. As employment opportunities within the federal government increased, concurrent reforms in the civil service system assured that more and more jobs were filled according to merit and not by patronage. By the late 1800s, reform efforts led to further increases in the size of the bureaucracy, as independent regulatory commissions were created. And in the wake of the Depression, many new agencies were created to get the national economy back on course as part of FDR's New Deal.

2. The modern bureaucracy is composed of nearly 3 million civilian workers from all walks of life. Most hold merit appointments and are very hard to discharge. In general, bureaucratic agencies fall into four general types: departments, government corporations, independent agencies, and regulatory boards or commissions.

3. Bureaucrats not only make, but implement public policy. Administrative discretion allows bureaucrats to decide how to implement congressional and presidential directives. Administrative discretion can be exercised on an informal basis, or more formally through rule making and administrative adjudication.

4. While agencies enjoy considerable discretion, they are subjected to many formal controls. The president, Congress, and the judiciary all exercise various degrees of control over the bureaucracy.

5. In spite of all of the direct and indirect checks and balances on the bureaucracy, it is still difficult to control. Iron triangles and issue networks make control more difficult. Accountability is made almost impossible by the vast size of the bureaucracy and several systems problems, including inadequate mechanisms for evaluation, decentralized authority, vague objectives and insufficient funding.

6. Presidents since Jefferson have called for reforms in the bureaucracy to cut waste and to make it more efficient. Few have succeeded.

Key Terms

bureaucracy

bureaucrats

patronage

spoils system

civil service system

Pendleton Act (Civil Service Reform Act of 1883)

merit system

regulatory commission

Hatch Act

Federal Employees Political Activities Act

clientele agencies

government corporations

independent agencies

implementation

administrative discretion

rule making

regulations

administrative adjudication

executive orders

iron triangles

issue networks

Sunshine laws

sunset laws

Suggested Readings

Derthick, Martha, and Paul J. Quirk. *The Politics of Deregulation*. Washington: Brookings Institution, 1985.

Dodd, Lawrence, and Richard Schott. *Congress and the Administrative State*. New York: Wiley, 1979.

Gormley, William T. Jr. *Taming the Bureaucracy: Muscles, Prayers and Other Strategies*. Princeton, NJ: Princeton University Press, 1989.

Knott, Jack H., and Gary J. Miller. *Reforming Bureaucracy: The Politics of Institutional Choice*. Englewood Cliffs, NJ: Prentice Hall, 1987.

Rourke, Francis E. *Bureaucracy, Politics and Public Policy*. Boston: Little, Brown, 1984.

Seidman, Harold, and Robert Gilmour. *Politics, Position, and Power*, 4th ed. New York: Oxford University Press, 1986.

Stillman, Richard J. *The American Bureaucracy*. New York: Nelson Hall, 1987.

Weiss, Carol H., and Allen H. Barton., ed. *Making Bureaucracies Work*. Beverly Hills: Sage Publications, 1980.

Wilson, James Q. *Bureaucracy: What Government Agencies Do and Why They Do It*. New York: Basic Books, 1989.

The Judiciary

When Alexander Hamilton wrote under the pen name of "Publius" to urge support of the U.S. Constitution in 1787, he firmly believed that the judiciary was the weakest of the three departments of government. And in its formative years, the judiciary was, in Hamilton's terms, "the least dangerous" branch. So seemingly inconsequential was the judicial branch that when the national government made its move to the District of Columbia, Congress forgot to include any space to house the justices of the Supreme Court! Last-minute conferences with the Capitol architects led to the allocation of a small area in the basement of the Senate wing of the Capitol Building for a courtroom. No other space was allowed for the justices, however. Noted one commentator, "A stranger might traverse the darkest avenues of the Capitol for a week, without finding the remote corner in which justice is served in the American Republic."[1]

Today, the role of the courts, particularly the U.S. Supreme Court, is significantly different from that envisioned in 1788, the year the national government came into being. The "least dangerous branch" is now perceived by many as having too much power. During different periods of the judiciary's history, the role and power of the federal courts have varied tremendously. They have often played a key role in creating a strong national government and have boldly led the nation in social reform. Yet at other times, the federal courts, especially the U.S. Supreme Court, have stubbornly stood as a major obstacle to important social and economic change.

In this chapter we explore the development of the national judiciary. The Framers could never have envisioned that the authority of the Supreme Court and other federal

> he judiciary, from the nature of its functions, will always
> be the least dangerous to the political rights of the
> Constitution; because it will be least in a capacity to
> annoy or injure them.
>
> *Alexander Hamilton*
> *Federalist No. 78*

The Framers worried about the tyranny of taxation, military despotism, a too-powerful presidency, and the balance of power between national and state governments. Because the judiciary was not expected to make policy in these areas, Hamilton feared the courts far less than he feared Congress or the president.

courts would grow to include issues as diverse as the right of married couples to use birth control, the right of parents to withdraw life-support systems from their children, and the question of whether a pregnant woman could be forced to undergo a caesarean section prior to going into natural labor. As some recent battles over nominations to the Supreme Court reveal, a growing segment of the public views the Court as the final word on many important, controversial issues.

We pay special attention to the political nature of the courts and examine how the power of the courts, especially that of the Supreme Court, has expanded over time. Many Americans have been raised to think of the Supreme Court as far above the fray

The Supreme Court does not operate in a vacuum. Here, protesters line up in front of the Court to comment on issues ranging from privacy to coerced confessions.

of politics. That is simply not the case. *Elected* presidents nominate justices to the Supreme Court, often to advance their personal politics, and *elected* Senators ultimately confirm (or decline to confirm) presidential nominees. Not only is the selection process political, but the process by which cases ultimately get heard by the Supreme Court is often political, too. Interest groups routinely seek out good test cases to advance their policy positions. Even the U.S. government, generally through the Justice Department and the U.S. Solicitor General (another political appointee), seeks to advance its version of the public interest in court. Interest groups then often line up on opposing sides, each in the form of an **amicus curiae** (friend of the court), and file briefs advancing their positions much in the same way that lobbyists do in Congress.

> **Amicus curiae** "Friend of the court"; a third party to a lawsuit who files a legal brief for the purpose of raising additional points of view in an attempt to influence a court's decision.

Moreover, as we will discuss, the justices of the Supreme Court don't make decisions in a vacuum. Not only do they read legal briefs and hear oral arguments, but they also read newspapers, watch television, and have some knowledge of public opinion—especially on controversial issues. In 1989, for example, pro-choice and right-to-life forces not only marched on Washington to highlight their respective causes, they also jammed the Court's phones and inundated the justices with mail. Similarly, in 1993, the Court's switchboard lit up like the national Christmas tree with calls about Baby Jessica, the two-year-old who was returned to her birth parents after they spent two years in legal wrangling with her custodial parents. Operators reported that some callers sobbed, others yelled, and others wanted to know how to impeach the Chief Justice. While actions like these probably have little impact on a particular justice's view of a particular case, they do make the Court aware of the intensity of public opinion on some issues.

A note on terminology before we start: When we refer to the Supreme Court, the Court, or high court here, we mean the U.S. Supreme Court, which sits at the pinnacle of the federal and state court systems. The Supreme Court is referred to by the name of the Chief Justice who presided over it during a particular period (e.g., the Marshall Court is the Court presided over by John Marshall from 1801 to 1835). When we use the term "courts," we refer to all federal or state courts unless otherwise noted.

The Creation of the Judicial Branch

At the Philadelphia Convention, James Madison took detailed notes that were released after his death. His notes make it clear that the Framers devoted little time to the writing or the content of Article III, which created the judicial branch of government. The Framers believed that it posed little of the threat of tyranny that they feared from the other two branches. One scholar has even suggested that for at least some delegates to the Constitutional Convention,

> provision for a national judiciary was a matter of theoretical necessity . . . more in deference to the maxim of separation [of powers] than in response to clearly formulated ideas about the role of a national judicial system and its indispensability.[2]

Anti-Federalists, however, did not agree about the need for a supreme court, in particular, or a federal judiciary, in general. They particularly objected to a judiciary whose members had life tenure and the ability to interpret what was to be "the supreme law of the land," a phrase that Anti-Federalists feared would give the Supreme Court too much power.

The Framers also debated the need for any federal courts below the level of the Supreme Court. Some argued in favor of deciding all cases in state courts, with only appeals going before the Supreme Court. Others argued for a system of federal courts. A compromise left the final choice to Congress, and Article III began simply by vesting "The judicial Power of the United States . . . in one supreme Court, and in such inferior Courts as the Congress may from time to time ordain and establish." Although there was some debate over whether the Court should have the power of judicial review (which allows the judiciary to review acts of the other branches of government and the states) the question was left unsettled in Article III (and not finally resolved until *Marbury* v. *Madison* [1803], discussed on page 276). This vagueness was not all that unusual, given the numerous compromises that took place in Philadelphia.

Had the Supreme Court been viewed as the potential policy maker it is today, it is highly unlikely that the Founders would have provided for life tenure with "good behavior" for federal judges in Article III. This feature was agreed upon because the Framers did not want the justices (or any federal judges) subject to the whims of politics, the public, or politicians. Moreover, Alexander Hamilton argued in *Federalist No. 78* that the "independence of judges" was needed "to guard the Constitution and the rights of individuals." Because the Framers viewed the Court as quite powerless, Hamilton stressed the need to place federal judges above the fray of politics. Yet although there is no denying that judges are political animals and carry the same prejudices and preferences to the bench that others do to the statehouse, Congress, or the White House, the provision of life tenure for "good behavior" has functioned well.

Some checks on the power of the judiciary were nonetheless included in the Constitution. Congress can alter the Court's jurisdiction (its ability to hear certain kinds of cases). Congress can also propose constitutional amendments that, if ratified, can effectively reverse judicial decisions, and it can impeach and remove federal judges. In one further check, it is the president who (with the "advice and consent" of the Senate) appoints all federal judges.

The Judiciary Act of 1789 and the Creation of the Federal Judicial System

In spite of the Framers' intentions, the pervasive role of politics in the judicial branch quickly became evident with the passage of the Judiciary Act of 1789. Congress spent nearly the entire second half of its first session deliberating the various provisions of the Act needed to give form and substance to the federal judiciary. As one early observer noted, "The convention has only crayoned in the outlines. It left it to Congress to fill up and colour the canvas."[3]

The Judiciary Act was drafted largely by U.S. Senator Oliver Ellsworth, a former member of the Constitutional Convention from Connecticut who later served on the Supreme Court as its second Chief Justice, from 1796 to 1800. The Act established the basic three-tiered structure of the federal court system. At the bottom were the federal district courts—one in each state (except Massachusetts and Virginia, with two apiece)—each staffed by a federal judge. Appeals from the district courts were to be made to one of the three circuit courts. Each circuit court was composed of one district court judge and two itinerant Supreme Court justices who joined them in twice-yearly meetings. Although the Constitution mentions "the supreme Court," it was silent on its size. In the Judiciary Act of 1789, Congress set the size of the Supreme Court at six—the Chief Justice plus five associate justices.

When the justices met in their first public session in New York City in 1790, they were magnificently garbed in black and scarlet robes in the English fashion, but they had discarded what Thomas Jefferson termed "the monstrous wig which makes English judges look like rats peeping through bunches of oakum!"[4] The elegance of their attire, however, could not make up for the relatively ineffective status of the Court. Its first session even had to be adjourned when not enough justices showed up. And the Jay Court only decided one really important case—*Chisholm* v. *Georgia* (1793), discussed on page 274. Moreover, in an indication of its status, one associate justice left the Court to become Chief Justice of the South Carolina Supreme Court. (Although such a move would be considered a step down today, keep in mind that in the early years of the United States, many viewed the states as more important than the new national government.)

Hampered by frequent changes in personnel, limited space for its operations, no clerical support, and no system of reporting its decisions, the Court and its meager activities did not impress many people. From the beginning, the circuit court duties of the Supreme Court justices presented problems for the prestige of the Court. Few good lawyers were willing to accept nominations to the high court because its circuit court duties entailed a substantial amount of travel—most of it on horseback over poorly maintained roads in frequently inclement weather. Southern justices often tallied up as much as 10,000 miles a year on horseback. George Washington tried to prevail upon several friends and supporters to fill vacancies on the Court as they appeared, but most refused the "honor." John Adams, the second president of the United States, ran into similar problems. When he asked John Jay, the first Chief Justice, to resume the position after he resigned to become governor of New York, Jay declined the offer. Jay had

Left: The Supreme Court held its first two sessions in this building, called the Exchange, in New York City. Right: The minutes from the first session of the Supreme Court of the United States, held on February 1, 1790. Not much went on—the session had to be adjourned when too few justices showed up.

John Jay (1745–1829), one of the authors of *The Federalist Papers,* was the first Chief Justice of the U.S. Supreme Court, a position he held from 1789 to 1795. While serving as Chief Justice, he left the country for a year to lead a diplomatic mission to Great Britain which resulted in an agreement that bears his name—the Jay Treaty. Jay was one of the architects of New York's first state constitution, and while still Chief Justice, he ran unsuccessfully for governor of that state. He was elected as governor in 1794 while in England. Jay resigned as Chief Justice in 1795 to assume the New York governorship.

once remarked of the Court that it had lacked "energy, weight and dignity" as well as "public confidence and respect." Given Jay's view of the Court and its performance statistics, his refusal was not surprising.

In spite of all its problems, in its first decade the Court took several actions to help mold the new nation. First, by declining to render advisory opinions, the justices attempted to establish the Supreme Court as an independent, nonpolitical branch of government. Although John Jay frequently gave the president advice in private, the Court refused to answer questions Washington posed to it concerning the construction of international laws and treaties. The justices wanted to avoid the appearance of prejudging an issue that could later arise before them.

The early Court also tried to advance principles of nationalism and to maintain the national government's supremacy over the states. As circuit court jurists, the justices rendered numerous decisions on such matters as national suppression of the Whiskey Rebellion and the constitutionality of the Alien and Sedition Acts, which made it a crime to criticize national governmental officials or their actions (see Chapter 4).

During the ratification debates, Anti-Federalists had warned that Article III extended federal judicial power to controversies "between a State and Citizens of another State," meaning that a citizen of one state could sue any other state in federal court, a prospect unthinkable to defenders of state sovereignty. Although Federalists, including Hamilton and Madison, had scoffed at the idea, the nationalist Supreme Court quickly proved them wrong in *Chisholm* v. *Georgia* (1793).[5] In *Chisholm*, the justices interpreted the Court's jurisdiction under Article III, Section 2, to include the right to hear suits brought by a citizen of one state against another state. Writing in *Chisholm*, Justice James Wilson, for example, denounced the "haughty notions of state independence, state sovereignty, and state independence." The states' reaction to this perceived attack on their authority led to speedy passage and ratification (in 1798) of the Eleventh Amendment, which specifically limited judicial power by stipulating that the federal courts' authority could not "extend to any suit . . . commenced or prosecuted against one of the United States by citizens of another State."

Finally, in a series of circuit and Supreme Court decisions, the justices paved the way for announcement of the doctrine of judicial review by the third Chief Justice, John Marshall. (Oliver Ellsworth served from 1796 to 1800.) Justices "riding circuit" frequently held state laws unconstitutional because they violated the U.S. Constitution. And in *Hylton* v. *United States* (1796),[6] the Court evaluated for the first time the constitutionality of an act of Congress. In *Hylton*, the Court ruled that a congressional excise tax on carriages was not a direct tax and was therefore valid even though it was not apportioned evenly among the states (as called for in the Constitution).

The Marshall Court (1801–1835)

John Marshall was appointed Chief Justice by President John Adams in 1801, three years after he declined to accept a nomination as associate justice. (See "People of the Past: John Marshall," p. 275.) An ardent Federalist who also earlier had declined Washington's offer to become Attorney General, Marshall later came to be considered the most important justice ever to serve on the high court. Part of his reputation is the result of the duration of his service and the historical significance of this period in our nation's history. Marshall also, however, brought much-needed respect and prestige to the Court through his leadership in a progression of cases and a series of innovations.

*P*EOPLE OF THE PAST

John Marshall

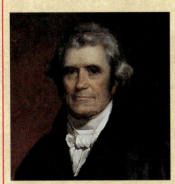

John Marshall (1755–1835) was born in a log cabin in Germantown, Virginia, the first of fifteen children of Welsh immigrants. Although tutored at home by two clergymen, Marshall's inspiration was his father, who introduced him to English literature and Sir William Blackstone's influential *Commentaries on the Laws of England*. After serving in the Continental Army and acquiring the rank of captain, Marshall taught himself the law. He attended only one formal course at the College of William and Mary before being admitted to the bar. Marshall practiced law in Virginia, where he and his wife lived and raised a family. Of their ten children, only six survived childhood.

Marshall served as a delegate to the Virginia legislature from 1782 to 1785, 1787 to 1790, and 1795 to 1796, and played an instrumental role in Virginia's ratification of the U.S. Constitution in 1787. As the leading Federalist in Virginia, Marshall was offered several positions in the Federalist administrations of George Washington and John Adams—including Attorney General and associate justice to the Supreme Court—but he refused them all. Finally, Washington persuaded him to run for the House of Representatives in 1799. Marshall was elected, but his career in the House was brief, for he became Secretary of State in 1800 under John Adams. When Oliver Ellsworth resigned as Chief Justice of the U.S. Supreme Court in 1800, Adams nominated Marshall.

Marshall was well suited to the leisurely pace of the Supreme Court in its early days. He enjoyed the outdoors and socializing in the clubs and saloons around Richmond, and he excelled at quoits (similar to horseshoes).

Marshall dominated the Court during his thirty-four years as Chief Justice. As one commentator noted, "Marshall found the Constitution paper; and he made it power. He found a skeleton, and he clothed it with flesh and blood."* In essence, Marshall transformed the Court into a co-equal branch of government through a series of key decisions that established:

- The practice by which the view of the Court is expressed in a single opinion instead of a series of opinions, as had previously been the case. Marshall insisted on unanimity, and discouraged dissenting and concurring opinions, thereby winning for the Court the prestige it needed to resolve many of the conflicts and controversies that came before it.
- The Court as the final arbiter of constitutional questions, with the right to declare congressional acts void (*Marbury* v. *Madison* [1803]).
- The authority of the Supreme Court over the judiciaries of the various states, including the Court's power to declare state laws invalid (*Fletcher* v. *Peck* [1810]; *Martin* v. *Hunter's Lessee* [1816]; *Cohens* v. *Virginia* [1821]).
- The supremacy of the federal government and Congress over state governments through a broad interpretation of the "necessary and proper" clause (*McCulloch* v. *Maryland* [1819]).

During the Marshall era, the Court operated like a family firm. The justices came to Washington for only a few months at a time, so they lived together in a boarding house where they often discussed cases at dinner over wine.

Personalities and individual characteristics had a tremendous influence on the Court. Although Marshall had had little experience in the practice of law and none as a judge prior to his appointment to Chief Justice, his personality and leadership capabilities allowed him to shape the Court and the federal judiciary into a branch of the government with authority and respect.

* Schwartz, *The Law in America*, p. 49.

One of Marshall's first innovations on the Court was to discontinue the practice of *seriatim* (Latin for "in a series") opinions, which was the custom of the King's Bench in Great Britain. Prior to the Marshall Court, the justices delivered their individual opinions in order. There was no single "opinion of the Court," as we are accustomed to today. For the Court to take its place as an equal branch of government, Marshall strongly believed, the justices needed to speak as a *Court* and not as six individuals. In fact, during Marshall's first four years in office, the Court routinely spoke as one, and the Chief Justice wrote twenty-four of its twenty-six opinions.

Judicial Review

During the Philadelphia Convention, the Framers debated and rejected the idea of judicial veto of legislation or executive acts, and they rejected the Virginia Plan's proposal to give the judiciary explicit authority over Congress. They did, however, approve Article VI, which contains the supremacy clause (see Chapter 3).

Judicial review The authority of a court to review the acts of the legislature, the executive, or states to determine their constitutionality; enunciated by Chief Justice John Marshall in *Marbury* v. *Madison* (1803).

In *Federalist No. 78,* Alexander Hamilton first publicly endorsed the idea of **judicial review,** noting, "whenever a particular statute contravenes the Constitution, it will be the duty of the judicial tribunals to adhere to the latter and disregard the former." Nonetheless, because the power of judicial review is not mentioned in the U.S. Constitution, the actual authority of the Supreme Court to review acts of Congress to determine their constitutionality was an unsettled question. During its first decade, the Supreme Court (or justices riding circuit) had often reviewed acts of Congress, but it had not found any unconstitutional. But in **Marbury v. Madison** (1803),[7] John Marshall claimed this sweeping authority for the Court by asserting the right of judicial review.

Marbury v. *Madison* The Court first asserted the power of judicial review in finding that the congressional statute extending the Court's original jurisdiction was unconstitutional.

In the final hours of the Adams administration, William Marbury was appointed a justice of the peace for the District of Columbia. But in the confusion of winding up matters, John Marshall, Adams's Secretary of State, failed to deliver Marbury's commission. Marbury then asked James Madison, Thomas Jefferson's Secretary of State, for the commission. Under direct orders from Jefferson, who was irate over the Adams administration's last-minute appointment of several federal judges (quickly ratified by the Federalist Congress), Madison refused to turn over the commission. Marbury and three other Adams appointees who were in the same situation then filed a writ of *mandamus* (a legal motion) asking the Supreme Court to order Madison to deliver their commissions.

Political tensions ran high as the Court met to hear the case. Jefferson threatened to ignore any order of the Court. Marshall realized that he and the prestige of the Court could be devastated by any refusal of the executive branch to comply with the decision. Responding to this challenge, in a brilliant opinion that in many sections reads more like a lecture to Jefferson than a discussion of the merits of Marbury's claim, Marshall concluded that although Marbury and the others were entitled to their commissions, the Court lacked the power to issue the writ sought by Marbury. Marshall further ruled that the parts of the Judiciary Act of 1789 that had extended the jurisdiction of the Court to allow it to issue writs was inconsistent with the Constitution and therefore unconstitutional.

Although the immediate effect of the decision was to deny power to the Court, its long-term effect was to establish the rule that "it is emphatically the province and duty of the judicial department to say what the law is." Through judicial review, the Supreme Court most dramatically exerts its authority to determine what the Constitution means. And since *Marbury*, the Court has routinely exercised the power of judicial review to determine the constitutionality of acts of Congress, the executive branch, and the states.

The Legal System

The judicial system in the United States can best be characterized as a dual system consisting of the federal court system and the judicial systems of the fifty states. Both are basically three-tiered. As depicted in Figure 9-1 (p. 278), at the bottom are district trial courts, where litigation begins. In the middle are appellate courts in the state systems and the Courts of Appeals in the federal system. And a supreme court sits at the top of the pyramid as the final word in each system (except New York, which calls its Supreme Court the Court of Appeals). The courts of appeal and supreme courts are **appellate courts** that, with few exceptions, review on appeal only cases that already have been decided in lower courts.

Jurisdiction

There are two kinds of jurisdiction; that is, authority of a court to decide a certain question: original and appellate. *Original jurisdiction* refers to a court's authority to hear disputes as a trial court. (The Menendez brothers' and O. J. Simpson's cases, for example, were heard in Los Angeles County, California, state trial courts.) The facts of a case are established at the trial court level. More than 90 percent of all cases end at this stage.

Appellate jurisdiction refers to a court's ability to review cases already decided by a trial court. Appellate courts do not review the factual record; instead, they review legal procedures to make certain that the law was applied properly to the issues presented in the case. *To appeal* means to take a case to a higher court.

Criminal and Civil Law

The body of law that grades, describes, and sets punishments for crimes is known as **criminal law**. A crime is an action considered to be an offense against authority, or a violation of a duty owed to the public. Crimes are graded as felonies, misdemeanors, or offenses, according to their severity. Some acts—for example, murder, rape, and robbery—are considered crimes in all states. Others—such as sodomy, and some forms of gambling, such as lotteries or bingo—are illegal only in some states. Moreover, although all states outlaw murder, their penal, or criminal, codes treat the crime quite differently; the penalty for murder differs considerably from state to state.

In contrast to civil law, criminal law assumes that society itself is the victim of the illegal act; therefore, the government prosecutes, or brings an action, on behalf of an injured party (acting as a plaintiff) in criminal but not civil cases. Thus, the murder charges against O. J. Simpson were styled as *The State of California* v. *O. J. Simpson*.

In criminal cases, a defendant is charged with violating a specific law. A state (or federal) prosecutor or district attorney then generally takes the case before a **grand jury** to see whether there are sufficient reasons to issue an **indictment**—a formal accusation—and proceed to trial. If an indictment is issued, the defendant can negotiate or plea-bargain with the prosecutor for reduced charges in exchange for a guilty plea.

The O. J. Simpson case, which involved many lawyers and millions of dollars to prosecute and defend, is not a usual criminal case. Most criminal trials take less than a week, and jurors are seldom sequestered, let alone the subject of constant media speculation.

Appellate courts Name given to courts of appeal and supreme courts that hear and review cases that already have been decided in lower courts.

Criminal law The branch of law dealing with crimes and their punishments.

Grand jury The body of persons selected to serve as an investigatory body of court; they decide whether or not to indict individuals whose cases are brought before them.

Indictment A formal accusation decided upon by a grand jury.

FIGURE 9-1
The American Court System

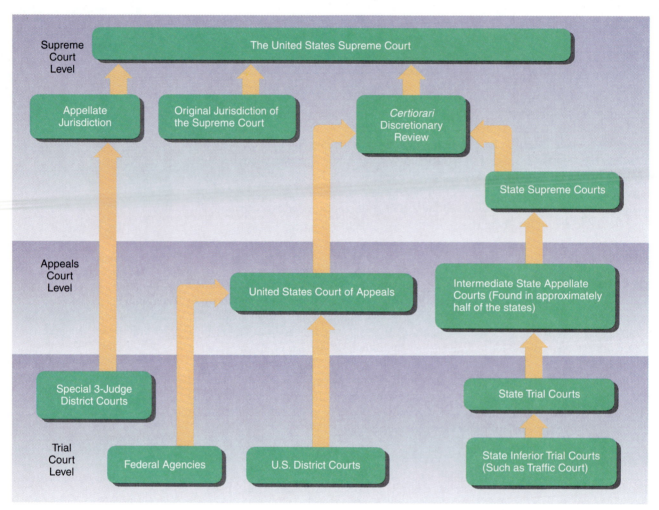

Civil law Noncriminal law, such as the law of property, commercial law, or family law.

Civil law is the body of law dealing with noncriminal matters, such as the laws of property, commercial law, and family law. It is used to regulate relationships between private individuals or companies. Because the actions at issue do not constitute a threat to society at large, persons who believe they have been injured by another party must take action on their own to seek judicial relief. Civil cases, then, involve lawsuits filed to recover something of value, whether it is the right to vote, fair treatment, or monetary compensation for an item or service that cannot be recovered. Most cases seen on the television program "The People's Court" are civil cases. Divorce and child-custody proceedings, employment discrimination claims, and disputes arising from contracts or accidents are all examples of civil law. Divorce and child-custody cases generally involve only issues of state law and so are not heard, except in rare cases, in the federal court system. Allegations of employment discrimination based on gender or race, however, are generally filed in federal court because such discrimination violates the Civil Rights Act of 1964, a federal statute.

Civil and criminal cases can involve state and federal offenses. Take the case of Rodney King, for example. At first, the Los Angeles police officers who beat King were tried in a state court on state criminal charges. When the officers were found not guilty by the jury, the U.S. federal government then brought different federal charges against them for basically the same actions, but this time they were charged with violating federal law. The officers were found guilty by the federal jury.[*]

Before a criminal or civil case gets to court, much has to happen. In fact, most legal disputes that arise in the United States never get to court. Individuals and companies involved in civil disputes routinely settle their disagreements out of court. Often these settlements are not reached until minutes before the case is to be tried. And many civil cases that go to trial are settled during the course of the trial—before the case can be handed over to the jury or submitted to a judge for a decision or determination of guilt. In 1993, silicon breast implant manufacturers, including Dow Chemical Company, agreed to create a $4.75 billion dollar fund to resolve all legal claims involving 800,000 American women, in effect settling the 8,000 lawsuits already filed in U.S. district courts.

Each civil and criminal case has a plaintiff who brings charges against a defendant. Sometimes the government is the plaintiff. The government may bring criminal or civil charges against a person or corporation for violating the law on behalf of the citizens of the state or the national government. Cases are known by the name of the plaintiff first, and of the defendant second. So in *Marbury* v. *Madison*, William Marbury was the plaintiff, suing the defendants, the U.S. government and James Madison as its Secretary of State, for not delivering his judicial commission.

During trials, judges must often interpret the intent of laws enacted by Congress and state legislatures as they bear on the issues at hand. To do so, they read reports, testimony, and debates on the relevant legislation and study the results of other similar legal cases. They also rely on the presentations made by lawyers in their briefs and at trial. If it is a jury trial, the jury ultimately is the finder of fact, while the judge is the interpreter of the law.

The Federal Court System

The federal district courts, circuit courts of appeal, and the Supreme Court are called **constitutional** (or Article III) **courts** because Article III of the Constitution authorizes Congress to establish them. Judges who preside over these courts are selected by the president (with the advice and consent of the Senate), and they serve lifetime terms, as long as they engage in "good behavior."

Constitutional courts Courts established by Article III of the Constitution or by congressional action authorized by the Constitution.

---

[*] The constitutional prohibition against double jeopardy does not apply in this case, because in the two trials King's assailants were charged with different crimes arising out of the same incident. In state court the officers were charged with using excessive criminal force; in federal court, they were charged with violating King's civil rights.

Legislative courts Courts established by Congress for specialized purposes, such as the Court of Military Appeals.

In addition to constitutional courts, **legislative courts** are set up by Congress, generally for special purposes. The U.S. Court of Military Affairs (which hears appeals of cases involving the military), the Court of Customs and Appeals (which hears appeals from decisions of customs courts and the Patent Office), and bankruptcy courts are examples of legislative courts. The judges who preside over these courts are appointed by the president (subject to Senate confirmation) and serve fixed, limited terms.

District Courts

As we saw earlier, Congress recognized the need for federal trial courts soon after ratification of the Constitution. The district courts were created by the Judiciary Act of 1789. By 1992 there were ninety-four federal district courts. Because of one of the compromises of the Judiciary Act of 1789, no district court cuts across state lines. Every state has at least one federal district court, and the largest states—California, New York, and Texas—each have four (see Figure 9-2, p. 281).[8]

Federal district courts have the authority, or jurisdiction, to hear only specific types of cases. (Cases involving other kinds of issues generally must be heard in state court.) Although the rules governing district court jurisdiction can be complex, cases heard there generally fall into one of three categories:

1. They present a federal question based on a claim under the U.S. Constitution, a treaty with another nation, or a federal statute. Federal question jurisdiction can involve criminal or civil law.
2. They involve the federal government as a party.*
3. They involve cases in which citizens are from different states, and the amount of money at issue is more than $50,000.**

Each federal judicial district has a U.S. Attorney, who is nominated by the president and confirmed by the Senate. The U.S. Attorney in each district is that district's chief law enforcement officer. The size of the staff and the number of Assistant U.S. Attorneys who work in each district depend on the amount of litigation in each district. U.S. Attorneys, like district attorneys within the states, have a considerable amount of discretion as to whether they pursue criminal or civil investigations or file charges against individuals or corporations.

The Courts of Appeal

The losing party in a case heard and decided in a federal district court can appeal the decision to the appropriate Circuit Court of Appeals, as illustrated in Figure 9-1 on page 278.

The Circuit Courts of Appeals, the intermediate appellate courts in the federal system, were established in 1789 to hear appeals from federal district courts. Originally

---

*   The most commonly filed cases in the federal district courts involve challenges to determinations made by the Social Security Administration concerning disability payments. In fact, more than 50 percent of the civil cases heard by some federal district courts involve these kinds of issues.
** Cases involving citizens from different states can generally be filed in either state or federal court.

FIGURE 9-2

The Federal Court System

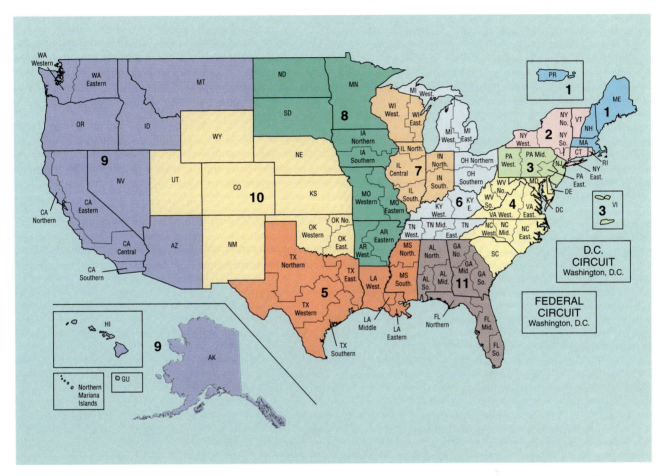

This map shows the locations of the Circuit Courts of Appeal and the boundaries of the Federal District Courts with more than one district.

called circuit courts, these courts with appellate jurisdiction are now officially known as the United States Court of Appeals for the [First–Eleventh] Circuit. There are eleven numbered circuit courts (see Figure 9-2). A twelfth, the D.C. Circuit, handles most appeals involving federal regulatory commissions and agencies, including, for example, the National Labor Relations Board and the Securities and Exchange Commission.

In 1994, the Courts of Appeals were staffed by 156 judges who are appointed by the president, subject to Senate confirmation. The number of judges within each circuit varies—depending upon the workload and the complexity of the cases—and ranges from fewer than ten to nearly thirty. Each circuit is supervised by a chief judge, the most senior judge in terms of service below the age of seventy. In deciding cases, judges are divided into rotating three-judge panels, made up of both the active judges within the circuit, visiting judges (primarily district judges from the same circuit), and retired judges. In rare cases, by majority vote all the judges in a circuit may choose to sit together (*en banc*) to decide a case.

The Courts of Appeals have no original jurisdiction. Rather, Congress has granted these courts appellate jurisdiction over two general categories of cases: appeals from criminal and civil cases from the district courts, and appeals from administrative agencies. Criminal and civil case appeals constitute about 90 percent of the workload of the Courts of Appeals. In contrast, appeals from administrative agencies make up only about 10 percent of their workload. And because so many agencies are located in Washington, D.C., the D.C. Circuit Court of Appeals hears an inordinate number of such cases. The D.C. Circuit Court of Appeals, then, is considered the second most important court in the nation because its decisions govern the regulatory agencies.

Once a decision is made by a federal Court of Appeals, a litigant no longer has an automatic right to an appeal. The losing party may submit a petition to the Supreme Court to hear the case, but the Court grants few of these requests, as illustrated in Figure 9-3. The Courts of Appeals, then, are the courts of last resort for almost all federal litigation. Keep in mind, however, that most cases, if they actually go to trial, go no further than the district court level.

In general, Courts of Appeals try to correct errors of law and procedure that have occurred in the lower court or administrative agency. Courts of Appeals hear no new

F I G U R E   9 - 3

Supreme Court Caseload, 1950–1994

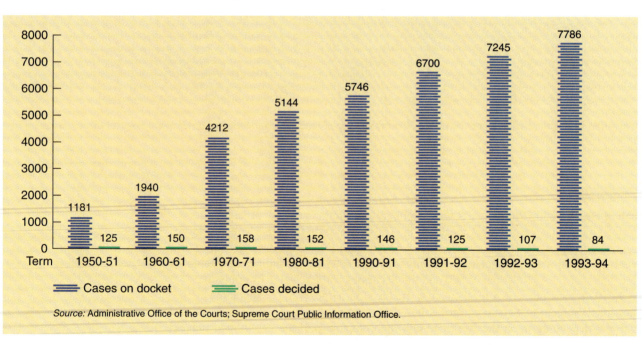

The figure shows the upward trend of case filings at the U.S. Supreme Court since 1950. Also shown is the fairly constant number of cases that the justices have actually accepted for full review and for which they have issued opinions. The Court usually decides only one or two cases a term under its original jurisdiction. Almost all the rest of its workload consists of petitions from lower federal or state courts.

testimony; instead, lawyers submit written arguments, in what is called a **brief** (also submitted in trial courts), and then appear to argue the case and orally present their arguments to the court. In deciding these cases, the judges rely on the briefs, oral argument, and **precedents** (past decisions) in making their decisions.

Although decisions of any Court of Appeals are binding on only the district courts within the geographic confines of the circuit, decisions of the U.S. Supreme Court are binding throughout the nation and establish precedents. This reliance on past decisions or precedents to formulate decisions in new cases is called *stare decisis* (a Latin phrase meaning "let the decision stand"). The principle of *stare decisis* allows for continuity and predictability in our judicial system. If a party goes to court, it is incumbent on the lawyer to know how a court has acted in similar cases. Although *stare decisis* can be helpful in predicting decisions, at times judges carve out new ground and ignore, decline to follow, or even overrule precedents in order to reach a different conclusion in a case involving similar circumstances. In one sense, that is why there is so much litigation in America today. Parties know that one cannot always predict the outcome of a case; if such prediction were possible, there would be little reason to go to court.

The Supreme Court

At the top of the judicial pyramid is the U.S. Supreme Court, which, as discussed below, has both original and appellate jurisdiction. (We discuss the details of the Supreme Court's jurisdiction later in this chapter.) In reviewing cases from the U.S. Courts of Appeals and state supreme courts, it acts as the final interpreter of the U.S. Constitution. It not only decides many major cases with tremendous policy significance each year, but it also ensures uniformity in the interpretation of national laws

Brief The collected legal written arguments in a case filed with a court by a party prior to a hearing or trial.

Precedents Prior judicial decisions that serve as rules for settling subsequent cases of a similar nature.

Stare decisis In court rulings, a reliance on past decisions or precedents to formulate decisions in new cases.

A *Washington Post* cartoon pokes fun at FDR's court packing plan and the changes that have occurred over the years in the Court's size.

HISTORICAL FIGURES

1789: CONGRESS DECIDED AT FIRST TO FIX THE NUMBER OF JUSTICES AT SIX.

1801: CONGRESS PLANNED ON A CHANGE TO FIVE, BUT THE SIX REMAINED VERY MUCH ALIVE.

1807: SIX HIGH JUDGES, SUPREME AS HEAVEN — AND JEFFERSON ADDED NUMBER SEVEN.

1837: SEVEN HIGH JUDGES, ALL IN A LINE — TWO MORE ADDED, AND THAT MADE NINE.

1863: NINE HIGH JUDGES WERE SITTING WHEN LINCOLN MADE THEM AN EVEN TEN.

1866: TEN HIGH JUDGES, VERY SEDATE; WHEN CONGRESS GOT THROUGH THERE WERE ONLY EIGHT.

1869: EIGHT HIGH JUDGES WHO WOULDN'T RESIGN; GRANT BROUGHT THE FIGURE BACK TO NINE.

1937: WOULD A JUSTICE FEEL LIKE A PACKED SARDINE IF THE NUMBER WAS RAISED TO — SAY — FIFTEEN?

From Herblock: A Cartoonist's Life (Lisa Drew Books/Macmillan Publishers, 1993).

and the Constitution, resolves conflicts among the states, and maintains the supremacy of national law in the federal system.

Since 1869, the U.S. Supreme Court has consisted of eight associate justices and one Chief Justice, who is nominated by the president specifically for that position. There is no special significance about the number nine, and the Constitution is silent about the size of the Court. Between 1801 and 1869, Congress altered the size of the Court several times. The lowest number of justices on the Court was six; the most, ten. In 1866, Congress reduced the size of the Court from ten to eight so that President Andrew Johnson, who was very unpopular with Congress (and who escaped being removed from office by the Senate by just one vote), could not fill two vacancies that existed. When the more popular former war hero Ulysses S. Grant took of-

THEN AND NOW

Law Clerks

As early as 1850, the justices of the Supreme Court had beseeched Congress to approve the hiring of an "investigating clerk" to assist each justice, particularly in copying opinions. Congress denied the request, so when Justice Horace Gray hired the first law clerk in 1882, he paid the clerk himself. Justice Gray's clerk was a top graduate of Harvard Law School whose duties included cutting Justice Gray's hair and running personal errands. Finally, in 1886, Congress authorized each justice to hire a "stenographer clerk" for $1,600 a year.

Today, clerks generally serve for periods of one to two years. In the past, however, some justices employed their clerks for longer periods. Pierce Butler's clerk, for example, served sixteen years.

Over time, the number of clerks employed by the justices has increased. Through the 1946 to 1969 terms, most justices employed two clerks. By 1970, most had three; and by 1980 all but three had four. In 1994, there were thirty-nine clerks serving the nine justices, whereas twenty years ago there were half as many. This growth in clerks has had many interesting ramifications for the Court. As noted by Richard A. Posner, "between 1969 and 1972—the period during which the justices each became entitled to a third law clerk—. . . the number of opinions increased by about 50 percent and the number of words tripled."[*] After the justices were authorized to hire a fourth clerk in 1980, a substantial growth in the number of citations and footnotes in each case occurred again.[**] And until recently, the number of cases decided annually increased as more help was available to the justices.

The justices have complete discretion over whom they hire and the nature and amount of the work they assign. Clerks are typically selected from candidates at the top of the graduating classes of prestigious law schools (see the accompanying figure). They perform a variety of tasks, ranging from searching every page of *United States Reports* for some particular information to playing tennis or taking walks with the justices. Clerks spend most of their time researching material relevant to particular cases, reading and summarizing cases, and helping justices write opinions. Just how much help they provide in the writing of opinions is not known. Although it is occasionally alleged that a particular clerk wrote a particular opinion delivered by a justice, no such allegation has ever been proved. The relationship between clerks and the justices for whom they work is close and confidential, and many aspects

[*] Richard A. Posner, *The Federal Courts: Crisis and Reform* (Cambridge, MA: Harvard University Press, 1985), p. 114.

[**] Ibid., p. 114.

fice, the number was increased to nine, where it has remained. Through 1994, only 108 justices had served on the Court and there had been fifteen chief justices.

The Chief Justice presides over public sessions of the Court, conducts the Court's conferences, assigns the writing of opinions (if he is in the majority; otherwise the most senior justice in the majority makes the assignment), and by custom administers the oath of office to the president and the vice president on Inauguration Day (any federal judge can administer the oath, as has happened when presidents have died in office). By law, the Chief Justice, like the rest of the justices, is authorized to hire four clerks. Chief Justice William H. Rehnquist, however, has a tradition of hiring only three. He also has several secretaries and a messenger to help him with his duties. In 1972, Congress authorized the position of administrative assistant to serve at the plea-

of the relationship are kept secret. Clerks may sometimes talk among themselves about the views and personalities of their justices, but rarely has a clerk leaked such information to the press.

Some former clerks try to exploit their connection to their justice, but at times this tactic can backfire. When North Dakota Attorney General Nicholas Spaeth, a former clerk to Justice Byron White, appeared before the Court, he did so sporting a necktie covered with buffaloes that White had given him years earlier. He jok-ingly referred to the tie, saying he had worn it because he particularly needed the vote of White, the only justice in the majority of an earlier, similar case still on the Court. White looked annoyed, the other justices did not laugh, and Justice Kennedy's later questioning revealed his obvious displeasure with Spaeth's theatrics.[†]

[†]Tony Mauro, "The Highs and Lows of the 1992 Court," *Legal Times* (December 28, 1992): 12.

Where Do Law Clerks Come From? Law Schools of 738 Supreme Court Clerks Between 1958 and 1985.

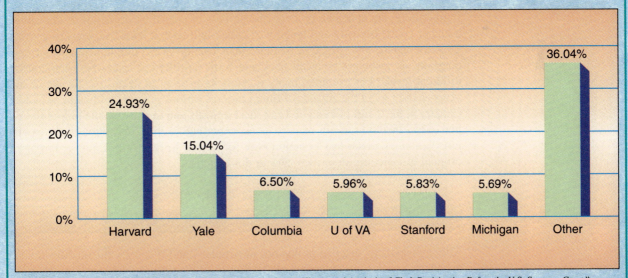

Source: Karen O'Connor and John R. Hermann, "The Clerk Connection: A History and Analysis of Clerk Participation Before the U.S. Supreme Court," paper prepared for delivery at the 1993 annual meeting of the Midwest Political Science Association.

sure of the Chief Justice. Chief Justice Warren E. Burger (1969–1986) used his assistant to help him in his nonlegal judicial duties by conducting research, monitoring judicial administration, supervising Court operations, and educating the public about the role of the Supreme Court.

In addition to their law clerks, justices are assisted in their duties by personal secretaries and other members of the Court's support staff, including

- The Clerk of the Court: In 1790, the justices authorized the appointment of the Clerk as the Court's official business manager. The Clerk accepts all filings, administers the Court's docket (all the cases it is asked to hear) receives all appeals, petitions, and motions, and prepares the Court's formal judgments; advises attorneys about Court rules, schedule, etc.
- The Marshal of the Court: In 1867, Congress authorized this position of the Court's chief security officer. Today, the duties of the Marshal and his staff include supervising physical facilities and grounds, and fiscal affairs including salaries, etc.
- The Reporter of Decisions: Originally this was an informal position. For several years, private individuals called "Reporters" published opinions of the Court and were compensated by sales. In 1817, Congress created the official position. The Reporter edits opinions and supervises their printing in the Court's official reporter, *The United States Reports*.
- The Public Information Officer: answers questions from the press and the public about the Court and the justices.
- The Legal Office: Created by the Court in 1973, it has two attorneys who serve four-year terms. They serve as in-house counsel on questions regarding the Court and also assist with screening petitions when necessary.

It is not uncommon to hear a disgruntled party emerge from a local courthouse and angrily vow to take his or her appeal "all the way to the Supreme Court." In reality, this seldom happens. Although the Court received a record 7,786 petitions for review in its 1993–1994 term, it handed down full opinions in only 84 cases for plenary (full) review—down from 146 in 1989 and 170 in 1988, as revealed in Figure 9-3 (p. 282). Furthermore, the appellate process (the process of appealing decisions of one court to a higher court) is costly and lengthy. A case could take at least five years to get to the Supreme Court, and litigation of more than twenty years' duration is not out of the question, as cases get bounced back and forth on different issues between courts of different levels. For example, many inmates have been on death row for ten or more years as they await the appeals of their cases on various grounds (although, as noted in Chapter 4, the Court is trying to limit these appeals and to expedite the process). Criminal cases, including death penalty cases, come before the Court through its appellate jurisdiction. A much less common way for a case to reach the Court is through its original jurisdiction (described later in this chapter).

How Federal Court Judges Are Selected

Although specific, detailed provisions in Articles I and II specify the qualifications for president, senator, and member of the House of Representatives, the Constitution is curiously silent on the qualifications for federal judge. This may have been because of an assumption that all federal judges would be lawyers, but to make such a requirement explicit might have marked the judicial branch as too elite for the tastes of common men and women. Also, it would have been impractical to require formal legal training, given that there were so few law schools in the nation, and the fact that most lawyers became licensed after clerking or apprenticing with another attorney.[9]

The selection of federal judges is often a very political process with important political ramifications, since they are nominated by the president and must be confirmed by the U.S. Senate. During the Reagan/Bush years, for example, 553 basically conservative Republican judges were appointed to the federal bench (see Figure 9-4, p. 288). The cumulative impact of this conservative block of judges led many liberal groups to abandon their efforts to expand rights through the federal courts. (See "The American Civil Liberties Union," p. 102.)

Typically, federal district court judges have held other political offices, such as those of state court judge or prosecutor, as illustrated in Table 9.1 (p. 289). Most have been involved in politics, which is what usually brings them into consideration for a position on the federal bench. Griffin Bell, Attorney General in the Carter administration and former federal circuit court judge, once remarked, "For me, becoming a federal judge wasn't very difficult. I managed John F. Kennedy's presidential campaign in Georgia. And I was campaign manager and special counsel for the governor [Carter]."[10]

Each year, a large number of federal district court judgeships become available through death and retirement, and other openings occur as Congress continually adds new positions in an effort to meet the increasing demands on the federal court system. Presidents Jimmy Carter and Ronald Reagan, for example, each appointed more than 200 judges to the federal district courts.

Presidents generally defer selection of district court judges to senators of their own party who represent the state in which a vacancy occurs on the federal bench, a practice called **senatorial courtesy**. By tradition, the Senate Judiciary Committee will not confirm a presidential nominee unless he or she has been agreed to by the senator(s) of the nominee's home state. This tradition is an important source of political patronage for senators.

Senatorial courtesy A practice by which senators can have near veto power over laws or appointments that affect their state in a specific way.

Presidents Reagan and Bush's insistence that candidates possess conservative "judicial philosophies" (see pp. 304–305) minimized home-state senators' roles in the confirmation process. President Bush, for example, requested that senators forward three choices to him for any district court vacancy. These names were reviewed by the president's Committee on Federal Judicial Selection after the prospective nominees had been interviewed by various Justice Department officials including the Deputy Attorney General and the Solicitor General (see pp. 298–299), to ascertain their judicial philosophy and position on controversial issues such as civil rights and abortion. One name was then selected for nomination. This practice incensed Republican senators, in particular, who viewed district court judgeships as an important way to reward friends and campaign workers. Moreover, the Bush administration's insistence on nominees who were "philosophically conservative"[11] resulted in a considerable number of vacancies on the federal bench. When President Bush left office, there were over 100 vacancies on the federal courts for President Clinton to fill.

Senatorial courtesy does not operate to the same degree in the selection of the more prestigious Courts of Appeals judgeships, largely because the jurisdiction of each circuit includes at least three states. When vacancies on the Courts of Appeals occur, presidents frequently consult senators of the various states in the circuit, but ultimately the Justice Department plays the key role in the selection process.

To ensure diverse representation of African-Americans, women, and other groups traditionally underrepresented on the federal bench, President Jimmy Carter established judicial nominating commissions (consisting of lawyers and laypersons selected

FIGURE 9-4
How a President Affects the Federal Judiciary

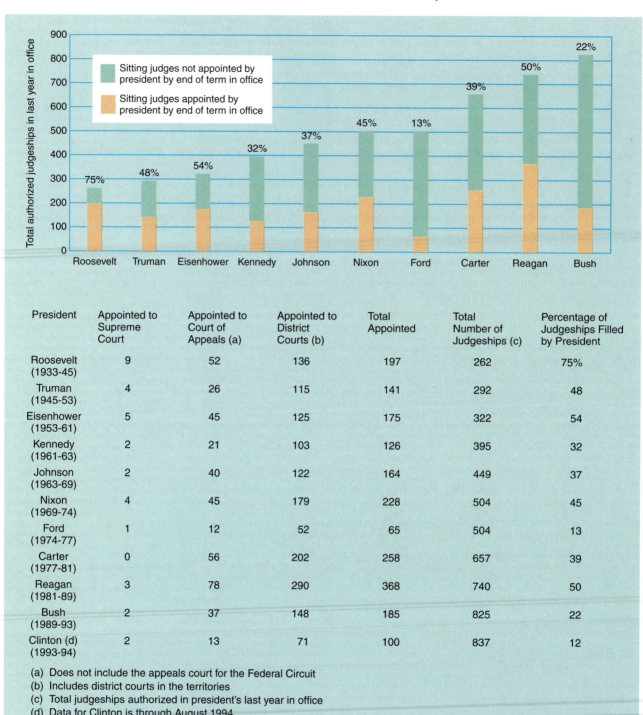

President	Appointed to Supreme Court	Appointed to Court of Appeals (a)	Appointed to District Courts (b)	Total Appointed	Total Number of Judgeships (c)	Percentage of Judgeships Filled by President
Roosevelt (1933-45)	9	52	136	197	262	75%
Truman (1945-53)	4	26	115	141	292	48
Eisenhower (1953-61)	5	45	125	175	322	54
Kennedy (1961-63)	2	21	103	126	395	32
Johnson (1963-69)	2	40	122	164	449	37
Nixon (1969-74)	4	45	179	228	504	45
Ford (1974-77)	1	12	52	65	504	13
Carter (1977-81)	0	56	202	258	657	39
Reagan (1981-89)	3	78	290	368	740	50
Bush (1989-93)	2	37	148	185	825	22
Clinton (d) (1993-94)	2	13	71	100	837	12

(a) Does not include the appeals court for the Federal Circuit
(b) Includes district courts in the territories
(c) Total judgeships authorized in president's last year in office
(d) Data for Clinton is through August 1994.

Source: "Imprints on the Bench," *CQ Weekly Report*, January 19, 1991, p. 173. Reprinted by permission. Data on Clinton and Bush provided by the Senate Judiciary Committee.

This figure shows the number of authorized federal judgeships in the last year of a president's term and the percent of those judgeships filled by appointees of the president. The table below the figure breaks down the president's appointments for each level of the judiciary.

Table 9.1 ◆ Characteristics of Appointees to the Lower Federal Courts from Carter to Clinton

	CARTER APPOINTEES	REAGAN APPOINTEES	BUSH APPOINTEES	CLINTON NOMINEES*
Occupation (percent)				
Politics/gov't	4.7%	11.4%	10.8%	9.1%
Judiciary	45.0	41.0	45.4	51.1
Lawyer	47.2	46.8	42.7	38.7
Other	0.8	0.8	0.1	1.1
Experience (percent)				
Judicial	54.3%	49.5%	49.7%	55.7%
Prosecutorial	37.2	40.8	37.3	44.3
Neither	30.2	29.6	31.9	23.9
Political Affiliation (percent)				
Democrat	90.3%	3.8%	5.4%	87.5%
Republican	5.0	94.0	88.6	3.4
Independent	4.7	1.9	5.9	6.8
ABA Rating				
Extremely/well qualified	56.2%	55.2%	58.9%	65.9%
Qualified	42.6	44.8	41.1	32.9
Not Qualified	1.2	—	—	1.1
Race/ethnicity (percent)				
White	78.7%	93.5%	89.2%	60.2%
Black	14.3	1.9	6.5	27.3
Asian-American	0.8	0.5	—	1.1
Hispanic	6.2	4.5	4.3	10.2
Native American	—	—	—	1.1
Gender				
Female	15.5%	7.6%	19.5%	32.9%
Male	84.5	92.4	80.5	67.0
White male (percent)	66.3	86.4	72.4	36.4
Net Worth (percent)				
Under $200,000	33.3%**	17.1%	9.2%	15.9%
200-499,999	38.4**	36.4	30.8	21.6
500-999,999	17.7**	24.2	25.4	33.0
1,000,000+	5.1**	22.0	34.6	29.5
Total number of appointees	238	36.8	18.5	88
Average age at nomination (years)	50.1	49.0	48.2	49.4

* Appointees through June 7, 1994.

**These figures are for appointees confirmed by the 96th Congress. Professor Elliot Slotnick of Ohio State University provided the net worth figures for all but six Carter district court appointees, for whom no data were available.

Source: Sheldon Goldman and Matthew D. Saranson, "Clinton's Nontraditional Judges: Creating a More Representative Bench," from *Judicature* The Journal of the American Judicature Society, 78 (September–October 1994): 72. Reprinted by permission.

by the president) in each circuit. Each commission was charged with submitting three to five names to the president for his consideration when vacancies occurred. According to political scientist Elliot E. Slotnick, in spite of President Carter's efforts to depoliticize the process, the judges selected in this manner were no different from those chosen more traditionally. Like those chosen in the past, they were overwhelmingly from the president's party and were likely to have been involved in party politics.[12] But Carter's efforts to open up the process did produce more women and minority judges than ever before.

The commissions were abandoned by President Reagan, whose Justice Department (and increasingly, the White House counsel) played a key role in selecting Court of Appeals judges. George Bush's administration followed in this tradition, as it searched for ideological conservatives who could further both administrations' political agendas through rulings from the bench. Bill Clinton created a three-member committee in the White House to help him fill federal court vacancies. He was criticized for taking so long to fill vacancies—by August 1993, only 14 nominations were forwarded to the Senate to fill the 136 existing vacancies. White House officials insisted that the delay occurred because it took Democratic senators so long to get their nominating commissions in place after 12 years of Republican rule. By July 1994, Clinton had appointed 100 federal judges. Nearly one-third were women, thirty-eight percent were members of minority groups and two of those minorities were Native Americans.

Appointments to the U.S. Supreme Court

The Constitution is silent on the qualifications for appointment to the Supreme Court (as well as to other constitutional courts), although Justice Oliver Wendell Holmes once remarked that a justice should be a "combination of Justinian, Jesus Christ and John Marshall."[13] In Great Britain, where the Lord Chancellor is the highest court official (formally appointed by the Crown but actually chosen by the prime minister), ideology is often not a concern in court appointments; experience as a trial judge is. In the United States, until recently Supreme Court justices generally have had little previous judicial experience on any level. Of the 108 justices who have served or are serving on the Court, only twenty-four had had ten or more years of experience on any bench, and forty-two had had no judicial experience at all.

Like other federal court judges, the justices of the Supreme Court are nominated by the president and must be confirmed by the Senate. Historically, however, because of the special place the Supreme Court enjoys in our constitutional system, its nominees have encountered more opposition than district or Court of Appeals judges. As the role of the Court has increased over time, so too has the amount of attention given to nominees. And with the increased attention has come greater opposition, especially to nominees with controversial views.

Nomination Criteria

Justice Sandra Day O'Connor once remarked that "You have to be lucky" to be appointed to the Court.[14] Although luck is certainly important, over the years nominations to the bench have been made for a variety of reasons. Depending on the timing of a vacancy, a president may or may not have a list of possible candidates or even a specific individual in mind. Until recently, presidents often have looked within their circle of friends or their administration to fill a vacancy. Nevertheless, whether the nominee

According to insurance company statistics, only conductors of symphony orchestras enjoy longer life spans than Supreme Court justices.

Anita Hill testifies before the then all-male Senate Judiciary Committee as it considered the appointment of Clarence Thomas to the Supreme Court.

The justices of the Court gather before the 1994–1995 term begins upon the occasion of the investiture of its newest member, Justice Stephen Breyer, the sixth new Justice since 1986. Left to right are Justices Clarence Thomas, Antonin Scalia, Sandra Day O'Connor, Anthony Kennedy, David Souter, Stephen Breyer, John Paul Stevens, Chief Justice William H. Rehnquist, and Ruth Bader Ginsburg.

is a friend or someone known to the president only by reputation, at least six criteria are especially important:

1. *Competence and ethical standards.* Most prospective nominees are expected to have had at least some judicial or governmental experience. John Jay, the first Chief Justice, was one of the authors of *The Federalist Papers* and was active in New York politics. John Marshall was a former Secretary of State. (See People of the Past: "John Marshall," p. 275.) Most recent appointees to the Court have had some prior judicial experience. Moreover, Justices John Paul Stevens, Anthony Kennedy, Antonin Scalia, David Souter, Clarence Thomas, and Ruth Bader Ginsburg all served on the U.S. Court of Appeals.

2. *Ideological or policy preferences.* Most presidents seek to appoint to the Court individuals who share their policy preferences, and almost all have political goals in mind when they appoint a justice. Presidents Franklin D. Roosevelt, Richard M. Nixon, and Ronald Reagan were very successful in molding the Court to their own political beliefs. Roosevelt was quickly able to appoint eight justices from 1937 to his death in 1945, solidifying support for his liberal New Deal programs. In contrast, Nixon and Reagan publicly proclaimed that they would nominate only individuals who favored a **strict constructionist** approach to constitutional decision making—that is, an approach emphasizing the initial intentions of the Framers (see p. 304). Justices William Rehnquist and Antonin Scalia, in particular, have been very vocal in support of this view, believing that it is inappropriate for the judiciary to make policy through broad or expansive interpretations of the Constitution.[15] Instead, they argue, the Court should construe the Constitution narrowly.

3. *Rewards.* Historically, many of those appointed to the Supreme Court have been personal friends of presidents. Abraham Lincoln, for example, appointed one of his

Strict constructionist An approach to Constitutional interpretation that emphasizes the Framers' initial intentions.

key political advisers to the Court. More recently, Lyndon B. Johnson appointed his longtime friend Abe Fortas to the bench. In addition, most presidents select justices of their own party affiliation. Chief Justice Rehnquist was long active in Arizona Republican Party politics, as was Justice O'Connor before her appointment to the bench; both were appointed by Republican presidents. Party activism can also be used by presidents as an indication of a nominee's commitment to certain ideological principles.

4. *Pursuit of political support.* During Ronald Reagan's successful campaign for the presidency in 1980, some of his advisers feared that the "gender gap" would hurt him. Polls repeatedly showed that he was far less popular with female voters than with men. Particularly troublesome was his vocal opposition to the pending Equal Rights Amendment. To gain support from women, Reagan announced during his campaign that should he win, he would appoint a woman to fill the first vacancy on the Court. When Justice Potter Stewart, a moderate, announced his early retirement from the bench, President Reagan nominated Sandra Day O'Connor of the Arizona State Court of Appeals to fill the vacancy. It probably will not hurt President Clinton that his first appointment was a woman *and* Jewish (at a time when no Jews served on the Court).

5. *Religion.* Ironically, religion, which historically has been an important issue, was hardly mentioned during the most recent Supreme Court vacancies. Some did, however, hail Clinton's appointment of Ginsburg, noting that the traditionally "Jewish" seat on the Court had been vacant for over two decades, since Abe Fortas's resignation in 1969.

Through 1994, of the 108 justices who have served on the Court, almost all have been members of traditional Protestant faiths. Only nine have been Catholic and only seven have been Jewish.[16] Twice during the Rehnquist Court, more Catholics—Brennan, Scalia, and Kennedy and then Scalia, Kennedy, and Thomas—have served on the Court at one time than at any other period in history. Today, however, it is clear that religion cannot be taken as a sign of a justice's conservative or liberal ideology: When William Brennan was on the Court, he and Antonin Scalia were at ideological extremes.

6. *Race and gender.* Only two African-Americans and two women have served on the Court. Race was undoubtedly a critical issue in the appointment of Clarence Thomas to replace Thurgood Marshall, the first African-American justice. But President Bush refused to acknowledge his wish to retain a "black seat" on the Court. Instead, he announced that he was "picking the best man for the job on the merits," a claim that was met with considerable skepticism by many observers.

In contrast, O'Connor was pointedly picked because of her gender. Ginsburg's appointment was more matter-of-fact, and her selection surprised many after the Clinton administration appeared to consider seriously several men for the appointment first. (See "Lobbying for a Top Spot?," p. 293.)

The Supreme Court Confirmation Process

Before 1900, about one-fourth of all presidential nominees to the Supreme Court were rejected by the Senate. In 1844, for example, President John Tyler sent six nominations to the Senate, and all but one were defeated. In 1866, Andrew Johnson nominated his brilliant Attorney General, Henry Stanberry, but the Senate's hostility to Johnson led it to *abolish* the seat to prevent Johnson's filling it.

As noted earlier, the Constitution gives the Senate the authority to approve all nominees to the federal bench, and the Senate takes this duty, given to it in the Advice and Consent clause, very seriously when considering nominees to the Supreme Court. Ordinarily, nominations are referred to the Senate Committee on the Judiciary. In the 103rd Congress, all but one member of the committee were lawyers. As detailed later, this committee investigates the nominees, holds hearings, and votes on its recommendation for Senate action. The full Senate then deliberates on the nominee before voting. A simple majority vote is required for confirmation.

Investigation. Once a president settles on a nominee to the Supreme Court, the nominee's name is sent to the Federal Bureau of Investigation. Some "investigation" actually occurs before the formal nomination process.

While the FBI conducts an extensive background check of the formal nominee, the Senate Judiciary Committee also begins to investigate his or her background. (The same process is used for nominees of the lower federal courts, although such investigations generally are not nearly as extensive as for Supreme Court nominees.)

To begin its task, the Senate Judiciary Committee asks each nominee to complete a lengthy questionnaire detailing previous work (dating as far back as high-school summer jobs), judicial opinions written, judicial philosophy, speeches, and even all inter-

Lobbying for a Top Spot?
◆ ◆ ◆

In their book on the Supreme Court, *The Brethren*, Bob Woodward and Scott Armstrong wrote critically of Court of Appeals Judge Warren Burger's apparent lobbying of Richard Nixon for the position of Chief Justice.[*] How times have changed. In 1993, Martin Ginsburg, the husband of Court of Appeals Judge Ruth Bader Ginsburg, unabashedly orchestrated a letter-writing campaign on behalf of his wife's nomination to the Supreme Court. Martin Ginsburg, a prominent tax attorney and Georgetown University law professor, contacted his wife's former students, the presidents of Stanford and Columbia, academics, legal scholars, and even Texas Governor Ann Richards to call or write the White House urging his wife's nomination. Said the nominee's husband of his campaign on his wife's behalf after her nomination, "If there was something I could have done to be helpful, I would have done it, because I think my wife is super, and the president couldn't have made a better appointment than the one he just made."[**]

Unconventional? Yes. Effective? You decide.

Lobbying on Ginsburg's behalf paid off when she became the second woman on the nation's highest court joining Sandra Day O'Connor.

[*] Bob Woodward and Scott Armstrong, *The Brethren* (New York: Simon and Schuster, 1979).

[**] Eleanor Randolph, "Ginsburg's spouse says he arranged letter campaign," *Washington Post* (June 17, 1993): A-17.

views ever given to members of the press. Committee staffers also contact potential witnesses who might offer testimony concerning the nominee's fitness for office.

At the same time, the president also forwards the name of the nominee to the American Bar Association (ABA), the politically powerful organization that represents the interests of the legal profession. After its own investigation, the ABA rates the nominee, based on his or her qualifications, as Highly Qualified (now called "Well-Qualified"), Qualified, or Not Qualified. (The same system is used for lower federal court nominees; over the years, however, the exact labels have varied.)

David Souter, Bush's first nominee to the Court, received a unanimous rating of Highly Qualified from the ABA, as did both of Clinton's nominees, Ruth Bader Ginsburg and Stephen Breyer. In contrast, another Bush nominee, Clarence Thomas, was given only a Qualified rating (well before the charges of sexual harassment became public), with two members voting Not Qualified. Of the twenty-two previous nominees rated by the ABA, he was the first to receive less than at least a unanimous Qualified rating.

Lobbying by Interest Groups.   The ABA is an organization that is asked formally to rate nominees, but other groups are also keenly interested in the nomination process.

Until recently, interest groups have played a minor and backstage role in most appointments to the U.S. Supreme Court. Although interest groups generally have not lobbied on behalf of any one individual, in 1981, women's rights groups successfully urged President Reagan to honor his campaign commitment to appoint a woman to the high court.

It is more common for interest groups to lobby *against* a prospective nominee. Even this, however, is a relatively recent phenomenon. In 1987, the nomination of Robert H. Bork to the Supreme Court produced an unprecedented amount of interest-group lobbying on both sides of the nomination. The Democratic-controlled Judiciary Commit-

The scrutiny by the public and press of President Reagan's Supreme Court nominee Robert H. Bork set a new standard of inquiry into the values—both political and personal—of future nominees. Bork's nomination was rejected by the Senate in 1987.

tee delayed the hearings, thus allowing liberal interest groups time to mobilize the most extensive radio, television, and print media campaign ever launched against a nominee to the U.S. Supreme Court. This opposition was in spite of the fact that Bork sat with distinction on the D.C. Court of Appeals, and was a former U.S. Solicitor General, a top-ranked law school graduate, and a Yale Law School professor. (His actions as Solicitor General, especially his firing of the Watergate Special Prosecutor— see "Watergate and Its Effect on the Presidency," [p. 210]—however, made him a special target for traditional liberals.)

The Senate Committee Hearings. As the uneventful Ginsburg hearings attest (she was confirmed by a Senate vote of ninety-seven to three), not all nominees inspire the kind of intense reaction that kept Bork from the Court and, more recently, almost blocked the confirmation of Clarence Thomas. Until 1929, all but one Senate Judiciary Committee hearing on a Supreme Court nominee was conducted in executive session—that is, closed to the public. The 1916 hearings on Louis Brandeis, the first Jewish justice, were conducted in public and lasted nineteen days, although Brandeis himself was never called to testify. In 1939, Felix Frankfurter became the first nominee to testify in any detail before the committee. Subsequent revelations about Brandeis's payment to Frankfurter for his participation in cases (while Brandeis was on the Court) raise questions about the fitness of both Frankfurter and Brandeis for the bench. Still, no information about Frankfurter's legal arrangements with Brandeis was unearthed during the committee's investigations or Frankfurter's testimony.[17]

Until recently, modern nomination hearings were no more thorough in terms of the attention given to nominees' backgrounds. In 1969, for example, Chief Justice Warren E. Burger was confirmed by the Senate on a vote of ninety-four to three, just nineteen days after he was nominated!

Since the 1980s, it has become standard for Senators to ask the nominees probing questions, but most nominees (with the notable exception of Robert Bork) have declined to answer most of them on the grounds that these issues might ultimately come before the Court.

The Vote in the Senate. After hearings are concluded, the Senate Judiciary Committee usually makes a recommendation to the full Senate. Any rejections of presidential nominees to the Supreme Court generally occur only after the Senate Judiciary Committee has recommended against a nominee's appointment. Few recent confirmations have been close; prior to Clarence Thomas's fifty-two to forty-eight vote, Rehnquist's nominations as associate justice (sixty-eight to twenty-six) and as Chief Justice (sixty-nine to thirty-three) were the closest in recent history.

The Supreme Court Today

Given the judicial system's vast size and substantial power (at least indirect) over so many aspects of our lives, it is surprising that so many Americans know next to nothing about the judicial system in general and the Supreme Court in particular. Until very recently, Senate Judiciary Committee hearings concerning nominees were conducted with little or no publicity, and little attention has been paid to the personnel of the Court. Even today, at a time when the Court is enjoying unprecedented media attention, few Americans can correctly name the Chief Justice, let alone the other eight justices. A *Washington Post* poll found that while more than 50 percent of Americans knew of Judge Joseph Wapner of the TV show "The People's Court," fewer than 10 percent knew of Chief Justice Rehnquist.[18] Another poll conducted in 1990 for the Court's 200th anniversary revealed that only 23 percent of Americans queried knew how many justices sit on the Court, and nearly two-thirds could not name a single member of the Court.[19]

Although much of this ignorance can be blamed on the American public's lack of interest, part of the problem stems from the Court itself. Its rites and rituals contribute to the Court's mystique and encourage a "cult of the robe." Consider, for example, the way judicial proceedings are conducted. Oral arguments are not televised, and deliberations concerning the outcome of cases are conducted in utmost secrecy. In contrast, C-SPAN brings us daily coverage of various congressional hearings and floor debate on bills and important national issues, and Court TV (and sometimes other networks) provides gavel-to-gavel coverage of many important state court trials.

Deciding to Hear a Case

Although more than 7,000 cases a year are now filed at the Supreme Court, this was not always the case. From 1790 to 1801, the Court heard only eighty-seven cases under its appellate jurisdiction.[20] In the Court's early years, the bulk of the justices' workload involved their circuit-riding duties. From 1862 to 1866, only 240 cases were decided. Creation of the Courts of Appeals in 1891 resulted in an immediate reduction in Supreme Court filings—from 600 in 1890 to 275 in 1892.[21] As recently as the 1940s, fewer than 1,000 cases were filed annually. Since that time, filings have increased at a dramatic rate as revealed in Figure 9-3 (p. 282).

Jurisdiction

The Constitution specifically sets out the scope of the Supreme Court's original jurisdiction; that is, cases for which the Court functions as a trial court having the first, or original, hearing in the case. The Court has original jurisdiction "over all Cases affecting Ambassadors, other public Ministers and Consuls, and those in which a State shall be a party." Most cases arising under the Court's original jurisdiction involve disputes between two states, usually over issues such as ownership of offshore oil deposits, territorial disputes caused by shifting river boundaries, or controversies caused by conflicting claims over water rights, such as when a river flows through two or more states.[22] In earlier days, the Court would actually sit as a trial court and hear evidence and argument. Today, the Court usually appoints a Special Master—often a retired judge or an expert on the matter at hand—to hear the case in a district court on behalf of the Supreme Court and then report his or her findings and recommendations to the Court. It is rare for more than two or three of these cases to come to the Court in a year.

Most cases arrive at the Court under its appellate jurisdiction; that is, its authority to hear appeals from other courts in the state or federal systems (see Figure 9-1, p. 278). The appellate jurisdiction of the Court can be changed by the Congress at any time, a power that has been a potent threat to the authority of the Court. The Judiciary Act of 1925 gave the Court discretion over its own jurisdiction, meaning that it does not have to accept all appeals that come to it. This so-called "Judge's Bill" was largely written by the Court itself under the direction of Chief Justice William Howard Taft (incidentally, the only member of the Court who also served as president of the United States). The idea behind the bill was that the intermediate Courts of Appeal should be the final word for almost all federal litigants, thus freeing the Supreme Court to concentrate on constitutional issues, unless the Court decided that it wanted to address other matters. The Court, then, is not expected to exercise its appellate jurisdiction simply to correct errors of other courts. Instead, appeal to the Supreme Court should be taken only if the case presents important issues of law, or what is termed "a substantial federal question." Since 1988, as illustrated in Figure 9-1, all appellate cases that come to the Supreme Court arrive there on a petition for a **writ of *certiorari*** (from the Latin "to be informed"), which are requests for the Supreme Court—at its discretion—to order up the records of the lower courts for purposes of review.

About one-third of all Supreme Court filings involve criminal law issues.[23] Many of these, in fact more than one-half of all petitions to the Court, are filed ***in forma pauperis*** (IFP) (literally from the Latin, "as a pauper"). About 80 percent of these are filed by indigent prison inmates seeking review of their sentences. Permission to proceed *in forma pauperis* allows the petitioner to avoid filing and printing costs. Any criminal defendant who has had a court-appointed lawyer in a lower court proceeding is automatically entitled to proceed in this fashion.

In recent years, the Court has tended more and more to deny requests to file *in forma pauperis*. In *In re Sindram* (1991), for example, the Rehnquist Court chastised Michael Sindram for filing his petition *in forma pauperis* to require the Maryland courts to expedite his request to expunge a $35 speeding ticket from his record. Sindram was no stranger to the Supreme Court: During the previous three years, he had filed forty-two separate motions on various legal matters, twenty-four of them in the 1990 term. In denying Sindram's request to file as an indigent, the majority noted that "[t]he goal of fairly dispensing justice . . . is compromised when the Court is forced to devote its limited resources to the processing of repetitious and frivolous requests." Along with the order denying the petition, the Court issued new rules to provide for denial of "frivolous" or "malicious" IFP motions.[24]

Writ of certiorari A formal document issued from the Supreme Court to a lower federal or state court that calls up a case. Four of the Court's nine justices must agree to accept the case before it is granted certiorari.
In forma pauperis Literally, "in the form of a pauper"; a way for an indigent or poor person to appeal a case to the U.S. Supreme Court.

The Rule of Four

Unlike other courts, the Supreme Court controls its own case load through the *certiorari* process and decides which cases it wants to hear, rejecting most cases that come to it. All petitions for *certiorari* must meet two criteria:

1. They must come from the U.S. Court of Appeals, special three-judge district courts, or a state court of last resort. Generally, this means that the case has already been decided by the state supreme court.
2. The case must involve a federal question. This means that the case must present questions of interpretation of federal constitutional law or involve a federal statute or treaty. The reasons why the Court should accept the case for review and legal argument supporting that position are set out in the petition (also called a brief).

The Clerk of the Court's office transmits petitions for writs of *certiorari* to the Chief Justice's office, where his clerks first review the petitions, and then to the individual justices' offices. All the justices on the Rehnquist Court except Justice John Paul Stevens participate in what is called the "cert pool."[25] As part of the pool, they review their assigned fraction of petitions and share their notes with each other. Those cases that the justices deem noteworthy are then placed on what is called the "discuss list"—a list of cases to be discussed—prepared by the Chief Justice's clerks and circulated to the chambers of the justices. Only about 30 percent of submitted petitions make it to this list. What helps a case make it onto the discuss list? Political scientists have interviewed justices and clerks, have conducted statistical analyses, and have concluded there are certain factors that increase the chances: (1) the U.S. government is a petitioning party; (2) conflict exists in the lower courts on an important point of law; and/or (3) the filing by an interest group of an *amicus curiae* brief urging the justices to accept the case for review.[26]

During one of the justices' weekly conference meetings, the cases on the discuss list are reviewed. The Chief Justice speaks first, then the rest of the justices, according to seniority. The decision process ends when the justices vote, and by custom, *certiorari* is granted according to the **Rule of Four**—when at least four justices vote to hear a case.

If *certiorari* is granted, the case is slated for oral argument and decision. Even under the Rule of Four, very few cases make it this far. Although the number of cases filed has increased, the number the Court accepts for oral argument and then decides has actually declined (see Figure 9-3, p. 282).

The content of the Court's docket is every bit as significant as its size. Prior to the 1930s, the Court generally heard cases of interest only to the immediate parties. In the 1930s, cases requiring the interpretation of constitutional law began to take a growing portion of its workload, leading the Court to take a more important role in the policymaking process. At that time, only 5 percent of the Court's cases involved questions concerning the Bill of Rights. By the late 1950s, one-third of filed cases involved such questions, and by the 1960s, half did.[27] In 1990, only 30 percent of the Court's caseload dealt with constitutional questions.

Characteristics of a Supreme Court Case

The reasons the Court decides to hear cases are many and diverse. The Court does not offer reasons, and "the standards by which the justices decide to grant or deny review are highly personalized and necessarily discretionary," noted former Chief Justice Earl Warren. Moreover, he continued, "those standards cannot be captured in rules or guidelines that would be meaningful."[28] Political scientists have nonetheless attempted to determine the characteristics of the cases the Court accepts; not surprisingly, they are similar to those that help a case get on the discuss list. Among the cues are the following:

- The federal government is the party asking for review.
- The case involves conflict among the circuit courts.
- The case presents a civil rights or civil liberties question.
- The case involves ideological and/or policy preferences of the justices.
- The case has significant social or political interest as evidenced by the presence of interest group *amicus curiae* briefs.

One of the most important cues for predicting whether the Court will hear a case is the position the U.S. **Solicitor General** takes on it. The Solicitor General, appointed by the president, is the fourth-ranking member of the Justice Department and is responsible for handling all appeals on behalf of the U.S. government to the Supreme Court. The Solicitor's staff is like a small, specialized law firm within the Justice

Rule of Four At least four justices of the Supreme Court must vote to consider a case before it can be heard.

Solicitor General The fourth-ranking member of the Justice Department; responsible for handling all appeals on behalf of the U.S. government to the Supreme Court.

As Solicitor General of the United States, Drew Day III is responsible for handling litigation on behalf of the United States government before the U.S. Supreme Court.

Department. But because this office has such a special relationship with the Supreme Court, even having a suite of offices within the Supreme Court, the Solicitor General is often referred to as the Court's "ninth and a half member."[29] Moreover, the Solicitor General appears as a party or as an *amicus curiae* in more than 50 percent of the cases heard by the Court each term.

This special relationship with the Court helps explain the overwhelming success the Solicitor General's office enjoys before the Supreme Court. The Court generally accepts 70 to 80 percent of the cases where the U.S. government is the petitioning party, compared to about 5 percent of all others.[30] But, because of this special relationship, the Solicitor General often finds himself playing two conflicting roles: representing both the president's policy interests and the broader interests of the United States in Court. At times, solicitors find these two roles difficult to reconcile. Former Solicitor General Rex E. Lee (1981–1985), for example, noted that on more than one occasion he refused to make in Court arguments that had been advanced by the Reagan administration (a stand that ultimately forced him to resign his position). Said Lee, "I'm not the pamphleteer general; I'm the solicitor general. My audience is not 100 million people; my audience is nine people. . . . Credibility is the most important asset that any solicitor general has."[31]

Conflict among the lower courts is apparently another reason why the justices take cases. When interpretations of constitutional or federal law are involved, the justices seem to want consistency throughout the federal court system.

Often, these conflicts occur when important civil rights or civil liberties questions arise. Then, the political ideology of the justices often is key. All but one of the justices through 1994 were appointed by (conservative) Republican presidents. The more conservative Burger and Rehnquist Courts were more likely to take cases when lower courts had ruled in favor of civil rights or civil liberties claims—generally to overrule those liberal decisions. As political scientist Lawrence Baum has commented, "justices' evaluations of lower court decisions are based largely on their ideological position."[32]

Interest group participation is another "quick" way for the justices to gauge the ideological ramifications of a particular case. Richard C. Cortner has noted that "cases do not arrive on the doorstep of the Supreme Court like orphans in the night."[33] Most cases heard by the Supreme Court involve either the government or an interest group—either as the sponsoring party or as an *amicus curiae*. Liberal groups such as the ACLU, People for the American Way, the NAACP Legal Defense Fund, and conservative groups including the Washington Legal Foundation, Concerned Women for America, or Americans United for Life Legal Defense Fund routinely sponsor cases or file *amicus* briefs either urging the Court to hear a case or asking it to deny *certiorari*. Research by political scientists has found that "not only does [an *amicus*] brief in favor of *certiorari* significantly improve the chances of a case being accepted, but two, three and four briefs improve the chances even more."[34] Clearly, it's more the merrier, whether or not the briefs are filed for or against granting review. Interest group participation may highlight lower court and ideological conflicts for the justices by alerting them to the amount of public interest in the issues presented in any particular case.

Starting the Case

Once the Court decides to hear a case, a flurry of activity begins. If a criminal defendant is proceeding *in forma pauperis*, the Court appoints an expert lawyer to prepare and argue the case. Unlike the situation in many state courts, where appointed lawyers are often novices, it is considered an honor to be asked to represent an indigent before the Supreme Court in spite of the fact that such representation is on a *pro bono*, or no fee, basis.

Whether they are being paid or not, lawyers on both sides of the case begin to prepare their written arguments for submission to the Court. In these briefs, lawyers cite prior case law and make arguments as to why the Court should find in favor of their client.

More often than not, these arguments are echoed or expanded in *amicus curiae* briefs filed by interested parties, especially interest groups. Often, lawyers will seek the support of sympathetic interest groups to buttress their claims before the Court, although most *amicus* briefs are filed independently, without requests from one of the two major parties in the case. In the 1987 term, 80 percent of the cases decided by the Court had at least one *amicus curiae* brief.

Since the 1970s, interest groups have increasingly used the *amicus* brief as a way to lobby the Court. Because litigation is so expensive, few individuals have the money (or time or interest) to pursue a perceived wrong all the way to the U.S. Supreme Court. All sorts of interest groups, then, find that joining ongoing cases through *amicus* briefs is a useful way of advancing their policy preferences. Major cases such as *Brown* v. *Board of Education* (1954), *Bowers* v. *Hardwick* (1986), and *Harris* v. *Forklift Systems* (1993), which involved the degree of psychological damage a victim of sexual harassment must show, all attracted large numbers of *amicus* briefs as part of interest groups' efforts to lobby the judiciary and bring about desired political objectives.[35] (See "*Amicus* Briefs in Support of *Harris*," p. 301.)

Interest groups also provide the Court with information not necessarily contained in the major-party briefs, help write briefs, and assist in practice moot-court sessions. In these sessions, the lawyer who will argue the case before the nine justices goes through a complete rehearsal, with prominent lawyers and law professors playing the roles of the various justices.

Oral Arguments by Attorneys

Once a case is accepted by the Court for full review and after briefs and *amicus* briefs are submitted on each side, oral argument takes place. The Supreme Court's annual term begins the first Monday in October, as it has since the late 1800s, and runs through early July. In the early nineteenth century, sessions of the Court lasted only a few weeks twice a year. Today, justices hear oral argument from the beginning of the term until early April. Special cases, such as *U.S.* v. *Nixon* (1974), have been heard even later in the year. During the term, "sittings," periods of about two weeks in which cases are heard, alternate with "recesses," also about two weeks long. Oral arguments are usually heard Monday through Wednesday during two-week sitting sessions.

Oral argument is generally limited to the immediate parties to the case, although it is not uncommon for the U.S. Solicitor General to appear to argue orally as an *amicus curiae*. Oral argument at the Court is fraught with time-honored tradition and ceremony. At precisely 10:00 every morning when the Court is in session, the Court Marshal (dressed in a cutaway) emerges to intone "Oyez! Oyez! Oyez!" as the nine justices emerge from behind a reddish-purple velvet curtain to take their places on the raised and slightly angled bench. (From 1790 to 1972, the justices sat on a straight bench. Chief Justice Burger modified it so that justices at either end could see and hear better.) There, the Chief Justice sits in the middle with the justices to his right and left, alternating in seniority.

Amicus Briefs in Support of *Harris*

❖ ❖ ❖

In *Harris* v. *Forklift Systems* (1993), the U.S. Supreme Court unanimously ruled that the federal civil rights laws created a "broad rule of workplace equality." In *Harris*, the Court found that Title VII of the Civil Rights Act was violated when Teresa Harris was subjected to "intimidation, ridicule, and insults" of a sexually harassing nature by her supervisor. The following groups or governments filed *amicus* briefs:

In support of *Harris*

1. United States
   Equal Employment Opportunity Commission

2. National Conference of Women's Bar Associations
   Women's Bar Association of District of Columbia

3. National Organization for Women Legal Defense and Education Fund
   Catherine MacKinnon
   American Jewish Committee
   American Medical Women Association
   Asian-American Legal Defense and Education Fund
   Association for Union Democracy
   Center for Women's Policy Studies
   Chicago Women in Trades
   Illinois Coalition Against Sexual Harassment
   National Organization for Women
   Northern Tradeswomen's Network
   Northern New England Tradeswomen Institute
   Puerto Rican Legal Defense and Education Fund
   Women's Law Project

4. NAACP Legal Defense and Education Fund
   National Conference of Jewish Women

5. Women's Legal Defense Fund
   National Women's Law Center
   AFL-CIO
   Ayuda, Inc.
   Bar Association of San Francisco
   California Women Lawyers
   Center for Women Policy Studies
   Coalition of Labor Union Women
   Committee for Justice for Women of North Carolina
   Federally Employed Women, Inc.
   Federation of Organizations for Professional Women
   Institute for Women's Policy Research
   Mexican American Women's National Association
   National Association of Female Executives

National Association of Social Workers, Inc.
National Center for Lesbian Rights
National Council of Negro Women, Inc.
9to5
National Association of Working Women
Older Women's League
Trial Lawyers for Public Justice
Wider Opportunities for Women
Women Employed
Women's Action Alliance
Women's Bar Association of the District of Columbia
Women's Law Center of Maryland
YWCA of the U.S.A.

6. Employment Law Center
   California Women Lawyer's Committee
   Equal Rights Advocates

7. National Employment Lawyers Association

8. American Civil Liberties Union
   American Jewish Congress

9. Feminists for Free Expression

10. Southern States Police Benevolent Association
    North Carolina Police Benevolent Association

11. National Conference of Women's Bar Associations
    Women's Bar Association of the District of Columbia

In Support of *Forklift Systems*

Equal Employment Advisory Council

For Neither Party

American Psychological Association

Teresa Harris celebrates her victory after the Supreme Court ruled that her employer's conduct was illegal sexual harassment.

Almost all attorneys are allotted one-half hour to present their cases, and this allotment includes the time taken by questions from the bench. Justice John Marshall Harlan once noted that there was "no substitute for this method in getting at the heart of an issue and in finding out where the truth lies."[36] As the lawyer for the appellee approaches the mahogany lectern, a green light goes on, indicating that the attorney's time has begun. A white light flashes when five minutes remain. When a red light goes on, Court practice mandates that counsel stop immediately. One famous piece of Court lore told to all attorneys concerns a counsel who continued talking and reading from his prepared argument after the red light went on. When he looked up, he found an empty bench—the justices had quietly risen and departed while he continued to talk. On another occasion, Chief Justice Charles Evans Hughes stopped a leader of the New York bar in the middle of the word "if."

Questions asked at oral argument can be very important. Lawyers are routinely interrupted as justices pepper them with questions and comments. Lawyers are now prohibited by formal rules from reading from prepared texts, but they may use notes. Other kinds of aids are usually barred, but the Court allowed the deaf lawyer in *Rowley Board of Education* v. *U.S.* (1982), a case involving the amount of assistance a public school district had to provide a deaf student, to use a video display screen from which he could read questions from the justices that were typed into it by a stenotypist.[37]

Questioning from the bench can become quite active, especially if the case is controversial. Until Justice Ginsburg joined the Court, Justice Scalia was considered the most loquacious jurist on the bench. Several justices have, in fact, privately expressed irritation over Scalia's "bull doggedness" from the bench. In one series of eight cases, Justice William J. Brennan did not ask a single question, whereas Justice Scalia asked 126. The Court also will often ask one side more questions than another. In the companion case to *Brown* v. *Board of Education*, for example, the lawyer defending segregation was interrupted only eleven times, whereas Thurgood Marshall, as counsel for the NAACP, was interrupted 127 times.[38] Continual interruptions can fluster even the most experienced lawyers. During the 1960 term, Justice Felix Frankfurter repeatedly questioned an obviously nervous lawyer, only to hear Justice William O. Douglas answer the questions. "I thought you were arguing the case," Frankfurter yelled to the lawyer, who answered, "I am, but I can use all the help I can get."[39]

Although many Court watchers have tried to figure out how a particular justice will vote based on the questioning at oral argument, most find that the nature and number of questions asked does not help much in predicting the outcome of a case. Nevertheless, many believe that oral argument has several important functions. Oral argument is the only opportunity for even a small portion of the public (who may attend the hearings) and the press to observe the workings of the Court. It assures lawyers that the justices have heard their case, and it forces lawyers to focus on arguments believed important by the justices.

Oral argument also provides the Court with additional information, especially concerning the Court's broader political role, an issue not usually addressed in written briefs. For example, the justices can ask how many people might be affected by its decision or where the Court (and country) would be heading if a case were decided in a particular way.

The Conference and Vote

The justices meet in closed conference on Wednesday afternoons and Fridays when the Court is hearing oral argument. The Wednesday conferences deal with cases heard on Mondays; the Friday conferences with cases heard on Tuesdays and Wednesdays and with *certiorari* petitions and appeals.

Since the ascendancy of Chief Justice Roger B. Taney to the Court in 1836, the justices have begun each session with a round of handshaking. Once the door to the Conference Room closes, no others are allowed to enter. The justice with the least seniority acts as the doorkeeper for the other eight, communicating with those waiting outside to fill requests for documents, water, and so on.

Conferences highlight the importance and power of the Chief Justice, who presides over them and makes the initial presentation of each case. Each individual justice then discusses the case in order of seniority on the Court, the most senior justice first. Most accounts of the decision-making process reveal that at this point some justices try to change the minds of others, but that most enter the conference room with a clear idea of how they feel. Although other Courts have followed different procedures, on the Rehnquist Court the justices generally vote at the same time they discuss the case. Initial conference votes are not final, allowing justices to change their minds before final votes are taken later.

Writing the Opinions of the Court

The Chief Justice, if he is in the majority, has the job of assigning the writing of the opinion, in which the reasons behind a decision are set forth. This privilege enables him to wield tremendous power. (If he is in the minority, the assignment falls to the most senior justice in the majority.) During the Burger Court years (1969–1986), the Chief Justice was heavily criticized for his tendency to wait to announce his vote at conference so that he could be in the majority (even when his initial comments indicated a different opinion) and thus assign the opinion. Burger could then, in essence, water down the force of the opinion and possibly weaken its overall impact. Today, however, the Chief Justice is regularly in the majority, so tactics like Burger's are no longer considered necessary.

The justice assigned to write the majority opinion circulates drafts of the opinion to all members of the Court. The Court must provide legal reasons for its positions. The reasoning behind any decision is often as important as the outcome, because, under our system of *stare decisis*, both are likely to be relied on later by lower courts confronted with cases involving similar issues. And the justice who drafts the opinion can have an important impact on how any issues are framed. Informal caucusing and negotiation then often take place as justices may "hold out" for word changes or other modifications as a condition of their continued support of the majority opinion. At the same time, **dissenting opinions**, disagreeing with the outcome, and/or **concurring opinions**, agreeing with the outcome but not the legal rationale for the opinion (or further clarifying support) also circulate through the various chambers. The justices are often assisted in their writing of opinions by their clerks, who also can serve as intermediaries between the justices as they talk among themselves.

A good example of how politics can be involved at the opinion-writing stage is evident in *Bowers* v. *Hardwick* (1986),[40] the Georgia sodomy case discussed in Chapters 4 and 5. Justices White and Burger voted for *certiorari* to state that the Constitution doesn't protect homosexual acts. The liberal Marshall and Brennan thought they had enough votes to overturn the law, but when Brennan perceived he would lose, he withdrew his vote for *certiorari*. Then, according to papers kept by Justice Thurgood Marshall, the opinion quickly became one of shifting coalitions. Justice Lewis Powell originally indicated at Conference that he would vote with the majority to find the law

Dissenting opinions Opinions written by judges who disagree with the opinion of the majority.
Concurring opinions Opinions written by judges who agree with the outcome of the case but do not agree with the legal rationale for the opinion.

unconstitutional. After drafts of the majority and minority opinions were circulated, however, he changed his mind, thus changing a five-to-four majority to strike down the law into a five-to-four majority to uphold it.[41]

This kind of communal work can result in poorly written opinions, as was the case with *U.S.* v. *Nixon* (1974).[42] Although the court order for Nixon to turn over tape recordings of his conversations (see "Watergate and Its Effect on the Presidency," p. 210) was issued under Chief Justice Burger's name, many believe that it was a combination of several justices' contributions and additions. Sensing the need for the Court to speak unanimously on such an important decision—one that pitted two branches of government against each other—Justice Burger apparently made concessions to get support.[43] This process led to sometimes confused prose.

Recently, tensions have grown on the Court concerning some issues, and dissents or concurring opinions have become quite pointed. The protocol of the Court has always been characterized by politeness, but this has not stopped some justices from openly ridiculing their brethren from the bench. Justice Scalia, for example, publicly criticized Justice O'Connor's opinion in *Webster* v. *Reproductive Health Services* (1989), saying that her "assertion that a fundamental rule of judicial restraint requires [the Court] to avoid reconsidering *Roe* [v. *Wade*] cannot be taken seriously."[44]

How the Justices Vote

Justices are human beings who do not make decisions in a vacuum. Principles of *stare decisis* dictate that the justices follow the law of previous cases in deciding cases at hand. But more factors are usually operating. A variety of legal and extra-legal factors have been shown to affect Supreme Court decision-making. For example, a number of scholars have tried to predict voting patterns by examining individual justices' social background characteristics (such as their education or party identification).[45] Others have attempted to predict voting based on the factual patterns in a case,[46] and others have relied on their perceptions of the justices' roles.[47] All of this research indicates to one degree or another that justices do not make decisions in a vacuum. Each is influenced by a variety of factors, and many in fact were appointed to the Court with the expectation that they would further a particular ideology or approach to interpreting the Constitution.

Legal Factors

Judicial Philosophy and Original Intent.   One of the primary issues of judicial power focuses on what is called the activism/restraint debate. Advocates of judicial restraint argue that courts should allow the decisions of other branches to stand, even when they offend a judge's own sense of principles.[48] Restraintists defend their position by asserting that the federal courts are composed of unelected judges, which makes the judicial branch the least democratic branch of government. Consequently, the courts should defer policy making to other branches of government as much as possible.

Restraintists refer to *Roe* v. *Wade* (1973), the case that liberalized abortion laws, as a classic example of judicial activism run amok. They maintain that the Court should have deferred policy making on this sensitive issue to the states or to the other branches of the federal government—the legislature and executive—because their officials are elected and therefore are more receptive to the majority's will.

Advocates of judicial activism contend that judges should use their power broadly to further justice, especially in the areas of equality and personal liberty. Activists argue that it is the courts' appropriate role to correct injustices committed by the other branches of government. Explicit in this argument is the notion that courts need to protect oppressed minorities.[49]

Activists point to *Brown* v. *Board of Education* (1954) as an excellent example of the importance of judicial activism. In *Brown*, the Supreme Court ruled that racial segregation in public schools violated the equal protection clause of the Fourteenth Amendment. Segregation was nonetheless practiced after passage of the Fourteenth Amendment, and an activist would point out that if the Court had not reinterpreted its provisions, many states probably would still have laws or policies mandating segregation in public schools.

The debate over activism versus restraint often focuses on how the Court should translate the meaning of the Constitution. Advocates of judicial restraint generally agree that judges should be strict constructionists; that is, they should interpret the Constitution as it was written and intended by the Framers. They argue that in determining the constitutionality of a statute or policy, the Court should rely on the explicit meanings of the clauses in the document, which can be found by looking at the intent of the Framers.

Edwin Meese III, the U.S. Attorney General in the Reagan administration, is a leading "interpretivist," who believes that judges should look to the Framers' original intent when interpreting the Constitution. As a "strict constructionist," Meese argues that judges should "resist any political effort to depart from the literal provisions of the Constitution."[50]

In contrast, "non-interpretivists" generally argue that the Framers intended the Constitution to be a flexible document whose provisions should be read in light of changing historical circumstances and needs. They believe that judges must move beyond the text of the Constitution and impart to it values that are not explicitly in the document, all the while explaining what the Constitution means for a developing and dynamic system.

Former Supreme Court Justice William J. Brennan Jr. is a leading "non-interpretivist." He believes the "Constitution was not intended to preserve a preexisting society but to make a new one, to put in place new principles that the prior political community had not sufficiently recognized."[51]

Of late, most non-interpretivist judges, such as Justice Brennan have tended to be liberal activists. There is, however, no necessary connection between activism and liberalism. Some believe, for example, that the conservative Rehnquist Court could adopt an activist approach as it puts its conservative stamp on its construction and interpretation of statutes and the Constitution.

Precedent. Most Supreme Court decisions are laced with numerous references to previous Court decisions. *Stare decisis* holds that once the Supreme Court has interpreted the Constitution or a statute in a certain way, that interpretation should be used to decide the case at hand. Adherence to *stare decisis* allows for stability and consistency in the law as justices look to past cases for guidance.

Some justices, however, believe that *stare decisis* and adherence to precedent is no longer as critical as it once was. Chief Justice Rehnquist, for example, has noted that

The 1989 pro-choice rally in Washington, D.C., was part of an intense lobbying effort to influence the Court's decision in the *Webster* case. Justice Sandra Day O'Connor, viewed as a swing vote on the case, was a particular target of the lobbying.

while "*stare decisis* is a cornerstone of our legal system . . . it has less power in constitutional cases."[52] In contrast, Justices O'Connor, Kennedy, and Souter explained their reluctance to overrule *Roe* v. *Wade* (1973) in *Planned Parenthood of Southeastern Pennsylvania v. Casey* (1992): "to overrule under fire in the absence of the most compelling reason to reexamine a watershed decision would subject this Court's legitimacy beyond any serious question."[53]

Interestingly, a 1990 study of the American public's knowledge and perceptions of the Court indicated that only 44 percent believed that the Court decides cases primarily on the basis of facts and law. Nearly 50 percent believe that the Court decides based on other factors, including political pressures (28 percent), political/personal beliefs (18 percent), and religious beliefs (1 percent). Although *theoretically* the Framers envisioned the Court to be above these pressures, the American public does not appear to be particularly upset about the role of politics and personal beliefs in the decision-making process. In fact, those polled want the Court to take a more active role in the areas of discrimination against women and minorities.

Extra-Legal Factors

Public Opinion. According to Chief Justice Rehnquist,

> Judges, so long as they are relatively normal human beings, can no more escape being influenced by public opinion in the long run than can people working at other jobs. And if a judge on coming to the bench were to decide to hermetically seal himself off from all manifestations of public opinion, he would accomplish very little; he would not be influenced by current public opinion, but instead would be influenced by the state of public opinion at the time he came to the bench.[54]

Public opinion can act as a check on the power of the courts as well as an energizing factor. Activist periods on the Supreme Court have generally corresponded to periods of social or economic crisis. For example, the Marshall Court supported a strong national government, much to the chagrin of a series of pro-states' rights Democratic-Republican presidents in the early crisis-ridden years of the republic. Similarly, the Court capitulated to political pressures and public opinion when, after 1936, it reversed many of its earlier decisions that had blocked President Roosevelt's New Deal legislation.

The courts also can be the direct target of public opinion. During the spring of 1989, when the case of *Webster* v. *Reproductive Health Services* was about to come before the Supreme Court, the Court was subjected to unprecedented lobbying as groups and individuals on both sides of the abortion issue marched and sent appeals to the Court. Earlier, in the fall of 1988, Justice Harry Blackmun, author of *Roe* v. *Wade*, had warned a law school audience in a public address that he feared that the decision was in jeopardy. This in itself was a highly unusual move; until recently, it was the practice of the justices never to comment on cases or the Court.

Speeches like Blackmun's put pro-choice advocates on guard, and many took advantage of the momentum that had built around their successful campaign against the nomination of Robert H. Bork. In 1989, their forces mounted one of the largest demonstrations in the history of the United States when more than 300,000 people marched from the White House to the Supreme Court. In addition, full-page advertisements appeared in prominent newspapers, and supporters of *Roe* v. *Wade* were urged to contact members of the Court to voice their support. Justice Sandra Day O'Connor, at the time the Court's lone woman, was targeted by many who viewed her as the crucial swing justice on the issue. Mail at the Court, which usually averages about 1,000 pieces a day, rose to an astronomical 46,000 pieces when *Webster* reached the Court, virtually paralyzing normal lines of communication. Several justices spoke out against this kind of "extra-judicial" communication and voiced their belief in its ineffectiveness. In *Webster* v. *Reproductive Health Services* (1989) Justice Scalia lamented,

> We can now look forward to at least another Term with carts full of mail from the public, and streets full of demonstrators, urging us—their unelected and life tenured judges who have been awarded those extraordinary, undemocratic characteristics precisely in order that we might follow the law despite the popular will—to follow the popular will.

But the fact remains that the Court *is* very dependent on the public for its prestige as well as for compliance with its decisions. In times of war and other emergencies, for example, the Court frequently has decided cases in ways that commentators have attributed to the sway of public opinion and political exigencies. In *Korematsu* v. *The United States* (1944),[55] for example, the high court upheld the obviously unconstitutional internment of Japanese-American citizens during World War II. Moreover, Chief Justice Rehnquist himself has suggested that the Court's restriction on presidential authority in *Youngstown Sheet & Tube Co.* v. *Sawyer* (1952),[56] which invalidated President Harry S Truman's seizure of the nation's steel mills, was largely attributable to Truman's unpopularity and that of the Korean War.[*] And, as Table 9.2 reveals, the public and the Court often are in agreement on many controversial issues.

Table 9.2 ◆ The Court versus the American Public

In recent years, the Court has agreed and disagreed with the public on various issues, such as:

ISSUE	COURT	PUBLIC
Should TV and other recording devices be permitted in the Supreme Court?	No	Yes (59%)
Should a parent be forced to reveal the whereabouts of a child even though it could violate Fifth Amendment rights?	Yes	Yes (50%) No (39%) Don't know (11%)
Should a family be allowed to decide to end life-support systems?	Yes	Yes (88%)
Before getting an abortion, whose consent should a teenager be required to gain?	One parent	Both parents (38%) One parent (37%) Neither parent (22%)
Is the death penalty constitutional?	Yes	Yes (72% favor)

Source: Table compiled from general social surveys and Gallup Poll data.

---

[*] In *Youngstown Sheet and Tube Co.* v. *Sawyer,* 343 U.S. 579 (1952), the Supreme Court had ruled that President Truman's seizure and operation of U.S. steel mills in the face of a strike threat were unconstitutional, because the Constitution implied no such broad executive power. See Alan Westin, *Anatomy of a Constitutional Law Case* (New York: Macmillan, 1958).

Behavioral Characteristics.   Many political scientists have concluded that a variety of behavioral characteristics motivate judicial decision making. Most notable of these are background characteristics and attitudes.

Some, for example, argue that social background differences, including childhood experiences, religious values, education, earlier political and legal careers, and political party loyalties are likely to influence how a judge evaluates the facts and legal issues presented in any given case. Harry Blackmun's service at the Mayo Clinic is often pointed to as a reason why his opinion for the Court in *Roe* v. *Wade* was so soundly grounded in medical evidence. Similarly, Justice Potter Stewart, who was generally considered a moderate on most civil liberties issues, usually took a more liberal position on cases dealing with freedom of the press. Why? It may be that Stewart's early job as a newspaper reporter made him more sensitive to these claims. Similarly, Justices Scalia and Thomas's Roman Catholic backgrounds often appear to affect their decisions dealing with abortion and First Amendment religion issues.

Ideology.   Critics of the social background approach argue that attitudes or ideologies can better explain the justices' voting patterns. Since the 1940s, the two most prevailing ideologies in the United States have been conservative and liberal. On the Supreme Court, justices with "conservative" views generally vote against affirmative action, abortion rights, expanded rights for criminal defendants, and increased power for the national government. In contrast, "liberals" tend to support the parties advancing these positions.

Over time, however, scholars have generally agreed that identifiable ideological voting blocs have occurred on the Court. During the New Deal period, for example, five justices, a critical conservative bloc, routinely voted to strike down the constitutionality of New Deal legislation. Traditionally, such voting blocs or coalitions have centered on liberal/conservative splits on issues such as states' rights (conservatives supporting and liberals opposing), economic issues (conservatives being pro-business; liberals, pro-labor), and civil liberties and civil rights (conservatives being less supportive than liberals). On death-penalty cases, for example, Justices William Brennan Jr. and Thurgood Marshall (sometimes joined by John Paul Stevens) consistently voted against the imposition of the death penalty. The current Rehnquist Court, however, has fewer of these blocs, because its members are ideologically more homogeneous than most courts in the past. All but John Paul Stevens, Ruth Bader Ginsburg, and Stephen Breyer usually take what could be termed conservative positions on most issues.

Judicial Policy Making and Implementation

When the Court decides to hear (or not to hear) a case, it takes its first step in policy making. Thus, it is through interpreting statutes or the Constitution that federal courts, and the Supreme Court in particular, make policy in several ways. Judges can interpret a provision of a law to cover matters not previously understood to be covered by the law or can "discover" new rights, such as that of privacy, from their reading of the Constitution.

This power of the courts to make policy presents difficult questions for democratic theory, as noted by Justice Scalia in *Webster*, because democratic theorists believe that the power to make law resides only in the people or their elected representatives. Yet

glance, but in practice it can be very difficult to understand. The implementing population in this case consists chiefly of state legislatures and local governments, which determine voting districts for federal, state, and local offices (see Chapter 6). If a state legislature draws districts in such a way that African-American voters are spread thinly across a number of separate constituencies, the chances are slim that any particular district will elect a representative who is especially sensitive to blacks' concerns. Does that violate "equal representation"? (In practice, the courts and the Justice Department have intervened in many cases to ensure that elected officials will include minority representation.)

The second requirement is that the implementing population must actually follow Court policy. Thus, when the Court ruled that men could not be denied admission to a state-sponsored nursing school, the implementing population—in this case, university administrators and the Board of Regents of the nursing school—had to enroll qualified male students.

Judicial decisions are most likely to be implemented smoothly if responsibility for implementation is concentrated in the hands of a few highly visible public officials, such as the president or a governor. By the same token, these officials can also thwart or impede judicial intentions. Recall from Chapter 5, for example, the effect of Governor Orval Faubus's initial refusal to allow black children to attend all-white public schools in Little Rock, Arkansas.

The third requirement for implementation is that the consumer population must be aware of the rights that a decision grants or denies them. Teenagers seeking an abortion, for example, are consumers of the Supreme Court's decisions on abortion. They need to know that most states require them to inform their parents of their intention to have an abortion or get parental permission to do so. Similarly, criminal defendants and their lawyers are consumers of Court decisions and need to know, for example, the implications of recent Supreme Court decisions for evidence presented at trial.

Toward Reform

Clearly, the American public regards the Supreme Court as a powerful policy maker. In a 1990 poll, most respondents said they believed that the Court was more powerful than the president (31 percent versus 21 percent) and that the Court was close to being as powerful as Congress (38 percent).

Considering how poorly informed the American public is about the Court, interest in its activities appears to be growing as more Americans come to understand the importance of the Court in shaping our social and economic agenda and as Court appointments continue to get extensive media coverage.

In the wake of the Clarence Thomas hearings, much was said about the need to reform the judicial selection process. Criticism was directed in particular at Senate confirmation hearings, special-interest groups, and ideological politics. As time has passed, however, little has been done in response to these concerns, and the Ruth Bader Ginsburg and Stephen G. Breyer hearings, which went like clockwork, seem to indicate that the Bork and Thomas hearings were anomalies.

Historically, in fact, there has been little inclination to tinker with the judicial system—even though the courts have grown in power—except when the Supreme Court has stepped on too many toes. Congress and the president have, from time to time, limited, or attempted to limit, the jurisdiction of the Court. When Democratic-Republicans were unable to get rid of Federalist judges by impeachment, they abolished the federal circuit courts. Following the Civil War, Radical Republicans cut the size of the Court and changed its appellate jurisdiction to prevent it from hearing a case involving the constitutionality of some Reconstruction legislation.[62] And in 1936, President Franklin D. Roosevelt tried unsuccessfully to change the size of the Court so that he could pack it with supporters of his New Deal.

More recently, proposals have been made to alter the Court's jurisdiction on matters such as abortion, but little has come of them. If the current Court continues its conservative pattern, it may someday find itself in conflict with a more liberal Democratic president and Congress. As revealed in Table 9.3, even with a Democratic Congress and president, if the present members of the Court retire at the same average age as their recent predecessors, it would still take many years for the Court to be re-made in a more liberal model.

The question may more properly be: Are the courts too political? Should their independence be curbed? The courts and the judiciary occupy a peculiar place in our democratic system. Not elected by the people, federal judges serve for life with no direct responsibility or accountability to those who can be affected so profoundly by their decisions. Yet, suggestions such as the one made by FDR to change the Supreme Court have not met with much enthusiasm by Congress or the public.

Table 9.3 ◆ The Future Composition of the Supreme Court			
JUSTICE	AGE IN 1995	PHILOSOPHY	PROJECTED YEAR OF RETIREMENT*
Stevens	75	Moderate	2001
Rehnquist	71	Conservative	2005
O'Connor	65	Conservative	2011
Scalia	59	Conservative	2017
Kennedy	59	Conservative	2017
Souter	56	Conservative	2020
Thomas	47	Conservative	2029
Ginsburg	63	Moderate/Liberal	2009
Breyer	57	Moderate	2019

* This is based on the last six Justices (Brennan, Burger, Marshall, Powell, White, and Blackmun) when they retired from 1986–1994—81 years of age.

Summary

The judiciary and the legal process—on both the national and state levels—are complex and play a far more important role in the setting of policy than the Framers ever envisioned. To explain the judicial process and its evolution, we have made the following points:

1. Many of the Framers viewed the judicial branch of government as little more than a minor check on the other two branches, ignoring Anti-Federalist concerns about an unelected judiciary and its potential for tyranny. The Judiciary Act of 1789 established the basic federal court system we have today. It was the Marshall Court (1801–1835), however, that interpreted the Constitution to include the Court's major power, that of judicial review.

2. Ours is a dual judicial system consisting of the federal court system and the separate judicial systems of the fifty states. In each system, there are two basic types of courts: trial courts and appellate courts. Each type deals with cases involving criminal and civil law. Original jurisdiction refers to a court's ability to hear a case as a trial court; appellate jurisdiction to a court's ability to review cases already decided by a trial court.

3. The federal court system is made up of constitutional and legislative courts. Federal district courts, courts of appeals, and the Supreme Court are constitutional courts.

4. District court and court of appeals judges are nominated by the president and subject to Senate confirmation. Senators often play a key role in "suggesting" district court appointees from their home state. Supreme Court justices are nominated by the president but must also win Senate confirmation. Presidents use different criteria for selection, but important factors include competence and ethical standards, ideology, rewards, pursuit of political support, religion, race, and gender.

5. Several factors go into the Court's decision to hear a case. Not only must the court have jurisdiction, but at least four justices must vote to hear the case, and cases with certain characteristics are most likely to be heard. Once a case is set for review, briefs and *amicus curiae* briefs are filed and oral argument scheduled. The justices meet after oral argument to discuss the case, votes are taken, and opinions written and circulated.

6. Several legal and extra-legal factors affect how the Court arrives at its decision. Legal factors include judicial philosophy, the original intent of the Framers, and precedent. Extra-legal factors include public opinion, and the behavioral characteristics and ideology of the justices.

7. The Supreme Court is an important participant in the policy-making process. The process of judicial interpretation gives the Court powers never envisioned by the Framers.

8. Unlike the other two branches of government, the Supreme Court and the federal judiciary have not been the subjects of many reform efforts, and periodic calls for change have met with little support.

Key Terms

amicus curiae

judicial review

Marbury v. *Madison*

appellate courts

criminal law

grand jury

indictment

civil law

constitutional courts

legislative courts

brief

precedents

stare decisis

senatorial courtesy

strict constructionist

writ of *certiorari*

in forma pauperis

Rule of Four

Solicitor General

dissenting opinions

concurring opinions

Suggested Readings

Abraham, Henry. *The Judicial Process*, 6th ed. New York: Oxford University Press, 1993.

Baum, Lawrence. *American Courts: Process and Policy,* 3rd ed. Boston: Houghton Mifflin, 1994.

———*The Supreme Court,* 4th ed. Washington: CQ Press, 1992.

Epstein, Lee, et. al. *The Supreme Court Compendium: Data, Decisions, and Developments*. Washington, DC: Congressional Quarterly Inc., 1994.

Hickock, Eugene and Gary McDowell. *Justice vs. Law: Courts and Politics in American Society*. New York: Macmillan, 1993.

Hall, Kermitt L. ed., *The Oxford Companion to the Supreme Court of the United States*. New York: Oxford University Press, 1992.

Levy, Leonard W., et al., eds. *American Constitutional History*. New York: Macmillan, 1989.

Marshall, Thomas. *Public Opinion and the Supreme Court*. Boston: Unwin and Hyman, 1989.

O'Brien, David M. *Storm Center: The Supreme Court in American Politics*, 2nd ed. New York: Norton, 1990.

O'Connor, Karen. *Women's Organizations' Use of the Courts*. Lexington, MA: Lexington Books, 1980.

Provine, Doris Marie. *Case Selection in the United States Supreme Court*. Chicago: University of Chicago Press, 1980.

Salokar, Rebecca Mae. *The Solicitor General: The Politics of Law*. Philadelphia: Temple University Press, 1992.

Wasby, Stephen. *The Supreme Court in the Federal Judicial System*, 4th ed. Chicago: Nelson-Hall, 1993.

Woodward, Bob, and Scott Armstrong. *The Brethren: Inside the Supreme Court*. New York: Simon and Schuster, 1979.

Public Opinion

When John Jay wrote so glowingly of the sameness of the American people in 1787, he and other writers of *The Federalist Papers* believed that Americans had more in common than not. Many of those who could vote were of English heritage; almost all were Christian. Moreover, most believed that certain rights such as freedom of speech, association, and religion were unalienable rights. This was part of the shared political culture that Jay celebrated in *Federalist No. 2.* There, he also spoke of shared public opinion and of the need for a national government reflecting American ideals. But Jay overstated the universality of the public's support for a strong national government. Moreover, even though Americans at the time generally shared one language, religion, and a common ancestry, existing class and philosophical differences were already producing the kind of factions that the Federalists feared.

The Federalist Papers were themselves one of the first major attempts to change public opinion—in this case, to gain public support for the newly drafted U.S. Constitution. Even prior to publication of *The Federalist Papers,* Thomas Paine's *Common Sense* and later his *Crisis* papers were widely distributed throughout the colonies in an effort to stimulate patriotic feelings and increase public support for the Revolutionary War. From the very early days of the republic, political leaders recognized the impor-

315

Like President Ronald Reagan, Bill Clinton has been a master manipulator of the media and public opinion. He regularly uses televised town hall meetings as a way to move public opinion.

> **I** have often taken notice that Providence has been pleased to give this one connected country to one united people—a people descended from the same ancestors, speaking the same language, professing the same religion, attached to the same principles of government, very similar in manners and customs. . . .
>
> *John Jay*
> *Federalist No. 2*

The Framers may have wished for all Americans to share a common culture. At no time, however, has the American public resembled Jay's description. Because public opinion is crucial to democracy and the formation of the policies and laws that govern our lives, it is extremely important to understand the makeup of the American people—what they think, what they believe, and what they say, in all their many voices.

tance of public opinion and used all the means at their disposal to manipulate it for their purposes.

In his first year in office, President Clinton revealed his understanding of the importance of public support. His major legislative victories—the budget bill, the North American Free Trade Agreement (NAFTA), and the Brady gun-control bill—were won with the support of very different groups of people. His efforts to mobilize public opinion included town hall meeting appearances and having his vice president, Al Gore Jr., debate Ross Perot on "Larry King Live" in order to bring the case for NAFTA directly to the American public.

The proper role of public opinion in the making of policy is just one question we explore in this chapter. Other areas of concern are how political attitudes and public opinion have been manipulated and measured over time, how opinions are formed, and what enduring issues have been important to politicians and the public.

What Is Public Opinion?

Public opinion What the public thinks about a particular issue or set of issues at any point in time.
Public opinion polls Interviews or surveys with a sample of citizens that are used to estimate public opinion of the entire population.

At first blush, **public opinion** seems to be a very straightforward term: It is what the public thinks about a particular issue or set of issues at a particular time. Since the 1930s, governmental decision makers have relied heavily on **public opinion polls**—interviews with a sample of citizens that are used to estimate public opinion of the entire population—to determine what the public is thinking. According to the founder of modern-day polling, George Gallup (see "People of the Past," p. 318), polls have played a key role in defining issues of concern to the public, shaping administrative decisions, and helping "speed up the process of democracy" in the United States.[1] But as we discuss later in this chapter, what the public thinks about various issues is difficult to know with certainty simply because public opinion can change so quickly. For example, two weeks before the United States bombed Iraq in January 1991, public opinion polls revealed that only 61 percent of the American public believed that the United States should engage in combat in Iraq. One week after the invasion, however, 86 percent reported that they approved of President Bush's handling of the situation.

Similarly, as revealed in Figure 10-1, public support for NAFTA soared from 34 percent to 57 percent after the vice president debated former presidential candidate Ross Perot. Not only did support for NAFTA go up 23 percent, but so did the public's favorable view of Al Gore Jr!

Throughout our nation's history, political thinkers have argued that a just government rests on the wishes of the people. In *Federalist No. 10*, for example, James Madison articulated this notion: "The public voice, pronounced by the representatives of the people, will be more consonant to the public good." Madison stressed that government should respond to the will of the people but not to momentary changes in opinion occasioned by dramatic events. Governments, he argued, need respond only to those enduring beliefs shared by the public. As we see throughout this book, many such enduring beliefs are reflected in the Declaration of Independence (see Appendix I) and in the Bill of Rights.

Not all commentators agree with Madison, however. According to pollster George Gallup, leaders must constantly take public opinion—no matter how short-lived—into

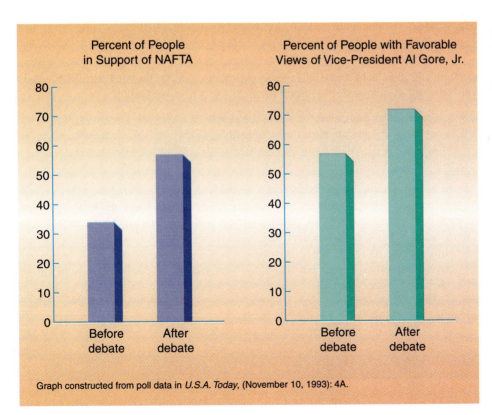

FIGURE 10-1

Public opinion on NAFTA and Al Gore Jr. before and after his televised debate on NAFTA with Ross Perot on "Larry King Live"

PEOPLE OF THE PAST

George Gallup

George Gallup

George Gallup earned a Ph.D. in journalism from the University of Iowa; his dissertation examined methods of measuring the readership of newspapers. He first became interested in polling when his mother-in-law ran for public office in 1932. She was running against a popular incumbent, and most observers considered her candidacy a lost cause. Nevertheless, because of the Democratic landslide of 1932, she was swept into office on Franklin D. Roosevelt's coattails.

Gallup's interest in politics, fostered by his experience in his mother-in-law's campaign and his academic background in journalism and advertising, led him to take a job at a New York advertising agency. In 1935 he founded the American Institute of Public Opinion, headquartered at Princeton University in New Jersey. At the Institute, Gallup refined a number of survey and sampling techniques to measure the public's attitudes on social, political, and economic issues. Weekly reports called the Gallup Polls were sent to more than forty subscribing newspapers.

Gallup attracted considerable national attention when he correctly predicted the outcome of the 1936 presidential election. Recognizing many flaws of the *Literary Digest*'s poll, he relied on a sample of a few thousand people who represented the voting population in terms of important demographic variables, such as age, gender, political affiliation, and region.

account. Like the Jacksonians of a much earlier era, Gallup was distrustful of leaders who were not in tune with the "common man." According to Gallup,

> in a democracy we demand the views of the people be taken into account. This does not mean that leaders must follow the public's view slavishly; it does mean that they should have an available appraisal of public opinion and take some account of it in reaching their decision.[2]

Even though Gallup undoubtedly had a vested interest in fostering reliance on public opinion polls, his sentiments accurately reflect the feelings of many political thinkers concerning the role of public opinion and governance. Majoritarians like Gallup believe that the government should do what a majority of the public wants done. In contrast, pluralists argue that the public as a whole doesn't have consistent opinions on day-to-day issues but that subgroups within the public often hold strong views on some issues. Pluralists believe that the government must allow for the expression of these minority opinions and that democracy works best when these different voices are allowed to fight it out in the public arena.

Early Efforts to Influence Public Opinion

You can hardly read a newspaper or a news magazine or watch television without hearing the results of the latest public opinion poll on health care, crime, AIDS, or some other social issue, or a report on the most recent presidential popularity rating. But long before modern polling, by the early 1800s, the term "public opinion" was frequently being used by the educated middle class. As more Americans became educated, they became more vocal about their opinions and were more likely to vote. A more educated, reading public led to increased demand for newspapers, which in turn provided more information about the process of government. And as the United States grew, there were more elections and more opportunities for citizens to express their political opinions through the ballot box. As a result of these trends, political leaders were more frequently forced to try to gauge public opinion in order to remain responsive to the wishes and desires of their constituents.

An example of the power of public opinion is the public's response to the 1851 through 1852 serialization of Harriet Beecher Stowe's *Uncle Tom's Cabin*. This novel was one of the most powerful propaganda statements ever issued about slavery, and by the time the first shots of the Civil War were fired at Fort Sumter in 1861 more than one million copies of the book were in print. Even though Stowe's words alone could not have caused the public outrage over slavery that contributed to Northern support for the war, her book convinced the majority of the American people of the justness of the abolitionist cause and solidified public opinion against slavery in the North.

During World War I, while some people argued that public opinion didn't matter at all, President Woodrow Wilson (1913–1921), like Taft, argued that public opinion would temper the actions of international leaders. Therefore, only eight days after the start of the war, Wilson created a Committee on Public Information. Run by a prominent journalist, the committee immediately undertook to unite U.S. public opinion behind the war effort. It used all of the tools available—pamphlets, posters, and speakers who exhorted the patrons of local movie houses during every intermission—in an effort to garner support and favorable opinion for the war. In the words of the committee's head, it was "the world's greatest adventure in advertising."[3]

In the wake of World War I, Walter Lippmann, a well-known journalist and author who was extensively involved in propaganda activities during the war, openly voiced his concerns about how easily public opinion could be manipulated and his reservations about the weight it should be given. In his seminal work, *Public Opinion* (1922), Lippmann wrote, "Since Public Opinion is supposed to be the prime mover in democracies, one might reasonably expect to find a vast literature. One does not find it."[4] By the 1920s, although numerous efforts had been made to manipulate public opinion, scientific measurement of the public opinion had yet to occur.

During World War I, as part of "The world's greatest adventure in advertising," the Committee on Public Information created a vast gallery of posters designed to shore up public support for the war effort.

Early Attempts to Gauge Public Opinion

Public opinion polling as we know it today did not begin to develop until the 1930s. Researchers in a variety of disciplines, including political science, heeded Lippmann's call to learn more about public opinion. Some tried to use scientific methods to measure political thought through the use of surveys or polls. As methods for gathering and interpreting data improved, survey data began to play an increasingly important role in all walks of life, from politics to retailing.

Even before the 1930s, many people had tried to forecast the results of political elections. As early as 1824, for example, one Pennsylvania newspaper tried to predict the winner of that year's presidential contest. Later, in 1883, the *Boston Globe* sent reporters to selected election precincts to poll voters as they exited voting booths in an

Not only did advance polls in 1948 predict that Republican nominee Thomas E. Dewey would defeat Democratic incumbent Harry S Truman, but based on early and incomplete vote tallies, some newspapers' early editions even on the day *after* the election declared Dewey to have won. Here a triumphant Truman holds aloft the *Chicago Tribune.*

effort to predict the results of key contests. And in 1916, *Literary Digest,* a popular magazine, began mailing survey postcards to potential voters in an effort to predict election outcomes. The *Literary Digest* drew its survey sample from "every telephone book in the United States, from the rosters of clubs and associations, from city directories, lists of registered voters [and] classified mail order and occupational data."[5] Using the data it received from the millions of postcard ballots sent out throughout the United States, the *Literary Digest* correctly predicted every presidential election from 1920 to 1932.

Straw polls Unscientific surveys used to gauge public opinion on a variety of issues and policies.

The *Literary Digest* used **straw polls** to predict the popular vote in those four presidential elections. Its polling methods were widely hailed as "amazingly right" and "uncannily accurate."[6] In 1936, however, its luck ran out. The *Literary Digest* predicted that Republican Alfred M. Landon (his daughter Nancy Kassebaum was elected to the U.S. Senate in 1984) would beat incumbent President Franklin D. Roosevelt by a margin of 57 percent to 43 percent. Roosevelt, however, won in a landslide election, receiving 62.5 percent of the popular vote and carrying every state except Vermont and Maine. The problems with the *Literary Digest*'s polling methods are discussed in "Then and Now: Straw Polls," p. 321).

Through the late 1940s, the number of polling groups and increasingly sophisticated polling techniques grew by leaps and bounds as new businesses and politicians relied on the information they provided to market products and candidates. In 1948, however, the polling industry suffered a severe, although fleeting, setback. George Gallup and many other pollsters incorrectly predicted that Thomas E. Dewey would defeat President Harry S Truman.

In spite of errors like these, pollsters have been quick to defend their craft. Gallup readily admitted the mistakes that affected his 1948 poll, including the early cutoff date of his sample, noting that he and his organization were learning continually. He consistently argued that the judgment of the masses was basically good and often far better than that of their leaders.

Political Socialization: The First Step Toward Forming Opinions

> **Political socialization** The process through which an individual acquires particular political orientations; the learning process by which people acquire their political beliefs and values.

Political scientists believe that many of our attitudes about issues are grounded in political values, which are acquired through a process called **political socialization.** Po-

THEN AND NOW

Straw Polls

In the early 1900s, polls like those conducted by the *Literary Digest* reached out to as many potential respondents as possible, with no regard for modern sampling techniques that require respondents be selected or sampled according to strict rules of cross-sectional representation. Respondents, in essence, were like "straws in the wind," hence the term "straw polls."

The *Literary Digest*'s sample had three fatal errors. First, its sample was drawn from telephone directories and lists of automobile owners. This technique oversampled the upper middle class and rich, groups heavily Republican in political orientation. In 1936, this oversampling proved to be particularly problematic because voting polarized along class lines. Thus, the oversampling of wealthy Republicans severely underestimated the Democratic vote. The *Literary Digest*'s second problem was timing: Questionnaires were mailed in early September. Thus, the changes in public sentiment that occurred as the election drew closer were not measured. Its third error occurred because of a problem we now call self-selection: Only highly motivated individuals sent back the cards—only 22 percent of those surveyed responded. Those who respond to mail surveys are quite different from the general electorate; they often are wealthier and better educated and care more fervently about issues. The *Literary Digest*, then, failed to observe one of the now well-known cardinal rules of survey sampling: "One cannot allow the respondents to select themselves into the sample."*

*Robert S. Erikson, Norman Luttbeg, and Kent Tedin, *American Public Opinion: Its Origin, Content and Impact* (New York: Wiley, 1980), p. 28.

Although these crude techniques are now looked on with disfavor by serious students of public opinion, straw polls are still in use today. Interest groups, for example, frequently poll their members on relevant issues. Perhaps the most common form of straw poll used today are those conducted by local television news programs. Many have nightly features asking viewers to call in their sentiments (with one phone number for pro and another for con). The results of these unscientific polls vary widely because individuals who feel very strongly about the issue often repeatedly call in their votes.

At least one pollster, however, correctly predicted the results of the 1936 election: George Gallup. (See "People of the Past," p. 318) Gallup had written his dissertation on how to measure the readership of newspapers and then expanded his methods to study public opinion about politics. He was so sure about his methods that he demonstrated his confidence when he gave all of his newspaper clients this money-back guarantee: If his poll predictions weren't closer to the actual election outcome than those of the highly acclaimed *Literary Digest* (remember that the *Literary Digest* had predicted every election correctly), he would refund their money. The *Digest* predicted Alf Landon; Gallup predicted Roosevelt to win. As a consequence, although he underpredicted Roosevelt's victory by nearly 7 percent, the fact that he got the winner right was what everyone remembered, especially given the *Literary Digest*'s dramatic miscalculations. And, as revealed in Figure 10-2 (p. 322), the Gallup Organization, now run by George Gallup's son, continues to be a successful predictor of elections today.

FIGURE 10-2

The Success of the Gallup Poll

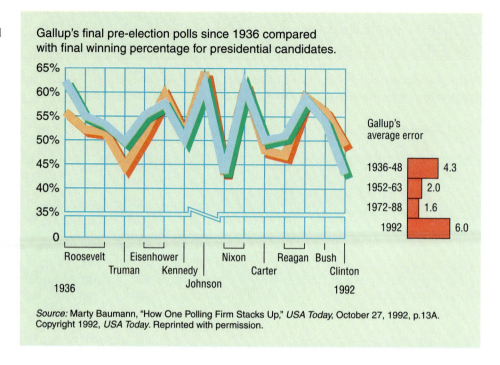

Gallup's final pre-election polls since 1936 compared with final winning percentage for presidential candidates.

Gallup's average error

1936-48	4.3
1952-63	2.0
1972-88	1.6
1992	6.0

Roosevelt Eisenhower Nixon Reagan Bush
Truman Kennedy Carter Clinton
Johnson
1936 1992

Source: Marty Baumann, "How One Polling Firm Stacks Up," *USA Today,* October 27, 1992, p.13A. Copyright 1992, *USA Today.* Reprinted with permission.

litical socialization "is the process through which an individual acquires his [or her] particular political orientations—his [or her] knowledge, feelings and evaluations regarding his [or her] political world."[7] Through the process of political socialization we become aware of political facts and events and form political values. Family, schools, houses of worship, peers, friends, and the media are often important influences or agents of political socialization. Try to remember your earliest memory of the president of the United States. For many of you it was probably Jimmy Carter or Ronald Reagan (older students probably remember earlier presidents). What did you think of him? Of the Republican or Democratic Party? It's likely that your earliest feelings or attitudes were shaped by what your parents thought about that particular president and his party. Similar processes also apply to your early attitudes about the flag of the United States, or even the police.

The Family

The influence of the family can be traced to two factors: communication and receptivity. Children, especially during their preschool years, spend tremendous amounts of time with their parents; early on they learn their parents' political values, even though these concepts may be vague. One study, for example, found that the most important visible public figures for children under the age of ten were police officers and, to a much lesser extent, the president. Children almost uniformly view both as "helpful." But by the age of ten or eleven, children become more selective in their perceptions of the president. By this age, children raised in Democratic households are much more likely to be critical of a Republican president than are those raised in Republican households.

In 1958, 72 percent of the children in Republican households adopted their parents' party identification. By 1988, 58 percent of children in Republican households identified themselves as Republicans, and many developed strong positive feelings toward

Ronald Reagan, the Republican president. Support for and the popularity of Ronald Reagan translated into strong support for the Republican Party through the 1988 presidential elections and also contributed to the growing conservative ideological self-identification of first-year college students depicted in Figure 10-3.

School

Researchers report mixed findings concerning the role of the schools in the political socialization process. There is no question that, in elementary school, children are taught respect for their nation and its symbols. Most school days begin with the Pledge of Allegiance, and patriotism and respect for country are important, although subtle, components of most school curricula. The importance of symbols that evoke our feelings of nationalism in development of our notions of political culture as they are taught at home and school. The terms "flag" and the "United States" evoke very posi-

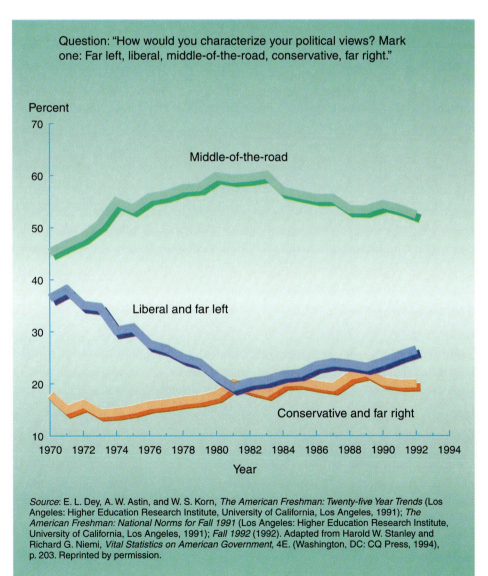

Question: "How would you characterize your political views? Mark one: Far left, liberal, middle-of-the-road, conservative, far right."

FIGURE 10-3

Ideological Self-Identification of College Students' First Year, 1970–1992

Source: E. L. Dey, A. W. Astin, and W. S. Korn, *The American Freshman: Twenty-five Year Trends* (Los Angeles: Higher Education Research Institute, University of California, Los Angeles, 1991); *The American Freshman: National Norms for Fall 1991* (Los Angeles: Higher Education Research Institute, University of California, Los Angeles, 1991); *Fall 1992* (1992). Adapted from Harold W. Stanley and Richard G. Niemi, *Vital Statistics on American Government*, 4E. (Washington, DC: CQ Press, 1994), p. 203. Reprinted by permission.

Throughout the United States, most school children start the day with a "Pledge to the Flag." From a very early age, children are taught respect for national symbols and ideals.

tive feelings from a majority of Americans. Support for these two icons serves the purpose of maintaining national allegiance and underlies the success of the U.S. political system in spite of relatively negative views about Congress, the courts, and the current government. In 1991, for example, few school children were taught to question U.S. involvement in the Persian Gulf. Instead, at almost every school in the nation, children were encouraged or even required to write servicemen and servicewomen stationed in the Gulf, involving these children with the war effort and implying school support for the war.

High schools are also important agents of political socialization. They continue the elementary school tradition of building good citizens and often reinforce textbook learning with trips to the state or national capital. They also offer courses on current U.S. affairs. Presentation of civic information is especially critical at the secondary school level because the formal education of many people in the United States ends with high school and because research shows that better-informed citizens vote more often as adults.

Learning at the college level is often different from that encountered in grade school or high school. Many college courses and texts like this one are designed in part to provide you with the information necessary to think critically about issues of major political consequence. It is common in college for students to be called on to question the appropriateness of certain political actions or to discuss underlying reasons for certain political or policy decisions. Therefore, most researchers believe that college has a liberalizing effect on students. Since the 1920s, studies have shown, students become more liberal each year they are in college.

Peers

Although the influence of the schools on political socialization is often called into doubt, a child's peers—that is, children about the same age as a young person—do seem to have an important effect on the socialization process. Whereas parental influences are greatest during the tender years from birth to age five, a child's peer group becomes increasingly more important as the child gets older.

The Impact of Events

While there is no doubt that parents—and, to a lesser degree, school and peers—play a role in a person's political socialization, the role of key political events is also very important. You probably do not have a single professor who cannot remember what she or he was doing on the day that President John F. Kennedy was killed—November 22, 1963. This dramatic event is indelibly etched in the minds of virtually all people who can remember it. In 1993, on the thirtieth anniversary of JFK's assassination, in fact, one major network televised a program in which celebrities recounted what they were doing when they learned of the tragedy.

President Richard M. Nixon's fall from grace and forced resignation in 1973 also had a profound impact on the socialization process of all Americans, possibly to the greatest extent on young people, who were forced to realize that their government was not always right or honest.

In fact, one problem in discussing political socialization is that many of the major studies on this topic were conducted in the aftermath of these and other crucial events,

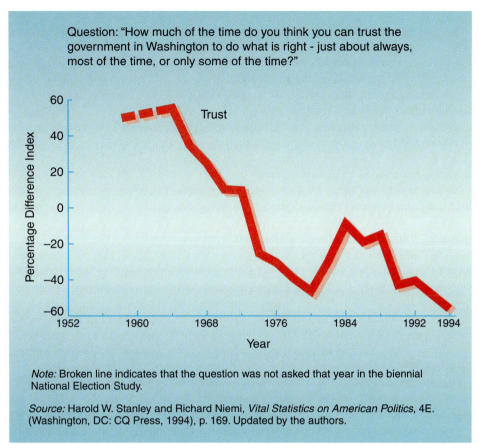

Question: "How much of the time do you think you can trust the government in Washington to do what is right - just about always, most of the time, or only some of the time?"

Trust

Note: Broken line indicates that the question was not asked that year in the biennial National Election Study.

Source: Harold W. Stanley and Richard Niemi, *Vital Statistics on American Politics*, 4E. (Washington, DC: CQ Press, 1994), p. 169. Updated by the authors.

FIGURE 10-4

Individual Trust in Government, 1952–1994

The percentage difference index is calculated by subtracting the number of those giving a trusting response to the question from the number of those giving a cynical response. A positive number in the index indicates an overall trust in government; a negative number indicates overall distrust.

including the civil rights movement and the Vietnam War, all of which produced a marked increase in Americans' distrust of government. The findings reported in Figure 10-4 reveal the dramatic dropoff of trust in government that began in the mid-1960s and continued through the election of Ronald Reagan in 1980. In a study of Boston children conducted in the aftermath of the Watergate scandal, for example, one political scientist found that children's perception of the president went from that of a benevolent to a "malevolent" leader.[8] These findings are indicative of the low confidence most Americans had in government in the aftermath of Watergate and President Nixon's ultimate resignation from office to avoid impeachment.

Social Groups

Also affecting the development and continuity of political beliefs and opinions are group effects, that is, certain characteristics that allow persons to be lumped into categories. Among the most important of these groups are religion, educational attainment, income, region, and race. More recently, researchers have learned that gender and age are becoming increasingly important determinants of public opinion, especially on certain issues.

Religion. Religion plays a very important role in the life of Americans. Many more Americans attend church regularly than do citizens of Great Britain. Moreover, in 1992, 56 percent of Americans identified themselves as Protestant, 25 percent as Catholic, 2 percent as Jewish, and 6 percent as other. Only 11 percent claimed to have no religious affiliation. Over the years, analysts have found continuing opinion differences among these groups, with Protestants being the most conservative on many issues and Jews the most liberal, as shown in Figure 10-5.

Shared religious attitudes tend to affect voting and stances on particular issues. Catholics tend to vote Democratic more than do Protestants, and they tend to vote for other Catholics. For example, Catholics overwhelmingly cast their ballots for John F. Kennedy, who became the first Catholic president, in 1960. Catholics as a group also favor aid to parochial schools, most Jews support aid to Israel, and many fundamentalist Protestants support organized prayer in public schools.

Region. Since colonial times, regional differences have been important to the development and maintenance of public opinion. As the United States grew and developed into a major industrial nation, waves of immigrants, with different religious traditions and customs, entered the United States and often settled in areas they viewed as hospitable to their way of life. For example, thousands of Scandinavians settled in cold, snowy, rural Minnesota, and many Irish settled in the urban centers of the Northeast, as did many Italians, and Jews. All brought with them unique views about many issues as well as about the role of government. Many of these regional differences continue to affect public opinion today, sometimes resulting in conflict at the national level.

Recall, for example, that during the Constitutional Convention most Southerners staunchly advocated a weak national government. The Civil War was fought in part because of basic differences in philosophy toward government (states' rights in the South versus national rights in the North) and the question of the moral and political validity of the institution of slavery.

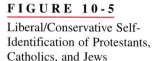

FIGURE 10-5

Liberal/Conservative Self-Identification of Protestants, Catholics, and Jews

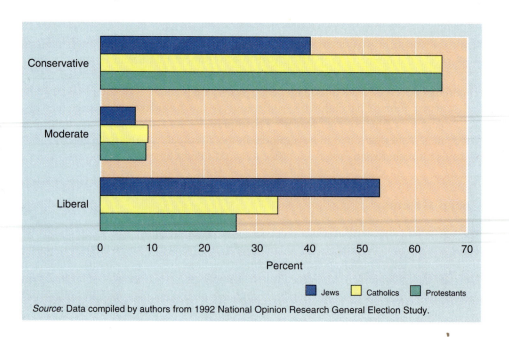

Source: Data compiled by authors from 1992 National Opinion Research General Election Study.

As we know from the results of modern political polling, the South has continued to lag behind the rest of the nation on support for civil rights, while continuing to favor return of power to the states at the expense of the national government, as revealed in Table 10.1.

During the drive to ratify the Equal Rights Amendment (1972–1981), Southern legislators made much about whether the national government should mandate how the states treat "their women." Not surprisingly, it was the Southern states that effectively blocked passage of the ERA.

Southerners also are much more supportive of a strong national defense. They accounted for 41 percent of the troops in the Persian Gulf in the early days of the war, even though they make up only 28 percent of the general population.

At one time, the South was so overwhelmingly Democratic that it was referred to as "the Solid South." Although they were conservative, Southerners' Democratic leanings stemmed from their negative reaction to the policies of Abraham Lincoln, a Republican. This Democratic bias has eroded recently because of massive migration to the South from the Northeast and Midwest (both hard hit by the economic recession of the 1970s), an escalating number of elderly people retiring from the North to warmer climates, and an increased perception that the Democratic Party is too liberal. Since 1972, for example, only the Southern Democratic candidates for president, Jimmy Carter and Bill Clinton, have been able to carry the South. Today, however, the Southern states have more Republican representatives in Congress than Democrats have, and those Democrats elected in the South are often more conservative than their Northern Republican colleagues.

Table 10.1 ◆ Does the South Differ?

Percentage giving "liberal" response among white Protestants living in different regions, 1988

ISSUE	EAST	MIDWEST	SOUTH	WEST
Economic and welfare issues:				
More government health care	48%	35%	37%	39%
Government job guarantees	19	19	22	21
Increase Social Security	56	50	59	53
Cut military spending	32	35	21	30
Civil rights and civil liberties issues:				
Aid to minorities	16	14	14	23
Homosexual rights	56	56	47	52
Women's equality	63	65	62	69
Right to abortion	65	49	45	60
Average percentage liberal, all issues	41%	37%	34%	41%

Source: Compiled by Daron Shaw. Reprinted with permission of the Center for Political Studies, University of Michigan.

Race.   Race is an exceptionally important factor in elections and in the study of public opinion. The direction and intensity of African-American political opinion is often quite different from that of whites. As revealed in Figure 10-6, whites oppose affirmative action plans at significantly higher levels than do African Americans. Likewise, significant differences arose in support for the Persian Gulf War and support for the death penalty.

Native Americans, Hispanics, and Asians/Pacific Islanders are other identifiable ethnic minorities in the United States (see Figure 10-7, p. 329). According to the last census, in 1991, Native Americans made up 1 percent of the population, Hispanics made up 9 percent, and Asian/Pacific Islanders represented 3 percent. These groups also often respond differently to issues than do whites. Generally, Native Americans and Hispanics hold similar opinions on many issues largely because significant proportions of these minority-group members belong to low-income groups and find themselves targets of discrimination. Within the Hispanic community itself, however, existing divisions often depend on national origin. Generally, Cuban Americans who cluster in Florida (and in the Miami-Dade County area in particular) are more likely to be conservative. They fled from communism and Fidel Castro in Cuba, and they generally vote Republican. In the 1976 presidential election, for example, only 40.2 percent of the Cuban Americans in the Miami-Dade area voted for Jimmy Carter.[9] In contrast, Chicanos (people of Mexican origin) voting in California, New Mexico, Arizona, Texas and Colorado cast 83.1 percent of their votes for Carter that year.[10]

Gender.   From the time that the earliest public opinion polls were taken, women have been known to hold more negative views about war and military intervention than do men and more strongly positive attitudes about issues touching on social welfare concerns, such as education, juvenile justice, capital punishment, and the environment. Many researchers have sought to explain this "gender gap." Some suggest that women's more "nurturing" nature and their prominent role as mothers lead women to have more liberal attitudes on issues affecting the family or the safety of their children. Research by Pamela Johnston Conover and Virginia Sapiro, however, finds no support for a maternal explanation.[11]

FIGURE 10-6

Black versus White Attitudes

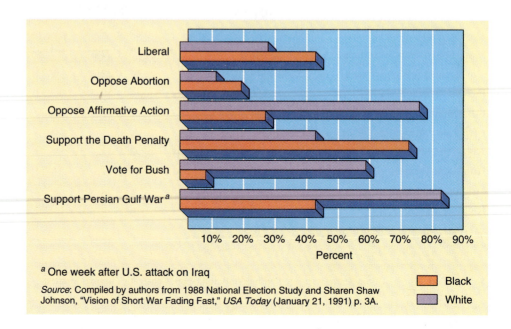

a One week after U.S. attack on Iraq

Source: Compiled by authors from 1988 National Election Study and Sharen Shaw Johnson, "Vision of Short War Fading Fast," *USA Today* (January 21, 1991) p. 3A.

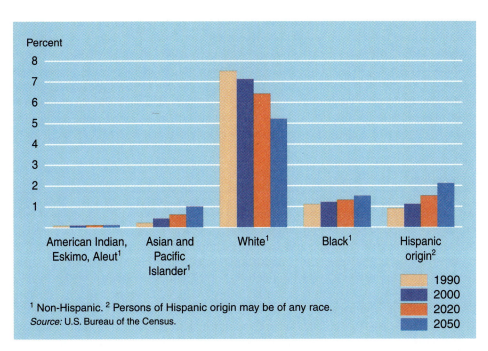

F I G U R E   1 0 - 7

Percentage Distribution of the
Population, by Race and
Hispanic Origin: 1990–2050

Polls taken in the late 1980s reveal that women continue to hold very different opinions from men on a variety of issues, as shown in Table 10.2. Ironically, however, during the debate over the Equal Rights Amendment, men supported the amendment more than did women voters. Men also appear today to support a woman's right to have an abortion to a greater extent than do women.

Age.   As Americans live longer, senior citizens are becoming a potent political force. In states such as Florida, to which many Northern retirees have flocked, seeking relief from cold winters and high taxes, the elderly have voted as a bloc to defeat school tax increases and to pass tax breaks for themselves. As a group, senior citizens are much

Table 10.2 ◆ Gender Differences on Issues of War, Peace, and Social Spending

ISSUES FAVORED	MALES	FEMALES
Increase defense spending	34	24
Aid to foreign military groups	42	21
"Star Wars" (defense) spending	24	10
No return to a peacetime draft	48	61
Initial sending of troops to Gulf	72	53
Increase spending on food stamps	18	24
Contract with America*	72	54

Source: Data supplied by Center for American Women and Politics.
*Data from Gallup Organization for CNN/*USA Today* (December 28–30, 1994).

more likely to favor an increased governmental role in the area of medical insurance while opposing any cuts in Social Security benefits.

In the future, the "graying of America" will have major social and political consequences. As we discuss in Chapter 12, the elderly under age 70 vote in much larger numbers than do their younger counterparts. Moreover, the fastest-growing age group in the United States is that of citizens over the age of sixty-five. Thus, not only are there more persons in this category, but they are also the most active at the ballot box and will undoubtedly continue to have their wishes heard and heeded.

Political Ideology

An individual's coherent set of values and beliefs about the purpose and scope of government is called his or her **political ideology.** Americans' attachment to, or evidence of, strong ideological positions has varied over time. In sharp contrast to spur-of-the-moment responses, these sets of values, often greatly affected by political socialization, can prompt citizens to favor a certain set of policy programs. "Conservative Versus Liberal" (p. 332) notes that conservatives are likely to support smaller, less activist governments. In contrast, liberals favor big governments that play active roles.

The terms "conservative" and "liberal" are difficult to define. Conservative and liberal ideologies focus on the function of liberty and equality in our society and on the proper role of government. These two terms reflect opposing attitudes on a wide range of economic, social, and political issues. Although many Americans continue to identify themselves as conservatives or liberals, over the years these terms have had very different meanings. During the nineteenth century, for example, conservatives supported governmental power and favored a role for religion in public life; in contrast, liberals supported freedom from undue governmental control. Today, these terms have very different meanings to the general public. **Conservatives** are thought to believe that a government is best that governs least and that big government can only infringe on individual personal and economic rights. Conservatives also believe that domestic problems like homelessness, poverty, and discrimination are better dealt with by the private sector than by the government. In contrast, **liberals** now are considered to favor extensive governmental involvement in the economy and the provision of social services and also to take an activist role in protecting the rights of women, the elderly, minorities, and the environment.

There are indications that college students are becoming more liberal as reflected in Figure 10-3, discussed earlier. The increase in the number of persons identifying themselves as liberals, as of the fall of 1992, may reflect identification with a younger presidential candidate, Bill Clinton.

While political scientists and politicians often talk in terms of conservative and liberal ideologies, the general public does not appear to be as enamored of this kind of labeling. When asked, most Americans respond that their political beliefs are "middle of the road" or moderate, although a substantial number call themselves conservatives, as revealed in Figure 10-8 (p. 331). In 1994, less than 30 percent of the American public labeled itself "liberal." As the United States became more conservative in recent years, the term "liberal" clearly came to be a label to be avoided in the 1980s. In the 1988 presidential election, George Bush was able to stick the label "liberal" on his opponent, Michael S. Dukakis. In the minds of the public, "liberal" was associated with big government, big spending, and support for affirmative action programs. The more the "liberal" label came to be associated with Dukakis, the more his support eroded.

Political ideology An individual's coherent set of values and beliefs about the purpose and scope of government.

Conservatives Those thought to believe that a government is best that governs least and that big government can only infringe on individual, personal, and economic rights.

Liberals Those considered to favor extensive governmental involvement in the economy and the provision of social services and to take an activist role in protecting the rights of women, the elderly, minorities, and the environment.

Democratic primary candidate Bill Clinton campaigned hard in Florida to attract the elderly vote.

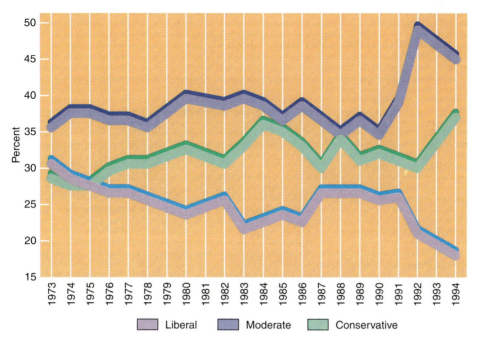

FIGURE 10-8
Self-Identification as Liberal,
Moderate, or Conservative,
1973–1994

☐ Liberal   ☐ Moderate   ☐ Conservative

Note: "Liberal" equals the combined percentages of those identifying themselves as extremely liberal, liberal, or slightly liberal; "conservative" equals the combined percentages of those identifying themselves as extremely conservative, conservative, or slightly conservative.

Source: General Society Survey, National Opinion Research Center, © Data from 1992 and 1994 from Everett Carl Ladd, *America at the Polls* (Storrs: Conn.: The Roper Center, 1995), p.16.

In 1993, the word "liberal" no longer seemed to be a "dirty word," and 67 percent of the U.S. public polled in that year believed that the national government under Clinton was becoming more liberal. Only 28 percent of those polled thought that this trend was a bad thing. But, by 1994, many liberal Democrats were ousted by conservative Republicans at the polls.

The labels "conservative" and "liberal" can be quite misleading. Studies reveal, for example, that many people who call themselves conservative actually take fairly liberal positions on many policy issues.[12] People who take conservative stances against "big government" often support increased government spending for the elderly, education, or health care. Thus, conservative or liberal ideology does not necessarily allow us to predict political opinions. In a "perfect" world, liberals would be liberal and conservatives would be conservative. Instead, Americans are inconsistent. Studies reveal that anywhere from 20 to 68 percent will take a traditionally "conservative" position on one issue and a traditionally "liberal" position on another.[13] Indeed, today, many people put differing emphases on the role of government in economic, social, and political spheres. It is, therefore, not unusual to encounter a person who could be considered liberal on social issues such as abortion and civil rights but who also holds conservative views on economic or "pocketbook" issues.

Despite their inconsistencies, most Americans believe that they do hold a political ideology. However, the political culture in the United States places a high premium on individual liberty, equality, and the right of self-government, values which lead people to hold a set of political beliefs that no longer allow them to be placed on a single liberal/conservative continuum.

"Conservative" Versus "Liberal"

♦ ♦ ♦

We often hear the terms "conservative" and "liberal" applied to politicians; but what do these ideological labels mean? The interpretations of both terms have evolved over the years. William Safire describes these changes in his *Political Dictionary*.

Conservative: A defender of the status quo who, when change becomes necessary in tested institutions or practices, prefers that it come slowly, and in moderation. . . .

Today the more rigid conservative generally opposes virtually all governmental regulation of the economy. He favors local and state action over federal action, and emphasizes fiscal responsibility, most notably in the form of balanced budgets. . . .

Liberal: Currently one who believes in more government action to meet individual needs; originally, one who resisted government encroachment on individual liberties.

In its present usage, the word acquired significance during the presidency of Franklin D. Roosevelt, who defined it this way during the 1932 campaign for his first term: ". . . say that civilization is a tree which, as it grows, continually produces rot and dead wood. The radical says: 'Cut it down.' The conservative says: 'Don't touch it.' The liberal compromises: 'Let's prune, so that we lose neither the old trunk nor the new branches.' "

Adlai Stevenson, the Democrats' presidential candidate in 1952 and 1956, once described a liberal as "one who has both feet firmly planted in the air."

Source: From *Safire's New Political Dictionary* by William Safire. Copyright © 1993 by The Cobbet Corporation. Copyright © 1968, 1972, 1978 by William Safire. Reprinted by permission of Random House, Inc.

How We Form Political Opinions

Many of us hold opinions on a wide range of political issues. In general, many of these ideas can be traced to the wide variety of social groups and different experiences each of us has had. Some individuals (called ideologues) think about politics and vote strictly on the basis of liberal or conservative ideology. Most people don't. In this section we explore how most people—those who are not ideologues—make up their minds on political issues. Chief among the factors that lead people to form political opinions are personal benefits, political knowledge, and cues from various leaders or opinion makers.

Personal Benefits

Most people choose policies that benefit them personally. You've probably heard the adage "People vote with their pocketbooks." Taxpayers generally favor lower taxes; hence, the popularity of candidates pledging "No new taxes." Similarly, the elderly usually support Social Security increases, and African Americans support strong civil rights laws and affirmative action programs.

Some government policies, however, don't really affect us *individually*. Legalized prostitution and the death penalty, for example are often perceived as moral issues that few citizens experience. Individuals often form attitudes toward issues such as these based on underlying values they have acquired through the years.

When individuals are faced with policies that don't affect them personally and don't involve moral issues, they often have difficulty forming an opinion. Foreign policy is an area in which this phenomenon is especially true. Most Americans often know little of the world around them. Unless moral issues such as apartheid in South Africa or human-rights violations in China are involved, American public opinion is likely to be quite volatile in the wake of any new information. For example, George Bush's popularity fell as soon as Americans viewed the results of Saddam Hussein's post-war ravaging of the Kurds.

Political Knowledge

Americans enjoy a relatively high literacy rate, and most Americans graduate from high school. And, unlike Great Britain, most Americans have access to a range of higher education opportunities. In spite of that access to education, however, Americans' level of actual political knowledge is low. As illustrated in Table 10.3, Americans, as a whole, don't know much about politics. In 1992, for example, 92 percent couldn't identify the Chief Justice of the United States and nearly three-quarters didn't know that Thomas Foley was the Speaker of the House. Moreover, after the 1986 elections, for example, only 22 percent of people surveyed could correctly identify their representative in Congress. One Gallup study done in 1988, moreover, found that 75 percent of all Americans were unable to locate the Persian Gulf on a map. Two-thirds couldn't find Vietnam. Americans aged eighteen to twenty-four scored the lowest, with two-thirds not being able to point to France on an outline map.[14]

One study of citizens' ability to recall the facts of recent major news stories revealed that less than 15 percent of those surveyed could get the facts right, prompting its authors to conclude that "ignorance is widespread, if not rampant."[15] Political scientist Doris Graber echoes that sentiment: "By and large . . . people do not seem to gain much specific information from the media,"[16] or elsewhere, it would seem.

In spite of their low levels of knowledge, Americans are still generally willing to offer opinions on a wide range of issues, from abortion to the budget to the North American Free Trade Agreement to the First Lady. Since her husband's election in 1992 (and even before), Hillary Rodham Clinton has been the object of unprecedented attention of pollsters.

Low levels of knowledge, however, can lead to the rapid opinion shifts on issues. The ebb and flow of popular opinion can be affected dramatically by political leaders. The president, especially, is often in a position to mold public opinion through effective use of the "bully pulpit," as discussed in Chapter 7.

Table 10.3 ◆ American Political Knowledge

PERCENTAGE UNABLE TO IDENTIFY

Name of vice president (1992)	12
Name of the Speaker of the House (1992)	74
Party with most members in Senate before election (1984)	70
Chief Justice of United States (1992)	92

Sources: National Opinion Research Center, General Social Surveys and Center for Political Studies, American National Election Studies.

Cues from Leaders

Given the visibility of political leaders and their access to the media, it is easy to see the important role they play in influencing public opinion. Political leaders, members of the news media, and a host of other experts have regular opportunities to influence public opinion, given the lack of deep conviction with which most Americans hold many of their political beliefs.

The president—particularly a popular one—can have an exceptionally powerful effect on public opinion. Political scientist John E. Mueller concludes, in fact, that there is a group of citizens—called followers—who are inclined to rally to the support of the president no matter what he does.[17] According to Mueller, the president's strength, especially in the area of foreign affairs (where public information is lowest), derives from the "majesty" of his office and his singular position as head of state.[18] Recognizing this phenomenon, presidents often take to television in an effort to drum up support for their programs.[19] President Clinton, like Reagan before him, has clearly realized the importance of mobilizing public opinion. He frequently takes his case directly to the public, urging the people to support his programs and to convey that support to their elected officials. He has also used his vice president to mobilize public opinion in order to help him get his programs through Congress.

How We Measure Public Opinion

To guide their policy decisions, public officials use a variety of measures as indicators of public opinion. These measures include election results, the number of telephone calls pro and con on any particular issue, letters to the editor in hometown papers, and the size of demonstrations or marches. But the most commonly relied on measure of public sentiment continues to be the public opinion survey, more popularly called a public opinion poll.

The polling process most often begins when someone says, "Let's find out about X and Y." Xs and Ys can be many things. Answers to questions including how to shape a candidate's campaign, how the public views the First Lady, how to market a new product, or how to package a new health care system can be partially acquired by knowing what the public wants at any given time. Potential candidates for local office may want to know how many people have heard of them (the device used to find out is called a name recognition survey). Better-known candidates contemplating running for higher office might want to know how they might fare against an incumbent. Polls can provide those answers. And news organizations routinely poll potential voters over the course of a campaign (or the duration of a war or presidential term, for example) to measure changes in public opinion and to measure the fluctuations in a candidate's popularity as Election Day nears.

According to the Federal Election Commission, former President George Bush spent $216,000 for public opinion polls in 1989 and 1990. In 1993 alone, President Clinton spent $1,986,410.

Determining the Content and Phrasing the Questions

Once a candidate, politician, or news organization decides to measure the public's attitudes via a poll, special care has to be taken in constructing the questions to be asked. For example, if your professor asked you, "Do you think my grading procedures are fair?" rather than asking, "In general, how fair do you think the grading is in your American Politics course?" you might give a slightly different answer. The wording of the first question tends to put you on the spot and personalize the grading style; the second question is more neutral. Even more obvious differences appear in the real world of polling, especially when interested groups want a poll to yield particular results. Responses to highly emotional issues such as abortion, busing, and affirmative action are often skewed depending on the wording of the question. As "Poll Wording" (p. 338) suggests, answers to questions about abortion appear to differ considerably depending on how the questions are worded. And, as revealed in Table 10.4, support for abortion can range from around 40 to 90 percent, depending on the question asked about abortion. Moreover, respondents often react to emotional cues in the question, which tends to skew survey results.

Selecting the Sample

Once the decision is made to take a poll, pollsters must determine the universe, or entire group whose attitudes they wish to measure. This universe could be all Americans, all voters, all city residents, all women, or all Democrats. Although in a perfect world each individual would be asked to give an opinion, this kind of polling is simply not practical. Consequently, pollsters take a sample of the universe in which they are interested. One way to obtain this sample is by **random sampling.** This method of selection gives each potential voter or adult the same chance of being selected. In theory, this sounds good, but it is actually impossible to achieve because no one has lists of every person in any group.

Random sampling A method of selection that gives each potential voter or adult the same chance of being selected.

Most national surveys and commercial polls use samples of from 1,000 to 1,500 individuals and use a variation of the random sampling method called **stratified** or **multi-stage area sampling.** Simple random samples aren't very useful at predicting voting because they may undersample (or oversample) key populations that are not likely to vote. The *Literary Digest* sample discussed earlier was a straw poll (see "Then and Now: Straw Polls," p. 321) and not a random sample. It suffered from an oversampling of voters whose names were drawn from telephone directories and car registrations; this group was hardly representative of the general electorate in the midst of the Depression.

Stratified or **multi stage sampling** A variation of random sampling; census data are used to divide a country into four sampling regions. Sets of counties and standard metropolitan statistical areas are then randomly selected in proportion to the total national population.

Table 10.4 ♦ Public Opinion on Abortion, 1962–1992 (in percentages) Abortion Should Be Legal Under These Circumstances

YEAR	MOTHER'S HEALTH	RAPE	BIRTH DEFECT	LOW INCOME	SINGLE MOTHER	AS A FORM OF BIRTH CONTROL	ANY REASON
1965	70	56	55	21	17	15	—
1973	91	81	82	52	47	46	—
1982	90	83	81	50	47	46	39
1992	92	87	84	49	45	45	43

Note: "—" indicates figures not available. Question: "Please tell me whether or not you think it should be possible for a pregnant woman to obtain a legal abortion [in the order asked in the survey] if there is a strong chance of serious defect in the baby? If she is married and does not want any more children? If the woman's own health is seriously endangered by the pregnancy? If the family has a very low income and cannot afford any more children? If she became pregnant as a result of rape? If she is not married and does not want to marry the man? The woman wants it for any reason?"

Sources: 1965: National Opinion Research Center surveys; 1973, 1983: General Social Survey. Compiled in Harold W. Stanley and Richard G. Niemi, *Vital Statistics on American Politics*, 4E (Washington, DC: CQ Press, 1994), p. 35. 1992 figures from National Opinion Research Center.

Former Virginia Governor L. Douglas Wilder's election in 1989 demonstrated some of the difficulties of polling. Despite advance surveys and exit polls that indicated a comfortable lead, Wilder's actual margin of victory was razor-thin. Apparently, voters, for fear of admitting racism, were unwilling to admit that they had voted against an African American.

Doonesbury

BY GARRY TRUDEAU

Nonprobability sampling
Unrepresentative sampling for surveys such as straw polls; this method often produces unreliable results.

Quota sample A type of nonprobability sample in which pollsters draw their sample based on known statistics.

To avoid these problems, stratified sampling uses census data, which provide the number of residences in an area and their location. Researchers divide the country into four sampling regions. They then randomly select a set of counties and standard metropolitan statistical areas in proportion to the total national population. Generally, about eighty primary sampling units are chosen. Once certain primary sampling units are selected, they are often used for many years because it is cheaper for polling companies to train interviewers to work in a fixed area.

About twenty respondents from each primary sampling unit are selected to be interviewed. Generally four or five city blocks or areas are selected, and then four or five target families from each district are used. Large, sophisticated surveys like the National Election Study and General Social Survey attempt to sample from lists of persons living in each household. The key to the success of this method is not to let people volunteer to be interviewed—volunteers as a group often have different opinions from those who don't volunteer.

Stratified sampling (the most rigorous sampling technique) is generally not used by most survey organizations. Instead, they randomly survey every 10th, 100th, or 1,000th person or household. If those individuals are not at home, they go to the home or apartment next door.

Not all polls are based on probability sampling. A less reliable but frequently used method is known as **nonprobability sampling.** The *Literary Digest* poll is one good example, as are the polls taken by local television stations. Such "straw polls" are not representative samples, because only those individuals who are aware of the poll and are highly motivated about it are included in the sample.

Another kind of nonprobability sample involves "surveys" taken by organized interests. Generally, these groups send "questionnaires" to their members. The tallies of these very biased polls are then sent to the press, members of Congress, and members of the executive branch to indicate support of group goals.

A more reliable nonprobability sample is a **quota sample,** in which pollsters draw their sample based on known statistics. Assume a citywide survey has been commissioned. If the city is 30 percent black, 15 percent Hispanic, and 55 percent white, interviewers will use those percentages to determine the proportion of particular groups they will sample in that city. These kinds of surveys are often conducted at local malls and shopping centers. Perhaps you've wondered why the man or woman with the clipboard has clearly passed you up to ask questions of other shoppers. Now you know it

A typical polling instrument.

```
                    NATIONAL STUDY

INTERVIEWER_____          STUDY #__5483____
TARRANCE & ASSOCIATES               CODING_____
GREENBERG-LAKE                      COMPUTER_____
PERSONAL/CONFIDENTIAL               FINANCE_____
                                    INTERVIEWING_____


Hello, I'm _____ of Tarrance & Associates, a national
research firm.  We're calling from our national telephone center.
We're talking to people in the nation today about public leaders
and issues facing us all.

A.    Are you registered to vote
      in your state and will you be
      able to vote in the election
      for President that will be
      held in 1992?


      _____
      IF "NO", ASK:  Is there someone
      else at home who is registered
      to vote?  (IF "YES", THEN ASK:
      MAY I SPEAK WITH HIM/HER?)
                              Yes (CONTINUE)

                              No  (THANK AND TERMINATE)
```

is likely that you did not fit into one of the categories of individuals that particular pollster was charged with locating. Although this kind of sampling technique can yield fairly impressive findings, the degree of accuracy falls short of that of surveys based on probability samples. Moreover, these polls generally oversample visible populations, such as shoppers. The views of stay-at-homes, who may be glued to CNN, C-SPAN, shopping networks, or soap operas are therefore underrepresented.

Kinds of Polls

Telephone Polls. The most common form of polls are random-digit dialing surveys, in which a computer randomly selects telephone numbers to be dialed. Because it is estimated that as many as 95 percent of the American public have telephones in their homes, samples selected in this manner are likely to be fairly representative. George Gallup observed in 1967 that the quickest and cheapest way to poll people is by telephone.

> But you run into a problem. . . . You're more likely to reach conservatives and more Republicans than Democrats. If you could reach people in theaters or bars or massage parlors, you'd find the Democrats.[20]

In spite of Gallup's obvious biases and stereotyping, he revealed one truth—some telephone polls can be less than accurate. But, today, modern pollsters have worked hard to refine their polling methods to remedy these shortcomings. Thus, today, in spite of some continued problems (such as the fact that many people don't want to be bothered, especially at dinner time), most polls done for newspapers and news magazines are conducted this way.

In-Person Polls. Individual, in-person interviews are conducted by some groups, such as by the University of Michigan for its National Election Studies. Some analysts

Poll Wording
♦ ♦ ♦

Polls, supported by each side in the abortion debate, differ depending on how the question is worded

One poll, partly paid for by the National Right to Life Committee, asked: "The U.S. Supreme Court recently ruled that the federal government is not required to use taxpayer funds for family planning programs to perform, counsel, or refer for abortion as a method of family planning. Do you favor or oppose this ruling?"

Favor
48 percent

Oppose
48 percent

Don't know/refuse
4 percent

Source: Wirthlin Group poll of 1,000 adults taken on June 17–19; margin of error is 3 percentage points.

Another poll, commissioned by Planned Parenthood, asked: "Do you favor or oppose that Supreme Court decision preventing clinic doctors and medical personnel from discussing abortion in family planning clinics that receive federal funds?"

Oppose percent	65
Favor percent	33
Not sure percent	2

Source: Lou Harris and Associates poll of 1,254 adults, May 31–June 5; margin of error: 3 percentage points

Source: "Words Affect Poll Numbers," *USA Today* (June 25, 1991): 7–A.

favor such in-person surveys, but others argue that the unintended influence of the questioner or pollster is very important and can lead to errors. How the pollster dresses, relates to the person being interviewed, and even asks the questions can affect responses. (Some of these factors, such as tone of voice, can also affect the results of telephone surveys.)

Exit Polls. **Exit polls** are polls conducted at selected polling places on Election Day. Generally, large news organizations send pollsters to selected precincts to sample every tenth voter as he or she emerges from the polling place. The results of these polls are used to help the television networks predict the outcome of key races, often just a few minutes after the polls close in a particular state and generally before voters in other areas—sometimes in a later time zone—have cast their ballots.

In 1980, his own polling and the results of network exit polls led President Jimmy Carter to concede defeat three hours before the polls closed on the West coast, leading many Democratic Party officials and candidates to criticize Carter and network predictions for harming their chances at victories. (Many Democrats argued that if the presidential election had already been "called," voters were unlikely to go to the polls.) In the aftermath of that controversy, all networks agreed not to predict the results of presidential contests until all polling places were closed.

Exit polls have also been faulted because it appears that not all voters are willing to reply truthfully to pollsters' questions. In 1989, for example, when L. Douglas Wilder ran for the Virginia governorship, the results of exit polls were way off. Surveys done before the race showed the African-American lieutenant governor winning by margins of 4 to 15 percent. A television exit poll showed him winning by 10 percent. Wilder won, but with a razor-thin margin (.0037 percent) of only 6,582 votes out of a record 1.78 million cast. Clearly, pollsters had been lied to or misled by "some Democratic-leaning white Virginians who could not bring themselves to vote for a black candidate . . . and few voters are secure enough in their bigotry to confess such blatant bias."[21] It seems that many white voters were unwilling to say that they had not voted for Wilder; therefore, they told pollsters that they *had* voted for Wilder, the African-American candidate, when they had not.

A similar phenomenon occurred during the Louisiana senatorial primary in 1990. Many whites who voted for David Duke, the former Ku Klux Klansman, apparently lied to pollsters, who underpredicted his support. Duke received a majority of the white vote, although he ultimately was soundly defeated in the general election.

Tracking Polls. During the 1992 presidential elections, "tracking polls," which were taken on daily basis by some news organizations (see Figure 10-9, p. 339), were introduced to allow candidates to monitor short-term campaign developments and the effects of their campaign strategy.

Tracking polls involve small samples of interviews conducted every twenty-four hours (usually of registered voters contacted at certain times of day) and are usually combined with some kind of a moving statistical average to boost the sample size and therefore the statistical reliability.[22] Even though such one-day surveys are fraught with reliability problems, most major news organizations used them during the 1992 election campaign, and, as a result, often provided the public with inaccurate views of the campaign.

Shortcomings of Polling

The accuracy of any poll depends on the quality of the sample that was drawn. Small samples, if properly drawn, can be very accurate if each unit in the universe has an

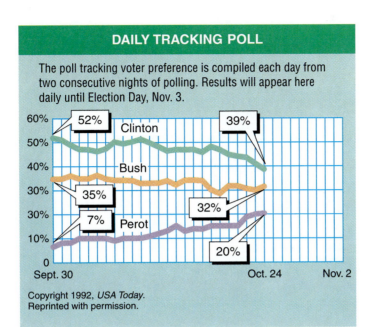

DAILY TRACKING POLL

The poll tracking voter preference is compiled each day from two consecutive nights of polling. Results will appear here daily until Election Day, Nov. 3.

Clinton — 52% ... 39%
Bush — 35% ... 32%
Perot — 7% ... 20%

Sept. 30 ... Oct. 24 ... Nov. 2

Copyright 1992, *USA Today*.
Reprinted with permission.

FIGURE 10-9

A Tracking Poll from *USA Today*'s Coverage of the 1992 Presidential Election

equal opportunity to be sampled. If a pollster, for example, fails to sample certain populations, his or her results may reflect that shortcoming. Often, the opinions of the poor and/or homeless are underrepresented because insufficient attention is given to making certain that these groups are representatively sampled. And, in the case of tracking polls, if you choose to sample only on weekends or from 5 P.M. to 9 P.M., you may get more Republicans, who are less likely to have jobs that require them to work in the evening or on weekends.

There comes a point in sampling, however, where increases in the size of the sample have little effect on a reduction of the **sampling error**, the difference between the actual universe and the sample.

All polls contain errors. Standard samples of approximately 1,500 individuals provide fairly good estimates of actual behavior (in the case of voting, for example). Typically, the **margin of error,** or sampling error, in a sample of 1,500 will be about 3 percent. If you ask "Do you like ice cream?" of 1,500 people and 52 percent say "yes" and 48 percent say "no," the results are too close to tell whether more people like ice cream than not. Why? Because the margin of error implies that somewhere between 55 percent (52 + 3) and 49 percent (52 − 3) of the people like ice cream while between 51 percent (48 + 3) and 45 percent (48 − 3) do not. The margin of error in a close election makes predictions very difficult.

Public opinion polls may also be "off" when they attempt to gauge attitudes about issues that some or even many individuals don't care about or about which the public has little information. For example, few Americans probably care about the elimination of the electoral college. If a representative sample were polled, many would answer pro or con without having given much consideration to the question.

Most academic public opinion research organizations, such as the National Election Study, for example, use some kind of filter question that first asks respondents whether or not they have thought about the question. These screening procedures generally allow surveyors to exclude as many as 20 percent of their respondents, especially on complex issues like the federal budget. Questions on more personal issues such as

Exit polls Polls conducted at selected polling places on election day.

Sampling error or **margin of error** A measure of the accuracy of a public opinion poll.

Exit polls can be undertaken by news networks, newspapers, polling organizations, or, as in this case, directly by a candidate's campaign staff.

moral values, drugs, crime, race, and women's role in society get far fewer "no opinion" or "don't know" responses, as indicated in Table 10.5 (p. 341).

Another shortcoming of polls concerns their inability to measure intensity of feeling about particular issues. Whereas a respondent might answer affirmatively to any question, it is likely that his or her feelings about issues such as abortion, the death penalty, or support for U.S. troops in the Gulf are much more intense than are his or her feelings about the electoral college.

How Polling and Public Opinion Affect Politicians, Politics, and Policy

The authors of *The Federalist Papers* noted that "all government rests on public opinion," and, as a result, public opinion inevitably influences the actions of politicians and public officials. The public's perception of crime as a problem, for example, was the driving force behind the comprehensive crime bill President Clinton submitted to Congress in 1994 and congressional passage of the Brady gun control bill in 1993. As Figure 10-10 (p. 341) shows, the public's concern with crime skyrocketed to an all-time high in 1994, and politicians at all levels were quick to convert that concern into a campaign issue.

Politicians and government officials spend millions of dollars each year taking the "pulse" of the public. Even the federal government spends millions annually on polls and surveys designed to evaluate programs and to provide information for shaping policies. But, as political scientist Benjamin Ginsburg noted, "the data reported by opinion polls are actually the product of an interplay between opinion and the survey instrument." They interact with each other and, in essence, often change the "charac-

Table 10.5 ◆	Public Opinion on Issues of Varying Public Prominence, 1990

"Would you favor or oppose a law which would require a person to obtain a police permit before he or she could buy a gun?"*

Favor: 79%   Oppose: 20%   Don't know: 2%

"The U.S. Supreme Court has ruled that no state or local government may require the reading of the Lord's Prayer or Bible verses in public schools. *What are your views on this—do you approve or disapprove of the court ruling?"*

Favor: 40%   Oppose: 56%   No opinion: 4%

"A proposed amendment to the Constitution would require Congress to approve a balanced federal budget each year. Government spending would have to be limited to no more than expected revenues, unless a three-fifths majority of the Congress voted to spend more than the expected revenues." *Would you favor or oppose this amendment to the Constitution?* (1989)

Favor: 59%   Oppose: 24%   No opinion: 17%

"The U.S. Supreme Court has required states to change their legislative districts so that each member of the upper house represents the same number of people. Some people would like to return to the earlier method of electing members of the upper house according to counties or other units regardless of population." *Would you favor continuing the present equal districting plan or returning to the earlier plan?*

Favor: 52%   Oppose: 23%   No opinion: 25%

* Numbers do not equal 100 percent due to rounding.

Source: Harold W. Stanley and Richard G. Niemi, *Vital Statistics on American Politics,* 4E (Washington, DC: CQ Press, 1994) pp. 20–22. Reprinted by permission.

ter of the views receiving public expression."[23] Polls can thus help transform public opinion.

We know that politicians rely on polls, but it's difficult to say just how much. Several political scientists have attempted to study whether public policy is responsive to public opinion, with mixed results.[24] As we have seen, public opinion can fluctuate, making it difficult for a politician or policy maker to assess. Some critics of polls and their use by politicians argue that polls hurt democracy and make leaders weaker. Some say that politicians are simply driven by the results of polls that do not reflect a serious debate of issues. In response to this argument, George Gallup retorted, "One might as well insist that a thermometer makes the weather."[25]

Polls can clearly distort the election process by creating what are called "bandwagon" and "underdog" effects. In a presidential campaign, an early victory in the Iowa caucuses or the New Hampshire primary, for example, can boost a candidate's standings in the polls as the rest of the nation begins to think of him or her in a more positive light. New supporters jump on the bandwagon. A strong showing in the polls,

FIGURE 10-10

Percentage of People Who Say Crime Is the Most Important Problem in the United States

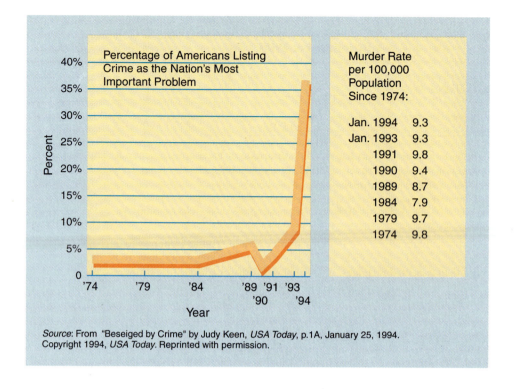

Source: From "Beseiged by Crime" by Judy Keen, *USA Today*, p.1A, January 25, 1994. Copyright 1994, *USA Today*. Reprinted with permission.

in turn, can generate more and larger donations, the lifeblood of any campaign. Political scientist Herbert Asher has noted that "bad poll results, as well as poor primary and caucus standings, may deter potential donors from supporting a failing campaign."[26]

Political scientist Benjamin Ginsburg argues that public opinion polls weaken democracy.[27] He claims that these polls allow governments and politicians to say they have considered public opinion in spite of the fact that polls don't always measure the intensity of feeling on an issue or might overreflect the views of the responders who lack sufficient information to make educated choices. Ginsburg further argues that democracy is better served by politicians' reliance on telephone calls and letters—active signs of interest—than on the passive voice of public opinion.

Toward Reform

When all the major television networks proclaimed that Ronald Reagan was going to easily defeat incumbent President Jimmy Carter, Carter went on television and conceded his defeat several hours before the polls closed on the west coast. Democrats, in particular, were furious, and they pressured the news media not to broadcast any winners in the future until all polls were closed—no matter what their exit polls indicated. This concession or reform was viewed as one that was good for democracy; after all, some voters were likely to stay home if they knew that the election had already been decided.

NOT A BAD STATE OF THE UNION SPEECH, ALTHOUGH YOU HATE TO SEE HIM PANDERING TO MASS HYSTERIA ON THE ISSUE OF CRIME.

Don Wright, the *Palm Beach Post.*

In the aftermath of the 1992 elections and their unprecedented use of polling—especially tracking polls—the use of those polls came under attack. There was "faulty polling" and "faulty tracking," which make analysis of the election difficult.[28] Some pollsters have called for either the American Association for Public Opinion Research or the National Council of Public Polls to conduct an open inquiry about the use and misuse of these kinds of polls.

Summary

Public opinion is a subject constantly mentioned in the media, especially in presidential election years or when important policies (such as health care, balancing the budget, or gun control) are under consideration. What public opinion is, where it comes from, how it's measured, and how it's used are aspects of a complex subject. To that end, this chapter has made the following points:

1. Public opinion is what the public thinks about an issue or a particular set of issues. Public opinion polls are used to estimate public opinion.

2. Almost since the beginning of the United States, various attempts have been made to influence public opinion about particular issues or to sway elections.

3. Modern-day polling did not begin until the 1930s. Over the years, polling to measure public opinion has become more and more sophisticated and more accurate because pollsters are better able to sample the public in their effort to determine their attitudes and positions on issues. Pollsters recognize that their sample must be re-flective of the population whose ideas and beliefs they wish to measure.

4. The first step in forming opinions occurs through a process called political socialization. The family, school, peers, and even the impact of events as well as the social groups of which one is a member—including religion, region, race, gender, and age—all affect how one views political events and issues, as do the major events themselves. Our political ideology—whether we are conservative, liberal, or moderate—also provides a lens by which we filter our political views.

5. All of these factors affect how we form our opinions. So does our level of personal benefit and our political knowledge of issues and events. Even the views of other people affect our ultimate opinions of a variety of issues, including race relations, the death penalty, abortion, and federal taxes.

6. Measuring public opinion can be difficult. The most frequently used measure is the public opinion poll. Determining the content, phrasing the questions, selecting

the sample, and choosing the right kind of poll are critical to obtaining accurate and useable data.

7. Knowledge of the public's views on these issues is often used by politicians to tailor campaigns or to drive policy decisions.

8. In the aftermath of problems that have occurred with the media's use of polls, projected winners—based on

exit polls—are no longer broadcast before the polls close. And, in the wake of the widespread use of tracking polls in the 1992 elections, calls for better study of their reliability and interpretation have been made.

Key Terms

public opinion

public opinion polls

straw polls

political socialization

political ideology

conservatives

liberals

random sampling

stratified sampling

multistage area sampling

nonprobability sampling

quota sample

exit polls

sampling error

margin of error

Suggested Readings

Asher, Herbert. *Polling and the Public: What Every Citizen Should Know.* Washington, DC: CQ Press, 1988.

Brace, Paul, and Barbara Hinckley. *Follow the Leader: Opinion Polls and Modern Presidents.* New York: Basic Books, 1992.

Campbell, Angus, et al. *The American Voter.* New York: Wiley, 1960.

Crespi, Irving. *Public Opinion, Polls, and Democracy.* Boulder, CO: Westview Press, 1989.

Ginsburg, Benjamin. *The Captive Public.* New York: Basic Books, 1986.

Graber, Doris. *Processing the News: How People Tame the Information Tide.* New York: Longman, 1984.

Jennings, M. Kent, and Richard Niemi. *Generations and Politics: A Panel Study of Young Adults and Their Parents.* Princeton, NJ: Princeton University Press, 1981.

Key, V. O. Jr. *Public Opinion and American Democracy.* New York: Alfred E. Knopf, 1961.

Niemi, Richard G., John Mueller, and Tom Smith. *Trends in Public Opinion: A Compendium of Survey Data.* New York: Greenwood Press, 1989.

Yeric, Jerry L., and John R. Todd. *Public Opinion: The Visible Politics,* 3rd ed. Itasca, IL: Peacock, 1994.

Political Parties

WHAT IS A POLITICAL PARTY?

THE EVOLUTION OF AMERICAN PARTY DEMOCRACY

THE ROLES OF THE AMERICAN PARTIES

ONE-PARTYISM AND THIRD-PARTYISM

THE BASIC STRUCTURE OF AMERICAN POLITICAL PARTIES

THE PARTY IN GOVERNMENT

THE MODERN TRANSFORMATION OF PARTY ORGANIZATION

THE PARTY-IN-THE-ELECTORATE

TOWARD REFORM

Ross Perot and his supporters would surely have agreed with *The Federalist Papers'* stand on the "mischiefs of faction," since they hold the excesses of modern Democrats and Republicans responsible for the massive national debt. Many of the Framers harbored a deep distrust of political parties and other "factions," fearing the divisiveness they might engender at a time when the success of the infant federal Constitution was still far from certain. In this regard we need only remember President George Washington's 1796 farewell address, in which he warned the new nation "in the most solemn manner against the baneful effects of the spirit of party generally." Judging by his arguments in *Federalist No. 10,* James Madison held the same views as far back as the 1780s. Yet Madison was wise enough to understand that the "cure" for factionalism—the absence of a citizen's liberty to join together with others freely—is far worse than the disease. Furthermore, Madison recognized that the formation of factions of various sorts, whether narrow special-interest groups or broad-based parties, was inevitable in any republic.

Madison also correctly foresaw that the mechanisms of the federal system would temper the "mischiefs of faction." The division of governmental powers among several branches; the layers of federal, state, and local governments; the numerous checks and balances in the Constitution; and the vigorous competition among and between the factions themselves all help to counteract or limit the ill effects of faction. In fact, for a variety of reasons that this chapter explains, the United States is the only highly developed democracy with only two parties of consequence.

> There are two methods of curing the mischiefs of faction: The one, by removing its causes; the other, by controlling its effects.
>
> *James Madison*
> *Federalist No. 10*

Of all the phenomena feared by the Framers, political parties have proved to be the most pervasive and lasting. In this famous passage, Madison expresses distrust of factions, by which he meant interest groups and parties—a distrust that arose from the fear that the divisiveness they represented would make it difficult to hold the new and fragile nation together.

In the centuries since Madison's and Washington's criticisms of faction, Americans have had a love/hate relationship with the political parties. While usually voting for either Democrats or Republicans, a sizable portion of the electorate has backed a third-party or independent candidate from time to time; Ross Perot in 1992 is the most recent example. Still, political scientists have come to see political parties in a light different from Madison's. Far from viewing parties as an evil to be tempered, political scientists believe that parties have provided our system of government with the stability and choice that preserve it. As this chapter explains, the political scientist E. E. Schattschneider was not exaggerating when he wrote, "modern democracy is unthinkable save in terms of the parties."[1]

In this chapter we first define our terms, then review the evolution of American party democracy, the roles played by the modern parties (including third parties), and the parties' basic structure. We attempt to help you understand political parties by examining them from several vantage points—the party as it operates in government, the

The major national parties are not always recognized as progressive forces, but in fact many advances in suffrage and voting rights have been spearheaded by the parties as they search for new sources of support. Although still seriously underrepresented, women in recent years have made inroads as delegates, candidates, and officeholders.

party as a campaign organization, and the party as a collection of supportive voters. Finally, we suggest some ways political parties might change to strengthen themselves—and American democracy.

What Is a Political Party?

Any definition of "political party" must be kept general, because there are so many kinds of parties in the United States. In some states and localities, party organizations are strong and well-entrenched, whereas in other places the parties exist more on paper than in reality. This diversity would probably please James Madison, validating as it does his vision of a varied federalism. But it also complicates our tasks of explaining and understanding the political parties.[2]

At the most basic level, a **political party** is a group of office holders, candidates, activists, and voters who identify with a group label and seek to elect to public office individuals who run under that label. Notice how pragmatic this concept of party is. The goal is to *win* office, not just compete for it. This objective is in keeping with the practical nature of Americans and the country's historical aversion to most ideologically driven, "purist" politics (as we discuss later in this chapter). Nevertheless, the group label—also called **party identification** for the voters who embrace the party as their own—can carry with it clear messages about ideology and issue positions. Although this is especially true of minor, less broad-based parties that have little chance of electoral success, it also applies to the national, dominant political parties in the United States—the Democrats and the Republicans.

The definition of "party" also identifies the three groups of individuals who make up any political party: (1) the office holders and candidates who run under the party's banner (the **governmental party**), (2) the workers and activists who staff the party's formal organization (the **organizational party**), and (3) the voters who consider themselves to be allied or associated with the party (the **party-in-the-electorate**). We examine each of these groups later in the chapter after first reviewing the history and development of political parties in the United States.

Political party A group of office holders, candidates, activists, and voters who identify with a group label and seek to elect to pubic office individuals who run under that label.

Party identification A citizen's personal affinity for a political party, usually expressed by his or her tendency to vote for the candidates of that party.

Governmental party The office holders and candidates who run under a political party's banner.
Organizational party The workers and activists who staff the party's formal organization.
Party-in-the-electorate The voters who consider themselves to be allied or associated with the party.

The Evolution of American Party Democracy

It is one of the great ironies of the early republic that George Washington's public farewell, which warned the nation against parties, marked the effective end of the brief era of partyless politics in the United States (see Figure 11–1). Washington's unifying influence ebbed as he stepped off the national stage, and his vice president and successor, President John Adams, occupied a much less exalted position. Adams was allied with Alexander Hamilton, and to win the presidency in 1796 he narrowly defeated Thomas Jefferson, Hamilton's former rival in Washington's Cabinet. Hamilton and Jefferson, before ratification of the Constitution, had been leaders of the Federalists and Anti-Federalists, respectively (see Chapter 2). Over the course of Adams's single term, two competing congressional party groupings (or caucuses) gradually organized around these clashing men and their principles: Hamilton's Federalists supported a strong central government, whereas the Democratic-Republicans of Thomas Jefferson and his ally James Madison inherited the mantle of the Anti-Federalists and preferred

FIGURE 11-1

American Party History
at a Glance

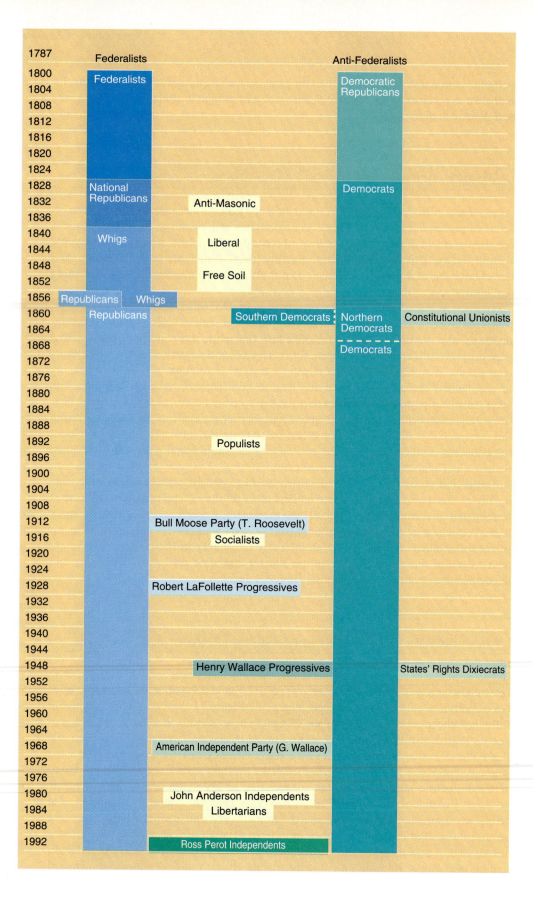

a federal system in which the states were relatively more powerful. (Jefferson actually preferred the simpler name "Republicans"—a very different group from today's party of the same name—but Hamilton insisted on calling them "Democratic-Republicans" to link them to the radical democrats of the French Revolution.) In the presidential election of 1800, the Federalists supported Adams's bid for a second term, but this time the Democratic-Republicans prevailed with their nominee, Jefferson, who became the first U.S. president elected as the nominee of a political party.

Jefferson was deeply committed to the ideas of his party, but not nearly as devoted to the idea of a party system. He regarded his party as a temporary measure necessary to defeat Adams and Hamilton. Neither Jefferson's party nor Hamilton's enjoyed widespread "party identification" among the citizenry akin to that of today's Democrats and Republicans. Although Southerners were overwhelmingly partial to the Democratic-Republicans and New Englanders to the Federalists, no broad-based party organizations existed on either side to mobilize popular support. Just as the nation was in its infancy, so, too, was the party system, and attachments to both parties were weak at first. The various eras of American political parties are summarized in Landmark Events in the American Party System (p. 350).

The Early Parties Fade

After the spirited confrontations of the republic's early years, political parties faded somewhat in importance for a quarter of a century. The Federalists ceased nominating presidential candidates by 1816, having failed to elect one of their own since Adams's victory in 1796, and by 1820 the party had dissolved. James Monroe's presidency from 1817 to 1825 produced the so-called Era of Good Feelings, when party politics was nearly suspended at the national level. Even during Monroe's tenure, though, party organizations continued to develop at the state level. Party growth was fueled in part by the enormous increase in the electorate that took place between 1820 and 1840,

This banner commemorates the inauguration of President Andrew Jackson in 1829. Jackson's Democratic Party was the successor to the Democratic-Republicans of Thomas Jefferson and James Madison. In the election of 1832, Jackson's Democrats won again, becoming the first party with a truly national base.

Landmark Events in the American Party System

1796	♦	Federalists v. Democratic-Republicans
1832	♦	Whigs v. Democrats
1860	♦	Republicans v. Democrats I (balance)
1896	♦	Republicans v. Democrats II (Republican dominance)
1932	♦	Republicans v. Democrats III (Democratic dominance)
1968	♦	Republicans v. Democrats IV (intermittent divided government)*

*Exceptions to this generalization occurred in 1977–1981 and 1993–current day.

as the United States expanded westward and most states abolished property requirements as a condition of white male suffrage. During this twenty-year period, the number of votes cast in presidential contests rose from 300,000 to more than 2 million.

At the same time, U.S. politics were being democratized in other ways. By the 1820s all the states except South Carolina had switched from state legislative selection of presidential electors to popular election of electoral college members. This change helped transform presidential politics. No longer just the concern of society's upper crust, the election of the president became a matter for all qualified voters to decide.

The party base broadened along with the electorate. Small caucuses of congressional party leaders had previously nominated candidates, but after much criticism of the process as elitist and undemocratic, this system gave way to nominations at large party conventions. The country's first major national presidential nominating convention was held in 1832 by the Democratic Party,[3] the successor to the old Jeffersonian Democratic-Republicans. (The shortened name had gradually come into use in the 1820s.) Formed around the charismatic populist President Andrew Jackson, the Democratic party attracted most of the newly enfranchised voters, who were drawn to Jackson's style. His strong personality helped to polarize politics, and opposition to the president coalesced into the Whig Party. The Whig Party was descended from the Federalists; its early leaders included Henry Clay, the Speaker of the House from 1811 to 1820. The incumbent Jackson defeated Clay in the 1832 presidential contest. He became the first chief executive who won the White House as the nominee of a truly national, popularly based political party. (See "People of the Past: Henry Clay," p. 177.)

The Whigs and the Democrats continued to strengthen after 1832, establishing state and local organizations almost everywhere. Their competition was usually fierce and closely matched, and they brought the United States the first broadly supported two-party system in the Western world.[4] Unfortunately for the Whigs, the issue of slavery sharpened the many existing divisive internal party tensions that led to its gradual dissolution and replacement by the new Republican Party. Formed in 1854 by anti-slavery activists, the Republican Party set its sights on the abolition (or at least the containment) of slavery. After a losing presidential effort for John C. Frémont in 1856, the party was able to assemble enough support primarily from the Whigs and anti-slavery Northern Democrats to win the presidency for Abraham Lincoln in a fragmented 1860 vote. In that year, the South voted solidly Democratic, beginning a habit so strong that not a single Southern state voted Republican for president again until 1920.

The British political system, which has been characterized by competition between two main political parties with significant third-party activity, provides an interesting contrast to the American case. In Britain, the massive extension of suffrage in 1867 prompted the emergence of two modern, mass political parties (the Liberals and the Conservatives), which were needed to organize and mobilize the now unwieldy electorate. In the aftermath of World War I, the Liberals gave way to the Labour Party as the Conservatives' principal contender for power.

Democrats and Republicans: The Golden Age

From the presidential election of 1860 to this day, the same two major parties—the Republicans and the Democrats—have dominated elections in the United States, and control of an electoral majority has seesawed between them. The dominance of the Republicans (now often called the Grand Old Party, or GOP) in the post–Civil War Reconstruction era eventually gave way to a closely competitive system from 1876 to 1896, in part because the Democrats were more successful at integrating new immigrants into U.S. society in port cities like New York, Boston, and Chicago. In the later years of the nineteenth century, however, the Republicans skillfully capitalized on fears of a growing anti-establishment, anti-big business sentiment in the Democratic Party. They fashioned a dominant and enduring majority of voters that essentially lasted until the early 1930s, when the Great Depression created the conditions for a Democratic resurgence.

President Franklin D. Roosevelt's New Deal coalition of 1932 (consisting of the South, racial and ethnic groups, organized labor, farmers, liberals, and big-city "machines"—as well-oiled party organizations are sometimes called) characterized both the Democratic Party and the prevailing national majority until at least the late 1960s. Since 1970, neither party has been clearly dominant, as more and more voters have seemed to be less committed to either of the two parties. In this same period, the Republicans have dominated presidential elections and Democrats have won most congressional contests. (The development of a "divided government" is discussed later in this chapter.)

The Modern Era Versus the Golden Age

The modern era seems very distant from the "golden age" of parties that existed from the 1870s to the 1920s. Emigration from Europe (particularly from Ireland, Italy, and Germany) fueled the development of big-city party organizations that ruled their domains with an iron hand. Party and government were virtually interchangeable, and the parties were the providers of much-needed services, entertainment, and employment. These big-city party organizations were a central element of life for millions of people: They sponsored community events, such as parades and picnics, and provided social services, such as helping new immigrants settle in and giving food and temporary housing to those in immediate need—all in exchange for votes.

The parties offered immigrants not just services but also the opportunity for upward social mobility as they rose in the organization. Because they held the possibility of

The Grand Old Party
♦ ♦ ♦

Ever since the 1880s, the term "Grand Old Party" has been used to refer to the Republican Party. The phrase seems to have taken its inspiration from Great Britain, where Prime Minister William Gladstone was dubbed "the Grand Old Man" or "GOM" in 1882. Soon after that, "GOP" made its debut in headlines appearing in the *New York Tribune* and the *Boston Post*.

With a wink, Mayor James M. Curley of Boston files his application to run for a fifth term. In many cities, the parties ruled over vast organizations, offering the growing population of recent immigrants a sense of cohesion, upward mobility, and "patronage"—jobs in exchange for loyalty and service to the party. These party "machines" were the target of liberal reform movements beginning in the 1920s.

Direct primary The selection of party candidates through the ballots of qualified voters rather than at party nomination conventions.

Civil service laws These acts removed the staffing of the bureaucracy from political parties and created a professional bureaucracy filled through competition.

Patronage Jobs, grants, or other special favors that are given as rewards to friends and political allies for their support.

Spoils system The firing of public-office holders of a defeated political party and their replacement with loyalists of the newly elected party.

social advancement, the parties engendered among their supporters and office holders intense devotion that helped to produce startlingly high voter turnouts—75 percent or better in all presidential elections from 1876 to 1900, compared with only about 50 to 55 percent today.[5] They also fostered the greatest party-line voting ever achieved in Congress and many state legislatures.[6] (See "People of the Past: Plunkitt of Tammany Hall," p. 357.)

Is the Party Over?

The heyday of the political party—at least this kind of party—has passed. In the twentieth century, many social, political, technological, and governmental changes have contributed to party decline. Historically, the government's gradual assumption of important functions previously performed by the parties—such as printing ballots, conducting elections, and providing social welfare services—had a major impact. Social services began to be seen as a right of citizenship rather than as a privilege extended in exchange for a person's support of a party. Also, as the flow of immigrants slowed dramatically in the 1920s, party organizations gradually withered in most places.

The **direct primary,** whereby party nominees were determined by the ballots of qualified voters rather than at party conventions, was widely adopted by the states in the first two decades of the twentieth century. The primary removed the power of nomination from party leaders and workers and gave it instead to a much broader and more independent electorate, thus loosening the tie between the party nominee and the party organization. **Civil service laws** also removed much of the patronage used by the parties to reward their followers. (Civil service laws require appointment on the basis of merit and competitive examinations, whereas **patronage**—also called the **spoils system**—awards jobs on the basis of party loyalty.) These changes were encouraged by the Progressive Movement (consisting of politically liberal reformers), which flourished in the first two decades of the twentieth century.

In the post–World War II era, extensive social changes led the movement away from strong parties. Broad-based education gave rise to **issue-oriented politics,** politics that focuses on specific issues, such as civil rights, tax cutting, environmentalism, or abortion, rather than on party labels. Issue politics tends to cut across party lines and encourages voters to **ticket-split,** that is, to vote for candidates of different parties for various offices in the same election. Another post–World War II social change that has affected the parties is the shift in the population. Millions of people have moved out of the cities, which are easily organizable because of population density, and into the sprawling suburbs, where a sense of privacy and detachment can deter the most energetic organizers.

Politically, many other trends have contributed to the parties' decline. Television, which has come to dominate U.S. politics, naturally emphasizes personalities rather than abstract concepts such as party labels. In addition, the modern parties have many rivals for the affections of their candidates, including **political consultants,** the hired guns who manage campaigns and design television advertisements. Both television and consultants have replaced the party as the intermediary between candidate and voter. It is little wonder that many candidates and office holders who have reached their posts without much help from their parties remain as free as possible of party ties.

The Parties Endure

The parties' decline can easily be exaggerated, however. Viewing parties in the broad sweep of U.S. history, it becomes clear that first, although political parties have evolved considerably and changed form from time to time, they usually have been reliable vehicles for mass participation in a representative democracy. In fact, the gradual but steady expansion of suffrage itself was orchestrated by the parties. As political scientist E. E. Schattschneider concluded, "In the search for new segments of the populace that might be exploited profitably, the parties have kept the movement to liberalize the franchise well ahead of the demand. . . . The enlargement of the practicing electorate has been one of the principal labors of the parties, a truly notable achievement for which the parties have never been properly credited."[7]

Second, the parties' journey through U.S. history has been characterized by the same ability to adapt to prevailing conditions that is often cited as the genius of the Constitution. Flexibility and pragmatism are characteristics of both and help ensure their survival and the success of the society they serve.

Third, despite massive changes in political conditions and frequent dramatic shifts in the electorate's mood, the two major parties have not only achieved remarkable longevity, but they also have almost consistently provided strong competition for each other and the voters at the national level. Of the twenty-eight presidential elections in the century-plus from 1884 to 1992, for instance, the Republicans won fifteen and the Democrats thirteen. Even when calamities have beset the parties—the Great Depression in the 1930s or the Watergate scandal of 1973–74 for the Republicans (see Chapter 7), the Civil War or left-wing McGovernism in 1972 for the Democrats—the two parties have proved tremendously resilient, sometimes bouncing back from landslide defeats to win the next election. After losing badly in 1988, for example, the Democrats managed to win in 1992, demonstrating again that the only constant in politics is change.

Perhaps most of all, history teaches us that the development of parties in the United States (outlined in Figure 11-1) has been inevitable, as James Madison feared. Human nature alone guarantees conflict in any society; in a free state, the question is simply how to contain and channel conflict productively without infringing on individual liberties. The Founders' utopian hopes for the avoidance of partisan faction have given way to an appreciation of the parties' constructive contributions to conflict definition and resolution during the years of the American republic.

Issue-oriented politics Politics that focus on specific issues rather than on party, candidate, or other loyalties.

Ticket split To vote for candidates of different parties for various offices in the same election.

Political consultants Professionals who manage campaigns and political advertisements for political candidates.

Although the parties have evolved—and in some ways weakened—over time, they continue to help define and resolve conflict in the national arena and provide consistently strong competition for each other. Here, James Carville and the Clinton-Gore campaign staff in the "war room" in Little Rock, on the eve of Democratic victory in 1992.

The Roles of the American Parties

The definition and resolution of conflict are two vital functions performed by the party system in the United States. But the parties play many other roles, too, and accomplish much for politics and society, as the following sampler suggests.

Mobilizing Support and Gathering Power

Party affiliation is enormously helpful to elected leaders. They can count on disproportionate support among their partisans in times of trouble and in close judgment calls. Therefore, the parties thus aid office holders by giving them room to develop their policies and by mobilizing support for them. When the president addresses the nation and requests support for his policies, for example, his party's activists are usually the first to respond to the call, perhaps by flooding Congress with telegrams urging action on the president's agenda.

Because there are only two major parties, pragmatic citizens who are interested in politics or public policy are mainly attracted to one or the other standard, creating nat-

Coalition A group of interests or organizations that join forces for the purpose of electing public officials.

ural majorities or near-majorities for party office holders to command. The party creates a community of interest that bonds disparate groups over time into a **coalition.** This continuing mutual interest eliminates the necessity of creating a new coalition for every campaign or every issue. Imagine the constant chaos and mad scrambles for public support that would ensue without the continuity provided by the parties.

A Force for Stability

As mechanisms for organizing and containing political change, the parties are a potent force for stability. They represent continuity in the wake of changing issues and personalities, anchoring the electorate in the midst of the storm of new political policies and people. Because of its unyielding, practical desire to *win* elections (not just to *contest* them), each party in a sense acts to moderate public opinion. The party tames its own extreme elements by pulling them toward an ideological center in order to attract a majority of votes on Election Day.

Another aspect of the stability the parties provide is found in the nature of the coalitions they forge. There are inherent contradictions in these coalitions that, oddly enough, strengthen the nation even as they strain party unity. Franklin D. Roosevelt's Democratic New Deal coalition, for example, included many African-Americans and most Southern whites—opposing elements nonetheless joined in common political purpose. This party union of the two groups, as limited a context as it may have been, provided a framework for acceptance of change and contributed to reconciliation of the races in the civil rights era. Nowhere can this reconciliation be more clearly seen than in the South, where most state Democratic parties remained predominant after the mid-1960s by building on the ingrained Democratic voting habits of both whites and blacks to create new, moderate, generally integrated societies.

Unity, Linkage, Accountability

Parties provide the glue that holds together the disparate elements of the fragmented U.S. governmental and political apparatus. The Founders designed a system that divides and subdivides power, making it possible to preserve individual liberty but difficult to coordinate and produce action in a timely fashion. Parties help compensate for this drawback by linking all the institutions of power one to another. Although rivalry between the executive and legislative branches of U.S. government is inevitable, the partisan affiliations of the leaders of each branch constitute a common basis for cooperation, as any president and his fellow party members in Congress usually demonstrate daily. Each time President Bill Clinton proposed a major new program (such as health care and crime control), for instance, Democratic members of the Congress were the first to speak up in favor of the program and to orchestrate efforts at its passage.

Even within each branch there is intended fragmentation, and the party once again helps narrow the differences between the House of Representatives and the Senate, or between the president and his chiefs in the executive bureaucracy. Similarly, the division of national, state, and local governments, while always an invitation to conflict, is made more workable and easily coordinated by the intersecting party relationships that exist among office holders at all levels. Party affiliation, in other words, is a basis for mediation and negotiation laterally among the branches and vertically among the layers.

The party's linkage function does not end there. Party identification and organization are natural connectors and vehicles for communication between the voter and the candidate as well as between the voter and the office holder. The party connection is one means of increasing accountability in election campaigns and in government. Candidates on the campaign trail and elected party leaders in office are required from time to time to account for their performance at party-sponsored forums, nominating primaries, and conventions.

Political parties, too, can take some credit for unifying the nation by dampening sectionalism. Because parties must form national majorities in order to win the presidency, any single, isolated region is guaranteed minority status unless it establishes ties with other areas. The party label and philosophy build the bridge that enables regions to join forces; and in the process, a national interest, rather than a merely sectional one, is created and served.

The Electioneering Function

The election, proclaimed author H. G. Wells, is "democracy's ceremonial, its feast, its great function," and the political parties assist this ceremony in essential ways. First, the parties funnel eager, interested individuals into politics and government. Thousands of candidates are recruited each year by the two parties, as are many of the candidates' staff members—the people who manage the campaigns and go on to serve in key governmental positions once the election has been won.

This function is even more crucial in the British parliamentary system. In the postwar period, the *only* avenue to national power (i.e., the prime minister's office or a choice seat on the Cabinet) has been through either the Conservative Party or the Labour Party. Ambitious politicians must work their way up through the party hierarchy and build a supporting coalition along the way.

Elections can have meaning in a democracy only if they are competitive, and in the United States they probably could not be competitive without the parties. Even in the South, traditionally the least politically competitive U.S. region, the parties today regularly produce reasonably vigorous contests at the state (and, increasingly, the local) level.

Party as a Voting and Issue Cue

A voter's party identification acts as an invaluable filter for information, a perceptual screen that affects how he or she digests political news. Therefore, party affiliation provides a useful cue for voters—particularly for the least informed and least interested, who can use the party as a shortcut or substitute for interpreting issues and events they may not fully comprehend. But even better-educated and more involved voters find party identification helpful. After all, no one has the time to study every issue carefully or to become fully knowledgeable about every candidate seeking public office.

Policy Formulation and Promotion

U.S. Senator Huey Long (D-La.), one of the premier spokesmen for "the people" of this century, was usually able to capture the flavor of the average person's views about politics. Considering an independent bid for president before his assassination in 1935,

Sen. Huey Long (D-La.) campaigned for the presidency in 1935 on a populist platform, arguing in fiery speeches that neither of the major parties' policies had the people's best interests at heart.

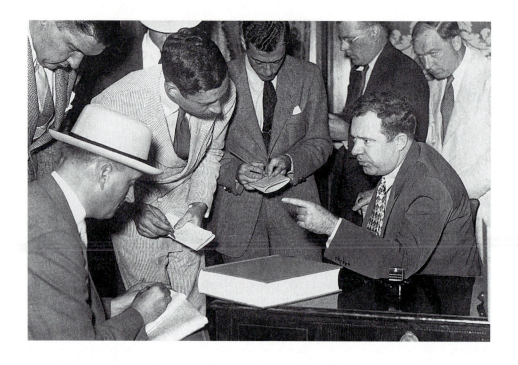

Long liked to compare the Republican and Democratic parties to the two patent medicines offered by a traveling salesman. Asked the difference between them, the salesman explained that the "High Populorum" tonic was made from the bark of the tree taken from the top down, while "Low Populorum" tonic was made from bark stripped from the root up. The analogous moral, according to Long, was this: "The only difference I've found in Congress between the Republican and Democratic leadership is that one of 'em is skinning us from the ankle up and the other from the ear down!"[8]

National party platforms A statement of the general and specific philosophy and policy goals of a political party, usually promulgated at the national convention.

Long would certainly have insisted that his fable applied to the **national party platforms,** the most visible instrument by which parties formulate, convey, and promote public policy. Every four years, each party writes for the presidential nominating conventions a lengthy platform explaining its positions on key issues. Most citizens in our own era undoubtedly still believe that party platforms are relatively undifferentiated, a mixture of pabulum and pussyfooting. Yet political scientist Gerald Pomper's study of party platforms from 1944 through 1976 has demonstrated that each party's pledges were consistently and significantly different, a function in part of the varied groups in their coalitions.[9] Interestingly, about 69 percent of the specific platform positions were taken by one party but not the other. On abortion, for example, the Democrats are strongly for abortion rights while the Republicans are firmly against them in their most recent platforms.

Granted, then, party platforms are quite distinctive as revealed in the box, "Selected Contrasts in the 1992 Party Platforms" (p. 409). Does this elaborate party exercise in policy formulation mean anything? One could argue that the platform is valuable, if only as a clear presentation of a party's basic philosophy and as a forum for activist opinion and public education. But platforms have much more impact than that. About two-thirds of the promises in the victorious party's presidential platform have been completely or mostly implemented; even more astounding, one-half or more of the pledges of the *losing* party find their way into public policy (with the success rate depending on whether the party controls one, both, or neither house of Con-

Plunkitt of Tammany Hall

Tammany Hall was a powerful New York City political organization during the mid–nineteenth and early twentieth centuries. Originally formed as a social club in 1797, it had been transformed into an influential political machine by 1850, with membership including most of the city's prominent Democrats.

Of all the organization's politicians, one of the most renowned at the turn of the twentieth century was ward boss George Washington Plunkitt. Starting as a teenager, this son of Irish immigrants worked his way up through the ranks of the organization to become the leader of the city's Fifteenth Assembly District. (An assembly district is made up of many smaller units, called election districts.) He is remembered as one of the shrewdest politicians of his time. Plunkitt was born poor but died a millionaire, acquiring most of his wealth through what he called "honest graft," a term best described in his own candid words:

> My party's in power in the city, and its goin' to make a lot of public improvements. Well, I'm tipped off, say, that they're going to lay out a new park at a certain place.
>
> I see my opportunity and I take it. I go to that place and I buy up all the land I can in the neighborhood. Then the board of this or that makes it public, and there is a rush to get my land, which nobody cared particular for before.
>
> Ain't it perfectly honest to charge a good price and make a profit on my investment and foresight? Of course, it is. Well, that's honest graft.

For Plunkitt there was a difference between dishonest and honest graft, "between [dishonest] political looters and [honest] politicians who make a fortune out of politics by keepin' their eyes wide open":

> The looter goes in for himself alone without considerin' his organization or his city. The politician looks after his own interests, the organization's interests, and the city's interests all at the same time.

Plunkitt certainly looked after his constituents' interests. During Tammany's reign, the population of New York City was made up predominantly of poor immigrants, mostly Irish, for whom Plunkitt and his fellow district leaders served as a bridge between the Old and New Worlds and also as a way out of the slums. Besides assimilating these newcomers to life in the United States and acquainting them with the processes of self-government, the ward bosses used the patronage at their disposal to provide tangible benefits. Be it a job, liquor, a pushcart license, or even cash, the ward boss was always happy to help out a needy constituent—in exchange, of course, for loyalty at the ballot box during election time.

In contrast to the issue-oriented or image-appeal politics we know today, Plunkitt's politics were *personal*. As Plunkitt put it, "[I] learned how to reach the hearts of the great mass of voters. I don't bother about reaching their heads." Plunkitt understood the value of this personalized, community-oriented politics to both voters and leaders. His advice to aspiring politicians was simply to know and study the members of their communities and to "study human nature and act accordin'."

Plunkitt's brand of politics had all but disappeared by the mid–twentieth century. First, a drastic decline of emigration during the 1920s strangled the fuel line that fed the fires of city machines. Second, many of the services the parties provided gradually came to be viewed as rights of citizenship rather than as rewards for supporting a particular party; therefore, government replaced party organizations as the dispensers of benefits. Most important, however, and much to the chagrin of Plunkitt himself, were the new civil service laws passed by reformers in the 1920s to combat the alleged corruption of machine politics. These laws, which struck at the heart and soul of machine politics—patronage and the spoils system—induced Plunkitt to deem the civil service laws "the biggest fraud of the age" and the ruin of the nation:

> There can't be no real patriotism while it lasts. How are you goin' to interest our young men in their country if you have no offices to give them when they work for their party? . . . I know more than one man in the past years who worked for the ticket and was just overflowin' with patriotism, but when he was knocked out by the civil service humbug he got to hate his country and became an anarchist.

For better or worse, however, the reformers prevailed, and by the mid–twentieth century, civil service had come to dominate government at every level, consigning Plunkitt's brand of politics to America's past.

Source: William L. Riordon, ed., *Plunkitt of Tammany Hall* (New York: Dutton, 1963), pp. 11, 89.

gress).[10] The party platform also has great influence on a new presidential administration's legislative program and on the president's State of the Union address. And while party affiliation is normally the single most important determinant of voting in Congress and in state legislatures,[11] the party–vote relationship is even stronger when party platform issues come up on the floor of Congress. Gerald Pomper concludes: "We should therefore take platforms seriously—because politicians appear to take them seriously."[12]

Besides mobilizing Americans on a permanent basis, then, the parties convert the cacophony of hundreds of identifiable social and economic groups into a two-part (semi)harmony that is much more comprehensible, if not always on key and pleasing to the ears. The simplicity of two-party politics may be deceptive given the enormous variety in public policy choices, but a sensible system of representation in the American context might be impossible without it. And the people who would suffer most from its absence would not be the few who are individually or organizationally powerful—their voices would be heard under almost any system. As political scientist Walter Dean Burnham has pointed out, the losers would be the many individually powerless for whom the parties are the only effective devices yet created that can generate collective power on their behalf.[13]

One-Partyism and Third-Partyism

The two-party system has not gone unchallenged. At the state level, two-party competition was severely limited or nonexistent in much of the country for most of this century.[14] Especially in the one-party Democratic states of the Deep South and the rock-ribbed Republican states of Maine, New Hampshire, and Vermont, the dominant party's primary nomination was often equivalent to election, and the only real contest was an unsatisfying intraparty one in which colorful personalities often dominated and a half-dozen major candidacies in each primary proved confusing to voters.[15] Even in most two-party states many cities and counties had a massive majority of voters aligned with one or the other party and thus were effectively one-party in local elections. In Britain, one-partyism at the subnational level is a relatively common phenomenon; for example, certain regions like the Northeast have voted overwhelmingly for the Labour Party in general election after general election.

Historical, cultural, and sectional forces primarily accounted for the concentration of one party's supporters in certain areas. The Civil War's divisions, for instance, were mirrored for the better part of a century in the Democratic predisposition of the South and the Republican proclivities of the Yankee Northern states. Whatever the combination of factors producing **one-partyism**—a political system in which one party dominates and wins virtually all contests—the condition has certainly declined precipitously in the last quarter century.[16]

The spread of two-party competition, while still uneven in some respects, is one of the most significant political trends of recent times, and virtually no one-party states are left. There are no purely Republican states any more, and the heavily Democratic contingent has been reduced to, at most, Louisiana, Arkansas, and Maryland. (Note, though, that in each of these states one or more Republicans have been elected to the governorship or U.S. Senate since 1970, and the Deep South states usually vote Republican in presidential contests as well, unless a Southerner heads the Democratic ticket.)

One-partyism A political system in which one party dominates and wins virtually all contests.

Ironically, the growth of two-party competition has been spurred less by the developing strength of the main parties than by party weakness, illustrated by the decline in partisan loyalty among the voters. In other words, citizens now are somewhat more inclined to cross party lines in order to support an appealing candidate regardless of party affiliation, thus making a victory for the minority party possible whether or not it has earned the victory through the party's own organizational hard work. It should also be noted that the elimination of pockets of one-party strength adds an element of instability to the system, since at one point, even in lean times of national electoral disaster, each party was assured of a regional base from which a comeback could be staged. Nonetheless, the increase in party competitiveness can be viewed positively, since it eliminates the effects of one-partyism and guarantees a comprehensible and credible partisan choice to a larger segment of the electorate than ever before.

Minor Parties

Third-partyism has proved more durable than one-partyism, though its nature is sporadic and intermittent, and its effects on the political system are on the whole less weighty. Given all the controversy third parties generate, one could be excused for thinking that they were extraordinarily important on the American scene. But as Frank Sorauf has concluded, third parties in fact "have not assumed the importance that all the [academic] attention lavished on them suggests."[17] No minor party has ever come close to winning the presidency, and only eight minor parties have won so much as a single state's electoral college votes (see Table 11.1). Just five third parties (the farmer-backed Populists in 1892, Theodore Roosevelt's Bull Moose Party in 1912, the reform-minded Progressives in 1924, former Alabama Governor George Wallace's racially-based American Independent Party in 1968, and Ross Perot's independents in 1992) have garnered more than 10 percent of the popular vote for president.* (Roosevelt, incidentally, abandoned the Republican Party—under whose banner he had won the presidency in 1904—in order to form the Bull Moose Party, composed mainly of reformist Republicans.)

Third parties find their roots in sectionalism (as did the South's states' rights Dixiecrats, who broke away from the Democrats in 1948); in economic protest (such as the agrarian revolt that fueled the Populists, an 1892 prairie-states party); in specific issues (such as the Prohibition Party's proposed ban on the sale of alcoholic beverages); in ideology (the Socialist, Communist, and Libertarian Parties are examples); and in appealing, charismatic personalities (Theodore Roosevelt is perhaps the best case). Many of the minor parties have drawn strength from a combination of these sources. The American Independent Party enjoyed a measure of success because of a dynamic leader (George Wallace), a firm geographic base (the South), and an emotional issue (civil rights). And in 1992 Ross Perot, the billionaire with a folksy Texas manner, was a charismatic leader whose campaign was fueled by the deficit issue (as well as by his personal fortune).

Above all, third parties make electoral progress in direct proportion to the failure of the two major parties to incorporate new ideas or alienated groups or to nominate at-

Third-partyism The tendency of third parties to arise with some regularity in a nominally two-party system.

The "Bull Moose" Party
♦ ♦ ♦

During his hunting expeditions in the Western United States, Theodore Roosevelt was so impressed with the great strength and stamina of the bull moose that "as strong as a bull moose" became one of his favorite expressions.

In 1912, when he refused to support Republican President William Howard Taft (1909–1913) for re-election, the "Bull Moose" became the nickname and symbol of the independent movement he led.

---

* Theodore Roosevelt's 1912 effort was the most successful; the Bull Moose Party won 27 percent of the popular vote for president (although only 17 percent of the electoral college votes). Roosevelt's is also the only third party to run ahead of one of the two major parties (the Republicans).

Table 11.1 ♦ Third Party and Independent Presidential Candidates Receiving 5 Percent or More of Popular Vote			
CANDIDATE (PARTY)	YEAR	PERCENTAGE OF POPULAR VOTE	ELECTORAL VOTES
Ross Perot (Independent)	1992	18.9	0
John B. Anderson (Independent)	1980	6.6	0
George C. Wallace (American Independent)	1968	13.5	46
Robert M. LaFollette (Progressive)	1924	16.6	13
Theodore Roosevelt (Bull Moose)	1912	27.4	88
Eugene V. Debs (Socialist)	1912	6.0	0
James B. Weaver (Populist)	1892	8.5	22
John C. Brekinridge (Southern Democrat)	1860	18.1	72
John Bell (Constitutional Union)	1860	12.6	39
Millard Fillmore (Whig-American)	1856	21.5	8
Martin Van Buren (Free Soil)	1848	10.1	0
William Wirt (Anti-Masonic)	1832	7.8	7

Source: Congressional Quarterly Weekly Report, October 18, 1980, p. 3147 (as adapted), and official election returns for 1992.

tractive candidates as their standard-bearers. Certainly in the media age, this latter qualification has grown in importance. The 1980 independent presidential bid of U.S. Representative John Anderson (R-Ill.) was spurred not by geography or specific issues or Anderson's persona but by intense dissatisfaction among some voters with the major-party nominees, Jimmy Carter and Ronald Reagan.*

Explanations

Third parties in the United States are akin to shooting stars that appear briefly and brilliantly but do not long remain visible in the political constellation. In fact, the United

* Anderson received only 7 percent of the vote in the end, although at times during the contest, polls had shown him with well above 20 percent.

States is the only major Western nation that does not have at least one significant, enduring national third party; there are a number of explanations for this. Unlike many European countries that use **proportional representation** (awarding legislative seats in proportion to the number of votes received) and that guarantee parliamentary seats to any faction securing as little as 5 percent of the vote, the United States has a "single-member, plurality" electoral system that requires a party to get one more vote than any other party in a legislative district or in a state's presidential election in order to win. To paraphrase the legendary football coach Vince Lombardi, finishing first is not everything, it is the only thing in U.S. politics; placing second, even by a smidgen, doesn't count. This condition encourages the grouping of interests into as few parties as possible (the democratic minimum being two).

Other institutional factors also undergird the two-party system:

- The laws in most states make it difficult for third parties to secure a place on the ballot by requiring large numbers of signatures, whereas the Democratic and Republican parties are often granted automatic access.
- Democrats and Republicans in the state legislatures may have little in common, but one shared objective is to make sure that the political pie is cut into only two sizable pieces, not three or more smaller slices.
- The public funding of campaigns (financing from taxpayer dollars), where it exists, is much more generous for the two major parties. At the national level, for instance, third-party presidential candidates receive money only *after* the general election, *if* they have garnered more than 5 percent of the vote, and *only* in proportion to their total vote; the major-party candidates, by contrast, get large, full general-election grants immediately upon their summer nominations. (This funding difference does not affect wealthy politicians like Perot.)
- The news media are biased—legitimately so—against minor parties; these parties are usually given relatively little coverage compared with that given to major-party nominees. The media are only reflecting political reality, of course, and it would be absurd to expect them to offer equal time to all comers. Still, this is a vicious cycle for minor-party candidates: A lack of broad-based support produces slight coverage, which minimizes their chances of attracting more adherents. Of course, once a third candidate such as Ross Perot becomes prominent, the media flock to his appearances and clamor to schedule him on their news shows.

Beyond the institutional explanations are historical, cultural, and social theories of two-partyism in the United States. The **dualist theory,** frequently criticized as overly simplistic, suggests that there has always been an underlying binary nature to U.S. politics. Whether it was the early conflict between Eastern financial interests and Western frontiersmen, the sectional division of North and South, the more current urban-versus-rural or urban-versus-suburban clashes, or even the natural tensions of democratic institutions (the government against the opposition, for instance), dualists believe that the processes and interests of politics inevitably push the players into two great camps.

Other political scientists emphasize the basic social consensus existing in U.S. life. Despite great diversity in our heritage, the vast majority of Americans accept without serious question the fundamental structures of our system: The Constitution, the governmental set-up, a lightly controlled free enterprise economy, for example. This consensus, when allied with certain American cultural characteristics developed over time (pragmatism, acceptance of the need for compromise, a lack of extreme and divisive social-class consciousness), produces the conditions necessary for relatively non-ideological, centrist politics that can naturally support two moderate alternative parties but has little need for more.

Proportional representation The practice of awarding legislative seats in proportion to the number of votes received.

Dualist theory The theory claiming that there has always been an underlying binary party nature to U.S. politics.

The passion for power and victory that drives both Democrats and Republicans overrides ideology and prevents rigidity. Unless a kind of rigor mortis takes hold in the future in one or both major parties—with, say, the capture of the party organization by unyielding extremists of right or left—it is difficult to imagine any third party becoming a major, permanent force in U.S. politics, although Ross Perot's organization bears watching. The corollary of this axiom, though, is that the major parties must be eternally vigilant if they are to avoid ideologically inspired takeovers; perhaps they can expand their participation in party activities to a group of voters that is as broad-based as possible.

For the foreseeable future, though, third parties likely will continue to play useful supporting roles similar to their historically sanctioned ones: They can popularize ideas that might not receive a hearing otherwise. They can serve as vehicles of popular discontent with the major parties and thereby induce change in major-party behavior and platforms. They may presage and assist party realignments in the future as they have sometimes done in the past. In a few states, third parties will also continue to take a unique part in political life, as the Conservative and Liberal Parties of New York State do.* But in a two-party system that is supplemented by generous means of expressing dissent and registering political opposition in other ways (court challenges, interest-group organizing, for example), third parties will probably continue to have a limited future in the United States.

The Basic Structure of American Political Parties

The structure of the two major parties is not elaborate. Figure 11-2 summarizes the levels of each party, from grassroots base to pinnacle.

National Committees

The first national party committees were skeletal and formed some years after the creation of the presidential nominating conventions in the 1830s. Every four years, each party holds a national convention to nominate its presidential and vice-presidential candidates. First the Democrats in 1848 and then the Republicans in 1856 established national governing bodies (the Democratic National Committee, or DNC, and the Republican National Committee, or RNC) to make arrangements for the conventions and to coordinate the subsequent presidential campaigns. The DNC and RNC were each composed of one representative from each state; this was expanded to two in the 1920s after the post of state committeewoman was established. The states had complete control over the selection of their representatives to the national committees. In addition, to serve their interests, the congressional party caucuses in both houses organized their own national committees, loosely allied with the DNC and RNC. The National Republican Congressional Committee (NRCC) was started in 1866 when the Radical Republican congressional delegation was feuding with Abraham Lincoln's moderate

---

* New York election law makes the Conservatives and Liberals (and, more recently, the Right to Life [anti-abortion] Party) potential power brokers because as an alternative to placing their own adherents on the ballot they can nominate the candidates of a major party to run under their labels, thus encouraging the major parties and their nominees to court them assiduously.

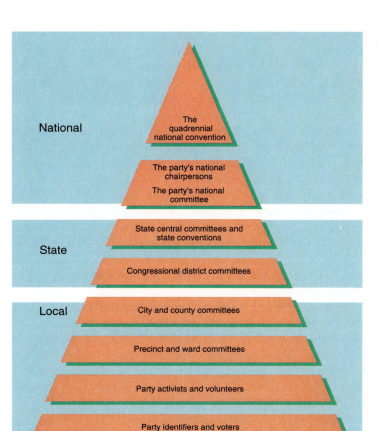

FIGURE 11-2

Political Party Organization in America: From Base to Pinnacle

successor, President Andrew Johnson, and wanted a counterweight to his control of the RNC. At the same time House and Senate Democrats set up a similar committee.

After the popular election of U.S. senators was initiated in 1913 with the ratification of the Seventeenth Amendment to the Constitution, both parties organized separate Senate campaign committees. This three-part arrangement of national party committee, House party committee, and Senate party committee has persisted in both parties until the present day, and each party's three committees are located together in Washington.

Leadership

The key national party official is the chairperson of the DNC or RNC. Although the chair is formally elected by the national committee, he or she is usually selected by the sitting president or newly nominated presidential candidate, who is accorded the right to name the individual for at least the duration of his or her campaign. Only the post-campaign out-of-power party committee actually has the authority to appoint a chairperson independently. The committee-crowned chairpersons generally have the greatest impact on the party because they come to their posts at times of crisis when a leadership vacuum exists. (A defeated presidential candidate is technically the head of the national party until the next nominating convention, but the reality is naturally otherwise as a party attempts to shake off a losing image.) The chair often becomes the prime spokesperson and arbitrator for the party during the four years between elections. He or she is called on to damp down factionalism, negotiate candidate disputes, raise money, and prepare the machinery for the next presidential election. Balancing the interests of all potential White House contenders is a particularly difficult job, and strict neutrality is normally expected from the chair.

In recent times both parties have benefited from adept leadership while out of power. William Brock, RNC chairman during the Carter presidency, and Ron Brown, DNC chairman—the first African-American to chair the DNC—during the Bush term, both skillfully used their positions to strengthen their parties organizationally and to polish the party images. Brock and Brown frequently appeared on news shows to give the out-of-power party's viewpoint. By contrast, party chairpersons selected by incumbent presidents and presidential candidates tend to be close allies of the presidents or candidates and often subordinate the good of the party to the needs of the campaign or White House. During the Carter presidency, for example, DNC Chairman Kenneth Curtis and his successor John White were creatures of the White House; they acted as cheerleaders for their chief executive but did little to keep the Democratic Party competitive with the then-strengthening GOP organization.

Because of their command of presidential patronage and influence, a few national-party chairpersons selected by presidents have become powerful and well known, such as Republican Mark Hanna during the McKinley presidency (1897–1901) and Democrat James Farley under President Franklin D. Roosevelt. Most presidentially appointed chairs, however, have been relatively obscure; the chance for a chairperson to make a difference and cut a memorable figure generally comes when there is no competition from a White House nominee or occupant. President Clinton originally named thirty-six-year-old national campaign manager, David Wilhelm, a veteran of Chicago politics, to head the DNC. Wilhelm served until mid-1994, when he resigned to return to his native Chicago. Clinton then chose the team of Connecticut U.S. Senator Christopher Dodd and South Carolina political activist Donald W. Fowler to head up the DNC. Dodd and Fowler's Republican counterpart is Haley Barbour, an ex-aide to Ronald Reagan; he was a Washington, D.C., lawyer and lobbyist at the time of his election by the RNC. Fowler has been credited with a superb job of organization for the GOP—one that paid off in November, 1994.

National Conventions

National convention A party conclave (meeting) held in the presidential election year for the purposes of nominating a presidential and vice-presidential ticket and adopting a platform.

Much of any party chairperson's work involves planning the presidential nominating convention, or **national convention,** the most publicized and vital event on the party's calendar. Until 1984, gavel-to-gavel coverage was standard practice on all national television networks. Even after the recent cutbacks by some news organizations, a substantial block of time is still devoted to the conventions. (In 1992, for example, all the networks devoted at least a couple of prime-time hours per night to convention coverage.) Although the nomination of the presidential ticket naturally receives the lion's share of attention, the convention also fulfills its role as the ultimate governing body for the party itself. The rules adopted and the platform passed at the quadrennial conclave are durable guidelines that steer the party for years after the final gavel has been brought down.

Most of the recent party chairpersons, in cooperation with the incumbent president or likely nominee, have tried to orchestrate carefully every minute of the conventions in order to project just the right image to voters. By and large, they have succeeded, though at the price of draining some spontaneity and excitement from the convention process.

From 1974 to 1982 the Democratic Party also held a **midterm convention** (also called a mini-convention). Designed to provide party activists a chance to express themselves on policy and presidential performance (whether the chief executive was a Democrat or a Republican), the midterm convention instead mainly generated worry among the party leadership and elected officials about the factional infighting and ideological posturing that might be on display before a national audience. Even though none of the midterm gatherings was a disaster, none was a roaring success, either. By 1986 the Democrats had decided to avoid potential divisiveness and save the $2 million necessary to hold the convention, and they canceled it.

Midterm convention A national party convention held in nonpresidential congressional election years, for the purposes of rallying the party and adopting new policies.

States and Localities

Although national committee activities of all kinds attract most of the media attention, the party is structurally based not in Washington but in the states and localities. Except for the campaign finance arena, virtually all governmental regulation of political parties is left to the states, for example, and most elected officials give their allegiance to the local party divisions they know best. Most important, the vast majority of party leadership positions are filled at subnational levels.

The pyramidal arrangement of party committees provides for a broad base of support. The smallest voting unit, the precinct, usually takes in a few adjacent neighborhoods and is the fundamental building block of the party. Each of the more than 100,000 precincts in the United States potentially has a committeeman or committeewoman to represent it in each party's councils. The precinct committeepersons are the key foot soldiers of any party, and their efforts are supplemented by party committees above them in the wards, cities, counties, towns, villages, and congressional districts.

The state governing body supervising this collection of local party organizations is usually called the state central (or executive) committee. It comprises representatives from all major geographic units, as determined by and selected under state law. Generally, state parties are free to act within the limits set by their state legislatures without interference from the national party, except in the selection and seating of presidential convention delegates. National Democrats have been particularly inclined to regulate this aspect of party life. With the decline of big-city political machines, few local parties have the clout to object to the national party's dictates. (See "Then and Now: The Political Machine," pp. 366–367).

U.S. Senator Christopher Dodd of Connecticut took over as the general chair of the Democratic National Committee in early 1995. Along with his co-chair, Donald Fowler of South Carolina, Dodd's objective was to reinvigorate the party after its disastrous 1994 election losses.

Informal Groups

The formal structure of party organization is supplemented by numerous official, semi-official, and unaffiliated groups that combine and clash with the parties in countless ways. Both the DNC and RNC have affiliated organizations of state and local party women (The National Federation of Democratic Women and the National Federation of Republican Women). The youth divisions (the Young Democrats of America and the Young Republicans' National Federation) have a generous definition of "young"—up to and including age thirty-five. The state governors in each party have their own party associations, too.

Just outside the party orbit are the supportive interest groups and associations that often provide money, labor, or other forms of assistance to the parties. Labor unions, progressive political action committees (PACs), teachers, African-American and liberal women's groups, and the Americans for Democratic Action are some of the Democratic Party's organizational groups. Business PACs, the Chamber of Commerce of the United States, fundamentalist Christian organizations, and some anti-abortion agencies work closely with the Republicans. Similar party-interest group pairings occur in Britain. Trade unions have aligned themselves with the Labour Party, providing the bulk of the party's contributions, and business has been closely allied with the Conservatives.

Each U.S. party also has several institutionalized sources of policy ideas. Though unconnected to the parties in any official sense, these so-called think tanks (institutional collections of policy-oriented researchers and academics) are quite influential. During the Reagan administration, for instance, the right-wing Heritage Foundation placed many dozens of its conservatives in important governmental positions, and its

THEN AND NOW

The Political Machines

Political machines played an important role in party politics in the United States, especially in the early-mid-twentieth century. In the 1950s and 1960s, for example, Chicago Mayor Richard J. Daley's legendary political machine dominated Chicago politics, controlling judges, politicians, municipal agencies, and the police and fire departments. The force behind the Daley machine was its control of municipal and county elections, in which supporters were rewarded with patronage and other tangible benefits, and opponents were disciplined accordingly. After more than two decades of command, the Daley machine gradually faded with the mayor's death in 1977, decimated by infighting, reformers, the institution of more civil service appointments, and court rulings that struck at the heart of the patronage system.

That all party organizations have gone the way of Chicago's is a commonly held belief, even among political observers. In fact, the weakening of the party organization is unmistakable in many cities and counties, and most county parties have no paid staff, central party headquarters, or even a telephone listing. But recent studies of the 7,300 county-level party organizations in the United States have revealed that many local parties—Democratic as well as Republican—are surprisingly active and have not really become less so over the decades. Some local parties appear to have a life of their own aided by substantial help from the state and (on the Republican side) national committees. These local organizations seem to

To many, Chicago Mayor Richard J. Daley personified old-style machine party politics. While ward politics continues to flourish in many cities, it is being replaced by a more modern (although less personal) style of direct-mail fund raising and issue management.

endure and sometimes prosper despite party reversals at state or national levels. In the most successful cases, this prosperity is due to one of two sources of strength: either a well-nourished grassroots organization fed by patronage or a technologically advanced party with a solid base of ideologically attuned contributors and supporters.

A present-day example of the former, more traditional local organization is the Republican Party of

issue studies on subjects ranging from tax reform to South Africa carried considerable weight with policy makers. The more moderate and bipartisan American Enterprise Institute also supplied the Reagan team with people and ideas. On the Democratic side, liberal think tanks proliferated during the party's Reagan- and Bush-induced exile. More than a half-dozen policy institutes formed after 1980 in an attempt to nurse the Democrats back to political health. The Center for National Policy and the Progressive Policy Institute, to cite two, sponsored conferences and published papers on Democratic policy alternatives.

Nassau County, New York. No doubt Mayor Daley would have found much to like about this rigid and hierarchical machine that controls more than 20,000 jobs and features an elaborate superstructure of ward chairpersons, precinct committee members, and block captains who turn out the vote on Election Day. Originally built on New York City's out-migration of blue-collar Irish and Italian ethnics who wanted to dissociate themselves from the city's liberal politics, the machine now takes great care to recruit young people, in part by distributing plum summer jobs. Many of these youths go on to base their whole careers on service to the party. In the best tradition of machine politics, aspiring office holders are expected to work their way up the ladder slowly, toiling for years in the back rooms and the neighborhoods, delivering votes for the party candidates and dollars for the party war chest.

But the Nassau County machine is not without its problems. Corruption charges against some of its leaders have been proven, and its command of so many patronage positions is under attack. Yet electoral success keeps the organization humming, and it regularly wins a large majority of the area's county, state legislative, and congressional posts. The machine has even produced one of New York's U.S. senators, Alfonse D'Amato. First elected in 1980, D'Amato was a supervisor of Nassau's Hempstead township and a top leader of the party organization prior to his Senate bid. Learning constituency-service politics well in the county machine, he attended assiduously to his state's interests just as he had done for his township, earning a landslide reelection in a 1986 campaign that even included an endorsement from the liberal *New York Times*. In 1992, D'Amato managed to win a narrow reelection that was nonetheless amazing in the face of a Democratic landslide in the state.

If Chicago and Nassau County represent the old-style political machine, then the Waxman-Berman machine in California may suggest the future directions of strong local parties. Named after its founders, liberal California Democratic Congressmen Henry Waxman and Howard L. Berman, this Los Angeles-based machine has built its success on direct mail and new campaign technologies rather than on patronage and ward committee members. In many ways, the Waxman-Berman machine is the polar opposite of the Nassau County organization: informal, candidate (not party) centered, and a creation of California's anti-party environment. Also unlike their Nassau brethren, who virtually ignore national politics and concentrate on local offices, Waxman, Berman, and their allies care little about local politics; most of their energies are devoted to electing congressional candidates and influencing national and international policy.

While the differences between the traditional and modern political machines are substantial, there is one fundamental link between them: they both accumulate power by helping friends gain elective and appointive office. The new technologically advanced model of strong local parties probably has more of a future than the older, ethnically based or patronage-fed machine. Yet the latter should not be dismissed so easily, not only because it has proven hardier in some places than many expected, but also because there is a great deal to be said for such personalized, neighborhood-oriented parties. Indeed, the ideal self-sustaining party might be a carefully crafted combination of modern technology and community service-centered organization.

Finally, there are extraparty organizations that form for a wide variety of purposes, including "reforming" a party or moving it ideologically to the right or left. In New York City, for example, Democratic reform clubs were established in the late 1800s to fight the Tammany Hall machine, the city's dominant Democratic organization at the time. About seventy clubs still prosper by attracting well-educated activists committed to various liberal causes. More recently, both national parties have been favored (or bedeviled) by the formation of new extraparty outfits. The Democrats have been pushed by both halves of the ideological continuum. The Democratic Leadership Council (DLC) was launched in 1985 by moderate-conservative Democrats concerned about what they perceived as the leftward drift of their party and its image as the captive of liberal special-interest groups. It is composed of more than one hundred current and former Democratic office holders (such as Senator Sam Nunn of Georgia and House Minority Leader Richard Gephardt of Missouri). The DLC has not always been popular with the national party leadership, which has sometimes viewed it as a potential rival, but it nurtured and strongly backed Bill Clinton's candidacy in 1992. Several DLC leaders have been appointed to positions in the Clinton administration.

The DLC formed in part to counter a left-leaning force organizing from within the partisan ranks, Jesse Jackson's National Rainbow Coalition. The Coalition is partly a vehicle for Jackson's ambitions. Beyond that, its goals of mass membership, hundreds of state and local charter affiliates, and endorsements of independent candidates when Democratic nominees are found to be "unacceptable" present a challenge to the Democratic Party in the eyes of at least some party officials.

Republicans have their extraparty agents too. The most prominent is GOPAC, the political action committee associated with U.S. House Speaker Newt Gingrich. GOPAC helped dozens of Republican congressional candidates prior to the 1994 elections by training them and their staffs and providing money at critical points in their campaigns. GOPAC and Gingrich were credited with helping to produce the Republican landslide of 1994.

The Party in Government

The structure of political parties reviewed so far has been organizational, self-contained, and apart from governing institutions. Another dimension of party exists—and thrives—*within* government as a critical, essential mechanism of all its branches and layers.

The Congressional Party

In no segment of U.S. government is the party more visible or vital than in the Congress. In this century, the political parties have dramatically increased the sophistication and impact of their internal congressional organizations. Prior to the beginning of every session, each party in both houses of Congress gathers (or "caucuses") separately to select party leaders (House Speaker or minority leader, Senate majority and minority leaders, party whips, and so on) and to arrange for the appointment of members of each chamber's committees. In effect, then, the parties organize and operate the Congress. Their management systems have grown quite elaborate; the web of deputy and assistant whips for House Democrats now extends to about one-fourth of the party's entire membership. Although not invulnerable to pressure from the minority, the majority party in each house generally holds sway, even fixing the size of its majority on all committees—a proportion frequently in excess of the percentage of seats it holds in the house as a whole.

Discipline.   Congressional party leaders have some substantial tools at their disposal to enforce a degree of discipline in their troops. Even though seniority usually determines most committee assignments, an occasional choice plum may be given to the loyal or withheld from the rebellious. A member's bill can be lovingly caressed through the legislative process, or it can be summarily dismissed without so much as a hearing. Pork barrel—government projects yielding rich patronage benefits that sustain many a legislator's electoral survival—may be included or deleted during the appropriations process. Small favors and perquisites (such as the allocation of desirable office space or the scheduling of floor votes for the convenience of a member) can also be useful levers. Then, too, there are the campaign aids at the command of the leadership: money from party sources, endorsements, appearances in the district or at fundraising events, and so on. On rare occasions, the leaders and their allies in the party caucus may even impose sanctions of various sorts (such as the stripping of seniority rights or prized committee berths) in order to punish recalcitrant law makers.[18]

In spite of all these weapons in the leadership's arsenal, the congressional parties lack the cohesion that characterizes parliamentary legislatures. This is not surprising, since the costs of bolting the party are much less in the United States than in, say, Great Britain. A disloyal English member of Parliament might be replaced as a party candidate at the next election; in the United States, it is more likely that the independent-minded member of Congress would be electorally rewarded—hailed as a free spirit, an individual of the people who stood up to the party bosses. Moreover, defections from the ruling party in a parliamentary system bring a threat of the government's collapse and with it early elections under possibly unfavorable conditions. Fixed election dates in the United States mean that the consequences of defection are much less dire. Also, a centralized, unicameral parliament (in which executive and legislative branches are effectively fused) permits relatively easy hierarchical control by party leaders.

There are other limits to coordinated, cohesive party action. For example, the separate executive branch, the bicameral power-sharing, and the extraordinary decentralization of Congress's work all constitute institutional obstacles to effective party action. Finally, party discipline is hurt by the individualistic nature of U.S. politics: campaigns that are candidate-centered rather than party-oriented; diverse electoral constituencies to which members of Congress must understandably be responsive; the largely private system of election financing that indebts legislators to wealthy individuals and nonparty interest groups more than to their parties; and the importance to law makers of attracting the news media's attention—often more easily done by showmanship than by quiet, effective labor within the party system.

Despite all of the barriers to cohesive party action, events occasionally move a party in that direction. One such example occurred in 1994, when most Republican U.S. House candidates signed onto the so-called "Contract with America"—a party platform for Congressional campaigns similar in some respects to a formal presidential platform. The Contract included such popular items as tax relief, term limits for congressmen, and welfare reform, and it became the basis for the House of Representatives' legislative activity in early 1995.

Results.   These are formidable barriers to the operation of responsible, potent legislative parties. Therefore, it is impressive to discover that party labels have consistently been the most powerful predictor of congressional roll-call voting, and in the last few years even more votes have closely followed the partisan divide. While not invariably predictive, as in strong parliamentary systems, a member's party affiliation has proven to be the indicator of his or her votes more than 70 percent of the time in recent years; that is, the average representative or senator sides with his or her party on about 70 percent of the votes that divide a majority of Democrats from a majority of Republicans. In most recent years, more than half of the roll-call votes in the House and Senate also found majorities of Democrats and Republicans on opposite sides.

High levels of party cohesion are especially likely when votes are taken in several areas. The votes that organize the legislative chambers (such as the election of a Speaker), set up the election machinery and campaign laws, and determine the results of disputed elections command nearly unanimous support on behalf of the party's basic interests. Votes involving key parts of the president's program also frequently divide along party lines. Finally, certain policy issues (such as Social Security, welfare programs, and union–management relations), as well as party platform issues that directly and manifestly affect the party's image or its key constituencies, produce substantial party voting.[19]

Until the 1980s there had been a substantial decline in party voting in Congress. At the turn of the century almost three-quarters of all the recorded votes saw a majority of one party voting against a majority of the other party, and astoundingly a third or more of a session's roll calls would pit at least 90 percent of one party against 90 percent or more of the other party. At this time two Speakers of the House (Republicans Thomas B. Reed and Joseph G. Cannon, who in succession controlled the Speakership most of the years between 1889 and 1911) possessed almost dictatorial authority and therefore could enforce strict voting discipline. But a rebellious House drastically curtailed the Speaker's powers between 1909 and 1911. This development, combined with internal GOP strains and splits, reduced party harmony and unity in congressional voting.

Two decades later, when the Democrats of the New Deal coalition held sway, they also had their own fractures and contradictions (African Americans versus whites, Northern liberals versus Southern conservatives, urban versus rural areas, and so forth). These tensions and other anti-party trends discussed earlier in this chapter left party majorities voting with each other on about 60 percent of recorded votes through the latter 1960s and the 1970s. This situation is reflected in Figure 11-3. In 1970, for example, neither the Democrats nor the Republicans were particularly unified; a majority of Democrats in Congress voted together on key votes less than 60 percent of the time, and the same was true for the Republicans.

In the past several years, however, party voting has increased noticeably, as reflected in the widening gap between Democrats and Republicans in Figure 11-3. In 1993, for instance, both the average Democratic member and Republican member voted with his or her party (on votes dividing party majorities) about 88 percent of the time. President Clinton's economic programs in his first year in office clearly polarized the Congress, and the proportion of party voting jumped considerably from the already high (79 percent) level recorded in 1992. Partisanship in 1994 was less evident than in 1993, but still high—83% among Democrats and 82% among Republicans.

There are many reasons for the recent growth of congressional party unity and cohesion. Some are the result of long-term political factors. Both congressional parties, for instance, have gradually become more ideologically homogeneous and internally consistent. Southern Democrats today are more moderate and much closer philosophically to their Northern counterparts than the South's legislative barons of old ever were. Similarly, there are few liberal Republicans left in either chamber of Congress,

FIGURE 11-3

Congressional Party Unity Scores, 1959–1994

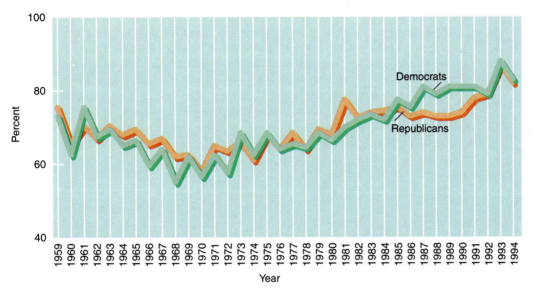

Source: *Congressional Quarterly Almanacs* (Washington: Congressional Quarterly, Inc).

and GOP House members from all regions of the country are—with a few exceptions—moderately to solidly conservative. At the same time, strong two-party competition has come to almost all areas of the nation. The electoral insecurity produced by vigorous competition seems to encourage party unity and cooperation in a legislature (perhaps as a kind of "circling the wagons" effect).[20]

The circumstances of contemporary politics are also producing greater party cohesion. There is renewed satisfaction on the Republican side of the House aisle with that party's return to majority status. The increased militancy of former Minority Whip and now Speaker of the House Newt Gingrich of Georgia has raised the partisan hackles of many Democrats, polarizing the House a bit more along party lines. In fact, Gingrich's Contract with America generated very strong party voting in the House in early 1995; most floor votes found virtually all Republicans supporting the provisions of the Contract, with most Democrats voting in opposition. On the other side of the Capitol, the continuing, close partisan struggle since 1980 over control of the Senate has appeared to increase the party consciousness of both groups of senators.

One of the least recognized but most enduring effects of the Watergate scandal was to stimulate the strengthening of the congressional parties long after Richard M. Nixon had departed the White House. The Watergate-spawned election of seventy-five reform-minded freshman Democrats in 1974 led to a revolt against the seniority system in early 1975. Three unresponsive senior chairmen were deposed, and the power of the committee system was diminished; a crucial barrier to the influence of party thus fell. When a rigid seniority system protected independent-minded members, committee chairs not surprisingly often voted against their party's wishes. After the 1975 display of caucus muscle, however, chairpersons dramatically increased their solidarity with the party majority, scoring even higher than backbenchers (junior members) on party unity scales.[21]

The political party campaign committees have also played a role in the renewed cohesiveness observed within Congress. Each national party committee has been recruiting and training House and Senate candidates as never before, and devising common themes for all nominees in election seasons—work that may help to produce a consensual legislative agenda for each party. The carrot and stick of party money and campaign services, such as media advertising production and polling, are also being used to convert candidates into party team players. Clearly, the more important the party organization can be to a legislator's election and reelection, the more attention a legislator is likely to pay to his or her party.

The Presidential Party

Political parties may be more central to the operation of the legislative branch than the executive branch, but it is the presidential party that captures the public imagination and shapes the electorate's opinion of the two parties. In our very personalized politics, voters' perceptions of the incumbent president and the presidential candidates determine to a large extent how citizens perceive the parties.

A chief executive's successes are his party's successes; the president's failures are borne by the party as much as by the individual. The image projected by a losing presidential candidate is incorporated into the party's contemporary portrait, whether wanted or not. As the highest elected candidate of the national party, the president naturally assumes the role of party leader, as does the White House nominee of the other party (at least during the campaign).

The juggling of contradictory roles is not always easy for a president. Expected to bring the country together as ceremonial chief of state and also to forge a ruling consensus as head of government, the president must also be an effective commander of a sometimes divided party. Along with the inevitable headaches party leadership brings, though, are clear and compelling advantages that accompany it. Foremost among them is a party's ability to mobilize support among voters for a president's program. Also, the executive's legislative agenda might be derailed more quickly without the common tie of party label between the chief executive and many members of Congress; all presidents appeal for some congressional support on the basis of shared party affiliation, and they generally receive it depending on circumstances and their executive skill.

In recent decades, as Figure 11-4 shows, the average legislator of the president's party has backed the chief executive two-thirds to three-quarters of the time, whereas the average member of the opposition has done so only one-third to one-half the time. In 1992, for example, George Bush had little pull among Democrats in the last year of his term: Senate Democrats backed him on only 32 percent of the votes and House Democrats on only 25 percent of the votes. (In fact, in 1992 Bush won just 43 percent of the congressional votes on his program, the lowest support level in the forty-one years *Congressional Quarterly* had compiled the information.) Ronald Reagan fared better, in part because his support among GOP senators was exceptionally high. By contrast, Jimmy Carter and Dwight D. Eisenhower (in his second term) had problems because of relatively little support from their House partisans.

In his first year in office, President Bill Clinton demonstrated exceptionally strong support among his fellow Democrats in Congress. House Democrats backed him 77

FIGURE 11-4

Average Support by Members of Congress on Votes
Related to the President's Program, 1953–1994

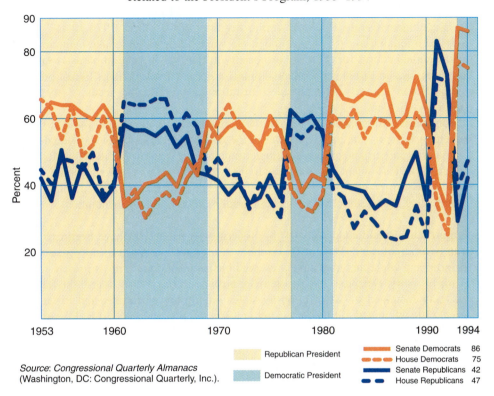

Republican President

Democratic President

Senate Democrats	86
House Democrats	75
Senate Republicans	42
House Republicans	47

Source: Congressional Quarterly Almanacs
(Washington, DC: Congressional Quarterly, Inc.).

percent of the time, and Senate Democrats, an impressive 87 percent. Of course, Republicans were much less accommodating: just 39 percent of the House GOP and 29 percent of the Senate Republicans backed Clinton on average. Overall, though, because Democrats controlled both houses of Congress, Clinton was quite successful, winning 86 percent of the 191 votes on which he had declared a position. That was double George Bush's congressional rating of 1992, and it was the highest presidential percentage since Lyndon Johnson's first full year in office (1964). These general trends continued in Clinton's second year, when he again won 86 percent of the 140 votes on which he had declared a position. With the GOP takeover of Congress in early 1995, however, Clinton's relative honeymoon with Congress came to an end.

These party gifts to the president are reciprocated in other ways. In addition to compiling a record for the party and giving substance to its image, presidents appoint many activists to office, recruit candidates, raise money for the party treasury, campaign extensively for party nominees during election seasons, and occasionally provide some "coattail" help to fellow office seekers who are on the ballot in presidential election years.

Pro-Party Presidents. Some presidents take their party responsibilities more seriously than others. In this century Democrats Woodrow Wilson and Franklin D. Roosevelt were exceptionally party-oriented and dedicated to building their party electorally and governmentally. In his first term, Wilson worked closely with Democratic congressional leaders to fashion a progressive and successful party program, and Roosevelt was responsible for constructing the enduring New Deal coalition for his party and breathing life into a previously moribund Democratic National Committee. Republican Gerald R. Ford, during his brief tenure from 1974 to 1977, also achieved a reputation as a party builder. He was willing to undertake campaign and organizational chores for the GOP (especially in fund raising and in barnstorming for nominees) that most other presidents minimized or shunned. Perhaps Ford's previous role as House minority leader made him more sensitive to the needs of his fellow party office holders.

Managing relations with the legislature is much less problematic in the British parliamentary system. The party in power in the government consists of individuals from the majority in Parliament, who continue to hold their seats in Parliament. Moreover, the life of the Parliament is tied intimately to the life of the government; should the latter fall, the former almost certainly will. This system provides the party in power with a compelling argument to use with recalcitrant partisans in the legislature.

Nonpartisan Presidents. Most U.S. modern chief executives have been cast in an entirely different mold. Dwight D. Eisenhower elevated "nonpartisanship" to a virtual art form, and while this may have preserved his personal popularity, it proved a disaster for his party. Despite a full two-term occupancy of the White House, the Republican Party remained mired in minority status among the electorate, and Eisenhower never really attempted to transfer his high ratings to the party. Lyndon B. Johnson kept the DNC busy with such trivial tasks as answering wedding invitations sent to the First Family. When many of the Democratic senators and representatives elected on his presidential coattails were endangered in the 1966 midterm election, LBJ canceled a major campaign trip on their behalf lest his policies get tied too closely to their possible defeats. Democrats lost forty-seven House seats, three Senate seats, and eight governorships in the 1966 debacle.

In 1972 the late Richard M. Nixon discouraged the GOP from nominating candidates against conservative Southern Democrats in order to improve his own electoral and congressional position, since the grateful unopposed legislators would presumably be less likely to cause Nixon trouble on the campaign trail or in Congress. Nixon also subordinated the party's agenda almost wholly to his own reelection. Shunting aside the Republican National Committee, Nixon formed the Committee to Re-Elect the President, which became known by the acronym, CREEP. So removed were party leaders from the Committee's abuses (see the box on Watergate in Chapter 7) that the Republican Party organization itself escaped blame during the Watergate investigations.

Jimmy Carter also showed little interest in his national party. Elected as an outsider in 1976, Carter and his top aides at first viewed the party as another extension of the Washington establishment they had pledged to ignore. Carter and his DNC chairmen failed to develop the Democratic Party organizationally and financially in order to keep it competitive during a critical period, while the Republicans were undergoing a dramatic revitalization stimulated by their desire to recover from the Watergate scandal. Later, during his fateful 1980 reelection campaign, Carter was properly criticized for diverting DNC personnel and resources to his presidential needs such as travel and Christmas cards rather than permitting them to pursue essential partywide electoral tasks.

Reagan and Bush. Carter's two Republican successors took a very different approach. Ronald Reagan was one of the most party-oriented presidents of recent times.[22] In 1983 and 1984, during his own reelection effort, Reagan made more than two dozen campaign and fund-raising appearances for all branches of the party organization and candidates at every level. More than 300 television endorsements were taped as well, including one for an obscure Honolulu city council contest. Reagan also showed a willingness to get involved in the nitty-gritty of candidate recruitment, frequently calling in strong potential candidates to urge them to run. During the intense and ultimately unsuccessful battle to retain Republican control of the U.S. Senate in 1986, Reagan played the good soldier, visiting twenty-two key states repeatedly and raising $33 million for the party and its candidates. Unlike Eisenhower, Reagan was willing to attempt a popularity transfer to his party and to campaign for Republicans whether or not they were strongly loyal to him personally. Unlike Johnson, Reagan was willing to put his prestige and policies to the test on the campaign trail. Unlike Nixon, Reagan spent time and effort helping underdogs and long-shot candidates, not just likely winners. Unlike Carter, Reagan signed more than seventy fund-raising appeals for party committees and took a personal interest in the further strengthening of the GOP's organizational capacity. George Bush, a former RNC chairman, emulated the Reagan model during his own presidency.

However, neither Reagan nor Bush had long enough coattails to help elect their party's nominees lower down on the ballot. Reagan's initial victory in 1980 was one factor in the election of a Republican Senate, but his landslide reelection in 1984 had, like Nixon's in 1972, almost no impact on his party's congressional representation. And Bush provided no coattails at all to the GOP in 1988. There is little question that the coattail effect—whereby party nominees lower on the ballot can receive additional votes generated by a popular presidential candidate—has diminished sharply compared with a generation ago.[23] Partly, the decreased competitiveness of congressional elections has been produced by artful redistricting and the growing value of incumbency.[24] But voters are also less willing to think and cast ballots in purely partisan terms—a development that limits presidential leadership and hurts party development. (We return to this subject in the next chapter.)

Clinton. Because Bill Clinton won with such a small plurality (43 percent) in 1992, he also produced little coattail for his party's candidates. Like Reagan and Bush, though, he has campaigned vigorously for many Democrats across the country since taking office. Unlike his predecessors, however, Clinton has had little success in transferring popularity. Democrats lost both governor's races in 1993 (Virginia and New Jersey) and a special Senate election in Texas since Clinton won the presidency. Clinton vigorously stumped for New York Mayor David Dinkins as well, but even in that heavily Democratic city, a Republican (Rudolph Guliani) triumphed in November 1993. Then came the Republican deluge in 1994, when the GOP won fifty-two House seats and nine Senate seats in an election widely regarded as a repudiation of Clinton's presidency.

The Parties and the Judiciary

Many Americans view the judiciary as "above politics" and certainly as nonpartisan, and many judges are quick to agree. Yet not only do members of the judiciary sometimes follow the election returns and allow themselves to be influenced by popular

President Clinton campaigned for U.S. Senator Harris Wofford (D-Pa.)
as election day neared in 1994. Despite this effort, Wofford lost his seat to
Republican Rick Santorum.

opinion, but they are also products of their party identification and possess the same partisan perceptual screens as all other politically aware citizens.

Legislators are much more partisan than judges, but it is wrong to assume that judges reach decisions wholly independent of partisan values. First, judges are creatures of the political process, and their posts are considered patronage plums. Judges who are not elected are appointed by presidents or governors for their abilities but also as members of the executive's party and increasingly as representatives of a certain philosophy of or approach to government. In this century, every president has appointed judges overwhelmingly from his own party; Jimmy Carter and Ronald Reagan, for instance, drew 95 percent or more of their judicial choices from their respective parties. Furthermore, Democratic executives are naturally inclined to select for the bench liberal individuals who may be friendly to the welfare state or critical of some business practices. Republican executives generally lean toward conservatives for judicial posts, hoping they will be tough on criminal defendants, anti-abortion, and restrained in the use of court power.

Research has long indicated that party affiliation is in fact a moderately good predictor of judicial decisions, at least in some areas.[25] In other words, party matters in the judiciary just as it does in the other two branches of government, although it certainly matters less on the bench than in the legislature and in the executive.

Many judges appointed to office have had long careers in politics as loyal party workers or legislators. Supreme Court Justice Sandra Day O'Connor, for example, was an active member of the National Republican Women's Club and is a former Republican state legislator. Some jurists are even more overtly political, since they are elected to office. In a majority of states at least some judicial positions are filled by election, and seventeen states hold outright partisan elections, with both parties nominating opposing candidates and running hard-hitting campaigns. In some rural counties across the United States, local judges are not merely partisanly elected figures; they are the key public officials, controlling many patronage jobs and the party machinery itself.

Obviously, therefore, in many places in the United States, judges by necessity and by tradition are not above politics but are in the thick of it. Although election of the judiciary is a questionable practice in light of its specially sanctioned role as impartial arbiter, partisan influence exerted both by jurists' party loyalties and by the appointment (or election) process is useful in retaining some degree of accountability in a branch often accused of being arrogant and aloof.

The Parties and State Governments

Most of the conclusions just discussed about the party's relationship to the legislature, the executive, and the judiciary apply to those branches on the state level as well. The national parties, after all, are organized around state units, and the basic structural arrangement of party and government is much the same in Washington and the state capitals. Remarkably, too, the major national parties are the dominant political forces in all fifty states. This has been true consistently; unlike Great Britain or Canada, the United States has no regional or state parties that displace one or both of the national parties in local contests. Occasionally in U.S. history a third party has proven locally potent, as did Minnesota's Farmer-Labor Party and Wisconsin's Progressives, both of which elected governors and state legislative majorities earlier in this century. But over time, no such party has survived,* and every state's two-party system mirrors national party dualism, at least as far as labels are concerned.

Parties and Governors.   There are some party-oriented differences at the state level, though. Governors in many states tend to possess even greater influence over their parties' organizations and legislators than do presidents. Many governors have many more patronage positions at their command than does a president, and these material rewards and incentives give governors added clout with activists and office holders. In addition, tradition in some states permits the governor to play a role in selecting the legislature's committee chairs and party floor leaders, and some state executives even attend and help direct the party legislative caucuses—activities no president would ever undertake. Moreover, forty-three governors possess a power denied the national executive until 1995—the item veto, which permits the governor to veto single items (such as individual pork barrel projects) in appropriations bills. Whereas many presidents prior to Clinton accepted objectionable measures as part of a bill too urgent or important to be vetoed, a governor could gain enormous leverage with legislators by means of the line-item veto. Thanks to a Republican-sponsored measure in the 104th Congress, the President now has a similar opportunity.

Parties and State Legislatures.   Just as the party relationship between the executive and the legislature tends to be stronger at the state level than in Washington, so also is the party role in the legislature itself more high-profile and effective. Most state legislatures surpass the U.S. Congress in partisan unity and cohesion. Even though fewer

---

Republicans and States' Rights
♦ ♦ ♦

The party names "Democrat" and "Republican" have remained constant since 1860, but the philosophies the names represent have not. The Republican Party first gained power in 1860, determined to preserve the federal Union and to battle those who believed that states had the right to secede. By the New Deal era, though, the GOP had become the advocate of states' rights, and the party's officials often sounded the alarm against federal encroachment on state prerogatives—a policy that continues today. Conversely, the Democratic Party has been transformed from the more conservative and states' rights-oriented party in the 1800s to the more liberal and pro-government party of today.

---

* The Farmer-Labor Party did survive in a sense; having endured a series of defeats, it merged in 1944 with the Democrats, and Democratic candidates still officially bear the standard of the Democratic-Farmer-Labor (DFL) Party. At about the same time, also having suffered severe electoral reversals, the Progressives stopped nominating candidates in Wisconsin. The party's members either returned to the Republican Party, from which it had split early in the century, or became Democrats.

than half of congressional roll calls in the post–World War II era have produced majorities of the two parties on opposite sides, a number of state legislatures (including Massachusetts, New York, Ohio, and Pennsylvania) have achieved party voting levels of 70 percent or better in some years. Not all states display party cohesion of this magnitude, of course. Nebraska has a nonpartisan legislature, elected without party labels on the ballot. In the South, the lack of two-party competition has left essentially one-party legislatures split into factions, regional groupings, or personal cliques. As real interparty competition reaches the legislative level in Southern states, however, party cohesion in the legislatures is likely to increase.

One other party distinction is notable in many state legislatures. Compared with the Congress, state legislative leaders have much more authority and power; this is one reason party unity is higher in the state capitols.[26] The strict seniority system that usually controls committee assignments in Congress is less absolute in most states, and legislative leaders often have considerable discretion in appointing the committee chairs and members. The party caucuses, too, are usually more active and influential in state legislatures than in their Washington counterparts. In some legislatures, the caucuses meet weekly or even daily to work out strategy and count votes, and nearly one-fourth of the caucuses bind all the party members to support the group's decisions on key issues (such as appropriations measures, tax issues, and procedural questions).

Not just the leaders and caucuses but the party organizations as well have more influence over legislators at the state level. State legislators are much more dependent than their congressional counterparts on their state and local parties for election assistance. Whereas members of Congress have large government-provided staffs and lavish perquisites to assist (directly or indirectly) their reelection efforts, state legislative candidates need party workers and, increasingly, the party's financial support and technological resources at election time.

The Modern Transformation of Party Organization

The parties are not just convenient labels for office holders; they are functioning organizations with bureaucracies in virtually every hamlet in the United States. However, the vitality of the organizations varies widely from place to place and from era to era.

Republican Strengths

Until 1992, the modern Republican Party thoroughly outclassed its Democratic rival in almost every category of campaign service and fund raising. There are a number of explanations for the disparity between the two major parties. Until 1980, the Republicans were almost perennially disappointed underdogs, especially in congressional contests; they therefore felt the need to give extra effort. The GOP had the willingness, and enough electoral frustrations, to experiment with new campaign technologies that might hold the key to elusive victories. Also, since Democrats held most of the congressional offices and thus had most of the benefits of incumbency and staff, Republican nominees were forced to rely more on their party to offset built-in Democratic advantages. The party staff, in other words, compensated for the Democratic congressional staff, and perhaps also for organized labor's divisions of election troops, which were usually at the beck and call of Democratic candidates. Then, too, one can argue that the business and middle-class base of the modern GOP has a natural managerial and entrepreneurial flair demonstrated by the party officers drawn from that talented pool of people.

Whatever the causes, the contemporary national Republican Party has organizational prowess unparalleled in American history. In fundraising the Republicans have surpassed the Democrats by large margins in recent election cycles—never by less than two to one and usually by a considerably higher ratio (see Figure 11-5). Democrats must struggle to raise enough money to meet the basic needs of most of their candidates, while, in the words of a past chairman of the Democratic Senatorial Campaign Committee, "The single biggest problem the Republicans have is how to legally spend the money they have."[27]

Most of the Republican money is raised through highly successful mail solicitation. This procedure started in the early 1960s and accelerated in the mid-1970s, when postage and production costs were relatively low. From a base of just 24,000 names in 1975, for example, the national Republican Party has expanded its mailing list of proven donors to several million in the 1990s. Mailings produce about three-quarters of total revenue, and they do so with an average contribution of less than $35. In this fashion, the GOP may have broadened its committed base, because contributing money usually strengthens the tie between a voter and any organization. Most of the rest of the GOP's funds come from donors of larger amounts who secure membership in various Republican contributor groups. For instance, the Republican National Committee designates any $10,000 annual giver an "Eagle."

The Republican cash is used to support a dazzling variety of party activities and campaign services, including the following.

1. **Party Staff.** Several hundred operatives are employed by the national GOP in election years, and even in the off years, many more than one hundred people hold full-time positions. There is great emphasis on field staff—that is, on staff members sent

FIGURE 11-5

Political Party Finances, 1976–1992: Total Receipts.

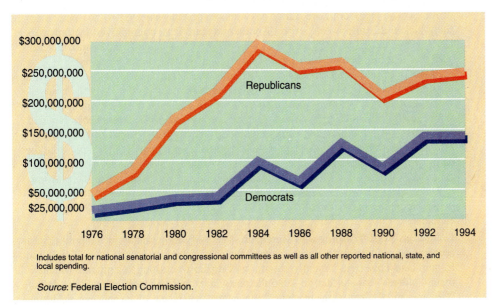

Includes total for national senatorial and congressional committees as well as all other reported national, state, and local spending.

Source: Federal Election Commission.

to and stationed in key districts and states who maintain close communication between local and national party offices.

2. **Voter Contact.** The Republicans frequently conduct massive telephone canvassing operations to identify likely Republican voters and to get them to the polls on Election Day. In 1986, for instance, the GOP used paid callers in seventeen phone centers across the country to reach 10.5 million prospective voters in twenty-five states during the general election campaign. Nearly 5.5 million previously identified Republicans were re-called just before Election Day, many of them hearing an automated message from the president: "This is Ronald Reagan and I want to remind you to go out and vote on Tuesday. . . . " In addition, 12 million pieces of "persuasive" (non-fund-raising) mail were sent to households in the last two weeks of the campaign.

3. **Polling.** The national Republican committees have spent millions of dollars for national, state, and local public opinion surveys, and they have accumulated an enormous storehouse of data on American attitudes generally and on marginal districts in particular. Many of the surveys are provided to GOP nominees at a cut-rate cost. In important contests, the party will frequently commission **tracking polls**—continuous surveys that enable a campaign to chart its daily rise or fall. The information provided in such polls is invaluable in the tense concluding days of an election.

4. **Media Advertising.** The national Republican Party operates a sophisticated in-house media division that specializes in the design and production of television advertisements for party nominees at all levels. About seventy to one hundred candidates are helped in an election cycle. They obtain expert and technically superior media commercials, and the party also offers its wares for a minimal fee, often including the actual buying of time—that is, the purchase of specific time slots on television shows for broadcasting the advertising spots. The candidates thus save the substantial commissions and fees usually charged by independent political consultants for the same services.

Perhaps of greater significance than the production of candidates' commercials is the GOP's advertising for the party itself. Since 1978, the Republicans have aired spots designed to support not specific candidates but the generic party label. Beginning with the 1980 election, the GOP has used institutional advertising to establish basic election themes. "Vote Republican—for a Change" spots attacked the Democratic Congress in 1980. In another spot, House Speaker Thomas P. O'Neill was lampooned by an actor who ignored all warning signs and drove a car until it ran out of fuel. ("The Democrats are out of gas," announced the narrator as the Speaker futilely kicked the automobile's tire.) Another ad starred an unemployed factory worker from Baltimore, a lifelong Democrat, who plaintively asked, "If the Democrats are so good for working people, then how come so many people aren't working?"

In the 1982 midterm congressional elections, the defensive focus of a $15-million institutional campaign was "give the guy [Reagan] a chance" and "stay the course" with the president in the midst of a deep recession and high unemployment. For instance, a white-haired mailman was seen delivering Social Security checks fattened with a cost-of-living increase, reminding elderly voters that Reagan had kept his promise, and urging, "For gosh sake, let's give the guy a chance." The spot, like the earlier 1980 ads, was highly rated by viewers. Although some moderate Republican candidates resisted being tied to Reagan during one of the most unpopular periods of his presidency, pre- and post-election surveys suggested that the GOP-sponsored media campaign had been, on the whole, helpful to the party and to individual candidates.

5. **Campaign Staff Training and Research.** The party trains many of the political volunteers and paid operatives who manage the candidates' campaigns. Since 1976 the Republicans have held annually about a half-dozen week-long "Campaign Management Colleges" for staffers. In 1986 the party launched an ambitious million-dollar "Congressional Campaign Academy" that offers two-week, all-expenses-paid training

Tracking polls Continuous surveys that enable a campaign to chart its daily rise or fall.

courses for prospective campaign managers, finance directors, and press relations staff. Early in each election cycle, the national party staff also prepares voluminous research reports on Democratic opponents, analyzing their public statements, votes, and attendance records. The reports are made available to GOP candidates and their aides.

Results

Despite its financial edge and service sophistication, all is not well in the Republican organization. Success has bred self-satisfaction and complacency, encouraged waste, and led the party to place too much reliance on money and technology, and not enough on the foundation of any party movement—people. As former U.S. Senator Paul Laxalt (R-Nev.), outgoing general chairman of the national Republican Party, was forced to admit in 1987:

> We've got way too much money, we've got way too many political operatives, we've got far too few volunteers. . . . We are substituting contributions and high technology for volunteers in the field. I've gone the sophisticate route, I've gone the television route, and there is no substitute for the volunteer route.[28]

As Laxalt's comments imply, technology and money can probably only add two or three percentage points to a candidate's margin. The rest is determined by the nominee's quality and positions, the general electoral tide prevailing in any given year, and the energy of party troops in the field. Republicans were to learn this anew in 1992, when George Bush's large warchest could not stave off defeat. Similarly, many Democratic U.S. Senators and Representatives outspent their opponents by a wide margin in the 1994 elections, but they tasted defeat nonetheless.

Democratic Party Gains

Parties, like people, change their habits slowly. The Democrats were reluctant to alter a formula that had been a winning combination for decades of New Deal dominance. The prevailing philosophy was, "Let a thousand flowers bloom"; candidates were encouraged to go their own way, to rely on organized labor and other interest groups allied with the Democrats, and to raise their own money, while the national party was kept subservient and weak.

The massive Democratic defeats suffered in 1980 forced a fundamental reevaluation of the party's structure and activities. Democrats, diverse by nature, came to an unaccustomed consensus that the party must change to survive, that it must dampen internal ideological disputes and begin to revitalize its organization. Thus was born the commitment to technological and fund-raising modernization, using the Republican Party's accomplishments as a model, that drives the Democratic Party today.

Comprehension of the task is the first step to realization of the goal, so even after more than a decade, Democrats still trail their competitors by virtually every significant measure of party activity. Yet the figures of party finances (receipts), graphed in Figure 11-6, can be read a different way. While the GOP has consistently maintained an enormous edge, the Democrats have considerably increased their total receipts, now raising many times more than just a few years ago. More importantly, Democrats are contributing much more to their candidates and have actually come close to the GOP's larger total recently (see Figure 11-6). Several national party chairs (Paul Kirk, Ronald

FIGURE 11-6

Political Party Finances, 1976–1992: Total Party Contributions to
and Expenditures for Candidates

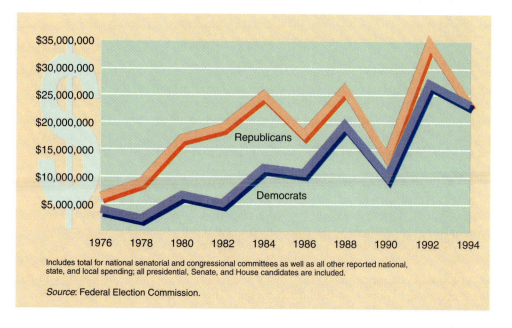

Includes total for national senatorial and congressional committees as well as all other reported national, state, and local spending; all presidential, Senate, and House candidates are included.

Source: Federal Election Commission.

Brown, and David Wilhelm) have aggressively sought more funds from party supporters and friendly interest groups.

With the 1992 elections, the Democrats reaped the benefits of their substantially increased receipts, winning the presidency for the first time in sixteen years. The Clinton administration also redoubled Democratic Party efforts as the midterm elections of 1994 approached, and their exertions again made the Democrats more competitive with the Republicans.

The decision in 1981 to begin a direct-mail program for the national party was a turning point. From a list of only 25,000 donors before the program began, the DNC's support base has grown to 500,000. The Democrats have imitated the Republicans not just in fund raising but also in the uses to which the money is put. For instance, in 1986 the party opened a $3-million media center that produces television and radio spots at rates much lower than those charged by independent political consultants. The Democratic Party is attempting to do more for its candidates and their campaign staffs, too, creating the Democratic National Training Institute in 1985. The Institute coordinates campaign schools for party workers from around the country. "Smart money" is a term used to describe campaign contributions that flow to the candidates and political party expected to win in an election year. With Bill Clinton leading every public opinion poll taken after mid-July during the 1992 campaign, Democrats were flooded with smart money. As Figures 11-5 and 11-6 show, the Democratic Party dramatically increased both its receipts and expenditures in 1992. The Republicans did equally well, but the GOP's well-oiled fund-raising machinery has regularly produced massive war chests. For the Democrats, being financially well-off was a new and delightful experience.

Thus, both party organizations have grown mightier in recent years—at the time when political parties have seemed to be in decline in some other ways. Most important, many voters appear to have less a sense of partisan identification and loyalty today than in generations past. Why is this so?

The Party-in-the-Electorate

A political party is much more than its organizational shell, however dazzling the technologies at its command, and its reach extends well beyond the relative handful of men and women who are the party-in-government. In any democracy, where power is derived directly from the people, the party's real importance and strength must come from the citizenry it attempts to mobilize. The party-in-the-electorate—the mass of potential voters who identify with the Democratic or Republican labels—is the most significant element of the political party, providing the foundation for the organizational and governmental parties. But in some crucial respects, it is the weakest of the components of U.S. political party system. In recent decades fewer citizens have been willing to pledge their fealty to the major parties (see Figure 11-7), and many of those who have declared their loyalties have done so with less intensity. Also, voters of each partisan stripe are increasingly casting ballots for some candidates of the opposing party, and partisan identification is a less reliable indicator of likely voting choices today than it once was.

FIGURE 11-7

Party Identification, 1952–1992

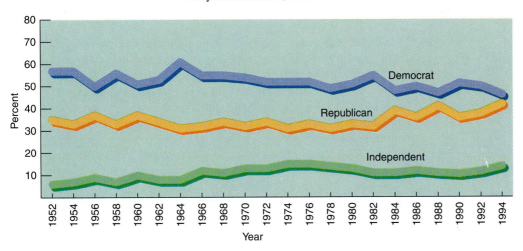

Partisan totals do not add to 100% since "apolitical" and "other" responses were deleted. Sample size from poll to poll varied, from a low of 1,130 to a high of 2,850.

Pure independents only. Independent "leaners" have been added to Democratic and Republican totals.

Source: Center for Political Studies/Survey Research Center of the University of Michigan, made available through the Inter-University Consortium for Political and Social Research. Also, Leon D. Epstein, *Political Parties in the American Mold* (Madison: University of Wisconsin Press, 1986), Table 8.1, p. 257. Data for 1994 provided by the Times-Mirror Center for the People and the Press (as of November 1994).

Party Identification

Most American voters *identify* with a party but do not *belong* to it. There is no universal enrolled party membership; there are no prescribed dues, no formal rules concerning an individual's activities, and no enforceable obligations to the party assumed by the voter. The party has no real control over or even an accurate accounting of its adherents, and the party's voters subscribe to few or none of the commonly accepted tenets of organizational membership, such as regular participation and some measure of responsibility for the group's welfare. Rather, party identification or affiliation is an informal and impressionistic exercise whereby a citizen acquires a party label and accepts its standard as a summary of his or her political views and preferences.

However, just because the acquisition is informal does not mean that it is unimportant. The party label becomes a voter's central political reference symbol and perceptual screen, a prism or filter through which the world of politics and government flows and is interpreted. For many Americans, party identification is a significant aspect of their political personality and a way of defining and explaining themselves to others. The loyalty generated by the label can be as intense as any enjoyed by sports teams and alma maters; in a few areas of the country, "Democrat" and "Republican" are still fighting words.

On the whole, though, Americans regard their partisan affiliation with lesser degrees of enthusiasm, viewing it as a convenience rather than a necessity. The individual identifications are reinforced by the legal institutionalization of the major parties. Because of restrictive ballot laws, campaign finance rules, the powerful inertia of political tradition, and many other factors, voters for all practical purposes are limited to a choice between a Democrat and a Republican in virtually all elections—a situation that naturally encourages the pragmatic choosing up of sides. The party registration process that exists in about half of the states, requiring a voter to state a party preference (or independent status) when registering to vote and thus restricting voter participation in primaries to party registrants, also is an incentive for voters to affiliate themselves with a party.[29]

Sources of Party Identification.   So from where do party loyalties come? Whatever the societal and governmental forces undergirding party identification, the explanations of partisan loyalty at the individual's level are understandably more personal. Not surprisingly, parents are the single greatest influence in establishing a person's first party identification. Politically active parents with the same party loyalty raise children who will be strong party identifiers, while parents without party affiliations or with mixed affiliations produce offspring more likely to be independents (see Chapter 10).

Early socialization is hardly the last step in the acquisition and maintenance of a party identity; marriage and other aspects of adult life can change one's loyalty. So can charismatic political personalities, particularly at the national level (such as Franklin D. Roosevelt and Ronald Reagan), cataclysmic events (the Civil War and the Great Depression are the best examples), and maybe intense social issues (for instance, abortion). Interestingly, social class is not an especially strong indicator of likely partisan choice in the United States, at least in comparison with Western European democracies. Not only are Americans less inclined than Europeans to perceive class distinctions—preferring instead to see themselves and most other people as members of an exceedingly broad middle class—but other factors, including sectionalism and candidate-oriented politics, tend to blur class lines in voting.

Declining Loyalty

Over the past two decades, many political scientists as well as other observers, journalists, and party activists have become increasingly anxious about a perceived decline in partisan identification and loyalty. Many public opinion surveys have shown a significant growth in independents at the expense of the two major parties. The Center for Political Studies/Survey Research Center (CPS/SRC) of the University of Michigan, for instance, has charted the rise of self-described independents from a low of 19 percent in 1958 to a peak of 38 percent twenty years later. Before the 1950s (although the evidence for this research is more circumstantial because of the scarcity of reliable survey research data), there are indications that independents were fewer in number, and party loyalties considerably firmer.

Yet the recent decline of party identification can be exaggerated, and in some ways there has been remarkable stability in the voters' party choices. Over more than thirty years, during vast political, economic, and social upheavals that have changed the face of the nation, the Democratic Party has nearly consistently drawn the support of a small majority and the Republican Party has attracted a share of the electorate in the low to mid-30-percent range. Granted, there have been peaks and valleys for both parties. The Lyndon B. Johnson landslide of 1964 helped Democrats top the 60 percent mark, and the Reagan landslide of 1984 and the post–Persian Gulf war glow of 1991 sent Democratic stock below the majority midpoint. The Barry Goldwater debacle of 1964 and the Watergate disaster of 1974 left the Republicans with less than one-third of the populace; Reagan's reelection brought the GOP to the threshold of 40 percent. Some slight average erosion over time in Democratic Party strength is certainly apparent, as is a small Republican gain during the Reagan and Bush eras. Yet these sorts of gradations are more akin to rolling foothills than towering mountain ranges. The steady nature of modern partisanship goes beyond the fortunes of each party. Identification with the two parties in modern times has never dipped below 83 percent of the U.S. electorate (recorded during the disillusionment spawned by Watergate in 1974) and can usually be found in the mid-to-upper-80-percent range.

When pollsters ask for party identification information, they generally proceed in two stages. First, they inquire whether a respondent considers himself or herself a Democrat, Republican, or independent. Then the party identifiers are asked to categorize themselves as "strong" or "not very strong" supporters, while the independents are pushed to reveal their leanings with a question such as, "Which party do you normally support in elections—the Democrats or the Republicans?" It may be true that some independent respondents are thereby prodded to pick a party under the pressure of the interview situation, regardless of their true feelings. But research has demonstrated that independent "leaners" in fact vote very much like real partisans, in some elections more so than the "not very strong" party identifiers. There is reason to count the independent leaners as closet partisans, though voting behavior is *not* the equivalent of real partisan identification.

In fact, the reluctance of "leaners" to admit their real party identities is in itself worrisome because it reveals a change in attitudes about political parties and their role in our society. Being a socially acceptable, integrated, and contributing member of one's community once almost demanded partisan affiliation; it was a badge of good citizenship, signifying that one was a patriot. Today, the labels are avoided as an offense to a thinking person's individualism, and a vast majority of Americans insist that they vote for "the person, not the party."

The reasons for these anti-party attitudes are not hard to find. The growth of an issue-oriented politics that cuts across party lines for voters who feel intensely about certain policy matters is partly the cause. So, too, is the emphasis on personality politics by the mass media (especially television) and political consultants. Underlying these causes, though, are two much more disturbing and destructive long-term phenomena: the perceived loss of party credibility and the decline of the party's tangible connections to the lives of everyday citizens. Although the underlying partisanship of the American people has not declined significantly since 1952, voter-admitted partisanship has dropped considerably. About three-quarters or more of the electorate volunteered a party choice without prodding from 1952 to 1964, but since 1970 an average of less than two-thirds has been willing to do so. Professed independents (including leaners) have increased from around one-fifth of the electorate in the 1950s to one-third or more in the 1970s and 1980s. Also cause for concern is the marginal decline in strong Democrats and strong Republicans. Strong partisans are a party's backbone, the source of its volunteer force, candidates, and dependable voters. Even a slight shrinkage in these ranks can be troublesome.

Group Affiliations

Just as individuals vary in the *strength* of their partisan choice, so, too, do groups vary in the degree to which they identify with the Democratic Party or the Republican Party. There are enormous variations in party identification from one region or demographic group to another. Consider the following examples:

- Geographic region: While all other geographic regions in the United States are relatively closely contested between the parties, the South still exhibits the Democratic Party affinity cultivated in the last century and hardened in the fires of the Civil War. This is changing rapidly, however; in the 1994 election, Southerners elected Republicans to a majority of the U.S. House seats in the states of the Old Confederacy. In all regions, party strengths vary by locality, with central cities almost everywhere heavily Democratic, the swelling suburbs serving as the main source of GOP partisans, and the small town and rural areas split evenly between the two major parties.

- Gender: Women and men differ somewhat in their partisan choice, a phenomenon called the **gender gap,** which has yawned at least since 1980. Women generally favor the Democratic Party by 5 to 10 percent, and men often give the GOP a similar edge. Besides abortion and women's rights issues, female concerns for peace and social compassion may provide much of the gap's distance. For instance, women are usually much less likely than men to favor American military action, and they are less inclined to support cuts in government funding of social welfare programs.

- Race and ethnicity: Blacks are the most dramatically different population subgroup in party terms. The 80-percent-plus advantage they offer the Democrats dwarfs the edge given to either party by any other segments of the electorate, and their proportion of strong Democrats (about 40 percent) is three times that of whites. Blacks account almost entirely for the slight lead in party affiliation that Democrats normally enjoy over Republicans, since the GOP has recently been able to attract a narrow plurality of whites to its standard. Perhaps as a reflection of the massive party chasm separating blacks and whites, the two races differ greatly on many policy issues, with blacks overwhelmingly on the liberal side and whites closer to the conservative pole. An exception, incidentally, is abortion, where religious beliefs may lead blacks to the more conservative stance. The much smaller population group of Hispanics supplements blacks as a Democratic stalwart; by more than three to one, Hispanics prefer the

Gender gap The difference between the partisan choices of women and men in the aggregate.

The "Gender Gap"

◆ ◆ ◆

Some political scientists argue that the difference in the way men and women vote first emerged in 1920, when newly enfranchised women registered overwhelmingly as Republicans. It was not until the 1980 presidential election, however, that a noticeable and possibly significant *gender gap* emerged. This time, the Democratic Party was the apparent beneficiary. While Ronald Reagan trounced incumbent Democratic President Jimmy Carter, he did so with the votes of only 46 percent of the women, compared to 54 percent of the men.

This gender gap continues to persist at all levels of elections. In 1990, exit polls conducted after seventy races revealed a gender gap in 61 percent of the races analyzed. In 1992, as in previous elections, more voters were women (54 percent) than men (46 percent). Again, more women—47 percent—voted for the Democrat (Clinton) than men—41 percent. Among working women the gap was even more pronounced—51 percent voted for Clinton, only 31 percent for Bush.

In 1994 the gender gap was also decisive. A plurality of women voted for Democratic congressional candidates, but men voted heavily for Republican candidates, thereby generating the GOP tsunami. (The gender gap in 1994 was ten percent, that is, 57 percent of men voted Republican while 47 percent of women did so.)

Democratic label. An exception is the Cuban-American population, whose anti–Fidel Castro tilt leads to Republicanism.

- Age: Young people are once again becoming more Democratic. Polls in 1972 indicated that the group of eighteen- to twenty-four-year-olds, and particularly students, was the only age group to support Democratic presidential nominee George McGovern.* But by the 1990s the eighteen-to-thirty-four-year-old age group was the most Republican of all. Much of this margin was derived from strong student affiliation with the Republicans. Perhaps because of the bad economy from 1990 to 1992, which limited job availability for college graduates, young people swung back to the Democrats in 1992. Bill Clinton ran strongly among eighteen- to twenty-four-year-olds, and they were among his best groups in the electorate.

- Social and economic factors: Some traditional strengths and weaknesses persist for each party by occupation, income, and education. The GOP remains predominant among executives, professionals, and white-collar workers, whereas the Democrats lead substantially among blue-collar workers and the unemployed. Labor union members are also Democratic by two-and-a-half to one. The more conservative, retired population leans Republican. Women who do not work outside the home are less liberal and Democratic than those who do. Occupation, income, and education are closely related, of course, so many of the same partisan patterns can be detected in all three classifications. Democratic support usually drops steadily as one climbs the income scale.

---

* Even the eighteen- to twenty-four-year-olds were very closely split between McGovern and Nixon in most polls, but McGovern ran more than a dozen percentage points better among the very young than among the electorate as a whole.

In order to continue to prosper, the parties must continually renew themselves by attracting young people as voters, campaign workers, and even as candidates.

Similarly, as years of education increase, identification with the Republican Party climbs—until graduate school, when the Democrats rally a bit and only narrowly trail GOP partisans.

- Religion: The party preferences by religion are also traditional, but with modern twists. Protestants—especially Methodists, Presbyterians, and Episcopalians—favor the Republicans by a few percentage points, whereas Catholics and, even more so, Jews are predominantly Democratic in affiliation. Less polarization is apparent all around, though.[30] Democrats have made inroads among many Protestant denominations over the past three decades, and Republicans can now sometimes claim up to 25 percent of the Jewish population and nearly 40 percent of the Catholics. The "born again" Christians, who have received much attention in recent years, are somewhat less Republican than commonly believed. The GOP usually has just about a 10 percent edge among them, primarily because so many blacks classify themselves as members of this group.

- Marital status: Even marital status reveals something about partisan affiliation. People who are married, a traditionally more conservative group, and people who have never married, a segment weighted toward the premarriage young who currently lean toward the Republicans, are closely divided in party loyalty. But the widowed are Democratic in nature, probably because there are many more widows than widowers; in this, the gender gap is again expressing itself. The divorced and the separated, who may be experiencing economic hardship and appear to be more liberal than the married population, are a substantially Democratic group.

- Ideology: Ideologically, there are few surprises. Lending credence to the belief that both parties are now relatively distinct philosophically, liberals are overwhelmingly Democratic and conservatives are staunchly Republican in most surveys and opinion studies.

As party identification has weakened, so, too, has the likelihood that voters will cast ballots predictably and regularly for their party's nominees. (Chapter 12 discusses this in some detail.) In the present day—as at the founding of the republic—Americans are simply not wedded to the idea or the reality of political parties.

The strong party system that prevails in Great Britain provides an illuminating contrast. A large majority of Britons strongly identifies with either the Conservatives (Tories) or the Labour Party, and voters rarely switch allegiances on Election Day. Of course, the British parliamentary system is party-based whereas U.S. politics is far more personality-oriented. In Britain, a voter essentially casts a ballot for a party rather than for a person who will serve as prime minister, who is elected by the parliament, not by the people directly; in the United States, many voters pick presidents more by their characters and personalities than on the basis of their party labels. The British parties also polarize the electorate because of the strong ideological cast of the Tories (free enterprise) and the Labour Party (socialist). While there are clear differences between a liberal Democratic Party and a conservative Republican Party, the American contrast is much less sharp than that of Great Britain. Nevertheless, observers of British politics point to recent developments that echo the U.S. experience. Within the past two decades, a general "dealignment" of the electorate has taken place, with stable party allegiances on the decline. Hardest hit has been the Labour Party, which has apparently lost its grip on traditional sources of support among the working class.

Toward Reform

Taking into account all the aspects and roles of parties that we discuss in this chapter, the following are a list of attributes that healthy political parties should possess and also some suggested means for helping them secure and maintain these attributes.

Philosophical Attributes	Possible Means
Fairness and legitimacy	Promote an open structure within the parties, which invites participation by *all* interested citizens.
Participation	Get local parties more involved in meeting the needs of the community and neighborhoods.
Accountability	Keep parties in closer touch with their constituents.
Incentives	Increase patronage positions so more party workers can be rewarded.

Operational Attributes	
Autonomy	"Deregulate" the parties; allow them to set their own rules as much as possible instead of having government do it for them.
Conflict control	Grant more power to party leaders so that they can control factional conflict within the party.
Broad electoral appeal	Prevent party takeover by ideological extremists.
Policy capacity	Establish an active policy council in each party to work on position papers year round.

Purposeful Attributes

Resources	Broaden the financial base of the parties.
Candidate assistance	Provide services such as television advertisement production and placement to the party's candidates.

The effect of all of these measures would be to strengthen the parties. Stronger parties would help bring apathetic voters back into the fold of electoral participation and would also provide a strong, unifying force to overcome regional disputes in Congress.

Before closing, let's look at one specific reform idea (related to the "participation" attribute above) and see how it would work and why it might be a good idea for political parties. A proposal has been made to build modern grassroots parties on an old-style model by designating party "ombudsmen" in key constituencies and establishing mobile party offices.[31]

Compared to European parties or even U.S. parties of a century ago, U.S. political parties today maintain remarkably little personal contact with average voters. Fully 77 percent of the electorate report that they have never "been helped with a problem by a member of a political party." A party representative would also be among the last individuals a voter in need of assistance would call: When asked, "if you had a problem or concern with the government, whom would you most likely contact for help—an elected official, or an official of your political party, or someone else?", only 14 percent of the respondents named the party.

This result should be no surprise. Party officials and scholars alike have long noted the atrophy of many local party organizations. Even when the local party committee rosters are at full strength, relatively few of the individual committee members tend to be active or particularly well known in the precinct they are charged with organizing. The rewards (social and political) for energetic service are often nonexistent or too small to encourage any other kind of behavior; committee posts are unpaid, and there are generally no sanctions (save expulsion) to be levied for indolence. The result, of course, is that the party becomes invisible in the community; people fail to see a useful connection between their party and their lives. Precisely this disjunction is cited by some scholars to explain the growing estrangement between voter and party.[32]

Both parties, in different ways, have recognized the problem and made some minor efforts to remedy it. The Republicans established the Working Partners program in 1982, which puts local GOP leaders to work on well-publicized community projects. In several hundred successful outings, party activists cleaned up litter in the Grand Canyon; refurbished a facility for autistic adults in Santa Rosa, California; held job fairs (with the NAACP) in Tulsa, Baltimore, and St. Paul; organized food banks for the needy in a half-dozen cities and towns, and sponsored safety fingerprinting of children in San Diego and La Mesa, California. The national Democratic party has no organizational counterpart, but individual local committees, often spurred by Democratic candidates and officeholders, have orchestrated similar events in scattered locales around the country.

Two questions might reasonably be asked: Do people really want the parties to strike out in the direction of community involvement? and, Would it make much difference to voters' partisan loyalties even if the parties did adopt an activist posture? An historical answer is certainly provided by the big-city machines of old; their devotion to their constituents' daily needs made them a dominant element of urban life and was richly rewarded at election time with votes from grateful beneficiaries. Evidence from modern public opinion also supports party activism. In one survey, respondents were asked this question:

> It has been suggested that there be a basic change in the role played by political parties in America. Some people want political parties to be more active as social and civic organizations to help people deal with government and better their communities. Do you believe that such a change should happen, or should political parties stay the way they are now?

A substantial majority (58 percent) favored a shift in party activity. The proposal was popular among all major segments of the population, and it was viewed especially favorably by groups that have sometimes been excluded from the party mainstream (women, blacks, and young people). Interestingly, Americans who live in the sprawling suburbs—the *least* organizable demographic unit, where parties are currently *least* in evidence—were *most* supportive of change, signaling both their desire for visible party assistance and an opening for the parties to appeal to them. Perhaps most important, the idea of a party role change appealed particularly to segments of the electorate who were more alienated from the parties and the political system: the unregistered and those who admitted becoming "less committed" to their political party over the last five years. This finding suggests at least the possibility that the least involved, most party-neutral citizens might establish or strengthen their partisan loyalties if a party tangibly contributed to their lives.

Summary

Political parties are an extra-constitutional invention that has proven essential to the successful organization of U.S. government. Despite the Framers' doubts about "factions," it is difficult to imagine our system without parties. In this chapter we have suggested some of the reasons—as well as reviewed the structure and operation of our political parties. Some of the basic points made here include these:

1. Political parties encompass three separate components: the governmental party comprises the office holders and candidates who run under the party's banner; the organizational party comprises the workers and activists who staff the party's formal organization; the party-in-the-electorate refers to the voters who consider themselves to be allied or associated with the party.

2. The evolution of U.S. political parties has been remarkably smooth, and the stability of the Democratic and Republican groupings—despite name changes—is a wonder considering all the social and political tumult in U.S. history.

3. The U.S. party system is uniquely a two-party system. While brief periods of third-party or independent activism (such as the Perot phenomenon) can prevail, the greatest proportion of all federal, state, and local elections are contests between the Republican and Democratic parties only.

4. Despite their lack of staying power, third parties have a vital role to play in our system, not least forcing the two established parties to adapt to changes in society and to tackle new issues and ideas.

5. Parties perform many functions. They create a community of interest that over time bonds disparate groups. They moderate extreme views into more pragmatic, stable, centrist positions. They offer voters a cue for judgment and allow them to hold politicians responsible for large policy questions. They also serve as incubators for new policy positions by creating national platforms every four years.

6. The basic structure of the major parties is simple and pyramidal. The state and local parties are more important than the national ones, though campaign technologies and fundraising concentrated in Washington are invigorating the national party committees.

7. Even though parties are most visible during their quadrennial national conventions, party activity is vital to the operation of Congress, the presidency, and state governments. The influence of party is even visible in the supposedly above-the-fray judiciary.

8. In recent years, the party-in-the-electorate seems to be declining, insofar as more and more voters prefer to call themselves independent. Moreover, voters have frequently chosen to elect Democratic Congresses and Republican presidents, suggesting that the voters' loyalty to neither party is strong. Nevertheless, party identification remains a critical element of most citizens' personal identity.

9. If political parties are to reverse the decline in voters' loyalty to them, they may have to regenerate grass-roots activities and services to people, rebuilding party strength neighborhood by neighborhood.

Key Terms

political party

party identification

governmental party

organizational party

party-in-the-electorate

direct primary

civil service laws

patronage

spoils system

issue-oriented politics

ticket-split

political consultants

coalition

national party platforms

one-partyism

third-partyism

proportional representation

dualist theory

national convention

midterm convention

tracking polls

gender gap

Suggested Readings

Broder, David S. *The Party's Over.* New York: Harper & Row, 1971.

Epstein, Leon. *Political Parties in the American Mold.* Madison: University of Wisconsin Press, 1986.

Kayden, Xandra, and Eddie Mahe. *The Party Goes On.* New York: Basic Books, 1985.

Key, V. O. Jr. *Politics, Parties, and Pressure Groups,* 5th ed. New York: Thomas Y. Crowell, 1964.

Maisel, L. Sandy, ed. *The Parties Respond.* Boulder, CO: Westview Press, 1990.

Polsby, Nelson W. *Consequences of Party Reform.* New York: Oxford University Press, 1983.

Pomper, Gerald M., ed. *Party Organizations in American Politics.* New York: Praeger, 1984.

Price, David E. *Bringing Back the Parties.* Washington, DC: CQ Press, 1984.

Riordan, William L., ed. *Plunkitt of Tammany Hall.* New York: Dutton, 1963. (First published in 1905.)

Sabato, Larry J. *The Party's Just Begun: Shaping Political Parties for America's Future.* Glenview, IL: Scott, Foresman/Little, Brown, 1988.

Schattschneider, E. E. *Party Government.* New York: Holt, Rinehart and Winston, 1942.

Sorauf, Frank J., and Paul Allen Beck. *Party Politics in America,* 6th ed. Glenview, IL: Scott, Foresman/Little, Brown, 1988.

Sundquist, James L. *Dynamics of the Party System,* rev. ed. Washington, DC: The Brookings Institution, 1983.

Wattenberg, Martin P. *The Decline of American Political Parties, 1952–1988.* Cambridge, MA: Harvard University Press, 1988.

Voting and Elections

THE PURPOSES SERVED BY ELECTIONS

DIFFERENT KINDS OF ELECTIONS

PRESIDENTIAL ELECTIONS

CONGRESSIONAL ELECTIONS

VOTING BEHAVIOR

TOWARD REFORM

Recall for a moment election night, November 3, 1992. A plurality of the voting electorate, simply by casting ballots peacefully across a continent-sized nation, removed from office the most powerful man on earth, commander-in-chief of the world's mightiest armed forces. We take this process for granted, but it is a marvel and a direct result of the Framers' design for the American system.

Despite the noble sentiments expressed in the quotation that opens this chapter, neither Alexander Hamilton nor James Madison desired a pure democracy, believing as they did that "mob rule" was an excess to be avoided at all costs. Nonetheless, they would surely have agreed with the novelist H. G. Wells, who, as noted in Chapter 11, declared an election to be "democracy's ceremonial, its feast, its great function." For it is through free and competitive elections that the consent of the people is obtained and the government gains its democratic legitimacy.

The United States of America is a democrat's paradise in many respects because it probably conducts more elections for more offices more frequently than any nation on earth. Moreover, in recent times the U.S. **electorate**—those citizens eligible to vote— has been the most universal in the country's history; no longer can one's race or sex or creed prevent participation at the ballot box.

But Hamilton's eloquent words in *Federalist No. 22* have been realized only after two centuries of struggle. In Hamilton's time, and long thereafter, women could not vote; slaves could not vote; members of certain religious groups could not vote in some jurisdictions; and people without property were barred from the ballot box in many places. The history of U.S. elections is in part a study of the contrast between Hamilton's high ideals and the harsh reality of a limited suffrage (as the right to vote is called). Although the denial of a basic right to millions of Americans throughout the country's history is a fact, the gradual but steady broadening of the voting franchise is

> **T**he fabric of the American empire ought to rest on the solid basis of THE CONSENT OF THE PEOPLE. The stream of national power ought to flow immediately from that pure, original fountain of legitimate authority.
>
> *Alexander Hamilton*
> *Federalist No. 22*

Both of the chief authors of The Federalist Papers *included passages designed to win over the hearts of the colonists. Here, Hamilton argues eloquently that the consent of the people is the linchpin of democracy. The consent of the people is best reflected in the results of elections at all levels of government.*

Electorate Those citizens eligible to vote.

a triumph for the people whose courage won them a full measure of freedom—and also for the U.S. system, which has repeatedly proven its ability to redeem itself by fulfilling Hamilton's vision.

The challenge of democracy is a challenge not just for the system but for the American people, too. After all the blood spilled and energy expended to expand the suffrage, only a little more than half the potentially eligible voters bother to go to the polls, a statistic we discuss later in the chapter. Also in this chapter we discuss the purposes served by elections, the various kinds of elections held in the United States, and patterns of voting over time. We concentrate in particular on presidential and congressional contests, both of which have rich histories that tell us a great deal about the American people and their changing hopes and needs.

The Purposes Served by Elections

Both the ballot and the bullet are methods of governmental change around the world, and surely the former is preferable to the latter. Although the United States has not escaped the bullet's awful effects, most change has come to this country through the election process. Regular elections guarantee mass political action and enable citizens to influence the actions of their government. Election campaigns may often seem unruly, unending, harsh, and even vicious, but imagine the stark alternatives: violence and social disruption. Societies that cannot vote their leaders out of office are left with little choice other than to force them out by means of strikes, riots, or *coups d'etat*.

Popular election confers on a government the legitimacy that it can achieve no other way. Even many authoritarian and communist systems around the globe recognize this and, from time to time, hold "referenda" to endorse their regimes or one-party elections even though these so-called elections offer no real choice that would ratify their rule. The *symbolism* of elections as mechanisms to legitimize change, then, is important, but so is their practical value. After all, elections are the means to fill public offices and staff the government. The voters' choice of candidates and parties helps to

Democrat Bill Clinton with his running mate Al Gore Jr. (left) and Republican President Bush with Vice President Dan Quayle (right) accept their parties' nominations during the presidential election campaign of 1992.

organize government as well. Because candidates advocate certain policies, elections also involve a choice of platforms and point the society in certain directions on a wide range of issues, from abortion to civil rights to national defense to the environment.

Regular elections also ensure that government is accountable to the people it serves. At fixed intervals the electorate is called on to judge those in power. If the judgment is favorable, and the incumbents are reelected, the office holders may continue their policies with renewed resolve. Should the incumbents be defeated and their challengers elected, however, a change in policies will likely result. Either way, the winners will claim a **mandate** (literally, a command) from the people to carry out their platform.

Sometimes the claim of a mandate is suspect because voters are not so much endorsing one candidate and his or her beliefs as rejecting his or her opponent. Frequently this occurs because the electorate is exercising **retrospective judgment;** that is, voters are rendering judgment on the performance of the party in power. This judgment makes sense because voters can evaluate the record of office holders much better than they can predict the future actions of the out-of-power challengers. Consider for a moment how voters retrospectively judged recent presidential administrations in reaching their ballot decisions:

Mandate A command, indicated by an electorate's votes, for the elected officials to carry out their platforms.

Retrospective judgment A voters evaluation of the performance of the party in power.

- *1968:* No one could know what Richard M. Nixon's promised "secret plan to end the Vietnam War" really was, but the electorate knew that President Lyndon B. Johnson had failed to resolve the conflict. Result: Republican Nixon elected over Johnson's Democratic vice president, Hubert H. Humphrey.
- *1972:* The American people were satisfied with Nixon's stewardship of foreign affairs, especially his good relationship with the Soviet Union, the diplomatic opening of China, and the "Vietnamization" of the war. The Watergate scandal (involving Nixon's coverup of his campaign committee's bugging of the Democrats' national headquarters) was only in its infancy, and the president was rewarded with a forty-nine-state sweep over Democrat George McGovern.

- *1976:* Despite confusion about Jimmy Carter's real philosophy and intentions, the relatively unknown Georgia Democrat was elected president as voters held President Gerald Ford responsible for an economic recession and deplored his pardon of Richard M. Nixon for Watergate crimes.
- *1980:* Burdened by difficult economic times and the Iranian hostage crisis (one year before Election Day, Iranian militants had seized fifty-three Americans, whom they held until January 20, 1981, Inauguration Day), Carter became a one-term president as the electorate rejected the Democrat's perceived weak leadership. At age sixty-nine, Ronald Reagan was not viewed as the ideal replacement by many voters, and neither did a majority agree with some of his conservative principles. But the retrospective judgment on Carter was so harsh that an imperfect alternative was considered preferable to another term of the Democrat.
- *1984:* A strong economic recovery from a midterm recession and an image of strength derived from a defense buildup and a successful military venture in Grenada combined to produce a satisfied electorate and a forty-nine-state landslide reelection for Reagan over Jimmy Carter's vice president, Walter Mondale.
- *1988:* Continued satisfaction with Reagan—a product of strong economic expansion and superpower summitry—produced an electoral endorsement of Reagan's vice president, George Bush. Bush was seen as Reagan's understudy and natural successor; the Democratic nominee, Michael Dukakis, offered too few convincing reasons to alter the voters' considered retrospective judgment.
- *1992:* A prolonged economic recession and weak growth in jobs plus Ross Perot's candidacy that split the Republican base denied a second term to George Bush, despite his many significant triumphs in foreign policy (the Persian Gulf War victory and arms control agreements, for example). In the end, voters preferred to gamble on a little-known governor, Bill Clinton, than order up more of the same by reelecting Bush.

Whether one agrees or disagrees with these election results, there is a rough justice at work here. When parties and presidents please the electorate, they are rewarded; when they preside over hard times, they are punished. A president is usually not responsible for all the good or bad developments that occur on his watch, but the voters nonetheless hold him accountable—not an unreasonable way for citizens to behave in a democracy.

On rare occasions, off-year congressional elections can produce mandates. In 1974 a tidal wave for Democrats produced a mandate to clean up politics after Watergate, while in 1994 Republicans enjoyed a similar wave and claimed a mandate for limiting government.

Different Kinds of Elections

Primary elections Elections in which voters decide which of the candidates within a party will represent the party in the general election.

Closed primary A primary election in which only a party's registered voters are eligible to vote.

Open primary A primary in which party members, independents, and sometimes members of the other party are allowed to vote.

So far we have referred mainly to presidential elections, but in the U.S. system, elections come in many varieties.

Primary Elections

In **primary elections,** voters decide which of the candidates *within* a party will represent the party's ticket in the general elections. The primaries themselves vary in kind. For example, **closed primaries** allow only a party's registered voters to cast a ballot, and **open primaries** allow independents and sometimes members of the other party to

By the end of the 1992 primary season Bill Clinton had secured the nomination of the Democratic Party for president, but polls suggested that he was poorly regarded by the electorate-at-large. In June, he appeared on "The Arsenio Hall Show" in what turned out to be the beginning of a campaign to improve his image.

participate. (Figure 12-1 shows the states with open and closed primaries for state offices. Closed primaries are considered healthier for the party system ballot, because they prevent members of one party from influencing the primaries of the opposition party.) In the **blanket primary,** voters are permitted to vote in either party's primary (but not both) on an office-by-office basis. When none of the candidates in the initial primary secures a majority of the votes, there is a **runoff primary,** a contest between the two candidates with the greatest number of votes. The **white primary,** in which all nonwhite voters were systematically excluded from voting, is no longer in existence. White primaries ended when the Supreme Court ruled in *Smith* v. *Allwright* 321 U.S. 649 (1944) that they violated the Fifteenth Amendment to the Constitution.

Blanket primary A primary in which voters may cast ballots in either party's primary (but not both) on an office-by-office basis.

Runoff primary A second primary election between the two candidates receiving the greatest number of votes in the first primary.

White primary A primary in which nonwhite voters are systematically denied participation (no longer practiced).

General elections Elections in which voters decide which candidates will actually fill elective public offices.

General Elections

Once the party candidates for various offices are chosen, **general elections** are held. In the general election, voters decide which candidates will actually fill the nation's elective public offices. These elections are held at many levels, including municipal, county, state, and national. While primaries are contests between the candidates *within* each party, general elections are contests between the candidates of *opposing* parties.

General elections come in many varieties because Americans perceive the various offices as substantially different from one another. In sizing up presidential candidates, voters look for leadership and character, and they base their judgments partly on foreign policy and defense issues that do not arise in state and local elections. Leadership qualities are vital for gubernatorial and mayoral candidates, as are the nuts-and-bolts issues (such as taxes, schools, and roads) that dominate the concerns of state and local governments. Citizens often choose their congressional representatives very differently than they select presidents. Knowing much less about the candidates, people will sometimes base a vote on simple name identification and visibility. This way of deciding one's vote obviously helps incumbents and therefore to some degree explains the high reelection rates of incumbent U.S. representatives: Since World War II, 92

FIGURE 12-1

Open and Closed Primaries for State Offices*

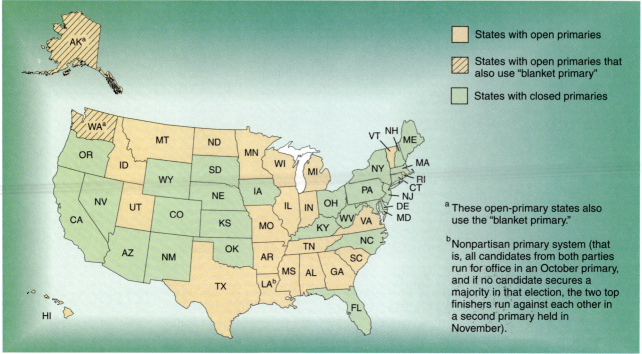

Legend:
- States with open primaries
- States with open primaries that also use "blanket primary"
- States with closed primaries

[a] These open-primary states also use the "blanket primary."

[b] Nonpartisan primary system (that is, all candidates from both parties run for office in an October primary, and if no candidate secures a majority in that election, the two top finishers run against each other in a second primary held in November).

* Many states employ the caucus method of nomination rather than a primary for *presidential delegate* selection.

percent of all U.S. House members seeking another term have won, and in several recent election years the proportion has been above 95 percent.

Initiative, Referendum, and Recall

Three other types of elections are the initiative, the referendum (plural, referenda), and the recall. Used in about twenty states, initiatives and referenda involve voting on *issues* (as opposed to voting for candidates). An initiative is a process that allows citizens to propose legislation and submit it to the state electorate for popular vote, as long as they have a certain number of signatures on petitions supporting the proposal. A referendum is a procedure whereby the state legislature submits proposed legislation to the state's voters for approval. Although both of these electoral devices provide for more direct democracy, they are not problem-free. In the 1990 elections, for instance, California had so many referenda and initiatives on its ballot that the state printed a lengthy two-volume guide in an attempt to explain them all to voters. Despite this, many Californians complained that it was virtually impossible for even a reasonably informed citizen to vote intelligently on so many issues.

The third type of election (or "de-election") found in many states is the recall, whereby an incumbent can be removed from office by popular vote. Recall elections are very rare, and sometimes they are thwarted by the official's resignation or impeachment prior to the vote. For example, Arizona Governor Evan Mecham was impeached and ousted in 1988 by the state legislature for mishandling campaign finances (among other offenses) just a few weeks before a recall election had been scheduled.

British election varieties pale in comparison. In Great Britain, one encounters national elections to the House of Commons, which must be called sometime during the five-year life of a Parliament; local elections, which are held every three years; elections to the European Parliament, which occur at five-year intervals; and three instances of national referenda.

Presidential Elections

Variety aside, no U.S. election can compare to the presidential contest. This spectacle, held every four years, brings together all the elements of politics and attracts the most ambitious and energetic politicians to the national stage. The election itself is a marathon—not a single election but a collection of fifty separate state elections in each party, held over a six-month period, to pick convention delegates. The election of delegates is followed in midsummer by the parties' grand national conventions and then by a final set of fifty separate state elections all held on the Tuesday after the first Monday in November. This lengthy process exhausts candidates and voters alike, but it allows the diversity of the United States to be displayed in ways a shorter, more homogeneous presidential election process could not. Every state has its moment in the sun, every local and regional problem a chance to be aired, every candidate an opportunity to break away from the pack.

The state party organizations use a number of methods to elect national convention delegates. There are six basic systems of delegate selection.

1. *Winner-take-all:* Under this system, the candidate who wins the most votes in a state secures all of that state's delegates. The Democrats moved away from this mode of delegate selection in 1976 and no longer permit its use because of the arguable unfairness to all candidates except the primary winner. Republicans do *not* prohibit winner-take-all contests, thus enabling a GOP candidate to amass a majority of delegates more quickly. This approach can give the GOP candidate a head start in planning for the general election.

2. *Proportional representation:* Under this system, candidates who secure a threshold percentage of votes (usually around 15 percent) are awarded delegates in proportion to the number of popular votes won. This system is now strongly favored by the Democrats and is used in many states' Democratic primaries. Although proportional representation is probably the most fair way of allocating delegates to candidates, its downfall is that it renders majorities of delegates more difficult to accumulate—and thus it can lengthen the contest for the nomination.

3. *Proportional representation with bonus delegates:* This system also awards delegates to candidates in proportion to the popular vote won and then gives one bonus delegate to the winner of each district. The appeal of this system is that it is a compromise between pure proportional representation and the winner-take-all method.

4. *Beauty contest with separate delegate selection:* The results of this type of primary have no bearing on actual delegate selection, which usually takes place in later conventions. The "beauty contest" serves as an indication of popular sentiment for the conventions to consider as they choose the actual delegates.

California Initiatives
♦ ♦ ♦

As the most populous state and a political powerhouse, California leads the nation in many ways, not least through its initiative process. (See text for definition of initiative.) In the late 1970s the California tax revolt was sparked by the success of Proposition 13, a ballot initiative to cut property taxes that passed easily.

Another initiative in 1994 to limit government services available to illegal aliens generated a national debate about the rights of illegals. The measure—Proposition 187—passed with almost 60 percent of the vote, and the conservative voter turnout that it spurred also helped to reelect the Proposition's chief booster, Republican Governor Pete Wilson.

Yet another controversial ballot initiative is scheduled for the 1996 California ballot. This one concerns affirmative action, which its sponsors want to abolish. (Affirmative action programs are explained in Chapter Five, pp. 155–157.) Whatever happens at the polls, California will again be at the forefront of the national discourse.

California's proposition 187 would have made it a crime to provide education, health care, or other services to illegal aliens.

5. *Delegate selection with no beauty contest:* Under this system the primary election chooses delegates to the national conventions who are not linked on the ballot to specific presidential contenders. Well-known names and party-endorsed delegates are often favored under this system.

6. *The caucus:* The caucus is the oldest, most party-oriented method of choosing delegates to the national conventions. Traditionally, the caucus was a closed meeting of party members in each state that selected the party's choice for presidential candidate. In the late nineteenth and early twentieth centuries, however, these caucuses came to be viewed by many people as elitist and anti-democratic, and reformers succeeded in replacing them with direct primaries in most states. While there are still presidential nominating caucuses today, as in Iowa, they are now more open and attract a wider range of the party's membership.

Primaries Versus Caucuses

The mix of preconvention contests has changed over the years, with the most pronounced trend being the shift to primaries: Only seventeen states held presidential primaries in 1968, compared with thirty-eight in 1992. The increase in the number of primaries is supported by some people who claim that this type of election is more democratic. The primaries are open not only to party activists, but also to anyone, wealthy or poor, urban or rural, Northern or Southern, who wants to vote. Theoretically, then, representatives of all these groups have a chance of winning the presidency. Related to this idea, advocates argue that presidential primaries are the most representative means by which to nominate presidential candidates. They are a barometer of a candidate's popularity with the party rank and file. Finally, the proponents of presidential primaries claim that they constitute a rigorous test for the candidates, a chance to display under pressure some of the skills needed to be a successful president.

Critics of presidential primaries, however, see the situation somewhat differently. First, they argue, although it may be true that primaries attract more participants than do caucuses, this quantity is more than matched by the quality of caucus participation. Compared with the unenlightening minutes spent at the primary polls, caucus attendees spend several hours learning about politics and the party, listening to speeches by candidates or their representatives, and taking cues from party leaders and elected officials. Moreover, voters may not know very much about any of the field of candidates in a primary, or they may be excessively swayed by popularity polls, television ads, and other media presentations, such as newspaper and magazine coverage.

Critics also argue that the scheduling of primaries unfairly affects their outcomes. For example, the earliest primary is in the small, atypical state of New Hampshire, which is heavily white and conservative, and it receives much more media coverage than warranted simply because it is first. Such excessive coverage undoubtedly skews the picture for more populous states that hold their primaries later. The critics also argue that the qualities tested by the primary system are by no means a complete list of those a president needs to be successful. For instance, skill at playing the media game is by itself no guarantee of an effective presidency. Similarly, the exhausting schedule of the primaries may be a better test of a candidate's stamina than of his or her brain power.

The primary proponents have obviously had the better of the arguments so far, though the debate continues, as do efforts to experiment with the schedule of primaries. From time to time, proposals are made for **regional primaries.** Under this sys-

Regional primaries A proposed system in which the country would be divided into five or six geographic areas and all states in each region would hold their presidential primary elections on the same day.

tem, the nation would be divided into five or six geographic regions (such as the South or the Midwest). All the states in each region would hold their primary elections on the same day, with perhaps one regional election day per month from February through June of presidential election years. This change would certainly cut down on candidate wear and tear. Moreover, candidates would be inspired to focus more on regional issues. On the other hand, regional primaries would probably cost candidates at least as much as the state-by-state system, and the system might needlessly amplify the differences and create divisive rifts among the nation's regions.

Occasionally a regional plan is adopted. In 1988, for instance, fourteen Southern and border South states joined together to hold simultaneous primaries on "Super Tuesday" (March 8) in order to maximize the South's impact on presidential politics. This was an attempt by conservative Democrats to influence the choice of the party nominee. Their effort failed, however, since the two biggest winners of Super Tuesday were liberals Jesse Jackson (who won six Southern states) and Michael Dukakis, who carried the mega-states of Texas and Florida. This outcome occurred because, in general, the kinds of citizens who vote in Democratic primaries in the South are not greatly different from those who cast ballots in Northern Democratic primaries—most tend toward the liberal side of the ideological spectrum.

The primary schedule has also been altered by a process called frontloading, the tendency of states to choose an early date on the primary calendar. Fully half or more of all the delegates to both party conventions are now chosen before the end of April. This trend is hardly surprising given the added press emphasis on the first contests and the voters' desire to cast their ballots before the competition is decided. Ever since 1976, when the then-unknown Jimmy Carter scored an upset win in the Iowa caucuses, Iowa's first-in-the-nation delegate selection in February has drawn enormous attention. So has the first primary state, New Hampshire, which holds its election shortly after the Iowa caucuses. In fact, except for 1992, the New Hampshire primary has the distinction of having voted for the eventual winner of the presidency in every election since 1952. Despite this record, the focus on early contests, coupled with frontloading, can result in a party's being saddled with a nominee too quickly, before press scrutiny and voter reflection are given enough time to separate the wheat from the chaff.

Kansas U.S. Senator Robert Dole, the Senate's Majority Leader, began campaigning for president early in 1995. Despite his defeats in two earlier presidential nominating contests (1980 and 1988), Dole was considered the frontrunner for the 1996 presidential ticket.

The Party Conventions

The seemingly endless nomination battle does have a conclusion: the national party convention held in the summer of presidential election years. The out-of-power party traditionally holds its convention first, in late July, followed by the party holding the White House in mid-August. Preempting some of prime-time television for four nights, these remarkable conclaves are difficult for the public to ignore; indeed, they are pivotal events in shaping the voters' perceptions of the candidates.

Yet the conventions once were much more: They were deliberative bodies that made actual decisions, where party leaders held sway and deals were sometimes cut in "smoke-filled rooms" to deliver nominations to little-known contenders (called "dark horses"—see "Then and Now: Dark Horses Versus Worn-out Horses," pp. 404–405). But this era pre-dated the modern emphasis on reform, primaries, and proportional representation, all of which have combined to make conventions mere ratifying agencies for pre-selected nominees.

In the 1830s the national nominating convention replaced the congressional caucus (an organization of all the party's members of Congress) as the means for selecting the

In 1836, Martin Van Buren became the first nonincumbent candidate nominated by a major party convention to win the presidency. Previously a loyal vice president to Andrew Jackson (and the last sitting vice president to win the presidency before George Bush in 1988), Van Buren proceeded to solidify the Democrats' party politics through patronage and active leadership. It is interesting that, just as Bush lost his 1992 reelection bid because of a rocky economy, so too did Van Buren fail in his 1840 race for a second term.

presidential ticket. The national convention consists of a delegation from each state. The delegation, whose size is determined by the national party, includes leaders from the state's various localities. Consequently, the nominee of the convention is, in effect, the choice of a congregation of state and local parties. Unlike the congressional caucus system, the convention is compatible with the federal separation of powers and provides for the broad participation of party members. In addition to selecting the party's presidential ticket, the convention drafts the party's platform (see Chapter 11) and establishes party rules and procedures.

The first national convention was held in 1831 by the Anti-Masonic Party. In 1832 Andrew Jackson's nomination for reelection was ratified by the first Democratic National Convention. Just four years later, in 1836, Martin Van Buren became the first non-incumbent candidate nominated by a major party convention (the Democrats) to win the presidency.

From the 1830s to the mid–twentieth century, the national conventions remained primarily under the control of the important state and local party leaders—the so-called bosses or kingmakers—who would bargain within a splintered, decentralized party. (See "Then and Now: Dark Horses Versus Worn-out Horses," pp. 404–405.) During these years state delegations in the convention consisted mostly of **uncommitted delegates** (that is, delegates who had not pledged to support any particular candidate). These delegates were selected by party leaders, a process that enabled the

Uncommitted delegates Delegates to a party convention whose support prior to the convention is not pledged to a particular candidate.

leaders to broker agreements with prominent national candidates. Under this system a state party leader could exchange delegation support for valuable political plums—for instance, a Cabinet position or even the vice presidency—for an important state political figure.

The convention today, however, is fundamentally different. First, its importance as a party conclave, at which compromises on party leadership and policies can be worked out, has diminished. Second, although the convention still formally selects the presidential ticket, most nominations are settled well in advance. New preconvention political processes have lessened the role of the convention in three areas.

1. *Delegate selection.* The selection of delegates to the conventions is no longer the function of party leaders but of primary elections and grassroots caucuses. Moreover, recent reforms, especially by the Democratic Party, have generally weakened any remaining control by local party leaders over delegates. A prime example of such reform is the Democrats' abolition of the **unit rule,** a traditional party practice under which the majority of a state delegation (say, twenty-six of fifty delegates) could force the minority to vote for its candidate. Another new Democratic Party rule decrees that a state's delegates be chosen in proportion to the votes cast in its primary or caucus (so that, for example, a candidate who receives 30 percent of the vote gains about 30 percent of the convention delegates). This change has had the effect of requiring delegates to indicate their presidential preference at each stage of the selection process. Consequently, the majority of state delegates now come to the convention already committed to a candidate. Again, this diminishes the discretionary role of the convention and the party leaders' capacity to bargain.

    In sum, the many complex changes in the rules of delegate selection have contributed to the loss of decision-making powers by the convention. And even though many of these changes were initiated by the Democratic Party, the Republicans were carried along as many Democrat-controlled state legislatures enacted the reforms as state laws. There have been new rules to counteract some of these changes, however. For instance, since 1984 the number of delegate slots reserved for elected Democratic Party officials—called **superdelegates**—has been increased, so that all Democratic governors and 80 percent of the congressional Democrats among others are now included as voting delegates at the convention.

2. *National candidates and issues.* The political perceptions and loyalties of voters are now influenced largely by national candidates and issues, a factor that has undoubtedly served to diminish the power of state and local party leaders at the convention. The national candidates have usurped the autonomy of state party leaders with their preconvention ability to garner delegate support. And issues, increasingly national in scope, are significantly more important to the new, issue-oriented party activists than to the party professionals, who, prior to the late 1960s, had a monopoly on the management of party affairs.

3. *The news media.* The mass media have helped to transform the national conventions into political extravaganzas for the television audience's consumption. They have also helped to preempt the convention, by keeping count of the delegates committed to the candidates; as a result, the delegates and even the candidates now have much more information about nomination politics well before the convention. From the strategies of candidates to the commitments of individual delegates, the media cover it all. Even the bargaining within key party committees—formerly done in secret—is now subject to some public scrutiny, thanks to open meetings. The business of the convention has been irrevocably shaped to accommodate television: Important roles are now assigned to attractive speakers, and most crucial party affairs are saved for prime-time viewing hours.

Unit rule A traditional party practice under which the majority of a state delegation can force the minority to vote for its candidate.

Superdelegates Delegate slots to the Democratic Party's national convention that are reserved for elected party officials.

Extensive media coverage of the convention has its pros and cons. On the one hand, such exposure helps the party launch its presidential campaign with fanfare. On the other hand, it can expose rifts within a party, as happened in 1968 at the Democratic convention in Chicago. Dissension was obvious when "hawks," supporting the Vietnam war and President Lyndon B. Johnson, clashed with the antiwar "doves" both on the convention floor and in street demonstrations around the convention hall. Whatever

THEN AND NOW

Dark Horses Versus Worn-out Horses

The national party convention of the present day is a different animal from that of the past. No longer is it a deliberative forum for choosing the party presidential nominee; rather, the convention now merely ratifies the choices of the preconvention state caucuses and primaries. A look at the Republican and Democratic Party conventions sixty years apart—in 1920 and 1980—illuminates one key contrast between the old-style and new-style conventions: the absence of dark horses—relatively unknown candidates who emerge at the convention and occasionally win a nomination as a compromise choice in order to break a deadlock.

The 1920 Republican convention featured a rift in the party. On one side was the party's old presidential faction, moderate and internationalist, with Abraham Lincoln and Theodore Roosevelt serving as its models. On the other side stood the more conservative wing of the party, with Senator Henry Cabot Lodge of Massachusetts at the helm and including most if not all of Capitol Hill's GOP leadership.

The "presidential" party during those days usually exerted more influence in presidential nominations than did the congressional party. But this changed in 1920 because Lodge's congressional party had garnered more power and influence during the latter part of Democratic President Woodrow Wilson's White House tenure (1913–21), when Wilson was seriously ill and his policies were under attack. Could the two wings of the party compromise on a presidential candidate for 1920? Any such compromise would undoubtedly be difficult to come by because most potential candidates were aligned firmly with one wing of the party or the other.

Senator Warren G. Harding of Ohio was one possible compromise candidate. A small-town politician and onetime editor of a staunchly Republican Ohio newspaper, Harding had a reputation in the Senate based primarily on his ability to win allies in all factions of the Republican Party. But Harding's chances appeared bleak at the outset of the convention, and after the first ballot, he was considerably behind a number of other Republican hopefuls. Yet, several frontrunners continued to deadlock in ballot after ballot, testing the patience of the delegates, who were baking in the hot Chicago summer.

The weather, combined with the seemingly unresolvable convention impasse, spurred a group of influential Senate leaders to meet at a nearby hotel room to attempt to hammer out a compromise—the classic gathering of party leaders behind the closed doors of a smoke-filled room. At the meeting, Harding's name continued to be floated. Although most of the party leaders questioned the Ohioan's convictions and leadership abilities, he did have some attractive qualities: He was handsome (it was said that Harding "looked like a president"), he hailed from a politically important state, and he could be expected to work with leaders of both party factions. The GOP kingmakers therefore decided to test the waters with Harding but agreed to reconvene later in the more likely event that the delegates rejected him. Harding soon went to work to ensure that no new meeting would be needed, however; he campaigned vigorously for his candidacy throughout the evening, roaming the halls and trying to convince any delegate he could find of his credibility as a candidate.

the case, it is obvious that saturation media coverage of pre-election events has led to the public's loss of anticipation and exhilaration about convention events.

Some reformers have spoken of replacing the conventions with national direct primaries, but it is unlikely that the parties would agree to this. Although its role in nominating the presidential ticket has often been reduced to formality, the convention is still a valuable political institution. After all, it is the only real arena where the national

The deadlock at the convention continued for a few more ballots, but the frazzled delegates gradually realized that Harding perhaps was the only candidate with the potential to secure a majority. This realization sent frontrunners scurrying around the convention to build a coalition to stop Harding. They failed, however, and dark-horse candidate Harding—on the tenth ballot—secured enough votes to win the nomination.

The Democrats also needed a candidate to unite the party in 1920, one who could emphasize Wilson's successes yet downplay his failures. After thirty-eight ballots at the Democratic National Convention, no majority candidate had yet emerged, instilling in Wilson a hope that the party might again turn to him as the nominee, despite his deteriorated physical condition. It was one thing for the Democrats to remain loyal to Wilson—which they did by endorsing his policies and paying him homage in the party platform—and another for the party to nominate him for a third term. A return to Wilson was ultimately unnecessary, as Ohio Governor James M. Cox finally secured the nomination on the forty-fourth ballot.

Conditions are very different today. Nominations are no longer decided in smoke-filled back rooms at the conventions; instead, the critical moments occur well beforehand in the highly visible primary-and-caucus obstacle course that creates not dark horses but worn-out horses by convention time. In 1980, for example, many Democrats were dissatisfied with the Carter presidency. The situation was so dismal for the incumbent president that a strong nomination challenge came from a prominent fellow Democrat, Senator Edward M. Kennedy of Massachusetts. At first, the polls were encouraging for Kennedy—he enjoyed a two-to-one margin over Carter in the summer of 1979. But the Iran hostage crisis—the seizing by Iranian militants of more than fifty Americans from the U.S. embassy in Tehran—led to a sharp rise in public support for Carter,

ultimately giving him a decisive margin over Kennedy in the vital early contests. Despite the initial strong challenge from Kennedy and the party's dissatisfaction with Carter's presidency, the incumbent's nomination was secured by April 1980, before the primaries had ended and four months before the Democratic convention opened. Even with a deep fissure in the Democratic Party, no dark-horse candidate emerged because most delegates arrived at the convention already bound by the rules of the party to either Carter or Kennedy.

No dark-horse candidate emerged in the Republican field in 1980, either. The most well-known of the Republicans was a former movie actor and California governor, Ronald Reagan, sixty-nine years old and a conservative who appealed to the right wing of the party. Moderate U.S. Senate Minority Leader Howard Baker of Tennessee and Senator Robert Dole of Kansas were both in the running, as were former Texas Governor John Connally, Representative John Anderson of Illinois (who would later declare himself an independent candidate for president), and George Bush, a former member of Congress from Texas and U.S. ambassador to China. Though Bush won the Iowa precinct caucuses (the first major contest in 1980), Reagan won handily in the next big challenge, New Hampshire, securing almost twice Bush's vote. Like the Democratic nomination, the Republican contest was settled four months before the party convention, and only the brokering over Reagan's choice of a vice-presidential running mate was left to generate excitement at the convention.

The 1980 conventions are typical of those in the modern era, where presidential candidates secure victory by appealing directly to the people, not the party leaders. For better or worse, the deliberative conventions at which dark-horse candidates flourished, such as those of 1920, are probably consigned to the American political past.

The Texas delegation to the 1992 Republican convention announces the votes that clinched the nomination of President Bush for a second term.

Women as Delegates
❖ ❖ ❖

Since 1980 Democratic Party rules have required that women comprise 50 percent of the delegates to its national convention. The Republican Party has no similar quotas. Nevertheless, both parties have tried to increase the role of women at the convention. Some "firsts" for women at conventions include:

1876 First women to address a national convention

1890 First women delegates to conventions of both parties

1940 First woman to nominate a presidential candidate

1951 First woman asked to chair a national party

1972 First woman keynote speaker

1984 First major party woman nominated for vice president (Democrat Geraldine Ferraro)

Source: Center for the Study of American Women in Politics.

political parties can command a nearly universal audience while they celebrate past achievements and project their hopes for the future.

Who Are the Delegates? In one sense, party conventions are microcosms of the United States: every state, most localities, and all races and creeds find some representation there. Yet delegates are an unusual and unrepresentative collection of people in many other ways. It is not just their exceptionally keen interest in politics that distinguishes delegates. These activists also are ideologically more pure and financially better off than most Americans.

In 1992, for example, both parties drew their delegates from an elite group that had income and educational levels far above the average American's. The distinctiveness of each party was also apparent. Democratic delegates tended to be younger and were more likely to be African American, female, divorced or single, and a member of a labor union. Republicans drew their delegates more heavily from people over forty-five years old, whites, married men, and Protestants. GOP conventioneers were also more likely to be elected or appointed officials and to have attended previous party conventions.

The contrast in the two parties' delegations is no accident; it reflects not only the differences in the party constituencies but also conscious decisions made by party leaders. After the tumultuous 1968 Democratic National Convention (which, as noted, was torn by dissent over the Vietnam War), Democrats formed the McGovern-Fraser Commission (named for Senator George McGovern and Representative Donald Fraser) to examine the condition of the party and to propose changes in its structure. As a direct consequence of the commission's work, the 1972 convention was the most broadly representative ever of women, African Americans, and young people, because the party required these groups to be included in state delegations in rough proportion to their numbers in the population of each state. (State delegations failing this test were not seated.) This new mandate was very controversial, and it has since been watered down considerably. Nonetheless, women and blacks are still more fully represented at Democratic conventions (as Table 12.1 shows) than at Republican conventions. GOP leaders have placed much less emphasis on proportional representation, and instead of procedural reforms, Republicans have concentrated on strengthening their state organiza-

| **Table 12.1** ♦ **A Comparison of Delegates to the 1992 Presidential Nominating Conventions[a]** |

	DEMOCRATIC DELEGATES	REPUBLICAN DELEGATES	ALL VOTERS IN NOV. 1992 PRESIDENTIAL ELECTION
Ideology			
Liberal	52	1	21
Moderate	42	28	49
Conservative	3	70	30
Age			
18–29	4%	3%	21
30–39	19	15	27
40–59	59	54	32
60 and older	18	28	20
Race/Ethnicity			
White	74%	89%	87
Black	17	4	8
Hispanic	6	4	2
Other	3	3	2
Labor Union			
Member	28%	3%	19
Not a member	72	97	81
Sex			
Male	50%	58%	48
Female	50	42	52

[a]Margin of sampling error is plus or minus 4.5 percentage points when figures do not include those who declined to answer the question; the margin of error is plus or minus 2 percentage points for all others. Other totals may not add up to 100 percent because of rounding.

Source: Figures in the first two columns are from a *Washington Post* telephone poll of 511 Republican delegates from July 29 to August 7, 1992, and 496 Democratic delegates from June 22 to July 8. Figures in the last column are adapted from the Voter Research & Surveys (VRS) poll of 15,232 Americans as they exited from their voting booths on November 3, 1992. VRS is an association of ABC News, CNN, CBS News, and NBC News.

tions and fund-raising efforts, a strategy that has clearly paid off at the polls in the elections of 1980, 1984, and 1988, which saw Republicans elected as President.

The delegates in each party also exemplify the philosophical gulf separating the two parties (see Table 12.2). Democratic delegates are well to the left of their own party's voters on most issues, and even further away from the opinions held by the nation's electorate as a whole. Republican delegates are a mirror image of their opponents—considerably to the right of GOP voters and even more so of the entire electorate. Although it is sometimes said that the two major parties do not present U.S. citizens with a "clear choice" of candidates, it is possible to argue the contrary. Our politics are perhaps too polarized, with the great majority of Americans—moderates and pragmatists overwhelmingly—left underrepresented by parties too fond of ideological purity.

Table 12.2 ◆ **Comparison of the Views of the Public with Those of Delegates to the 1992 Presidential Nominating Conventions**[a]

Question: "I am going to read a few statements. After each, please tell me if you agree with the statement or disagree with it, or if, perhaps, you have no opinion about the statement." (Figures show percentage who agreed with the statement.)

	ALL VOTERS	DEMOCRATIC DELEGATES	DEMOCRATS VOTERS	REPUBLICAN DELEGATES	REPUBLICANS VOTERS
A. Parents should have the right to send their children to any public school that they want to.	85%	56%	86%	86%	82%
B. Black people in the United States are still a long way from having the same chance in life that white people have.	53	87	57	44	43
C. The government should raise taxes now as one means of dealing with the federal budget deficit.	20	47	21	7	19
D. Large corporations have too much power for the good of the country.	73	66	79	14	76
E. Taxes on businesses should be cut to stimulate the economy.	74	74	65	96	82
F. There should be a constitutional amendment outlawing abortion.	25	3	24	28	30
G. The United States can meet its national security obligations with a much smaller military budget than we have today.	60	93	66	44	53

[a]Margins of sampling error are plus or minus 5 percentage points for figures based on delegates (Republicans and Democrats) and 3 points for figures based on all voters.

Source: Figures are from a *Washington Post* telephone poll of 511 Republican delegates from July 29 to August 7, 1992; 496 Democratic delegates from June 22 to July 8; and a *Washington Post*-ABC News telephone poll of 1,506 registered voters from July 1 to 8.

The philosophical divergence is usually reflected in the party platforms, even in years such as 1992, when one party attempts to water down its rhetoric and avoid specifics (see "Selected Contrasts in the 1992 Party Platforms," p. 409). (The Democrats did so in 1992; the Republicans have done so in earlier years, as in 1968.)

The Electoral College: How Presidents Are Elected

Given the enormous output of energy, money, and time expended to nominate two major-party presidential contenders, it is difficult to believe that the general election could be more arduous than the nominating contests—but it usually is. The actual campaign for the presidency (and other offices) is described in Chapter 13, but the object of the

Selected Contrasts in the 1992 Party Platforms

◆ ◆ ◆

Domestic Policy

	REPUBLICANS	DEMOCRATS
Abortion	"Support human life amendment to the Constitution . . . oppose the use of public revenues for abortion"	"Stand behind the right of every woman to choose . . . regardless of ability to pay"
Gay rights	"Oppose efforts . . . to include sexual preference as a protected minority"	"Provide civil rights protection for gay men and lesbians"
Taxes	"Oppose any attempts to increase taxes"	"Forc[e] the rich to pay their fair share"
Campaign reform	"Oppose arbitrary spending limits for congressional candidates"	"We must limit overall campaign spending [for congressional candidates]"

Foreign and Defense Policy

South Africa	"Condemn all violence . . . and applaud those who seek reconciliation"	"Consider reimposing [U.S. government] sanctions against South Africa"
China	"Maintain the relationship with China so that we can effectively encourage [democratic] reform"	"Condition . . . favorable trade terms for China on respect for human rights"

Sources: 1992 Democratic and Republican Party Platforms.

exercise is clear: winning a majority of the electoral college. This uniquely American institution consists of representatives of each state who cast the final ballots that actually elect a president.

The electoral college was the result of a compromise between Framers like Roger Sherman and Elbridge Gerry, who argued for selection of the president by the Congress, and those such as James Madison, James Wilson, and Gouverneur Morris, who favored selection by direct popular election. The electoral college compromise, while not a perfect solution, had practical benefits. Since there were no mass media in those days, it is unlikely that common citizens, even reasonably informed ones, would know much about a candidate from another state. This situation could have left voters with no choice but to vote for someone from their own state, thus making it improbable that any candidate would secure a national majority. On the other hand, the **electors** (members of the electoral college) would be men of character with a solid knowledge of national politics who were able to identify, agree on, and select prominent national statesmen. There are three essentials to understanding the Founders' design of the electoral college: (1) It was meant to work *without* political parties, (2) it was designed

Electors Members of the electoral college chosen by methods determined in each state.

Landmark Events in Voting and Elections

1804 ◆ Twelfth amendment ratified (provides for separate election for president and vice president in Electoral College)

1830s ◆ Nominating conventions replace congressional caucuses as means of selecting presidential ticket

1850s ◆ Critical elections period: Whig Party dissolves, Republican Party develops

1890s ◆ Critical elections period: Republicans strengthen majority status and voter attachments that last until the 1930s

1932 ◆ Electorate decisively rejects Republicans and propels Democrats to power during Great Depression

to cover both the nominating *and* electing phases of presidential selection, and (3) it was constructed to produce a nonpartisan president.

The machinery of the electoral college was somewhat complex. Each state designated electors (through appointment or popular vote) equal in number to the sum of its representation in the House and Senate. The electors met in their respective states. Each elector has *two* votes for president, an attempt by the Founders to ensure that at least one candidate would secure a majority of electoral votes needed for victory. The candidate with the most votes, providing he received votes from a majority of the total number of electors, won the presidency; the candidate securing the second greatest number of votes won the vice presidency. If two candidates received the same number of votes and both had a majority of electors, the election was decided in the House of Representatives, with each state delegation acting as a unit and having one vote to cast. In the event that no candidate secured a majority, the election would also be decided in the House, with each state delegation having one vote to cast for any of the top five electoral vote-getters. In both of these scenarios a majority of the total number of states was necessary to secure victory.

But the Framers' idea of nonpartisan presidential elections lasted barely a decade, ending for the most part after George Washington's two terms. In 1796, their arrangement for presidential selection produced a president and vice president with markedly different political philosophies, which, as we noted in Chapter 7, is a circumstance unthinkable in modern times. This occurred when a tie in the electoral college sent the election into the House of Representatives, which selected Federalist John Adams as president and his political opponent, the Democratic-Republican Thomas Jefferson, as vice president.

The Election of 1800.   By the election of 1800, both of the two emerging national parties—the Federalists and the Democratic-Republicans—nominated presidential and vice presidential candidates through their respective congressional caucuses before electors had even been chosen in the states. At the same time, the national parties were also gaining influence in the states, and this resulted in the selection of electors committed to their presidential and vice-presidential nominees. In other words, the once-deliberative electors lost their independent judgment and assumed the less important role of instructed party agents. This was, of course, a far cry from the nonpartisan system envisioned by the Founders.

The republic's fourth presidential election also revealed a flaw in the Framers' plan. In 1800, when Thomas Jefferson and Aaron Burr were, respectively, the Democratic-Republican Party's candidates for president and vice president, supporters of the Democratic-Republican Party controlled a majority of the electoral college. Accordingly, each Democratic-Republican elector in the states cast one of his two votes for Jefferson and the other one for Burr, a situation that resulted in a tie for the presidency between Jefferson and Burr, since there was no way under the constitutional arrangements for electors to earmark their votes separately for president and vice president. And even though most understood Jefferson to be the actual choice for president, the Constitution mandated that a tie be decided by the House of Representatives. And so it was, of course, and in Jefferson's favor—but only after much energy was expended to persuade lame-duck Federalists not to give Burr the presidency.

The Twelfth Amendment, ratified in 1804 and still the constitutional foundation for presidential elections, was an attempt to remedy the confusion between the selection of vice presidents and presidents that beset the election of 1800. The amendment provided for separate elections for each office, with each elector having only *one* vote to cast for each. In the event of a tie or when no candidate received a majority of the total number of electors, the election still went to the House of Representatives; now, however, each state delegation would have one vote to cast for one of the *three* candidates who had received the greatest number of electoral votes.

The electoral college modified by the Twelfth Amendment fared better than the college as originally designed, but it has not been problem-free. For example, in the 1824 election between John Quincy Adams and Andrew Jackson, neither presidential candidate secured a majority of electoral votes, once again throwing the election into the House. Despite the fact that Jackson had more electoral and popular votes than Adams, the House voted for the latter as president. On two other occasions in the nineteenth century the presidential candidate with fewer popular votes than his opponent won the presidency. In the 1876 contest between Republican Rutherford B. Hayes and Democrat Samuel J. Tilden, no candidate received a majority of electoral votes; the House decided in Hayes's favor even though he had only one more (disputed) electoral vote and 250,000 fewer popular votes than Tilden (see the "People of the Past" box below). In the election of 1888, President Grover Cleveland secured about 100,000 more popular votes than did Benjamin Harrison, yet Harrison won a majority of the electoral college vote, and with it the presidency.

The Electoral College in the Twentieth Century.   Although generally more stable than the previous two centuries, the twentieth century has also witnessed a number of near crises pertaining to the electoral college. For instance, in the turbulent year of 1968, the possibility that the presidential election would be decided in the House increased considerably with the entrance into the race of third-party candidate George Wallace. And the election of 1976 was almost a repeat of those nineteenth-century contests in which the candidate with fewer popular votes won the presidency: Even though Democrat Jimmy Carter received about 1.7 million more popular votes than

Republican Gerald Ford, a switch of some 8,000 popular votes in Ohio and Hawaii would have secured for Ford enough votes to win the electoral college, and hence the presidency. Had Ross Perot stayed in the 1992 presidential contest without his summer hiatus, it is possible that he could have thrown the election into the House of Representatives. His support had registered from 30–36 percent in the polls for much of the spring and early summer of 1992. When he reentered the race, some of that backing had evaporated, and he finished with 19 percent of the vote and carried no states, as Figure 12.2 shows. However, Perot drained a substantial number of Republican votes from George Bush, thus splitting the GOP base. This enabled Clinton to win many normally GOP-leaning states such as Georgia, Nevada, and Montana—although he carried them with well less than a majority of the votes.

PEOPLE OF THE PAST

How Rutherford B. Hayes Was Elected President in 1876

The story of Rutherford B. Hayes's ascent to the presidency is a fascinating one. It began with the dismal record of Republican President Ulysses S. Grant's administration, the corruption and incompetence of which was so well established by 1876 that the Republican Party's only hope of winning that year's presidential election was probably in running an obscure candidate. It was under these circumstances that Hayes, a little-known former governor of Ohio, received his party's nomination over James G. Blaine of Maine by only five votes on the seventh ballot at the Republican National Convention in Cincinnati. Conversely, Hayes's Democratic opponent, New York Governor Samuel J. Tilden, easily secured his party's nomination on the second ballot.

National prominence aside, both candidates considered themselves reformers. Having played a crucial role in the breakup of the Democrats' New York City machine run by party boss William M. Tweed, Tilden staked his reputation on reform. And Hayes went so far as to vow that, if elected, he would not seek a second term, ensuring that patronage would not be used to secure his reelection.

Again, however, the Grant administration's record, combined with the nation's depressed economy, made Democrat Tilden the likely victor. Accepting this seemingly inevitable conclusion, Hayes retired to bed early on election evening, and with good reason: Early,

unofficial election returns indicated that Tilden had carried New York, New Jersey, Connecticut, Indiana, and most of the South, apparently giving him 203 electoral votes, 18 more than the 185 needed to win. The contest was not yet finished, though. Hayes carried most of the Western United States, and he could still win if he captured the Southern states that had Republican governors. In these states the vote leaned to Tilden but was extremely close. Not ready to concede, Republican Party operative General Daniel E. Sickles telegraphed Republican leaders in Florida, Louisiana, and South Carolina, explaining that "with your state for Hayes, he is elected," and admonishing them to "Hold your state." The Republicans responded with newfound assurance of a Hayes victory, which fueled the ensuing controversy.

In the three Southern states contacted by Sickles, Republican-dominated election boards disputed the legitimacy of many Democratic votes. During the late nineteenth century, voter fraud was rampant, as many states had no registration laws and political parties printed their own ballots. Therefore, each state had an election board charged with counting ballots and discounting fraudulent votes. In South Carolina the five-member board discarded enough allegedly fraudulent votes to give Hayes a narrow 600-vote victory. Florida's election board, too, ultimately pruned enough supposedly fraudulent votes to secure for

Superdelegates

Occasionally, a political party finds a new idea in an old one. Such is the case with the Democrats and "superdelegates." Before 1972 most delegates to a Democratic National Convention were not bound by primary results to support a particular candidate for president. This freedom to maneuver meant that conventions could be exciting and somewhat unpredictable gatherings, where last-minute events and deals could sway wavering delegates. Since 1972, however, all the Democratic conventions have been predetermined by primary elections and the party has been committed to a nominee for weeks or months prior to the convention.

Hayes a 900-vote victory. Even in Louisiana—where Tilden ostensibly won by 6,300 votes—the election board threw out 15,000 votes, 13,000 of which were Democratic. This allowed Hayes to carry the state by 3,000 votes.

On December 6, 1876, each state's electors formally cast their ballots and sent them to Congress for official tallying. In most states the process occurred without incident. But the exceptions—Florida, Louisiana, Oregon, and South Carolina—each forwarded conflicting electoral votes to Washington. Consequently, the result of the initial Washington count included twenty disputed electoral votes—all, of course, claimed by both the candidates—along with 184 electoral votes for Tilden and 165 for Hayes.

How could this crisis be resolved? The Constitution states only that electoral votes be "directed to the President of the Senate," who "shall, in the presence of the Senate and House of Representatives, open all the certificates and the Votes shall then be counted." The document makes no mention of who decides which votes to include when a state's votes are in dispute. Enjoying a majority in the Senate, the Republicans argued that Michigan Republican Thomas W. Ferry, the president of the Senate, should decide. (Henry Wilson, who as vice president of the United States would have been the Senate's presiding officer, had died in office in 1875.) The Democrats, who controlled the House and commanded a comfortable majority in Congress as a whole, contended that the House and the Senate combined should decide. Neither side was able to persuade the other, so in the end a compromise was forged: A bipartisan commission was set up to decide the fate of the disputed electoral votes, the results of which would be final unless *both* houses of Congress vetoed them.

The parties turned next to the issue of the commission's composition, with the result being another moderate compromise. The commission would include four Supreme Court justices—two Democrats and two Republicans—who would in turn select a fifth judge. Most observers assumed the fifth judge would be Judge David Davis, an independent. Additionally, the commission would include ten members of Congress—five representatives and five senators, of whom half would be Republicans and half Democrats. Unexpectedly, however, Judge Davis refused the invitation to sit on the commission, and Republican Supreme Court Justice Joseph Bradley was chosen instead, giving the Republicans an eight-to-seven majority on the commission.

The commission's partisan colors became obvious as it decided which electoral votes to accept from the four disputed states. In all cases, the Republican majority gave Hayes the disputed electoral votes and, therefore, a 185 to 184 overall electoral college victory. Thus was the presidency awarded to Rutherford B. Hayes in 1876—despite his having received fewer popular votes than Tilden, even after accounting for voter fraud. Despite encouragement from some supporters to march on Washington and seize control of the government, Tilden accepted the results and permitted Hayes to enter the White House. But Hayes was never regarded as a legitimate occupant of 1600 Pennsylvania Avenue by many Tilden backers, and he was frequently referred to as "His Fraudulency" throughout his single term in office from 1877 to 1881.

FIGURE 12-2
The States Drawn in Proportion to Their Electoral College Votes

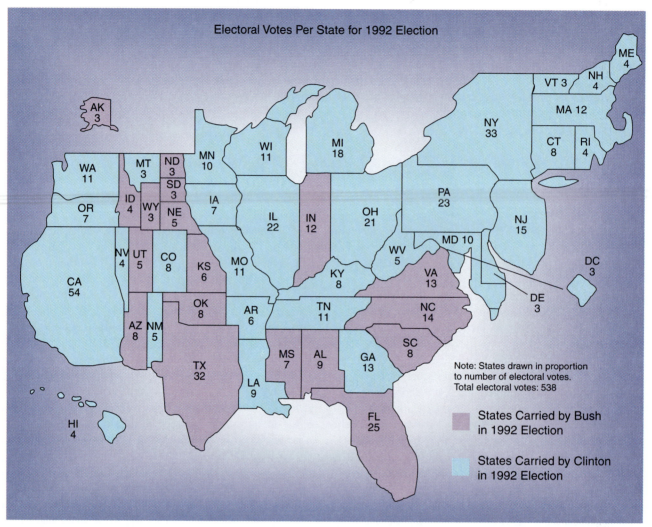

The states are pictured here with the size merited by their number of electoral college votes. Some states (such as New Jersey and California) are much larger than they appear on a regular map, while others (such as Alaska and Nevada) are much smaller.

Democrats attempted to add more flexibility to their 1984, 1988, and 1992 conventions and to add the "peer review" of potential nominees that used to take place when party bosses made decisions behind closed doors by allotting several hundred superdelegate slots—positions reserved for the party's high elected and appointed officials. To this point, though, superdelegates have made little practical difference, because they usually support the candidate who has won the primaries. However, if the primary results are ever split and a convention is deadlocked, superdelegates could prove to be critical in the selection of the party's presidential candidate, just as the bosses of old were.

Before the election of 1876, Cartoonist Nast was quite confident the Republican Party would easily trample Samuel Tilden and Thomas Hendricks, the Democratic nominees for president and vice president.

After the election: Nast's elephant, battered and bandaged, moans with Pyrrhus, "Another such victory and I am undone." Hayes was elected by a margin of a single electoral vote.

Patterns of Presidential Elections

The electoral college results reveal more over time than simply who won the presidency. They show which party and which region(s) are coming to dominance and how voters may be changing party allegiances in response to new issues and generational changes.

Party Realignments.   Usually such movements are gradual, but occasionally the political equivalent of a major earthquake swiftly and dramatically alters the landscape. During these rare events, called **party realignments,**[1] existing party affiliations are subject to upheaval: Many voters may change parties, and the youngest age group of voters may permanently adopt the label of the newly dominant party. Until recent times, at least, party realignments have been spaced about thirty-six years apart in the U.S. experience.

> **Party realignments** A shifting of party coalition groupings in the electorate that remains in place for several elections.

A major realignment is precipitated by one or more **critical elections,** which may polarize voters around new issues and personalities in reaction to crucial developments, such as a war or an economic depression. In Britain, for example, the first postwar election held in 1945 was critical, since it ushered the Labour Party into power for the first time and introduced to Britain a new interventionist agenda in the fields of economic and social welfare policies.

> **Critical elections** An election that signals a party realignment through voter polarization around new issues.

In the entire history of the United States, there have been six party alignments, as indicated by "Landmark Events in Voting and Elections" (p. 410). Three tumultuous eras in particular have produced significant critical elections (see Figure 12-3). First, during the period leading up to the Civil War, the Whig Party gradually dissolved and the Republican Party developed and won the presidency. Second, the populist radicalization of the Democratic Party in the 1890s enabled the Republicans to greatly

FIGURE 12-3
Electoral College Results for Three Realigning Presidential Contests

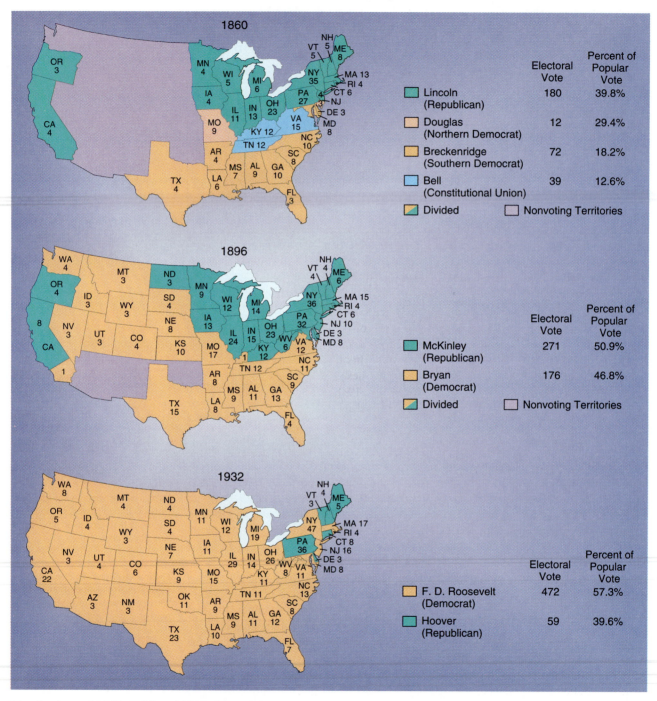

The elections of 1860, 1896, and 1932 changed the way many Americans viewed their politics and partisan alignments. The victories of Abraham Lincoln and William McKinley pushed the country in a Republican direction, while Franklin D. Roosevelt's triumph began a long period of Democratic rule.

strengthen their majority status and make lasting gains in voter attachments. Third, the Great Depression of the 1930s propelled the Democrats to power, causing large numbers of voters to repudiate the GOP and embrace the Democratic Party. In each of these cases, fundamental and enduring alterations in the party equation resulted.

The last confirmed major realignment, then, happened in the 1928–36 period, as Republican Herbert Hoover's presidency was held to one term because of voter anger about the Depression. In 1932, Democrat Franklin D. Roosevelt swept to power as the electorate decisively rejected Hoover and the Republicans. This dramatic vote of "no confidence" was followed by substantial changes in policy by the new president, who demonstrated in fact or at least in appearance that his policies were effective. The people responded to his success, accepted his vision of society, and ratified their choice of the new president's party in subsequent presidential and congressional elections.

Simultaneously, the former majority party (Republican) reluctantly but inevitably adjusted to its new minority role. So strong was the new partisan attachment for most voters that even when short-term issues and personalities that favored the Republican Party dislodged the Democrats from power, the basic distribution of party loyalties did not shift significantly. In 1952, 1956, 1968, and 1972, then, Republicans won the presidency, but the New Deal Democratic coalition was still visible in the voting patterns, and it survived to emerge again in future elections.

The elections of 1952, 1956, 1968, and 1972 are examples of alignment-*deviating* presidential elections. In these elections, the results (the victories of Republicans Dwight D. Eisenhower and Richard M. Nixon) were at odds with what would be expected, given the underlying Democratic voting majority in the electorate at the time. (Eisenhower won mainly because of his war record and appealing personality, and Nixon gained the White House thanks to internal splits in the Democratic Party over the Vietnam War and racial issues.) We can contrast these four deviating elections with the alignment-*maintaining* elections of 1940, 1944, 1948, 1960, 1964, and 1976. In these six elections, the New Deal coalition prevailed in the presidential contests, as Democrats Franklin D. Roosevelt, Harry S Truman, John F. Kennedy, Lyndon B. Johnson, and Jimmy Carter won office.

With the aid of timely circumstances, realignments are accomplished in two primary ways.[2] Some voters are simply converted from one party to the other by the issues and candidates of the time. New voters may also be mobilized into action: Immigrants, young voters, and previous nonvoters may become motivated and then absorbed into a new governing majority. However vibrant and potent party coalitions may be at first, as they age, tensions increase and grievances accumulate. The majority's original reason for existing fades, and new generations neither remember the traumatic events that originally brought about the realignment nor possess the stalwart party identifications of their ancestors. New issues arise, producing conflicts that can be resolved only by a breakup of old alignments and a reshuffling of individual and group party loyalties. Viewed in historical perspective, party realignment has been a mechanism that ensures stability by controlling unavoidable change.

A critical realigning era is by no means the only occasion when changes in partisan affiliation are accommodated. In truth, every election produces realignment to some degree, since some individuals are undoubtedly pushed to change parties by events and by their reactions to the candidates. Recent research suggests that partisanship is much more responsive to current issues and personalities than had been believed earlier, and that major realignments are just extreme cases of the kind of changes in party loyalty registered every year.[3]

Secular realignment The gradual rearrangement of party coalitions, based more on demographic shifts than on shocks to the political system.

Secular Realignment.   Although the term "realignment" is usually applied only if momentous events such as war or depression produce enduring and substantial alterations in the party coalitions, political scientists have long recognized that a more gradual rearrangement of party coalitions could occur.[4] Called **secular realignment,** this piecemeal process depends not on convulsive shocks to the political system but on slow, almost barely discernable demographic shifts—the shrinking of one party's base of support and the enlargement of the other's, for example, or simple generational replacement (that is, the dying off of the older generation and the maturing of the younger generation). A recent version of this theory, termed "rolling realignment,"[5] argues that in an era of weaker party attachments (such as we currently are experiencing), a dramatic, full-scale realignment may not be possible. Still, a critical mass of voters may be attracted for years to one party's banner in waves or streams, if that party's leadership and performance are consistently exemplary. Something of this nature began in Britain when Margaret Thatcher led the Conservatives to victory in 1979; thereafter, the Labour Party has lost its hold on traditional sources of support, and the party now faces a difficult road to restored political viability.

Some scholars and political observers also contend that the decline of party affiliation has in essence left the electorate *dealigned* and incapable of being realigned as long as party ties remain tenuous for so many voters. Voters shift with greater ease between the parties during de-alignment, but little permanence or intensity exists in identifications made and held so lightly. If nothing else, the obsolescence of realignment theory may be indicated by the calendar; if major realignments occur roughly every thirty-six years, then we are long overdue. The last major realignment took place between 1928 and 1936, and so the next one might have been expected in the late 1960s and early 1970s.

As the trends toward ticket-splitting, partisan independency, and voter volatility suggest, there is little question that we have been moving through an unstable and somewhat "de-aligned" period at least since the 1970s. The foremost political question today is whether de-alignment will continue (and in what form) or whether a major realignment is in the offing. Each previous de-alignment has been a precursor of realignment,[6] but realignment need not succeed dealignment, especially under modern conditions. It may be that the outlines of the Democratic New Deal coalition will continue to be seen and to prevail in U.S. politics, or that the system may be so dealigned that only short-term and transitory majority coalitions are possible. The other alternative—plausible but without hard evidence to support it—is one more to the liking of Republican activists: a full-scale or rolling realignment of the electorate that builds on the electoral successes of the Reagan and Bush years and produces a stable GOP majority.

Of course, Republican analysts attempted to convince the political world of the reality of major realignment after Ronald Reagan's decisive presidential victory in 1980, just as another contingent had tried to do following Richard M. Nixon's successes in 1968 and 1972. As evidence, GOP boosters pointed to increased levels of Republican identification, especially by the young, and to a string of presidential victories that supposedly imply a Republican "lock" on an electoral college majority.

Democrats insisted all along that the Republican claims were nothing more than wishful thinking. Resurrecting a popular advertising slogan used as a 1984 campaign retort, Democrats again asked, "Where's the beef?," noting their overwhelming edge in local offices, continuous firm control of the House of Representatives, and recapture of the Senate in 1986. The 1992 presidential election served as a vindication of sorts for these Democratic arguments—although the 43-percent victory of Bill Clinton really proved nothing except that the Republicans were too optimistic. What goes around comes around, and the 1994 congressional elections showed that Democrats were too optimistic in suggesting that a Republican realignment was impossible. Of course, it is too soon to know whether 1994 was actually the beginning of a realignment that will favor the GOP.

Clearly, major changes in the U.S. electorate have been occurring, but these changes may or may not constitute a major critical realignment of party balance. The Democrats are not the dominant party they once were, but the GOP has not obtained majority status, either. The struggle between the parties for dominance continues, and the outcome is as yet uncertain.

Congressional Elections

Senator Robert Byrd (D-W.V.) making a speech. Former majority leader of the Senate, Byrd has become a master at promoting himself to his state. His pork-barrel tactics have included legislation that relocates federal offices to West Virginia, bringing lots of jobs with them for the citizens of his state.

Incumbency The condition of already holding elected office.

Many similar elements are present in different kinds of elections: Candidates, voters, issues, and television advertisements are constants. But there are distinctive aspects of each kind of election as well. Compared with presidential elections, congressional elections are a different animal.

First, most candidates for Congress labor in relative obscurity. While there are some celebrity nominees for Congress—television stars, sports heroes, even local TV news anchors—the vast majority of party nominees are little-known state legislators and local office holders. For them, just getting known, establishing name identification, is the biggest battle. No major-party presidential nominee need worry about this elementary stage because so much media attention is focused on the race for the White House. This is not so for most congressional contests; elections for spots in the House of Representatives receive remarkably little coverage in many states and communities.

The Incumbency Advantage

Under these circumstances, the advantages of **incumbency** (that is, already being in office) are enhanced, and a kind of electoral inertia takes hold: Those people in office tend to remain in office. Every year the average member of the U.S. House of Representatives expends about $750,000 in taxpayer funds to run the office. Much of this money directly or indirectly promotes the legislator by means of mass mailings and constituency services—the term used to describe a wide array of assistance provided by a member of Congress to voters in need (for example, tracking a lost Social Security check, helping a veteran receive disputed benefits, or finding a summer internship for a college student). In addition to these institutional means of self-promotion, most incumbents are highly visible in their districts. They have easy access to local media, cut ribbons galore, attend important local funerals, and speak frequently at meetings and community events. Nearly a quarter of the people in an average congressional district claim to have met their representative, and about half recognize their legislator's name without prompting.

This spending and visibility pays off: reelection rates for sitting House members range well above 90 percent in most election years.

Frequently the reelection rate for senators is as high, but not always. In a "bad" year for House incumbents, "only" 88 percent will win (as in the Watergate year of 1974), but the senatorial reelection rate can drop much lower on occasion (to 60 percent in the 1980 Reagan landslide, for example). There is a good reason for this lower senatorial reelection rate. A Senate election is often a high-visibility contest; it receives much more publicity than a House race. So while House incumbents remain protected and insulated in part because few voters pay attention to their little-known challengers, a Senate-seat challenger can become well known more easily, and thus be in a better position to defeat an incumbent.

Incidentally, the 1994 congressional elections are yet another example of the power of incumbency. The press focused on the Republican takeover of both houses of Congress, naturally enough, but another perspective is provided by the reelection rates for incumbents. More than 90 percent of the sitting representatives and senators who sought reelection won another term, despite electoral conditions that were termed a tidal wave.

Redistricting, Scandals, and Coattails

For the relatively few incumbent members of Congress who *do* lose their reelection bids, three explanations are paramount: redistricting, scandals, and coattails. Every ten years, after the census, all congressional district lines are redrawn (in states with more than one congressperson) so that every legislator represents about the same number of citizens. Redistricting inevitably puts some incumbents in the same districts as other incumbents, and weakens the base of other congresspersons by adding territory favorable to the opposition party. In 1992 ten incumbents were paired together—five therefore lost—and about a dozen more incumbents were defeated in part because of unfavorable redistricting.

Scandals come in many varieties in this age of the investigative press. The old standby of financial impropriety (bribery and payoffs, for example) has been supplemented by other forms of career-ending incidents, such as personal improprieties (sexual escapades, for instance). The power of incumbency is so strong, however, that many legislators survive even serious scandal to win reelection. Congressman Barney Frank (D-Mass.), for instance, an acknowledged homosexual, hired a male prostitute who ran a prostitution service out of Frank's apartment in Washington. This situation became public knowledge in 1989. Though Frank claimed ignorance of the man's activities, he admitted having some of his parking tickets "fixed." Despite the sordid nature of this arrangement, most of Frank's constituents were satisfied with his representation of them and easily reelected him in 1990, and again in 1992.

The defeat of a congressional incumbent can also occur as a result of the presidential coattail effect. As Table 12.3 shows, successful presidential candidates usually carry into office a substantial number of congressional candidates of the same party in the year of their election. Notice the overall decline in the strength of the coattail effect in modern times, however, as party identification has weakened and the powers and perks of incumbency have grown. Whereas Harry S Truman's party gained seventy-six House seats and nine additional Senate seats in 1948, George Bush's party actually *lost* three House seats and one Senate berth in 1988, despite Bush's handsome 54 percent majority. The gains can be minimal even in presidential landslide reelection years such as 1972 (Nixon) and 1984 (Reagan). Occasionally, though, when the issues are emotional and the voters' desire for change is strong enough, as in Reagan's original 1980 victory, the coattail effect can still be substantial.

Table 12.3 ♦ **Congressional Election Results, 1948–1992**

GAIN (+) OR LOSS (–) FOR PRESIDENT'S PARTY

Presidential Election Years			Off-Year Elections		
President/Year	*House*	*Senate*	*Year*	*House*	*Senate*
Truman (D): 1948	+76	+9	1950	−29	−6
Eisenhower (R): 1952	+24	+2	1954	−18	−1
Eisenhower (R): 1956	−2	0	1958	−48	−13
Kennedy (D): 1960	−20	−2	1962	−4	+3
Johnson (D): 1964	+38	+2	1966	−47	−4
Nixon (R): 1968	+7	+5	1970	−12	+2
Nixon (R): 1972	+13	−2	Ford: 1974	−48	−5
Carter (D): 1976	+2	0	1978	−15	−3
Reagan (R): 1980	+33	+12	1982	−26	+1
Reagan (R): 1984	+15	−2	1986	−5	−8
Bush (R): 1988	−3	−1	1990	−9	−1
Clinton (D): 1992	−10	0	1994	−52	−9*

*Includes the switch from Democrat to Republican of Alabama U.S. Senator Richard Shelby.

Off-Year Elections

Elections in the middle of presidential terms—**off-year elections**—present a different threat to incumbents. This time it is the incumbents *of the president's party* who are most in jeopardy. Just as the presidential party usually *gains* seats in presidential election years, it usually *loses* seats in off years. The problems and tribulations of governing normally cost a president some popularity, alienate key groups, or cause the public to want to send the president a message of one sort or another. An economic downturn or a scandal can underline and expand this circumstance, as the Watergate scandal of 1974 and the recession of 1982 demonstrated.

What is most apparent from the off-year statistics of Table 12.3, however, is the frequent tendency of voters to punish the president's party much more severely in the sixth year of an eight-year presidency (1958, 1966, 1974).[7] After only two years voters are still willing to "give the guy a chance," but after six years voters are often restless for change. (Interestingly, for the first time in this century, the United States in 1994 experienced a "sixth-year itch" in the second year of a presidency, such was the dissatisfaction with the Clinton Administration.) Finally, notice in the table that Senate elections are less inclined to follow these rules than are House elections. The idiosyncratic nature of Senate contests is due to both their intermittent scheduling (only one-third of the seats come up for election every two years) and the existence of well-funded celebrity candidates who can sometimes swim against whatever political

In November, 1994, Iran-*Contra* scandal figure Oliver North narrowly lost a U.S. Senate seat to Virginia's incumbent Democrat Charles Robb. North received 43 percent of the vote to Robb's 46 percent. An independent Republican candidate, Marshall Coleman, garnered the remaining 11 percent.

Off-year elections Elections that take place in the middle of a presidential term.

tide is rising. Also worth remembering is that midterm elections in recent history have a much lower voter turnout than presidential elections. As Figure 12-4 shows, a midterm election may draw only 35 to 40 percent of adult Americans to the polls, while a presidential contest attracts 50–55 percent.

The 1994 Midterm Congressional Elections

As noted, the 1994 congressional elections were extraordinary—a massacre for the Democrats and a dream come true for the Republicans. Not since Harry Truman's loss in 1946 had a Democratic president lost both houses of Congress in a midterm election; but such was President Clinton's fate. For the first time since popular elections for the U.S. Senate began in the early 1900s, the entire freshman Senate class was Republican. Moreover, every Democratic incumbent House member, senator, and governor was defeated for reelection. Even the House Speaker, Thomas Foley (D-Wa.), fell in the onslaught. Republican George Nethercutt became the fiirst person to unseat a House Speaker since 1862 (see Table 12-4).

Republicans had just as much success at the state level. The GOP took control of nineteen houses in state legislatures, securing a majority of the legislative bodies. From just nineteen governors before the election, Republicans wound up with thirty governorships, including eight of the nine largest. (Only Florida, which reelected Democratic governor Lawton Chiles, resisted the trend.)

Where did the GOP margins at the polls come from? Men voted strongly Republican, overwhelming women's narrow preference for Democrats. Whites cast 58 percent

FIGURE 12-4

Voter Turnout in American Presidential and Midterm Congressional Elections

Voter turnouts have varied dramatically in the course of U.S. history, but since the 1830s, presidential elections have always drawn more voters to the polls than midterm congressional elections.

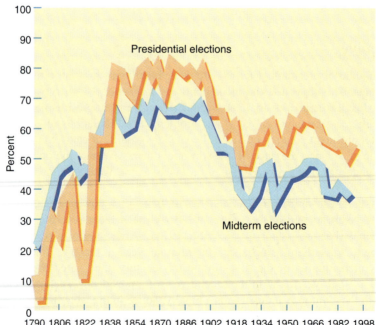

Source: Adapted from Harold W. Stanley and Richard G. Niemi, *Vital Statistics on American Politics*, 3rd ed. (Washington: CQ Press, 1992), Figure 3–1, p. 85.

Table 12.4 ♦ Results of Some Key Races—1994 Midterm Elections

STATE	CONTEST	WINNER	LOSER	SIGNIFICANCE
California	U.S. Senate	Incumbent Dianne Feinstein (D)	U.S. Rep. Michael Huffington (R)	Huffington spent a record $28 million from his own fortune.
California	Governor	Incumbent Pete Wilson (R)	Kathleen Brown (D)	Brown failed to become Calif.'s first woman governor.
Florida	Governor	Incumbent Lawton Chiles (D)	Jeb Bush (R)	Son of former President Bush lost.
Maine	U.S. Senate	U.S. Rep. Olympia Snowe (R)	U.S. Rep. Tom Andrews (D)	Snowe succeeded Majority leader George Mitchell (D).
Massachusetts	U.S. Senate	Incumbent Edward Kennedy (D)	Mitt Romney (R)	Kennedy dynasty continues.
Missouri	U.S. Senate	Ex-Gov. John Ashcroft (R)	U.S. Rep. Alan Wheat (D)	African-American Wheat lost.
New York	Governor	George Pataki (R)	Mario Cuomo (D)	Three-term governor lost to unknown.
Pennsylvania	U.S. Senate	U.S. Rep. Rick Santorum (R)	Incumbent Harris Wofford (D)	"Senator Health Care" lost seat after Clinton health plan failed.
Tennessee	U.S. Senate	Bill Frist (R) and Fred Thompson (R)	Incumbent Jim Sasser (D) and U.S. Rep. Jim Cooper (D)	GOP swept Gore's Tennessee and won all major posts.
Texas	Governor	George W. Bush (R)	Incumbent Ann Richards (D)	Eldest son of ex-president won.
Virginia	U.S. Senate	Incumbent Charles Robb (D)	Oliver North (R) and Marshall Coleman (I-R)	GOP split enabled Robb to win narrowly despite a sex scandal.
Washington	U.S. Representative	George Nethercutt (R)	Incumbent Thomas Foley (D)	House Speaker Foley lost, symbolizing end of Democratic rule.

of their ballots for the GOP, overwhelming the 88 percent of African Americans and 70 percent of Hispanics, who voted Democratic. Americans who backed Ross Perot in 1992 also shifted heavily to the GOP column in 1994. And the once solidly Democratic South continued a decades-long trend to the Republican party. For the first time since Reconstruction, the GOP captured a majority of all Sourthern U.S. House seats, Senate seats, and governorships.

All across the United States, but in the South in particular, voters seemed to be rejecting the Clinton presidency. Of the majority of Americans who disapproved of Clinton's performance as president, 82 percent cast ballots for GOP candidates for Congress, according to the networks' exit poll on election day. Only the 1996 presidential election would reveal whether this reaction among voters was a temporary rebuke or a permanent repudiation.

Voting Behavior

Whether they are casting ballots in congressional or presidential elections, voters behave in certain distinct ways and exhibit unmistakable patterns to political scientists who study them.

Voting Rights
♦ ♦ ♦

Both the Civil Rights Act of 1964 and the Voting Rights act of 1965 were intended to guarantee voting rights to African Americans nearly a century after passage of the Fifteenth Amendment. Since 1965, African-American voters have used their strength at the ballot box to elect black officials at all levels. Only seventy African Americans held public office in the eleven Southern states covered by the Act in 1965; by the early 1980s more than 2,500 held elected office in those states.

Today, most Voting Rights Act cases deal not with bars to voting by African Americans but with the drawing of election lines. As amended in 1982, the Voting Rights Act not only prohibits state legislatures from diluting African-American voting strength by distributing black voters among white districts or packing them into one black district, it also *requires* states to create as many African-American districts as possible. But, as discussed in Chapter 6, the constitutionality of this provision is under serious legal question.

The redrawing of election-district lines comes under careful scrutiny after each national census. Most Southern states must have all revisions in their districts "pre-cleared" by the U.S. Justice Department, which is charged with enforcing the Voting Rights Act. After the 1980 and 1990 censuses, the Republican-controlled Justice Department insisted that the maximum number of African-American districts be drawn, recognizing that the more black districts there are, the more likely it will be to gain Republican districts elsewhere in a state (since 90 percent of African Americans are Democrats).

In 1980, not only African Americans but Hispanics, too, closely watched the redistricting process. In 1981, for example, the nation's largest Hispanic organization, League of United Latin American Citizens (LULAC) revived its political action and played an active role along with the Mexican American Legal Defense Fund (MALDEF) (see pp. 152–153) to get additional Hispanic seats, especially in Texas, which experienced a spectacular growth in its Hispanic population.

The results of the 1990 census have given rise to numerous lawsuits. African Americans, however, are no longer at the forefront of this movement. White Republicans are challenging the new "black" districts (see p. 164). And throughout the Southwest, Hispanic voters are increasingly going to court to protect their voting rights, which they frequently see as diluted by unfavorable drawing of legislative district lines by state legislatures.

The first clear division is between citizens who vote and those who do not. About 40 percent of the eligible adult population in the United States vote regularly, whereas 25 percent are occasional voters. Thirty-five percent rarely or never vote. There are many differences, including socioeconomic and attitudinal, between voters and nonvoters. First, people who vote are usually more highly educated than nonvoters. A high percentage of registered voters have four or more years of college, whereas many nonvoters tend to have less schooling. This fact suggests that institutions of higher education provide citizens with opportunities to learn about and become interested in politics.

There is also a relationship between income and voting. A considerably higher percentage of citizens with annual incomes over $40,000 vote than do citizens with incomes under $10,000. Income level is, to some degree, connected to education level, as wealthier people tend to have more opportunities for higher education and more education also may lead to higher income. Wealthy citizens are also more likely than poor ones to think that the "system" works for them and that their votes make a difference. By contrast, lower-income citizens often feel alienated from politics, possibly believing that conditions will remain the same no matter for whom they vote.

There is also a correlation between age and voter participation rates. A much higher percentage of citizens age thirty and older vote than do citizens younger than thirty, although voter turnout decreases over the age of seventy, primarily because of physical infirmity, which makes it difficult to get to the polling location. Regrettably, less than half of the eligible eighteen- to twenty-four-year age group is even registered to vote. The most plausible reason for this is that younger people are more mobile; they have not put down roots in a community. Because voter registration is not automatic, people who relocate have to make an effort to register.

Another voter difference is related to race: Whites vote more regularly than do blacks. This is due in part to the relative income and educational levels of the two racial groups. African Americans tend to be poorer and have less formal education than whites, and, as mentioned earlier, both of these are factors in voter turnout. Significantly, though, highly educated and wealthier African Americans tend to participate in elections to a *greater* degree than their white counterparts.

Race also explains why the South has long had a lower turnout than the rest of the country (see Figure 12.5). In the wake of Reconstruction, the Southern states made it extremely difficult for African Americans to register to vote, and only a small percentage of the eligible African-American population was registered throughout the South. The Voting Rights Act of 1965 changed this situation, and gradually the South's vot-

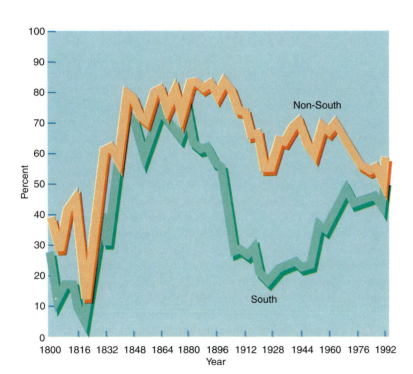

FIGURE 12-5

The South Versus the Non-South for Presidential Voter Turnout

Mainly because of racially discriminatory registration restrictions, the South had dramatically lower voter turnout than the rest of the nation from the post–Civil War period until the 1960s, when civil rights laws (especially the Voting Rights Act of 1965) eliminated much of the turnout difference. Note that voter participation in the South still remains somewhat below that of the other regions.

Source: Harold W. Stanley and Richard G. Niemi, *Vital Statistics on American Politics*, 4th ed. (Washington: CQ Press, 1993), Figure 3–2, p. 86.

ing participation has approached that of the rest of the nation, although the region still lags behind.

Although socioeconomic factors undoubtedly weigh heavily in voter participation rates, an interest in politics must also be included as an important factor. Many citizens who vote have grown up in families interested and active in politics, and they in turn stimulate their children to take an interest. Conversely, many nonvoters simply do not care about politics or the outcome of elections, never having been taught their importance at a younger age.

People who are highly interested in politics constitute only a small minority of the U.S. populace. For example, the most politically active Americans—party and issue-group activists—make up less than 5 percent of the country's 250 million people. And those who contribute time or money to a party or a candidate during a campaign make up only about 10 percent of the total population. On the other hand, although these percentages appear low, they translate into millions of Americans who contribute more than just votes to the system.

Why Is Voter Turnout So Low?

There is no getting around the fact that the United States has the lowest voter participation rate of any nation in the industrialized world, and it has declined somewhat (see "Voter Turnout around the World," p. 427). Only about half of the eligible electorate (that is, those age eighteen and over) voted in the 1988 general presidential election and 55 percent in 1992, compared with 62 percent in 1960. In contrast, turnout for British postwar elections has fluctuated between 72 and 84 percent.

There are a number of reasons for the low U.S. rates. First, unlike the United States, some nations—such as Australia and Belgium—have *compulsory* voting laws; not surprisingly, they enjoy voter turnout rates in excess of 95 percent. (In some nations, citizens pay a tax if they do *not* vote.) Second, many nations automatically register all of their citizens to vote. In the United States, however, citizens must jump the extra hurdle of voter registration. Indeed, it is no coincidence that voter participation rates dropped markedly after reformers pushed through strict voter registration laws in the early part of the twentieth century. Also a factor in the United States' low voter turnout are stringent absentee ballot laws. Many states, for instance, require citizens to apply in person for absentee ballots, a burdensome requirement given that one's inability to be present in his or her home state is often the reason for absentee balloting in the first place. Another explanation for low voter turnout in this country are the sheer number and frequency of elections, which few if any other democracies can match. Yet an election cornucopia is the inevitable result of federalism and the separation of powers, which result in layers of often separate elections on the local, state, and national levels.

Although some of the reasons for low voter participation are due to the institutional factors we have just reviewed, voter attitudes play an equally important part. As noted previously, alienation afflicts some voters, and others are just plain apathetic—possibly because of a lack of pressing issues in a particular year, satisfaction with the status quo, or uncompetitive (even uncontested) elections. Furthermore, many citizens may be turned off by the quality of campaigns in a time when petty issues and personal mudslinging are more prevalent than ever.

Reformers have suggested many ideas to increase voter turnout in the United States. Always on the list is raising the political awareness of young citizens, a reform that in-

In 1992, the "Rock the Vote" campaign (partially funded—and heavily promoted—by MTV) set out to register record numbers of young voters who traditionally are among the lowest demographics of voter turnout.

Voter Turnout around the World

❖ ❖ ❖

Almost all democracies around the globe have a higher percentage of voter turnout than the United States, as this table shows. Only Switzerland has a voter turnout lower than that of the United States. One reason for a poor U.S. showing is our requirement that citizens *register* to vote before being able to participate in elections. In all other nations listed in this table (except for France) citizens are *automatically* registered by the government or, in the cases of Australia and New Zealand, are compelled by law both to register and to vote.

PERCENT OF AVERAGE TURNOUT IN NATIONAL ELECTIONS, BY COUNTRY[a]

Italy, 93	Netherlands, 81
Austria, 85	Norway, 82
Belgium, 87	France, 77
Sweden, 85	Ireland, 76
Denmark, 84	United Kingdom, 74
Australia, 83	Japan, 71
West Germany, 79	Canada, 69
New Zealand, 80	United States, 51
Finland, 78	Switzerland, 41
Israel, 82	

[a]Either all parliamentary elections or, for France and the United States, presidential elections held from 1981 to 1990.

Source: Robert W. Jackman and Ross A. Miller, "Voter Turnout in the Industrial Democracies During the 1980's," *Comparative Political Studies* 27 (January 1995): 485.

evitably must involve our nation's schools. No less important, and perhaps simpler to achieve, are the institutional reforms, though many of these reforms, if enacted, may result in only a marginal increase in turnout.

To begin, many observers propose making it easier for citizens to register to vote. The typical thirty-days-before-an-election registration deadline could be shortened to a week or ten days. After all, most people become more interested in voting as Election Day nears. Better yet, all U.S. citizens could be registered automatically at the age of eighteen. Absentee ballots could also be made easier to obtain by eliminating the in-person requirement. A more concise and clear ballot might help, too. A short ballot, listing only a few offices up for election, keeps a sharper election focus for easily distracted citizens; the long ballot, on which few offices are appointive and a dozen or more statewide posts are elective, pleases populists but usually results in uninformed voting.

In her 1994 California Gubernatorial campaign, Kathleen Brown failed to extend her family's dynasty in that state, losing to incumbent Governor Pete Wilson. Both Brown's father and brother are former Governors of California.

Another worthwhile idea is the proposal to make Election Day a holiday. Besides removing an obstacle to voting (the busy workday), this might focus more voter attention on the contests in the critical final hours. Finally, reformers have long argued that strengthening the political parties would increase voter turnout, because parties have historically been the organizations in the United States best suited for and most successful at mobilizing citizens to vote. During the late 1800s and early 1900s, the country's "Golden Age" of powerful political parties, one of their primary activities was getting out the vote on Election Day. And even today, the parties' Election Day get-out-the-vote drives increase voter turnout by as many as several million in national contests.

Other ideas to increase voter turnout are less practical or feasible. For example, holding fewer elections might sound appealing, but it is difficult to see how this could be accomplished without diluting many of the central tenets of federalism and separation of powers that the Founders believed essential to the protection of liberty.

In 1993 a major advance toward easier registration was achieved with the passage by Congress of the so-called "motor voter" bill, which required states to permit individuals to register by mail, not just in person. The law, strongly backed by President Clinton, also allows citizens to register to vote when they visit any motor vehicles office, public assistance agency, or military recruitment division.

A New Voting Pattern: Ticket-Splitting

Among citizens who do cast their ballots, an important voting trend cannot be ignored. Citizens have been increasingly deserting their party affiliations in the polling booths. The practice of ticket-splitting—voting simultaneously for candidates of both parties for different offices—has soared dramatically.

The evidence of this development abounds. As already reviewed in this chapter, Republican presidential landslides in 1956, 1972, 1980, and 1984 were accompanied by the election of substantial Democratic majorities in the House of Representatives. Divided government, with the presidency held by one party and one or both houses of Congress held by the other party, has never been as frequent in U.S. history as it has been recently. From 1920 to 1944 about 15 percent of the congressional districts voted for presidential and House candidates of different parties, but from 1960 to 1988, at least 25 percent of the districts cast split tickets in any presidential year, and in 1984 nearly 50 percent of the districts did so. Similarly, at the statewide level only 17 percent of the states electing governors in presidential years between 1880 and 1956 elected state and national executives from different parties. Yet from 1960 to 1992 almost 40 percent of states holding simultaneous presidential and gubernatorial elections recorded split results. (In 1992 the proportion was somewhat lower, just 25 percent.)

These percentages actually understate the degree of ticket-splitting by individual voters. The Gallup Poll has regularly asked its respondents, "For the various political offices, did you vote for all the candidates of one party, that is, a straight ticket, or did you vote for the candidates of different parties [ticket-splitting]?" Since 1968 the proportion of voters who have ticket-split in presidential years has consistently been around 60 percent of the total.[8] Other polls and researchers have found reduced straight-ticket balloting and significant ticket-splitting at all levels of elections, especially since 1952.

Not surprisingly, the intensity of party affiliation is a major determinant of a voter's propensity to split the ticket. Strong party identifiers are the most likely to cast a straight-party ballot; pure independents are the least likely. Somewhat greater proportions of ticket-splitters are found among high-income and better-educated citizens, but there is little difference in the distribution by gender or age. Blacks exhibit the highest straight-party rate of any population subgroup; about three-quarters of all black voters stay in the Democratic Party column from the top to the bottom of the ballot.

There are a number of explanations for the modern increase in ticket-splitting, many of them similar to the perceived causes of the dip in party identification levels (see Chapter 11). The growth of issue-oriented politics, the mushrooming of single-interest groups, the greater emphasis on candidate-centered personality politics, and broader-based education are all often cited. A strong independent presidential candidacy such as Ross Perot's also helps to loosen party ties among many voters. So, too, does the marked gain in the value of incumbency. Thanks in part to the enormous fattening of congressional constituency services, incumbent U.S. representatives and senators have been able to attract a steadily increasing share of the other party's identifiers.[9]

Toward Reform

Most proposals for electoral reform center on the electoral college, starting with the *faithless elector*—that is, the elector who does not vote for the candidate to whom he or she is committed. In the twentieth century alone, electors have been faithless in seven elections: 1948, 1956, 1960, 1968, 1972, 1976, and 1988. In 1960 Alabama and Mississippi harkened back to the original design of the electoral college by electing a considerable number of "unpledged" electors, rather than supporting either Democrat John F. Kennedy or Republican Richard M. Nixon.

Electors in about half the states are required by law to cast a ballot for the presidential and vice-presidential candidates who win the most votes in the state. While some legal scholars have questioned the constitutionality of these laws, the Supreme Court has upheld them, though the laws are obviously difficult to enforce. Any law to remedy the problem of the faithless elector would therefore have to be in the form of a constitutional amendment, either mandating that electors vote for the candidate who wins a state's popular vote or removing altogether the office of elector and automatically awarding a state's electoral votes to the winner of its popular vote.

Other proposals for reforming the electoral college include getting rid of it altogether—that is, holding a direct national election. Such a change would have three major consequences: (1) The popular vote would be the only determinant for winning the presidency. (2) The slight advantage given to states with small populations under the electoral college would be eliminated. Currently, each state (from lightly populated Wyoming, Vermont, and populous Rhode Island to California) is given the same two additional electoral votes on top of the votes it receives to match the number of representatives it sends to the U.S. House of Representatives. (3) More minor-party candidates would run, since they would no longer be encumbered by the winner-take-all rules of the states and could accumulate votes nationally. In order to preclude a candidate with only a small plurality of the popular vote from winning the election, however, any reasonable plan for a direct national contest would have to stipulate that the winner must receive a certain percentage of the popular vote (perhaps 40 percent), with a runoff election necessary between the top two contenders if no one secures that proportion. A constitutional amendment proposing this reform was passed by a wide margin in the House of Representatives in 1969. However, in a vote ten years later, the Senate failed to come up with the two-thirds majority needed to send the proposal on to the states for ratification.

Defenders of the electoral college concede its problems, but argue that they are not serious enough to warrant change. Moreover, many observers still see value in the electoral college. To begin with, the electoral college helps preserve the contours of federalism by stressing states as the building blocks of presidential victories. Its elimination would hurt less populous states, which enjoy slight overrepresentation. Also, the electoral college magnifies the victory of presidents, helping them claim a mandate to govern. For example, in 1992 Bill Clinton received only a 43 percent plurality of the popular vote, but his landslide 100-vote edge in the electoral college gave him a needed boost as he prepared to take the reins of leadership. Finally, opponents of reform argue against an important component of direct popular elections: the *recount* (another count and tally of all votes cast on election day). In extremely close elections, such as the 1960 contest between John F. Kennedy and Richard M. Nixon, recounts in a few states with sizable blocs of electoral votes are inevitable, but at least under the electoral college system, recounts can be limited to the states in which the numbers are close. With a direct popular election, where only the national vote total matters, a close count would mean the daunting task of recounting every ballot in the nation.

Overall, although individual elections may sometimes be predictable, the electoral system in the United States is anything but static. New generations—and party-changers in older generations—constantly remake the political landscape. At least every other presidential election brings a change of administration and a focus on new issues. Every other year at least a few fresh personalities and perspectives infuse the Congress, as newly elected U.S. senators and representatives claim mandates and seek to shake up the established order. Each election year the same tumult and transformation can be observed in the fifty states and in thousands of localities.

The welter of elections may seem like chaos, but from this chaos come the order and often explosive productivity of a democratic society. For the source of all change in the United States, just as Hamilton and Madison predicted, is the individual citizen who goes to the polls and casts a ballot.

In most societies, there are an insatiable itch for change and a desire to better the conditions of life. In authoritarian countries, repression and violent revolution are the only avenues open to check or provide for change. In democratic nations such as the United States, however, the voters have the opportunity to orchestrate a peaceful revolution every time they visit their polling places.

Elections take the pulse of average people and gauge their hopes and fears; the study of elections permits us to trace the course of the American revolution over 200 years of voting. Much good and some harm have been accomplished by this explosion of balloting—but all of it has been done, as Hamilton insisted, "on the solid basis of THE CONSENT OF THE PEOPLE."

Summary

An old bumper sticker from the cynical 1970s captures one view of voting: "I don't vote—it only encourages 'em." Fortunately, most Americans, though not enough, reject this perspective, and understand why and how elections serve their interests. As we have reviewed, however, the U.S. electoral system is multilayered and often complex. In an effort to explain it, we covered these points in this chapter:

1. Regular elections guarantee mass political action and governmental accountability. They also confer legitimacy on regimes better than any other method of change.

2. When it comes to elections, the United States has an embarrassment of riches. There are various types of primary elections in the country, as well as general elections, initiatives, referenda, and recall elections. In presidential elections, primaries are sometimes replaced by caucuses in which party members choose a candidate in a closed meeting, but recent years have seen fewer caucuses and more primaries.

3. After the primary and caucus season finishes, parties hold their national conventions to choose candidates—who generally have been determined in advance by the nominating elections—for the general election.

4. In the general election that follows, statewide popular votes are used to determine the composition of the electoral college, which ultimately makes the formal choice of a president. The electoral college is a controversial institution, and frequent proposals for reform of it are aired. But it also has its staunch defenders, especially the lightly populated states that benefit from it.

5. Voters tend to vote retrospectively—that is, they judge candidates based on their past performance, or on the past performance of the party in power.

6. There are voting patterns over time that are evident to election scholars. Approximately every thirty-two or thirty-six years, voters have realigned into coalitions that redefine the parties and their candidates. These major realignments are precipitated by one or more critical elections, which polarize voters around new issues and personalities in reaction to crucial developments, such as wars or depressions. We are long overdue for a critical election, but it may not be possible in an age of lesser party loyalties.

7. Voter participation tends to follow certain patterns: the more educated, affluent, and older the citizens are, the more often they vote; also, whites tend to vote more often than non-whites; Southerners vote less often than non-Southerners.

8. The incumbency advantage in congressional elections is so significant and powerful that relatively few sitting legislators are ever defeated for reelection. Those who do lose usually are victims of redistricting, scandal, or presidential coattail effects.

9. The United States has exceptionally low voter turnout. The reasons include voter registration and absentee ballot barriers, alienation, and voter indifference (due to everything from apathy to satisfaction). Remedies for low turnout are many, ranging from an election day holiday to better civic education in the schools.

10. The practice of ticket-splitting has become commonplace during an era of issue-oriented, candidate-centered politics with weaker partisan loyalties. One consequence is the greater likelihood of split party control of the executive and legislative branches both in Washington and the state capitals.

Key Terms

electorate

mandate

retrospective judgment

primary elections

closed primaries

open primaries

blanket primary

runoff primary

white primary

general elections

regional primaries

uncommitted delegates

superdelegates

unit rule

electors

party realignments

critical elections

secular realignment

incumbency

off-year elections

Suggested Readings

Asher, Herbert B. *Presidential Elections and American Politics,* 4th ed. Chicago: Dorsey Press, 1988.

Bartels, Larry M. *Presidential Primaries and the Dynamics of Public Choice.* Princeton, NJ: Princeton University Press, 1988.

Berelson, Bernard R., Paul F. Lazarsfeld, and William N. McPhee. *Voting: A Study of Opinion Formation in a Presidential Campaign.* Chicago: University of Chicago Press, 1954.

Burnham, Walter Dean. *Critical Elections and the Mainsprings of American Politics.* New York: Norton, 1970.

Campbell, Angus, Philip E. Converse, Warren E. Miller, and Donald E. Stokes. *The American Voter.* New York: Wiley, 1960.

Ceaser, James W. *Presidential Selection: Theory and Development.* Princeton, NJ: Princeton University Press, 1979.

Fiorina, Morris P. *Retrospective Voting in American National Elections.* New Haven, CT: Yale University Press, 1981.

Jacobson, Gary C. *The Politics of Congressional Elections,* 2nd ed. Boston: Little, Brown, 1987.

———. *The Electoral Origins of Divided Government.* Boulder, CO: Westview Press, 1990.

Kelley, Stanley Jr. *Interpreting Elections.* Princeton, NJ: Princeton University Press, 1983.

Key, V. O. Jr., with the assistance of Milton C. Cummings. *The Responsible Electorate.* Cambridge, MA: Harvard University Press, 1966.

Nie, Norman H., Sidney Verba, and John R. Petrocik. *The Changing American Voter.* Cambridge, MA: Belknap Press of Harvard University, 1966.

Polsby, Nelson W., and Aaron Wildavsky. *Presidential Elections: Contemporary Strategies of American Electoral Politics,* 7th ed. New York: Free Press, 1988.

Wayne, Stephen J. *The Road to the White House,* 2nd ed. New York: St. Martin's Press, 1984.

The Campaign Process

What might James Madison have said about the relentlessly vicious presidential and congressional campaigns of recent years? Of course, even in his day, politics could get down and dirty, with gossip and slander ruling the day. But Madison could not have conceived of television, much less negative attack commercials used to sully the reputations of all contenders in modern campaigns—so we can forgive him for assuming that every winner is awarded the esteem of his or her constituents. Yet in another sense Madison is correct. Each victorious candidate manages to obtain the votes of a plurality of those people going to the polls on Election Day. The candidate accomplishes this personal triumph by means of the campaign, the process of seeking and winning votes in the run-up to an election.

So far we have focused on the election decision itself and have said little about the campaign conducted prior to the balloting. Although modern electioneering is advanced, with dazzling technologies and strategies used to attract voters, its basic purpose is primitive: one person asking another for support, an approach unchanged since the dawn of democracy.

The art of campaigning involves the science of polls, the planning of sophisticated mass mailings, and the coordination of electronic telephone banks to reach voters. More important, it also involves the diplomatic skill of unifying disparate individuals and groups to achieve a fragile but election-winning majority. How candidates perform this exquisitely difficult task is the subject of this chapter. First we examine how campaigns are organized, with a special eye on media—both the press and the separate television advertising that is so dominant today. The money chase—the ways in which candidates raise and spend the enormous sums necessary to win office—is discussed in some detail. Last, an extended look at the ins and outs of the 1992 presidential election attempts to bring together the main lessons of both Chapters 12 and 13.

433

> **P**eople will enter into the public service under circumstances which cannot fail to produce a temporary affection at least to their constituents. There is in every breast a sensibility to marks of honor, of favor, of esteem, and of confidence, which, apart from all considerations of interest, is some pledge for grateful and benevolent returns.
>
> *James Madison*
> *Federalist No. 57*

In this passage Madison expresses his belief that public servants will be held in high esteem and honor by the constituents who have elected them—at least for a while—and that those public servants will in return be true to the voters who put them in office.

At the Starting Block: Ambition and Strategy

In Federalist No. 57 James Madison suggests one of the vital motivations that lead candidates to seek public office: the desire for "marks of honor" and "esteem." Fortunately for U.S. democracy, a fair number of people find the often intangible rewards of public service to be sufficient inducement to enter the public arena. They are willing to

Appealing to various groups: During the first week of March 1992, Governor Bill Clinton campaigned hard in Florida. A densely populated state with a wide range of voters, Florida has been a key early contest for several recent election cycles. On March 4 in Miami, Clinton reiterated a pledge for tax cuts for working people, a position that helped him gain a plurality of both black and white Democratic voters in the statewide contest on March 10.

"Next time, why don't you run? You're a well-known figure, people seem to like you, and you haven't had an original idea in years."

put up with abuse from citizens, criticism from the press, invasion of their privacy, and frequently a lessening of income in order to win the honor of office. Despite the common notion that "the office seeks the man or woman," it is personal *ambition* that leads most candidates to the starting gate.[1] The ambition is not always selfish. In addition to a desire for power, a candidate may wish to push an issue or cause dear to his or her heart.

Whatever their motivation, candidates quickly recognize the realities of running for office. The candidate's campaign must be geared to appeal to both rank-and-file voters and the leaders of various groups and voting blocs (such as business, labor, and key ethnic populations). The candidate must find issues that motivate voters and must take defensible stands on the controversies of the day. Unavoidably, the candidate must also raise large sums of money in order to compete, as we discuss later.

The Structure of a Campaign

A campaign for high office (such as the presidency, a governorship, or a U.S. Senate seat) is a highly complex effort akin to running a multimillion-dollar business, while campaigns for local offices are usually less complicated mom-and-pop operations. But all campaigns, no matter what their size, have certain aspects in common. Indeed, each campaign really consists of several campaigns that are run simultaneously, including the following:

Nomination campaign That part of a political campaign aimed at winning a primary election.

General election campaign That part of a political campaign following a primary election, aimed at winning a general election.

Personal campaign That part of a political campaign concerned with presenting the candidate's public image.

Organizational campaign That part of a political campaign involved in fund raising, literature distribution, and all other activities not directly involving the candidate.

Media campaign That part of a political campaign waged in the broadcast and print media.

Paid media Political advertisements purchased for a candidate's campaign.

Free media Coverage of a candidate's campaign by the news media.

1. The **nomination campaign.** The target is the party elite, the leaders and activists who choose nominees in primaries or conventions. Party leaders are concerned with electability, while activists are often ideologically and issue oriented, so a candidate must appeal to both bases.

2. The **general election campaign.** A far-sighted candidate never forgets the ultimate goal: winning the general election. Therefore, the candidate tries to avoid taking stands that, however pleasing to party activists in the primary, will alienate a majority of the larger general election constituency.

3. The **personal campaign.** This is the public part of the campaign. The candidate and his or her family and supporters make appearances, meet voters, hold press conferences, and give speeches.

4. The **organizational campaign.** Behind the scenes, another campaign is humming. Volunteers telephone voters and distribute literature, staffers organize events, and everyone raises money to support the operation.

5. The **media campaign.** On television and radio the candidate's advertisements (termed **paid media**) air frequently in an effort to convince the public that the candidate is the best person for the job. Meanwhile, campaigners attempt to influence the press coverage of the campaign by the print and electronic news reporters—the **free media.**

British election campaigns are very different from those in the United States. In the first place, candidate selection is controlled by local party organizations, not by any sort of primary system. Second, the national parties control key facets of the campaign, for example, providing the financing, which is regulated by national statute, and executing the campaign strategy. As a result, national party platforms—not candidate personalities—play a dominant role in British campaigns. Finally, the power of the prime minister to call elections at his or her discretion—literally at a moment's notice—produces campaigns of a mere four to five weeks in duration instead of the two years (for a Senate seat) to four-year campaigns (for president) we endure in the United States.

In order to better comprehend the various campaigns, let's examine a few aspects of each, remembering that they must all mesh successfully for the candidate to win.

The Nomination Campaign

A new candidate gets sea legs early on, as he or she adjusts to the pressures of being in the spotlight day in and day out. This is the time for the candidate to learn that a single careless phrase could end the campaign or guarantee a defeat. This is also the time to seek the support of party leaders and interest groups and to test out themes, slogans, and strategies. The press and public take much less notice of shifts in strategy at this time than they will later in the general election campaign.

At this time, there is a danger not widely recognized by candidates: Surrounded by friendly activists and ideological soulmates in the quest to win the party's nomination, a candidate can move too far to the right or the left and become too extreme for the November electorate. Conservative Barry Goldwater, the 1964 Republican nominee for president, and liberal George McGovern, the 1972 Democratic nominee for president, both fell victim to this phenomenon in seeking their party's nomination, and they were handily defeated in the general elections by Presidents Lyndon B. Johnson and Richard M. Nixon, respectively.

The General Election Campaign

Once the choice between the two major-party nominees is clear, both candidates can get to work. Most significant interest groups are courted for money and endorsements, although the results are mainly predictable: liberal, labor, and minority groups usually back Democrats, while conservative and business organizations support Republicans. The most active and intense groups are often coalesced around emotional issues such as abortion and gun control, and these organizations can produce a bumper crop of money and activists for favored candidates.

Virtually all candidates adopt a brief theme, or slogan, to serve as a rallying cry in their quest for office. (The first to do so was William Henry Harrison in 1840 (see "William Henry Harrison and the Media Campaign of 1840," p. 441). Some presidential campaign slogans have entered national lore (see the box below), but most are nondescript and can fit many candidates ("She thinks like us," "He's on our side," "She hears you," "You know where he stands"). Candidates try to avoid controversy in their selection of slogans, and some openly eschew ideology. (An ever-popular one of this genre: "Not left, not right—forward!") The clever candidate also attempts to find a slogan that cannot be lampooned easily. In 1964 Barry Goldwater's handlers may

---

Famous Presidential Campaign Slogans
◆ ◆ ◆

William Henry Harrison (Whig, 1840)	"Tippecanoe and Tyler, Too"[a]
Calvin Coolidge (Republican, 1924)	"Keep Cool with Coolidge"
Herbert Hoover (Republican, 1928)	"A Chicken in Every Pot, a Car in Every Garage."
Dwight D. Eisenhower (Republican, 1952)	"I Like Ike"
Lyndon B. Johnson (Democrat, 1964)	"All the Way with LBJ"
Barry Goldwater (Republican, 1964)	"In Your Heart You Know He's Right"
George Wallace (Independent, 1968)	"Send Them a Message"
Richard M. Nixon (Republican, 1968)	"Nixon's the One!"
Richard M. Nixon (Republican, 1972)	"Now More Than Ever"
Jimmy Carter (Democrat, 1976)	"Why Not the Best?"
Ronald Reagan (Republican, 1984)	"It's Morning in America"
George Bush (Republican, 1992)	"Annoy the Media. Re-elect Bush"
Bill Clinton (Democrat, 1992)	"It's the economy, stupid."[b]

[a]Tippecanoe was a nickname given to Harrison—a reference to his participation in the battle of Tippecanoe—and Tyler was Harrison's vice-presidential candidate, John Tyler of Virginia.

[b]This was a sign posted in Clinton's Little Rock headquarters, and it became the guiding philosophy of his general election campaign.

have regretted their choice of "In your heart you know he's right" when Lyndon B. Johnson's supporters quickly converted it into "In your guts you know he's nuts." (Democrats were trying to portray Goldwater as a warmonger after the Republican indicated a willingness to use nuclear weapons in Vietnam and elsewhere under some conditions.)

The Personal Campaign

In the effort to show voters that they are hard working, thoughtful, and worthy of the office they seek, candidates try to meet personally as many citizens as possible in the course of a campaign. A candidate for high office may deliver up to a dozen speeches a day, and that is only part of the exhausting schedule most contenders maintain. The day may begin at 5:00 A.M. at the entrance gate to an auto plant with an hour or two of handshaking, followed by similar gladhanding at subway stops until 9:00 A.M. Strategy sessions with key advisers and preparation for upcoming presentations and forums may fill the morning. A luncheon talk, afternoon fund raisers, and a series of television and print interviews crowd the afternoon agenda. The light fare of cocktail parties is followed by a dinner speech, perhaps telephone or neighborhood canvassing of voters, and a civic-forum talk or two. More meetings with advisers and planning for the next day's events can easily take a candidate past midnight. Following only a few hours of sleep, the candidate starts all over again. After months of this grueling pace, the candidate may be functioning on automatic pilot and unable to think clearly.

Beyond the strains this fast-lane existence adds to a candidate's family life, the hectic schedule leaves little time for reflection and long-range planning. Is it any wonder that under these conditions many candidates commit gaffes and appear to have foot-in-mouth disease?

Of course considerable rewards are to be had on the campaign trail that balance the personal disadvantages. A candidate can affect the course of the government and community and in so doing become admired and respected by peers. Meeting all kinds of

On February 12, 1992, President Bush formally announced his candidacy in Washington and then quickly flew to New Hampshire to begin campaigning with voters at the Bedford, New Hampshire Mall.

Right-wing 1964 Republican candidate Barry Goldwater's famous slogan, "In your heart, you know he's right" was quickly lampooned by incumbent Democratic opponent President Lyndon B. Johnson's campaign as "In your guts you know he's nuts."

Media consultants arrange everything from paid advertising to daily photo opportunities, such as this Oval Office setting for President Clinton.

people, solving problems, gaining exposure to every facet of life in one's constituency—these experiences help a public person live life fully and compensate for the hardships of the campaign trail.

The Organizational Campaign

If the candidate is the public face of the campaign, the organization behind the candidate is the private face. Depending on the level of the office sought, the organizational staff can consist of a handful of volunteers or hundreds of paid specialists supplementing and directing the work of thousands of volunteers. The most elaborate structure is found in presidential campaigns. Tens of thousands of volunteers distribute literature and visit neighborhoods. They are directed by paid staff that may number three hundred or more, including a couple of dozen lawyers and accountants. At the top of the organizational chart are the campaign manager and the key political consultants, the hired handlers who provide technologies, services, and strategies to the campaign. The best-known consultants for any campaign are usually the **media consultant,** who produces the candidate's television and radio advertisements; the **pollster,** who takes the public opinion surveys that guide the campaign; and the **direct mailer,** who supervises direct-mail fund raising. After the candidate, however, the most important person in the campaign is probably the finance chair, who is responsible for bringing in the large contributions that pay most of the salaries of the consultants and staff.

In addition to raising money, the most vital work of the candidate's organization is to get in touch with voters. Some of this is done in person by volunteers who walk the neighborhoods going door to door to solicit votes. Some is accomplished by telephone as volunteers use computerized telephone banks to call targeted voters with scripted messages. Both contact methods are termed **voter canvass.** Most canvassing takes place in the month before the election, when voters are paying attention. Close to Election Day, the telephone banks begin the vital **get-out-the-vote** (GOTV) effort, reminding supporters to vote and arranging for their transportation to the polls if necessary. (See Figure 13-1 for a summary graph of a campaign's basic organization.)

Media consultant A professional who produces political candidate's television, radio, and print advertisements.

Pollster A professional who takes public opinion surveys that guide political campaigns.

Direct mailer A professional who supervises a political campaign's direct-mail fund-raising strategies.

Voter canvass The process by which a campaign gets in touch with individual voters, either by door-to-door solicitation or by telephone.

Get-out-the-vote A push at the end of a political campaign to encourage supporters to go to the polls.

FIGURE 13-1
The Organizational Campaign

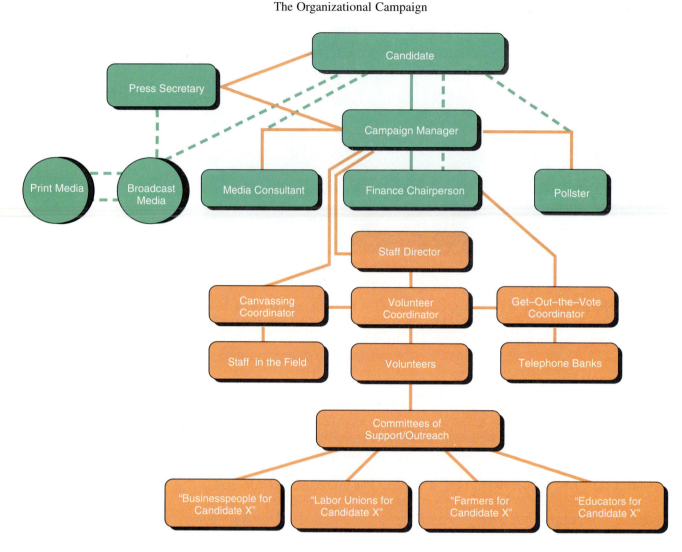

The Media Campaign

Positive ads Advertising on behalf of a candidate that stresses the candidates qualifications, family and issue positions without reference to the opponent.

Negative ads Advertising on behalf of a candidate that attacks the opponents platform or character.

What voters actually see and hear of the candidate is primarily determined by the paid media (such as television advertising) accompanying the campaign and the free media (newspaper and television coverage). The two kinds of media are fundamentally different: Paid advertising is completely under the control of the campaign, whereas the press is totally independent. Great care is taken in the design of the television advertising, which takes many approaches. **Positive ads** stress the candidate's qualifications, family, and issue positions with no direct reference to the opponent. **Negative ads** attack the opponent's character and platform and (except for a brief legally required identification at the ad's conclusion) may not even mention the candidate who is paying for their airing. **Contrast ads** compare the records and proposals of the candidates—obviously with a bias toward the sponsor. And whether the public likes them or not, all three kinds of ads can inject important (as well as trivial) issues into a campaign.

Contrast ads Political campaign advertisements that compare the records of the candidates, favoring the ads sponsor.

PEOPLE OF THE PAST

William Henry Harrison and the Media Campaign of 1840

The political historian Keith Melder, among others, has argued that William Henry Harrison's 1840 run for the presidency was the first media campaign, complete with the creation of an image and the means for selling it to the public.

Harrison's campaign began with his pursuit of the Whig Party's nomination, for which Harrison—an accomplished general but a political novice—ran against Henry Clay and Daniel Webster, both experienced politicians. In the first Whig national convention, party leaders unfriendly to Clay and Webster rigged the rules in Harrison's favor, guaranteeing his nomination. For geographic balance, they also added Virginian John Tyler to the ticket as the vice-presidential candidate. (Harrison, although also a native of Virginia, was governor of Indiana.) Moreover, since the party was divided over many issues, the leadership decided early on that waging a colorful and unsubstantial campaign would be the best route to victory in a year when the incumbent Democratic president, Martin Van Buren, was already weakened by a severe economic depression.

Ironically, Harrison's key image was provided not by his own party but by a Democratic newspaper in Baltimore, which caricatured Harrison as a cider-swilling, log cabin-dwelling simpleton. Unfortunately for the Democrats, the Whig Party took hold of this sarcasm and converted it into a powerful campaign theme for the candidate. Harrison, the Whig Party claimed, resided in a log cabin (actually, only the original structure of his home was made from logs) and supposedly possessed all the virtuous qualities of the hard-working frontiersman.

The log cabin issue was pushed vigorously by the Whigs, who used banners, ribbons, songs, and cabin raisings—the construction of log cabins in many communities to serve as the local Whig Party headquarters—to get their message to the public. The Whig Party created a campaign newspaper—named, of course, the *Log Cabin*—that featured speeches by eloquent Whigs and, in a true harbinger of things to come, peddled campaign banners and log cabin souvenirs considered indispensable to the loyal Harrison supporter. In another first, the candidate himself spoke often (a total of twenty-three speeches) on behalf of his candidacy. Before 1840, it had been considered improper for a candidate to participate directly in the electioneering process.

The Harrison campaign of 1840, then, was the first to sell a candidate as a national product, and it became the model for many presidential campaigns to follow. The Democrats complained loudly about Whig showboating, but when Harrison easily defeated Van Buren, the Whig methods seemed vindicated. As for the voters, they clearly preferred the new style of campaigning. Not only did Harrison win handsomely, but nearly 80 percent of those eligible to vote also turned out at the polls—a remarkable proportion at that time, or in ours. (In 1992 only 55 percent of the eligible voters cast a ballot for president.) Tragically for Harrison, his election was the high point of the briefest of all presidencies. After catching cold at his March 1841 inauguration, Harrison died in April, serving as president for only one month.

Spot ads Television advertising on behalf of a candidate that is broadcast in sixty-, thirty-, or ten-second durations.

The infamous "Willie Horton" ad (held up here by the candidate) portrayed Democratic nominee Michael Dukakis as soft on crime by implying that Horton's escape from a Massachusetts prison work-release program and his subsequent terrorizing of a Florida family were a result of Governor Dukakis's liberal policies. Critics charged that this ad, in particular, was both misleading and racist; nevertheless, it seemed to resonate with voters.

Occasionally, advertisements are relatively long (ranging from four-and-one-half-minute ads up to thirty-minute documentaries). Usually, however, the messages are short **spot ads** of sixty-, thirty-, or ten-second durations.

There is little question that negative advertisements have shown the greatest growth in the past two decades. While voters normally need a reason to vote *for* a candidate, they also frequently vote *against* the other candidate—and negative ads can provide the critical justification for such a vote.

Prior to the 1980s, well-known incumbents usually ignored negative attacks from their challengers, believing that the proper stance was to be above the fray. But after some well-publicized defeats of incumbents in the early 1980s in which negative television advertising played a prominent role,* incumbents began attacking their challengers with relish. The new rule of politics became "An attack unanswered is an attack agreed to." In a further attempt to stave off brickbats from challengers, incumbents even began anticipating the substance of their opponents' attacks and airing inoculation advertising early in the campaign to protect themselves in advance of the other side's spots. (Inoculation advertising attempts to counteract an *anticipated* attack from the opposition *before* the attack is even launched.) For example, a senator who fears a broadside about her voting record on Social Security issues might air advertisements featuring senior citizens praising her support of Social Security.

The Candidate or the Campaign: Which Do We Vote For?

One important point needs to be made about media and organizational techniques. Much is said and written about them during the campaign, and they are often presented as political magic. Yet although campaign methods have clearly become very sophisticated, the technologies still often fail the candidates and their campaigns. The political consultants who develop and master the technologies of polling, media, and other techniques frequently make serious mistakes in judgment. Despite popular lore and journalistic legend, few candidates are the creations of their clever consultants and dazzling campaign techniques. Partly, this is because politics always has been (and always will be) much more art than science, not subject to precise manipulation or formulaic computation. *In the end—in most cases—the candidate wins or loses the race according to his or her abilities, qualifications, communication skills, issues, and weaknesses.* Although this simple truth is warmly reassuring, it has been remarkably overlooked by election analysts and reporters seemingly mesmerized by the exorbitant claims of consultants and the flashy computer lights of their technologies.[2] Of course, campaign techniques can enhance the candidate's strengths and downplay his or her weaknesses, and in that respect, technique certainly matters.

The voter deserves much of the credit for whatever encouragement we can draw from this candidate-centered view of politics. Granted, citizens are often inattentive to politics and, in effect, force candidates to use empty slogans and glitz to attract their attention. But it is also true that most voters want to take the real measure of candi-

---

* Five liberal Democratic U.S. senators, including George McGovern of South Dakota, were defeated in this fashion in 1980, for example.

dates and retain a healthy skepticism about the techniques of running for office. The political cartoonist Tom Toles suggested as much when he depicted the seven preparatory steps the modern candidate takes: (1) Set out to discover what voters want, (2) Conduct extensive polling, (3) Study demographic trends, (4) Engage in sophisticated interpretation of in-depth voter interviews, (5) Analyze results, (6) Discover that what the voters want is a candidate who doesn't need to do steps one through five, (7) Pretend you didn't. The chastened politician then tells his assembled throng, "I follow my conscience."[3]

Modern Campaign Challenges

The modern candidate faces two major challenges: communicating through the media and raising the money needed to stay in the race. We consider each challenge in turn.

The News Media

The news media present quite a challenge to candidates. Although politicians and their staffs cannot control the press, they nonetheless try to manipulate press coverage. They use three techniques to accomplish this aim. First, the staff often seeks to isolate the candidate from the press, thus reducing the chances that reporters will bait a candidate into saying something that might damage the candidate's cause. Naturally, the media are frustrated by such a tactic and insist on as many open press conferences as possible. Second, the campaign stages media events—activities designed to include brief, clever quotes called "soundbites" and staged with appealing backdrops so that they are all but irresistible, especially to television news. In this fashion the candidate's staff can successfully fill the news hole reserved for campaign coverage on the evening news programs and in the morning papers. Third, the handlers and consultants have perfected the technique termed "spin"—that is, they put the most favorable possible interpretation for their candidate on any circumstance occurring in the campaign, and they work the press to sell their point of view or at least to ensure that it is included in the reporters' stories. **Candidate debates,** especially the televised presidential variety, are showcases for the consultants' spin patrol, and teams of staffers from each side swarm the press rooms to declare victory even before the candidates finish their closing statements.

Candidate debates Forums in which political candidates face each other to discuss their platforms, records, and character.

In Great Britain, where the House of Commons is structured to provide continuous debate between government and opposition, resorting to such media extravaganza is for the most part superfluous. To be sure, television plays an increasingly important role as a forum for party clashes in British politics, but in no way does it achieve the prominence of television coverage in the United States.

Televised Debates. Candidate debates are media extravaganzas that are a hybrid of free and paid media. As with ads, much of the candidate dialogue (jokes included) is canned and prepackaged. Yet spontaneity cannot be completely eliminated, and gaffes, quips, and slips of the tongue can sometimes be revealing. President Gerald Ford's insistence during an October 1976 debate with Jimmy Carter that Poland was not under Soviet domination may have cost him a close election. Ronald Reagan's refrain, "Are

Democratic candidate Bill Clinton makes a point during the second of three presidential debates in the 1992 election campaign. This debate, held in Richmond, Virginia, had an unusually informal format that allowed the candidates to move about the stage as they responded to questions from an audience of uncommitted voters.

you better off today than you were four years ago?" neatly summed up his case against Carter in 1980. Moreover, Reagan's easygoing performance reassured a skeptical public that wanted Carter out of the White House but was not certain it wanted Reagan in.

Senator John F. Kennedy's visually impressive showing in the first 1960 presidential debate dramatically reduced the utility of two-term Vice President Richard M. Nixon's experience edge. Not only was Nixon ill at the time, but he also was poorly dressed and poorly made up for television. Interestingly, most of those who heard the debate on radio—and therefore could not see the contrast between the pale, anxious, sweating Nixon and the relaxed, tanned Kennedy—thought that Nixon had won.

The importance of debates can easily be overrated, however. A weak performance by Reagan in his first debate with Walter Mondale in 1984 had little lasting effect, in part because Reagan did better in the second debate. And most of the debates in 1960, 1976, 1980, and 1988 were unmemorable and electorally inconsequential. Debates usually just firm up voters' predispositions and cannot change the fundamentals of an election (the state of the economy, scandal, and presidential popularity, for example). This is what appeared to happen in 1992, when none of the three presidential debates and one vice-presidential debate changed the underlying pro-Clinton trends in the election. Nonetheless, because debates are potentially educational and focus the public's mind on the upcoming election, they are useful. Since they have been held in every presidential campaign from 1976, debates are now likely to be an expected and standard part of the presidential election process.* They are also an established feature of campaigns for governor, U.S. senator, and many other offices.

Can the Press Be "Handled"?   Whether in debates or elsewhere, efforts by candidates to manipulate the news media often fail because the press is wise to their tactics

---

* Incumbents or frontrunners refused to participate in suggested presidential debates in 1964, 1968, and 1972, but precedent would now probably make such a decision a costly one for any presidential contender, even an incumbent.

and determined to thwart them. Not even the candidates' paid media are sacrosanct anymore. The press, especially major newspapers throughout the country, has taken to analyzing the accuracy of the television advertisements aired during the campaign—a welcome and useful addition to journalists' scrutiny of politicians.

Less welcome are some other news media practices in campaigns. Many studies have shown that the media are obsessed with the horse race aspect of politics—who's ahead, who's behind, who's gaining—to the detriment of the substance of the candidates' issues and ideas. Public opinion polls, especially tracking polls, many of them taken by the news outlets themselves, dominate coverage, especially on network television, where only a few minutes a night are devoted to politics. (Tracking polls were discussed in Chapter 10.)

Related to the proliferation of polls is the media's expectations game in presidential primary contests. With polls as the objective backdrop, journalists set the margins by which contenders are expected to win or lose—so much so that even a clear victory of five percentage points can be judged a setback if the candidate had been projected to win by twelve or fifteen points. Finally, the news media often overemphasize trivial parts of the campaign, such as a politician's minor gaffe, and give too much attention to the private lives of candidates. This superficial coverage and the resources needed to generate it are displacing serious journalism on the issues. These subjects are taken up again in the next chapter, which deals with the news media.

Raising the Money

To run all aspects of a campaign successfully requires a great deal of money. In 1992 alone, more than $675 million was raised and spent in U.S. House and Senate races.[4] This amount was an increase of 40 percent over the 1990 elections, mainly owing to greater competition because of a large number of open seats—one of the effects of redistricting. Because of a vacancy, there were also simultaneous elections in 1992 for

Fund Raising for 1996
❖ ❖ ❖

No one knows in advance the winner of the 1996 presidential race, but one prediction is certain: the winner will have raised and spent more money in the primary season than any candidate in previous election years.

Republican candidates are each planning to raise $20-25 million for the nomination process, and raising money has been termed "the first primary." Texas U.S. Senator Phil Gramm raised an estimated $4 million at a single fundraiser in his state in March 1995, for example.

In the general election, each of the major-party candidates will be given more than $50 million in public funds to finance their campaigns. In addition, the Democratic and Republican National Committees will raise tens of millions of dollars to spend on party activities related to the presidential campaign.

Political action committees
Federally mandated, officially registered fund-raising committees that represent interest groups in the political process.
Public funds: Donations from general tax revenues to the campaigns of qualifying presidential candidates.

two U.S. Senate seats in California, the largest and most expensive state for campaigns. On average, a House incumbent who was seriously challenged and received less than 55 percent of the vote spent nearly $750,000, while his or her opponent spent nearly $400,000. As humorist Will Rogers once remarked early in the twentieth century, "Politics has got so expensive that it takes lots of money even to get beat with."

All this political money is regulated by the federal government under the terms of the Federal Election Campaign Act of 1971, first passed in 1971 and substantially strengthened after Watergate in 1974 and again in 1976. (Still more amendments were passed in 1979.) Table 13.1 summarizes some of the important provisions of this law, which limits what individuals, interest groups, and political parties can give to candidates for president, U.S. senator, and U.S. representative. These limits on contributions are discussed in the passages that follow, but the goal of all limits is the same: to prevent any single group or individual from gaining too much influence over elected officials, who naturally feel indebted to campaign contributors.

Given the cash flow required by a campaign and the legal restrictions on political money, raising the funds necessary to run a modern campaign is a monumental task.

Table 13.1 ◆   **Current Contribution Limits for Congressional Candidates (under the Federal Election Campaign Act)**

CONTRIBUTIONS FROM	GIVEN TO CANDIDATE (PER ELECTION)[a]	GIVEN TO NATIONAL PARTY (PER CALENDAR YEAR)	TOTAL ALLOWABLE CONTRIBUTIONS (PER CALENDAR YEAR)
Individual	$1,000	$20,000	Limited to $25,000
Political action committee[b]	$5,000	$15,000	No limit
Any political party committee[c]	$5,000	No limit	No limit
All national and state party committees taken together	To House candidates: $30,000 plus "coordinated expenditures"[d] (of $55,240 per candidate in 1992) To Senate candidates: $27,500 plus "coordinated expenditures"[d] (of $110,480 per candidate in smallest states to $2.5 million in California in 1992)		

[a]Each of the following is considered a *separate* election: primary (or convention), run-off, general election.

[b]Multi-candidate PACs only. Multi-candidate committees have received contributions from at least fifty persons and have given to at least five federal candidates.

[c]Multi-candidate party committees only. Multi-candidate committees have received contributions from at least fifty persons and have given to at least five federal candidates.

[d]Coordinated expenditures are party-paid general election campaign expenditures made in consultation and coordination with the candidate.

Consequently, presidential and congressional campaigns have squads of fund raisers on staff. These professionals rely on several standard sources of campaign money.

Individual Contributions.   Individual contributions are donations from individual citizens. The maximum allowable contribution under federal law for congressional and presidential elections is $1,000 per election to each candidate, with primary and general elections considered separately. Individuals are also limited to a total of $25,000 in gifts to all candidates combined in each calendar year. Most candidates receive a majority of all funds directly from individuals, and most individual gifts are well below the maximum level.

Political Action Committee (PAC) Contributions.   Donations from **political action committees** are those from interest groups (labor unions, corporations, trade associations, and ideological and issue groups). Under federal law these organizations are required to establish officially recognized fund-raising committees, called PACs, in order to participate in federal elections. (Some but not all states have similar requirements for state elections.) Approximately 4,000 PACs are registered with the Federal Election Commission—the governmental agency charged with administering the election laws—and in 1994 all PACs together gave $179 million to Senate and House candidates. (By contrast, individual citizens donated nearly $336 million.) On average, PAC contributions account for 33 percent of the war chests (campaign funds) of House candidates and 20 percent of the treasuries of Senate candidates. (Interest groups are treated in more detail in Chapter 15.)

Political Party Contributions.   Candidates also receive donations from the national and state committees of the Democratic and Republican parties. As is mentioned in Chapter 11, political parties can give substantial contributions to their congressional nominees. In 1994 both the Republican and the Democrats funneled over $23 million to their standard-bearers. In competitive races the parties may provide 15 to 17 percent of their candidates' total war chests.

Candidates' Personal Contributions.   Candidates and their families may donate to the campaign. The Supreme Court ruled in 1976 in *Buckley* v. *Valeo* that no limit could be placed on the amount of money candidates can spend from their own families' resources, since such spending is considered a First Amendment right of free speech [424 U.S.1 (1976)]. For wealthy politicians such as U.S. Senators John D. Rockefeller IV (D-W.Va.) or Herbert H. Kohl (D-Wisc.), this allowance may mean personal spending in the millions. Most candidates, however, commit much less than $100,000 in family resources to their election bids. Ross Perot, who publicly committed to spend millions, was not the usual candidate. In 1994 House and Senate candidates loaned or contributed almost $82 million to their own campaigns.

Public Funds.   **Public funds** are donations from general tax revenues. Only presidential candidates (and a handful of state and local contenders) receive public funds. Under the terms of the Federal Election Campaign Act of 1971 (which first established public funding of presidential campaigns), a candidate for president can become eligible to receive public funds during the nominating contest by raising at least $5,000 in individual contributions of $250 or less in each of twenty states. Once the receipt of

---

Women's PACs Continue to Make a Difference
◆ ◆ ◆

Women's political action committees have made a real difference in recent elections. In 1990, women's PACs contributed over 2.6 million to candidates and in 1992 nearly triple that.

EMILY's List, which stands for Early Money Is Like Yeast (it makes the dough rise), is the largest contributor to women's campaigns. Founded in 1985, its members contributed nearly 1.5 million to liberal female candidates in 1990. Ann Richards, who ran a hotly contested race for the Texas governorship in 1990, credits EMILY's List with providing crucial funding at a key time. In 1992, EMILY's List provided $6.2 million to 55 pro-choice Democratic women candidates of whom 25 won. EMILY's list also spent more than $8.2 million to support 38 candidates in the 1994 election cycle.

Sources: Center for the American Woman and Politics, *CAWP News & Notes* (Winter 1991), pp. 10–11, *The Times-Picayune,* "EMILY's List Dough Helps Women Rise," January 26, 1994, p. A1; and, EMILY's List.

Matching funds Donations to presidential campaigns from the federal government that are determined by the amount of private funds a qualifying candidate raises.

this money is certified, the candidate can apply for federal **matching funds,** whereby every dollar raised from individuals in amounts less than $251 is matched by the federal treasury on a dollar-for-dollar basis. This assumes there is enough money in the Presidential Election Campaign Fund to do so. The fund is accumulated by taxpayers who designate $1.00 of their taxes for this purpose each year when they send in their federal tax returns. (Only about 20 percent of taxpayers check off the appropriate box, even though participation does not increase their tax burden.)

For the general election, the two major-party presidential nominees are given a lump-sum payment in the summer before the election ($55 million each in 1992), from which all their general election campaign expenditures must come. A third-party can-

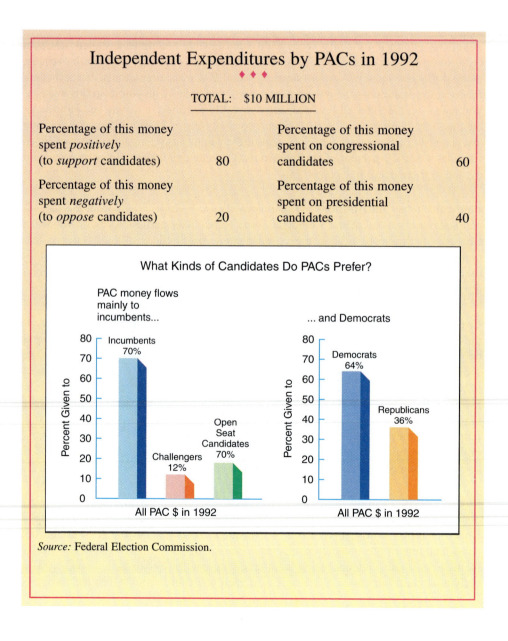

Independent Expenditures by PACs in 1992

◆ ◆ ◆

TOTAL: $10 MILLION

Percentage of this money spent *positively* (to *support* candidates)	80	Percentage of this money spent on congressional candidates	60
Percentage of this money spent *negatively* (to *oppose* candidates)	20	Percentage of this money spent on presidential candidates	40

What Kinds of Candidates Do PACs Prefer?

PAC money flows mainly to incumbents...

Incumbents 70%
Open Seat Candidates 70%
Challengers 12%

Percent Given to

All PAC $ in 1992

... and Democrats

Democrats 64%
Republicans 36%

Percent Given to

All PAC $ in 1992

Source: Federal Election Commission.

didate receives a smaller amount proportionate to his or her November vote total *if* that candidate gains a minimum of 5 percent of the vote. Note that in such a case the money goes to third-party campaigns only *after* the election is over; no money is given in advance of the general election. The only third-party candidate to qualify for general election funds so far has been John Anderson, the Independent candidate for president in 1980, who garnered 7 percent of the national vote. Ross Perot chose not to take public funds for his campaign, which was largely self-financed.

Independent Expenditures.   Individuals, groups, and PACs also spend money independent of any campaign or candidate. This spending is *not* under the direction or control of the campaign staff and is unlimited because First Amendment free speech is involved. Sometimes the spending is positive and advocates the election of a candidate; on other occasions it is negative, urging the defeat of a targeted candidate. (See "Independent Expenditures by PACs in 1992," p. 448.) Liberals, conservatives, environmentalists, supporters of Israel, and trade groups representing realtors, doctors, and car dealers are some organizations that have used this supplementary method of campaign spending over the years. In addition, untold millions are spent by labor, corporate, and community groups for grassroots organizing, voter registration, volunteer participation, and internal political communications with their members and employees. Depending on the sponsoring group, all of this activity has a political effect—favoring one candidate or party and hurting others—but that is not always obvious or well publicized. Also, unlike all the other forms of contributions discussed earlier, it is usually not necessary for these indirect gifts to be disclosed to the Federal Election Commission.*

It is often alleged that campaign contributions are used illegally. Republican Christine Todd Whitman is shown here with Jesse Jackson and Al Sharpton after her narrow election to the New Jersey governorship as she attempts to counter her campaign manager's contention that the Republicans conspired to lower African-American turnout on election day. Ed Rollins, Whitman's campaign manager, said that the campaign contributed to African-American churches to encourage ministers to refrain from backing Whitman's Democratic opponent, incumbent James Florio, and to encourage others to stay home on election day. An investigation into Rollins' statements found no evidence of wrong-doing.

---

* All *direct* contributions over $100 must be disclosed to the Federal Election Commission, and the report is supposed to include the name, address, and occupation of each donor.

Are PACs a Good or Bad Part of the Process?

Of all these forms of spending, probably the most controversial is that involving PAC money. Some observers claim that PACs are the embodiment of corrupt special interests that use campaign donations to buy the votes of legislators. Most political scientists in the field of campaign finance have a quite different opinion, viewing PACs as a natural manifestation of interest-group politics in a diverse democracy.

Although a good number of PACs of all persuasions existed prior to the 1970s, it was during this decade—the decade of campaign reform—that the modern PAC era began. Spawned by the Watergate-inspired revisions of the campaign-finance laws, PACs grew in number from 113 in 1972 to 4,100 by the early 1990s, and their contributions to congressional candidates multiplied almost eighteenfold, from $8.5 million in 1971–72 to $180.5 million in 1991–92 (see Figures 13-2 and 13-3). The rapid rise of PACs has inevitably proved controversial, yet many of the charges made against political action committees are exaggerated and dubious.

Some people argue that PACs are newfangled inventions that have flooded the political system with money. Although the widespread use of the PAC structure is new, the fact remains that special-interest money of all types has *always* found its way into politics. Before the 1970s it did so in less traceable and much more disturbing and unsavory ways because, before PACs, little of the money given to candidates was regularly disclosed to public inspection. And although it is true that PACs contribute a massive sum to candidates in absolute terms, it is not clear that there is *proportionately* more interest-group money in the system than before. The proportion of House and Senate campaign funds provided by PACs has certainly increased since the early 1970s, but *individuals,* most of whom are unaffiliated with PACs, together with the political parties still supply more than 60 percent of all the money spent by or on behalf of House candidates and 75 percent of the campaign expenditures for Senate contenders (see Figure 13-4). So while the importance of PAC spending has grown, PACs clearly remain secondary as a source of election funding and therefore pose no overwhelming threat to the system's legitimacy.

It can be argued that contemporary political action committees are another manifestation of what James Madison called "factions." Through the flourishing of competing

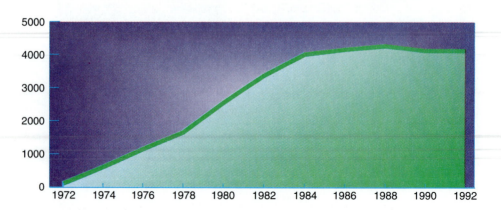

FIGURE 13-2

Growth in Total Number of PACs[a]

[a]As of December 31st of every other year, starting in 1972.
Source: Federal Election Commission.

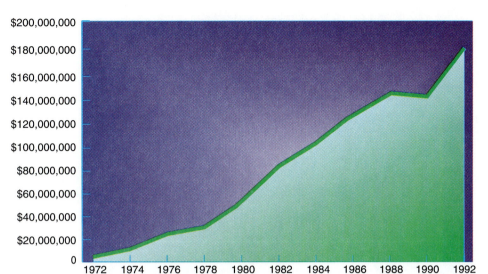

FIGURE 13-3

Growth in Total Contributions by PACs to House and Senate Candidates[a]

a For two-year election cycles ending in years shown.
Source: Federal Election Commission.

interest groups or factions, said Madison in *Federalist No. 10,* liberty would be preserved. In any democracy, and particularly in one as pluralistic as that of the United States, it is essential that groups be relatively unrestricted in advocating their interests and positions. Not only is unrestricted political activity by interest groups a mark of a free society, but it also provides a safety valve for the competitive pressures that build on all fronts in a democracy. It also supplies a means of keeping representatives responsive to legitimate needs.

The election outlays of PACs, like the total amount expended in a single election season, seem huge. But the cost of elections in the United States is less than or approximately the same as in some other nations, measured on a per voter basis.[5] Moreover, the cost of all elections in the United States taken together is less than the annual advertising budgets of many individual private corporations to sell cereals, dog food, cars, and toothpaste. These days it is expensive to communicate, whether the message is political or commercial. The costs of television time, polling, consultants, and other items have soared over and above the inflation rate.

A Summary of Contributions and Expenses

Figure 13-4 gives an idea of where all the money comes from and goes. A typical U.S. Senate candidate in 1992 received most of his or her war chest (about 60 percent) from relatively small individual donations. PACs supplied about 22 percent, the political party committees 15 percent, and the candidates about 3 percent.

The single greatest outlay (40 percent of the total) was for television advertising; the next-largest item, staff and consultant salaries, was half television's cost (20 percent). The other 40 percent of the budget was spent on everything from polls to travel expenses. Keep in mind that in a large state with a dozen or more media markets (concentrated population centers with many television and radio stations), expenditures often balloon to $5 million, $10 million, and even more.

FIGURE 13-4

Campaign for U.S. Senate, 1994: A "Typical" Candidate's Budget of $2 Million

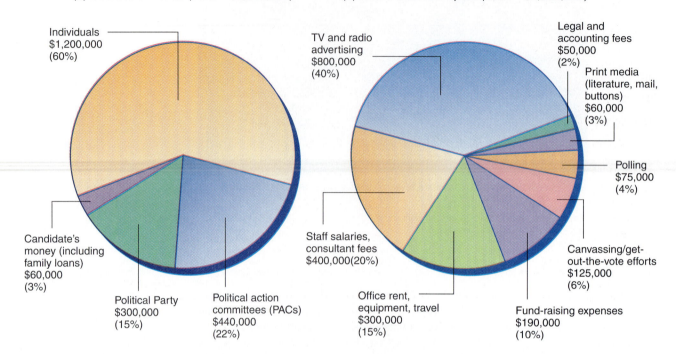

(a) Sources of Funds (Total = $2,000,000)

Individuals
$1,200,000
(60%)

Candidate's
money (including
family loans)
$60,000
(3%)

Political Party
$300,000
(15%)

Political action
committees (PACs)
$440,000
(22%)

(b) How Funds Are Spent (Total = $2,000,000)

TV and radio
advertising
$800,000
(40%)

Legal and
accounting fees
$50,000
(2%)

Print media
(literature, mail,
buttons)
$60,000
(3%)

Polling
$75,000
(4%)

Canvassing/get-
out-the-vote efforts
$125,000
(6%)

Fund-raising expenses
$190,000
(10%)

Office rent,
equipment, travel
$300,000
(15%)

Staff salaries,
consultant fees
$400,000(20%)

Some candidates have more difficulty than others in raising the necessary dollar amounts. Those in power—the incumbents—have the least trouble, although challengers who face incumbents weakened by scandal can also find the task of financing the campaign relatively easy. The size of a challenger's war chest is really the key variable. There is a point of diminishing returns for incumbent spending, since most office holders are already well known to the voters. But the challenger's name and platform are likely to be obscure. If the challenger can raise and spend enough to get his or her basic message across, there is a reasonable chance that the election will be at least moderately competitive. As is more common, though, if the challenger is starved for funds, the contest will probably turn into a romp for the well-heeled incumbent.

Bringing It Together: The 1992 Presidential Campaign and Election

A year before the November 1992 presidential election, it looked likely to be a rather boring, predictable affair, much like the 1984 contest that had resulted in a landslide reelection for President Reagan. Most of the strongest potential Democratic candidates, such as New York Governor Mario Cuomo and New Jersey U.S. Senator Bill Bradley, decided not to run for president, and President Bush was still riding a wave of popularity from the Persian Gulf war. In the end, however, 1992 produced one of the most exciting and competitive contests for the White House in modern times (see Figure 13-5).

The Party Nomination Battle

President Bush's hopes for an uncontested renomination were shattered when he was challenged by conservative television commentator Patrick J. Buchanan. Buchanan attacked Bush on the economy, on his 1990 abandonment of his 1988 "no new taxes" campaign pledge, and on National Endowment of the Arts funding of such controversial projects as a film about African-American gay males. Buchanan achieved his high watermark on February 19, receiving 37 percent of the vote in the first primary, New Hampshire. (Bush won the primary with 53%.) This state had saved Bush's candidacy in 1988 after his third-place finish in the Iowa caucuses. In 1992, however, many of the state's citizens felt Bush had abandoned them during the recession, which was much more severe in their state than in the country as a whole. Buchanan also won 36 percent of the vote in Georgia on March 3, but he faded thereafter. Although Bush eventually collected nearly all of the delegates to the Republican convention, his overall showing in the primaries was anemic compared to most of his Republican predecessors. Bush won just 73 percent of all the votes cast in GOP contests in 1992, much less than Presidents Eisenhower (86 percent), Nixon (87 percent), and Reagan (99 percent) in their reelection years.

FIGURE 13-5

Landmarks in 1992 Campaign

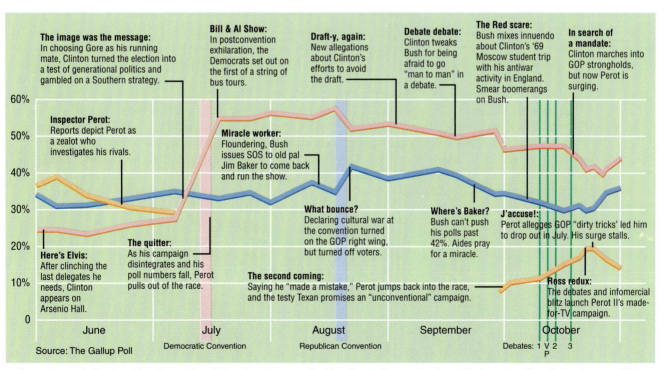

Percentages indicate percentage of registered voters sampled by the Gallup poll who said they would vote for the candidates.

Democrats sponsored one of their standard free-for-alls for the presidential nomination in 1992. The leading announced candidate from the beginning was Governor Bill Clinton of Arkansas, although his status as frontrunner was shaky. He was plagued by mini-scandals that threatened to drive him from the race: an alleged affair with an Arkansas woman named Gennifer Flowers, his possible evasion of the draft during the Vietnam War, and his youthful experimentation with marijuana (self-admitted, but with the explanation that he had "never inhaled").

Clinton survived and managed to outflank all his rivals, one by one. The most serious threat was former Massachusetts U.S. Senator Paul Tsongas, whose tough fiscal message—"no more Santa Claus"—attracted white middle- and upper-class Democrats concerned about the budget deficit and the country's deep-seated economic problems. Tsongas won the New Hampshire primary, with Clinton a respectable second. Senator Tom Harkin of Iowa, Senator Robert Kerrey of Nebraska, and former Governor of California Jerry Brown each won other early contests, but starting with Georgia on March 3, Clinton began to generate unstoppable momentum. On "Super Tuesday" (March 10), he swept the Southern contests, but Tsongas did well outside the South. Then, on March 17, Clinton won both Illinois and Michigan decisively. Short of

ᴛHEN AND NOW

The Television Advertising Campaigns of 1952 and 1992

Forty years—and a world of difference—separate the presidential campaigns of 1952 and 1992 when viewed through the camera lens of television advertising.

The initial, landmark year for political television was 1952. Television had become truly national, not just regional, and portions of the political parties' national conventions were telecast for the first time. With 45 percent of the nation's households owning television sets, the presidential campaign was forced to take notice. Republican presidential nominee Dwight D. Eisenhower's advisers were particularly intrigued with the device, seeing it as a way to counter Eisenhower's stumbling press-conference performances and to make him appear more knowledgeable.

Eisenhower's advertising campaign was a glimpse of the future. Two associates of the Ted Bates and Company advertising agency of New York designed the spots, targeted them to play in key swing areas of the country, and arranged a television and radio saturation blitz in the last three weeks of the campaign along with the Batten, Barton, Durstine, and Osborn (BBD&O) advertising agency, which actually bought the air time. The three primary themes of the commercials (corrup-

tion, high prices, and the Korean War) were chosen after consultation with pollster George Gallup. There was an extraordinarily large number of spots (forty-nine produced for television, twenty-nine for radio). Most spots were twenty seconds in length; the rest, sixty seconds. They played repeatedly in forty-nine selected counties in twelve non-Southern states as well as in a few targeted Southern states. On the day before the election in New York City alone, 130 Eisenhower television ads were shown at station breaks. The GOP's media strategy appeared to have been successful, and the Nielsen ratings showed that Eisenhower's telecasts consistently drew higher ratings than those of his Democratic opponent, Adlai Stevenson.

The commercials themselves were simplistic and technically very primitive in comparison with modern fare. Eisenhower had a peculiarly stilted way of speaking while reading cue cards, and his delivery was amateurish, albeit sincere and appealing. If nothing else, the GOP commercials from 1952 reveal that the issues in U.S. politics never seem to change. Eisenhower's slogan, "It's Time for a Change," is a perennial production, for example. One advertisement was a clever

money, Tsongas joined Harkin and Kerrey on the inactive list. Brown persisted, winning a few more contests, but Clinton effectively ended his challenge with a decisive win in New York on April 7. From then on, Clinton scored relatively easy victories everywhere, even in Brown's home state of California on June 2. Voter turnouts were low, however—overall just 12 percent of the voting-age population—and Democrats appeared more resigned than enthusiastic as they looked to a Clinton candidacy. Nonetheless, Clinton's 51.9 percent of the total Democratic primary votes was a solid showing.

The Third Force: Ross Perot

On February 20, 1992, Texas billionaire Ross Perot, appearing on CNN's "Larry King Live," announced that if Americans in all fifty states put him on their ballots, he would run for president. Capitalizing on widespread discontent with the two major party nominees, he then launched a most improbable pseudo-candidacy that derived in good part from his intense dislike of fellow Texan Bush.

---

adaptation of the "March of Time" newsreel series that preceded the main features in U.S. movie theaters of the period, and various news clips of Eisenhower accompanied the audio.

Narrator: The man from Abilene. Out of the heartland of America, out of this small-frame house in Abilene, Kansas, came a man, Dwight D. Eisenhower. Through the crucial hours of historic D-Day, he brought us to the triumph and peace of VE-Day. Now, another crucial hour in our history. The big question . . .

Man's voice: General, if war comes, is this country really ready?

Eisenhower: It is not. The administration has spent many billions of dollars for national defense. Yet today we haven't enough tanks for the fighting men in Korea. It is time for a change.

Narrator: The nation, haunted by the stalemate in Korea, looks to Eisenhower. Eisenhower knows how to deal with the Russians. He has met with Europe's leaders, has got them working with us. Elect the number-one man for the number-one job of our time. November fourth, vote for peace, vote for Eisenhower.

Yet this spot had an odd ring to it, perhaps because the approach ignored the intimate nature of television, which reaches its viewers in the home's cozy quarters as opposed to the blare of a newsreel in an auditorium. Some other Eisenhower commercials used an even less effective format wherein a film showed Eisenhower mechanically responding to off-camera questions.

By the best estimates this first media blitz cost the Republicans close to $1.5 million. During that campaign the Democrats spent only about $77,000 on television, and the new spots they produced played on New Deal themes and Republican responsibility for the Great Depression: "Sh-h-h-h. Don't mention it to a soul, don't spread it around . . . but the Republican party was in power back in 1932 . . . 13 million people were unemployed . . . bank doors shut in your face. . . ." The Democrats, who had wanted to run an ad blitz but could not raise the money to pay for it, turned instead to broadsides about the GOP's "soap campaign." Stevenson's supporters charged that the Republican ad managers conceived a multimillion-dollar production designed to sell a political party ticket to the American people in precisely the way they sell soap.

The poet Marya Mannes was moved to write "Sales Campaign" in reaction to the Eisenhower advertising effort. Her poem read, in part: "Phillip Morris, Lucky Strike, Alka Seltzer, I Like Ike."

For better or worse, the pattern was set for future campaigns, although 1992's television advertising was far more sophisticated in both presidential camps.

Independent candidate Ross Perot garnered 19% of the popular vote in the 1992 Presidential election. As election day neared, billionaire Perot bought network TV time and staged a series of half-hour infomercials to bring his message directly to voters.

Although Perot declared a willingness to spend "whatever it takes"—estimates ranged from $100 to $300 million—of his own fortune to be competitive, he actually spent little in the early months of his unannounced candidacy. Instead, he cleverly used the free media, especially the soft-edged talk shows and morning TV ("Larry King Live," "Donahue," "Today"), to advance himself while offering little of detailed substance. With the political press at bay, he could project accessibility with little risk; with party identification on the decline, his independent stand was a magnet for many alienated voters eager for "change" and an end to politics as usual; and with nearly unlimited resources, he was not forced to waste time in a money chase. His folksy image and "can-do" approach to gridlocked government proved popular, and he rocketed to the top of the opinion polls.

Gradually, though, some less flattering facts about Perot began to filter out. The tycoon's autocratic, authoritarian manner unsettled some people, as did his penchant for conspiracy theories and alleged investigations of adversaries' private lives. Still, with a seemingly firm hold on millions of Americans, Perot cast a long shadow over both parties—until he abruptly declined to run on July 16, 1992, the last day of the Democratic National Convention. Unable to work with the feisty Texan, his campaign manager and other key aides had resigned just prior to the withdrawal. Feeling outraged and betrayed, many of Perot's supporters abandoned him, while others urged him to reverse his decision. Stung by the label of "quitter," and claiming disappointment that Bush and Clinton had not adopted his debt-reduction platform, Perot abruptly changed course again on October 1 and announced his independent candidacy. But his luster was clearly gone, and his appeal sharply diminished.

The Party Conventions

Democrats gathered first in convention, in New York City from July 13–17. The week before, Clinton had named Tennessee Senator Al Gore Jr. as his running mate. The privileged son of a senator and unsuccessful candidate for president in 1988, Gore struck many people as similar to Clinton: young (44), Southern, and moderate-liberal. The unusual pairing of two Southerners on the ticket signaled the Democrats' determination to fight for GOP-leaning Dixie's electoral votes, and the match of two post-World War II "baby boom" generation candidates guaranteed a vigorous campaign and an appeal for change (as in so many campaigns in history). Gore's strengths in foreign policy and the environment as well as his Vietnam-era military service balanced several of Clinton's prominent weaknesses.

Democrats were enormously pleased and encouraged by the course of their convention, which they used to showcase a "new" Democratic Party more to the liking of mainstream America. With the exception of Jerry Brown, all of Clinton's former rivals for the nomination warmly embraced him; New York Governor Mario Cuomo gave a stirring nomination speech; the party adopted a platform incorporating important centrist positions on economics and government (for example, that government programs were not the solution to every problem); and the Clinton–Gore ticket was given a rousing sendoff. Following Perot's stunning announcement that he would not run for president, most Perot voters appeared to switch to Clinton as the other "change" candidate, and as the convention concluded, the nominee skyrocketed to a twenty-four point lead over President Bush in a CNN–Gallup survey. Buoyed by this large convention "bounce" and armed with the opportunities provided by a weak economy, Democrats looked forward to the coming campaign and tried not to look back to 1988, when nominee Michael S. Dukakis had squandered a smaller 17-point advantage and lost to George Bush.

In the months before the 1992 election, candidate Clinton was a tireless campaigner. Here he consults with strategist Paul Begala aboard his campaign jet "Longhorn One," while in flight on a 33-hour, cross-country campaign marathon on November 2, the eve of the election.

Clinton quickly proved that he had learned from Dukakis's mistakes. Setting a pattern he would follow to Election Day, he campaigned vigorously and nearly continuously between the Democratic and Republican conventions, much of the time on a bus tour with his running mate, aggressively countering every attack made by the Bush forces and launching many attacks of his own. Combined with more bad economic news and a listless Bush response, these techniques helped him maintain his lead through the GOP convention and beyond.

Republicans prepared for their party conclave with trepidation. A few conservative activists and columnists called for Bush to step aside and not seek reelection, while other Republicans suggested that Vice President Quayle should step aside. Instead, Bush reaffirmed his ticket, and then delighted his party by moving Secretary of State James Baker— one of the architects of his 1988 victory—out of the State Department and over to the White House to serve as chief of staff and campaign manager.

On that upbeat note, the Republican National Convention opened in Houston, Texas, on August 17. That evening Pat Buchanan enthusiastically endorsed President Bush, but his harsh address, reflecting the influence of the right wing on the tone and substance of the convention, alienated many moderate Americans. Framing the November battle from the Republican perspective, the convention organizers emphasized "family values," foreign policy, and Congress bashing. President Bush gave a generally well regarded closing address on these themes.

In retrospect, many observers concluded that the convention had been poorly organized and, in particular, that giving prominence to the negative messages of Buchanan and others may have been a mistake. Most polls showed Bush achieved some "bounce" from his convention, but much less than Clinton had secured from his. Bush, it became increasingly clear, would be hard pressed to catch up.

The Fall Campaign and General Election Results

As the campaign developed in the months following the Republican convention, each of the more than 275 pre-election public opinion polls showed Bill Clinton ahead. Without question, he ran a technically superb campaign; his strategy, television adver-

1992 Party Primaries

❖ ❖ ❖

DEMOCRATS

	Number of Primaries Won	Percent of Total Votes
Clinton	32	51.9
Brown	2	19.9
Tsongas	4	18.1
Uncommitted/ others	1	10.1

A total of 20,179,973 votes were cast in 39 primaries.

REPUBLICANS

	Number of Primaries Won	Percent of Total Votes
Bush	39	73.0
Buchanan	0	22.4
Uncommitted/ others	0	3.6
Duke	0	1.0

A total of 13,025,824 votes were cast in 39 primaries.

Source: Congressional Quarterly Weekly Supplements 50, July 4, 1992, p. 71 and August 8, 1992, p. 67.

Ideological opposites and determined rivals during the 1992 Presidential campaign, Clinton strategist James Carville and Bush manager Mary Matalin were married in 1993.

tising, use of the media, and energetic stumping (frequently on a bus) were on target and exceptionally clever. Fielding the best Democratic campaign team in a generation, he successfully projected a moderate image that appealed to a wide range of voters. Keeping his message focused on the weak economy, he was able to win back many so-called "Reagan" Democrats—registered Democrats who had voted for Republican presidential candidates since 1980. Appearing on MTV and—with saxophone in hand—on "The Arsenio Hall Show," Clinton also appealed directly and effectively to young voters. Clinton campaigners were quick to respond to Republican attacks, faxing counterstatements and "truth sheets" almost instantaneously to networks and print reporters.

Bush's campaign, in contrast, was slow to organize and even slower to focus on consistent themes. It hopped, skipped, and jumped among topics as diverse as "family values," experience, trust, Clinton's draft evasion and anti-war demonstrating, and the Arkansas record. Even Republicans admit their party had rarely, if ever, mismanaged a presidential campaign so badly. It reminded most observers of the inept effort made by Michael S. Dukakis in 1988—the same year that a finely crafted and executed campaign by George Bush won him the presidency.

Although the differences between the two campaigns was certainly a factor in the outcome of the election, it is also true that any election involving an incumbent president is essentially a referendum on his incumbency, and, in that sense, George Bush lost the election every bit as much as Bill Clinton won it. Here are some of the reasons—beyond his lackluster campaign—that Bush forfeited his second term:

- *The economy.* The U.S. economy, the most basic of all forces in presidential elections, suffered a serious recession in 1990–91 and recovered only fitfully and painfully in the months leading up to the election. In many ways relating to their pocketbooks, voters simply did not believe they were better off than four years earlier, which predisposed them to change the status quo. Clinton and Perot continually hammered away at Bush about the recession and the rising national debt, making the economy the most important issue in the campaign.

- *Presidential domestic inaction and the end of the Cold War.* Known as a "foreign policy president" because of his love of international relations, Bush often seemed disinterested in domestic affairs. His repeated declarations that the economy was improving—designed to increase consumer confidence—made him appear out of touch. Meanwhile, festering problems across the United States (decaying inner cities, infrastructure deterioration, a perceived decline in the quality of health care and education) caused many voters to yearn for a candidate who placed domestic matters at the top of his agenda. The end of the Cold War and the collapse of communism also helped focus the election squarely on domestic policy, leaving foreign affairs on the periphery.

- *Vice-presidential candidates.* Bush's vice president, Dan Quayle, was certainly more competent than the news media and the late-night comics portrayed him, but his public image was so negative that he undoubtedly hurt Bush. By contrast, Clinton's vice-presidential pick, Al Gore Jr., was widely viewed as an asset, and the news media gave him extremely positive reviews.

- *The Perot factor.* The billionaire Independent had an intense hatred for his fellow Texan Bush and aimed most of his fire at the President—even charging late in the campaign (with absolutely no evidence) that the GOP planned to disrupt his daughter's wedding. Most of Perot's support was drawn from the white, suburban upper-middle class, a predominantly Republican constituency, and Bush likely suffered disproportionately as a result.

- *Scandals.* Two scandals haunted Bush's reelection effort: Iran-Contra and Iraq-gate. The Iran-Contra scandal, which had begun in the Reagan administration, involved the illegal sale of U.S. arms to Iran, with some of the profits improperly diverted to fund the anti-communist *contras* fighting a civil war in the Central American country of Nicaragua. Bush, who was vice president at the time, had repeatedly claimed he was "out of the loop" on this policy, but the release of a memorandum written by Reagan Defense Secretary Casper Weinberger just days before the election suggested that he was very much in the loop. The revelation cost Bush the last-minute campaign momentum he had generated. The Iraq-gate scandal took some of the luster off of Bush's leadership in the Persian Gulf war. It referred to the U.S. policy of arming Iraq's leader, Saddam Hussein, in the years leading up to his invasion of Kuwait in 1990 and the possible postwar coverup of the Bush administration's decisions in this matter. Both scandals hampered efforts by the Bush team to raise questions about Clinton's character (marital infidelity, youthful marijuana use, and draft evasion).
- *News media bias.* Republicans claimed that the national media, particularly the television networks, the *Washington Post,* and the *New York Times,* were tilting heavily to Clinton and putting Bush and the economy in the worst possible light. Although there is some truth to this criticism, it is questionable how much media bias affected the final election outcome. The other factors discussed here weighed more heavily in leading to Bush's defeat.

Election Results. The Reagan–Bush majority coalition that had governed for twelve years simply buckled under the weight of all these burdens. "Reagan" Democrats returned en masse to the Democratic fold. Young people between the ages of eighteen and thirty also moved into Clinton's column after supporting the GOP in 1980, 1984, and 1988. Many women also shifted to Clinton, a result of a bad economy, the Democrat's pro-abortion position, and the Anita Hill–Clarence Thomas hearings of the U.S. Senate when Thomas's nomination to the Supreme Court was under consideration in 1991. Some exit poll findings suggested women comprised as much as 54 percent of the voters on November 3, 1992, so Clinton's edge among women was especially important.

Voter turnout was up in 1992 after a long and worrisome decline. About 55 percent of Americans aged eighteen and over turned up at the polling places in 1992 (and about 80 percent of those *registered* to vote did so). These numbers were a significant increase over 1988, when just 50 percent of those eighteen and older voted. But it is still well below the 62 percent of 1960 and the even higher turnouts regularly recorded in the last century.

Clinton's Electoral College victory (370 for Clinton, 168 for Bush, and 0 for Perot) was much broader than his popular vote plurality (43 percent for Clinton, 38 percent for Bush, and 19 percent for Perot) (see Figure 13-6). He was thus to be a "minority president"—elected by less than half the popular vote*—but one whose win was nonetheless impressive. After all, since World War II only two other challengers— Jimmy Carter in 1976 and Ronald Reagan in 1980—had ousted incumbents from the

---

* Fifteen of our forty-two chief executives were elected with less than a majority. The most recent prior to Clinton was Richard Nixon, who (like Clinton) garnered 43 percent of the votes in 1968's three-way race.

FIGURE 13-6

Results of 1992 Election

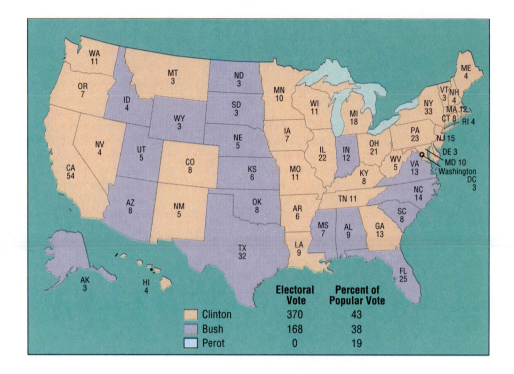

	Electoral Vote	Percent of Popular Vote
Clinton	370	43
Bush	168	38
Perot	0	19

White House, and no president had been as popular as Bush was earlier in his term. Bush became the tenth president to lose a bid for reelection.*

The Democrats won states in every region of the country. They swept the economically hard-hit Northeast, winning even reliably Republican New Hampshire. Except for Indiana, home of Dan Quayle, the Midwest was solidly Democratic, as was the Pacific Coast. (The Republicans ceded giant California's fifty-four electoral votes to the Democrats months before the election, when polls showed them in a hopeless position there.)

President Bush achieved a respectable showing only in the South. But even in this region, which had long been solidly Republican, Florida and Texas stayed loyal to Bush by only narrow margins, and the Democrats stole Georgia and Louisiana as well as Clinton's Arkansas and Gore's Tennessee. Bush also held onto some Rocky Mountain and Plains states, but significantly, he forfeited four states that had nearly consistently voted Republican in modern times: Colorado, Montana, Nevada, and New Mexico.

By the standards of recent history, Clinton's Electoral College majority was the most impressive and diverse for a Democrat since Lyndon Johnson's landslide election in 1964. And Bush's collapse from his 427 Electoral College votes in 1988 to 168 in 1992 was stunning. Bush fared far worse than Gerald Ford, who won 240 Electoral

---

*   The other defeated presidents (and year of defeat) were John Adams (1800), John Quincy Adams (1828), William Howard Taft (1912), Herbert Hoover (1932), Gerald Ford (1976), and Jimmy Carter (1980).

Bill Clinton and Al Gore Jr., with their wives Hillary and Tipper, acknowledge victory in Little Rock, Arkansas on election night.

College votes in his losing 1976 bid. Still, Jimmy Carter, who captured just forty-nine Electoral College votes in his 1980 reelection bid, holds the post-World War II record for the most decisive defeat of an incumbent.

Toward Reform

In response to the growing concern about the amounts of money spent on federal elections, both Republicans and Democrats have sponsored major campaign-finance reform bills in Congress. But changing the rules of the game can alter the results of elections, and not surprisingly the Democratic proposals favor Democratic candidates and the Republican proposals favor Republican candidates. For many years now, as a consequence, Congress has been at an impasse on campaign reform.

Democrats favor setting a limit on the amount of money any congressional candidate can spend in an effort to win office. (For the House a candidate might be limited to $600,000; the Senate limit would depend on each state's population, with a more heavily populated state having a higher limit.) Republicans are adamantly against these spending caps, arguing that the limits mainly hurt challengers who are not as well known as incumbents are and who need to spend more money to increase their name identification. For example, from 1978 to 1988 only seven of the thirty-two winning Senate challengers remained within the spending limits proposed by the Democrats. Republicans also claim that they must spend more than Democrats do because they do not have access to any volunteer group comparable to organized labor, which aids Democrats overwhelmingly, and hence the GOP candidates normally must pay campaign workers.

Of course, both parties' positions on this issue are rooted in self-interest. The Republicans are more successful than are Democrats at raising money, and the Democrats want to limit that advantage. Moreover, the cost to either party of conceding too much on this issue is the possibility of relinquishing control of Congress for a long time to come. This makes campaign spending an issue that does not easily lend itself to compromise.

Yet many experts inside and outside of Congress argue that there are other ideas concerning campaign finance that would create a more wholesome system without resorting to spending limits. One idea is to limit the influence of political action committees (PACs). Critics charge that PACs reduce political competition by giving overwhelmingly to incumbents—usually about two-thirds to three-quarters of their warchests—while at the same time they corrupt the system by indebting legislators to the special interests that form PACs. Abolishing PACs altogether, however, is probably unconstitutional, since doing so would violate the First Amendment's guarantee of free political association. Restricting their contribution limits too greatly would only divert their money into other forms of political spending that are not easily revealed (such as funneling cash to state and local parties in states that do not require full campaign-finance disclosure). As reformers through the years have discovered, it is nearly impossible to dam the flow of political money in a free and open democratic system in which participation is encouraged.

A better way to control PACs and special-interest groups is to increase the influence and level of spending by political parties. This would limit PACs *indirectly* by augmenting the power of a rival source of campaign funds. As is discussed in Chapter 11, parties can be strengthened in many ways, especially by loosening or eliminating current restrictions on what citizens may give to a party or what a party may donate to its candidates. In addition, parties ought to receive some free broadcast time on all television and radio stations. This air time could then be allocated to the most needy nominees—incumbents who are in trouble, as well as promising challengers. Since candidates spend a major portion of their campaign funds for media advertising time—up to 60 percent in some Senate races—such a reform could conceivably help to cut the burgeoning costs of campaigns. And it would aid challengers and less wealthy candidates in particular, balancing some of the advantages of incumbency. The United States, incidentally, is the only major democratic country that does not provide some free media time to parties or candidates.

Campaign-finance reform is a favorite Washington topic, but for all the good (and bad) ideas that are proposed, little legislation is ever passed. Many incumbents prefer not to alter the system that, whatever its faults, elected them. Democrats and Republicans are also at loggerheads over the partisan effects of various reforms. The American people also remain skeptical of political parties, and little popular support can be found for their cause. The last set of campaign-finance reforms passed in the wake of Watergate, and it may take more scandal to generate enough momentum to pass a successor package of reforms in the Congress.

Summary

As the analysis of the 1992 election suggests, the campaign process in the United States is far from perfect. Campaigns stretch out seemingly interminably, unlike in Great Britain, where the entire parliamentary election process is confined to four or five weeks. Moreover, candidates in the United States are often judged on trivial issues, voters cast many ballots for the lesser of two evils, and some contenders for lower office never raise enough money to get a fair hearing. But those who follow campaigns would also do well to remember the wise words of one of this century's greatest political scientists, V. O. Key Jr. Key's central observation was simple but powerful: "Voters are not fools."* Not every citizen devotes enough time to politics, and many people are woefully uninformed at times. But virtually all voters know their basic interests and cast their ballots accordingly. They are not always right in their judgments, yet over time there is a rough justice to election results. Parties and office holders who produce a measure of prosperity and happiness for the electorate are usually rewarded, and those who do not keep the home folks satisfied may be forced to find another line of work.

In this chapter, we have stressed the following observations:

1. Campaigns, the process of seeking and winning votes in the run-up to an election, consist of five separate components: the nomination campaign, in which party leaders and activists are courted to ensure that the candidate is nominated in primaries or conventions; the general election campaign, in which the goal is to appeal to the nation as a whole; the personal campaign, in which the candidate and his or her family make appearances, meet voters, hold press conferences, and give speeches; the organizational campaign, in which volunteers telephone voters, distribute literature, organize events, and raise money; and the

* See V. O. Key Jr., *The Responsible Electorate* (Cambridge, MA: Harvard University Press, 1966).

broadcast media campaign waged on television and on the radio.

2. Campaign staffs combine volunteers with a manager at the top and key political consultants—including media consultants, a pollster, and a direct mailer. In recent years, media consultants have assumed greater and greater importance, partly because the cost of advertising has skyrocketed, so that campaign media budgets consume the lion's share of available resources.

3. Despite the dazzle of technology and the celebrity of well-known consultants, the candidate remains the most important component of any campaign. The candidate's strengths, weaknesses, and talents are central to the success or failure of the campaign.

4. Candidates tell their story directly in paid broadcast media advertising. They are much less successful in managing and directing their *press* coverage. (This topic is taken up again in Chapter 14.)

5. Campaigns receive money from several sources. Individual contributions are currently limited to $1,000 per candidate per election; political action committees, which represent interest groups, are limited to $5,000. In addition, candidates can receive large supplements from their party, and they can spend as much of their own money as they like.

6. Campaign finance is regularly a reform issue, because candidates who outspend their opponents tend to win, and raising money is easier for some candidates than for others. Incumbents enjoy a fund-raising edge as well as advantages related to name recognition and some of the perks of office, such as mailing privileges.

Key Terms

nomination campaign	media consultant	contrast ads
general election campaign	pollster	spot ads
personal campaign	direct mailer	candidate debates
organizational campaign	voter canvass	political action committees
media campaign	get-out-the-vote	public funds
paid media	positive ads	matching funds
free media	negative ads	

Suggested Readings

Abramson, Paul R., John H. Aldrich, and David W. Rohde. *Change and Continuity in the 1988 Elections.* Washington, DC: CQ Press, 1990.

Alexander, Herbert E., and Monica Bauer. *Financing the 1988 Election.* Boulder, CO: Westview Press, 1991.

Goldenberg, Edie, and Michael W. Traugott. *Campaigning for Congress.* Washington, DC: CQ Press, 1984.

Jackson, Brooks. *Honest Graft: Big Money and the American Political Process.* Washington, DC: Farragut, 1990.

Kern, Montague. *30-Second Politics: Political Advertising in the Eighties.* New York: Praeger, 1989.

Nelson, Michael, ed. *The Elections of 1992.* Washington, DC: CQ Press, 1993.

Orren, Gary R., and Nelson W. Polsby, eds. *Media and Momentum: The New Hampshire Primary and Nomination Politics.* Chatham, NJ: Chatham House, 1987.

Patterson, Thomas E. *The Mass Media Election.* New York: Praeger, 1980.

Pomper, Gerald M., ed. *The Election of 1992: Reports and Interpretations.* Chatham, NJ: Chatham House, 1993.

Sabato, Larry J., ed. *Campaigns and Elections: A Reader in Modern American Politics.* Glenview, IL: Scott, Foresman, 1989.

———. *PAC Power: Inside the World of Political Action Committees.* New York: Norton, 1985.

———. *Paying for Elections: The Campaign Finance Thicket.* New York: Priority Press for the Twentieth Century Fund, 1989.

———. *The Rise of Political Consultants: New Ways of Winning Elections.* New York: Basic Books, 1981.

Salmore, Barbara G., and Stephen Salmore. *Candidates, Parties, and Campaigns,* 2nd ed. Washington, DC: CQ Press, 1989.

Sorauf, Frank J. *Money in American Elections.* Glenview, IL: Scott, Foresman, 1988.

The News Media

THE AMERICAN PRESS OF YESTERYEAR

THE CONTEMPORARY MEDIA SCENE

HOW THE MEDIA COVER POLITICIANS AND GOVERNMENT

THE POST-WATERGATE ERA

THE MEDIA'S INFLUENCE ON THE PUBLIC

HOW POLITICIANS USE THE MEDIA

GOVERNMENT REGULATION OF THE ELECTRONIC MEDIA

TOWARD REFORM

The press is now, and has always been, controversial. Whether it is publication of the name of a rape victim or of unsubstantiated rumors about a presidential candidate, or the use of ambush journalism made famous by the television program "60 Minutes," the news media are sure to generate public outcry and criticism with regularity.

The passage by Alexander Hamilton that opens this chapter is a pointed reminder that many of the Framers did not share the belief that guaranteed freedom of the press is fundamental to American democracy. Actually, Federalists such as Hamilton agreed to include freedom of the press and the other amendments in the Bill of Rights only to satisfy states' righters and secure passage of the Constitution. In fact, there is not much evidence that even the staunchest advocates of the Bill of Rights favored *absolute* freedom of the press—that is, a free press unbalanced by other legitimate rights, such as those of personal privacy, fair trial, copyright protection, and national security.[1] The surprising truth is that the Framers devoted little thought and debate to the free press clause because it was not considered a matter of the highest importance. Even its position as the *First* Amendment is deceptive. Originally the rights of free speech and press were included in the third amendment to the proposed Bill of Rights, but the first two amendments were not ratified by the original states. So what we now herald as the all-powerful, preeminent First Amendment was a product of political compromise, relative inattention, and historical accident!

Nonetheless, the simple words *"Congress shall make no law . . . abridging the freedom of speech, or of the press"* have shaped the American republic as much as or

465

> hat is the liberty of the press? Who can give it any
> definition which would not leave the utmost latitude
> for evasion? . . . [I]ts security, whatever fine
> declarations may be inserted in any constitution respecting it,
> must altogether depend on public opinion, and on the general
> spirit of the people and of the government.
>
> *Alexander Hamilton*
> *Federalist No. 84*

Hamilton asserted that the rights of a free press, like all other democratic rights,
ultimately depend on the support of the public.

Print press The traditional form of
mass media, comprising newspapers,
magazines, and journals.

Electronic media The newest form
of broadcast media including
television, radio, and cable.

more than any others in the Constitution and its amendments. With the Constitution's
sanction, as interpreted by the Supreme Court over two centuries, a vigorous and
highly competitive press has emerged. Composed of **print press** (newspapers, magazines, journals) and **electronic media** (television and radio), the news media in the
United States arguably have more freedom and are less controlled today than any other
press in the world. How this freedom evolved, the ways in which it is manifested, and
whether press freedom is used responsibly are subjects we examine in this chapter.[2]
We first review the history and development of the press in the colonies and the United
States, and then survey the contemporary media scene. We look closely at how journalists cover politicians and government (president, Congress, and the courts), especially the modern emphasis on investigation of private lives. Among other questions
addressed are these: Are the news media biased? How much does the press influence
the public's voting choice? In what ways do politicians attempt to influence the mass
media? Finally, we explain how the government regulates the news business—a deli-
cate matter in a free society.

The American Press of Yesteryear

Journalism—the process and profession of collecting and disseminating the news
(that is, new information about subjects of public interest)—has been with us in some
form since the dawn of civilization.[3] Yet its practice has often been remarkably un-
civilized, and it was much more so at the beginning of the American republic than
it is today.

A hint of future directions appeared in the first newspaper published in the North
American colonies in 1690, which carried a report that the king of France "used to lie
with" his son's wife. George Washington escaped most press scrutiny but detested
journalists nonetheless; his battle tactics in the Revolutionary War had been much criticized in print, and an early draft of his "Farewell Address to the Nation" at the end of

Landmark Events in the History of the American Media

1690 ◆ First newspaper published

1789 ◆ First party newspapers circulated

1833 ◆ First penny press

1890 ◆ Yellow journalism spreads

1900 ◆ Muckraking in fashion

1928 ◆ First radio broadcast of an election

1948 ◆ First election results to be covered by television

1952 ◆ First presidential campaign advertisements aired on television

1960 ◆ First televised presidential campaign debates

1979 ◆ The Cable Satellite Public Affairs Network (C-SPAN) is founded, providing live round-the-clock coverage of politics and government.

1980 ◆ Cable News Network (CNN) is founded by media mogul Ted Turner, making national and international events available instantaneously around the globe.

1992 ◆ Talk-show television circumvents the news, allowing candidates to go around journalists to reach the voting public directly.

his presidency (1796) contained a condemnation of the press that has often been described as savage.[4] Thomas Jefferson was treated especially harshly by elements of the early U.S. press. For example, one Richmond newspaper editor, angered by Jefferson's refusal to appoint him as postmaster, concocted a falsehood that survives to this day: that Jefferson kept a slave as his concubine and had several children by her.[5] One can understand why Jefferson, normally a defender of a free press, commented that "even the least informed of the people have learned that nothing in a newspaper is to be believed."

Jefferson probably did not intend that statement literally, since he himself was instrumental in establishing the *National Gazette,* the newspaper of his political faction and viewpoint. The *Gazette* was created to compete with a similar paper (called the *Gazette of the United States*) founded earlier by Alexander Hamilton and his anti-Jefferson Federalists. The era of party newspapers extended from Washington's tenure through Andrew Jackson's presidency. The editor of Jackson's party paper, *The Globe,* was included in the president's influential "kitchen cabinet" (a group of informal advisers), and all of Jackson's appointees with annual salaries greater than $1,000 were required to buy a subscription. (Incidentally, from George Washington through James Buchanan, who left office in 1861, all government printing contracts were awarded to the newspaper associated with the incumbent administration).

A Less Partisan Press

The partisan press eventually gave way to the penny press. In 1833 Benjamin Day founded the *New York Sun,* which cost a penny at the newsstand. It was politically a more independent publication than the party papers, and it was not tied to one party. The *Sun* was the forerunner of the modern press built on mass circulation and commercial advertising to produce profit. By 1861 the penny press had so supplanted partisan papers that President Abraham Lincoln (who succeeded Buchanan) announced that his administration would have no favored or sponsored newspaper.

The press thus became markedly less partisan but not necessarily more respectable. Mass-circulation dailies sought wide readership, and, then as now, readers were clearly attracted by the sensational and the scandalous. The sordid side of politics became the entertainment of the times. One of the best-known examples occurred in the presidential campaign of 1884, when the *Buffalo Evening Telegraph* headlined "A Terrible Tale" about Grover Cleveland, the Democratic nominee.[6] In 1871, while sheriff of Buffalo, the bachelor Cleveland had allegedly fathered a child. Even though the woman in question had been seeing other men, Cleveland willingly accepted responsibility since all the other men were married, and he had dutifully paid child support for years. Fortunately for Cleveland, another newspaper, the *Democratic Sentinel,* broke a story that helped to offset this scandal: Republican presidential nominee James G. Blaine and his wife had had their first child just three months after their wedding. There is a lesson for politicians in this double-edged morality tale. Cleveland acknowledged his responsibility forthrightly and took his lumps, whereas Blaine told a fabulously elaborate, completely unbelievable story about having had two marriage

"Uncle Sam's Next Campaign— the War Against the Yellow Press." In this 1898 cartoon in the wake of the Spanish American War, yellow journalism is attacked for its threats, insults, filth, grime, blood, death, slander, gore, and blackmail, all of which are "lies." The cartoonist suggests that, after winning the foreign war, the government ought to attack its own yellow journalists at home.

ceremonies six months apart. Cleveland won the election (although other factors also played a role in his victory).

The era of the intrusive press was in full flower. First **yellow journalism** and then **muckraking** were in fashion. Pioneered by prominent publishers such as William Randolph Hearst and Joseph Pulitzer, yellow journalism[7] featured pictures, comics, and color designed to capture a share of the burgeoning immigrant population market. These newspapers also oversimplified and sensationalized many news developments. The front-page editorial crusade became common, the motto for which frequently seemed to be "Damn the truth, full speed ahead."

The muckrakers—so named by President Theodore Roosevelt after a special rake designed to collect manure[8]—took charge after the turn of the century in a number of newspapers and nationally circulated magazines. Journalists such as Upton Sinclair and David Graham Phillips searched out and exposed real and apparent misconduct by government, business, and politicians in order to stimulate reform.[9] There was no shortage of corruption to reveal, of course, and much good came from these efforts. But an unfortunate side effect of the emphasis on crusades and investigations was the frequent publication of gossip and rumor without sufficient proof.

The modern press corps may also be guilty of this offense, but it has achieved great progress on another front. Throughout the nineteenth century, payoffs to the press were not uncommon. Andrew Jackson, for instance, gave one in ten of his early appointments to loyal reporters,[10] and during the 1872 presidential campaign the Republicans slipped cash to about three hundred newsmen.[11] Wealthy industrialists also sometimes purchased editorial peace or investigative cease-fire for tens of thousands of dollars. Examples of such press corruption are exceedingly rare today, and not even the most extreme of the modern media's critics believe otherwise.

As the news business grew, its focus gradually shifted from passionate opinion to corporate profit. Newspapers, hoping to maximize profit, were more careful to avoid alienating the advertisers and readers who produced their revenues, and the result was less harsh, more objective reporting. Meanwhile, media barons became pillars of the establishment; for the most part, they were no longer the anti-establishment insurgents of yore.

Technological advances obviously had a major impact on this transformation in journalism. High-speed presses and more cheaply produced paper made mass-circulation dailies possible. The telegraph and, later, the telephone made news gathering easier and much faster. And, of course, nothing else could compare to the invention of radio and television. Radio became widely available in the 1920s, and, for the first time, millions of Americans were hearing national politicians instead of merely reading about them. With television—first introduced in the late 1940s and nearly a universal fixture in U.S. homes by the mid-1950s—citizens could see and hear candidates and presidents. The removal of newspapers and magazines as the foremost conduits between politicians and voters had profound effects on the electoral process, as we discuss shortly.

The Contemporary Media Scene

The editors of the first partisan newspapers could scarcely have imagined what their profession would become more than two centuries later. The number and diversity of media outlets existing in the 1990s are stunning: many thousands of daily and weekly

Yellow journalism A form of newspaper publishing in vogue in the late nineteenth century that featured pictures, comics, color, and sensationalized, oversimplified news coverage.

Muckraking A form of newspaper publishing, in vogue in the early twentieth century, concerned with reforming government and business conduct.

Almost from the beginning of his 1992 presidential campaign, Bill Clinton attracted intense media coverage. After placing second in the New Hampshire primary in February, he quickly jumped to front-runner status. Whether this status was real or media-appointed finally mattered little as Clinton made adept use of press scrutiny right up to election day.

newspapers, periodicals (magazines, newsletters, computerized information services), and radio and television stations and networks. In some ways the news business is more competitive than at any time in history, yet, paradoxically, the news media have expanded in some ways and contracted in others, dramatically changing the ways in which they cover politics.

The growth of the political press corps is obvious to anyone familiar with government or campaigns. Since 1983, for example, the number of print (newspaper and magazine) reporters accredited at the U.S. Capitol has jumped from 2,300 to more than 4,100; the gain for broadcast (television and radio) journalists was equally impressive and proportionately larger, from about 1,000 in 1983 to more than 2,400 by 1990.[12] On the campaign trail a similar phenomenon has been occurring. In the 1960s a presidential candidate in the primaries would attract a press entourage of at most a couple of dozen reporters, but in the 1990s a hundred or more print and broadcast journalists can be seen tagging along with a frontrunner. Consequently, a politician's every public utterance is reported and intensively scrutinized and interpreted in the media.

Although there are more journalists, they are not necessarily attracting a larger audience, at least on the print side. Daily newspaper circulation has been stagnant for twenty years at 62 to 63 million papers per day (see Figure 14-1). On a per household basis, circulation has actually fallen 44 percent over these two decades.[13] Barely half of the adult population reads a newspaper every day. Among young people age eighteen to twenty-nine, only one-third are daily readers—a decline of 50 percent in two decades.

FIGURE 14-1
Circulation of Daily Newspapers, 1850–1991

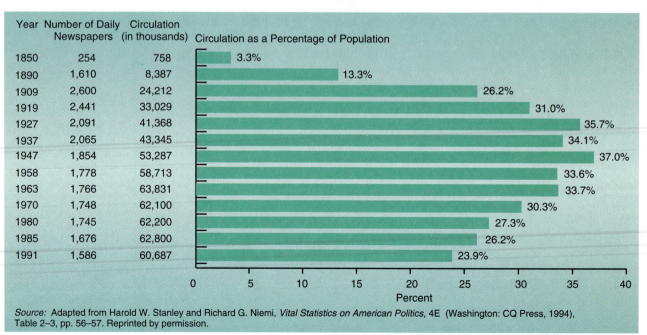

Year	Number of Daily Newspapers	Circulation (in thousands)	Circulation as a Percentage of Population
1850	254	758	3.3%
1890	1,610	8,387	13.3%
1909	2,600	24,212	26.2%
1919	2,441	33,029	31.0%
1927	2,091	41,368	35.7%
1937	2,065	43,345	34.1%
1947	1,854	53,287	37.0%
1958	1,778	58,713	33.6%
1963	1,766	63,831	33.7%
1970	1,748	62,100	30.3%
1980	1,745	62,200	27.3%
1985	1,676	62,800	26.2%
1991	1,586	60,687	23.9%

Source: Adapted from Harold W. Stanley and Richard G. Niemi, *Vital Statistics on American Politics*, 4E (Washington: CQ Press, 1994), Table 2–3, pp. 56–57. Reprinted by permission.

Along with the relative decline of readership has come a drop in the overall level of competition. In 1880, 61 percent of U.S. cities had at least two competing dailies, but by 1990 a mere 2 percent of cities did so. Not surprisingly, the number of dailies has declined significantly, from a peak of 2,600 in 1909 to 1,611 today.[14] Most of the remaining dailies are owned by large media conglomerates called chains. In 1940, 83 percent of all daily newspapers were independently owned, but by 1990 just 24 percent remained independent of a chain (such as Gannett, Hearst, Knight-Ridder, and Newhouse). Chain ownership usually reduces the diversity of editorial opinions and can result in the homogenization of the news.

Part of the cause of the newspapers' declining audience has been the increased numbers of television sets and cable subscribers (see Figure 14-2) and the increased popularity of television as a news source. As Table 14.1 shows, at the dawn of the 1960s a substantial majority of Americans reported that they got most of their news from newspapers, but by the latter half of the 1980s television was the people's choice by an almost two-to-one margin.[15] Moreover, by a margin of 55 to 21 percent, Americans now say that they are inclined to believe television over newspapers when conflicting reports about the same story arise. Of course, most individuals still rely on *both* print and broadcast sources,[16] but there can be little question that television news is increasingly important. Despite its many drawbacks (such as simplicity, brevity, and entertainment orientation) television news is "news that matters."[17] Although not totally eclipsing newspapers, television frequently overshadows them, even as it often takes its agenda and lead stories from the headlines produced by print reporters (especially those working for the print elite, such as the *New York Times,* the *Washington Post,* the *Wall Street Journal,* the Associated Press, United Press International, *Time, Newsweek,* and *U.S. News & World Report*). Regrettably, busy people today appear to have less time to review the printed word, and consequently they rely more on television's brief headline summaries to stay in touch.

The television news industry differs from its print counterpart in a variety of ways. The number of outlets has been increasing, not declining, as with newspapers. The

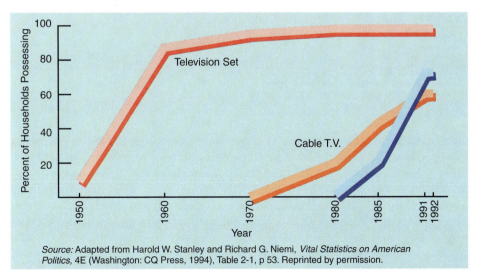

FIGURE 14-2

Television in the American Home

Source: Adapted from Harold W. Stanley and Richard G. Niemi, *Vital Statistics on American Politics,* 4E (Washington: CQ Press, 1994), Table 2-1, p 53. Reprinted by permission.

Table 14.1 ◆ Use and Trustworthiness of News Media

In the 1950s, newspapers provided most of the average American's news, and papers were more "believable" than television. By the 1980s, television had triumphed over newspapers in both categories, and TV had also eclipsed the influence of radio and magazines.

Source of most news (by percent)

Question: *"First, I'd like to ask you where you usually get most of your news about what's going on in the world today—from the newspapers or radio or television or magazines or talking to people or where?"* (more than one answer permitted)

	1959	1963	1967	1972	1976	1982	1986	1992	
Television	51%	55%	64%	64%	64%	64%	66%	69%	(1)
Newspapers	57	53	55	50	49	44	36	43	(2)
Radio	34	29	28	21	19	18	14	16	(3)
Magazines	8	6	7	6	7	6	4	4	(5)
People	4	4	4	4	5	4	4	6	(4)

Most believable (by percent)

Question: *"If you got conflicting or different reports of the same news story from radio, television, the magazines, and the newspapers, which of the versions would you be most inclined to believe—the one on the radio or television or magazines or newspapers?"* (only one answer permitted)

	1959	1963	1967	1972	1976	1982	1986	1992	
Television	29%	36%	41%	48%	51%	53%	55%	56%	(1)
Newspapers	32	24	24	21	22	22	21	22	(2)
Radio	12	12	7	8	7	6	6	7	(3)
Magazines	10	10	8	10	9	8	7	4	(4)
Don't know/ no answer	17	18	20	13	11	11	12	12	(5)

Source: Adapted from Harold W. Stanley and Richard G. Niemi, *Vital Statistics on American Politics,* 4th ed. (Washington, DC: CQ Press, 1994), Table 2-12, p. 74.

three major networks now receive broadcast competition from Cable Network News (CNN), "Headline News," Cable Satellite Public Affairs Network (C-SPAN), and PBS's "MacNeil/Lehrer NewsHour." Although the audiences of all the alternate shows are relatively small compared with those of the network news shows, they are growing while the networks' audience shares contract. The potential for cable expansion is still large, too; fewer than half of all U.S. households are currently wired for cable. Adding to television's diversity, the national television news corps is often outnumbered on the campaign trail by local television reporters. Satellite technology has provided any of the 1,300 local stations willing to invest in the hardware an opportunity to beam back reports from the field. On a daily basis, local news is watched by more people (67 percent of adults) than is network news (49 percent), so increased local attention to politics has some real significance.

The decline of the major networks' audience shares and the local stations' decreasing reliance on the major networks for news—coupled with stringent belt tightening ordered by the networks' corporate managers—resulted in severe news staff cutbacks at NBC, CBS, and ABC during the 1980s. These economy measures have affected the quality of broadcast journalism. Many senior correspondents bemoan the loss of desk assistants and junior reporters, who did much of the legwork necessary to get less superficial, more in-depth pieces on the air. As a consequence, stories requiring extensive research are often discarded in favor of simplistic, eye-catching, "sexy" items that increasingly seem to dominate campaign and government coverage.

Media That Matter

Every newspaper, radio station, and television station is influential in its own area, but only a handful of media outlets really are influential in a national sense. The United States has no nationwide daily newspapers to match the influence of Great Britain's *The Times,* the *Guardian,* and the *Daily Telegraph,* all of which are avidly read in virtually every corner of the United Kingdom. The national orientation of the British print media can be traced to the smaller size of the country and also to London's role as both the national capital and the largest cultural metropolis. The vastness of the United States and the existence of many large cities, such as New York, Los Angeles, and Chicago, effectively preclude a nationally united print medium in this country.

However, national distribution of the *New York Times,* the *Wall Street Journal, USA Today,* and the *Christian Science Monitor* does exist, and other newspapers, such as the *Washington Post* and the *Los Angeles Times,* have substantial influence from coast to coast. These six newspapers also have a pronounced effect on what the four national **networks** (ABC, CBS, NBC, and CNN) broadcast on their evening news programs—or, in the case of CNN, air on cable around the clock. A major story that breaks in one of these papers is nearly guaranteed to be featured on one or more of the network news shows. These news shows are carried by hundreds of local stations—called **affiliates**—that are associated with the national networks and may choose to carry their programming. A **wire service,** the Associated Press (AP), also nationalizes the news. Most newspapers subscribe to the service, which not only produces its own news stories but also puts on the wire major stories produced by other media outlets. The AP was established in 1848.

The national newspapers, wire service, and broadcast networks are supplemented by a number of national news magazines, whose subscribers number in the millions. *Time, Newsweek,* and *U.S. News & World Report* bring the week's news into focus and headline one event or trend for special treatment. Other news magazines stress commentary from an ideological viewpoint, including *The Nation* (left-wing), *The New Republic* (moderate-liberal), and *The National Review* (conservative). These last three publications have much smaller circulations, but their readerships are composed of activists and opinion leaders, and therefore they have disproportionate influence.

Circumstances can conspire to make a less important publication into a relative giant. For example, the *Manchester Union-Leader* in New Hampshire and the *Des Moines Register* in Iowa are closely read by a national political audience in the months leading up to the early presidential contests in these states. (In presidential election

This television picture of O.J. Simpson in his white Ford Bronco with Los Angeles police in pursuit was broadcast live around the globe. The murder trial of Simpson that followed became a media extravaganza, covered daily by virtually every major news organization in the world.

Network An association of broadcast stations (radio or television) that shares programming through a financial arrangement.

Affiliates Local television stations that carry the programming of a national network.

Wire service An electronic delivery of news gathered by the news services' correspondents and sent to all member news media organizations.

PEOPLE OF THE PAST

Pioneers of the Broadcasting Industry

One of the first and most prominent broadcast journalists in the United States was the CBS radio anchor Edward R. Murrow. Trained in language and public speaking through childhood Bible readings and endowed with a richly textured voice, Murrow was a superb radio reporter who later adapted his skills to the new medium of television.

Murrow joined CBS in 1935 as director of "talks and education," a position that entailed setting up radio speeches by prominent public officials. In 1937 he became European director of "talks," stationed in London, a move that would prove to be the catalyst for his career as a radio newscaster. When Germany invaded Austria on March 11, 1938, Murrow was on assignment in Poland, but he was soon directed to go to Vienna. Once he was in Austria, which he reached only with great difficulty, Murrow's dramatic eyewitness accounts of Adolf Hitler's takeover mesmerized both Europe and the United States.

Murrow's finest moment, however, came in the 1940 Battle of Britain—the German bombing campaign that

Edward R. Murrow

years, New Hampshire holds the nation's first scheduled primary, and Iowa has the first caucus.)

How the Media Cover Politicians and Government

Covering the Presidency

The three branches of the U.S. government—the executive, the legislative, and the judicial—are roughly equal in power and authority, but in the world of media coverage, the president is first among equals. All television cables lead to the White House, and a president can address the nation on all networks almost at will. On television, Congress and the courts appear to be divided and confused institutions—different segments contradicting others—whereas the commander-in-chief is in clear focus as chief of state and head of government. The situation is scarcely different in other democra-

flattened much of London. Probably more than any other broadcast journalist, Murrow brought the air battle to the forefront of U.S. public attention. Murrow was so respected by British authorities that only he and two other reporters—NBC's Fred Bates and John Mac-Vane—were permitted to broadcast without first clearing their information with British censors. Murrow, Bates, and MacVane all did rooftop broadcasts during Germany's bombing raids, but CBS's were the most listened to because of Murrow's special talents.

After the war, in 1946, Murrow became vice president of news and public affairs at CBS. His task was to set the course of that network's radio newscasting, and one of his achievements was the development of CBS's first documentary unit. Yet Murrow did not really enjoy administration, and a few years later he returned to the field as a journalist, this time on television. Among his many accomplishments were hard-hitting CBS programs on the right-wing extremism of U.S. Senator Joseph R. McCarthy (R.-Wis.) and on the poverty and exploitation of migrant workers. In 1961 Murrow was appointed director of the United States Information Agency by President John F. Kennedy. He died of cancer in 1965.

Meanwhile, NBC television was establishing the first broadcast news anchor team for its evening news show. Chet Huntley and David Brinkley hosted "The Huntley-Brinkley Report" each night for fifteen minutes. The two had first been paired to cover the 1956 Democratic and Republican presidential conventions, and it was obvious from the start that they were compatible and appealing. Huntley, a North Carolina native who got his start with United Press International, had a solemn, serious style of reporting. Brinkley, a Montanan who began his media career working for KPCB-AM in Seattle while a senior at the University of Washington (he was at once a disc jockey, a writer, a salesman, and a janitor), had a sharp, witty tone that complemented Huntley nicely. Americans quickly became accustomed to their style and their signature signoff at program's end: "Goodnight, David." "Goodnight, Chet." "And goodnight for NBC News."

"The Huntley-Brinkley Report" ran for fourteen years, from 1956 to 1970. In 1963 its time slot was increased to a half hour, mostly in response to competition from CBS, which had initiated the first half-hour news show on network television, anchored by another rising star, Walter Cronkite. In 1970 the team broke up when Chet Huntley decided to retire. Chet Huntley has since died; David Brinkley still broadcasts a Sunday talk show, "This Week with David Brinkley," although he has changed networks, working now for ABC News.

cies. In Great Britain, all media eyes are on No. 10 Downing Street, the office and residence of the prime minister.

Since Franklin D. Roosevelt's time, chief executives have used the presidential press conference to shape public opinion and explain their actions (see Figure 14-3). The presence of the press in the White House enables a president to appear even on very short notice and to televise live, interrupting regular programming. The White House's press-briefing room is a familiar sight on the evening news, not just because presidents use it so often but also because the presidential press secretary has almost daily question-and-answer sessions there.

The press secretary's post has existed only since Herbert Hoover's administration (1929–33), and the individual holding it is the president's main conduit of information to the press. For this vital position, a number of presidents have chosen close aides who were very familiar with their thinking. For example, John F. Kennedy had Pierre Salinger (now an ABC News foreign correspondent), Lyndon B. Johnson had Bill Moyers (who now hosts many PBS documentaries), and Jimmy Carter chose his longtime Georgia associate Jody Powell. Probably the most famous recent presidential

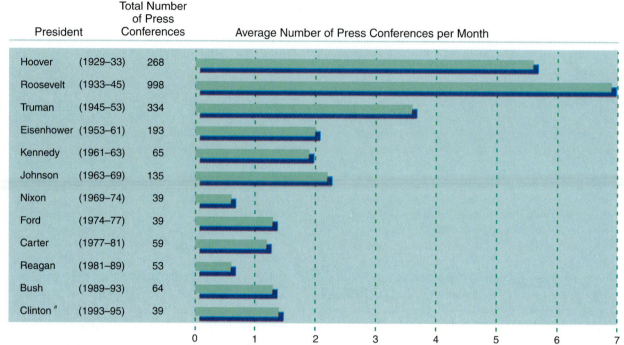

FIGURE 14-3
Presidential News Conferences, 1929–1995

[a] As of May 15, 1995.

Source: Adapted from Harold W. Stanley and Richard G. Niemi, *Vital Statistics on American Politics*, 4E. (Washington: CQ Press, 1994) Table 2–4, p. 59. Reprinted by permission.

press secretary is James Brady, who was wounded and disabled in the March, 1981, assassination attempt on President Ronald Reagan. President Bill Clinton's press secretary Dee Dee Myers, also became an instantly recognizable figure.

Covering Congress

Press coverage of Congress is very different from media coverage of the president. The size of the institution alone (535 members) and its decentralized nature (bicameralism, the committee system, and so on) make it difficult for the media to survey. Nevertheless, the congressional press corps has more than 3,000 members (Figure 14-4). Most news organizations solve the size and decentralization problems by concentrating coverage on three groups of individuals. First, the leaders of both parties in both houses receive the lion's share of attention because only they can speak for a majority of their party's members. Usually the majority and minority leaders in each house and the Speaker of the House are the preferred spokespersons, but the whips also receive a substantial share of air time and column inches. Second, key committee chairs command center stage when subjects in their domain are newsworthy. Heads of the most prominent committees (such as Ways and Means or Armed Services) are guaranteed frequent coverage, but even the chairs and members of minor committees or subcommittees can achieve fame when the time and issue are right. For example, the U.S. Senate Subcommittee on Surface Transportation is not normally a hotbed of media interest, but in 1989 when the subjects before it were drug dealing and prostitution at

The White House Press Corps
♦ ♦ ♦

Perhaps the most visible part of the national press corps is the group of correspondents who work at the White House. Every network, many large television stations, and virtually all big-city daily newspapers have at least one representative who works in the White House to cover the president and his chief advisers. Other media outlets representing foreign countries are also given access to the White House and are included in the presidential press corps.

White House reporters do not have the run of the place, of course. They are usually restricted to the press room, where the president makes announcements and holds informal question-and-answer sessions. Small cubicles adjoining the press room are also provided for many news outlets. Although presidential appearances in the press room rarely occur more than once or twice a week, the president's news secretary appears daily to brief reporters on the chief executive's current schedule and activities. Frequently the press secretary also makes announcements on behalf of the president (perhaps the chief executive's comments on just-released economic statistics, for example).

Formal presidential news conferences, often held in the East Room of the White House, are an elaborate production, especially if held during prime-time hours. All the networks carry them live and in full, and correspondents jockey to attract the president's attention. The best-known reporters are nearly guaranteed to be selected to ask a question, and these are prime opportunities for them and for the news organizations they represent. Over the years, many of the networks' most prominent professionals have served on the White House beat, including CBS's Dan Rather and Lesley Stahl, NBC's Tom Brokaw, and ABC's Sam Donaldson. Many print journalists, such as United Press International's Helen Thomas, also become well known while on the White House beat. In fact, these reporters become celebrities, and they are often asked to appear on the late-night David Letterman and Jay Leno shows. On occasion, they have played themselves in movies (such as *Dave*).

It is not always easy for the president to have reporters literally underfoot. But the instantaneous access to the American people they give the president is essential to his work, and the scrutiny of the chief executive they offer the American people is vital to the voters as well.

highway truck stops, reporters and cameras packed the hearing room, showering attention on an obscure Nebraska senator, James Exon (the subcommittee chairman). Third, local newspapers and broadcast stations will normally devote some resources to covering their local senators and representatives, even when these legislators are junior and relatively lacking in influence. Most office holders, in turn, are mainly concerned with meeting the needs of their local media contingents, since these reporters are the ones who directly and regularly reach the voters in their home constituencies.

One other kind of congressional news coverage is worth noting: investigative-committee hearings. Occasionally, a sensational scandal leads to televised congressional committee hearings that transfix and electrify the nation. In the early 1950s Senator Joseph R. McCarthy (R-Wis.) held a series of hearings to expose and root out what he claimed were communists in the State Department and other U.S. government agencies, as well as Hollywood's film industry. The senator's style of investigation, which involved many wild charges made without proof and the smearing and labeling of some innocent opponents as communists, gave rise to the term *McCarthyism.*

The Watergate hearings of 1973 and 1974 made heroes out of two committee chairs, Senator Sam Ervin (D-N.C.) and U.S. Representative Peter Rodino (D-N.J.). They un-

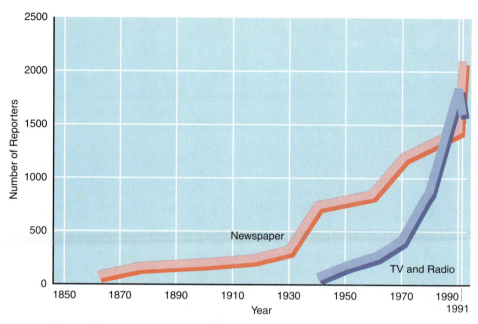

FIGURE 14-4

Growth of Congressional
Press Corps, 1964–1991

Source: Adapted from Harold W. Stanley and Richard G. Niemi, *Vital Statistics on American Politics,*
4E (Washington: CQ Press, 1994), Figure 2–1, p. 58. Reprinted by permission.

covered many facts behind the Watergate scandal and then pursued the impeachment of President Richard M. Nixon. (Nixon resigned in August 1974 before the full House could vote on his impeachment.)

In 1987 the Iran-Contra hearings—set up to investigate a complicated Reagan administration scheme in which arms were sold to Iran and the profits were then diverted to the Nicaraguan anti-communist *contras*—also created a popular hero. This time, however, the hero was not the committee chair but a witness, Lieutenant Colonel Oliver North, a White House aide deeply involved in the plot. North's boyish appeal and patriotic demeanor projected well on television, on which all the hearings were carried live (as were the McCarthy and Watergate hearings). North capitalized on his fame and in 1994 launched a campaign for a U.S. Senate seat from Virginia. More recently, in October 1991, the nation viewed another televised committee spectacle when Supreme Court nominee Clarence Thomas was accused of sexual harassment (see "The Clarence Thomas Hearings," p. 480).

Coverage of Congress has been greatly expanded through use of the cable industry channel C-SPAN, the Cable Satellite Public Affairs Network, founded in 1979. C-SPAN1 and C-SPAN2 provide gavel-to-gavel coverage of House and Senate sessions as well as many committee hearings. For the first time Americans can watch their representatives in action (or inaction as the case may be), and do so 24 hours a day.

Covering the Courts

The branch of government that is the most different, in press coverage as in many other respects, is the judicial branch. Cloaked in secrecy—because judicial deliberations and decision making are conducted in private—the courts receive scant coverage under most circumstances. However, a volatile or controversial issue, such as abortion, can change usual type of coverage, especially when the Supreme Court is rendering the decision. Each network and major newspaper has one or more Supreme Court reporters, who are usually well schooled in the law and whose instant analysis of court opinions interprets the decisions for the millions of people without legal training. Gradually, the admission of cameras into state and local courtrooms across the United States is offering people a more in-depth look at the operation of the judicial system. As yet, though, the Supreme Court does not permit televised proceedings.

Even more than the Court's decisions, presidential appointments to the high court are the focus of intense media attention. As the judiciary has assumed a more important role in modern times, the men and women considered for the post are being subjected to withering scrutiny of their records and even of their private lives. The media's disclosure that Douglas Ginsberg had smoked marijuana extensively as an adult forced President Reagan to withdraw his Supreme Court nomination in 1987, for example.

Watergate and the Era of Investigative Journalism

The Watergate scandal of the Nixon administration—which stemmed from White House efforts to eavesdrop on officials of the Democratic National Committee and then to cover up presidential involvement in the scheme—had the most profound impact of any modern event on the manner and substance of the press's conduct. In many respects Watergate began a chain reaction that today allows for intense scrutiny of public officials' private lives. Moreover, coupled with the civil rights movement and the Vietnam War, Watergate shifted the orientation of journalism away from mere description (providing an account of happenings) and toward prescription—helping to set the campaign's (and society's) agenda by focusing attention on the candidates' shortcomings as well as on certain social problems.

A new breed and a new generation of reporters were attracted to journalism, particularly to its investigative role. As a group they were idealistic, although aggressively mistrustful of authority, and they shared a contempt for "politics as usual." The Vietnam and Watergate generation dominates journalism today. They and their younger colleagues hold sway over most newsrooms, with two-thirds of all reporters now under the age of thirty-six and an ever-increasing number of editors and executives who had their start in journalism in the Watergate era.[18]

Of course, many people who found journalism newly attractive in the wake of Watergate were not completely altruistic. Young and ambitious journalists saw the happy fate of the *Washington Post*'s youthful Watergate sleuths Bob Woodward and Carl Bernstein, who gained fame, fortune, and big-screen portrayals by Robert Redford and Dustin Hoffman in the movie *All the President's Men*. The young were attracted not just to journalism but to a particular *kind* of journalism. Their role models were not respected, established reporters but two unknowns who succeeded by refusing to play by the rules their seniors had accepted. Whatever their motives, though, journalism's new breed has been determined to get to the bottom of each new scandal.

In the post-Watergate press a volatile mix of guilt and fear is at work. The guilt stems from regret that experienced Washington reporters failed to detect the telltale signs of the Watergate scandal early on; that even after the story broke, most journalists underplayed the unfolding disaster until forced to take it more seriously by the two young *Post* reporters; that over the years journalism's leading lights had become too close to the politicians they were supposed to check and therefore for too long failed to

The Clarence Thomas Hearings
◆ ◆ ◆

As with Watergate and the Iran-Contra scandal, Clarence Thomas's nomination to the Supreme Court in 1991 gave rise to a television extravaganza that mesmerized the American people. The U.S. Senate Judiciary Committee hearings on allegations of sexual harassment that were lodged against Thomas drew a large audience for three full days in early October 1991.

The intense media attention focused on the Senate Judiciary Committee's confirmation hearings of Judge Clarence Thomas created a three-way spectacle: the senators, the testifiers (pictured at right is Thomas), and the media themselves.

A few months earlier, President George Bush had nominated Thomas, a black conservative, to succeed retiring Justice Thurgood Marshall, a pillar of the civil rights movement. Thomas appeared to be heading for an easy Senate confirmation when National Public Radio's correspondent Nina Totenberg reported the harassment charges just days before Thomas's scheduled confirmation vote. The all-male Senate Judiciary Committee had earlier disregarded the charges, in part because the chief accuser, University of Oklahoma Law School Professor Anita Hill, was reluctant to come forward publicly. But after the information was leaked to National Public Radio and other news outlets, the Senate was forced to postpone its confirmation vote and hold an additional Judiciary Committee hearing to investigate the allegations, which dated back to Thomas's chairmanship of the Equal Employment Opportunity Commission (EEOC) during the Reagan administration. (Hill had also been an EEOC employee and one of Thomas's subordinates.)

The hearings became a national obsession—a real-life soap opera made for television. Hill's graphic accusations of Thomas's advances and vivid sexual allusions shocked many Americans, who were equally riveted by Thomas's angry denial of the charges and denouncement of the Judiciary Committee inquiry as "a high-tech lynching." Convincing and sincere character witnesses for both sides were produced, leaving most viewers puzzled about the truth. In the absence of hard evidence, a substantial majority of people (as measured by public opinion polls) eventually sided with Thomas, and he managed to win confirmation in the full Senate by a vote of fifty-two to forty-eight — the narrowest affirmative vote for a Supreme Court justice in this century.

The most damaging political consequences of the hearings were visited on the senators themselves. Both sides agreed that the Senate handled the matter poorly—first, by not treating Hill's accusations seriously, then by conducting a public spectacle. The Watergate hearings made heroes of many of the participating legislators (such as U.S. Senator Sam Ervin [D-N.C.], the folksy chairman of the Senate Watergate panel). But the Thomas hearings only diminished the reputations of most senators who had the misfortune to be in the spotlight. Democrats not known to have a spotless private life, such as Senator Edward M. Kennedy (D-Mass.), were derided for hypocrisy, while Republicans such as Arlen Specter (R-Pa.) and Alan Simpson (R-Wyo.) were criticized for their often harsh questioning of Anita Hill.

The contrast between the Watergate and Thomas hearings demonstrates that intense media coverage is a double-edged sword: When the television cameras are trained on elected officials, these officials can easily emerge as national heroes—or as national objects of scorn.

tell the public about dangerous excesses in the government. The press's ongoing fear is deep-seated and complements the guilt. Every political journalist is apprehensive about missing the next big story, of being left on the platform when the next scandal train leaves Union Station.

The Post-Watergate Era

In the post-Watergate era, the sizable financial and personnel investments many major news organizations have made in investigative units almost guarantee that greater attention will be given to scandals and that probably more of them—some real and some manufactured—will be uncovered.

The Character Issue in Media Coverage of Politicians

Another clear consequence of Watergate has been the increasing emphasis by the press on the character of candidates. The issue of character has always been present in U.S. politics—George Washington was not made the nation's first president for his policy positions—but rarely if ever has character been such an issue as it has in elections from 1976 onward. Jimmy Carter's 1976 presidential campaign was characterized by moral posturing in the wake of Watergate. Edward M. Kennedy's 1980 presidential candidacy was destroyed in part by lingering character questions. The 1988 race witnessed an explosion of character concerns so forceful that several candidates (including Gary Hart) were badly scarred by it. And the 1992 contest for the White House became a tawdry debate about the alleged mistresses of Bill Clinton and George Bush. (The evidence in both of the 1992 cases was less than convincing, but that did not stop the media.)

The character issue may in part have been an outgrowth of the "new journalism" popularized by author Tom Wolfe in the 1970s.[19] Contending that conventional journalism was sterile and stripped of color, Wolfe and others argued for a reporting style that expanded the definition of news and, novel-like, highlighted all the personal details of the newsmaker. Then, too, reporters had witnessed the success of such books as Theodore H. White's "Making of the President" series and Joe McGinniss's *The Selling of the President 1968,* which offered revealing, behind-the-scenes vignettes of the previous election's candidates.[20] Why not give readers and viewers this information before the election? the press reasoned. There was encouragement from academic quarters as well. "Look to character first" when evaluating and choosing among presidential candidates, wrote Duke University political science professor James David Barber in a widely circulated 1972 volume, *The Presidential Character* (see - Chapter 7).[21]

Whatever the precise historical origins of the character trend in reporting, it is undergirded by certain assumptions. First, the press sees that it has mainly replaced the political parties as the screening committee that winnows the field of candidates and filters out the weaker or more unlucky contenders. (This fact may be another reason to support the strengthening of the political parties. Politicians are in a much better position than the press to provide professional peer review of colleagues who are seeking the presidency.) Second, many journalists believe it necessary to tell people about any of a candidate's foibles that might affect his or her public performance. The press's

$\mathcal{T}$HEN AND NOW

The Character Issue from Grover Cleveland to Bill Clinton

The character issue—which focuses press attention on the private-life activities and personalities of candidates—has been with us throughout U.S. history, as this text's reference to President Grover Cleveland's out-of-wedlock child suggests. Yet the intensity and the reach of the character issue have grown over the centuries, and particularly in recent years, as Democratic presidential candidate Gary Hart discovered to his chagrin in 1987. The press corps had long heard stories about Hart's alleged extramarital affairs, but no usable evidence had come to light. The situation changed dramatically in May 1987, shortly after Hart declared his candidacy for a second run at the White House.

The *Miami Herald* received an anonymous tip that Hart would be meeting an attractive model for a weekend tryst in Washington, D.C. This tip closely followed Hart's public insistence that the womanizing rumors about him were false and that his once-rocky marriage was again on firm ground. Hart had said to one reporter, E. J. Dionne of the *New York Times,* "Follow me around. . . . [You'll] be very bored."

Bored the *Miami Herald* was not when it decided to stake out Hart's Washington townhouse. The paper's reporters apparently observed Hart and Donna Rice, the model, inhabiting the townhouse, although the journalists' surveillance was not continuous and both house entrances were not always covered. Despite the flaws in the investigation, the circumstances were suspicious enough to generate a major scandal that dominated Hart's campaign.

When other indiscretions surfaced in an overwhelming media maelstrom, Hart withdrew from the race on May 8, 1987, with a bitter blast at the "intrusive" press that had brought him down. He briefly reentered the presidential contest in December, but by then Hart was a spent force and received only a handful of votes in the early 1988 primaries.

Probably no event from the 1988 presidential campaign has proved to be as memorable as the undoing of Gary Hart. The Hart episode also marked a milestone for the news media. They had helped eliminate the Democratic Party's frontrunner before a single ballot had been cast in the primaries, and they had done it by ag-

gressively investigating the private life of the unlucky candidate.

Four years later Bill Clinton learned from Gary Hart's mistakes. Before formally announcing his presidential candidacy, he admitted unspecified extramarital indiscretions, but—with the support of his spouse, Hillary Rodham Clinton—Clinton stressed that his marriage had weathered its storms. When lounge singer Gennifer Flowers claimed a past relationship with Clinton in January 1992, the candidate was able to point to his previous revelation (while denying Flowers's specific charge). With a well-timed visit to CBS's "60 Minutes" right after the Super Bowl, the Clintons were able to demonstrate marital solidarity at a moment of crisis. And the mainstream press itself was embarrassed to follow the lead of a supermarket tabloid, *The Star,* which had first carried—and hyped—Flowers's allegations.

With a strong organization behind him, Clinton managed a second-place finish in the New Hampshire primary and dubbed himself "the comeback kid." Clinton earned the title, overcoming an obstacle that had unhorsed frontrunner Hart earlier. Unfortunately for Clinton, various allegations about his involvement with women continued to be made during his presidency, but none threatened seriously to cut short his term—just as Flowers failed to derail his candidacy.

third supposition is that it is giving the public what it wants and expects, more or less. Perhaps television has conditioned voters to think about the private lives of the rich and famous. The rules of television prominence now seem to apply to all celebrities equally, whether they reside in Hollywood or Washington. And, perhaps more important, scandal sells papers and attracts television viewers.

Loosening of the Libel Law.   Another factor permits the modern press to undertake character investigations. In the old days, a reporter would think twice about filing a story critical of a politician's character, and the editors probably would have killed the story had the reporter been foolish enough to do so. The reason? Fear of a libel suit. (Recall from Chapter 4 that libel is published defamation of character that unjustly injures a person's reputation.) The first question editors would ask about even an ambiguous or suggestive phrase about a public official was, "If we're sued, can you prove beyond a doubt what you've written?"

Such inhibitions were ostensibly lifted in 1964, when the Supreme Court ruled in ***New York Times Co. v. Sullivan***[22] that simply publishing a defamatory falsehood is not enough to justify a libel judgment. Henceforth a public official would have to prove "actual malice," a requirement extended three years later to all public figures, such as Hollywood stars and prominent athletes.[23] The Supreme Court declared that the First Amendment requires elected officials and candidates to prove that the publisher either believed the challenged statement was false or at least entertained serious doubts about its truth and acted recklessly in publishing it in the face of those doubts. The actual malice rule has made it very difficult for public figures to win libel cases.

Despite *Sullivan,* the threat of libel litigation (and its deterrent effect on the press) persists for at least two reasons. First, the *Sullivan* protections do little to reduce the expense of defending defamation claims. The monetary costs have increased enormously, as have the required commitments of reporters' and editors' time and energy. Small news organizations without the financial resources of a national network or the *New York Times* are sometimes reluctant to publish material that might invite a lawsuit because the litigation costs could threaten their existence. The second reason for the continuing libel threat is a cultural phenomenon of heightened sensitivity to the harm that words can do to an individual's emotional tranquility. As a result, politicians are often more inclined to sue their press adversaries, even when success is unlikely.

But high costs and the politicians' propensity to sue cut both ways. The overall number of libel suits filed in recent years has dropped because plaintiffs also incur hefty legal expenses, and—perhaps more important—they have despaired of winning. Some news outlets have added another disincentive by filing countersuits charging their antagonists with bringing frivolous or nuisance actions against them.

In practice, then, the loosening of libel law has provided journalists with a safer harbor from liability in their reporting on elected officials and candidates. Whether it has truly diminished press self-censorship, especially for financially less well-endowed media outlets, is a more difficult question to answer. However, at least for the wealthy newspapers and networks, the libel laws are no longer as severe a restraint on the press as they once were.

The Question of Bias

Whenever the media break an unfavorable story about a politician, the politician usually counters with a cry of "biased reporting"—a claim that the press has told an untruth, has told only part of the truth, or has reported facts out of the complete context

New York Times Co. v. *Sullivan*
Supreme Court decision ruling that simply publishing a defamatory falsehood is not enough to justify a libel judgment.

Immediately after George Bush's 1988 surprise choice of Senator Dan Quayle to be his running mate, the media swarmed over Quayle's political track record, National Guard service record, and even his academic record. Here, reporters surround Quayle in his home state of Indiana.

Conservative talk-show host Rush Limbaugh became the symbol for the talk-radio phenomenon of the 1990s. In addition to his daily three-hour radio broadcast, Limbaugh also has a nightly, syndicated television show.

of the event. Who is right? Are the news media biased? The answer is simple and unavoidable: Of course they are. Journalists are fallible human beings who inevitably have values, preferences, and attitudes galore—some conscious, others subconscious, but all reflected at one time or another in the subjects selected for coverage or the slant of that coverage. Given that the press is biased, it is important to know in what ways it is biased and when and how the biases are shown.

Truth be told, most journalists lean to the left. First of all, those in the relatively small group of professional journalists (not many more than 100,000, compared with more than 4 million teachers in the United States) are drawn heavily from the ranks of highly educated social and political liberals, as a number of studies, some conducted by the media themselves, have shown.[24] Journalists are substantially Democratic in party affiliation and voting habits, progressive and anti-establishment in political orientation, and well to the left of the general public on most economic, foreign policy, and social issues (such as abortion, affirmative action, gay rights, and gun control). Second, dozens of the most influential reporters and executives entered (or reentered) journalism after stints of partisan involvement in campaigns or government, and a substantial majority worked for Democrats.[25]

Third, this liberal press bias does indeed show up frequently on screen and in print. A study of reporting on the abortion issue, for example, revealed a clear slant to the pro side on network television news, matching in many ways the reporters' own abortion-rights views.[26] Additionally, the media list to the left on the agenda of topics they choose to cover.[27] In the latter half of the 1980s, for instance, television gave enormous attention to the homelessness issue; in the process, some experts in the field believe, the broadcasters both exaggerated the problem and grossly overstated the role of unemployment in creating the condition of homelessness.[28]

The right wing is not alone in its disgruntlement with the news media. For very different reasons, the left wing joins in the condemnation. Liberals, while acknowledging the press's early tough line on Quayle, have taken the media to task for not keeping the pressure on him throughout the 1988 campaign. The failure of the media to analyze and criticize the sometimes exaggerated claims made in George Bush's anti-Dukakis advertisements is also cited. To the left, the perceived press kindness toward Bush was merely a continuation of its genuflection to Ronald Reagan during his presidency. "Because of the government manipulation and voluntary self-censorship the major American news organizations too often abdicated their responsibility . . . during the Reagan years," wrote the left-wing media critic Mark Hertsgaard.[29] Like others of his persuasion over the years, Hertsgaard points to the conservative status-quo interests of the corporate elites who run most media organizations to explain why a Ronald Reagan would be pampered by the press.

The question of media bias surfaces frequently in Great Britain, too. Many of the national newspapers sport openly acknowledged editorial lines. For example, the *Daily Telegraph* generally supports the position of the Conservative Party, the *Daily Mirror* sides with Labour, and the *Manchester Guardian* tends to adopt a Social Democratic position. Precisely because of these open political loyalties, the appearance in 1987 of *The Independent* as a self-declared nonpartisan newspaper created quite a splash. The broadcast media are by law required to maintain political impartiality, although they have been a frequent target of conservative criticism for their supposedly leftist leanings.

Other Sources of Bias. From left to right, all of these criticisms have some validity in different times and circumstances, in one media forum or another. But these cri-

Campaigning provides candidates with a host of carefully arranged photo opportunities that sometimes don't turn out quite as planned. Is the capturing and replaying of such gaffes a form of non-ideological media bias or just an unintended, but natural, consequence of candidates' reliance on media coverage?

tiques ignore some non-ideological factors probably more essential to an understanding of press bias. Owing to competition and the reward structure of journalism, the deepest bias most political journalists have is the desire to get to the bottom of a good campaign story—which is usually negative news about a candidate. The fear of missing a good story, more than bias, leads all media outlets to the same developing headlines and encourages them to adopt the same slant. One newspaper that broke important negative information about Dan Quayle in 1988 was the Quayle family-owned paper, the *Indianapolis News.* (The story concerned Quayle's service in the National Guard rather than in the military during the Vietnam War.)

A related non-ideological bias is the effort to create a horse race where none exists. Newspeople, whose lives revolve around the current political scene, naturally want to add spice and drama, minimize their boredom, and increase their audience. Other human, not just partisan, biases are also at work. Whether the press likes or dislikes a candidate personally is often vital. Former Governor Bruce Babbitt and U.S. Representative Morris K. Udall, both wisecracking, straight-talking Arizona Democrats, were press favorites in their presidential bids (in 1988 and 1976, respectively), and both enjoyed favorable coverage. Richard M. Nixon, Jimmy Carter, and Gary Hart—all aloof politicians—were disliked by many reporters who covered them, and they suffered from a harsh and critical press.

Finally, in their quest to avoid bias, reporters frequently seize on non-ideological offenses such as gaffes, ethical violations, and campaign-finance problems. These objective items are intrinsically free of partisan taint and can be pursued without guilt.

For all the emphasis here on bias, it is undeniably true that the modern U.S. news media are much fairer than their predecessors ever were. News blackouts of the editors' enemies, under which all positive information about the targeted politicians was banned from print, were once shockingly common but are now exceedingly rare and universally condemned. No longer do organized groups of reporters take out advertisements to support or oppose candidates or send telegrams to the president and members of Congress advocating certain public policies—events that occurred as recently as the 1970s.

In sum, then, press bias of all kinds—partisan, agenda-setting, and non-ideological—can and does influence the day-to-day coverage of politicians. But bias is not the be-all and end-all that critics on both the right and left often insist it is. Press tilt has a marginal to moderate effect, and it is but one piece in the media's news mosaic.

The Media's Influence on the Public

Some bias in media coverage clearly exists, as we have just discussed. But how does this bias affect the public that reads or views or listens to biased reporting?

In most cases the press has surprisingly little effect. To put it bluntly, people tend to see what they want to see; that is, human beings will focus on parts of a report that reinforce their own attitudes and ignore parts that challenge their core beliefs. Most of us also selectively tune out and ignore reports that contradict our preferences in politics and other fields. Therefore, a committed Democrat will remember certain portions of a televised news program about a current campaign—primarily the parts that reinforce his or her own choice—and an equally committed Republican will recall very different sections of the report or remember the material in a way that supports the GOP position. In other words, most voters are not empty vessels into which the media can pour their own beliefs. This fact dramatically limits the ability of news organizations to sway public opinion.

Media effects The influence of news sources on public opinion.

And yet the news media *do* have some influence (called **media effects**) on public opinion. Let's examine how this is so.

- First, reporting can sway people who are uncommitted and have no strong opinion in the first place. On the other hand, this sort of politically unmotivated individual is probably unlikely to vote in a given election, and therefore the media influence is of no particular consequence.

- Second, the press has a much greater impact on topics far removed from the lives and experiences of its readers and viewers. News reports can probably shape public opinion about events in foreign countries fairly easily. Yet what the media say about rising prices, neighborhood crime, or child rearing may have relatively little effect because most citizens have personal experience of and well-formed ideas about these subjects.

- Third, news organizations can help tell us what to think *about,* even if they cannot determine *what* we think. As mentioned earlier, the press often sets the agenda for government or a campaign by focusing on certain issues or concerns. For example, in the week following the *Exxon Valdez*'s massive oil spill off the Alaska coast in 1989, every national network devoted extensive coverage to the accident. And sure enough, concern about the environment quickly began to top the list of national problems considered most pressing by the public, as measured by opinion polls. Without the dramatic pictures and lavish media attention that accompanied the spill, it is doubtful that the environment would have risen so quickly to the forefront of the country's political agenda.

How Politicians Use the Media

The Clinton administration has set the pace for shrewd political use of the television media. President Clinton, First Lady Hillary Rodham Clinton, and Vice President Albert Gore Jr. have all appeared on CNN's "Larry King Live." The president has gone on MTV to speak directly to young voters, and the vice president has been a featured guest on David Letterman's late-night CBS show. Journalists, individually and in groups, are wined and dined at numerous White House receptions and intimate gatherings.

Our emphasis so far has been mainly on the ways and means of press coverage of politicians. But, as suggested by the Clinton example, the other side of the story is every bit as interesting: how politicians use the media to achieve their own ends. In Chapter 13, we discuss media events (press conferences at picturesque locations, for example) that are staged to attract coverage. Other manipulations of the press can be more subtle, however. Frequently, elected officials pass along tips to reporters, seeking to curry favor or produce stories favorable to their interests. (Reporters and editors usually decide whether to publish a tip based on its newsworthiness rather than on the motivations of their sources.)

On other occasions, candidates and their aides will go on background to give trusted newspersons juicy morsels of negative information about rivals. **On background**—meaning that none of the news can be attributed to the source—is one of several journalistic devices used to solicit and elicit information that might otherwise never come to light. **Deep background** is another such device; whereas background talks can be attributed to unnamed senior officials, deep background news must be completely unsourced, with the reporter giving the reader no hint about the origin of the information.

On background A term for when sources are not included in a news story.

Deep background Information gathered for news stories that must be completely unsourced.

Left: President Franklin D. Roosevelt during a fireside chat in 1941. Roosevelt's skillful use of radio boosted his popularity throughout his tenure in the White House. **Right:** Today, President Bill Clinton (shown with Bryant Gumbel on the "Today" show) typifies the pro-active stance many politicians take toward controlling their media coverage.

Off-the-record Information gathered for a news story that cannot be used at all.

On-the-record Information gathered for a news story that can be used and cited.

An even more drastic form of obtaining information is the **off-the-record** discussion, in which nothing the official says may be printed. (If a reporter can obtain the same information elsewhere, however, he or she is free to publish it.) By contrast, in an **on-the-record** session, such as a formal press conference, every word an official utters can be printed—and used against that official. It is no wonder that office holders often prefer the nonpublishable alternatives!

Clearly, these rules are necessary for reporters to do their basic job—informing the public—but ironically, the same rules keep the press from fully informing their readers and viewers. Every public official knows that journalists are pledged to protect the confidentiality of their sources, and therefore the rules can sometimes be used to an official's own benefit—by, say, giving reporters derogatory information to print about a rival without having to be identified as the source. However regrettable the manipulation, it is an unavoidable part of the process.

Government Regulation of the Electronic Media

Not only do politicians manipulate the media, but the U.S. government also *regulates* the electronic component of the media. Unlike radio or television, the print media are exempt from most forms of government regulation, although even print media must not violate community standards for obscenity, for instance. There are two reasons for this unequal treatment. First, the airwaves used by the electronic media are considered public property; they are leased by the federal government to private broadcasters. Second, those airwaves are in limited supply, and without some regulation, the nation's many radio and television stations would interfere with one another's frequency signals. It was not, in fact, the federal government but rather private broadcasters, frustrated by the numerous instances in which signal jamming occurred, that initiated the call for government regulation in the early days of the electronic media. Newspapers, of course, are not subject to these technical considerations.

The first government regulation of the electronic media came in 1927, when Congress enacted the Federal Radio Act, which established the Federal Radio Commission (FRC) and declared the airwaves to be public property. In addition, the act required that all broadcasters be licensed by the FRC. In 1934 the Federal Communications Commission (FCC) replaced the FRC as the electronic media regulatory body. The FCC is composed of five members, of whom not more than three can be from the same political party. These members are selected by the president for five-year terms on an overlapping basis. Because the FCC is shielded from direct, daily control by the president or Congress—although both have influence over the FCC commissioners—it is an independent regulatory agency (see Chapter 8). In addition to regulating public and commercial radio and television, the FCC oversees telephone, telegraph, satellite, and foreign communications in the United States.

Under the FCC's rules, television stations must apply for license renewal every five years; radio stations, every seven years. Until the 1980s, the FCC's criteria for license renewal were how well a station served its community, how judiciously it used the public airwaves, and how much time it devoted to public affairs. In fact, though, few licenses were ever withdrawn, and the tests for license renewal were never truly rigorous. Regulation of the broadcast industry became even looser—nearly non-existent, in fact—during the Reagan administration. For example, license renewal became something of a formality, with most stations able to complete the process simply by dropping a postcard in the mail. The FCC holds a formal hearing only if the license is challenged by a competing group of individuals who want to operate a station at the assigned frequency.

The FCC also regulates private ownership of broadcast stations. For instance, in the 1940s it said that a single person or corporation could own only one radio and one television station in any one community or media market. In the 1950s it enacted the 7-7-7 rule, limiting to seven each the number of AM, FM, and television stations a single company could own throughout the nation. In addition, the FCC forbids ownership of a daily newspaper and a television station in the same media market. Yet deregulation has recently prevailed in the area of ownership rules, too. During the Reagan years, the FCC expanded the limits on ownership of AM, FM, and television stations from 7 to 12, thereby making the 7-7-7 rule the 12-12-12 rule. In 1992, the FCC further expanded the limits of ownership of AM and FM stations, such that the 12-12-12 rule became a new 12-30-30 rule.

Content Regulation

The government also subjects the electronic media to substantial **content regulation** that, again, does not apply to the print media. Charged with ensuring that the airwaves "serve the public interest, convenience, and necessity," the FCC has attempted to promote equity in broadcasting. For example, the **equal time rule** requires that broadcast stations sell campaign air time equally to all candidates *if* they choose to sell it to any, which they are under no obligation to do. An exception to this rule is a political debate: Stations may exclude from this event less well-known and minor-party candidates.

Another noteworthy FCC regulation is the **right-of-rebuttal rule,** which requires that a person who is attacked on a radio or television station be offered the opportunity to respond. This rule was sanctioned judicially in the 1969 Supreme Court case *Red Lion Broadcasting Company* v. *FCC,* 395 U.S. 367 (1969), in which the Court ruled that Fred Cook, the author of a book on U.S. Senator Barry Goldwater (R-Ariz.) (the 1964 Republican nominee for president), must be afforded the chance to answer an attack on him aired by a Pennsylvania radio station.

Perhaps the most controversial FCC regulation was the **fairness doctrine.** Implemented in 1949 and in effect until 1985, the fairness doctrine required broadcasters to be "fair" in their coverage of news events—that is, they had to cover the events adequately and present contrasting views on important public issues. Many broadcasters disliked this rule, however, claiming that fairness is simply too difficult to define and that the rule abridged their First Amendment freedoms. They also argued that it ultimately forced broadcasters to decrease coverage of controversial issues out of fear of a deluge of requests for air time from interest groups involved in each matter.

In a hotly debated 1985 decision, the FCC, without congressional consent, abolished the fairness doctrine, arguing that the growth of the electronic media in the United States during the preceding forty years had created enough diversity among the stations to render unnecessary the ordering of diversity within them. In 1986 a federal circuit court of appeals vindicated the FCC decision, holding that the FCC did not need congressional approval to abolish the rule. Seeking to counter the FCC's decision, Congress attempted to write the fairness doctrine into law, which, if successful, would have forced the FCC to implement it. Although both the House and the Senate passed the bill, President Reagan ended the controversy for the moment

Content regulation Governmental attempts to regulate the electronic media.

Equal time rule The rule that requires broadcast stations to sell campaign air time equally to all candidates if they choose to sell it to any.

Right-of-rebuttal rule A Federal Communications Commission regulation that people attacked on a radio or television broadcast be offered the opportunity to respond.

Fairness doctrine Rule in effect from 1949 to 1985 requiring broadcasters to cover events adequately and to present contrasting views on important public issues.

Extreme left- or right-wing candidates such as Republican David Duke often battle for equal time on the major networks. In reality, however, air time is so expensive and fringe candidates have such a hard time raising large sums of money, that the networks can offer equal time without the candidates' being able to take advantage of it.

by vetoing it, citing his First Amendment concerns about government regulation of the news media.

The abolition of the fairness doctrine has by no means ended debate over its merit, however. Proponents, still trying to reinstate the doctrine, argue that its elimination results in a reduction of quality programming on public issues. In their view, deregulation means more advertisements, soap operas, and situation comedies wasting air time and leaving less room for public discourse on important matters. Opponents of the fairness doctrine, on the other hand, continue to call for decreased regulation, arguing that the electronic media should be as free as the print media—especially because the electronic media are now probably more competitive than are the print media.

Confidentiality of Sources

Another vital aspect of news media practice, both print and electronic, has been influenced by legal statutes and court decisions: the confidentiality of sources. How much a reporter can learn from a source often depends on the journalist's guarantees of confidentiality to that source, that is, a pledge not to reveal the origin of information the journalist may print or air.

Only a small number of states have laws protecting the confidentiality of reporters' sources, and no federal law provides such protection. Therefore, the courts have decided the degree to which confidentiality is protected, largely on a case-by-case basis. For example, in *Branzburg* v. *Hayes* (1972), the Supreme Court ruled that the First Amendment does not protect reporters from having to testify and possibly divulge sources before state or federal grand juries. "The investigation of crime by grand juries," the Court held, "implements a fundamental governmental role of securing the safety of the person and property of the [citizen]."[30] Compared with this overriding governmental interest, the protection of sources is an insufficient reason to treat reporters subpoenaed by grand juries differently from other citizens—or so the high court held.

Journalists have maintained that rulings such as that in *Branzburg* hinder the press's efforts at gathering the news—that without a guarantee of confidentiality, sources will be reluctant to provide crucial information. In response, the Court has noted that although confidentiality of sources does not outweigh the government's interest in prosecuting criminals, a journalist's confidentiality pledge is protected in most cases.

Censorship

While not free of government regulation, the media in the United States enjoy considerably more liberty than do their counterparts in Great Britain. One of the world's oldest democracies, Great Britain nonetheless owns that nation's main electronic medium, the British Broadcasting Company (BBC). And the BBC, along with the privately owned media, is subjected to unusually strict regulation on the publication of governmental secrets. For example, the sweeping Official Secrets Acts of 1911 makes it a criminal offense for a Briton to publish any facts, material, or news collected in that person's capacity as a public minister or civil servant. The act was invoked recently when the British government banned the publication of a 1987 novel, *Spy Catcher,* written by Peter Wright, a former British intelligence officer, who undoubtedly collected much of the book's information while on the job.

In the United States, only government officials can be prosecuted for divulging classified information; no such law applies to journalists. Nor can the government, except under extremely rare and confined circumstances, impose prior restraints on the press—that is, the government cannot censor the press. This principle was clearly established in *New York Times* v. *United States* (1971).[31] In this case the Supreme Court ruled that the government could not prevent publication by the *New York Times* of the "Pentagon Papers," classified government documents about the Vietnam War that had been stolen, photocopied, and sent to the *Times* and the *Washington Post* by Daniel Ellsberg, an anti-war activist. "Only a free and unrestrained press can effectively expose deception in the government," Justice Hugo Black wrote in a concurring opinion for the Court. "To find that the President has 'inherent power' to halt the publication of news by resort to the courts would wipe out the First Amendment."

To assist the media in determining what is and is not publishable, Great Britain provides a system called D-notice, which allows journalists to submit questionable material to a review committee before its publication. But D-notice has not quelled argument over media freedom in the United Kingdom. Indeed, the debate came to the fore during the 1982 Falkland Islands war between Great Britain and Argentina, when it centered on questions of how much information the public had a right to know and whether the media should remain neutral in covering a war in which the nation is involved. Once again, however, the British government prevailed in arguing for continued strict control of the media, declaring, "There can be sound military reasons for withholding the whole truth from the public domain, [or] for using the media to put out 'misinformation.' "[32]

Similar questions and arguments arose in the United States during the 1991 Persian Gulf war. Reporters were upset that the military was not forthcoming about events on and off the battlefield, while some Pentagon officials and many persons in the general public accused the press of telling the enemy too much in their dispatches. Unlike the case in Great Britain, however, the U.S. government had little recourse but to attempt to isolate offending reporters by keeping them away from the battlefield. Even this maneuver was highly controversial and very unpopular with news correspondents because it directly interfered with their job of reporting the news.

Such arguments are an inevitable part of the landscape in a free society. Whatever their specific quarrels with the press, most Americans would probably prefer that the media tell them too much rather than not enough. Totalitarian societies have a tame journalism, after all, so press excesses may be the price of unbridled freedom. Without question, a free press is of incalculable value to a nation, as the recent revolution in the Soviet Union (now the Commonwealth of Independent States) has shown. The 1991 coup against then-Soviet President Mikhail Gorbachev failed in part because the coup leaders could not smother the public's continued desire for freedom, stoked by the relatively uncensored television and print journalism that existed in the final years of Gorbachev's rule.

In the United States, freedom is secured mainly by the Constitution's basic guarantees and institutions. But freedom is also ensured by the thousands of independently owned and operated newspapers, magazines, and broadcast stations. The cacophony of media voices may often be off-key and harsh, but its very lack of orchestration enables us all to continue to sing the sweet song of freedom.

Toward Reform

The phenomenal growth of cable television during the past two decades has given new competition to the three major commercial television networks (ABC, CBS, and NBC). With half of all U.S. households now wired for cable television, the networks' share of the national television audience has declined steadily. Today fewer than six in every ten viewers are watching the three networks during many prime-time hours, compared with the networks' near-monopoly twenty years ago.

Some aspects of cable television's recent growth have been undesirable, at least in the eyes of critics. A case in point is the trend toward cross ownership—the possession of commercial and cable stations by the same people and corporations. As cable has become more popular and therefore more threatening to the commercial networks, these networks have been buying some cable franchises, and other media giants, such as Time Warner Communications and Times-Mirror, have done the same. The concentration of commercial and cable television ownership in relatively few hands can be troubling, not least because this arrangement can reduce the diversity of programming that was originally cable's great promise.

So far, though, any fair observer would conclude that cable television has greatly increased consumer choice and made available many new options for the U.S. public. The large number of cable channels and information services suggests as much. In March 1988, for instance, 77 percent of all homes that subscribed to cable had access to thirty or more channels, and 90 percent had access to twenty or more channels.

One vital difference between cable and commercial television is the emergence of interactive systems—cable systems that allow interaction between the sender and the consumer. These interactive systems permit viewers to respond instantly to televised polls by using hand-held devices, for example. Potentially, such an arrangement could lead to televised town meetings on issues of general interest. (Both Ross Perot and Bill Clinton have talked about holding electronic "town halls" in the future.) Of course, such developments must be viewed with caution as well as enthusiasm: Instant polls are unscientific and imprecise, since participants are not randomly selected, and those who respond to such public affairs programming constitute only a minute and usually unrepresentative proportion of the population.

The rise of cable television is also having a significant effect on political campaigns. For example, cable systems carry a large number of debates by local candidates. Although debates for state and national offices are televised frequently by the commercial stations, campaigns for local offices have often been neglected, largely because they are of interest to only a relatively small audience. Cable channels are so numerous that access for local candidates is much less of a problem. Cable channels also permit candidates to target paid political advertisements at small, select audiences. Such narrowcasting to targeted groups—as opposed to broadcasting to a large, diversified audience—enables candidates to tailor a message to Hispanics watching a Spanish-language channel, sports fans who watch ESPN, or younger voters who watch MTV, for example.

In general, then, cable means more choice in media and less influence for the commercial networks. These changes can prove to be beneficial, a frequent result of diversity and decentralization, or cable could turn out to be just more wasted fluff in programming that is distinct only because it is packaged a bit differently. Consumers of television—all of us who make up the audience—will help to determine cable television's quality.[33]

Summary

The U.S. press is constantly evolving, including in its relationship with the public. Television talk shows, such as CNN's "Larry King Live," came to prominence in 1992 in part because both the voters and the candidates wanted to communicate directly, without the news media's filter. Yet there will always be a prominent role for a vigorous press to play. As we have reviewed, only the media have the credibility and the resources to inform the public about the government and elected officials. At the same time the press can do its job better, and journalists must constantly strive to minimize bias and reduce the investigative and competitive excesses that have cost them some respect in recent years.

In surveying the news media, we have made a number of general observations about press operations and practices in American life:

1. The modern media consist of print press (newspapers, magazines, journals) and electronic media (television and radio). In the United States the media are relatively uncontrolled and free to express many views, although that has not always been the case. Until the mid- to late-1800s, when independent papers first appeared, newspapers were partisan; that is, they openly supported a particular party.

2. In this century, first radio in the late 1920s and then television in the late 1940s revolutionized the transmission of political information, leading to more candidate-centered, entrepreneurial politics in the age of television.

3. The media have shifted focus in recent years, first toward investigative journalism in the Watergate era and then toward character issues. While these are useful aspects of both kinds of coverage, excesses have been noted, especially unnecessary invasions of privacy and the publication and broadcast of unsubstantiated rumor.

4. Studies have shown that by framing issues for debate and discussion, the media have clear and recognizable effects on voters. For example, people who are relatively uninformed about a topic can be more easily swayed by press coverage about that topic. However, in most cases the press has surprisingly little effect on people's views.

5. Politicians constantly try to manipulate and influence press coverage. One method many officials use is passing along tips (information) on an off-the-record basis.

6. The press is a business—big business, in the case of the networks and large newspapers—and as such it is regulated to some extent by the government. The government has gradually loosened its restrictions on the media. Officially, the Federal Communications Commission (FCC) licenses and regulates broadcasting stations, although in practice it has been quite willing to grant and renew licenses, and recently it has reduced its regulation of licensees. Additionally, cable transmission was first allowed on a widespread basis in the late 1970s, from whence it has grown into a large supplier of information. Finally, content regulations have loosened, with the courts using a narrow interpretation of libel.

Key Terms

print press

electronic media

yellow journalism

muckraking

network

affiliates

wire service

New York Times Co. v. *Sullivan*

media effects

on background

deep background

off the record

on the record

content regulation

equal time rule

right-of-rebuttal rule

fairness doctrine

Suggested Readings

Arterton, F. Christopher. *Media Politics: The News Strategies of Presidential Campaigns.* Lexington, MA: Lexington Books, 1984.

Berkman, Ronald, and Laura W. Kitch. *Politics in the Media Age.* New York: McGraw-Hill, 1986.

Broder, David S. *Behind the Front Page.* New York: Simon & Schuster, 1987.

Cook, Timothy E. *Making Laws and Making News: Media Strategies in the U.S. House of Representatives.* Washington, DC: The Brookings Institution, 1989.

Crouse, Timothy. *The Boys on the Bus.* New York: Ballantine, 1973.

Entman, Robert M. *Democracy Without Citizens: Media and the Decay of American Politics.* New York: Oxford University Press, 1989.

Epstein, Edward Jay. *News from Nowhere: Television and the News.* New York: Random House, 1973.

Graber, Doris A. *Mass Media and American Politics,* 3rd ed. Washington, DC: CQ Press, 1989.

Iyengar, Shanto, and Donald R. Kinder. *News That Matters.* Chicago: University of Chicago Press, 1987.

Lichter, S. Robert, Stanley Rothman, and Linda S. Lichter. *The Media Elite.* Bethesda, MD: Adler & Adler, 1986.

Press, Charles, and Kenneth VerBurg. *American Politicians and Journalists.* Glenview, IL: Scott, Foresman, 1988.

Ranney, Austin. *Channels of Power: The Impact of Television on American Politics.* New York: Basic Books, 1983.

Sabato, Larry J. *Feeding Frenzy: How Attack Journalism Has Transformed American Politics,* updated ed. New York: Macmillan/The Free Press, 1993.

Stephens, Mitchell. *A History of News: From the Drum to the Satellite.* New York: Viking, 1989.

Interest Groups

WHAT ARE INTEREST GROUPS?

THE ROOTS OF AMERICAN INTEREST GROUPS

WHAT DO INTEREST GROUPS DO?

WHAT MAKES AN INTEREST GROUP SUCCESSFUL?

TOWARD REFORM

From his days in the Virginia Assembly, James Madison knew that factions occurred in all political systems and that the struggle for influence and power among such groups was inevitable in the political process. This knowledge led him and the other Framers to tailor a governmental system of multiple pressure points to check and balance these factions, or what today we call interest groups, in the natural course of the political process. As we discuss in Chapter 2, Madison and many of the other Framers were intent on creating a government of many levels—local, state, and national—the national government consisting of three branches. It was their belief that this division of power would prohibit any one individual or group of individuals from becoming too powerful. Decentralizing power also would neutralize the effect of special interests, who would not be able to spread their efforts throughout so many different levels of government. Thus, the "mischief of faction" could be lessened.

Ironically, *The Federalist Papers* were a key component of one of the most skillful and successful examples of interest-group activity in the history of this nation. As discussed in Chapter 2, if "the Federalists [themselves an interest group] had not been as shrewd in manipulation as they were sound in theory, their arguments could not have prevailed."[1]

The Federalists were only one of many interest groups that existed in the era following the Revolutionary War. And, as we discuss in the following sections, interest groups have proliferated over the years. In 1831–1832, Alexis de Tocqueville, a French aristocrat and philosopher, toured the United States extensively. A keen observer of American politics, he was very much impressed by the tendency of Americans to join groups in order to participate in the policy-making process. "Whenever at the head of some new undertaking you see government in France, or a man of rank in England, in the United States you will be sure to find an association,"[2] wrote

> **A**zeal for different opinions concerning religion, concerning government, and many other points . . . have, in turn, divided mankind . . . inflamed them with mutual animosity, and rendered them more disposed to vex and oppress each other than to cooperate for the common good.
>
> *James Madison*
> *Federalist No. 10*

Madison believed that one principal purpose of government is to control the possibly divisive effects of groups of people, each of which wants to advance its own special interests and each of which competes with the others for the attentions and resources of the government. The Framers hoped to avoid the formation of official political parties; at the private level, however, they realized that the formation of interest groups was inevitable.

de Tocqueville. He was especially impressed by the ability of groups to influence the formal institutions of government, noting:

> It is true that they [representatives of these associations] have not the right, like the others, of making the laws; but they have the power of attacking those which are in force and of drawing up beforehand those which ought to be enacted.[3]

The United States is still a nation of joiners, and many interest groups play important roles as laws or policies are being negotiated. Think of the number of interest groups or voluntary associations to which you belong. It's likely that you belong to some kind of organized religion; a political party; a town, college, or university social, civic, athletic, or academic group; a more general special-interest group, such as Greenpeace, the National Rifle Association, the National Right-to-Life Committee, or Amnesty International. Even if you don't belong to one of these groups, you undoubtedly have heard of their activities or know someone who is a member of one of these groups.

Not all groups are political, but they may become politically active when their members feel that a government policy threatens or affects group goals. Most politically active groups use a technique called **lobbying** to make their interests heard and understood by those who are in a position to influence or cause change in governmental policies. Depending on the type of group and on the role it is looking to play, lobbying can take many forms. You probably have never thought of the Boy Scouts or Girl Scouts of America as "political." Yet, when Congress began debating the passage of legislation dealing with discrimination in private clubs, representatives of both organizations testified in an attempt to persuade Congress to allow each one to remain a single-sex organization. Similarly, you probably don't often think of garden clubs as political. Yet, when issues of highway beautification come before a legislature, representatives from numerous garden clubs are likely to be there to lobby, or to advance, their interests.

Lobbying The activities of groups and organizations that seek to influence legislation and persuade political leaders to support the group's position.

In this chapter, we examine what interest groups are, their development since the days of the Founders, and what they do. We also look to see why people join groups, why groups flourish, and the kinds of tactics they use as they attempt to pressure government to achieve their policy objectives.

What Are Interest Groups?

Interest groups go by a variety of names: special interests, pressure groups, organized interests, political groups, lobby groups, and public interest groups are among the common ones. These various terms have produced a diverse collection of operational definitions. Originally, most political scientists talked about "pressure groups"; today, most political scientists use the more neutral terms "interest group" or "organized interest."[4]

Definitions of interest groups vary as much as groups do themselves:

- "any association of individuals, whether formally organized or not, that attempts to influence public policy";[5]
- "an organization which seeks or claims to represent people or organizations which share one or more common interests or ideals";[6]
- "any group that, on the basis of one or more shared attitudes, makes certain claims upon other groups in society for the establishment, maintenance, or enhancement of forms of behavior that are implied by the shared attitudes."[7]

Some definitions stress what a group does. This definition is offered by political scientist Robert H. Salisbury:

- "an interest group is an organized association which engages in activity relative to governmental decisions."[8]

And, distinguished political scientist V. O. Key Jr. tries to differentiate political parties from interest groups by arguing that

- [interest groups] "promote their interests by attempting to influence government rather than by nominating candidates and seeking responsibility for the management of government."[9]

In this book we use **interest group** as a generic term to describe the numerous political activities of organized groups as they try to influence government policy.

Interest groups Organized groups that try to influence public policy.

Types of Interest Groups

Interest groups generally can be characterized by the kinds of interests they represent or the number of issues in which they are involved.

Economic Interest Groups.   Most groups have some sort of "economic" agenda, even if it only involves acquiring enough money in donations to pay the telephone bill or send out the next mailing. **Economic interest groups** are, however, a special type of interest

Economic interest groups Groups with the primary purpose of promoting the financial interests of their members.

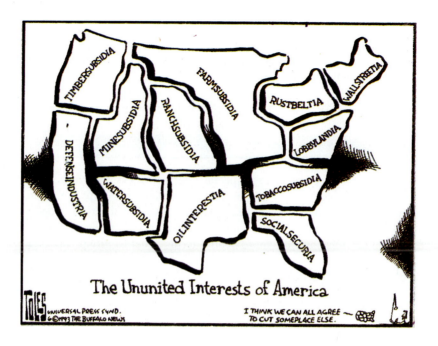

group: Their primary purpose is to promote the economic interests of their members. Historically, business groups (including trade and professional groups), labor organizations (unions), and organizations representing the interests of farmers have been considered the "big three" of economic interest groups.

As discussed below, however, unions and agricultural organizations no longer have the large memberships or the political clout they once held in governmental circles. In contrast, trade and professional associations such as the Chamber of Commerce or the American Medical Association are usually more powerful and find few doors closed to them in Washington.

Groups that mobilize to protect particular economic interests generally are the most fully and effectively organized of all the types of interest groups.[10] They exist to make profits and to obtain economic benefits for their members. To achieve these goals, however, they often find that they must resort to political means rather than trust the operation of economic markets to produce outcomes favorable to their members.

Public-interest group A group that seeks a collective good that will not selectively and materially benefit the members of the organization.

Public Interest Groups.   Political scientist Jeffrey Berry defines **public interest groups** as groups "that seek a collective good, the achievement of which will not selectively and materially benefit the membership or activists of the organization."[11] Unlike economic-interest groups, public-interest groups do not tend to be particularly motivated by the desire to achieve goals that would benefit their members. As Berry notes, the public interest has many faces. In the past, for example, many Progressive Era groups, perhaps as best personified by the settlement house movement (see pp. 504–505) that began to sweep the United States in the late 1800s, were created to solve the varied problems (such as poor quality housing) of new immigrants and the poor. Today, civil and constitutional rights groups, environmental groups, good-government groups such as Common Cause, peace groups, church groups, and groups that speak out for those who cannot (such as children, the mentally ill, or animals) are examples of public-interest groups. The American Civil Liberties Union (ACLU) (see "The American Civil Liberties Union," p. 102), for example, is a public-interest organization that fights against, among other things, government entanglement with religion. Group members realize no financial gain when ACLU lawyers argue that the government should not allow nativity scenes to be erected on public lands. Similarly, its members derive no direct economic benefits when the ACLU challenges the constitutionality of New York State's practice of awarding college scholarships to students based on their SAT scores. (The ACLU successfully argued that the SATs discriminate against women.)[12]

Multi-Issue *versus* Single-Issue Groups.   Many of the economic- and public-interest groups discussed above are **multi-issue groups,** that is, they are concerned with more than just a single issue. For example, the AFL-CIO, the largest labor union in the United States, which was formed to represent the interests of organized labor, is also concerned with health care, Social Security, and civil rights, among other issues. In 1993, it lobbied hard against passage of the North American Free Trade Agreement (NAFTA), arguing that jobs of union workers would be lost to Mexico. Similarly, the NAACP is interested primarily in race relations, but it is also involved in other areas, including education, the criminal justice system, housing, and welfare rights—all areas of potential concern to its members.

Multi-issue groups Groups that are concerned with more than just a single issue (e.g., the AFL-CIO).

In the 1800s various abolitionist groups opposed to slavery could be classified as single-issue groups. The 1980s witnessed a substantial growth of **single-issue groups,** those organized to influence policy in only one area. Single-issue groups differ from multi-issue groups both in the range and intensity of their interests. Concentration on one area generally leads to greater zeal in a group's lobbying efforts. Probably the most visible single-issue groups today are those organized on each side of the abortion and gun control debates. Anti-abortion groups like Operation Rescue and pro-choice groups like the National Abortion and Reproductive Rights Action League (NARAL) are good examples of single-issue groups, as are the National Rifle Association (NRA) and Handgun Control, Inc. Today, people single-mindedly pursue all kinds of interests.

Single-issue groups Groups that are concerned with only one issue (e.g., National Abortion and Reproductive Rights Action League).

The AFL-CIO, the largest and among the oldest labor unions in the country, rallied its members to campain against NAFTA. It lost with the passage of NAFTA in late 1993.

Drug- or AIDS-awareness groups, environmental groups, and anti-nuclear power groups, for example, can each be classified as a single-issue group. Table 15.1 describes several prominent interest groups active today.

The Roots of American Interest Groups

Disturbance theory The theory offered by political scientist David Truman that posits that interest groups form in part to counteract the efforts of other groups.

Political scientists have long debated how and why interest groups arise. Robert H. Salisbury, for example, argues that resource scarcity leads to group formation.[13] Jack L. Walker contends that without what he terms "patrons" (those who often finance a group) few organizations could begin.[14] And, one of the first political scientists to study interest groups, David B. Truman, posed what he termed **disturbance theory** to explain why interest groups form.[15] He hypothesizes that groups form in part to counteract the activities of other groups or of organized special interests. According to Truman, the government's role is to provide a forum in which the competing demands of groups and the majority of the U.S. population can be heard and balanced. He argues that the government's role in managing competing groups is to balance their conflicting demands. Nevertheless, when examining the evolution and growth of interest groups in the United States, we are not always looking at clashes of one group against another, but of one group against the majority of the American public. As with the many different definitions of interest groups, a variety of sound reasons have been offered to explain why interest groups form.

Generally, however, interest groups tend to arise in response to changes. They can be political or economic changes, changes in the population, technological changes, or even changes in society itself. During the 1770s, for example, many groups (such as the Sons of Liberty) arose to fight for political and economic independence from Great Britain. From the 1820s, in a period called the Second Great Awakening, prominent preachers stressed the moral need to end sinful practices. Large revival meetings focused on the sinfulness and evils of slavery, providing a major impetus to the founding of several anti-slavery societies. After the Civil War, trade unions flourished, and the Grange was founded to help farmers. Business associations proliferated in the 1880s and 1890s as revealed in "Landmark Events in the History of Early National Interest Groups" (p. 502). In the early 1900s, other groups were created in reaction to big business and other social and economic forces. And, the 1960s saw the rapid growth of public-interest groups.

The Early Years: The Colonial Period to 1830

Many of the first colonists who came to America in the early seventeenth century were escaping religious persecution. They organized themselves into colonies based on their own religious preference. Catholics founded Maryland, the Puritans founded Massachusetts, and the Quakers founded Pennsylvania, for example. In essence, these colonies became some of the first special-interest groups in the New World: They were governmental units organized along religious lines and designed to further certain religious, moral, and policy preferences.

Once the new nation was formed, its highly agricultural nature was reflected in some of its earliest regional societies. In 1785 the Philadelphia Society for Promoting Agriculture was created. Its goal was to advance "products of the land within the American states." Benjamin Franklin was an active member, and George Washington

Table 15.1 ♦ Profiles of Selected Interest Groups

NAME (FOUNDED)	SINGLE- OR MULTI-ISSUE	1993 BUDGET (MILLIONS)	MEMBERS	PAC
Economic Groups				
AFL-CIO	M	62	14.1 million	AFL-CIO PAC
American Medical Association (AMA)	M	205	300,000	AMA PAC
Association of Trial Lawyers of America	M	19	60,000	Association of Trial Lawyers of America PAC
National Association of Manufacturers (NAM) (1895)	M	16	12,500	no
Tobacco Institute	S	38	13 (cigarette companies)	no
U.S. Chamber of Commerce (1912)	M	70	180,000 companies	National Chamber Alliance for Politics
Public Interest Groups				
American Association of Retired Persons (AARP) (1958)	M	305	33,000,000	no
Amnesty International U.S.A. (1961)	S	22.3	386,000	no
Handgun Control, Inc. (1974)	S	8	360,000	Handgun Control Voter Education Fund
League of United Latin American Citizens (LULAC) (1929)	M	N/A	110,000	no
National Abortion and Reproductive Rights Action League (NARAL) (1969)	S	9.3	450,000	NARAL PAC
National Association for the Advancement of Colored People (NAACP) (1909)	M	16	345,000	no
National Gay and Lesbian Task Force (1973)	S	1.4	17,000	no
National Rifle Association (NRA) (1871)	S	86.9 (1990)	2,650,000	Political Victory Fund
National Right to Life Committee (1973)	S	13.5	400,000	National Right to Life PAC
Environmental Groups				
Environmental Defense Fund (EDF) (1967)	S	16	150,000	no
Greenpeace USA (1971)	S	35 (1990)	2,100,000	no
Sierra Club (1892)	S	39	650,000	Sierra Club Political Committee
Good Government Groups				
Common Cause (1970)	S	11.3	270,000	no
Public Citizen, Inc. (1971)	M	6.2	100,000	no

Source: Public Interest Profiles, 1993–1994 (Washington, D.C.: Congressional Quarterly, 1993). Reprinted by permission. "Profiles of Interest Groups," *Health Line,* October 13, 1993, "Legal Times: Profiles of Interest Groups Part II," *Health Line,* October 14, 1993,

Landmark Events in the History of Early National Interest Groups	
1830s ◆	Early trade associations formed
1833 ◆	American Anti-Slavery Society founded
1848 ◆	Seneca Falls Convention for women's rights
1851 ◆	Young Men's Christian Association (YMCA) founded
1869 ◆	National Woman Suffrage Association (NWSA) formed Grange founded
1874 ◆	Women's Christian Temperance Union (WCTU) founded
1886 ◆	American Federation of Labor (AFL) formed
1896 ◆	National Association of Manufacturers begins operation
1897 ◆	AFL and other union membership increases 360 percent (pro-labor)
1904 ◆	NAM budget increases to fight unions

was an honorary member. The Society for Promoting and Improving Agriculture and Other Rural Concerns was founded around the same time in Charleston, South Carolina. A lack of communications networks prevented any of these associations from becoming national in scope, and none was particularly political in nature. Yet, all worked for the economic benefit of their members.

National Groups Emerge (1830–1880)

In the 1830s, as the nation began to industrialize, communications networks improved, and the first groups national in scope began to emerge. It is interesting to note that an identical flowering of associational activity occurred in Britain at the same time.

Many of these early national organizations were single-issue in scope. Often they were deeply rooted in the Christian religious revivalism that was sweeping the nation. Concern with humanitarian issues such as temperance (total abstinence from alcoholic beverages), peace, capital punishment, education, and, most important, slavery led to the founding of numerous associations dedicated to solving social problems. Among the first of these groups was the American Anti-Slavery Society, founded in 1833 by William Lloyd Garrison. The only woman allowed to speak at its first meeting, Lucretia Mott, went on to organize the first large gathering of women's rights activists in Seneca Falls, New York, in 1848. But no national women's groups were formed until after the Civil War.

In the wake of continued immigration and growing poverty in large, increasingly industrialized cities, concern for the fate of the poor led to the founding of the Young Men's Christian Association (YMCA) in Boston in 1851. Although today many people associate the YMCA with sports and recreation, its founders initially viewed these kinds of activities only as a means of reaching out to the children of immigrants and the poor in urban centers to help integrate them into U.S. society and a Christian lifestyle.

The Civil War (1861–1865) fostered the creation of a national communications network of telegraph lines and railroads. It also brought people together in a variety of new groups, such as sanitary commissions, the Red Cross and, later, veteran's associations. After the war, for the first time in history, railroads, radio, and telegraphs brought people, manufactured goods, agricultural products, and information to the far corners of the nation. And, better methods of communication allowed more people to stay in touch. Right after the Civil War, for example, the National Woman Suffrage Association was founded. Many of its early members and leaders had met while volunteers in the war effort.

Other women founded the Women's Christian Temperance Union (WCTU) in 1874, with the goal of outlawing the sale of liquor. Its members, many of them quite religious, believed that the consumption of alcohol was an evil that was injurious to family life because many men drank away their paychecks, leaving no money to feed or clothe their families. Many women who believed that the national suffrage associations (whose aims were to get women the right to vote) were too radical joined the WCTU to do good for others. Churches and Southerners, in particular, supported the WCTU's goal of prohibiting the manufacture and sale of all alcoholic beverages. The WCTU's activities included conventional and nonconventional forms of activity: organizing prayer groups, lobbying for prohibition legislation, conducting peaceful marches, and engaging in more violent protests that included the destruction of saloons. By the 1890s, the WCTU had more than 200,000 female members at a time when the total U.S. population was 63 million. (In contrast, in 1993, the membership of the National Organization for Women was 280,000 when the total population was more than 250 million.)

While the WCTU and the YMCA were clearly public-interest groups, the Grange, which was also formed during the period following the Civil War, was more concerned with the economic interests of its members. In fact, it was created by six government employees as an educational society for farmers in order to teach them about the latest agricultural developments. Although its charter formally stated that the Grange was not to become involved in "politics," in 1876 it formulated a detailed plan to pressure Congress to enact legislation favorable to farmers. In response to the growth of large businesses and monopolies that affected the prices of livestock and harvests, the Grange's members banded together to influence the traditional political parties to deal more effectively with big-business interests. In essence, government became the mediator between the interests of farmers who belonged to the Grange and big business.

After the Civil War, the demand grew for more railroads to meet the needs of an expanding and united country. In fact, the railroad industry was perhaps the most effective interest group of the day. In a move that couldn't take place today because of its illegality, the Central Pacific Railroad sent its own lobbyist to Washington, DC as early as 1861, before the Civil War ended. There, he eventually became the administrator of both committees of Congress charged with overseeing regulation of the railroad industry. Subsequently, the Central Pacific Railroad received vast grants of land from Congress along its route and large subsidized loans from the national government. The railroad became so important that it later went on to have nearly total political control of the California state legislature.

Business interests soon began to play even larger roles in both state and national politics. A popular saying of the day noted that the Standard Oil Company did every-

At the turn of the century, Carry Nation was one of the fiercest advocates of the temperance movement. Unlike some of her fellow prohibitionists, Nation favored direct action over peaceful demonstrations. More than once she was arrested and jailed for breaking up a saloon with an axe.

thing to the Pennsylvania legislature except refine it. Increasingly, large trusts, monopolies, business combinations, and corporate conglomerations in the oil, steel, and sugar industries became sufficiently powerful to control many representatives in the state and national legislatures.

National Groups Increase (1890–1920)

By the 1890s, a profound change had occurred in the nation's political and social outlook. Rapid industrialization and an influx of immigrants had contributed to a host of problems, including crime, poverty, squalid and unsafe working conditions, widespread political corruption, and high prices and low wages caused by monopolistic business practices. Many Americans began to believe that new measures would be necessary to impose order on this growing chaos and to curb some of the more glaring problems. The political and social movement that grew out of these concerns was called progressivism.

The Progressive Movement and Public Interest Groups. Not even the progressives themselves could agree on what the term "progressive" actually meant. To some it was a broad societal vision. Others believed that it encompassed a set of moral and humanitarian goals. And to others it was a set of particular good-government reforms. Desire for reform led to an explosion of all types of interest groups. Politically, the movement took the form of the Progressive Party, which sought on the electoral front to run and elect candidates pledged to limit or end the power of the industrialists' near-total control of the steel, oil, railroad, and other key industries.

During its formative stages, the Progressive Movement was epitomized by the rapid growth of settlement houses across the United States. Settlement houses were welfare centers that provided community services such as child care, reading and English language lessons, and job training for the less fortunate. Jane Addams, a young social worker, established one of the first settlement houses, Hull House, in Chicago in 1889. By 1900, there were more than 400 such houses across the nation.

Here a cartoon shows a U.S. Senator receiving a paycheck from "two masters"— Uncle Sam *and* a railroad representative.

In addition to providing many services to the poor, settlement houses provided room and board for innumerable progressive activists. Here, prominent thinkers met and exchanged ideas; settlement house residents, in essence, were the Progressive Movement. They were active in women's suffrage, in reform of the treatment of juvenile offenders, in education systems (including implementation of a system of kindergartens), and in the reform of corrupt city governments. Many settlement house residents went on to found groups that would later form the core of the civil rights and public-interest movements of the 1960s.

Progressive groups relied heavily on the support of the public for various appeals to legislators for reform. For example, the National Consumers' League (NCL) was founded in 1899 by wealthy women to work for improved working conditions for women and children. At that time, many women and children worked for long hours at low wages in substandard buildings lacking proper ventilation or safety features. In addition to extensive lobbying (at the state and national levels) for maximum hour and minimum wage laws for women and children, the NCL's local organizations published a list of approved retailers who treated their employees well by providing them fair wages for reasonable hours in a safe environment. It also allowed companies complying with their conditions to use the NCL label. The NCL also started the "shop early" movement at Christmas time to encourage consumers to do their holiday shopping before the Christmas rush. The League believed that such a campaign would prompt consumers to shop early, thereby reducing the burden placed on shop girls.

Many members of the NCL were also members of the National American Woman Suffrage Association, which was the key organization pushing for a constitutional amendment to give women the right to vote. During the Progressive era, women's organizations were second only to trade organizations in number and influence on Capitol Hill.

In response to the pressure applied by progressive groups, the national government began to regulate business. Because businesses had a vested interest in keeping wages

Jane Addams founded Hull House in 1889 in Chicago and helped launch the Progressive Movement. She is pictured here in 1914.

low and costs down, more business groups organized to consolidate their strength and to counter progressive organizations. Not only did governments have to mediate progressive and business demands, but they also had to accommodate the role of organized labor, which often allied itself with progressive groups against big business.

Organized Labor. While wealthy industrialists and large corporations had no problems getting the ear of most politicians, employees generally had little clout. Several early attempts to maximize their bargaining power by organizing local labor groups into national unions were unsuccessful. Not until the creation of the American Federation of Labor (AFL) in 1886 was there any real national union activity. The AFL brought together skilled workers from several trades into one stronger national organization. By 1902, its membership exceeded one million workers. However, its effectiveness in mobilizing for higher wages for workers triggered more and better business organization. As business interests pushed states for "open shop" laws (which allowed employees not to join unions in unionized factories), the AFL became increasingly political. It was also forced to react to the success of big businesses' use of legal injunctions to prohibit union organization.

In Britain, labor organized at the national level much earlier: The Trades Union Congress (TUC), a federation of individual unions, formed in 1868. Conversely, organized business appeared somewhat later in Britain than in the United States: The Federation of

PEOPLE OF THE PAST

Florence Kelley

Florence Kelley (1859–1932) was the third of eight children born to William Darrah Kelley, a self-educated lawyer who later enjoyed a long career in Congress. Kelley's five sisters died in infancy, and since she was ill quite often herself, her early schooling took place at home. She read her father's entire library and developed strong interests in social reform at an early age. Kelley's father, a strong believer in women's suffrage, encouraged her to enter Cornell University. There, Kelley earned a bachelor's degree in 1876 and applied to the University of Pennsylvania to study law, but she was refused admittance because of her sex.

The National Consumers' League used this "White Label" in the early 1900s to certify that goods were produced under working conditions that were acceptable as stipulated by the NCL.

While traveling in Europe, Kelley met M. Carey Thomas, the first American woman to earn a Ph.D., who urged Kelley to attend her alma mater, the University of Zurich. There, Kelley translated several major works by Karl Marx and Friedrich Engels, and she met and married a Polish medical student and socialist. They had three children before returning to New York City. Kelley's husband abused her, however, and finally

British Industry (FBI) opened its doors in 1916, some twenty-one years after its U.S. counterpart, the National Association of Manufacturers (NAM), began operations.

In 1914, massive lobbying by the AFL and its members led to passage of the Clayton Act, which labor leader Samuel Gompers hailed as the "Magna Carta" of the labor movement. This law allowed unions to organize free from prosecution and also guaranteed their right to strike, a powerful weapon against employers.

Business Groups and Trade Associations.   The National Association of Manufacturers (NAM) was founded in 1895 by manufacturers who had suffered business reverses in the economic panic of 1893 and who believed that they were being affected adversely by the growth of organized labor. NAM first became politically active in 1913, when a major tariff bill was under congressional consideration. NAM's tactics were "so insistent and abrasive" and its expenditures of monies so lavish that President Woodrow Wilson was forced to denounce its lobbying tactics as creating an "unbearable situation."[16] Congress immediately called for an investigation of NAM's activities but found no member of Congress willing to testify that he had ever even encountered a member of NAM (probably because many of them had been "bought" with illegal contributions and gifts).

The second major business organization came into being in 1912, when the National Chamber of Commerce was created with the assistance of the Secretary of Commerce

in 1891, she took her children and fled to Chicago, where she obtained a divorce and went back to using her maiden name.

In Chicago, Kelley joined Jane Addams and other women reformers at Hull House, one of the nation's first social settlements. Concerned with child labor, she published a pamphlet in 1892, *Our Toiling Children*. Three years later she published *Hull House Maps and Papers* based on her investigations of the "sweatshops" in garment factories and a survey of the condition of city slums. Described as a "guerilla warrior" in the "wilderness of industrial wrongs" by the local press, Kelley pushed to get legislation limiting the number of hours a woman could work, prohibiting child labor, and controlling tenement sweatshops. Frustrated by her inability to get cases prosecuted, Kelley took night classes in 1894 and earned a law degree from Northwestern University.

To attack child labor from another angle, Kelley eagerly accepted the position of general secretary of the newly established National Consumers' League (NCL), a position she held from 1899 until her death in 1932. The NCL used consumer pressure to ensure that goods were manufactured under acceptable working conditions. Kelley spoke to groups all over the country on behalf of her cause. She established sixty Consumers' Leagues in twenty states and organized two international conferences.

Kelley pursued a number of other interests as well. She was a founding member of the National Association for the Advancement of Colored People and served as vice president of the National Woman Suffrage Association for several years.

Under Kelley's leadership, the NCL launched a successful defense of protective legislation in the courts. Kelley's efforts were also key to congressional passage of the Sheppard-Towner Maternity and Infancy Act in 1921, which provided federal funds to the states that offered pre- and postnatal care for women and for their babies (see "Then and Now," p. 71).

and Labor. Like the Grange several years before, government workers served as patrons for the new organization. (This was before that Cabinet post was split into the Department of Commerce and the Department of Labor.) The administration of President William Howard Taft believed that the government should have one body to consult with concerning the interests of business. Also, regional chambers of commerce saw the need to operate on the national level. They had been distressed by the progressive, seemingly anti-business, anti-monopoly policies of President Theodore Roosevelt (who left office in 1909) and were alarmed by the increased political activity of organized labor.

Trade associations Groups that represent specific industries.

NAM, the Chamber of Commerce, and **trade associations,** groups that represent specific industries, were effective spokespersons for their member companies. They were unable to defeat passage of the Clayton Act, but groups such as the Cotton Manufacturers planned successful elaborate court campaigns to overturn key provisions of the act in the courts.[17] And, the Clayton Act aside, innumerable pieces of pro-business legislation were passed by Congress, whose members continued to insist that they had never been contacted by business groups.

In 1928 the bubble burst for some business interests. At the Senate's request, the Federal Trade Commission (FTC) undertook a massive investigation of the lobbying tactics of the business community. The FTC's examination of Congress revealed extensive illegal lobbying by another group, the National Electric Light Association (NELA). Not only did the NELA lavishly entertain members of Congress, but it also went to great expense to educate the public on the virtues of electric lighting. Books and pamphlets were produced and donated to schools and public libraries to sway public opinion. Needy teachers and ministers who were willing to advocate electricity were "helped" with financial grants. These tactics were considered unethical by many people, and business was held in public disfavor. It was these kinds of activities that led the public to view lobbyists in a negative light.

Though issues changed and the Progressive Movement gave way under the weight of the Depression and World War II, the general balance of groups maintained itself until well past the mid-twentieth century.

The Modern Era of Interest-Group Activity (1960 to the Present)

After the Depression, the New Deal, and the country's entry into World War II, many progressive groups fell into disarray. Others remained active, but with less vitality. Many business, labor, and professional groups, however, continued to flourish. According to a study conducted by Kay Lehman Schlozman and John Tierney, nearly 70 percent of today's Washington, D.C.-based political organizations established their offices after 1960.[18] Nearly half opened their offices after 1970. Not surprisingly, given the social and economic thrust of President Lyndon B. Johnson's "Great Society" programs, most of the new groups were formed to take advantage of the money and opportunities those programs offered.

From 1960 to 1992, the number of interest-group representatives registered (as required by law) in Washington increased from fewer than 500 to 6,083. The federal government had clearly become the primary target of policy change, and it was natural for groups to concentrate their resources in the nation's capital. Numerous interest groups and law firms that are hired as lobbyists, in fact, are clustered together in a small section of Washington, D.C.

Public-Interest Groups.   During the 1960s and 1970s, the progressive spirit found renewed vigor in the rise of public-interest groups. Generally, these groups devoted themselves to representing the interests of African Americans, women, the elderly, the poor, and consumers or to working on behalf of the environment. Many of their leaders and members had been active in the civil rights and anti-Vietnam War movement efforts of the 1960s. Other groups, like the ACLU and NAACP, which had survived for nearly a century, gained renewed vigor. Many of them had as their patron the liberal Ford Foundation, which helped to bankroll numerous groups, including the Mexican-American Legal Defense and Education Fund, the Puerto Rican Legal Defense and Education Fund, and the Native American Rights Fund. Another group that came to prominence in this era was the American Association of Retired Persons (AARP). The elderly are the fastest growing group in the United States, and AARP is the largest single interest group in the country, with thirty-three million members in 1994.

Common Cause and the Nader Network.   The civil rights and anti-war movements of the 1960s and 1970s left many Americans feeling cynical about a government that they believed failed to respond to the will of the majority. They also believed that if citizens banded together, they could make a difference. Thus, two major new public interest groups—Common Cause and Ralph Nader's Public Citizen, Inc.—were founded during this period. Common Cause, a "good government" group similar to some of the early progressive good-government groups, has effectively challenged aspects of the congressional seniority system, successfully urged the passage of sweeping campaign-financing reforms, and played a major role in the enactment of legislation authorizing federal financing of presidential campaigns. It continues to lobby for accountability in government and for more efficient and responsive governmental structures and practices.

Perhaps more well known than Common Cause is the collection of groups headed by Ralph Nader under the name Public Citizen, Inc. In 1965 Nader, a young lawyer, was thrust into the limelight with the publication of his book *Unsafe at Any Speed.* In it he charged that the Corvair, a General Motors (GM) car, was unsafe to drive; he produced voluminous evidence of how the car could flip over at average speeds on curved roads. In 1966 he testified about auto safety in front of Congress and then learned that General Motors had spied on him in an effort to discredit his work. The $250,000 that GM subsequently paid to Nader in an out-of-court settlement allowed him to establish the Center for the Study of Responsive Law in 1969. The Center analyzed the activities of regulatory agencies and concluded that few of them enforced anti-trust regulations or cracked down on deceptive advertising practices. Nader then turned again to lobbying Congress, which led him to create Public Citizen, Inc., which would act as an umbrella organization for what was to be called the "Nader Network" of groups.

These good-government groups have had a significant impact on governmental policy making, as have other public interest groups, including those concerned with the environment and women's issues. Good-government groups and other public-interest groups have enjoyed considerable success in the legislative forum.

Conservative Backlash: Religious and Ideological Groups.   The growth and successes that various public-interest groups had in the 1960s and 1970s ultimately led to a conservative backlash. Many of these liberal groups' advances were made through litigation, that is, by challenging existing laws and practices through the courts. As discussed in detail in Chapter 9, since the days of the progressive National Consumers' League, liberal groups had targeted the courts, especially the Supreme Court, in an effort to secure their goals. Women and African Americans won many rights through expanded readings of the equal protection clause of the Fourteenth Amendment and judicial interpretation of the requirements of the Civil Rights Act of 1964 (such as the

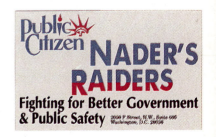

*T*HEN AND NOW

Lobbying

The exact origin of the term "lobbying" is disputed. In the mid-seventeenth century there was a room located near the floor of the English House of Commons where members of Parliament would congregate and could be approached by their constituents and other people who wanted to plead a particular cause. Similarly, in the United States, people often waited outside the chambers of the House and Senate to speak to members of Congress as they emerged. Because they waited in the lobbies to argue their cases, by the nineteenth century they were commonly referred to as "lobbyists." Another piece of folklore explains that when Ulysses S. Grant was president he would frequently walk from the White House to the Willard Hotel on Pennsylvania Avenue just to relax in its comfortable and attractive lobby. Interest-group representatives and people seeking favors from Grant would crowd into that lobby and try to press their claims. Soon they were nicknamed "lobbyists."

Lobbying reached an infamous peak in the late 1800s, when railroads and other big businesses openly bribed state and federal legislators to obtain the passage of favorable legislation. Congress finally began regulating some aspects of lobbying in 1946 with the Regulation of Lobbying Act. The Act required paid lobbyists to register with the House and Senate and to file quarterly financial reports, including an account of all contributions and expenditures as well as the names and addresses of individuals to whom they gave $500 or more. Organizations also were required to submit financial reports, although they did not have to register officially. The purpose of the Act was to publicize the activities of lobbyists, thus removing some uncertainty surrounding the influence of lobbying on legislation.

In 1954, however, a lower court ruled the Act unconstitutional. Although the Supreme Court reversed the decision, the Court's narrow interpretation undermined the effectiveness of the Act. The Court ruled that the Act was applicable only to persons or organizations who solicited, collected, or received money for the principal purpose of influencing legislation by directly lobbying members of Congress. Consequently, many lobbyists do not register at all. The National Association of Manufacturers, for example, was formed in 1895 but did not register as a lobbying group until 1975. Of the organizations that do register, more than 90 percent do not file complete financial reports.

Congress continually considers legislation creating a unified lobbying disclosure law in an effort to reduce many loopholes in the current regulations. While lobbyists are currently required to disclose all meetings with House and Senate members, time spent with personal or committee staff is not counted. And while the expenses incurred during those meetings with members of Congress must be reported, the total spending of lobbyists remains unknown. Stricter regulations on lobbying will reveal a more accurate picture of who is trying to influence legislation and with how much money.

end of segregated public schools and the right to a job free from discrimination), and the Nader groups and environmentalists secured many governmental regulations that adversely affected business interests. Conservative groups quickly took notice of these successes and began responding to them.

By the mid- to late 1970s, conservatives became very concerned about the successes of liberal groups in shaping and defining the public agenda, and religious and ideological conservatives became a potent force in U.S. politics. The largest new religious conservative group was the Reverend Jerry Falwell's Moral Majority, founded in 1978. At one time, the Moral Majority had an extensive television ministry and in its peak year, 1984, raised $11 million for political lobbying. It was widely credited with assisting Ronald Reagan's 1980 presidential victory as well as the defeats of several liberal Democratic senators that same year. Falwell claimed to have sent from three to four million newly registered voters to the polls.[19] In June 1989, Falwell announced that he was terminating the Moral Majority after the group suffered from a series of financial and sexual scandals involving television evangelists. To some extent, the end of the Reagan era seemed to trigger an end to the effectiveness of the religious right in national politics. Other conservatives, however, were not so daunted.

In 1973, friends of Ronald Reagan, who was then the governor of California, were dismayed by the repeated successes in the courts of liberal public-interest groups. Liberal groups were continually victorious in challenging the "reforms" of the Reagan administration—particularly those concerning welfare and the environment. Reaganites were incensed that these liberal groups continually went to court claiming to represent the "public interest." Therefore, Reagan supporters in California founded the Pacific Legal Foundation, the chief aim of which was to present the conservative side of the public interest in court. In the late 1970s, the Pacific Legal Foundation was sufficiently successful to justify the creation of several regional law centers throughout the United States.[20] The conservative law centers' goal was to bring to court cases that would secure the reversal of liberal decisions involving the environment, affirmative action, and other issues of concern to conservatives. As the Supreme Court took a more conservative turn, these conservative public-interest firms renewed their efforts to bring to the Court test cases on issues involving civil rights, affirmative action, the environment, and prayer in schools.

Impressed by the successes of these groups in court, other conservatives moved to fill the void left by the demise of the Moral Majority. In 1990, the televangelist Pat Robertson, host of the popular "The 700 Club," formed a new group, the Christian Coalition (see "Conservatives Reorganize," p. 512), which again is giving conservatives new clout at the ballot box.

Business Groups. Conservative public-interest groups were not the only ones organized to advance conservative views beginning in the 1970s. Many members of the business community believed that both the Chamber of Commerce and the National Association of Manufacturers were too reactionary and shrill in their condemnation of governmental policies and practices. In addition, some members of the business community believed that both were too slow to act and therefore were ineffective representatives of big business. To fill this perceived void and to counter the effects of the Nader Network, the Business Roundtable was created in 1972. Largely made up of the chief executive officers of major businesses, the Roundtable uses its members for direct lobbying and policy formation. It is "a fraternity of powerful and prestigious business leaders that tells 'business's side of the story' to legislators, bureaucrats, White

Conservatives Reorganize

♦ ♦ ♦

The Christian Coalition which aims to have 450,000 dues-paying members and another 300,000 volunteers says it is gaining 10,000 members a month. This growth is translating into political victories as Christian Coalition candidates win local races such as school and library boards, state legislatures, and city and county Republican organizations all over the country. Success has been possible largely through a complex grass-roots organizing and loyal church-based workers. In 1994, polls indicated that religious conservatives accounted for one-third of all voters, up from only 18 percent in 1988.

"Clinton may control the White House; we control the grass roots," says coalition president Ralph Reed, Jr. "By the end of the decade we'll be the mainstream."

It's easy to see how. Thirty-three million voter guides were distributed by the Conservative Coalition in 1994. As many as forty abortion rights supporters lost their seats in the House of Representatives, for example, after being targeted by the Coalition.

Source: Adapted from Richard Benedetto, "Religious Right to Flex Muscles," *USA Today* (September 10, 1993): 6A. Copyright 1993, USA TODAY. Reprinted by permission.

House personnel, and other interested public officials."[21] One of its first battles led to the defeat of legislation backed by the Carter administration that would have created a federal consumer protection agency, a pet project of Ralph Nader's.

Unlike public-interest groups, organizations like the Chamber of Commerce and the Business Roundtable enjoy many of the benefits other businesses do as lobbyists: They already have extensive organization, expertise, large numbers, a strong financial base, and a longstanding relationship with key actors in government. Such natural advantages have led to a huge number of business groups. One observer describes their proliferation this way:

> If you want to understand government, don't begin by reading the Constitution. It conveys precious little of today's statecraft. Instead, read selected portions of the Washington Telephone Directory, such as pages 354–58, which contain listings for all of the organizations with titles beginning with the word "National." . . . There are, of course, the big ones, like the National Association of Manufacturers, and the National Association of Broadcasters. But the pages teem with others, National Cigar Leaf Tobacco Association, National Association of Mirror Manufacturers, National Association of Miscellaneous Ornamental and Architectural Product Contractors, National Association of Margarine Manufacturers.[22]

Many of these national groups devote tremendous resources to fighting government regulation. And quite often, they find themselves on the opposite side of organized labor on any issue.

Organized Labor.   Labor became a stronger force in U.S. politics when the American Federation of Labor and the Congress of Industrial Organizations merged in 1955.

The new AFL-CIO immediately turned its energies to pressuring the government to protect concessions won from employers at the bargaining table. Concentrating its efforts largely on the national level, the AFL-CIO and other unions have been active in a wide range of issues, including minimum wage laws, the environment, civil rights, medical insurance, and consumer and education issues.

But the once-fabled political clout of organized labor has been on the wane. By the late 1970s it was clear that even during a Democratic administration (Carter's), organized labor lacked the impact it had had during earlier decades. During the Reagan administration, organized labor's influence fell to an all-time modern-day low. In spite of the tremendous resources behind the AFL-CIO and other unions, membership has dropped and continues to do so, as revealed in Figure 15-1. In 1983, 20.1 percent of workers were unionized; in 1992 only 15.8 percent were. President Clinton backs legislation banning companies from permanently replacing striking employees. Labor leaders hope that its passage will reverse the decline in union membership.

Professional Associations. In contrast to the labor union situation, the political influence of professional societies continues to expand. The American Medical Association (AMA), for example, waged an all-out battle to fend off President Clinton's proposed system of national guaranteed health care. In the early 1960s, the AMA spent millions of dollars in an unsuccessful effort to fight Medicare. Once some sort of medical assistance for the elderly was inevitable, the AMA turned its efforts toward the drafting and implementation of legislation and regulations, an effort that produced considerable financial rewards for physicians. It will probably try to play a similar role in a national health care system.

The National Education Association (NEA), which represents the interests of teachers, professors, and administrators, is another influential professional association. It

FIGURE 15-1

Labor Union Membership, 1900–1993

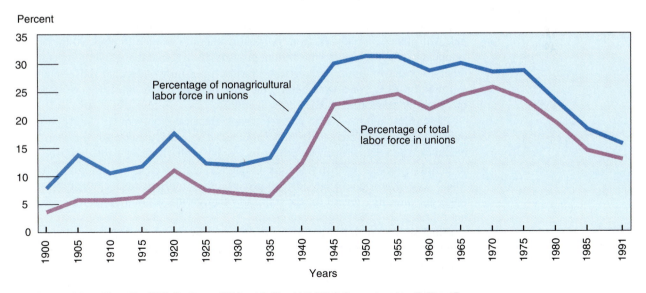

Source: Adapted from Harold W. Stanley and Richard G. Niemi, *Vital Statistics on American Politics*, 4E. (Washington, DC: CQ Press, 1994) Table 6-11, p. 190. Reprinted by permission.

was instrumental in the establishment of the Department of Education during the Carter administration. Also influential is the American Bar Association (ABA), which represents many of the nation's lawyers. As discussed in Chapter 9, the ABA plays a key role in nominations to the federal bench via its rating of judicial nominees.

What Do Interest Groups Do?

Americans have long debated the nature of interest groups and their role in a democratic society. Do interest groups contribute to the betterment of society, or are they an evil best controlled by government?

Interest groups often fill voids left by the traditional political parties and give Americans another opportunity to take their claims directly to the government. Interest groups give the unrepresented or underrepresented an opportunity to have their voices heard, thereby making the government and its policy-making process more representative of diverse populations and perspectives.

Interest groups also enhance political participation by motivating like-minded individuals to work toward a common goal. Legislators are often much more likely to listen to or be concerned about the interests of a group as opposed to the interests of any one individual. The congressional testimony of Kimberly Bergalis, the first known individual who claimed to have contracted HIV from a dentist, was given heavy media coverage. Yet the likelihood is slim that Congress will approve mandatory HIV testing of all health care workers without the backing of one or more organized groups to support Bergalis's requests for mandatory testing.

Just as members of Congress are assumed to represent the interests of their constituents in Washington, D.C., interest groups are assumed to represent the interests of their members to policy makers at all levels of government. In the 1950s, for example, the National Association for the Advancement of Colored People (NAACP) was able to articulate and present the interests of African Americans to national decision makers even though as a group they had little or no electoral clout, especially in the South. Without the efforts of the civil rights groups discussed in Chapter 5, it is unlikely that either the courts or Congress would have acted as quickly to make discrimination illegal. All sorts of individuals, from railroad workers to women to physical therapists to campers to homosexuals to mushroom growers, have found that banding together with others who have similar interests and hiring a person to advocate those interests in Washington, D.C., or a state capital increase the likelihood that issues of concern to them will be addressed and acted on favorably.

There is also a downside to interest groups. Because groups make claims on society, they can increase the cost of public policies. The elderly can push for more costly health care and Social Security programs, people with disabilities for improved access to public buildings, industry for tax loopholes, and veterans for improved benefits. Many Americans believe that interest groups exist simply to advance their own selfish interests, with little regard for the rights of other groups or, more important, of people not represented by any organized group.

Whether good or bad, interest groups play an important role in U.S. politics. In addition to *enhancing* the democratic process by providing increased representation and participation, they increase public awareness about important issues, help frame the public agenda, and often monitor programs to guarantee effective implementation. Most often they accomplish these things through some sort of lobbying or informational campaign.

"Lobbying" is generally at the top of the agendas of most interest groups. Lobbying is the process by which interest groups attempt to assert their influence on the policy process. The term **lobbyist** refers to any representative of a group who attempts to influence a policy maker by one or more of the tactics illustrated in Table 15.2. It is important to note that not only do large, organized interests have their own lobbyists, but

Lobbyist Interest group representative who seeks through political persuasion to influence legislation that will benefit his or her organization.

Table 15.2   ◆   Percentage of Groups Using Each Lobbying Technique to Exercise Influence

LOBBYING TECHNIQUE USED	PERCENTAGE
Testifying at hearings	99%
Contacting government officials directly to present your point of view	98
Engaging in informal contact with officials—at conventions, over lunch, etc.	95
Presenting research results or technical information	92
Sending letters to members of your organization to inform them about your activities	92
Entering into coalitions with other organizations	90
Attempting to shape the implementation of policies	89
Talking with people from the press and the media	86
Consulting with government officials to plan legislative strategy	85
Helping to draft legislation	85
Inspiring letter-writing or telegram campaigns	84
Shaping the government's agenda by raising new issues and calling attention to previously ignored problems	84
Mounting grassroots lobbying efforts	80
Having influential constituents contact their member of Congress	80
Helping to draft regulations, rules, or guidelines	78
Serving on advisory commissions and boards	76
Alerting members of Congress to the effects of a bill on their districts	75
Filing suit or otherwise engaging in litigation	72
Making financial contributions to electoral campaigns	58
Doing favors for officials who need assistance	56
Attempting to influence appointments to public office	53
Publicizing candidates' voting records	44
Engaging in direct-mail fund raising for your organization	44
Running advertisements in the media about your position on issues	31
Contributing work or personnel to electoral campaigns	24
Making public endorsements of candidates for office	22
Engaging in protests or demonstrations	20

Source: Adapted from Kay Lehman Schlozman and John T. Tierney, "More of the Same: Washington Pressure Group Activity in a Decade of Change," *Journal of Politics* 45 (1988): 351–375.

other groups, including colleges, trade associations, cities and even foreign nations, also hire lobbying firms (some law firms have lobbying specialists) to represent them in the halls of Congress or to get through the bureaucratic maze.

As Table 15.2 (p. 515) indicates, there are at least twenty-seven ways to lobby. Lobbying allows interest groups to try to convince key governmental decision makers *and* the public of the correctness of their positions. Almost all interest groups lobby by testifying at hearings and contacting legislators. Other groups also provide information that decision makers might not have the time, opportunity, and/or interest to gather on their own. Of course, information these groups provide is designed to present the group's position in a favorable light, although a good lobbyist for an interest group will also note the downside to proposed legislation. Interest groups also file lawsuits to lobby the courts, and some even engage in protests or demonstrations as a form of "lobbying" public opinion or decision makers.

Lobbying Congress. Members of Congress are the targets of a wide variety of lobbying activities: individual letters from interested constituents, campaign contributions, or the outright payment of money for votes. Of course, the last item is illegal, but there are numerous documented instances of money changing hands for votes.

Lobbying Congress is a skill that many people have developed over the years. In 1869, for example, women meeting in Washington, D.C., for the second annual meeting of the National Woman Suffrage Association marched to Capitol Hill to hear one of their members (unsuccessfully) ask Congress to pass legislation to enfranchise women under the terms of the Fourteenth Amendment.

Practices such as these floor speeches are no longer permitted. Some interest groups do, however, still try mass marches to Congress. For example, after the Supreme Court ruled in 1976 that discrimination against a pregnant woman was not prohibited by the Civil Rights Act of 1964, hordes of lobbyists from various women's rights groups descended on Congress at one time. In response, Congress quickly enacted the Pregnancy Discrimination Act of 1978.

Today, lobbyists try to develop close relationships with senators and representatives in an effort to enhance their access to the policy-making process. A symbiotic relationship between members and interest-group representatives often develops. Representatives and their staff members, who face an exhausting workload and legislation they know little about, frequently look to lobbyists for information. "Information is the currency on Capitol Hill, not dollars," said one lobbyist.[23] According to one aide:

> My boss demands a speech and a statement for the *Congressional Record* for every bill we introduce or co-sponsor—and we have a lot of bills. I just can't do it all myself. The better lobbyists, when they have a proposal they are pushing, bring it to me along with a couple of speeches, a *Record* insert, and a fact sheet.[24]

Not surprisingly, lobbyists work most closely with representatives who share their interests. A lobbyist from the National Rifle Association (NRA), for example, would be unlikely to try to influence a liberal representative who was on record as strongly in favor of gun control. Instead, it is much more effective for a group like the NRA to provide useful information for its supporters and to those who are undecided. Good lobbyists can also encourage members to file amendments to bills favorable to their interests. They can also urge their supporters in Congress to make speeches (often written by the group) and to pressure their colleagues in the chamber.

Personal Gifts from Lobbyists
❖ ❖ ❖

In his 1995 state of the Union message, Bill Clinton called on members of Congress—who had yet to pass restrictions on taking gifts from lobbyists—simply to stop taking gifts. By February 1995, 10 percent of all members of Congress had voluntarily signed a pledge drafted by Common Cause and Public Citizen pledging to stop taking free gifts, meals, and trips from lobbyists.

By permission of Mike Luckovich and Creators Syndicate.

A lobbyist's effectiveness depends largely on his or her reputation for fair play and provision of accurate information. No member of Congress wants to look uninformed. As one member noted:

> It doesn't take very long to figure out which lobbyists are straightforward, and which ones are trying to snow you. The good ones will give you the weak points as well as the strong points of their case. If anyone ever gives me false or misleading information, that's it—I'll never see him again.[25]

Because lobbying plays such an important role in Congress, many effective lobbyists often are former members of that body, former staff aides, former White House officials or Cabinet officers, or Washington insiders. This type of lobbyist frequently drops in to visit members of Congress or their staff members and often takes them to lunch, golf, or parties.

While much of that activity may be ethically questionable, most is not illegal (see "Ethics in Government Act," p. 518). There are well-publicized exceptions, however. Michael K. Deaver, once a top aide to President Ronald Reagan, was convicted of perjury in connection with a grand jury investigation of his use of his former government contacts to help clients in his public relations firm.

Lobbying the Executive Branch and Executive Agencies.   As the scope of the federal government has expanded, lobbying the executive branch has increased in importance and frequency. Groups often target one or more levels of the executive branch because there are so many potential access points—the president and White House staff, the numerous levels of the bureaucracy, and the independent regulatory commissions. Groups try to work closely with the administration in an effort to influence policy decisions at their formulation and implementation stages. And, like the situation with congressional lobbying, the effectiveness of a group often lies in its ability to provide decision makers with important information and a sense of where the public stands on the issue.

Ethics in Government Act

◆ ◆ ◆

In 1978, in the wake of Watergate, Congress passed the Ethics in Government Act. Its key provisions dealt with financial disclosure and employment after government service:

Financial disclosure: The president, vice president, and top-ranking executive employees must file annual public financial disclosure reports that list:

- The source and amount of all earned income; all income from stocks, bonds, and property; any investments or large debts; and the source of a spouse's income, if any.

- Any position or offices held in any business, labor, or nonprofit organizations.

Employment after government services: Former executive branch employees may not:

- Represent anyone before any agency for two years after leaving government service on matters that came within the former employees' sphere of responsibility (even if they were not personally involved in the matter).

- Represent anyone on *any* matter before their former agency for one year after leaving it, even if the former employees had no connection with the matter while in the government.

Sources: National Journal (November 19, 1977): 1796–1803; and *Congressional Quarterly Weekly Report* (October 28, 1978): 3121–3127. Reprinted by permission.

Historically, group representatives have met with presidents or their staff members to urge policy directions. In 1992, representatives of the auto industry even accompanied President Bush to lobby the Japanese for more favorable trade regulations. Most presidents also specifically set up staff positions "explicitly to serve as brokerages or clearinghouses to provide greater access to presidential attention for professional, demographic or specialized organizations."[26] Political scientist Thomas Cronin has suggested that "presidents have appointed either an aide or an office for every American dilemma."[27] Among these are offices of domestic policy, economic policy, science and technology, consumer affairs, the environment, and minority affairs. At various times, special liaison offices have been created to deal with women, Jews, African Americans, and bankers, among others.

An especially strong link exists between interest groups and the regulatory agencies (see Chapter 8). Because of the highly technical aspects of much regulatory work, many groups employ Washington attorneys to deal directly with the agencies. So great is interest-group influence in the decision-making process of these agencies that many people charge that the agencies have been captured by the interest groups.

Even after the extensive deregulation that took place during the Carter and Reagan administrations, some groups still complained that certain agencies were unduly influenced by some groups. The National Coal Association (NCA), for example, has argued that the Interstate Commerce Commission (ICC) has granted excessive increases in rail freight rates that adversely affect the coal industry. The head of the NCA once remarked: "I used to say that the ICC is a wholly owned subsidiary of the Association of American Railroads. But now I'm older and wiser and as a consequence of these

Members of the American Association of Retired Persons (AARP) meet with President Clinton in 1993.

outrageous decisions I now contend that the ICC is a wholly owned subsidiary of the coal-carrying railroads."[28]

With or without former government officials on their staffs, interest groups strive to form stable and cozy relationships with Congress and the bureaucracy to achieve their goals. The term "iron triangle" is commonly used to describe the informal yet semi-permanent relationship of these three actors in the policy process (see Chapter 8).

Similar group behavior can be observed in Britain. Because interest groups tend to concentrate their lobbying efforts where it will do them the most good, this practice leads to perceptibly different patterns of interaction. In the British case, however, since Parliament lacks the institutional power of the U.S. Congress, interest groups tend to cluster around the bureaucracy and the occasional government minister who is known to be open to influence. As a result, one rarely observes classic iron triangles in the British system.

Lobbying the Courts. Finally, the courts have proved a useful target for interest groups.[29] Although you might think that the courts decide cases that affect only the parties involved or that they should be immune from political pressures, interest groups have for years recognized the value of lobbying the courts, especially the Supreme Court. As shown in Table 15-2, 72 percent of the Washington-based groups surveyed participated in litigation as a lobbying tool. Richard C. Cortner has noted that "Cases do not arrive on the doorstep of the Supreme Court like orphans in the night."[30] Most major cases noted in this book have either been sponsored by an interest group or one or both of the parties in the case have been supported by a friend of the court brief.

Generally, interest group lobbying of the courts can take two forms: direct sponsorship and *amicus curiae* (friend of the court) briefs. Groups such as the liberal Native American Rights Fund or the Natural Resources Defense Council routinely represent clients to advance the interests of their groups.

The American Association of Retired Persons
◆ ◆ ◆

The American Association of Retired Persons (AARP) was founded in 1958 and today counts more than thirty-three million members over the age of fifty-five. It is not only the fastest-growing interest group in the United States, but it is also the second largest not-for-profit organization in the world. Like other minority groups, it frequently resorts to traditional lobbying as well as litigation to achieve its objectives. In conjunction with the National Senior Citizens' Law Center, founded in 1972, AARP often participates in litigation involving the concerns of senior citizens, including pension and retirement issues, Medicaid benefits, Social Security disability benefits, and mandatory retirement.

When cases come to the Supreme Court that raise issues a particular organization is interested in but not actually sponsoring, often the organization will file an *amicus* brief—either alone or with other like-minded groups — to inform the Justices of their policy preference, generally offered in the guise of legal arguments. (See "Amicus Briefs in Support of Harris," p. 301). Over the years, as the number of groups viewing litigation as a useful tactic has increased, so has the number of briefs submitted to the Court, as revealed in Figure 15-2 below.

In addition to litigating, interest groups try to influence who is nominated to the federal courts. They also have played an important role of late in Senate confirmation hearings, as discussed in Chapter 9. As highlighted in Table 15.3 (p. 521), in 1991 numerous groups lined up in favor of the nomination of Clarence Thomas to the U.S. Supreme Court—and many other groups lined up against his nomination.

Grassroots Lobbying. As this term implies, "grassroots lobbying" is a form of pressure-group activity that attempts to involve those people at the bottom level of the political system. It often involves door-to-door informational or petition drives—a tried and true method of lobbying. As early as the 1840s, for example, women (who could not vote) used petition campaigns to persuade state legislators to enact Married Women's Property Acts that gave women control of their earnings and a greater legal say in the custody of their children. Today, environmentalists frequently go door-to-door to alert their friends and neighbors about pending legislation, the creating or locating of hazardous waste materials, or other perceived threats.

When these forms of pressure-group activity are unsuccessful or appear to be too slow to achieve results, some groups resort to more forceful measures to attract attention to their cause. During the civil rights movement, as discussed in Chapter 5, Martin Luther King Jr. and his followers frequently resorted to nonviolent marches to draw attention to the plight of African Americans in the South. These forms of organized group activity were legal. Proper parade permits were obtained, and government officials notified. The protesters who tried to stop the freedom marchers, however, were

FIGURE 15-2

Interest Group Participation in Supreme Court Litigation

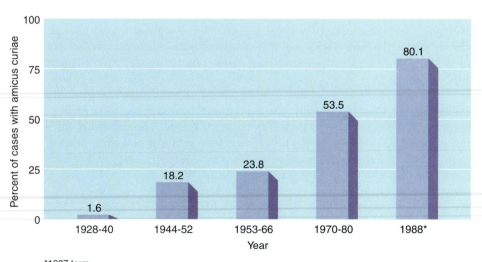

*1987 term

Source: Figures compiled by the authors. See also, Karen O'Connor and Lee Epstein, "Amicus Curiae Participation in U.S. Supreme Court Litigation: An Appraisal of Hakman's 'Folklore,' " *Law & Society Review* 16(1981-82): pp. 318-319.

Table 15.3 ♦ Interest Groups Taking Sides on the Nomination of Clarence Thomas to the U.S. Supreme Court	
FOR THOMAS	**AGAINST THOMAS**
U.S. Chamber of Commerce	NAACP
Coalition for Self-Reliance	AFL-CIO
Coalitions for America	National Organization for Women
American Conservative Union	National Abortion Rights Action League
Concerned Women for America	United Church of Christ
Eagle Forum	League of United Latin American Citizens
Family Research Council	Congressional Black Caucus
The Council of 100	National Women's Political Caucus
Simon Wiesenthal Center	National Education Association
Women For Judge Thomas*	Americans for Democratic Action
	The Women's Legal Defense Fund
	People for the American Way
	Service Employees International Union
	Alliance for Justice

*Group created expressly to support Thomas.

Source: "The Opposition Mounts," *USA Today,* August 8, 1991: A–1.

engaging in illegal protest activity, another form of activity sometimes resorted to by interest groups.

Today, interest groups regularly try to stir up their members, hoping that lawmakers will respond to those pressures and the attendant publicity. For example, when Congress was debating the "Brady Bill" (to limit the sale of handguns) in the early 1990s, groups on both sides of the debate used mass mailings and print ads to educate the public. In essence, the goal of many organizations is to persuade ordinary voters to serve as their advocates. In the world of lobbying, there are few things more useful than a list of committed supporters.

Lobbyists now use electronic technologies to quickly reach and recruit thousands of Americans at the grassroots level, causing "Congress to govern more by fear and an intense desire for simple, easy answers,"[31] said Representative Steve Gunderson (R-Wis.). Today, the simple grassroots campaigns of just a few years ago (fill-in-the-blank post cards and forms torn out of the newspaper) have grown much more sophisticated and become more effective.

To mobilize their members, many interest groups and trade groups have installed banks of computerized fax machines to send faxes automatically around the country overnight, instructing each member to ask his or her employees, customers, or other people to write, call, or fax their members of Congress. Other lobbyists now run carefully targeted and costly television advertisements pitching one side of an argument. Their opponents must generally respond or lose. Many of these advertisements end with a toll-free phone number that viewers can call if they find the pitch convincing. New telemarketing companies answer these calls and transfer the callers directly to the offices of the appropriate members of Congress.[32]

Contacting Government Officials Through the Internet
♦ ♦ ♦

The White House, the House of Representatives, the Senate, Federal and State courts, as well as a host of government agencies are all accessible through the internet. All you need are a computer, a modem, and an electronic mailbox. Database information is available by "Gopher," a search and retrieval function. A partial listing of government database gophers includes the Agency for International Development (USAID) gopher; the Congressional Directory, which lists House and Senate members by State, District, address, phone, fax, and e-mail; the Housing and Urban Development (HUD) gopher; the White House gopher, as well as databases of historical documents and speeches. The World Wide Web provides a graphically sophisticated information map that users access one "page" at a time. In the realm of government and politics there are over 1700 home pages of information, each of which is linked to a multitude of other sources. As a starting point, try exploring the web site **http://www. yahoo.com/government/**. This dauntingly long address is actually just a starting point that will lead you down untold information pathways.

The American Trucking Association uses a satellite network to advise its affiliates and members when and how to lobby legislators.

Election Activities

When interest groups are unable to achieve their goals through conventional forms of lobbying, they may decide to become involved more directly in the electoral process. Many groups claim to be nonpartisan, that is, nonpolitical. Usually they try to have friends in both political parties to whom they can look for assistance and access. Some organizations, however, routinely endorse candidates for public office, pledging money, group support, and often even campaign volunteers. Endorsements from some groups may be used by a candidate's opponent to attack the candidate. When several labor unions endorsed Walter Mondale in his 1984 campaign against President Ronald Reagan, he was labeled a "tool of the labor unions" by Republicans.

Some liberal or conservative ideological groups rate candidates in order to help their members (and the general public) evaluate the voting records of members of Congress. The American Conservative Union (conservative) and the Americans for Democratic Action (liberal)—two groups at ideological polar extremes—routinely rate candidates and members of Congress based on their votes on key issues of importance to the group, as illustrated in Table 15.4 (p. 523).

Other groups target certain individuals and campaign against them to show their clout and to scare other elected officials into paying more attention to them. Beginning in 1970, for example, Environmental Action (EA) labeled twelve members of the House of Representatives "the dirty dozen" because of their votes against bills that the group believed were necessary to protect the environment. Over the years, the designation of more than thirty members of Congress with a similar label was widely publicized by the media and through direct-mail campaigns to voters interested in the environment. To date, only seven members to earn EA's anti-environmental nickname have stayed in office.

Similarly, in 1980, the Moral Majority targeted several liberal Democratic senators who were up for reelection and saw all of them defeated. Its clout, although short-lived, clearly made many vulnerable senators think twice about risking the wrath of what seemed to be a very powerful group able to produce results at the polls. More recently, the Conservative Coalition has made substantial inroads by taking over local party organizations and running its own candidates (often in "non-partisan" elections) for local school boards and town councils in order to get its views about school prayer, homosexuality, sex education, and other items on its agenda implemented at the local level.

Another interest-group strategy is to form a political party in order to publicize a cause and even possibly win a few public offices. In 1848, the Free Soil Party was formed to publicize the crusade against slavery; twenty years later, the Prohibition Party was formed to try to ban the sale of alcoholic beverages. Similarly, in 1976, the National Right-to-Life Party was formed to publicize the anti-abortion position.

The effectiveness of an interest group in the election arena has often been overrated by members of the news media. In general, it is very difficult to assess the effect of a particular group's impact on any one election because of the number of other factors present in any election or campaign. However, the one area in which interest groups do seem able to affect the outcome of elections directly is through a relatively new device called the political action committee.

Interest Groups and Political Action Committees. Throughout most of history, powerful interests and individuals have often used their money to "buy" politicians or their votes. Even if outright bribery was not involved, huge corporate or other interest-

Table 15.4 ◆ 1992 Interest Group Ratings of Select Members of Congress*

MEMBER	AMERICAN CONSERVATIVE UNION	AMERICANS FOR DEMOCRATIC ACTION	AFL-CIO	CHAMBER OF COMMERCE
Senate				
Sen. Jesse Helms (R-N.C.)	100	5	13	100
Sen. Nancy Kassebaum (R-Kans.)	67	25	25	100
Sen. Edward M. Kennedy (D-Mass.)	0	100	92	20
Sen. Robert Kerrey (D-Nebr.)	0	100	83	10
House				
Rep. Vic Fazio (D-Calif.)	8	90	75	50
Rep. E. (Kika) de la Garza (D-Tex.)	19	70	75	43
Rep. Newt Gingrich (R-Ga.)	100	10	58	50
Rep. Olympia Snowe (R-Maine) (now in the Senate)	60	50	58	50

*Members are rated on a scale from 1 to 100, with 1 being the lowest and 100 being the highest support of a particular group's policies.

group donations certainly made some politicians look as if they were in the "pocket" of certain special interests. Congressional passage of the Federal Election Campaign Act began to change most of that. The 1971 Act required candidates to disclose all campaign contributions and limited the amount of money that they could spend on media advertising. In 1974, in the wake of the Watergate scandal (see Chapter 7), amendments to the Act made it more far-reaching. They sharply limited the amount of money any interest group could give to a candidate for federal office. However, they also made it legal for corporations, labor unions, and interest groups to form **political action committees,** often referred to as PACs, that could make contributions to candidates for national elections. (See Chapter 13 for more on this subject.)

Technically, a "PAC" is a political arm of a business, labor, trade, professional, or other interest group legally authorized to raise funds on a voluntary basis from employees or members in order to contribute to a political candidate or party. These monies have changed the face of U.S. elections. Unlike some contributions to interest groups, however, contributions to PACs are not tax deductible, and PACs generally don't have members who call legislators; instead, PACs have contributors who write checks specifically for the purpose of campaign donations. For many congressional incumbents, for example, PAC money plays a significant role in their campaigns—averaging 35 percent of a House candidate's total campaign spending. PACs generally contribute to those who have helped them before and who serve on committees or subcommittees that routinely consider legislation of concern to that group.

The number of PACs is increasing rapidly. Roughly 3,000 PACs contributed in the 1992 congressional elections, making about 180,000 contributions in that election cy-

Political action committee (PAC)
Federally mandated, officially registered fund-raising committees that represent interest groups in the political process.

By permission of Mike Luckovich and Creators Syndicate.

cle (see Figure 15-3).[33] In light of the 1992 campaign's focus on health care reform, it is not surprising that health care industry PACs increased their giving to congressional candidates by 32 percent over 1990. The American Trial Lawyers of America PAC gave 2.3 million dollars to candidates, hoping to head off tort reform legislation that would affect lawyers by limiting the amounts of money awarded by juries (and therefore lawyers' fees) in negligence cases. One of the biggest increases in PAC contributions came from women's groups, which experienced a 314 percent increase over 1990. Especially important was EMILY's List, which stands for "Early Money Is Like Yeast—it makes the dough rise"; this group was the largest single contributor to Democratic women congressional candidates in 1992 and 1994. Its early successes even spawned a Republican counterpart—WISH (Women in the Senate and House).

Protest Activity.   When other forms of lobbying activity don't seem to be getting an interest group very far quickly enough, some groups resort to protest activity. Over the years, organized interests have engaged in both legal (sit-ins, for example) and illegal forms of mass protest. Since the Revolutionary War, violent, illegal protest has been one tactic of organized interests. The Boston Tea Party, for example, involved breaking all sorts of laws although no one was hurt physically. Other forms of protest such as Shays's Rebellion ended in tragedy for some participants.

Groups on both ends of the political spectrum historically have resorted to violence. Abolitionists, anti-nuclear activists, anti-war activists, animal-rights advocates, and other groups on the "left" have broken laws, damaged property, and even injured or killed innocent bystanders. On the "right," groups such as Operation Rescue and the Ku Klux Klan have broken the laws and even hurt or killed people in the furtherance of their objectives. From the early 1900s until the 1960s, African Americans were routinely lynched by KKK members. Today, Operation Rescue members regularly block the entrances to abortion clinics; others active in the anti-abortion movement have taken credit for clinic bombings.

Table 15.5 ◆ Doling out PAC Dollars

While organized labor's political action committees contributed the most money to 1992 congressional races, health-care industry PACs showed the sharpest increase in activity since 1990.

SECTOR	TOTAL	CHANGE FROM '90	PAC MONEY SPLIT	
			DEM.	REP.
Agriculture	$15,027,605	10%	51%	49%
Communications/electronics	$9,334,146	14%	56%	44%
Construction	$4,575,364	–5%	38%	62%
Defense	$7,228,724	–2%	55%	45%
Energy/natural resources	$13,113,938	8%	48%	52%
Finance/insurance/real estate	$28,792,287	13%	56%	44%
Health	$14,406,370	32%	61%	39%
Labor	$42,557,697	17%	94%	6%
Lawyers/lobbyists	$5,590,745	22%	80%	20%
Transportation	$11,992,988	22%	52%	48%

Source: Center for Responsive Politics. Reprinted in Richard Benedetto, "Health PACs' Giving Rises," *USA Today,* March 12, 1993: 4A.

FIGURE 15-3

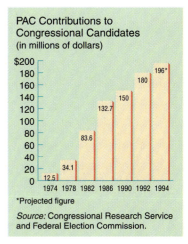

PAC Contributions to Congressional Candidates (in millions of dollars)

*Projected figure

Source: Congressional Research Service and Federal Election Commission.

Most groups, however, have few members so devoted as to put everything on the line for their cause. It is much more usual for a group's members to opt for more conventional forms of lobbying or to influence policy through the electoral process.

What Makes an Interest Group Successful?

Throughout our nation's history, all kinds of interests in society have organized to pressure the government for policy change. Some have been successful, and some have not. E. E. Schattschneider once wrote, "Pressure politics is essentially the politics of small groups. . . . Pressure tactics are not remarkably successful in mobilizing general interests."[34] He was correct; historically, corporate interests often prevail over the concerns of public interest groups such as environmentalists.

To understand this point better, it's important to distinguish between an actual and a potential group and to understand that most groups seek only members who agree with them on most (if not all issues) (see Table 15.6). Theoretically, all women could be members of a women's rights group, all campers members of a conservation group, or all gun owners members of the National Rifle Association. Potential groups include *all* people who might be group members because they share a common trait or interest.[35] An actual group consists of only those people who actually join, and it is almost *always* smaller than the potential group. No group can ever attract all potential members; no one group is so monolithic that it could appeal to all people in the potential group. All farmers won't want to belong to the Grange, and all pro-life activists don't want to join Operation Rescue.

Table 15.6 ◆ Potential versus Actual Interest Groups

The goal of most groups is to mobilize all potential members. Often that task is impossible. As Mancur Olson Jr. points out, the larger the group, the more difficult it is to mobilize. To illustrate the potential versus actual membership phenomenon, here are several examples of groups and their potential memberships.

POPULATION	GROUP	NUMBER OF POTENTIAL MEMBERS	NUMBER OF ACTUAL MEMBERS
Governors	National Governor's Association	55	55 (includes territories)
Political Science Faculty	American Political Science Association	17,000	8,250
Doctors	American Medical Association (AMA)	548,000	288,000
Women	National Organization for Women (NOW)	127,000,000	250,000
African Americans	National Association for the Advancement of Colored People (NAACP)	30,600,000	345,000

Collective good Something of value that cannot be withheld from a non-interest group member, e.g., a tax write-off, a good feeling, etc.

Free-rider problem A problem that occurs when those who don't join or work for the benefit of the group still reap the rewards of the group's activity.

Groups vary tremendously in their ability to enroll potential members, as revealed in Table 15.6. Economist Mancur Olson Jr. notes that all groups, whether economic or non-economic, provide some **collective good**—that is, something of value, such as money, a tax write-off, a good feeling, or a better environment—that can't be withheld from a non-group member.[36] If one union member at a factory gets a raise, for example, all other workers at that factory will, too. Therefore, those who don't join or work for the benefit of the group still reap the rewards of the group's activity. This phenomenon is called the **free rider problem.** Consequently, Olson asserts, potential members are unlikely to join a group because they realize that they will receive many of the benefits the group achieves regardless of their participation. Not only is it irrational for free riders to join any group, but the bigger the group, the greater the free rider problem. Small groups like the AMA or the American Political Science Association have an organizational advantage because in a small group, any individual's share of the collective good may be great enough to make it rational to join. The "patrons" deemed important by political scientist Jack L. Walker often eliminate the free rider problem for public interest groups by making the "costs" of joining minimal.[37]

The Role of Leaders

Interest-group theorists frequently acknowledge the key role that leaders play in the formation and viability of groups. The role of an interest-group leader is similar to that of an entrepreneur in the business world. As in the marketing of a new product, an interest-group leader must have something attractive to offer in order to persuade members to join. Potential members of the group must be convinced that the benefits of joining outweigh the costs. Union members, for example, must be persuaded that the cost of their union dues will be offset by the union's winning higher wages for them.

How Events Can Affect Interest Groups
◆ ◆ ◆

In the wake of the Clarence Thomas hearings in 1991, liberal women's interest groups attempted to capitalize on women's anger through a variety of well-written pleas for funds to prevent any other women from being treated as Anita Hill was treated by the all-male Senate Judiciary Committee. The results:

ORGANIZATION	RESULT
EMILY's List	$300,000 raised in a direct-mail solicitation sent out two weeks after the hearings
Fund for the Feminist Majority	30% increase in direct-mail contributions
National Organization for Women (NOW)	Direct-mail contributions up 25%–30%; threefold increase in paid memberships
National Women's Political Caucus	$85,000 raised from one newspaper ad
Women's Campaign Fund	50% increase in direct-mail contributions

Source: Jill Abramson, "Women's Anger About Hill–Thomas Hearings Has Brought Cash into Female Political Causes," *Wall Street Journal* (January 6, 1992): A–16. Reprinted by permission of the *Wall Street Journal* © copyright 1992 Dow Jones & Company, Inc. All rights reserved worldwide.

Without the powerful pen of William Lloyd Garrison in the 1830s, would the abolitionist movement have been as successful? Similarly, Frances Willard was the prime mover behind the Women's Christian Temperance Union (WCTU), as were Marian Wright Edelman of the Children's Defense Fund in 1968, and the Reverend Jerry Falwell of the Moral Majority in the 1980s. Most successful groups, especially public-interest groups, are led by charismatic individuals who devote most of their energies to "the cause." Moreover, leaders often differ from the rank and file of the group in that they are usually more future oriented, better educated, and affluent.

Funding

Funding is crucial to all interest groups. In a 1983 study, political scientist Jack L. Walker found that patrons—those who fund groups—were key to many interest-group successes.[38] Government, foundations, and wealthy individuals all serve as patrons providing crucial start-up funds for groups, especially public-interest groups.

Groups also rely heavily on membership contributions, dues, and other fund-raising activities. During the 1980s, conservative groups, for example, relied on the direct mail skills of marketing wizard Richard Viguerie to raise monies for a variety of conservative causes. In the 1990s, pro-choice groups have successfully appealed to sup-

Suffrage leader Susan B. Anthony in later life. Although she died before passage of the Nineteenth Amendment, her efforts on its behalf were critical.

porters by requesting funds to campaign for legislation in anticipation of the Supreme Court's reversal of *Roe* v. *Wade.* When the Supreme Court's decision in *Casey* v. *Planned Parenthood of Southeastern Pennsylvania* (1992)[39] did not overrule *Roe* v. *Wade* (1973) and then when Ruth Bader Ginsburg was appointed to the Supreme Court, contributions to pro-choice groups such as NARAL and Planned Parenthood dropped precipitously.

Membership

Organizations are usually composed of three kinds of members. At the top are a relatively small number of leaders who devote most of their energies to the single group. The second tier of members are generally involved psychologically as well as organizationally. They are the workers of the group—they attend meetings, pay dues, and chair committees to see that things get done. In the bottom tier are the rank and file, members who don't actively participate. They pay their dues and call themselves group members, but they do little more. Most group members fall into this last category.

E. E. Schattschneider has noted that the interest-group system in the United States has a decidedly "upper class bias," and he concluded that 90 percent of the population does not participate in an interest-group, or what he called the pressure-group, system.[40] Since the 1960s, survey data have revealed that group membership is drawn primarily from people with higher income and education levels. Individuals who are wealthier can afford to belong to more organizations because they have more money and, often, more leisure time. Money and education are also associated with greater confidence that one's actions will bring results, a further incentive to devote time to organizing or supporting interest groups.

People who do belong to groups often belong to more than one. This overlapping membership can often affect the cohesiveness of a group. Imagine, for example, that you are an officer in the college Young Republicans. If you call a meeting, people may not attend because they have academic, athletic, or social obligations. Divided loyalties and multiple group memberships can often affect the success of a group, especially if it has too many members who simply fall into the dues-paying category.

Getting Ideas on the Public Agenda.   Throughout this chapter, we discuss a variety of groups. Most of them have been the "successful" ones—the ones that were lucky enough to have committed leaders, adequate financing or patrons, and ideas that appealed to enough people to make those ideas viable in the political process.

A successful group usually can use its resources to put its ideas on the government's policy agenda. As groups mobilize to push their policy goals, they often bring into the public forum issues that might not have otherwise surfaced at that time. The Humane Society, for example, has been in existence since the turn of the century, but it was not until more aggressive groups such as People for the Ethical Treatment of Animals (PETA) made the public aware of the widespread testing of many products on animals did the pressure of the general public effectively forced many manufacturers to alter their testing programs. For many groups, simply getting their issues on the public agenda equals success. Government responses may not be forthcoming, but their activities can mean that the public is made sufficiently aware of a certain practice or policy to work for changes to be made (or, at the very least, to make the changes themselves).

Program Monitoring.   Successful groups, to stay successful, must often monitor how the laws or policies they advocated are implemented. Thus, successful interest groups often find it useful, once a law is passed or a regulation written that affects them, to monitor how that law or regulation is implemented. The National Organization for Women (NOW), for example, created the Project on Educational Equity Review (PEER) to monitor the enforcement of Title IX, the purpose of which is to ban sex discrimination in schools receiving federal funding. Its newsletter, *PEER Perspective,* provides detailed analyses of Title IX legislative and administrative activity. Moreover, PEER staffers are in regular contact with government officials to discuss enforcement and to lobby against regulations that would hinder the enforcement of Title IX.

Toward Reform

Since the turn of the century, when good-government groups formed in response to blatant political corruption and the conflicts of interest between big business and government, the public has been uniform in its support of reforming and reducing the influence of "special interests." But, as James Madison pointed out two centuries earlier in *Federalist No. 10,* it may be dangerous for governments to regulate factions too strictly, for such actions could limit liberty itself. Madison optimistically believed that competition among factions could be balanced by governments; but as we have seen in this chapter, all groups are not created equal. Generally, wealthy and powerful people, and the groups that represent them, have more political sway than do the poor and disenfranchised.

In 1946, in an effort to limit the power of lobbyists, Congress passed the Federal Regulation of Lobbying Act, which required anyone hired to lobby any member of Congress to register and file quarterly financial reports. Few lobbyists actually file these reports, and the Justice Department has not even opted to try to enforce the provisions of the Act, believing its vagueness makes it virtually unenforceable. While some good-government groups argue that the laws should be strengthened, civil liberties groups such as the American Civil Liberties Union (ACLU) (see p. 102) argue that registration provisions violate the First Amendment's freedom of speech and the right of citizens to petition the government.

Good government groups continue to press for national legislation to regulate lobbyists. Such legislation, however, is not one of the major planks in the Republicans' Contract with America.

IN 1992, HANDGUNS KILLED
33 PEOPLE IN GREAT BRITAIN
36 IN SWEDEN
97 IN SWITZERLAND
60 IN JAPAN
13 IN AUSTRALIA
128 IN CANADA
AND 13,220 IN THE UNITED STATES.

GOD BLESS AMERICA.

STOP HANDGUNS BEFORE THEY STOP YOU.

Handgun Control, Inc. (HCI) is a national, non-profit lobbying organization that is working to enact a national gun control policy. HCI has worked to pass the Brady Bill as well as a ban on semi-automatic assault weapons. In addition, HCI has introduced comprehensive legislation, the Gun Violence Prevention Act of 1994 or Brady II, that looks to overhaul the way we buy and sell guns in this country. But the powerful National Rifle Association is vigorously opposing its efforts with renewed vigor after its 1993 defeat, when the Brady Bill was passed.

Summary

The United States has always been a nation of joiners. National groups first emerged in the country in the 1830s. Since that time, the type, nature, sophistication, and tactics of groups have changed dramatically. To that end, we have made the following points:

1. Those who study interest groups have offered a variety of definitions to explain what they are. Most definitions revolve around notions of "associations or groups of individuals" who "share" some sort of "common" "interest" or "attitude" and who try to "influence" or "engage in activity" to effect "governmental policies" or the people in "government." In general, interest groups represent economic or the public interest and are single- or multi-issue.

2. The history of interest groups in this country is longer than that of the nation itself. Groups national in scope, however, did not begin until around the 1830s as communications networks improved to facilitate their development. After the Civil War, the number of groups increased as groups that had never organized before, including African Americans and women, began to form

associations. Industrialization also brought about fledg-ling attempts by employees to form labor unions.

3. The dawn of the Progressive era (1890–1920) brought with it more new groups. Settlement houses were often a gathering spot for people active in all kinds of public interest groups. During this period organized labor be-gan to gain political clout, and the National Association of Manufacturers (NAM) and the Chamber of Com-merce became some of its biggest enemies.

4. After the Progressive era, some groups faltered while others continued to flourish. Beginning in the 1960s, however, hundreds of new interest groups were formed; many of them were Washington, D.C.–based in order to better advance their interests in the nation's capitol. Many of these groups are similar, but larger, versions of the socially concerned or good-government groups that were the hallmark of the Progressive era. This time, however, a new, more effective breed of conserva-tive groups arose to counter their claims before legisla-tures, as well as in the courts. Professional associations, too, became an active presence in Washington, D.C.

5. Interest groups often fill voids left by the major politi-cal parties and give Americans opportunities to make claims, as a group, on government. The most common activity of interest groups is lobbying, which takes many forms. Groups routinely pressure members of

Congress and their staffs, the president and the bureau-cracy, and the courts; they use a variety of techniques to educate and stimulate the public also to pressure key governmental decision makers. Interest groups also at-tempt to influence the outcome of elections; some even run their own candidates for office. Others "rate" elected officials to inform their members how particular legislators stand on issues of importance to them. Polit-ical action committees (PACs), a way for some groups to contribute money to candidates for office, are an-other method of gaining support from elected officials and ensuring that their "friends" stay in office.

6. Just as groups are diverse, so are the ways in which they become successful and measure their success. Strong leaders or patrons are critical to the success of most interest groups, as are adequate resources, whether in the form of a dedicated membership or a re-liable source of funds. Leaders and funds allow groups to engage in a variety of lobbying activities and, once they get the programs or laws they seek, to monitor their implementation.

7. Adverse reaction to the potential power of interest groups and the possibility of inappropriate influence have led Congress periodically to draft legislation to regulate lobbying. PACs, in particular, have come under an increasing amount of criticism.

Key Terms

lobbying	multi-issue groups	lobbyist
interest groups	single-issue groups	political action committee (PAC)
economic-interest groups	disturbance theory	collective good
public-interest groups	trade associations	free rider problem

Suggested Readings

Berry, Jeffrey M. *The Interest Group Society,* 2nd ed. Glenview, IL: Scott, Foresman/Little, Brown, 1989.

——. *Lobbying for the People: The Political Behavior of Public Interest Groups.* Princeton, NJ: Princeton University Press, 1977.

Cigler, Allan J., and Burdett A. Loomis, eds. *Interest Group Politics,* 4th ed. Washington, DC: CQ Press, 1991.

Hrebenar, Ronald J., and Ruth K. Scott. *Interest Group Politics in America,* 2nd ed. Englewood Cliffs, NJ: Prentice-Hall, 1990.

McGlen, Nancy E., and Karen O'Connor. *Women, Politics and American Society.* Englewood Cliffs, NJ: Prentice-Hall, 1995.

Olson, Mancur Jr. *The Logic of Collective Action: Public Good and the Theory of Groups.* Cambridge, MA: Harvard University Press, 1965.

Sabato, Larry J. *PAC Power: Inside the World of Political Action Committees.* New York: Norton, 1984.

Schlozman, Kay Lehman, and John T. Tierney. *Organized Interests and American Democracy.* New York: Harper & Row, 1986.

Truman, David B. *The Governmental Process: Political Interests and Public Opinion.* (New York: Knopf, 1951).

Policy Portfolio

As James Madison indicated in *Federalist No. 44,* the Framers heatedly debated how strictly to limit the federal government. The necessary and proper, or elastic clause, discussed in Chapters 2 and 6, was viewed with particular distrust by many Anti-Federalists because it allowed Congress broad and undefined authority to pass what were termed "necessary" laws. Madison and the Federalists prevailed, however, and the elastic clause was made part of Article I.

The necessary and proper clause, along with the commerce clause, and the Supreme Court's interpretation of these clauses and others, ultimately gave the national government—as well as the states—sweeping powers to regulate, influence and, some would say, interfere in the lives and well-being of the country's inhabitants through a variety of social welfare, economic, and foreign policies.

The Policy-Making Process

A good workable definition of a **public policy** states that it is a purposive course of action followed by government in dealing with some problem or matter of concern.[1] Public policies are thus governmental policies; based on law, they are authoritative and binding on people. Individuals, groups, and even government agencies that do not comply with policies can be penalized through fines, loss of benefits, or even jail terms. As the phrase "course of action" implies, policies develop or unfold over time. They involve more than a legislative decision to enact a law or a presidential decision to issue an executive order. Also important is how the law or executive order is carried out. Whether a policy is vigorously enforced, enforced only in some instances, or not enforced at all helps determine its meaning and impact on people. Although their intentions are important, it is what governments actually do that constitutes public policy and that really counts in shaping or influencing people's behavior.

531

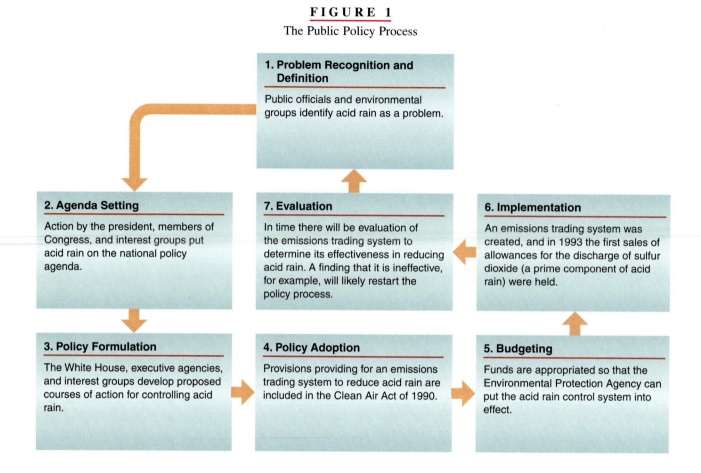

FIGURE 1

The Public Policy Process

1. Problem Recognition and Definition

Public officials and environmental groups identify acid rain as a problem.

2. Agenda Setting

Action by the president, members of Congress, and interest groups put acid rain on the national policy agenda.

7. Evaluation

In time there will be evaluation of the emissions trading system to determine its effectiveness in reducing acid rain. A finding that it is ineffective, for example, will likely restart the policy process.

6. Implementation

An emissions trading system was created, and in 1993 the first sales of allowances for the discharge of sulfur dioxide (a prime component of acid rain) were held.

3. Policy Formulation

The White House, executive agencies, and interest groups develop proposed courses of action for controlling acid rain.

4. Policy Adoption

Provisions providing for an emissions trading system to reduce acid rain are included in the Clean Air Act of 1990.

5. Budgeting

Funds are appropriated so that the Environmental Protection Agency can put the acid rain control system into effect.

public policy A purposive course of action followed by government in dealing with some problem or matter of concern.

Here, we present a widely used model of the policy-making process that views it as a sequence of stages or functional activities. Collectively, the sequence constitutes a policy cycle. As illustrated in Figure 1 above, which uses the issue of acid rain, a *problem* that disturbs or distresses people gives rise to demands for relief, often through governmental action. Individual or group efforts are then made to get the problem placed on a governmental *agenda*. If successful, this step is followed by the *formulation* of alternatives for dealing with the problem. *Policy adoption* involves the formal enactment or approval of an alternative. *Budgeting* provides financial resources to carry out the approved alternative, which can now be called a "policy." *Policy implementation,* the actual administration or application of the policy to its targets, may then be followed by *policy evaluation* to determine the policy's actual accomplishments or consequences. Evaluation may restart the policy cycle by touching off an attempt to modify or terminate the policy. With this overview in mind, let's now look in more detail at the various stages of the policy process or cycle.

Problem Definition

A problem involves some condition or situation in society that causes distress or dissatisfaction or generates needs for which some kind of relief or corrective action is sought—often from the government (national, state, or local). At any given time there are many conditions that disturb or distress people—polluted air, unsafe workplaces, earthquakes and hurricanes, too much or too little rain, the rising cost of medical care, the poor academic performance of high school students, too many handguns, too few "dedicated" public officials, or no prayers in the public schools, for example. All disturbing conditions do not automatically become problems; some of them may be accepted as trivial, appropriate, inevitable, or beyond the control of government.

Usually there is not a single agreed-on definition of a problem. Indeed, political struggle often occurs over defining the problem because how the problem is defined helps determine what sort of action is appropriate. If access to transportation for people with disabilities is defined as a transportation problem, then an acceptable solution is to provide the people with transportation by adapting the regular transportation system or by establishing other means of transport, such as a special van service. If access to transportation is defined as a civil rights problem, however, then people with disabilities are entitled to equal access to the regular transportation system. The solution to the problem defined as a civil rights problem might require extensive and expensive alterations to make *all* public transport accessible to people with disabilities. After some wavering between these definitions in the 1980s the national government appeared to be moving toward the transportation view of the problem. But congressional passage of the Americans with Disabilities Act forced local governments to take a civil rights perspective when they were compelled to provide accessible transportation to the elderly and to all people with disabilities.

Problems differ not only in terms of how they are defined but also in terms of their tractability, that is, in terms of how easy they are to ameliorate or resolve. For instance, problems that affect large numbers of people or require widespread behavioral changes are more difficult to resolve. The Voting Rights Act of 1965, intended to ensure equal voting rights for African Americans, was easier to implement than was policy requiring desegregation of public schools. Only a small number of voting registrars were directly affected in the first instance; vast numbers of school officials, students, and parents were affected by school desegregation. Tangible problems, such as low incomes or potholes in streets often are more amenable to solutions than are more intangible problems, such as racism or sexism.

One additional point needs to be made. Public policies are frequently viewed as problems or the causes of problems. Thus, for some people, gun control legislation is a solution to the handgun problem. To the National Rifle Association (NRA), however, any laws that restrict gun ownership are a problem because of the NRA's view that such laws inappropriately restrict an individual's right to keep and bear arms. To conservatives, overly generous welfare programs are a problem, whereas for many liberals laws restricting the right to abortion fall into the problem category.

Agenda Setting

Once a problem is recognized and defined, it must be brought to the attention of public officials and it must secure a place on an agenda.

An **agenda** is a set of problems to which policy-makers believe they should be attentive. Professors Roger W. Cobb and Charles D. Elder have identified two basic agenda types: the **systemic agenda** and the governmental or institutional agenda.[2] The systemic agenda is essentially a discussion agenda; it comprises "all issues that are commonly perceived by the members of the political community as meriting public attention and as involving matters within the legitimate jurisdiction" of governments.[3] Every political community—national, state, and local—has a systemic agenda.

agenda A set of problems to which policy makers believe they should be attentive.

systemic agenda All public issues that are viewed as requiring governmental attention; a discussion agenda.

governmental agenda The changing list of issues to which governments believe they should address themselves.

institutional agenda The problems to which legislators or other public officials feel obliged to devote active and serious attention.

agenda setting The constant process of forming the list of issues to be addressed by government.

A **governmental** or **institutional agenda** includes only problems to which legislators or other public officials feel obliged to devote active and serious attention. Not all the problems that attract the attention of officials are likely to have been widely discussed by the general public, or even the "attentive" public—those who follow certain issues closely. Acid rain was a widely discussed public problem in the 1980s that was addressed by the Clean Air Act of 1990, but there was little public awareness of the Pollution Prevention Act, also adopted in 1990. This Act set priorities for pollution control programs in an attempt to improve their effectiveness.

It is useful to think of **agenda setting** as a competitive process. Congress, for instance, does not have the time or resources to take on all the problems and issues it is called on to handle. Whether because of their influence, skill in developing political support, or presentation of more attractive issues, some players are more successful than others in steering items onto the agenda. Chance plays a small role in agenda setting, except in cases of accidents or natural disasters.

Policy Formulation

policy formulation The crafting of appropriate and acceptable proposed courses of action to ameliorate or resolve public problems.

Policy formulation involves the crafting of appropriate and acceptable proposed courses of action to ameliorate or resolve public problems. It has both political and technical components. The political aspect of policy formulation encompasses determining generally what should be done to reduce acid rain, for example—whether standard setting and enforcement or emissions testing should be used. The technical facet involves correctly stating in specific language what one wants to authorize or accomplish, so as to adequately guide those who implement policy and to prevent distortion of legislative intent.

Policy formulation may be undertaken by various players in the policy process—the president and his aides, agency officials, specially appointed task forces and commissions, interest groups, private research organizations (or "think tanks"), and legislators and their staffs. The Bush administration's version of the Clean Air Act of 1990, for example, was drafted by White House aides working with officials in the Environmental Protection Agency. In Congress, professional aides played a major role in drafting the detailed provisions of the law. Several competing alternatives may be formulated to address a problem, as is the case concerning calls for reform of the health care system.

The people engaged in formulation are usually looking down the road toward policy adoption. Particular provisions may be included or excluded from a proposal in an attempt to enhance its likelihood of adoption. To the extent that formulators think in this strategic manner, the formulation and adoption stages of the policy process often become muddled. Political feasibility is always on the mind of the wise policy formulators; they are more interested in getting action on a problem than in creating political issues.

Policy Adoption

policy adoption The approval of a policy proposal by the people with requisite authority, such as a legislature.

Policy adoption involves the approval of a policy proposal by the people with requisite authority, such as a legislature or chief executive. This approval gives the policy legal force. Because most public policies in the United States are based on legislation, policy adoption frequently requires the building of majority coalitions necessary to secure the enactment of legislation.

In Chapter 6, we discuss how power is diffused in Congress and how the legislative process comprises a number of roadblocks or obstacles—House subcommittee, House Committee, House Rules Committee, and so on—that a bill must successfully navigate before it becomes law. A majority is needed to clear a bill through each of these obstacles; hence, not one majority, but a series of majorities are needed for congressional policy adoption. To secure the needed votes, a bill may be watered down or modified at each of these decision points. Or, the bill may fail to win a majority at one of them and die, at least for the time being.

Not all policy adoption necessitates the forming of majority coalitions. Presidential decision making on foreign affairs, military actions, and other matters is often a one-man affair. Although the president has many aides and advisers and is bombarded with much information and advice, the power of final decision rests with him. Ultimately, too, it is the president who decides whether to veto a bill passed by Congress. President Clinton's decision not to intervene militarily in 1993 in Bosnia, for example, was ultimately his responsibility.

Budgeting

Most policies require money in order to be carried out; some policies, such as those involving income security, essentially involve the transfer of money from taxpayers to the government and back to individual beneficiaries. Funding for most policies and agencies is provided through the budgetary process. Whether a policy is well funded or poorly funded has a significant effect on its scope, impact, and effectiveness.

A policy can be nullified by an absence of funding or refusal to fund, which was the fate of the Noise Control Act. In 1981, the Reagan administration decided not to seek funds for the Office of Noise Abatement and Control, the unit within EPA that enforced the Act. Because Congress followed the president's lead, this decision ended implementation of noise control policy.

Other policies or programs often suffer from inadequate funding. Thus, the Occupational Safety and Health Administration (OSHA) can afford to inspect only a small fraction of the workplaces within its jurisdiction annually. Similarly, the Department of Housing and Urban Development has funds sufficient to provide rent subsidies only to approximately 20 percent of the eligible low-income families.

The budgetary process also gives the president and the Congress an opportunity to review the government's many policies and programs, to inquire into their administration, to appraise their value and effectiveness, and to exercise some influence on their conduct. All of the government's hundreds of programs are not fully examined every year. But, over a period of several years, most programs come under scrutiny. Some agencies, moreover, may come under sharp attack and experience cutbacks and restraints. In recent years, for example, conservatives in Congress have used the budget as a venue for attacking the activities of the National Endowment for the Arts (NEA). Charging that some of the art projects funded by the Endowment are obscene or pornographic, they have sought to reduce funding for the NEA. Their actions have apparently made NEA officials more cautious and circumspect in the funding of art projects.

Policy Implementation

Most public policies are carried out or implemented primarily by administrative agencies (see Chapter 8). Some, however, are enforced in other ways. Product liability and product dating are two examples. Product liability laws are usually enforced by lawsuits initiated in the courts by injured consumers or their survivors. In contrast, state product-dating laws are implemented more by voluntary compliance when grocers take out-of-date products off their shelves or by consumers when they choose not to buy products af-

policy implementation The process of carrying out public policy through governmental agencies and the courts.

ter the use dates stamped on them. The courts also get involved in **policy implementation** when they are called on to interpret the meaning of legislation, review the legality of agency rules and actions, and determine whether the administration of institutions such as prisons and mental hospitals conforms to legal and constitutional standards.

Administrative agencies may be authorized to use a number of different techniques to implement the public policies within their jurisdictions. These techniques can be categorized as authority, incentive, capacity, and hortatory techniques, depending on the behavioral assumptions on which they are based.[4]

Authoritative techniques for policy implementation rest on the notion that people's actions must be directed or restrained by government in order to prevent or eliminate activities or products that are unsafe, unfair, evil, or immoral. Thus, people who drive while intoxicated can, by law, have their licenses revoked. On the federal level, consumer products must meet certain safety regulations and radio stations can have their licenses revoked if they broadcast obscenities.

Incentives for policy implementation are based on the assumption that people are utility maximizers who act in their own best interest and must be provided with payoffs or financial inducements to get them to comply with public policies. Tax deductions may be given to encourage charitable giving, or grants awarded to companies for the installation of pollution control equipment. Subsidies given to farmers make their production (or nonproduction) of wheat, cotton, and other commodities more profitable. Conversely, sanctions such as high taxes may be adopted to discourage the purchase and use of such products as tobacco or liquor, and pollution fees may be levied to reduce the discharge of pollutants by making this action more costly to businesses.

Capacity techniques provide persons with information, education, training, or resources that will enable them to undertake desired activities. The assumption underlying the provision of these techniques is that people have the incentive or desire to do what is right but lack the capacity to act accordingly. Job-training may enable able-bodied people to find employment, and accurate information on interest rates will enable people to protect themselves against interest-rate gouging. Financial assistance can help the needy acquire better housing and warmer winter coats and perhaps lead more comfortable lives.

Hortatory techniques encourage people to comply with policy by appealing to peoples' "better instincts" in an effort to get them to act in desired ways. In this instance, the policy implementors assume that people decide how to act on the basis of their personal values and beliefs on matters such as right and wrong, equality, and justice. In the mid-1960s and late 1970s, the Johnson and Carter administrations, respectively, instituted voluntary (i.e., there were no "punishments" for noncompliance) wage and price control programs to control inflation. Presidential appeals were made to individuals, labor unions, and businesses to avoid inflation-causing behavior. Hortatory techniques also include the use of highway signs that tell us "Don't Be a Litterbug" and "Don't Mess with Texas" to discourage littering. And slogans such as "Only You Can Prevent Forest Fires" are meant to encourage compliance with fire and safety regulations in national parks and forests.

The capacity of agencies to administer public policies effectively depends partly on whether the agencies are authorized to use appropriate implementation techniques. Many other factors also come into play, including the clarity and consistency of the policies' statutory mandates, adequacy of funding, political support, and the will and skill of agency personnel. There is no easy formula that will guarantee successful policy implementation; in actuality, many policies only partially achieve their goals.

Policy Evaluation

Essentially, practitioners of **policy evaluation** are concerned with determining whether a policy is accomplishing its goals or, perhaps, anything at all. They may also try to determine whether a policy is being fairly or efficiently administered. In the case of welfare programs, for instance, uncovering evidence of "waste, fraud, or abuse" in their administration has often been of more interest to official evaluators than whether the programs are meeting the needs of the poor.

policy evaluation The process of determining whether a course of action is achieving its intended goals.

Policy evaluation may be engaged in by a variety of players: congressional committees, through investigations and other oversight activities; presidential commissions; administrative agencies themselves; university researchers; private research organizations such as the Brookings Institution and the American Enterprise Institute; and the General Accounting Office (GAO). The GAO, for example, originally created in 1921, is an important evaluator of public policies. Every year the GAO undertakes hundreds of studies of government agencies and programs either at the request of members of Congress or on its own initiative.

Evaluation research and studies can stimulate attempts to modify or terminate policies and thus restart the policy process. Legislators and administrators may formulate and advocate amendments designed to correct revealed problems or shortcomings in a policy.

Social Welfare Policy

Social welfare policy is a term for any of the broad and varied range of government policies designed to provide people with protection against want and deprivation, to improve their health and physical well-being, to provide educational and employment training opportunities, and otherwise to enable them to lead more satisfactory, meaningful, and productive lives. In a nutshell, social welfare policies are intended to enhance the quality of life. They benefit all segments of society, but they are especially helpful for the less fortunate members, who often find it more difficult to provide for themselves and their families. More specifically, social welfare policies focus on such matters as public education, income security, medical care, sanitation and disease prevention, public housing, employment training, children's protective services, and improvements in human nutrition.

Social welfare policy Governmental program designed to enhance an individual's quality of life.

State and local governments in the United States have long operated public schools and provided assistance to the needy members of society, though often in a tight-fisted and mean-spirited fashion. The twentieth century, however, has witnessed a great expansion in social welfare policies and spending for their support at all levels of government—local, state, and national—although the United States has tended to act more cautiously than most other democracies in this arena (see Figure 2). Universal, compulsory public education became firmly established in the early decades of the century. Public health, income security, and other social welfare programs multiplied and expanded. And, since the 1930s (as discussed in Chapter 3), the national government has become a major, and sometimes dominating, participant in this policy area, which was once largely the domain of the state and local governments.

Public Education

Historically, public education was the province of the state and local governments. From the founding of the United States through the nineteenth century, local govern-

FIGURE 2

Enactment of National Social
Programs in Ten Nations

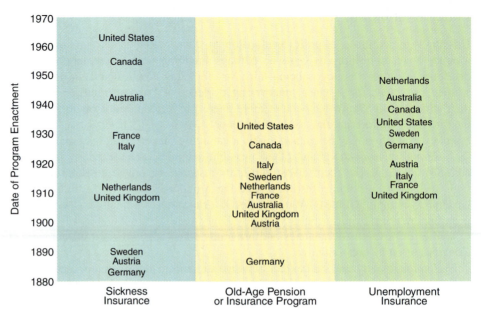

Source: D. B. Robertson and D. R. Judd, *The Development of American Public Policy* (Glenview,IL:
Scott, Foresman, 1989), p. 59.

FIGURE 3

Sources of Public School
Spending, 1990

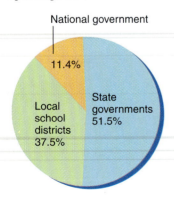

Source: *Statistical Abstract of the
United States, 1993.* (Washington,
DC: U.S. Government Printing Office,
1993), p. 150.

ments bore most of the responsibility for public education. In the twentieth century the
state governments have continually expanded their involvement until, at present, they
are the largest source of funding for the public schools. The states have also created an
extensive legal framework for local school systems; they have exerted control over
such aspects of school administration as curricula, textbook selection, graduation requirements, eligibility for extracurricular activity, and teacher certification and competence. Nonetheless, local independent school districts, governed by appointed or
elected boards, continue to exercise much control over the daily operation of the public schools. The school districts are responsible, for example, for constructing and
maintaining school buildings, hiring teachers, transporting students, operating school
lunch programs, and designing educational programs.

In 1990, national, state, and local governments in the United States spent nearly
$273 billion on public (elementary and secondary) education (see Figure 3). Of this
amount, 51.5 percent came from the state governments, 37.5 percent from local school
districts, and 11.4 percent from the national government. Private citizens and parochial
and private schools spent another $103 billion. There is much variation among states,
and among school districts within states, on educational expenditures, as measured by
spending on a per-student basis. Some states spend two or three times as much as other
states according to this measure. Although federal dollars are the smallest share of
public school funding, these dollars are still vital to school systems that are usually financially strapped and sometimes in dire need of additional revenue.

The revenues raised by most local school districts come almost entirely from property taxes. Because of substantial differences among districts in the value of the tax-
able property within their boundaries, some communities are able to generate much
more revenue than others, even with lower tax rates. This variation is then reflected in
spending disparities among schools when measured on a per-pupil basis. Within a

given state some districts may spend more than twice as much per pupil as others. Many parents, educators, and public officials believe that such unequal spending results in significant disparities in the quality of the education that students receive.

Most conflicts concerning the quality of education that a state must provide have been solved through state administrative procedures. In some situations, however, disputes have ended up in the U.S. Supreme Court. In 1993, for example, the Court ruled that a school district must provide a sign language interpreter for a deaf child attending a Roman Catholic school.[5] In 1994, however, the U.S. Supreme Court ruled that a New York school district had gone too far to accommodate religious needs. The creation of a new school district to educate the special-needs children of the Satmar Hasidim, a strict Jewish sect, was declared to be a violation of the First Amendment's establishment clause.[6]

Since the early 1970s, school finance has been a priority item on the policy agendas in many states. In some states, inequality in expenditures among districts has been held to violate the state constitution. In New Jersey, the state court practically forced the state legislature to adopt an income tax to finance the schools.[7] School finance has been a volatile and vexing issue in many other states. Most people want good schools; paying for good schools, particularly if this requires raising taxes, stirs up much opposition in a time when "no new taxes" is a mantra with wide popular appeal.

Income Security

Income security programs protect people against loss of income because of retirement, disability, unemployment, or death or absence of the family breadwinner. Although cases of total deprivation are now rare, many people are unable to provide a minimally decent standard of living for themselves and their families. They are poor in a relative if not an absolute sense. In 1993 an urban family of four earning $14,350 or less per year was officially below the poverty line. Millions of families do not fare that well.

Income security programs fall into two general categories. Social insurance programs are non-means-based programs that provide cash assistance to qualified beneficiaries. **Means-tested programs** require that people must have incomes below specified levels in order to be eligible for benefits. Benefits of means-tested programs may take the form either of cash assistance or in-kind benefits, such as food stamps.

> **means-tested programs** Programs intended to assist those whose incomes fall below a designated level.

Social Insurance.   Social insurance programs operate in a manner somewhat similar to private automobile or life insurance. Contributions are made to the programs by or on behalf of the prospective beneficiaries, their employers, or both. When a person becomes eligible for benefits, the monies are paid as a matter of right, regardless of how much wealth or unearned income (for example, from dividends and interest payments) the recipient has. (For Social Security, a limit is imposed on earned income. There is no means test.)

Old Age, Survivors, and Disability Insurance.   This program began as old-age insurance, providing benefits only to retired workers. Its coverage was extended to survivors of covered workers in 1939 and to the permanently disabled in 1956. This is the program customarily called "Social Security." It is not, as many people believe, a pension program that collects contributions from workers, invests them, and then returns them with interest to beneficiaries. In essence, as the program actually operates, the current generation of workers pays taxes to provide benefits for the previous generation. Presently, a payroll tax of 7.5 percent on the first $60,600 of wages or salaries is paid by the employee and another 7.5 percent is paid by the employer into the Social Security trust fund. Nearly all employees and most of the self-employed (who pay a 12.8 percent tax) are now covered by the Social Security program. People earning less money pay a greater share of their income into the Social Security program than do workers earning more.

People are eligible to receive retirement benefits at age sixty-five. Individuals who opt to retire earlier, at age sixty-two, receive a reduced benefit. In the early 1990s the average retired worker received $674 a month. The maximum benefit in 1994 for a retired worker was $1,147 per month. An additional 50 percent was paid if the worker had a spouse. For many retired people, Social Security payments are their primary source of income; were it not for Social Security they would likely be living in poverty. However, eligible people are entitled to Social Security benefits regardless of how much *unearned* income (e.g., dividends and interest payments) they also receive. Until they reach the age of seventy, there is a limit of $11,160 on the annual *earned* income they can receive without a reduction in their benefits. A dollar of benefits is lost for every three dollars by which one exceeds that limit.

Expenditures for Social Security have greatly increased during the last couple of decades because the number of beneficiaries is growing, they are living longer, and benefit levels are rising. More than forty million people, including some three million workers with disabilities, currently receive Social Security benefits. Total program expenditures were $304 billion in 1993, making Social Security by far the national government's largest entitlement program (see Figure 4, p. 541).

Unemployment Insurance. Financed by a payroll tax paid by employers, the unemployment insurance program pays benefits to covered workers who are unemployed through no fault of their own; for example, by being laid off during a recession. The Social Security Act provided that if a state set up a comparable program and levied a payroll tax for its support, most of the federal tax would be forgiven (not collected). The states were thus accorded a choice—either they could set up and administer an acceptable unemployment program, or they could let the national government handle the matter. Within a short period of time all of the states had established their own programs.

Unemployment insurance covers employers of four or more persons, but not part-time or occasional workers. Benefits are paid to unemployed workers who have neither been fired nor quit their jobs and who are willing and able to accept suitable employment. The fifty state unemployment programs differ considerably in levels of benefits, length of benefit payment, and eligibility for benefits. Average weekly benefit payments, for example, range from $222 in Massachusetts and $212 in Michigan to $116 in Mississippi and $111 in Louisiana. The most generous programs exist in the northern industrial states, where labor unions are more powerful and influence the nature of these programs. Nationwide, only about half of the people counted as unemployed at any given time will be receiving benefits.

Means-Tested Programs. Means-tested income security programs are intended to help the needy, that is, persons or families whose incomes fall below specified levels, such as a percentage of the official poverty line. Included in this category are the Supplementary Security Income (SSI), Aid to Families with Dependent Children (AFDC), and Food Stamp programs.

Supplementary Security Income. This program began under the Social Security Act as a categorical grant-in-aid program to aid the needy aged or blind. Financed jointly by

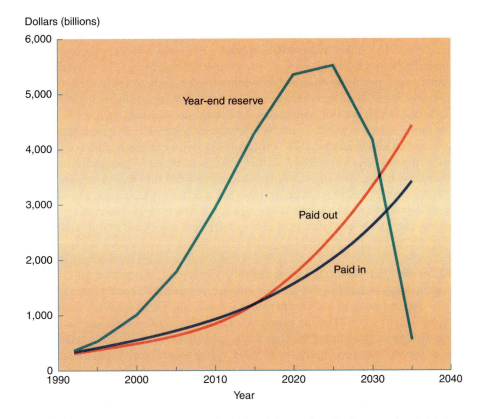

Dollars (billions)

Year-end reserve

Paid out

Paid in

FIGURE 4

Social Security Receipts, Spending, and Reserve Estimates, 1992–2035

Note: The combined OASI and DI Trust Funds (Social Security) are estimated to become exhausted during 2035 under alternative II projections. For details see source.

Source: U.S. Congress, House, House Committee on Ways and Means, "1992 Report of The Board of Trustees of the Federal Old-Age and Survivors Insurance and Disability Insurance Trust Funds," 102d Cong., 2d sess., April 2, 1992, p. 182.

the national and state governments from general revenues, the states played a major role in determining standards of eligibility and benefit levels. In 1950 Congress adopted legislation extending coverage to people who were permanently and totally disabled and could demonstrate a need for assistance.

With the support of the Nixon administration, Congress converted these programs into the Supplementary Security Income (SSI) programs in 1974. Primary funding for SSI is provided by the national government, which prescribes benefit levels that are uniform throughout the nation. To be eligible, beneficiaries can own only a limited amount of possessions. Maximum monthly payments for 1994 were $446 for an individual and $669 for a couple. The states may choose to supplement the federal benefits, and forty-six states do. This program generates little controversy as the modest benefits go to people who obviously cannot provide for themselves.

Aid to Families with Dependent Children (AFDC). In the early 1930s nearly all of the states had programs of cash assistance for mothers (mostly widows) with dependent children under the Social Security Act. A federal grant-in-aid program called Aid to Dependent Children was initiated to supplement the assistance provided by the states. The program was renamed Aid to Families with Dependent Children (AFDC) in 1950, when coverage was expanded to include not only dependent children but also mothers themselves or other adults with whom dependent children were living.

Initially, AFDC was a small program because there were few unmarried mothers in 1935. Most mothers of covered dependents were widows. Much has changed since this program began. The AFDC rolls have expanded greatly since 1960 because of the increasing numbers of children born to unwed mothers, the growing divorce rate, and the migration of poor people to cities, where they are more likely to apply for and be provided benefits. Now, most families covered by the AFDC program are headed by single mothers. Assistance for needy families with unemployed fathers was made optional for the states in 1962; many states opted not to provide this coverage.

Because of its clientele, the AFDC program is the focus of much controversy and is frequently stigmatized as "welfare." Critics claim that it encourages promiscuity and out-of-wedlock births, that it encourages dependency, and that it is creating a permanent class of welfare families. There is, however, a lack of research and little hard evidence to document these claims fully. Much effort has been expended by public officials to restrict the availability of aid, to ferret out fraud and abuse, and to hold down the AFDC program's cost.

Earned Income Tax Credit Program (EITC). Designed to help the working poor, this program was created in 1975 at the insistence of Senator Russell Long (D-La.). It helps the working poor by subsidizing their wages, and it also provides an incentive for people to go to work. Drawing extensive support from both Democrats and Republicans in Congress, the Earned Income Tax Credit (EITC) is frequently described as being "pro-work and pro-family." The EITC program has been expanded several times, most recently in 1993 at the request of the Clinton administration.

When the latest version of EITC is fully phased in, working-poor families with two or more children will receive a $4 tax credit for every $10 of the first $8,425 that they earn. The maximum EITC is $3,370. When a family's income reaches $11,000, the credit will begin to be reduced and will be totally eliminated at an income level of $27,000. Lesser tax credits are available to one-child families and single workers. It is expected that in 1996 around nineteen million families will qualify for the tax credit at a total cost of $25 billion. The EITC program is administered by the Internal Revenue Service through the income tax system.

Food Stamp Program. Initially, recipients of food stamps had to make a cash payment for them, but this practice was halted by the Carter Administration in 1977. The program gradually was extended to all counties in each state in the nation. Benefiting poor and low-income families, the program has helped to combat hunger and reduce malnutrition. Spending for the program was reduced somewhat in the early years of the Reagan administration, but its growth has since resumed. Food stamps were provided to more than thirteen million beneficiaries in 1994 at a cost of $24 billion, and they are expected to increase by three billion people over the next five years.

Several other food programs targeted at the needy are also operated by the national government. These programs include a state child nutrition program; a special nutritional program for women, infants, and children (WIC); a school breakfast and lunch program; and an emergency food assistance program. These programs cost the national government several billions of dollars a year.

Medical Care

Governments in the United States have long been active in the health field. Local governments began to establish public health departments in the first half of the nineteenth

century and were followed by state health departments in the second half. As knowledge of the bacteriological causes of diseases and human ailments and of the adverse
effects of urbanization and industrialization expanded in the late nineteenth and early
twentieth centuries, significant advances were made in improving public health. Public
sanitation and clean water programs, pasteurization of milk, immunization programs,
and other health activities reduced the incidence of infectious and communicable diseases. The increase in life expectancy at birth in the United States from forty-seven
years in 1900 to seventy-five years in 1990 is mostly due to public health programs.

Most medical research currently is financed by the national government, primarily
through the National Institutes of Health (NIH). The National Cancer Institute, the National Heart, Lung, and Blood Institute, The National Institute of Allergy and Infectious Diseases, and the other NIH institutes and centers expend more than $10 billion
annually on biomedical research. The research is conducted both by NIH scientists and
by scientists at universities, medical schools, and other research centers receiving NIH
research grants.

In recent years national government spending for AIDS research has expanded
greatly, exceeding a billion-and-a-half dollars in 1993. In the early 1980s, however,
many public officials were disinclined to do much on the AIDS problem, regarding it
as a condition afflicting a narrow segment of the population. In part, at least, the decision to hold back on funding AIDS research reflected conservative, anti-homosexual
sentiments.[8] Research scientists and advocates for the gay community, however, were
able to convince policy makers that AIDS constituted a dire public health problem and
that a major governmental response was required. Some critics now assert that too
large a share (around one-sixth) of medical research dollars is being channeled into
AIDS research, while others still believe that not enough is being done.

A different situation exists in government programs that assist individuals in paying
the costs of their own medical care. In helping people defray their medical costs, the
United States continues to provide less assistance than other western industrial democracies as shown in Figure 5, "Rising Medicare and Medicaid Costs"; all of them have
long had some sort of national health insurance program (see Table 1, p. 545).

Medicare, which covers persons receiving Social Security benefits, is administered
by the Health Care Financing Administration in the Department of Health and Human
Services. Medicare coverage is divided into two parts, called Parts A and B. Benefits
under Part A come to all Americans automatically at age sixty-five when they qualify
for Social Security. Part A covers hospitalization, some skilled nursing care, and home
health services. In 1994 individuals had to pay $696 in medical bills before they were
eligible for Part A benefits. Medicare is financed by a payroll tax of 1.45 percent paid
each by both employees and employers on the total amount of one's wages or salary.

> **Medicare** The federal program established in the Johnson administration that provides medical care to elderly Social Security recipients.

Part B, which is optional, covers payment of physicians' services, outpatient and diagnostic services, x-rays, and some other items not covered by Part A. Excluded from
coverage are prescription drugs, eyeglasses, hearing aids, and dentures. This portion of
the Medicare program is financed partly by monthly payments from beneficiaries and
partly by general tax revenues. Almost all of the eligible people have opted for Part B
coverage, which in 1994 cost $41.10 a month.

Enacted into law at the same time as Medicare, the **Medicaid** program provides
comprehensive health care, including hospitalization, physicians' services, prescription drugs, and long-term nursing home care (unlike Medicare). This care is provided
for all persons who qualify as needy under AFDC and SSI.

> **Medicaid** An expansion of Medicare, this program subsidizes medical care for the poor.

In 1986 Congress acted to provide Medicaid coverage for pregnant women and for
children under age six in families with incomes of less than 133 percent of the official

F I G U R E   5

Rising Medicare and
Medicaid Costs

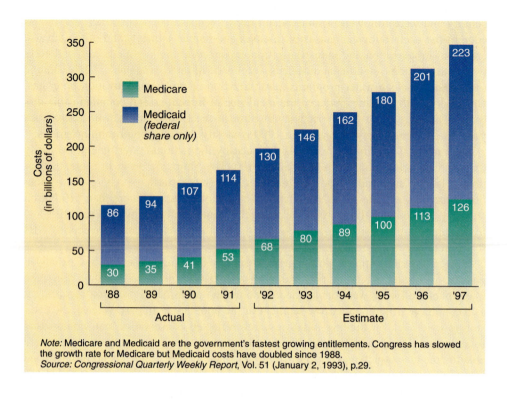

Note: Medicare and Medicaid are the government's fastest growing entitlements. Congress has slowed
the growth rate for Medicare but Medicaid costs have doubled since 1988.
Source: Congressional Quarterly Weekly Report, Vol. 51 (January 2, 1993), p.29.

poverty level. The states were also accorded the option of extending coverage to all
pregnant women and to all children under one year of age in families with incomes below 185 percent of the poverty level. By 1993, twenty-nine of the states had chosen to
provide this coverage.

Table 1 ◆ Government Expenditures as a Percent of Total Health Expenditures, 1991, by Country			
United States	43.9%	Italy	81.1%
Australia	62.9	Japan	70.8
Austria	68.8	Luxembourg	92.8
Belgium	83.4	Netherlands	74.7
Canada	74.7	New Zealand	83.6
Denmark	85.2	Norway	98.4
Finland	79.0	Portugal	72.4
France	78.8	Spain	79.9
Germany (West)	75.0	Sweden	92.5
Greece	82.2	Switzerland	67.5
Iceland	88.2	Turkey	27.3
Ireland	82.2	United Kingdom	89.6

Source: Statistical Abstract of the United States 1993 (Washington, D.C.: Government Printing
Office, 1993), p. 849.

Medicaid covered 32.6 million people in 1992. Most of the benefits paid out under the program went to elderly people. Approximately one-seventh of the benefits went to children under the AFDC program.

Vastly exceeding early estimates, the costs of Medicare and Medicaid have been major contributors to the ballooning costs of health care. In 1993 national expenditures for Medicare were $143 billion and for Medicaid, $76 billion (see Table 2 below). The states collectively spent another $50 billion on Medicaid. Barring any changes, costs of these programs are expected to rise sharply over the next decade (see Figure 5, p. 544).

Total health care expenditures in the United States have also soared in recent decades, growing from $27.1 billion in 1960 to $250.1 billion in 1980, to $838.5 billion in 1992.[9] In 1992 health care costs comprised 14 percent of the gross domestic product. The national government's health spending for Medicare, Medicaid, medical research, and other purposes amounted to 40 percent of total health spending.

A number of factors have contributed to the high and rising costs of health care. First, more people are living longer and are requiring costly and extensive care in their declining years. Second, the range and sophistication of diagnostic practices and therapeutic treatments, which are often quite expensive, have increased. Third, the expansion of private health insurance, along with Medicare and Medicaid, has reduced the direct costs of health care to most people and increased the demand for services. More people, in short, can afford needed care. They may also be less aware of the costs of care. Fourth, the costs of health care have also increased because of its higher quality and because labor costs have outpaced productivity in the provision of hospital care.[10] Fifth, U.S. medicine focuses less on preventing illnesses and more on curing them, which is more costly.

Public opinion polls indicate that the major cause of Americans' dissatisfaction with the health care system is its cost. While most people indicate that they are satisfied with the quality of health care services provided by physicians and hospitals, a substantial majority express dissatisfaction over the costs of health care.[11] There is, as a consequence, a strong belief in the need to improve the nation's health care system, and this task is viewed as appropriate for the government to handle.

Table 2 ◆ Entitlements and Projections

THE BIGGEST ENTITLEMENTS IN 1993 (IN BILLIONS)		PROJECTIONS FOR 1999 (IN BILLIONS)	
1. Social Security	$302	1. Social Security	$408
2. Medicare	143	2. Medicare	264
3. Medicaid	76	3. Medicaid	151
4. Federal civilian retirement	39	4. Federal civilian retirement	51
5. Unemployment compensation	35	5. Supplemental Security Income	35
6. Military retirement	26	6. Military retirement	35
7. Food stamps	25	7. Food stamps	30
8. Supplemental Security Income	21	8. Unemployment compensation	26
9. Veterans' benefits	17	9. Earned Income Tax Credit	22
10. Farm price supports	16	10. Family support	20

Source: Congressional Budget Office and *The Atlanta Journal Constitution,* February 7, 1994, p. A7.

Economic Policy

To many people politics and economics seem to be separate and distinct spheres of activity. Economics is concerned with the production, distribution, and exchange of goods and services. Economic decisions, which are made primarily through markets governed by prices, involve action by private consumers, workers, and firms pursuing their self-interest. Politics, in comparison, centers on government and the development of policies by which a people are governed. Political decisions in a democracy are made by majorities in elections and legislatures, and by bureaucrats who service power legislatively delegated to them. Although politics is by no means devoid of self-interested behavior, its basic concern is promotion of the broader public interest.

In actuality, government and the economy in the United States have always been closely intertwined. The U.S. economic system would be unable to survive and thrive in the absence of such government activities as the definition and protection of property rights, the maintenance of law and order, the enforcement of contracts, the provision of a common monetary system, and granting of corporate charters, the issuance of patents and copyrights, and the adoption of legislation to handle bankruptcy. This core of government activities, many of which are the responsibility of the state governments, provide the foundation for the U.S. capitalist (or free enterprise) economy.

Stabilizing the Economy

Until the early 1930s the prevailing view in the United States was that the country's economy was controlled by natural economic laws that could be disrupted but not improved on by the government. Fluctuations in the economy were accepted with a sense of inevitability. At the time, it was thought that the best things the government could do if a depression struck would be to increase taxes, cut spending, and balance the budget, or the situation might be made worse by a lack of public confidence in the government's financial condition. This was the tack taken by Herbert Hoover and, for a time, by Franklin D. Roosevelt during the early years of the Great Depression.

The policy change represented by the Employment Act of 1946, which committed the government to maintaining "maximum employment, production and purchasing power," stemmed from a confluence of several factors.[12] First, the massive scale and persistence of the Great Depression refuted the notion that depressions were "self-correcting." Second, new techniques of economic measurement and analysis enabled people to better understand the operation of the economy.

Third, the ideas of the famed English economist, John Maynard Keynes, had gained acceptance and influence. In his *General Theory of Employment, Interests, and Money* (1936) Keynes argued that deficit spending by a government could supplement the total or aggregate demand for goods and services. Government spending would offset a decline in private spending and thus help maintain high levels of spending, production, and employment. During the New Deal the national government engaged in limited deficit spending, which was sometimes referred to as "pump-priming," but it was not sufficient to bring economic recovery. Fourth, World War II brought with it a tremendous increase in government spending and large budget deficits. The economy expanded, production rose, and unemployment fell below 2 percent. The interaction of these factors contributed to the national government's assuming responsibility for maintaining economic stability.

Economic stability can be defined as a situation in which there is economic growth and a rising national income along with high employment and steadiness in the general level of prices. Conversely, economic instability may involve inflation or recession. **Inflation** occurs when there is too much demand for the available supply of goods and services, so that general price levels rise as buyers compete for the available supply. Prices may also rise if large corporations and unions have sufficient economic power to push prices and wages above competitive levels. A **recession** involves a decline in the economy. Investment sags, production falls off, and unemployment increases.

The primary means available to government to maintain economic stability or, if one prefers, to combat instability, are monetary and fiscal policy. Our attention now turns to a discussion of these concepts.

Monetary Policy. **Monetary policy,** which is a form of macroeconomic regulation, involves regulating a nation's money supply and interest rates. A modern industrial economy operates on the basis of money, which is the medium through which nearly all income and all buying and selling transactions take place. When money is mentioned, most of us think of currency and coins, items we can feel, count, and carry in our pockets. But currency and coins are only a small portion of the nation's money supply. The term "money" also includes bank deposits and other financial assets. The Federal Reserve Board has three definitions of **money** based on this broader conception. *M1* (the first definition) includes currency, checking accounts, travelers checks, NOW accounts, and other checkable deposits. *M2* includes all of *M1* plus savings and small time deposits and money market account balances. *M3* includes *M2* plus large time deposits and institutional money market fund balances. The *M2* definition is of the most concern to the Federal Reserve Board.

The Federal Reserve Board has responsibility for the formation and implementation of monetary policy because of its ability to control the credit-creating and lending activities of the nation's banks. When individuals and corporations deposit their money in financial institutions such as commercial banks (which accept deposits and make loans) and savings and loan associations, these deposits serve as the basis for loans to borrowers. In effect, the loaning of money creates new deposits or financial liabilities—new money that did not previously exist. But, we are getting ahead of our story. A look at the Federal Reserve System and its authority is needed at this point.

The Federal Reserve System. Created in 1913 to adjust the money supply to the needs of agriculture, commerce, and industry, the Federal Reserve System comprises the Federal Reserve Board (FRB) (formally, the Board of Governors of the Federal Reserve System; informally, the "Fed"), the Federal Open Market Committee, and the twelve Federal Reserve Banks in regions throughout the country (see Figure 6, p. 548). The Fed represents a mixture of private interests and governmental authority.

The seven members of the Federal Reserve Board, who direct the system, are appointed by the president for fourteen-year, overlapping terms with the approval of the Senate. A member can be removed from office by the president for stated causes, but this has never occurred. One board member is designated by the president to serve as chair for a four-year term, which runs from the midpoint of one presidential term to the midpoint of the next to ensure economic stability during a change of administrations. Formally, the FRB has much independence from the executive branch, ostensibly so that monetary policy will not be influenced by political considerations. Defenders of the FRB's independent position assert that monetary policy is too important, complex, and technical to be under the day-to-day control of elected public offi-

economic stability A situation in which there is economic growth, rising national income, high employment, and steadiness in the general level of prices.

inflation A rise in the general price levels of an economy.

recession A short-term decline in the economy that occurs as investment sags, production falls off, and unemployment increases.

monetary policy A form of government regulation in which the nation's money supply and interest rates are controlled.

money A system of exchange for goods and services that includes currency, coins, and bank deposits.

FIGURE 6
Inside the Federal Reserve System

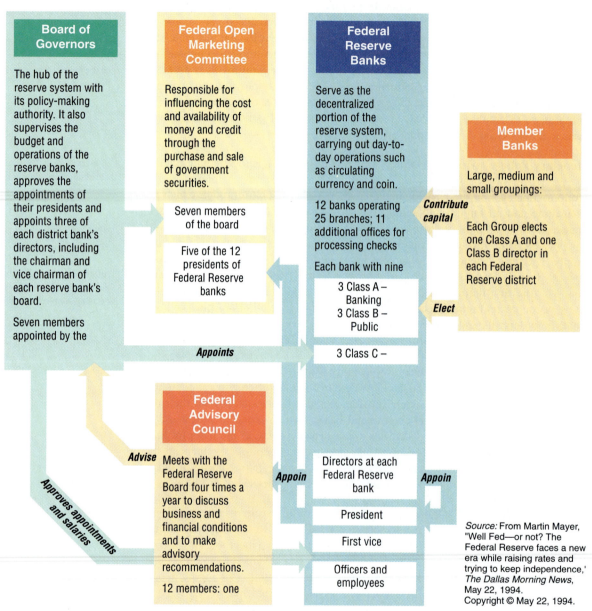

Board of Governors

The hub of the reserve system with its policy-making authority. It also supervises the budget and operations of the reserve banks, approves the appointments of their presidents and appoints three of each district bank's directors, including the chairman and vice chairman of each reserve bank's board.

Seven members appointed by the

Federal Open Marketing Committee

Responsible for influencing the cost and availability of money and credit through the purchase and sale of government securities.

Seven members of the board

Five of the 12 presidents of Federal Reserve banks

Federal Reserve Banks

Serve as the decentralized portion of the reserve system, carrying out day-to-day operations such as circulating currency and coin.

12 banks operating 25 branches; 11 additional offices for processing checks

Each bank with nine

3 Class A – Banking
3 Class B – Public

3 Class C –

Member Banks

Large, medium and small groupings:

Each Group elects one Class A and one Class B director in each Federal Reserve district

Contribute capital

Elect

Appoints

Federal Advisory Council

Advise Meets with the Federal Reserve Board four times a year to discuss business and financial conditions and to make advisory recommendations.

12 members: one

Approves appointments and salaries

Appoin

Directors at each Federal Reserve bank

President

First vice

Officers and employees

Appoin

Source: From Martin Mayer, "Well Fed—or not? The Federal Reserve faces a new era while raising rates and trying to keep independence,' *The Dallas Morning News*, May 22, 1994. Copyright © May 22, 1994.

The Federal Reserve system is the central banking system of the United States. It consists of 12 privately owned regional reserve banks subject to close control by the board of governors in Washington, an agency of the U.S. government. The Federal Reserve banks are not profit-seeking institutions, and they do not deal directly with the general public. They perform services for the U.S. treasury and for deposit institutions—commercial banks, savings banks, savings and loan associations, and credit unions—the operations of which they also regulate. The banks issue the country's paper currency. Through their influence on reserve positions, they control the supply of money and credit.

cials, who might be inclined to make monetary decisions to advance their own short-term political interests (such as being reelected).

At the base of the Federal Reserve System are the twelve Federal Reserve Banks. These are "bankers' banks"; they are formally owned by the Federal Reserve System member banks in each region and they do not do business with the public. A majority of the board of directors of each Federal Reserve Bank is elected by the commercial member banks in its region. The president of a Federal Reserve Bank is selected by its board of directors, not by the president of the United States.

The middle of the Federal Reserve System is occupied by the Federal Open Market Committee (FOMC). This committee consists of twelve members—all seven FRB members, plus five presidents from the Federal Reserve Banks. The representatives from the reserve banks rotate among the twelve regions, except for the New York Federal Reserve Bank. Because of its importance in the financial world, the New York Federal Reserve Bank is always represented on the FOMC.

The primary monetary policy tools are the setting of reserve requirements for member banks, control of the discount, and open market operations. **Reserve requirements** designate the portion of the banks' deposits that must be retained as backing for their loans. Raising the reserve requirement limits the capacity of banks to make new loans; lowering it enables them to expand their loans. Hypothetically, if the reserve requirement is 10 percent, banks can make more loans on a given amount of deposits than they can if the requirement is raised to 15 percent. When the FRB wants to increase the money supply in circulation it can lower the reserve requirements; to reduce the money supply, it can raise the reserve requirement.

The **discount rate** is the rate of interest at which member banks can borrow money from their regional Federal Reserve Bank when they need additional reserves to support their loans. Raising the discount rate should discourage borrowing by banks to make loans and, in turn, will make loans more costly to persons wanting to borrow money. Conversely, lowering the discount rate should expand the money supply and encourage borrowing both by member banks and by people wanting money to expand business and for other purposes. The assumption here is that what people do will be directly affected by whether interest rates are higher or lower.

Open market operations involve the buying and selling of government securities by the FRB in the market, that is, wherever government securities are bought and sold. Government securities are interest-bearing bonds that are regularly bought and sold by investors in their quest for profits. When the FRB buys securities in the market, it ultimately pays for them by creating deposits for the sellers in the federal reserve banks. These deposits serve as additional reserves for commercial banks and enable them to expand their loans to borrowers. On the other hand, when the FRB sells government securities in the market, the buyers' payments for them are deducted from commercial banks reserve accounts, reducing these reserves and thus the capacity of banks to lend money to their customers. As a rule of thumb, when the FRB buys securities, it expands the money supply; when the FRB sells securities, it restricts, or "tightens," the money supply. Open market operations are the tools the FRB uses most frequently because of their flexibility and direct impact.

Moral suasion refers to the capacity of the FRB to influence the actions of banks and other members of the financial community by suggestion, exhortation, and informal agreement. Because of its commanding position as a monetary policy maker, much attention and respect are given by the media, economists and market observers to verbal signals about economic trends and conditions emitted by the FRB and its chair.

reserve requirements
Governmental requirement that a portion of member banks' deposits must be retained to back loans made.

discount rate The rate of interest at which member banks can borrow money from their regional Federal Reserve Bank.

open market operations The buying and selling of government securities by the Federal Reserve Bank in the securities market.

How the FRB uses these policy tools depends in part on how they perceive the state of the economy. If inflation appears to be the problem, then the Fed would likely restrict or tighten the money supply. If a recession with rising unemployment appears to threaten the economy, then the FRB would probably act to loosen or expand the money supply in order to stimulate the economy.

Fiscal Policy.   Fiscal policy involves the deliberate use of the national government's taxing and spending policies to influence the overall operation of the economy and maintain economic stability. Fiscal policy is formulated by the president and Congress and is conducted through the federal budget process. The powerful instruments of fiscal policy are budget surpluses and deficits. These are achieved by manipulating the overall or "aggregate" levels of revenue and expenditures.

According to standard fiscal policy theory, at some level of total or aggregate spending, the economy will operate at full employment. Total spending is the sum of consumer spending, private investment spending, and government spending. If consumer and business spending does not create demand sufficient to cause the economy to operate at full employment, then the government should make up the shortfall by increasing spending in excess of revenues. This was essentially what Keynes recommended that the national government should do during the Great Depression. If inflation is the problem confronting policy makers, then government can reduce demand for goods and services by reducing its expenditures and running a budget surplus.[13]

Discretionary fiscal policy involves deliberate decisions by the president and Congress to run budget surpluses or deficits. This can be done by increasing or decreasing spending while holding taxes constant; by increasing or cutting taxes while holding spending stable; or by some combination of changes in tax and expenditure.

Discretionary fiscal policy is so called because public officials must make overt decisions concerning its use. There are also some automatic stabilizers that have been built into the economy, whether intentionally or unintentionally, that operate without decisions by policy makers. These automatic stabilizers "act as buffers when the economy weakens by automatically reducing taxes and increasing government spending."[14] When the economy declines, for example, mandatory spending for such programs as unemployment insurance, food stamps, and Medicaid increases because eligibility for benefits depends on people's income or employment status. The tax system also acts as an automatic stabilizer. When the economy slows down and personal income and corporate profits decline, tax payments fall and help reduce the decline in after-tax incomes that would otherwise occur.[15] Conversely, when the economy revives, taxes begin to take a bigger bite out of incomes and thus help hold down spending. Although the automatic stabilizers are helpful in mitigating economic fluctuations, they are by themselves inadequate to stabilize the economy.

The Budgetary Process

The Budget and Accounting Act of 1921 gave the president authority to prepare an annual budget and submit it to Congress for approval. A staff agency now called the Office of Management and Budget (OMB) was created to assist the president and handle the details of budget preparation (see also Chapter 7). The budget runs for a single fiscal year, now beginning on October 1 of one calendar year and running through September 30 of the following calendar year. The fiscal year takes its name from the calendar year in which it ends; thus, the time period from October 1, 1995, through September 30, 1996, is designated fiscal year (FY) 1996.

The president sends his budget to Congress in January or February of each year. Work on the budget within the executive branch will have begun nine or ten months earlier, however. Acting in accordance with presidential decision on the general structure of the budget, the OMB provides the various departments and agencies with instructions and guidance on presidential priorities to help them in preparing their budget requests. The departments and agencies then proceed to develop their detailed funding requests. Each agency believes in the value and necessity of its set of programs and seeks to expand or at least maintain its budget. The OMB's role, on the other hand, is to put together a budget that reflects the president's preferences and priorities. Consequently, agency budget requests are frequently modified and revised downward by the OMB. Agencies that are aggrieved by OMB reductions may try to appeal these decisions to the president. If this happens, the president usually agrees with the OMB. During the early years of the Reagan administration this traditional "bottom-up" process of preparing the budget, in which the agencies' requests shape the budget, was replaced by a "top-down" process. In "top-down" budgeting, directives from the president and the OMB dominate the budgetary process.[16]

Conflicts often develop between Congress and the president over both the details of the budget and its overall dimensions, such as the size of the deficit or the balance between military and domestic spending. Throughout the 1980s there was conflict between the Democrats in Congress, who favored more domestic spending and less military spending, and President Ronald Reagan and his administration, whose spending preferences leaned in the opposite direction. In 1993 the Clinton administration touched off a titanic partisan political struggle in Congress with its budget deficit-reduction plan involving a combination of spending cuts and tax increases. Drawing almost unanimous opposition from the Republicans in Congress and also from some conservative Democrats, the Clinton proposal was passed by Vice President Albert Gore Jr.'s tie-breaking vote in the Senate and by a margin of two votes in the House.[17] The Clinton administration, moreover, had to make many deals with members of Congress in order to secure the votes needed to adopt its budget proposal.

As with other legislation, appropriations bills passed by Congress need the president's approval to become law. Conventional wisdom once held that appropriations bills were "veto proof" because they provided the funds necessary to keep the government in operation. However, Presidents Richard M. Nixon and Gerald R. Ford both vetoed appropriations bills that they called "budget-busting" and inflationary because more funds were appropriated for some programs than the presidents wanted. These bills were later enacted into law after appropriations were reduced in an effort to meet presidential preferences.

To provide itself with more control over the budget process, Congress initiated and enacted the Budget and Impoundment Control Act of 1974. The Act establishes a budget process that includes setting overall levels of revenues and expenditures, the size of the budget surplus or deficit, and priorities among different "functional" areas (e.g., national defense, transportation, agriculture, foreign aid, and health). New budget committees were established in the House and Senate to perform these tasks. The Congressional Budget Office (CBO), a professional staff of technical experts, was created to assist the budget committees and to provide members of Congress with their own source of budgetary information so they would be more independent of OMB.

The budget committees hold hearings on the president's proposed budget, soliciting advice from the OMB and CBO, executive agencies, and other members of Congress. The committees then formulate a concurrent budget resolution that set targets for overall levels of revenues and spending, and ceilings for each functional area in the budget.

The budget resolution is supposed to be completed by April 15, although this deadline is often missed. Once the concurrent budget resolution is adopted (it does not require the president's approval), the House and Senate appropriations committees and their subcommittees are expected to act within its limits when making their decisions on the details of appropriations requests by various agencies. In most years, reconciliation legislation is necessary to ensure that the revenue and spending targets in the budget resolution are actually met. The reconciliation process requires the taxation and legislative committees to propose changes in existing tax laws and entitlement programs, such as Medicare and food stamps. Typically, these changes involve cutting spending and increasing taxes by specified amounts. The budget committees then consolidate these proposed changes into a single reconciliation bill, which must be passed by both houses. Unlike the budget resolution, which is an internal congressional matter, the reconciliation bill requires presidential approval. Reconciliation legislation makes permanent changes in the laws involving the affected policies and program. For instance, taxes may be increased or the benefits available under an entitlement program may be lowered.[18] Overall growth in both entitlements and discretionary spending are shown in Figure 7 below.

FIGURE 7

Entitlements and Discretionary Spending

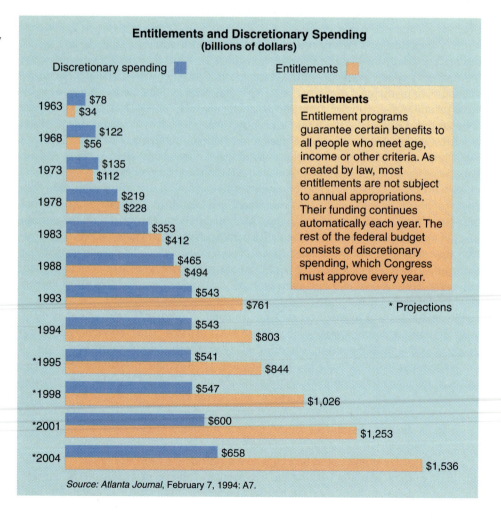

Entitlements and Discretionary Spending
(billions of dollars)

Discretionary spending ■   Entitlements ■

Year	Discretionary	Entitlements
1963	$78	$34
1968	$122	$56
1973	$135	$112
1978	$219	$228
1983	$353	$412
1988	$465	$494
1993	$543	$761
1994	$543	$803
*1995	$541	$844
*1998	$547	$1,026
*2001	$600	$1,253
*2004	$658	$1,536

Entitlements

Entitlement programs guarantee certain benefits to all people who meet age, income or other criteria. As created by law, most entitlements are not subject to annual appropriations. Their funding continues automatically each year. The rest of the federal budget consists of discretionary spending, which Congress must approve every year.

* Projections

Source: *Atlanta Journal*, February 7, 1994: A7.

Legislative action on all appropriations bills is supposed to be completed by October 1, the start of the fiscal year. More often than not, however, some appropriations bills have not emerged from Congress by this date. When this happens the Congress must pass a continuing resolution, which authorizes agencies to continue operating on the basis of last year's appropriation until their new appropriation is enacted. This procedure can cause some uncertainty in agency operations.

The budget process put in place in 1974 was intended to make the national budgetary process more rational, comprehensive, and coherent. To some extent it has done that. It has also compelled members of Congress to consider the overall dimensions of the budget and to directly confront the deficit. It has not done much to help Congress balance the budget, however.

The Deficit and the Debt

Large annual budget deficits and a rapidly growing national debt (which is the cumulation of the annual budget deficits) have characterized government finance during the past decade and a half. Several factors have contributed to this situation: a severe recession in the early 1980s; the large tax cut enacted in 1981; sharply increased spending for national defense during the 1980s; and continuously expanding spending on such entitlement programs as Social Security, Medicare, and Medicaid.[19] National budget deficits, which rarely exceeded $60 billion before 1980 and usually were much less than that, averaged $150 billion during the decade of the 1980s (see Table 3, p. 554). These dollar figures have increased in part because of inflation. One way to control for inflation when comparing budget deficits is to view the deficits as a percentage of **gross domestic product** (GDP). (GDP is the total market value of all goods and services produced in the United States during a year.) During the 1960s the budget deficit typically was less than 1 percent of GDP, compared with between 3 to 5 percent of GDP during the 1980s. This comparison also reveals a major increase in absolute budget deficit levels.

gross domestic product The total market value of all goods and services produced in a country during a year.

The national debt tripled during the 1980s. Standing at $908 billion in 1980, it soared beyond $2.87 trillion in 1989. (In 1994 the national debt was nearly $4.7 trillion.) Measured against GDP, the national debt increased from 34 to 55 percent of GDP during the 1980s. Interest payments on the national debt now account for about 15 percent of the national budget. It may make the reader feel better to know that, while the national debt has grown, so has the value of the national government's assets—including land, buildings, military installations, and equipment. According to one calculation, the government's assets approximately equaled its liabilities in 1960; by 1980 assets exceeded liabilities by $279 billion.[20] But a massive selloff of assets is highly unlikely. (See Table 3 on page 554 and Figure 8 on page 555.)

Strong partisan conflict and policy differences between the Democrats in Congress and the Reagan administration over the size and composition of the budget made reduction of the budget deficit impossible through conventional budgetary procedures. The alarming size of the deficits and public concern over them pushed Congress into taking extraordinary action in 1985. Called "a bad idea whose time had come," the Balanced Budget and Emergency Deficit Reduction Act created a procedure for automatic deficit reduction. This Act is better known as the Gramm-Rudman-Hollings Act after its three Senate sponsors—Phil Gramm (R-Tex.), Warren Rudman, (R-N.H.), and Ernest Hollings, (D-S.C.). There were three basic components to the Act:

Table 3 ◆ National Government Finances, Selected Years, 1940–1994 (billions of current dollars)

YEAR	RECEIPTS	OUTLAYS	SURPLUS OR DEFICIT	NATIONAL DEBT
1940	6.5	9.5	–2.9	50.7
1945	45.2	92.7	–47.6	260.1
1950	39.4	42.6	–3.1	256.9
1955	65.5	68.4	–3.0	274.4
1960	92.5	92.2	0.3	290.5
1965	116.8	118.2	–1.4	322.3
1970	192.8	195.6	–2.8	380.9
1975	279.1	332.3	–53.2	541.9
1980	517.1	590.9	–72.7	908.5
1985	734.1	946.4	–212.3	1817.0
1988	909.0	1064.1	–155.2	2600.8
1989	990.7	1143.2	–152.5	2867.5
1990	1031.3	1252.7	–221.4	3206.2
1991	1054.3	1323.8	–269.5	3598.3
1992	1090.5	1380.9	–290.4	4001.9
1993	1153.5	1408.2	–254.7	4351.2
1994*	1249.1	1483.8	–234.8	4676.0

*Estimates

Source: Annual Report of the Council of Economic Advisers, 1994 (Washington, DC: Government Printing Office, 1994), p. 359.

1. Budget deficit goals of $171.9 billion and $144 billion were set for 1986 and 1987. After that, the deficit goal would be lowered annually by $36 million decrements until it reached zero in 1991.

2. Several programs were exempted from automatic budget cuts, including Social Security, Medicaid, veterans' benefits, food stamps, Aid to Families with Dependent Children, child nutrition, and interest on the national debt.

3. If at the *beginning* of a fiscal year the deficit target was not met, then, by a process called sequestration (Congress seems to like these clumsy terms), automatic, across-the-board budget cuts, divided equally between nonexempt domestic and military programs, would be levied, sufficient to meet the deficit target.

   In 1987 Congress and the Reagan administration were confronted with the need to reduce the deficit by $45 billion to meet the Gramm-Rudman-Hollings Act target. Most members of Congress found this disagreeable, as did the Reagan administration because of the military spending cuts that would be required. Consequently, the Act was amended to revise the budget deficit targets and make them easier to meet. The zero target date then became 1993, a year that, in reality, saw a deficit of $254.7 billion.

F I G U R E 8

The National Debt as a
Percentage of GDP,
1940–1998

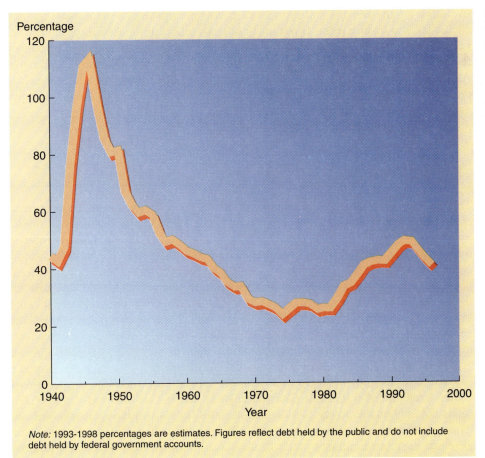

Percentage

Note: 1993-1998 percentages are estimates. Figures reflect debt held by the public and do not include debt held by federal government accounts.

Sources: 1940–1992: Office of Management and Budget, *Budget Baselines, Historical Data, and Alternatives for the Future* (Washington, DC: U.S. Government Printing Office, 1993), p. 1346. 1993–1998: Office of Management and Budget, *Budget of the U.S. Government Fiscal Year 1994* (Washington, DC: U.S. Government Printing Office, 1993), p. 32.

The Gramm-Rudman-Hollings Act did not accomplish much deficit reduction, although arguably budget deficits might have been larger had not the Act been in effect. In this sense, the Act may have imposed some restraint. It was, however, possible for Congress to avoid the requirements of the Act. Deficit targets set by Congress can be altered by Congress, as they were in 1987.

The Gramm-Rudman-Hollings Act was extensively revised and extended by the Budget Enforcement Act of 1990, which was negotiated by Bush administration officials and congressional leaders. As amended in 1993, the Budget Enforcement Act (BEA) runs through fiscal year 1998.[21] It seeks to lower deficits by imposing controls on spending. The BEA distinguishes between discretionary spending, which is controlled through annual appropriations, and direct spending, which is also called mandatory spending. Approximately two-thirds of national spending falls into the direct or mandatory category, with monies going mostly for entitlement programs and interest on the national debt.

Most likely, however, the BEA, or any similar effort, will not eliminate the budget deficit. Such approaches essentially involve an attempt to contrive a procedural solution for a substantive problem. The deficit exists because people in the United States like receiving the benefits and services of government programs more than they like paying taxes to finance them. Government officials reflect this ambivalence in their behavior. There is no easy, painless way to balance the budget, although the alternatives can be quickly stated: increase taxes, cut spending, or use a combination of the two. All the decision makers have to determine is which taxes to raise or which spending programs to cut. The difficulties in doing that account for the existing budget situation and continue to handicap the quest for a solution.

Foreign and Military Policy

nation-state Nation-states are based on the idea that one government should have sole authority over a well-defined territory.

The Federalists' views on the importance of national unity derived from the emergence of the **nation-state,** (ideally, a country where almost all of the people of one nationality govern themselves) as the most powerful political organization. With its roots in the Reformation and the political system of Europe in the 1600s, the nation-state was and is the dominant form of political organization in international politics. This form of political organization is based on the idea that one government should have sole authority over a well-defined territory. By appeals to nationalism, the government could support large military forces to defend its interests. These national interests include preserving its territorial boundaries, maintaining a relatively sovereign (independent) form of government, and promoting economic prosperity.

Nation-states range in size and resources from micro-states, such as Grenada, Monaco, and Tuvalu, to superpowers like the United States and the former Soviet Union. International power (the power of any one nation-state relative to another) depends not only on the power of other nation-states but also on the issue involved. International power also varies over time. Although the collapse of the Soviet Union increased the relative military power of the United States in the 1990s, many scholars argue that the overall power of the United States has been in decline since the early 1970s, similar to the rise and fall of other great powers over the last four centuries.

Recent debates about military intervention in Bosnia, Haiti, Somalia, and elsewhere are really about building a consensus on the most appropriate role for the United States in the world. This debate takes place in every era, particularly when key political, technological, or economic changes have taken place either at home or abroad.

The Machinery of Modern Foreign Policy Making

National Security Acts of 1947 and 1949 These acts consolidated the army, the navy, and the new air force into one department under civilian leadership.

In *Federalist No. 8,* John Jay noted that "it is the nature of war to increase the executive at the expense of the legislative authority." One consequence of World War II and the Cold War was the creation of a foreign policy-making process in the United States in which the president plays the major role. Congress supported a larger role for the United States in global military affairs with the **National Security Acts of 1947 and 1949.** These Acts consolidated the army, the navy, and the new air force into one department under civilian leadership, with the name the Department of Defense. (Previously the military office in the Cabinet had been named the War Department.) The legislation also set up two agencies: (1) the Central Intelligence Agency (CIA), which would collect and analyze the information deemed necessary to meet national security threats, and (2) the National Security Council (NSC), made up of the president, the vice president, the Secretaries of State and Defense, the chair of the Joint Chiefs of Staff, and the Director of the Central Intelligence Agency. The NSC, along with the newly created post of Assistant to the President for National Security Affairs (the National Security Advisor), would advise the president on foreign and military affairs.

This policy-making process differed sharply from the process the United States had followed in the past. The president now commanded a vast military-industrial complex supported by a large foreign policy and intelligence network. The NSC, set up to institutionalize the system by which the U.S. government had conducted World War II, was used in later years to coordinate foreign policy issues, such as dealing with the fall of the shah of Iran or negotiating a new canal treaty with Panama.

In most critical military and foreign policy matters, direction is provided by the president with advice from the members of the NSC, the National Security Advisor, and the NSC staff with input from other executive departments and agencies as the president desires. For foreign economic policy, President Bill Clinton created a National Economic Council (NEC) with a role parallel to the NSC's influence on security policy. The inner core of the NEC includes a presidential advisor who chairs the council, the Secretaries of Labor, Treasury, and Commerce, the Director of the Office of Management and Budget, the U.S. Trade Representative, and the head of the Council of Economic Advisors. The NSC and the NEC work together, even share staff, on a number of issues, including trade. They also work with the Domestic Policy Council on some non-economic issues.

Congress and interest groups have a smaller role in making foreign and military policy than domestic policy. Their role in foreign economic and military funding policies is somewhat larger, but not as large as their role in purely domestic policies. In foreign policy, it is often the president who speaks for the nation. President Harry S Truman and his successors have been able to win support for their foreign and military policies so often that we must conclude that success flows *not* from the president but from the *office itself.* The U.S. political system bestows tremendous formal and informal powers on the president in the policy areas of foreign relations and defense. The question then is, how and why has this happened?

The nature of foreign and military policy often differs from the nature of domestic policy in ways that reinforce the power of the president. Alexander Hamilton, in *Federalist No. 75,* recognized that foreign policy was different from domestic policy because it required

1. Accurate and comprehensive knowledge of foreign politics

2. A steady and systematic adherence to the same views

3. A nice and uniform sensibility to national character

4. Decision, secrecy, and despatch [sic].

On each point, the office of the president has an advantage over Congress. The advantage is captured neatly by the story of the Cuban Missile Crisis, which brought the United States and the Soviet Union very close to nuclear war. In foreign affairs, crises often arise in which the country faces a great threat with little time for decision making. In late summer of 1962, the Soviet Union secretly began placing nuclear missiles in Cuba. President John F. Kennedy knew, through the resources of the executive branch, what the Soviets were doing—although the Soviets did not know that he knew. (Without secrecy, the Soviets might have sped up their construction of missile bases, thus increasing the likelihood of war.) At most, Kennedy had a few weeks before Soviet preparations in Cuba were complete. After three days of deliberation, Kennedy and his advisers decided on a blockade to force the missiles out. Soviet vessels stopped short of U.S. naval forces surrounding Cuba, and the Soviet leader, Nikita Khrushchev, agreed to remove the missiles.

By confining his decision making to a small group of trusted advisers, Kennedy gained time. It is unlikely that within a larger body the secret could have been kept. Kennedy was also able to decide quickly, while Congress would have had many opportunities for delay. As the only federal official elected by the nation as a whole, President Kennedy could more easily consider the national interest than could members of Congress, who were responsible to a particular district or state. Finally, Kennedy had all of the executive branch at his command while Congress had few resources directly under its control.

A president's command of the executive branch is an important reason the president dominates foreign policy making: The president has great access to and control over information. This situation is quite unlike that of domestic politics, in which many people, including Congress, the media, and interest groups, often have important information that bears on policy decisions. Such information is a source of power.

When dealing with foreign affairs, the president has exclusive sources of information—diplomats working for the State Department, military attachés working for the Defense Department, agents controlled by the CIA, and technical devices (such as satellites) controlled by the National Security Agency (NSA), which is in charge of electronic intelligence gathering. Private citizens, companies, interest groups, even Congress cannot balance the president's information with their own on issues such as the number of Soviet missiles in Cuba or the extent of Iraq's nuclear weapons program. Even the one source of information available to the president's critics, the news media, is dominated by the president (see Chapter 14).

The president's authority is enhanced by the aura of secret information available to him: diplomatic cables, CIA reports, and NSA intercepts. Sometimes, to win points in debates against rivals, the president will declassify secret information. Virtually any other citizen could be prosecuted for revealing classified material, but the president may do so freely. In 1962 the presence of Soviet missiles in Cuba was a tightly held secret until President John F. Kennedy chose to reveal it in a dramatic nationwide broadcast. In the 1980 election campaign, President Jimmy Carter, under attack from Republican opponents for neglecting U.S. defenses, authorized his Secretary of Defense to reveal that the United States had been developing a plane that would be invisible to radar, the Stealth bomber.

Challenges to Presidential Power

The president is powerful in the field of foreign policy but not omnipotent. International factors place limits on the power of the president. The foreign and military policy of the United States is often criticized as simply a reaction to the policies of other countries. In addition, all presidents face domestic constraints on their power from Congress, the bureaucracy, the media, and the public as well.

Congress. The most consistent restraint on presidential power in foreign affairs comes from Congress. The Constitution gives a lesser role to Congress in foreign affairs than in domestic affairs, but much of the modern-day power of the president comes from broad authority granted the executive through legislation, not through the Constitution. Congress also exercises its oversight powers on the foreign policy and military activities of the president and the executive branch.

Congressional oversight is a relatively new check on the president's power to set foreign and military policy. During and after World War II, weapons became more and more complex, and Congress was willing to defer to presidential recommendations and military advice on what weapons the country needed. But in 1969, Congress for the first time challenged a president on a major defense expenditure. President Richard M. Nixon proposed a nationwide system of radar and interceptor missiles to defend against incoming missiles, known at the time as Anti-Ballistic Missiles (ABMs). The Senate, relying on expert testimony by Defense Department officials who had actually tried to develop such systems and believed they would not work, came within a single vote of turning down Nixon's request. Since 1969 the U.S. public has become accustomed to congressional scrutiny of weapon development and deployment.

The Constitution gives the Senate explicit power to approve treaties; the defeat of the Versailles Peace Treaty and the League of Nations in 1919 reminded everyone that this power was real. Even though in U.S. history treaties have been rejected outright only sixteen times, the power is effective because presidents try to avoid direct defeats.

As head of state and government, the president appoints ambassadors and other persons involved in the formation and implementation of foreign and defense policy. The Constitution gives the Senate the right to provide advice and consent. As in the domestic arena, important political appointees for foreign and defense policy frequently have close connections to Congress.

Congress can also try to control foreign policy through its power to appropriate funds. The power to go to war is shared between the executive and legislative branches, but the power to appropriate funds belongs to the legislature alone. Congress has been cautious about applying this power. In the case of Vietnam, it concentrated its efforts on keeping the war from widening into the neighboring country of Cambodia.

Frustrated with their failure to influence policy on Vietnam, members of Congress tried in 1973 to prevent intervention overseas without congressional approval by passing the **War Powers Act**. Under the Act, the president was limited in his deployment of troops overseas to a sixty-day period in peacetime (which could be extended for an extra thirty days to permit withdrawal) unless Congress explicitly gave its approval for a longer period. Under the Act, the president could respond to an emergency, such as rescue of endangered Americans abroad, but not engage in a prolonged struggle without congressional approval.

The War Powers Act has been an issue in the struggle for control of foreign policy between the president and Congress ever since its passage. When first passed, it was vetoed by President Richard M. Nixon. Congress overrode the veto in March 1973, but Nixon called the Act unconstitutional and said he was not bound by it. No issue arose to test the competing claims before Nixon was forced to resign in 1974, but such issues did arise under his successors. President Gerald R. Ford dispatched troops to rescue the crew of the merchant ship *Mayaguez,* captured as it sailed near Cambodia in 1975; in 1980 President Carter dispatched troops in an abortive attempt to rescue U.S. diplomats held hostage in Iran. In neither case did the action last sixty days, but the presidents notified Congress, as the Act required, although in both instances after some delay.

The first serious test of the War Powers Act came under President Ronald Reagan. In 1982 Reagan ordered Marines into Lebanon as part of a peacekeeping mission. Because the troops were not in combat, Congress did not object. But after a year, the Marines came under increasing fire from various factions in Lebanon's civil war. Although Marines were being killed, Congress was slow to invoke the War Powers Act.

War Powers Act Under this Act, passed by Congress in 1973, the president was limited in his deployment of troops overseas to a sixty-day period in peacetime (which could be extended for an extra thirty days to permit withdrawal) unless Congress explicitly gave its approval for a longer period.

In the midst of a drawn out debate over U.S. involvement in Lebanon, a Lebanese terrorist drove an explosive-filled truck into the Marine barracks in Beirut, killing 241 servicemen. Shortly thereafter, all Marines were withdrawn on the president's initiative. In this and subsequent actions, presidents have usually complied with parts of the War Powers Act, especially the requirements for notifying key members of Congress. More important, President George Bush solicited congressional approval for the use of force in the Persian Gulf War, recognizing the importance of bringing Congress into the decision-making process. In January 1994 President Bill Clinton, for example, told NATO leaders that he would seek congressional approval before agreeing to the use of U.S. air strikes or ground troops in Bosnia.

The Bureaucracy.   One major check on the foreign policy and military powers of the president comes from inside the executive branch itself. The president is recognized as the ultimate executive authority, but, as noted in Chapter 8, the federal bureaucracy must implement those decisions. Without full support of career bureaucrats, who usually have expert knowledge of the issues and procedures, policy decisions and actions can be ignored or delayed, and information can be leaked to Congress or the media to raise issues on the political agenda or to embarrass the president. Since many bureaucrats have strong ties to Congress or interest groups such as the defense industries, their loyalties may be divided.

The News Media.   With Congress and the bureaucracy, the press provides some check on presidential power in foreign and military affairs. During World War II and the early Cold War years, the press tended to support the president. As a rule, editors assumed that government statements were true and printed them as unquestioned fact. In the mid-1960s, the press's role as a prop for foreign policy began to change.

The Public.   How U.S. public opinion is divided on general dimensions of foreign policy also constrains the president. Many scholars argue that public opinion has two dimensions, militarism/nonmilitarism and isolationism/internationalism, creating four basic opinion groups. Others argue that a third dimension, unilateralism/multilateralism (essentially the difference between acting alone and acting in concert with other countries), is also important. Although the public is not equally divided among different opinion groups, U.S. foreign policies usually have to appeal across these dimensions to two or more groups in order to achieve widespread popular support. At the same time, the existence of these various dimensions mean that almost every U.S. foreign policy will have a core group of opponents who are likely to try to limit the impact of the policy.

The Declaration of Independence

In Congress, July 4, 1776

THE UNANIMOUS DECLARATION OF THE THIRTEEN UNITED STATES OF AMERICA

When in the Course of human events it becomes necessary for one people to dissolve the political bands which have connected them with another, and to assume, among the powers of the earth, the separate and equal station to which the Laws of Nature and of Nature's God entitle them, a decent respect to the opinions of mankind requires that they should declare the causes which impel them to the separation.

We hold these truths to be self-evident, that all men are created equal, that they are endowed by their Creator with certain unalienable Rights, that among these are Life, Liberty and the pursuit of Happiness. That to secure these rights, Governments are instituted among Men, deriving their just powers from the consent of the governed. That whenever any Form of Government becomes destructive of these ends, it is the Right of the People to alter or to abolish it, and to institute new Government, laying its foundation on such principles and organizing its powers in such form, as to them shall seem most likely to effect their Safety and Happiness. Prudence, indeed, will dictate that Governments long established should not be changed for light and transient causes; and accordingly all experience hath shewn that mankind are more disposed to suffer, while evils are sufferable, than to right themselves by abolishing the forms to which they are accustomed. But when a long train of abuses and usurpations, pursuing invariably the same Object evinces a design to reduce them under absolute Despotism, it is their right, it is their duty, to throw off such Government, and to provide new Guards for their future security.—Such has been the patient sufferance of these Colonies; and such is now the necessity which constrains them to alter their former Systems of Government. The history of the present King of Great Britain is a history of repeated injuries and usurpations, all having in direct object the establishment of an absolute Tyranny over these States. To prove this, let Facts be submitted to a candid world.

He has refused his Assent to Laws, the most wholesome and necessary for the public good.

He has forbidden his Governors to pass Laws of immediate and pressing importance, unless suspended in their operation till his Assent should be obtained; and when so suspended, he has utterly neglected to attend to them.

He has refused to pass other Laws for the accommodation of large districts of people, unless those people would relinquish the right of Representation in the Legislature, a right inestimable to them and formidable to tyrants only.

He has called together legislative bodies at places unusual, uncomfortable, and distant from the depository of their Public Records, for the sole purpose of fatiguing them into compliance with his measures.

He has dissolved Representative Houses repeatedly, for opposing with manly firmness his invasions on the rights of the people.

He has refused for a long time, after such dissolutions, to cause others to be elected; whereby the Legislative Powers, incapable of Annihilation, have returned to the People at large for their exercise, the State remaining in the mean time exposed to all the dangers of invasion from without, and convulsions within.

He has endeavored to prevent the population of these States; for that purpose obstructing the Laws of Naturalization of Foreigners; refusing to pass others to encourage their migration hither, and raising the conditions of new Appropriations of Lands.

He has obstructed the Administration of Justice, by refusing his Assent to Laws for establishing Judiciary powers.

He has made Judges dependent on his Will alone, for the tenure of their offices, and the amount and payment of their salaries.

He has erected a multitude of New Offices, and sent hither swarms of Officers to harass our people, and eat out their substance.

He has kept among us, in times of peace, Standing Armies without the Consent of our legislatures.

He has affected to render the Military independent of and superior to the Civil power.

He has combined with others to subject us to a jurisdiction foreign to our constitution, and unacknowledged by our laws, giving his Assent to their Acts of pretended Legislation:

For quartering large bodies of armed troops among us:

For protecting them, by a mock Trial, from punishment for any Murders which they should commit on the Inhabitants of these States:

For cutting off our Trade with all parts of the world:

For imposing Taxes on us without our Consent:

For depriving us in many cases, of the benefits of Trial by Jury:

For transporting us beyond Seas to be tried for pretended offences:

For abolishing the free System of English Laws in a neighboring Province, establishing therein an Arbitrary government, and enlarging its Boundaries so as to render it at once an example and fit instrument for introducing the same absolute rule into these Colonies:

For taking away our Charters, abolishing our most valuable Laws, and altering fundamentally the Forms of our Governments:

For suspending our own Legislatures, and declaring themselves invested with power to legislate for us in all cases whatsoever.

He has abdicated Government here, by declaring us out of his Protection and waging War against us.

He has plundered our seas, ravaged our Coasts, burnt out towns, and destroyed the lives of our people.

He is at this time transporting large Armies of foreign Mercenaries to compleat the works of death, desolation and tyranny, already begun with circumstances of Cruelty and perfidy scarcely paralleled in the most barbarous ages, and totally unworthy the Head of a civilized nation.

He has constrained our fellow Citizens taken Captive on the high Seas to bear Arms against their Country, to become the executioners of their friends and Brethren, or to fall themselves by their Hands.

He has excited domestic insurrections amongst us, and has endeavored to bring on the inhabitants of our frontiers, the merciless Indian Savages, whose known rule of warfare, is an undistinguished destruction of all ages, sexes and conditions.

In every stage of these Oppressions We have Petitioned for Redress in the most humble terms: Our repeated Petitions have been answered only by repeated injury: A Prince, whose character is thus marked by every act which may define a Tyrant, is unfit to be the ruler of a free people.

Nor have We been wanting in attention to our British brethren. We have warned them from time to time of attempts by their legislature to extend an unwarrantable jurisdiction over us. We have reminded them of the circumstances of our emigration and settlement here. We have appealed to their native justice and magnanimity; and we have conjured them by the ties of our common kindred to disavow these usurpations, which would inevitably interrupt our connections and correspondence. They too have been deaf to the voice of justice and consanguinity. We must, therefore, acquiesce in the necessity, which denounces our Separation, and hold them, as we hold the rest of mankind, Enemies in War, in Peace Friends.

We, therefore, the Representatives of the United States of America, in General Congress, Assembled, appealing to the Supreme Judge of the world for the rectitude of our intentions, do, in the Name, and by Authority of the good People of these Colonies, solemnly publish and declare, That these

United Colonies are, and of Right ought to be Free and Independent States; that they are Absolved from all Allegiance to the British Crown, and that all political connection between them and the State of Great Britain, is and ought to be totally dissolved: and that as Free and Independent States, they have full power to levy War, conclude Peace, contract Alliances, establish Commerce, and to do all other Acts and Things which Independent States may of right do. And for the support of this Declaration, with a firm reliance on the protection of divine Providence, we mutually pledge to each other our Lives, our Fortunes and our sacred Honor.

JOHN HANCOCK

NEW HAMPSHIRE
Josiah Bartlett,
Wm. Whipple,
Matthew Thornton.

MASSACHUSETTS BAY
Saml. Adams,
John Adams,
Robt. Treat Paine,
Elbridge Gerry.

RHODE ISLAND
Step. Hopkins,
William Ellery.

CONNECTICUT
Roger Sherman,
Samuel Huntington,
Wm. Williams,
Oliver Wolcott.

NEW YORK
Wm. Floyd,
Phil. Livingston,
Frans. Lewis,
Lewis Morris

NEW JERSEY
Richd. Stockton,
In. Witherspoon,
Fras. Hopkinson,
John Hart,
Abra. Clark.

PENNSYLVANIA
Robt. Morris,
Benjamin Rush,
Benjamin Franklin,
John Morton,
Geo. Clymer,
Jas. Smith,
Geo. Taylor,
James Wilson,
Geo. Ross.

DELAWARE
Caesar Rodney,
Geo. Read,
Tho. M'kean.

MARYLAND
Samuel Chase,
Wm. Paca,
Thos. Stone,
Charles Caroll of Carollton.

VIRGINIA
George Wythe,
Richard Henry Lee,
Th. Jefferson,
Benjamin Harrison,
Thos. Nelson, jr.,
Francis Lightfoot Lee,
Carter Braxton.

NORTH CAROLINA
Wm. Hooper,
Joseph Hewes,
John Penn.

SOUTH CAROLINA
Edward Rutledge,
Thos. Heyward, Junr.,
Thomas Lynch, jnr.,
Arthur Middleton.

GEORGIA
Button Guinnett,
Lyman Hall,
Geo. Walton.

The Constitution of the
United States of America

*W*e the People of the United States, in Order to form a more perfect Union, establish Justice, insure domestic Tranquility, provide for the common defence, promote the general Welfare, and secure the Blessings of Liberty to ourselves and our Posterity, do ordain and establish this Constitution for the United States of America.

ARTICLE I

SECTION 1. All legislative Powers herein granted shall be vested in a Congress of the United States, which shall consist of a Senate and House of Representatives.

SECTION 2. The House of Representatives shall be composed of Members chosen every second Year by the People of the several States, and the Electors in each State shall have the Qualifications requisite for Electors of the most numerous Branch of the State Legislature.

No person shall be a Representative who shall not have attained to the Age of twenty five Years, and been seven Years a Citizen of the United States, and who shall not, when elected, be an Inhabitant of that State in which he shall be chosen.

Representatives and direct Taxes shall be apportioned among the several States which may be included within this Union, according to their respective Numbers which shall be determined by adding to the whole Number of free Persons, including those bound to Service for a Term of Years, and excluding Indians not taxed, three fifths of all other Persons. The actual Enumeration shall be made within three Years after the first Meeting of the Congress of the United States, and within every subsequent Term ten Years, in such Manner as they shall by Law direct. The Number of Representatives shall not exceed one for every thirty Thousand, but each State shall have at Least one Representative; and until such enumeration shall be made, the State of New Hampshire shall be entitled to chuse three, Massachusetts eight, Rhode-Island and Providence Plantations one, Connecticut five, New-York six, New Jersey four, Pennsylvania eight, Delaware one, Maryland six, Virginia ten, North Carolina five, South Carolina five, and Georgia three.

When vacancies happen in the Representation from any State, the Executive Authority thereof shall issue Writs of Election to fill such Vacancies.

The House of Representatives shall chuse their speaker and other Officers; and shall have the sole Power of Impeachment.

SECTION 3. The Senate of the United States shall be composed of two Senators from each State chosen by the Legislature thereof, for six Years; and each Senator shall have one Vote.

Immediately after they shall be assembled in Consequence of the first Election, they shall be divided as equally as may be into three Classes. The Seats of the Senators of the first Class shall be vacated at the Expiration of the second year, of the second Class at the Expiration of the fourth Year, and of the third Class at the Expiration of the sixth Year, so that one third may be chosen every second Year and if Vacancies happen by Resignation, or otherwise, during the Recess of the Legislature of any State, the Executive thereof may make temporary Appointments until the next Meeting of the Legislature, which shall then fill such Vacancies.

No Person shall be a Senator who shall not have attained to the Age of thirty Years, and been nine Years a Citizen of the United States, and who shall not, when elected, be an Inhabitant of that State for which he shall be chosen.

The Vice President of the United States shall be President of the Senate, but shall have no Vote, unless they be equally divided.

The Senate shall chuse their other Officers, and also a President pro tempore, in the Absence of the Vice President, or when he shall exercise the Office of President of the United States.

The Senate shall have the sole Power to try all Impeachments. When sitting for that Purpose, they shall be on Oath or Affirmation. When the President of the United States is tried, the Chief Justice shall preside: And no Person shall be convicted without the Concurrence of two thirds of the Members present.

Judgment in Cases of Impeachment shall not extend further than to removal from Office, and disqualification to hold and enjoy any Office of honor, Trust or Profit under the United States; but the Party convicted shall nevertheless be liable and subject to Indictment, Trial, Judgment and Punishment, according to Law.

Section 4. The Times, Places and Manner of holding Elections for Senators and Representatives, shall be prescribed in each State by the Legislature thereof; but the Congress may at any time by law make or alter such Regulations, except as to the Places of chusing Senators.

The Congress shall assemble at least once in every Year, and such Meeting shall be on the first Monday in December, unless they shall by Law appoint a different Day.

Section 5. Each House shall be the Judge of the Elections, Returns and Qualifications of its own Members, and a Majority of each shall constitute a Quorum to do Business; but a smaller Number may adjourn from day to day, and may be authorized to compel the Attendance of absent Members, in such Manner, and under such Penalties as each House may provide.

Each House may determine the Rules of its Proceedings, punish its Members for disorderly Behaviour, and with the Concurrence of two thirds, expel a Member.

Each House shall keep a journal of its Proceedings, and from time to time publish the same, excepting such Parts as may in their judgment require Secrecy; and the Yeas and Nays of the Members of either House on any question shall, at the Desire of one fifth of those present, be entered on the Journal.

Neither House, during the Session of Congress, shall, without the Consent of the other, adjourn for more than three days, nor to any other Place than that in which the two Houses shall be sitting.

Section 6. The Senators and Representatives shall receive a Compensation for their Services, to be ascertained by Law, and paid out of the Treasury of the United States. They shall in all Cases, except Treason, Felony and Breach of the Peace, be privileged from Arrest during their Attendance at the Session of their respective Houses, and in going to and returning from the same; and for any Speech or Debate in either House, they shall not be questioned in any other Place.

No Senator or Representative shall, during the Time for which he was elected, be appointed to any civil Office under the Authority of the United States, which shall have been created, or the Emoluments whereof shall have been encreased during such time; and no Person holding any Office under the United States, shall be a Member of either House during his Continuance in Office.

Section 7. All Bills for raising Revenue shall originate in the House of Representatives; but the Senate may propose or concur with Amendments as on other Bills.

Every Bill which shall have passed the House of Representatives and the Senate, shall, before it become a Law, be presented to the President of the United States; If he approves he shall sign it, but if not he shall return it, with his Objections to that House in which it shall have originated, who shall enter the Objections at large on their journal, and proceed to reconsider it. If after such Reconsideration two thirds of that House shall agree to pass the Bill, it shall be sent, together with the Objections, to the other House, by which it shall likewise be reconsidered, and if approved by two thirds of that House, it shall become a Law. But in all such Cases the Votes of both Houses shall be determined by Yeas and Nays, and the Names of the Persons voting for and against the Bill shall be entered on the Journal of each House respectively. If any Bill shall not be returned by the President within ten Days (Sundays excepted) after it shall have been presented to him, the Same shall be a Law, in like Manner as if he had signed it, unless the Congress by their Adjournment prevent its Return, in which Case it shall not be a Law.

Every Order, Resolution, or Vote to which the Concurrence of the Senate and House of Representatives may be necessary (except on a question of Adjournment) shall be presented to the President of the United States; and before the Same shall take Effect, shall be approved by him, or being disapproved by him, shall be repassed by two thirds of the Senate and House of Representatives, according to the Rules and Limitations prescribed in the Case of a Bill.

Section 8. The Congress shall have Power To lay and collect Taxes, Duties, Imposts and Excises, to pay the Debts and provide for the common Defence and general Welfare of the United States; but all Duties, Imposts and Excises shall be uniform throughout the United States;

To borrow Money on the credit of the United States;

To regulate Commerce with foreign Nations, and among the several States, and with the Indian Tribes;

To establish a uniform Rule of Naturalization, and uniform Laws on the subject of Bankruptcies throughout the United States;

To coin Money, regulate the Value thereof, and of foreign Coin, and fix the Standard of Weights and Measures;

To provide for the Punishment of counterfeiting the Securities and current Coin of the United States;

To establish Post Offices and post Roads;

To promote the Progress of Science and useful Arts, by securing for limited Times to Authors and Inventors the exclusive Right to their respective Writings and Discoveries;

To constitute Tribunals inferior to the supreme Court;

To define and punish Piracies and Felonies committed on the high Seas, and Offences against the Law of Nations;

To declare War, grant Letters of Marque and Reprisal, and make Rules concerning Captures on Land and Water;

To raise and support Armies, but no Appropriation of Money to that Use shall be for a longer Term than two Years;

To provide and maintain a Navy;

To make Rules for the Government and Regulation of the land and naval Forces;

To provide for calling forth the Militia to execute the Laws of the Union, suppress Insurrections and repel Invasions;

To provide for organizing, arming, and disciplining, the Militia, and for governing such Part of them as may be employed in the Service of the United States, reserving to the States respectively, the Appointment of the Officers, and the Authority of training the Militia according to the discipline prescribed by Congress;

To exercise exclusive Legislation in all Cases whatsoever, over such District (not exceeding ten Miles square) as may, by Cession of particular States, and the Acceptance of Congress, become the Seat of the Government of the United States, and to exercise like Authority over all Places purchased by the Consent of the Legislature of the State in which the Same shall be for the Erection of Forts, Magazines, Arsenals, dock-Yards, and other needful Buildings;—And

To make all Laws which shall be necessary and proper for carrying into Execution the foregoing Powers, and all other Powers vested by this Constitution in the Government of the United States, or in any Department or Officer thereof.

SECTION 9. The Migration or Importation of such Persons as any of the States now existing shall think proper to admit, shall not be prohibited by the Congress prior to the Year one thousand eight hundred and eight, but a Tax or duty may be imposed on such Importation, not exceeding ten dollars for each Person.

The Privilege of the Writ of Habeas Corpus shall not be suspended, unless when in Cases of Rebellion or Invasion the public Safety may require it.

No Bill of Attainder or ex post facto Law shall be passed.

No Capitation, or other direct, Tax shall be laid, unless in Proportion to the Census or Enumeration herein before directed to be taken.

No Tax or Duty shall be laid on Articles exported from any State.

No Preference shall be given by any Regulation of Commerce or Revenue to the Ports of one State over those of another; nor shall Vessels bound to, or from, one State, be obliged to enter, clear, or pay Duties in another.

No Money shall be drawn from the Treasury, but in Consequence of Appropriations made by Law; and a regular Statement and Account of the Receipts and Expenditures of all public Money shall be published from time to time.

No Title of Nobility shall be granted by the United States: And no Person holding any Office of Profit or Trust under them, shall, without the Consent of the Congress, accept of any present, Emolument, Office, or Title, of any kind whatever, from any King, Prince, or foreign State.

SECTION 10. No state shall enter into any Treaty, Alliance, or Confederation; grant Letters of Marque and Reprisal; coin Money; emit Bills of Credit; make any Thing but gold and silver Coin a Tender in Payment of Debts; pass any Bill of Attainder, ex post facto Law, or Law impairing the Obligation of Contracts, or grant any Title of Nobility.

No State shall, without the Consent of the Congress, lay any Imposts or Duties on Imports or Exports, except what may be absolutely necessary for executing its inspection Laws: and the net Produce of all Duties and Imposts, laid by any State on Imports or Exports, shall be for the Use of the Treasury of the United States, and all such Laws shall be subject to the Revision and Controul of the Congress.

No State shall, without the Consent of Congress, lay any Duty of Tonnage, keep Troops, or Ships of War in time of Peace, enter into any Agreement or Compact with another State, or with a foreign Power, or engage in War, unless actually invaded, or in such imminent Danger as will not admit of delay.

ARTICLE II

SECTION 1. The executive Power shall be vested in a President of the United States of America. He shall hold his Office during the Term of four Years, and, together with the Vice President, chosen for the same Term, be elected as follows.

Each State shall appoint, in such Manner as the Legislature thereof may direct, a Number of Electors, equal to the whole Number of Senators and Representatives to which the State may be entitled in the Congress; but no Senator or Representative, or Person holding an Office of Trust of Profit under the United States, shall be appointed an Elector.

The Electors shall meet in their respective States, and vote by Ballot for two Persons, of whom one at least shall not be an Inhabitant of the same State with themselves. And they shall make a List of all the Persons voted for, and, of the Number of Votes for each; which List they shall sign and certify, and transmit sealed to the Seat of the Government of the United States, directed to the President of the Senate. The

President of the Senate shall, in the Presence of the Senate and House of Representatives, open all the Certificates, and the Votes shall then be counted. The Person having the greatest Number of Votes shall be the President, if such Number be a Majority of the whole Number of Electors appointed; and if there be more than one who have such Majority, and have an equal Number of Votes, then the House of Representatives shall immediately chuse by Ballot one of them for President; and if no Person have a Majority, then from the five highest on the List the said House shall in like Manner chuse the President. But in chusing the President, the Votes shall be taken by States, the Representation from each State having one Vote; A quorum for this Purpose shall consist of a Member or Members from two thirds of the States, and a Majority of all the States shall be necessary to a Choice. In every Case, after the Choice of the President, the Person having the greatest Number of Votes of the Electors shall be the Vice President. But if there should remain two or more who have equal Votes, the Senate shall chuse from them by Ballot the Vice President.

The Congress may determine the Time of chusing the Electors, and the Day on which they shall give their Votes; which Day shall be the same throughout the United States.

No Person except a natural born Citizen, or a Citizen of the United States, at the time of the Adoption of this Constitution, shall be eligible to the Office of President; neither shall any Person be eligible to that Office who shall not have attained to the Age of thirty five Years, and been fourteen Years a Resident within the United States.

In Case of the Removal of the President from Office, or of his Death, Resignation, or Inability to discharge the Powers and Duties of the said Office, the Same shall devolve on the Vice President, and the Congress may by Law provide for the Case of Removal, Death, Resignation or Inability, both of the President and Vice President, declaring what Officer shall then act as President, and such Officer shall act accordingly, until the Disability be removed, or a President shall be elected.

The President shall, at stated Times, receive for his Services, a Compensation, which shall neither be encreased nor diminished during the Period for which he shall have been elected, and he shall not receive within that Period any other Emolument from the United States, or any of them.

Before he enter on the Execution of his Office, he shall take the following Oath or Affirmation—"I do solemnly swear (or affirm) that I will faithfully execute the Office of President of the United States, and will to the best of my Ability, preserve, protect and defend the Constitution of the United States."

SECTION 2. The President shall be Commander in Chief of the Army, and Navy of the United States, and of the Militia of the several States, when called into the actual Service of the United States; he may require the Opinion, in writing, of the principal Officer in each of the executive Departments, upon any Subject relating to the Duties of their respective Offices, and he shall have Power to grant Reprieves and Pardons for Offences against the United States, except in Cases of Impeachment.

He shall have Power, by and with the Advice and Consent of the Senate, to make Treaties, provided two thirds of the Senators present concur; and he shall nominate, and by and with the Advice and Consent of the Senate, shall appoint Ambassadors, other public Ministers and Consuls, Judges of the supreme Court, and all other Officers of the United States, whose Appointments are not herein otherwise provided for, and which shall be established by Law: but the Congress may by Law vest the Appointment of such inferior Officers, as they think proper, in the President alone, in the Courts of Law, or in the Heads of Departments.

The President shall have Power to fill up all Vacancies that may happen during the Recess of the Senate, by granting Commissions which shall expire at the end of their next Session.

SECTION 3. He shall from time to time give to the Congress Information of the State of the Union, and recommend to their Consideration such Measures as he shall judge necessary and expedient; he may, on extraordinary Occasions, convene both Houses, or either of them, and in Case of Disagreement between them, with Respect to the Time of Adjournment, he may adjourn them to such Time as he shall think proper; he shall receive Ambassadors and other public Ministers; he shall take Care that the Laws be faithfully executed, and shall Commission all the Officers of the United States.

SECTION 4. The President, Vice President and all civil Officers of the United States, shall be removed from Office on Impeachment for, and Conviction of, Treason, Bribery, or other high Crimes and Misdemeanors.

ARTICLE III

SECTION 1. The judicial Power of the United States, shall be vested in one supreme Court, and in such inferior Courts as the Congress may from time to time ordain and establish. The Judges, both of the supreme and inferior Courts, shall hold their Offices during good Behaviour, and shall, at stated Times, receive for their Services, a Compensation, which shall not be diminished during their Continuance in Office.

SECTION 2. The judicial Power shall extend to all Cases, in Law and Equity, arising under this Constitution, the Laws of the United States, and Treaties made, or which shall be made, under their Authority;—to all Cases affecting Ambassadors, other public Ministers and Consuls;—to all Cases of admiralty and maritime Jurisdiction;—to Controversies to which the United States shall be a Party;—to Controversies between two or more States;—between a State and Citizens of another State;—between Citizens of different States,—between Citizens of the same State claiming Lands under Grants of different States,—and between a State, or the Citizens thereof, and foreign States, Citizens of Subjects.

In all Cases affecting Ambassadors, other public Ministers and Consuls, and those in which a State shall be Party, the supreme Court shall have original Jurisdiction. In all the other Cases before mentioned, the supreme Court shall have appellate Jurisdiction, both as to Law and Fact, with such Exceptions, and under such Regulations as the Congress shall make.

The Trial of all Crimes, except in Cases of Impeachment, shall be by Jury; and such Trial shall be held in the State where the said Crimes shall have been committed; but when not committed within any State, the Trial shall be at such Place or Places as the Congress may by Law have directed.

SECTION 3. Treason against the United States, shall consist only in levying War against them, or in adhering to their Enemies, giving them Aid and Comfort. No Person shall be convicted of Treason unless on the Testimony of two Witnesses to the same overt Act, or on Confession in open Court.

The Congress shall have Power to declare the Punishment of Treason, but no Attainder of Treason shall work Corruption of Blood, or Forfeiture except during the Life of the Person attainted.

ARTICLE IV

SECTION 1. Full Faith and Credit shall be given in each State to the public Acts, Records, and judicial Proceedings of every other State. And the Congress may by general Laws prescribe the Manner in which such Acts, Records and Proceedings shall be proved, and the Effect thereof.

SECTION 2. The Citizens of each State shall be entitled to all Privileges and Immunities of Citizens in the several States.

A Person charged in any State with Treason, Felony, or other Crime, who shall flee from Justice, and be found in another State, shall on Demand of the executive Authority of the State from which he fled, be delivered up, to be removed to the State having Jurisdiction of the Crime.

No Person held to Service or Labour in one State under the Laws thereof, escaping into another, shall, in Consequence of any Law or Regulation therein, be discharged from such Service or Labour, but shall be delivered up on Claim of the Party to whom such Service or Labour may be due.

SECTION 3. New States may be admitted by the Congress into this Union; but no new State shall be formed or erected within the Jurisdiction of any other State; nor any State be formed by the Junction of two or more States, or Parts of States, without the Consent of the Legislatures of the States concerned as well as of the Congress.

The Congress shall have Power to dispose of and make all needful Rules and Regulations respecting the Territory or other Property belonging to the United States; and nothing in this Constitution shall be so construed as to Prejudice any Claims of the United States, or of any particular State.

SECTION 4. The United States shall guarantee to every State in this Union a Republican Form of Government, and shall protect each of them against Invasion, and on Application of the Legislature, or of the Executive (when the Legislature cannot be convened) against domestic Violence.

ARTICLE V

The Congress, whenever two thirds of both Houses shall deem it necessary, shall propose Amendments to this Constitution, or, on the Application of the Legislatures of two thirds of the several States, shall call a Convention for proposing Amendments, which, in either Case, shall be valid to all Intents and Purposes, as Part of this Constitution, when ratified by the Legislatures of three fourths of the several States, or by Conventions in three fourths thereof, as the one or the other Mode of Ratification may be proposed by the Congress; Provided that no Amendment which may be made prior to the Year One thousand eight hundred and eight shall in any Manner affect the first and fourth Clauses in the Ninth Section of the first Article; and that no State, without its Consent, shall be deprived of its equal Suffrage in the Senate.

ARTICLE VI

All Debts contracted and Engagements entered into, before the Adoption of this Constitution, shall be as valid against the United States under this Constitution, as under the Confederation.

This Constitution, and the laws of the United States which shall be made in Pursuance thereof; and all Treaties made, or which shall be made, under the Authority of the United States, shall be the supreme Law of the Land; and the Judges in every State shall be bound thereby, any Thing in the Constitution or Laws of any State to the Contrary notwithstanding.

The Senators and Representatives before mentioned, and the Members of the several State Legislatures, and all executive and judicial Officers, both of the United States and of the several States, shall be bound by Oath or Affirmation, to support this Constitution; but no religious Test shall ever be required as a Qualification to any Office or public Trust under the United States.

ARTICLE VII

The Ratification of the Conventions of nine States, shall be sufficient for the Establishment of this Constitution between the States so ratifying the Same.

Done in Convention by the Unanimous Consent of the States present the Seventeenth Day of September in the Year of our Lord one thousand seven hundred and Eighty seven and of the Independence of the United States of America the Twelfth. IN WITNESS whereof we have hereunto subscribed our Names,

Go. WASHINGTON
Presid't. and deputy from Virginia

Attest
WILLIAM JACKSON
Secretary

DELAWARE
Geo. Read
Gunning Bedford jun
John Dickinson
Richard Basset
Jaco. Broom

MASSACHUSETTS
Nathaniel Gorham
Rufus King

CONNECTICUT
Wm. Saml. Johnson
Roger Sherman

NEW YORK
Alexander Hamilton

NEW JERSEY
Wh. Livingston
David Brearley
Wm. Paterson
Jona. Dayton

PENNSYLVANIA
B. Franklin
Thomas Mifflin
Robt. Morris
Geo. Clymer
Thos. FitzSimons
Jared Ingersoll
James Wilson
Gouv. Morris

NEW HAMPSHIRE
John Langdon
Nicholas Gilman

MARYLAND
James McHenry
Dan of St. Thos. Jenifer
Danl. Carroll

VIRGINIA
John Blair
James Madison, Jr.

NORTH CAROLINA
Wm. Blount
Richd. Dobbs Spaight
Hu. Williamson

SOUTH CAROLINA
J. Rutledge
Charles Cotesworth Pinckney
Charles Pinckney
Pierce Butler

GEORGIA
William Few
Abr. Baldwin

Articles in addition to, and amendment of the Constitution of the United States of America, proposed by Congress and ratified by the Legislatures of the several states, pursuant to the Fifth Article of the original Constitution.

(The first ten amendments were passed by Congress on September 25, 1789, and were ratified on December 15, 1791.)

Amendment I

Congress shall make no law respecting an establishment of religion, or prohibiting the free exercise thereof; or abridging the freedom of speech, or of the press; or the right of the people peaceably to assemble, and to petition the Government for a redress of grievances.

Amendment II

A well regulated Militia, being necessary to the security of a free State, the right of the people to keep and bear Arms, shall not be infringed.

Amendment III

No Soldier shall, in time of peace be quartered in any house, without the consent of the Owner, nor in time of war, but in a manner to be prescribed by law.

Amendment IV

The right of the people to be secure in their persons, houses, papers, and effects, against unreasonable searches and seizures, shall not be violated, and no warrants shall issue, but upon probable cause, supported by Oath or affirmation, and particularly describing the place to be searched, and the persons or things to be seized.

Amendment V

No person shall be held to answer for a capital, or otherwise infamous crime, unless on a presentment or indictment of a Grand Jury, except in cases arising in the land or naval forces, or in the Militia, when in actual service in time of War or public danger; nor shall any person be subject for the same offence to be twice put in jeopardy of life or limb; nor shall be compelled in any criminal case to be a witness against himself, nor be deprived of life, liberty, or property, without due process of law; nor shall private property be taken for public use, without just compensation.

Amendment VI

In all criminal prosecutions, the accused shall enjoy the right to a speedy and public trial, by an impartial jury of the State and district wherein the crime shall have been committed, which district shall have been previously ascertained by law, and to be informed of the nature and cause of the accusation; to be confronted with the witnesses against him; to have compulsory process for obtaining witnesses in his favor, and to have the assistance of counsel for his defence.

Amendment VII

In Suits at common law, where the value in controversy shall exceed twenty dollars, the right of trial by jury shall be preserved, and no fact tried by a jury, shall be otherwise re-examined in any Court of the United States, than according to the rules of the common law.

Amendment VIII

Excessive bail shall not be required, nor excessive fines imposed, nor cruel and unusual punishments inflicted.

Amendment IX

The enumeration in the Constitution, of certain rights, shall not be construed to deny or disparage others retained by the people.

Amendment X

The powers not delegated to the United States by the Constitution, nor prohibited by it to the States, are reserved to the States respectively, or to the people.

Amendment XI   *(Ratified on February 7, 1795)*

The Judicial power of the United States shall not be construed to extend to any suit in law or equity, commenced or prosecuted against one of the United States by Citizens of another State, or by Citizens or Subjects of any Foreign State.

Amendment XII   *(Ratified on June 15, 1804)*

The Electors shall meet in their respective states, and vote by ballot for President and Vice-President, one of whom, at least, shall not be an inhabitant of the same state with themselves; they shall name in their ballots the person voted for as President, and in distinct ballots the person voted for as Vice-President, and they shall make distinct lists of all persons voted for as President, and of all persons voted for as Vice-President, and of the number of votes for each, which lists they shall sign and certify, and transmit sealed to the seat of the government of the United States, directed to the President of the Senate;—The President of the Senate shall, in the presence of the Senate and House of Representatives, open all the certificates and the votes shall then be counted;—The person having the greatest number of votes for President, shall be the President, if such number be a majority of the whole number of Electors appointed; and if no person have such majority; then from the persons having the highest numbers not exceeding three on the list of those voted for as President, the House of Representatives shall choose immediately, by ballot, the President. But in choosing the President, the votes shall be taken by states, the representation from each state having one vote; a quorum for this purpose shall consist of a member or members from two-thirds of the states, and a majority of all the states shall be necessary to a choice. And if the House of Representatives shall not choose a President whenever the right of choice shall devolve upon them, before the fourth day of March next following, then the Vice-President shall act as President, as in the case of the death or other constitutional disability of the President.—The person having the greatest number of votes as Vice-President, shall be the Vice-President, if such number be a majority of the whole number of Electors appointed, and if no person have a majority, then from the two highest numbers on the list, the Senate shall choose the Vice-President; a quorum for the purpose shall consist of two-thirds of the whole number of Senators, and a majority of the whole number shall be necessary to a choice. But no person constitutionally ineligible to the office of President shall be eligible to that of Vice-President of the United States.

Amendment XIII   *(Ratified on December 6, 1865)*

SECTION 1. Neither slavery nor involuntary servitude, except as a punishment for crime whereof the party shall have been duly convicted, shall exist within the United States, or any place subject to their jurisdiction.

SECTION 2. Congress shall have power to enforce this article by appropriate legislation.

Amendment XIV   *(Ratified on July 9, 1868)*

SECTION 1. All persons born or naturalized in the United States, and subject to the jurisdiction thereof, are citizens of the United States and of the State wherein they reside. No State shall make or enforce any law which shall abridge the privileges or immunities of citizens of the United States; nor shall any State deprive any person of life, liberty, or property, without due process of law; nor deny to any person within its jurisdiction the equal protection of the laws.

SECTION 2. Representatives shall be apportioned among the several States according to their respective numbers, counting the whole number of persons in each State, excluding Indians not taxed. But when the right to vote at any election for the choice of electors for President and Vice President of the United States, Representatives in Congress, the Executive and Judicial officers of a State, or the members of the Legislature thereof, is denied to any of the male inhabitants of such State, being twenty-one years of age, and citizens of the United States, or in any way abridged, except for participation in rebellion, or other crime, the basis of representation therein shall be reduced in the proportion which the number of such male citizens shall bear to the whole number of male citizens twenty-one years of age in such State.

SECTION 3. No person shall be a Senator or Representative in Congress, or elector of President and Vice President, or hold any office, civil or military, under the United States, or under any State, who, having previously taken an oath, as a member of Congress, or as an officer of the United States, or as a member of any State legislature, or as an executive or judicial officer of any State, to support the Constitution of the United States, shall have engaged in insurrection or rebellion against the same, or given aid or comfort to the enemies thereof. But Congress may by a vote of two-thirds of each House, remove such diability.

SECTION 4. The validity of the public debt of the United States, authorized by law, including debts incurred for payment of pensions and bounties for services in suppressing insurrection or rebellion, shall not be questioned. But neither the United States nor any State shall assume or pay any debt or obligation incurred in aid of insurrection or rebellion against the United States, or any claim for the loss or emancipation of any slave, but all such debts, obligations and claims shall be held illegal and void.

SECTION 5. The Congress shall have power to enforce, by appropriate legislation, the provisions of this article.

Amendment XV   (Ratified on February 3, 1870)

SECTION 1. The right of citizens of the United States to vote shall not be denied or abridged by the United States or by any State on account of race, color, or previous condition of servitude.

SECTION 2. The Congress shall have power to enforce this article by appropriate legislation.

Amendment XVI   (Ratified on February 3, 1913)

The Congress shall have power to lay and collect taxes on incomes, from whatever source derived, without apportionment among the several States, and without regard to any census or enumeration.

Amendment XVII   (Ratified on April 8, 1913)

The Senate of the United States shall be composed of two Senators from each State, elected by the people thereof, for six years; and each Senator shall have one vote. The electors in each State shall have the qualifications requisite for electors of the most numerous branch of the State legislatures.

When vacancies happen in the representation of any State in the Senate, the executive authority of such State shall issue writs of election to fill such vacancies: Provided, That the legislature of any State may empower the executive thereof to make temporary appointments until the people fill the vacancies by election as the legislature may direct.

This amendment shall not be so construed as to affect the election or term of any Senator chosen before it becomes valid as part of the Constitution.

Amendment XVIII   (Ratified on January 16, 1919)

SECTION 1. After one year from the ratification of this article the manufacture, sale, or transportation of intoxicating liquors within, the importation thereof into, or the exportation thereof from the United States and all territory subject to the jurisdiction thereof for beverage purposes is hereby prohibited.

SECTION 2. The Congress and the several States shall have concurrent power to enforce this article by appropriate legislation.

SECTION 3. This article shall be inoperative unless it shall have been ratified as an amendment to the Constitution by the legislatures of the several States, as provided in the Constitution, within seven years from the date of the submission hereof to the States by the Congress.

Amendment XIX   (Ratified on August 18, 1920)

The right of citizens of the United States to vote shall not be denied or abridged by the United States or by any State on account of sex.

Congress shall have power to enforce this article by appropriate legislation.

Amendment XX   (Ratified on February 6, 1933)

SECTION 1. The terms of the President and Vice President shall end at noon on the 20th day of January, and the terms of Senators and Representatives at noon on the 3d day of January, of the years in which such terms would have ended if this article had not been ratified; and the terms of their successors shall then begin.

SECTION 2. The Congress shall assemble at least once in every year, and such meeting shall begin at noon on the 3d day of January, unless they shall by law appoint a different day.

SECTION 3. If, at the time fixed for the beginning of the term of the President, the President elect shall have died, the Vice President elect shall become President. If a President shall not have been chosen before the time fixed for the beginning of his term, or if the President elect shall have failed to qualify, then the Vice President elect shall act as President until a President shall have qualified; and the Congress may by law provide for the case wherein neither a President elect nor a Vice President elect shall have qualified, declaring who shall then act as President, or the manner in which one who is to act shall be selected, and such person shall act accordingly until a President or Vice President shall have qualified.

SECTION 4. The Congress may by law provide for the case of the death of any of the persons from whom the House of Representatives may choose a President whenever the rights of choice shall have devolved upon them, and for the case of the death of any of the persons from whom the Senate may choose a Vice President whenever the right of choice shall have devolved upon them.

SECTION 5. Sections 1 and 2 shall take effect on the 15th day of October following the ratification of this article.

SECTION 6. This article shall be inoperative unless it shall have been ratified as an amendment to the Constitution by the legislatures of three-fourths of the several States within seven years from the date of its submission.

Amendment XXI *(Ratified on December 5, 1933)*

SECTION 1. The eighteenth article of amendment to the Constitution of the United States is hereby repealed.

SECTION 2. The transportation or importation into any State, Territory, or possession of the United States for delivery or use therein of intoxicating liquors, in violation of the laws thereof, is hereby prohibited.

SECTION 3. This article shall be inoperative unless it shall have been ratified as an amendment to the Constitution by conventions in the several States, as provided in the Constitution, within seven years from the date of the submission hereof to the States by the Congress.

Amendment XXII *(Ratified on February 27, 1951)*

No person shall be elected to the office of the President more than twice, and no person who has held the office of President, or acted as President, for more than two years of a term to which some other person was elected President shall be elected to the office of the President more than once. But this Article shall not apply to any person holding the office of President when this Article was proposed by the Congress, and shall not prevent any person who may be holding the office of President, or acting as President, during the term within which this Article becomes operative from holding the

office of President or acting as President during the remainder of such term.

Amendment XXIII *(Ratified on March 29, 1961)*

SECTION 1. The District constituting the seat of Government of the United States shall appoint in such manner as the Congress may direct:

A number of electors of President and Vice President equal to the whole number of Senators and Representatives in Congress to which the District would be entitled if it were a State, but in no event more than the least populous State; they shall be in addition to those appointed by the States, but they shall be considered, for the purposes of the election of President and Vice President, to be electors appointed by a State; and they shall meet in the District and perform such duties as provided by the twelfth article of amendment.

SECTION 2. The Congress shall have power to enforce this article by appropriate legislation.

Amendment XXIV *(Ratified on January 23, 1964)*

SECTION 1. The right of citizens of the United States to vote in any primary or other election for President or Vice President, for electors for President or Vice President, or for Senator or Representative in Congress, shall not be denied or abridged by the United States or any State by reason of failure to pay any poll tax or other tax.

SECTION 2. The Congress shall have power to enforce this article by appropriate legislation.

Amendment XXV *(Ratified on February 10, 1967)*

SECTION 1. In case of the removal of the President from office or of his death or resignation, the Vice President shall become President.

SECTION 2. Whenever there is a vacancy in the office of the Vice President, the President shall nominate a Vice President who shall take office upon confirmation by a majority vote of both Houses of Congress.

SECTION 3. Whenever the President transmits to the President pro tempore of the Senate and the Speaker of the House of Representatives his written declaration that he is unable to discharge the powers and duties of his office, and until he transmits to them a written declaration to the contrary, such powers and duties shall be discharged by the Vice President as Acting President.

SECTION 4. Whenever the Vice President and a majority of either the principal officers of the executive departments or of such other body as Congress may by law provide, transmit to the President pro tempore of the Senate and the Speaker of the House of Representatives their written declaration that the President is unable to discharge the powers and duties of his office, the Vice President shall immediately assume the powers and duties of the office as Acting President.

Thereafter, when the President transmits to the President pro tempore of the Senate and the Speaker of the House of Representatives his written declaration that no inability exists, he shall resume the powers and duties of his office unless the Vice President and a majority of either the principal officers of the executive department or of such other body as Congress may by law provide, transmit within four days to the President pro tempore of the Senate and the Speaker of the House of Representatives their written declaration that the President is unable to discharge the powers and duties of his office. Thereupon Congress shall decide the issue, assembling within forty-eight hours for that purpose if not in session. If the Congress, within twenty-one days after receipt of the latter written declaration, or, if Congress is not in session, within twenty-one days after Congress is required to assemble, determines by two-thirds vote of both Houses that the President is unable to discharge the powers and duties of his

office, the Vice President shall continue to discharge the same as Acting President; otherwise, the President shall resume the powers and duties of his office.

Amendment XXVI   *(Ratified on July 1, 1971)*

SECTION 1. The right of citizens of the United States, who are eighteen years of age or older, to vote shall not be denied or abridged by the United States or by any State on account of age.

SECTION 2. The Congress shall have power to enforce this article by appropriate legislation.

Amendment XXVII   *(Ratified on May 7, 1992)*

No law varying the compensation for the services of Senators and Representatives shall take effect until an election of Representatives shall have intervened.

Presidents, Congresses and Chief Justices: 1789–1992

TERM	PRESIDENT AND VICE PRESIDENT	PARTY OF PRESIDENT	CONGRESS	Majority Party		CHIEF JUSTICE OF THE UNITED STATES
				HOUSE	SENATE	
1789–1797	**George Washington** John Adams	None	1st 2d 3d 4th	(N/A) (N/A) (N/A) (N/A)	(N/A) (N/A) (N/A) (N/A)	John Jay (1789–1795) John Rutledge (1795) Oliver Ellsworth (1796–1800)
1797–1801	**John Adams** Thomas Jefferson	Federalist	5th 6th	(N/A) Fed	(N/A) Fed	Oliver Ellsworth (1796–1800) John Marshall (1801–1835)
1801–1809	**Thomas Jefferson** Aaron Burr (1801–1805) George Clinton (1805–1809)	Democratic-Republican	7th 8th 9th 10th	Dem-Rep Dem-Rep Dem-Rep Dem-Rep	Dem-Rep Dem-Rep Dem-Rep Dem-Rep	John Marshall (1801–1835)
1809–1817	**James Madison** George Clinton (1809–1812)[a] Elbridge Gerry (1813–1814)[a]	Democratic-Republican	11th 12th 13th 14th	Dem-Rep Dem-Rep Dem-Rep Dem-Rep	Dem-Rep Dem-Rep Dem-Rep Dem-Rep	John Marshall (1801–1835)
1817–1825	**James Monroe** Daniel D. Tompkins	Democratic-Republican	15th 16th 17th 18th	Dem-Rep Dem-Rep Dem-Rep Dem-Rep	Dem-Rep Dem-Rep Dem-Rep Dem-Rep	John Marshall (1801–1835)
1825–1829	**John Quincy Adams** John C. Calhoun	National-Republican	19th 20th	Nat'l Rep Dem	Nat'l Rep Dem	John Marshall (1801–1835)
1829–1837	**Andrew Jackson** John C. Calhoun (1829–1832)[b] Martin Van Buren (1833–1837)	Democrat	21st 22d 23d 24th	Dem Dem Dem Dem	Dem Dem Dem Dem	John Marshall (1801–1835) Roger B. Taney (1836–1864)
1837–1841	**Martin Van Buren** Richard M. Johnson	Democrat	25th 26th	Dem Dem	Dem Dem	Roger B. Taney (1836–1864)
1841	**William H. Harrison**[a] John Tyler (1841)	Whig				Roger B. Taney (1836–1864)
1841–1845	**John Tyler** (VP vacant)	Whig	27th 28th	Whig Dem	Whig Whig	Roger B. Taney (1836–1864)
1845–1849	**James K. Polk** George M. Dallas	Democrat	29th 30th	Dem Whig	Dem Dem	Roger B. Taney (1836–1864)
1849–1850	**Zachary Taylor**[a] Millard Fillmore	Whig	31st	Dem	Dem	Roger B. Taney (1836–1864)

| TERM | PRESIDENT AND VICE PRESIDENT | PARTY OF PRESIDENT | CONGRESS | Majority Party | | CHIEF JUSTICE OF THE UNITED STATES |
				HOUSE	SENATE	
1850–1853	**Millard Fillmore** (VP vacant)	Whig	32d	Dem	Dem	Roger B. Taney (1836–1864)
1853–1857	**Franklin Pierce** William R.D. King (1853)[a]	Democrat	33d 34th	Dem Rep	Dem Dem	Roger B. Taney (1836–1864)
1857–1861	**James Buchanan** John C. Breckinridge	Democrat	35th 36th	Dem Rep	Dem Dem	Roger B. Taney (1836–1864)
1861–1865	**Abraham Lincoln**[a] Hannibal Hamlin (1861–1865) Andrew Johnson (1865)	Republican	37th 38th 38th	Rep Rep Rep	Rep Rep Rep	Roger B. Taney (1836–1864) Salmon P. Chase (1864–1873)
1865–1869	**Andrew Johnson** (VP vacant)	Republican	39th 40th	Union Rep	Union Rep	Salmon P. Chase (1864–1873)
1869–1877	**Ulysses S. Grant** Schuyler Colfax (1869–1873) Henry Wilson (1873–1875)[a]	Republican	41st 42d 43d 44th	Rep Rep Rep Dem	Rep Rep Rep Rep	Salmon P. Chase (1864–1873) Morrison R. Waite (1874–1888)
1877–1881	**Rutherford B. Hayes** William A. Wheeler	Republican	45th 46th	Dem Dem	Rep Dem	Morrison R. Waite (1874–1888)
1881	**James A. Garfield**[a] Chester A. Arthur	Republican	47th	Rep	Rep	Morrison R. Waite (1874–1888)
1881–1885	**Chester A. Arthur** (VP vacant)	Republican	48th	Dem	Rep	Morrison R. Waite (1874–1888)
1885–1889	**Grover Cleveland** Thomas A. Hendricks (1885)[a]	Democrat	49th 50th	Dem Dem	Rep Rep	Morrison R. Waite (1874–1888) Melville W. Fuller (1888–1910)
1889–1893	**Benjamin Harrison** Levi P. Morton	Republican	51st 52d	Rep Dem	Rep Rep	Melville W. Fuller (1888–1910)
1893–1897	**Grover Cleveland** Adlai E. Stevenson	Democrat	53d 54th	Dem Rep	Dem Rep	Melville W. Fuller (1888–1910)
1897–1901	**William McKinley**[a] Garret A. Hobart (1897–1899)[a] Theodore Roosevelt (1901)	Republican	55th 56th	Rep Rep	Rep Rep	Melville W. Fuller (1888–1910)
1901–1909	**Theodore Roosevelt** (VP vacant, 1901–1905) Charles W. Fairbanks (1905–1909)	Republican	57th 58th 59th 60th	Rep Rep Rep Rep	Rep Rep Rep Rep	Melville W. Fuller (1888–1910)
1909–1913	**William Howard Taft** James S. Sherman (1909–1912)[a]	Republican	61st 62d	Rep Dem	Rep Rep	Melville W. Fuller (1888–1910) Edward D. White (1910–1921)
1913–1921	**Woodrow Wilson** Thomas R. Marshall	Democrat	63d 64th 65th 66th	Dem Dem Dem Rep	Dem Dem Dem Rep	Edward D. White (1910–1921)
1921–1923	**Warren G. Harding**[a] Calvin Coolidge	Republican	67th	Rep	Rep	William Howard Taft (1921–1930)

| TERM | PRESIDENT AND VICE PRESIDENT | PARTY OF PRESIDENT | CONGRESS | Majority Party | | CHIEF JUSTICE OF THE UNITED STATES |
				HOUSE	SENATE	
1923–1929	**Calvin Coolidge** (VP vacant, 1923–1925) Charles G. Dawes (1925–1929)	Republican	68th 69th 70th	Rep Rep Rep	Rep Rep Rep	William Howard Taft (1921–1930)
1929–1933	**Herbert Hoover** Charles Curtis	Republican	71st 72d	Rep Dem	Rep Rep	William Howard Taft (1921–1930) Charles Evans Hughes (1930–1941)
1933–1945	**Franklin D. Roosevelt**[a] John N. Garner (1933–1941) Henry A. Wallace (1941–1945) Harry S Truman (1945)	Democrat	73d 74th 75th 76th 77th 78th	Dem Dem Dem Dem Dem Dem	Dem Dem Dem Dem Dem Dem	Charles Evans Hughes (1930–1941) Harlan F. Stone (1941–1946)
1945–1953	**Harry S Truman** (VP vacant, 1945–1949) Alben W. Barkley (1949–1953)	Democrat	79th 80th 81st 82d	Dem Rep Dem Dem	Dem Rep Dem Dem	Harlan F. Stone (1941–1946) Frederick M. Vinson (1946–1953)
1953–1961	**Dwight D. Eisenhower** Richard M. Nixon	Republican	83d 84th 85th 86th	Rep Dem Dem Dem	Rep Dem Dem Dem	Frederick M. Vinson (1945–1953) Earl Warren (1953–1969)
1961–1963	**John F. Kennedy**[a] Lyndon B. Johnson (1961–1963)	Democrat	87th	Dem	Dem	Earl Warren (1953–1969)
1963–1969	**Lyndon B. Johnson** (VP vacant, 1963–1965) Hubert H. Humphrey (1965–1969)	Democrat	88th 89th 90th	Dem Dem Dem	Dem Dem Dem	Earl Warren (1953–1969)
1969–1974	**Richard M. Nixon**[c] Spiro T. Agnew (1969–1973)[b] Gerald R. Ford (1973–1974)[d]	Republican	91st 92d	Dem Dem	Dem Dem	Earl Warren (1953–1969) Warren E. Burger (1969–1986)
1974–1977	**Gerald R. Ford** Nelson A. Rockefeller[d]	Republican	93d 94th	Dem Dem	Dem Dem	Warren E. Burger (1969–1986)
1977–1981	**Jimmy Carter** Walter Mondale	Democrat	95th 96th	Dem Dem	Dem Dem	Warren E. Burger (1969–1986)
1981–1989	**Ronald Reagan** George Bush	Republican	97th 98th 99th 100th	Dem Dem Dem Dem	Rep Rep Rep Dem	Warren E. Burger (1969–1986) William H. Rehnquist (1986–)
1989–1993	**George Bush** J. Danforth Quayle	Republican	101st 102nd	Dem Dem	Dem Dem	William H. Rehnquist (1986–)
1993–	**William J. Clinton** Albert Gore Jr.	Democrat	103d 104th	Dem Rep	Dem Rep	William H. Rehnquist (1986–)

[a]Died in office.
[b]Resigned from the vice presidency.
[c]Resigned from the presidency.
[d]Appointed vice president.

APPENDIX IV

The Federalist No. 10

James Madison

November 22, 1787

TO THE PEOPLE OF THE STATE OF NEW YORK

Among the numerous advantages promised by a well constructed Union, none deserves to be more accurately developed than its tendency to break and control the violence of faction. The friend of popular governments, never finds himself so much alarmed for their character and fate, as when he contemplates their propensity to this dangerous vice. He will not fail therefore to set a due value on any plan which, without violating the principles to which he is attached, provides a proper cure for it. The instability, injustice and confusion introduced into the public councils, have in truth been the mortal diseases under which popular governments have every where perished; as they continue to be the favorite and fruitful topics from which the adversaries to liberty derive their most specious declamations. The valuable improvements made by the American Constitutions on the popular models, both ancient and modern, cannot certainly be too much admired; but it would be an unwarrantable partiality, to contend that they have as effectually obviated the danger on this side as was wished and expected. Complaints are every where heard from our most considerate and virtuous citizens, equally the friends of public and private faith, and of public and personal liberty; that our governments are too unstable; that the public good is disregarded in the conflicts of rival parties; and that measures are too often decided, not according to the rules of justice, and the rights of the minor party; but by the superior force of an interested and over-bearing majority. However anxiously we may wish that these complaints had no foundation, the evidence of known facts will not permit us to deny that they are in some degree true. it will be found indeed, on a candid review of our situation, that some of the distresses under which we labor, have been erroneously charged on the operation of our governments; but it will be found, at the same time, that other causes will not alone account for many of our heaviest misfortunes; and particularly, for that prevailing and increasing distrust of public engagements, and alarm for private rights, which are echoed from one end of the continent to the other. These must be chiefly, if not wholly, effects of the unsteadiness and injustice, with which a factious spirit has tainted our public administrations.

By a faction I understand a number of citizens, whether amounting to a majority or minority of the whole, who are united and actuated by some common impulse of passion or of interest, adverse to the rights of other citizens, or to the permanent and aggregate interests of the community.

There are two methods of curing the mischiefs of faction: the one, by removing its causes; the other, by controlling its effects.

There are again two methods of removing the causes of faction: the one by destroying the liberty which is essential to its existence; the other, by giving to every citizen the same opinions, the same passions, and the same interests.

It could never be more truly said than of the first remedy, that it is worse than the disease. Liberty is to faction, what air is to fire, an aliment without which it instantly expires. But it could not be a less folly to abolish liberty, which is essential to political life, because it nourishes faction, than it would be to wish the annihilation of air, which is essential to animal life, because it imparts to fire its destructive agency.

The second expedient is as impracticable, as the first would be unwise. As long as the reason of man continues fallible, and he is at liberty to exercise it, different opinions will be formed. As long as the connection subsists between his reason and his self-love, his opinions and his passions will have a reciprocal influence on each other; and the former will be objects to which the latter will attach themselves. The diversity in the faculties of men from which the rights of property originate, is not less an insuperable obstacle to a uniformity of interests. The protection of these faculties is the first object of Government.

From the protection of different and unequal faculties of acquiring property, the possession of different degrees and kinds of property immediately results: and from the influence of these on the sentiments and views of the respective proprietors, ensues a division of the society into different interests and parties.

The latent causes of faction are thus sown in the nature of man; and we see them every where brought into different degrees of activity, according to the different circumstances of civil society. A zeal for different opinions concerning religion, concerning Government and many other points, as well of speculation as of practice; an attachment to different leaders ambitiously contending for pre-eminence and power; or to persons of other descriptions whose fortunes have been interesting to the human passions, have in turn divided mankind into parties, inflamed them with mutual animosity, and rendered them much more disposed to vex and oppress each other, than to co-operate for their common good. So strong is this propensity of mankind to fall into mutual animosities, that where no substantial occasion presents itself, the most frivolous and fanciful distinctions have been sufficient to kindle their unfriendly passions, and excite their most violent conflicts. But the most common and durable source of factions, has been the various and unequal distribution of property. Those who hold, and those who are without property, have ever formed distinct interests in society. Those who are creditors, and those who are debtors, fall under a like discrimination. A landed interest, a manufacturing interest, a mercantile interest, a monied interest, with many lesser interests, grow up of necessity in civilized nations, and divide them into different classes, actuated by different sentiments and views. The regulation of these various and interfering interests forms the principal task of modern Legislation, and involves the spirit of party and faction in the necessary and ordinary operations of Government.

No man is allowed to be a judge in his own cause; because his interest would certainly bias his judgment, and, not improbably, corrupt his integrity. With equal, nay with greater reason, a body of men, are unfit to be both judges and parties, at the same time; yet, what are many of the most important acts of legislation, but so many judicial determinations, not indeed concerning the rights of single persons, but concerning the rights of large bodies of citizens, and what are the different classes of legislators, but advocates and parties to the causes which they determine? Is a law proposed con-

cerning private debts? It is a question to which the creditors are parties on one side, and the debtors on the other. Justice ought to hold the balance between them. Yet the parties are and must be themselves the judges; and the most numerous party, or, in other words, the most powerful faction must be expected to prevail. Shall domestic manufactures be encouraged, and in what degree, by restrictions on foreign manufactures? are questions which would be differently decided by the landed and the manufacturing classes; and probably by neither, with a sole regard to justice and the public good. The apportionment of taxes on the various descriptions of property, is an act which seems to require the most exact impartiality; yet, there is perhaps no legislative act in which greater opportunity and temptation are given to a predominant party, to trample on the rules of justice. Every shilling with which they over-burden the inferior number, is a shilling saved to their own pockets.

It is in vain to say, that enlightened statesmen will be able to adjust these clashing interests, and render them all subservient to the public good. Enlightened statesmen will not always be at the helm: Nor, in many cases, can such an adjustment be made at all, without taking into view indirect and remote considerations, which will rarely prevail over the immediate interest which one party may find in disregarding the rights of another, or the good of the whole.

The inference to which we are brought, is, that the *causes* of faction cannot be removed; and that relief is only to be sought in the means of controlling its *effects*.

If a faction consists of less than a majority, relief is supplied by the republican principle, which enables the majority to defeat its sinister views by regular vote: it may clog the administration, it may convulse the society; but it will be unable to execute and mask its violence under the forms of the Constitution. When a majority is included in a faction, the form of popular government on the other hand enables it to sacrifice to its ruling passion or interest, both the public good and the rights of other citizens. To secure the public good, and private rights, against the danger of such a faction, and at the same time to preserve the spirit and the form of popular government, is then the great object to which our enquiries are directed: Let me add that it is the great desideratum, by which alone this form of government can be rescued from the opprobrium under which it has so long labored, and be recommended to the esteem and adoption of mankind.

By what means is this object attainable? Evidently by one of two only. Either the existence of the same passion or interest in a majority at the same time, must be prevented; or the majority, having such co-existent passion or interest, must be rendered, by their number and local situation, unable to concert and carry into effect schemes of oppression. If the impulse and the opportunity be suffered to coincide, we well know that neither moral nor religious motives can be relied on as an adequate control. They are not found to be such on the injustice and violence of individuals, and lose their efficacy in proportion to the number combined together; that is, in proportion as their efficacy becomes needful.

From this view of the subject, it may be concluded, that a pure Democracy, by which I mean, a Society, consisting of a small number of citizens, who assemble and administer the Government in person, can admit of no cure for the mischiefs of faction. A common passion or interest will, in almost every case, be felt by a majority of the whole; a communication and concert results from the form of Government itself; and there is nothing to check the inducements to sacrifice the weaker party, or an obnoxious individual. Hence it is, that such Democracies have ever been spectacles of turbulence and contention; have ever been found incompatible with personal security, or the rights of property; and have in general been as short in their lives, as they have been violent in their deaths. Theoretic politicians, who have patronized this species of Government, have erroneously supposed, that by reducing mankind to a perfect equality in their political rights, they would, at the same time, be perfectly equalized and assimilated in their possessions, their opinions, and their passions.

A republic, by which I mean a government in which the scheme of representation takes place, opens a different prospect, and promises the cure for which we are seeking. Let us examine the points in which it varies from pure democracy, and we shall comprehend both the nature of the cure and the efficacy which it must derive from the union.

The two great points of difference, between a democracy and a republic, are, first, the delegation of the government, in the latter, to a small number of citizens, elected by the rest; secondly, the greater number of citizens, and greater sphere of country, over which the latter may be extended.

The effect of the first difference is, on the one hand, to refine and enlarge the public views, by passing them through the medium of a chosen body of citizens, whose wisdom may best discern the true interest of their country, and whose patriotism and love of justice, will be least likely to sacrifice it to temporary or partial considerations. Under such a regulation, it may well happen, that the public voice, pronounced by the representatives of the people, will be more consonant to the public good, than if pronounced by the people themselves, convened for the purpose. On the other hand the effect may be inverted. Men of factious tempers, of local prejudices, or of sinister designs, may by intrigue, by corruption, or by other means, first obtain the suffrages, and then betray the interest of the people. The question resulting is, whether small or extensive republics are most favorable to the election of proper guardians of the public weal, and it is clearly decided in favor of the latter by two obvious considerations.

In the first place, it is to be remarked that, however small the republic may be, the representatives must be raised to a certain number, in order to guard against the cabals of a few; and that however large it may be, they must be limited to a certain number, in order to guard against the confusion of a multitude. Hence, the number of representatives in the two cases not being in proportion to that of the constituents, and being proportionally greatest in the small republic, it follows, that if the proportion of fit characters be not less in the large than in the small republic, the former will present a greater option, and consequently a greater probability of a fit choice.

In the next place, as each Representative will be chosen by a greater number of citizens in the large than in the small Republic, it will be more difficult for unworthy candidates to practise with success the vicious arts, by which elections are too often carried; and the suffrages of the people being more free, will be more likely to center on men who possess the most attractive merit, and the most diffusive and established characters.

It must be confessed, that in this, as in most other cases, there is a mean, on both sides of which inconveniences will be found to lie. By enlarging too much the number of electors, you render the representative too little acquainted with all their local circumstances and lesser interests; as by reducing it too much, you render him unduly attached to these, and too little fit to comprehend and pursue great and national objects. The Federal Constitution forms a happy combination in this respect; the great and aggregate interests being referred to the national, the local and particular, to the state legislatures.

The other point of difference is, the greater number of citizens and extent of territory which may be brought within the compass of Republican, than of Democratic Government; and it is this circumstance principally which renders factious combinations less to be dreaded in the former, than in the latter. The smaller the society, the fewer probably will be the distinct parties and interests composing it; the fewer the distinct parties and interests, the more frequently will a majority be found of the same party; and the smaller the number of individuals composing a majority, and the smaller the compass within which they are placed, the more easily will they concert and execute their plans of oppression. Extend the sphere, and you take in a greater variety of parties and interests; you make it less probable that a majority of the whole will have a common motive to invade the rights of other citizens; or if such a common motive exists, it will be more difficult for all who feel it to discover their own strength, and to act in unison with each other. Besides other impediments, it may be remarked, that where there is a consciousness of unjust or dishonorable purposes, communication is always checked by distrust, in proportion to the number whose concurrence is necessary.

Hence it clearly appears, that the same advantage, which a Republic has over a Democracy, in controlling the effects of faction, is enjoyed by a large over a small Republic—is enjoyed by the Union over the States composing it. Does this advantage consist in the substitution of Representatives, whose enlightened views and virtuous sentiments render them superior to local prejudices, and to schemes of injustice? It will not be denied, that the Representation of the Union will be most likely to possess these requisite endowments. Does it consist in the greater security afforded by a greater variety of parties, against the event of any one party being able to outnumber and oppress the rest? In an equal degree does the increased variety of parties, comprised within the Union, increase this security? Does it, in fine, consist in the greater obstacles opposed to the concert and accomplishment of the secret wishes of an unjust and interested majority? Here, again, the extent of the Union gives it the most palpable advantage.

The influence of factious leaders may kindle a flame within their particular States, but will be unable to spread a general conflagration through the other States: a religious sect, may degenerate into a political faction in a part of the Confederacy but the variety of sects dispersed over the entire face of it, must secure the national Councils against any danger from that source: a rage for paper money, for an abolition of debts, for an equal division of property, or for any other improper or wicked project, will be less apt to pervade the whole body of the Union, than a particular member of it; in the same proportion as such a malady is more likely to taint a particular county or district, than an entire State.

In the extent and proper structure of the Union, therefore, we behold a Republican remedy for the diseases most incident to Republican Government. And according to the degree of pleasure and pride, we feel in being Republicans, ought to be our zeal in cherishing the spirit, and supporting the character of Federalists.

PUBLIUS

The Federalist No. 51

James Madison

February 6, 1788

TO THE PEOPLE OF THE STATE OF NEW YORK

To what expedient then shall we finally resort for maintaining in practice the necessary partition of power among the several departments, as laid down in the constitution? The only answer that can be given is, that as all these exterior provisions are found to be inadequate, the defect must be supplied, by so contriving the interior structure of the government, as that its several constituent parts may, by their mutual relations, be the means of keeping each other in their proper places. Without presuming to undertake a full development of this important idea, I will hazard a few general observations, which may perhaps place it in a clearer light, and enable us to form a more correct judgment of the principles and structure of the government planned by the convention.

In order to lay a due foundation for that separate and distinct exercise of the different powers of government, which to a certain extent, is admitted on all hands to be essential to the preservation of liberty, it is evident that each department should have a will of its own; and consequently should be so constituted, that the members of each should have as little agency as possible in the appointment of the members of the others. Were this principle rigorously adhered to, it would require that all the appointments for the supreme executive, legislative, and judiciary magistracies, should be drawn from the same fountain of authority, the people, through channels, having no communication whatever with one another. Perhaps such a plan of constructing the several departments would be less difficult in practice than it may in contemplation appear. Some difficulties however, and some additional expense, would attend the execution of it. Some deviations therefore from the principle must be admitted. In the constitution of the judiciary department in particular, it might be inexpedient to insist rigorously on the principle; first, because peculiar qualifications being essential in the members, the primary consideration ought to be to select that mode of choice, which best secures these qualifications; secondly, because the permanent tenure by which the appointments are held in that department, must soon destroy all sense of dependence on the authority conferring them.

It is equally evident that the members of each department should be as little dependent as possible on those of the others, for the emoluments annexed to their offices. Were the executive magistrate, or the judges, not independent of the legislature in this particular, their independence in every other would be merely nominal.

But the great security against a gradual concentration of the several powers in the same department, consists in giving to those who administer each department, the necessary constitutional means, and personal motives, to resist encroachments of the others. The provision for defense must in this, as in all other cases, be made commensurate to the danger of attack. Ambition must be made to counteract ambition. The interest of the man must be connected with the constitutional right of the place. It may be a reflection on human nature, that such devices should be necessary to control the abuses of government. But what is government itself but the greatest of all reflections on human nature? If men were angels, no government would be necessary. If angels were to govern men, neither external nor internal controls on government would be necessary. In framing a government which is to be administered by men over men, the great difficulty lies in this: You must first enable the government to control the governed; and in the next place, oblige it to control itself. A dependence on the people is no doubt the primary control on the government; but experience has taught mankind the necessity of auxiliary precautions.

This policy of supplying by opposite and rival interests, the defect of better motives, might be traced through the whole system of human affairs, private as well as public. We see it particularly displayed in all the subordinate distributions of power; where the constant aim is to divide and arrange the several offices in such a manner as that each may be a check on the other; that the private interest of every individual, may be a sentinel over the public rights. These inventions of prudence cannot be less requisite in the distribution of the supreme powers of the state.

But it is not possible to give to each department an equal power of self defense. In republican government the legislative authority, necessarily, predominates. The remedy for this inconveniency is, to divide the legislature into different branches; and to render them by different modes of election, and different principles of action, as little connected with each other, as the nature of their common functions, and their common dependence on the society, will admit. It may even be necessary to guard against dangerous encroachments by still further precautions. As the weight of the legislative authority requires that it should be thus divided, the weakness of the executive may require, on the other hand, that it should be fortified. An absolute negative, on the legislature, appears at first view to be the natural defense with which the executive magistrate should be armed. But perhaps it would be neither altogether safe, nor alone sufficient. On ordinary occasion, it might not be exerted with the requisite firmness; and on extraordinary occasions, it might be perfidiously abused. May not this defect of an absolute negative be supplied, by some qualified connection between this weaker department, and the weaker branch of the stronger department, by which the latter may be led to support the constitutional rights of the former, without being too much detached from the rights of its own department?

If the principles on which these observations are founded be just, as I persuade myself they are, and they be applied as a criterion, to the several state constitutions, and to the federal constitution, it will be found, that if the latter does not perfectly correspond with them, the former are infinitely less able to bear such a test.

There are moreover two considerations particularly applicable to the federal system of America, which place that system in a very interesting point of view.

First. In a single republic, all the power surrendered by the people, is submitted to the administration of a single government; and usurpations are guarded against by a division of the government into distinct and separate departments. In the compound republic of America, the power surrendered by the people, is first divided between two distinct governments, and then the portion allotted to each, subdivided among distinct and separate departments. Hence a double security arises to the rights of the people. The different governments will control each other; at the same time that each will be controlled by itself.

Second. It is of great importance in a republic, not only to guard the society against the oppression of its rulers; but to guard one part of the society against the injustice of the other part. Different interests necessarily exist in different classes of citizens. If a majority be united by a common interest, the rights of the minority will be insecure. There are but two methods of providing against this evil: The one by creating a will in the community independent of the majority, that is, of the society itself, the other by comprehending in the society so many separate descriptions of citizens, as will render an unjust combination of a majority of the whole, very improbable, if not impracticable. The first method prevails in all governments possessing an hereditary or self appointed authority. This at best is but a precarious security; because a power independent of the society may as well espouse the unjust views of the major, as the rightful interests, of the minor party, and may possibly be turned against both parties.

The second method will be exemplified in the federal republic of the United States. While all authority in it will be derived from and dependent on the society, the society itself will be broken into so many parts, interests and classes of citizens, that the rights of individuals or of the minority, will be in little danger from interested combinations of the majority. In a free government, the security for civil rights must be the same as for religious rights. It consists in the one case in the multiplicity of interests, and in the other, in the multiplicity of sects. The degree of security in both cases will depend on the number of interests and sects; and this may be presumed to depend on the extent of country and number of people comprehended under the same government. This view of the subject must particularly recommend a proper federal system to all the sincere and considerate friends of republican government: Since it shows that in exact proportion as the territory of the union may be formed into more circumscribed confederacies or states, oppressive combinations of a majority will be facilitated, the best security under the republican form, for the rights of every class of citizens, will be diminished; and consequently, the stability and independence of some member of the government, the only other security, must be proportionally increased. Justice is the end of government. It is the end of civil society. It ever has been, and ever will be pursued, until it be obtained, or until liberty be lost in the pursuit. In a society under the forms of which the stronger faction can readily unite and oppress the weaker, anarchy may as truly be said to reign, as in a state of nature where the weaker individual is not secured against the violence of the stronger: And as in the latter state even the stronger individuals are prompted by the uncertainty of their condition, to submit to a government which may protect the weak as well as themselves: So in the former state, will the more powerful factions or parties be gradually induced by a like motive, to wish for a government which will protect all parties, the weaker as well as the more powerful. It can be little doubted, that if the state of Rhode Island was separated from the confederacy, and left to itself, the insecurity of rights under the popular form of government within such narrow limits, would be displayed by such reiterated oppressions of factious majorities, that some power altogether independent of the people would soon be called for by the voice of the very factions whose misrule had proved the necessity of it. In the extended republic of the United States, and among the great variety of interests, parties and sects which it embraces, a coalition of a majority of the whole society could seldom take place on any other principles than those of justice and the general good; and there being thus less danger to a minor from the will of the major party, there must be less pretext also, to provide for the security of the former, by introducing into the government a will not dependent on the latter; or in other words, a will independent of the society itself. It is no less certain than it is important, notwithstanding the contrary opinions which have been entertained, that the larger the society, provided it lie within a practicable sphere, the more duly capable it will be of self government. And happily for the *republican cause,* the practicable sphere may be carried to a very great extent, by a judicious modification and mixture of the *federal principle.*

PUBLIUS

E N D N O T E S

Chapter 1

1. The English and Scots often signed covenants with their churches in a pledge to defend and further their religion. In the Bible, covenants were solemn promises made to humanity by God. In the colonial context, then, covenants were formal agreements sworn to a new government to abide by its terms.

2. The term *men* is used here because only males were considered fit to vote.

3. Jefferson ultimately and without explanation changed these words to "Life, Liberty, and the pursuit of Happiness," although most of the signers were far more concerned with property.

4. Margaret Carlson, "Where Is 'My Center'?" *Time* (June 14, 1993): 22.

5. Harold D. Lasswell, *Politics: Who Gets What, When, and How* (New York: McGraw-Hill, 1938).

6. David B. Truman, *The Governmental Process* (New York: Knopf, 1951).

7. See also Robert Dahl, *Dilemmas of Pluralist Democracy: Autonomy vs. Control* (New Haven, CT: Yale University Press, 1982) and Iris Marion Young, *Justice and the Politics of Difference* (Princeton, NJ: Princeton University Press, 1990).

8. Theodore S. Lowi, *The End of Liberalism* (New York: Norton, 1979), Chapter 3.

9. Modern disciples of *laissez-faire* are called libertarians. Libertarians adamantly oppose all forms of government regulation and action unless it is critical to the protection of life, liberty, or property. They argue that while governments are at best an evil necessity, governments are best when they govern least.

10. Karl Marx, "Critique of the Gotha Program," in *Marx Selections,* ed. Allen W. Wood (New York: Macmillan, 1988), p. 190.

11. Hannah Arendt, *The Origins of Totalitarianism* (Cambridge, MA: Harvard University Press, 1958).

Chapter 2

1. Sir William Blackstone attempted to codify the common law's most widely accepted principles. His multi-volume *Commentaries on the Law of England* remain the single best source of English law.

2. For an account of the early development of the colonies, see D.W. Meining, *The Shaping of America,* Vol. 1: *Atlantic America, 1492–1800* (New Haven, CT: Yale University Press, 1986).

3. For an excellent chronology of the events leading up to the writing of the Declaration of Independence and the colonists' break with Great Britain, see Calvin D. Linton, ed., *The Bicentennial Almanac* (Nashville, TN: Thomas Nelson, 1975).

4. See Garry Wills, *Inventing America: Jefferson's Declaration of Independence* (New York: Random House, 1978). Wills argues that the Declaration was signed solely to secure foreign aid for the ongoing war effort.

5. For John Locke's influence on the Declaration of Independence, see Carl L. Becker, *The Declaration of Independence: A Study in the History of Political Ideas* (New York: Random House, 1942).

6. See Gordon Wood, *The Creation of the American Republic, 1776–1787* (Chapel Hill: University of North Carolina Press, 1969).

7. For more about the Articles of Confederation, see Merrill Jensen, *The Articles of Confederation* (Madison: University of Wisconsin Press, 1940).

8. Quoted in Selma R. Williams, *Fifty-Five Fathers: The Story of the Constitutional Convention* (New York: Dodd, Mead, 1970), p. 10.

9. See Samuel Beer, "Federalism, Nationalism and Democracy in America," *American Political Science Review*, 72 (March 1978): 9–21.

10. Quoted in Doris Faber and Harold Faber, *We the People* (New York: Charles Scribner's Sons, 1987), p. 25.

11. Ibid., p. 31.

12. For more on the political nature of compromise at the Convention, see Calvin C. Jillson, *Constitution Making: Conflict and Consensus in the Federal Constitution of 1787* (New York: Agathon, 1988).

13. This kind of assumption about slaves was never specifically spelled out in the Constitution. In fact, slavery is nowhere specifically mentioned in that document. Although many of the Framers were morally opposed to slavery, they recognized that if the convention attempted to abolish or seriously restrict it in the short term, the Southern states would walk away from the new Union (as they eventually did, resulting in the Civil War).

14. Quoted in Faber and Faber, *We the People,* p. 43. (See n. 10.)

15. Quoted in Richard N. Current, T. Harry Williams, Frank Freidel, and Alan Brinkley, *American History: A Survey*, 6th ed. (New York: McGraw-Hill, 1983), p. 168.

16. Bernard Bailyn, *The Ideological Origins of the American Revolution* (Cambridge, MA: Harvard University Press, 1967).

17. Richard E. Neustadt, *Presidential Power: The Politics of Leadership from FDR to Carter* (New York: Macmillan, 1980), p. 26.

18. See E.P. Panagopoulos, *Essays on the History and Meaning of Checks and Balances* (Landham, MD: University Press of America, 1985).

19. Quoted in Faber and Faber, *We the People,* pp. 51–52. (See n. 10.)

20. Federal Republicans favored a republican or representative form of government (do not confuse this term with the modern Republican Party, which came into being in 1854; see Chapter 11). Ultimately the word *federal* came to mean the form of government embodied in the new Constitution, just as *confederation* meant the "league of states" under the Articles, and later came to mean the "Confederacy" of 1861–1865.

21. Numerous editions of *The Federalist Papers* exist. One of the most commonly used is: Clinton Rossiter, ed., *The Federalist* (New York: New American Library, 1961).

22. See Ralph Ketcham, ed., *The Anti-Federalist Papers and the Constitutional Debates* (New York: New American Library, 1986).

23. See Alan P. Grimes, *Democracy and the Amendments to the Constitution* (Lexington, MA: Lexington Books, 1978).

24. David E. Kyvig, *Repealing National Prohibition* (Chicago: University of Chicago Press, 1978).

25. See Jane J. Mansbridge, *Why We Lost the ERA* (Chicago: University of Chicago Press, 1986).

26. Eleanor Flexner, *Century of Struggle: The Woman's Rights Movement in the United States* (New York: Atheneum, 1974).

27. Speech by Attorney General Edwin Meese III before the American Bar Association, July 9, 1985, Washington, DC.

28. Speech by William J. Brennan Jr. at Georgetown University, Text and Teaching Symposium, October 10, 1985, Washington, DC.

29. James Bryce. *The American Commonwealth*, vol. I, (New York: Macmillan, 1889), pp. 293–295.

30. For a full critique of these proposals see Mark P. Petracca with Lance Bailey and Pamela Smith, "Proposals for Constitutional Reform: An Evaluation of the Committee on the Constitutional System," *Presidential Studies Quarterly*, 20 (Summer 1990): 503–532.

31. James L. Sundquist, "Needed: A Political Theory for the New Era of Coalition Governments in the United States," *Political Science Quarterly*, 103 (1988): 613–635.

32. Ibid. 631.

33. Hedrick Smith, "The Politics of Blame," *The New York Times,* October 7, 1984: 36.

Chapter 3

1. In *City of Burbank* v. *Lockheed*, 411 U.S. 624 (1973), the U.S. Supreme Court ruled that the city could not impose curfews on plane takeoff or landing times. The Court said that one uniform *national* standard was critical for safety and the national interest.

2. *McCulloch* v. *Maryland*, 4 Wheat. 316 (1819).

3. The Constitution does not specifically mention slaves. It does, however, contain the mandate that "No Person held to Service or Labour in one State . . . escaping into another, shall . . . be discharged from such service . . . but shall be delivered up."

4. *Kentucky* v. *Dennison*, 65 U.S. 66 (1861).

5. *Puerto Rico* v. *Branstad,* 483 U.S. 219 (1987).

6. 252 U.S. 416 (1920).

7. John A. Garraty, ed., *Quarrels That Have Shaped the Constitution* (New York: Harper & Row, 1987), Chapter 3.

8. *McCulloch* v. *Maryland*, 4 Wheat. 316 (1819).

9. *Gibbons* v. *Ogden*, 22 U.S. 1 (1824).

10. 19 How. 393 (1857).

11. 16 Wall. 36 (1873); see Chapter 5.

12. *Lane County* v. *Oregon*, 74 U.S. 71 (1869).

13. 163 U.S. 537 (1896).

14. *Panhandle Oil Co.* v. *Knox*, 277 U.S. 218 (1928).

15. *Indian Motorcycle Co.* v. *United States*, 238 U.S. 570 (1931).

16. *Pensacola Telegraph* v. *Western Union*, 96 U.S. 1 (1877).

17. Lee Epstein, *Conservatives in Court* (Knoxville: University of Tennessee Press, 1985).

18. *NLRB* v. *Jones & Laughlin Steel Co.*, 301 U.S. 1 (1937).

19. *United States* v. *Darby*, 312 U.S. 100 (1941).

20. *Wickard* v. *Filburn*, 317 U.S. 111 (1942).

21. Morton Grodzins, "Centralization and Decentralization in the American Federal System," *A Nation of States*, ed. Robert A. Goldwin (Chicago: Rand McNally, 1963), pp. 3–4.

22. Alice M. Rivlin, *Reviving the American Dream*, (Washington, DC, Brookings Institution, 1992), p. 92.

23. Ibid., p. 98.

24. Advisory Commission on Intergovernmental Relations, "The Federal Role in the Federal System: The Dynamics of Growth" (Washington, DC: 1980), pp. 120–121.

25. Aaron Wildavsky, "Birthday Cake Federalism," in Robert E. Hawkins, ed. *American Federalism: A New Partnership for the Republic* (New Brunswick, NJ: Transaction Press, 1982), p. 182.

26. Samuel H. Beer, "The Modernization of American Federalism," *Publius* 3 (Fall 1973): 74–79.

27. Edward I. Koch, "The Mandate Millstone," *The Public Interest* 61 (Fall 1980): 43.

28. Richard P. Nathan et al. *Reagan and the States* (Princeton, NJ: Princeton University Press, 1987), p. 4.

29. John Kincaid, "From Cooperation to Coercion in American Federalism: Housing, Fragmentation, and Preemption, 1789–1992," *Journal of Law and Politics* 9 (Winter 1993): 333–430.

30. This discussion of preemption relies heavily on Joseph F. Zimmerman, *Contemporary American Federalism: The Growth of National Power* (New York: Praeger, 1992), pp. 55–81.

31. Timothy J. Conlan and David R. Beam, "Federal Mandates: The Record of Reform and Future Prospects," *Intergovernmental Perspective* (Fall, 1992): 9.

32. Ibid.

33. William Claiborne, "States Demand an Explanation; Federal Lawmakers Summoned to Justify Unfunded Mandates," *Washington Post*, July 5, 1993: A17.

34. When senators were directly elected by state legislatures, senators were much more responsive to state legislators than they are today. In fact, these summonses have no legal force. But it is unlikely they can be ignored without a high political cost.

35. "Vice President Al Gore Calls for New Federalism to Meet Concerns, Goals," *Government Employee Relations Report*, 31 (August 23, 1993): 1119.

36. Quoted in David E. Anderson, "Conservative Think Tanks Go Local," *UPI* (June 10, 1991), BC Cycle.

37. *Harper* v. *Virginia Board of Elections*, 383 U.S. 663 (1966).

38. *Gregory* v. *Ashcroft*, 111 S.Ct. 2395 (1991).

39. 426 U.S. 833 (1976).

40. 469 U.S. 528 (1985).

41. *United States* v. *Lopez*, 1995 LEXIS 3039.

42. Marianne Arneberg, "Cuomo Assails Judicial Hodgepodge," *Newsday,* August 15, 1990, p. 15.

43. 492 U.S. 490 (1989).

44. 112 S. Ct. 931 (1992).

45. Maralee Schwartz, "Louisiana Lawmakers Override Abortion Bill Veto," *Washington Post,* June 19, 1991: A4.

46. *Missouri* v. *Jenkins*, 495 U.S. 33 (1990).

47. *Perpich* v. *Department of Defense*, 110 S. Ct. 2418 (1990).

48. David Osborne, "A New Federal Compact: Sorting Out Washington's Proper Role," in Will Marshall and Martin Schram, *Mandate for Change* (New York: Berkeley Books, 1993), p. 239.

49. David S. Broder, "The Right Time for a Test of Ideas," *The Washington Post* (February 1, 1995) A-19.

50. David B. Walker, *The Rebirth of Federalism* (New Jersey: Chatham House, 1994).

Chapter 4

1. The absence of a bill of rights led Mason to refuse to sign the proposed Constitution, noting that he "would sooner chop off his right hand than put it to the constitution as it now stands." Quoted in Eric Black, *Our Constitution: The Myth That Binds Us* (Boulder, CO: Westview Press, 1988), p. 75.

2. Alexander Hamilton, *Federalist No. 84*.

3. Quoted in Jack N. Rakove, "Madison Won Passage of the Bill of Rights But Remained a Skeptic," *Public Affairs Report* (March 1991), p. 6.

4. Continental Congress to the People of Great Britain, October 21, 1774, in Philip Kurland and Ralph Lerner, eds., *The Founders' Constitution,* Vol. 5 (Chicago: University of Chicago Press, 1987), p. 61.

5. 310 U.S. 296 (1940).

6. *Reynolds* v. *U.S.,* 98 U.S. 145 (1879).
7. 330 U.S. 1 (1947).
8. *McCollum* v. *Board of Education,* 333 U.S. 203 (1948).
9. *Tilton* v. *Richardson,* 403 U.S. 672 (1971).
10. *Board of Education* v. *Allen,* 392 U.S. 236 (1968).
11. *Mueller* v. *Allen,* 463 U.S. 388 (1983).
12. *Zobrest* v. *Catalina Foothills School District,* 1993 U.S. LEXIS 4211.
13. 370 U.S. 421 (1962).
14. 403 U.S. 602 (1971).
15. Ibid.
16. *Stone* v. *Graham,* 449 U.S. 39 (1980).
17. 472 U.S. 38 (1985).
18. 482 U.S. 578 (1987).
19. 112 S. Ct. 2649 (1992).
20. *Widmar* v. *Vincent,* 454 U.S. 263 (1981).
21. 110 S. Ct. 2356 (1990).
22. *Lamb's Chapel* v. *Center Moriches Union Free School District,* 113 S. Ct. 2141 (1993).
23. *Sherbert* v. *Verner,* 374 U.S. 398 (1963).
24. 406 U.S. 208 (1972).
25. *Minnesota* v. *Hershberger,* 110 S. Ct. 1918 (1990).
26. *Goldman* v. *Weinberger,* 475 U.S. 503 (1986).
27. *Lyng* v. *Northwest Indian Cemetery Protective Association,* 485 U.S. 439 (1988).
28. 494 U.S. 872 (1990).
29. *Church of the Lukumi Babalu Aye* v. *Hialeah,* 113 S. Ct. 2217 (1993).
30. 380 U.S. 163 (1965).
31. *Cruz* v. *Beto,* 405 U.S. 319 (1972).
32. *O'Lone* v. *Shabazz,* 482 U.S. 342 (1987).
33. See, for example, the opinion in *Boissonneault* v. *Flint City Council,* 392 Mich. 685 (1974).
34. 7 Wall. 506 (1869).
35. David M. O'Brien, *Constitutional Law and Politics, Vol. Two* (New York: Norton, 1991), p. 345.
36. See Frederick Siebert, *The Rights and Privileges of the Press* (New York: D. Appleton-Century, 1934), pp. 886, 931–940.
37. 249 U.S. 47 (1919).
38. *Frohwerk* v. *United States,* 249 U.S. 204 (1919).
39. 249 U.S. 211 (1919).
40. 250 U.S. 616 (1919).
41. 395 U.S. 444 (1969).
42. 7 Pet. 243 (1833).
43. *Gitlow* v. *New York,* 268 U.S. 652 (1925).
44. 283 U.S. 697 (1931).
45. For more about *Near,* see Fred W. Friendly, *Minnesota Rag* (New York: Random House, 1981).
46. 302 U.S. 319 (1937).
47. *Abrams* v. *United States,* 250 U.S. 616 (1919).
48. 283 U.S. 359 (1931).
49. *West Virginia State Board of Education* v. *Barnette,* 319 U.S. 503 (1943).
50. 393 U.S. 503 (1969).
51. *Texas* v. *Johnson,* 491 U.S. 397 (1989).
52. *U.S.* v. *Eichman,* 496 U.S. 310 (1990).
53. 403 U.S. 713 (1971).
54. 427 U.S. 539 (1976).
55. "Penn Students Drop Racism Charge," *Facts on File, World News Digest* (June 10, 1993): 427, A1.
56. 376 U.S. 254 (1964).
57. *Masson* v. *New Yorker Magazine,* 111 S. Ct. 2419 (1991).
58. 315 U.S. 568 (1942).
59. L.R. 2 Q.B. 360 (1868).
60. *Butler* v. *Michigan,* 352 U.S. 380 (1957).
61. 354 U.S. 476 (1957).
62. *Ginzburg* v. *United States,* 383 U.S. 463 (1968).
63. 413 U.S. 15 (1973).
64. *Jenkins* v. *Georgia,* 418 U.S. 153 (1974).
65. *Jacobellis* v. *Ohio,* 378 U.S. 184 (1964).
66. *Barnes* v. *Glen Theater,* 111 S. Ct. 2456 (1991).
67. *Stein* v. *N.Y.,* 346 U.S. 156 (1953).
68. *Minnesota* v. *Dickerson,* 113 S. Ct. 2130 (1993).
69. *Terry* v. *Ohio,* 392 U.S. 1 (1968).
70. *U.S.* v. *Sokolov,* 490 U.S. 1 (1989).
71. *U.S.* v. *Matlock,* 415 U.S. 164 (1974).
72. *Johnson* v. *U.S.,* 333 U.S. 10 (1948).
73. *Winston* v. *Lee,* 470 U.S. 753 (1985).
74. *South Dakota* v. *Neville,* 459 U.S. 553 (1983).
75. *Michigan* v. *Tyler,* 436 U.S. 499 (1978).
76. *Hester* v. *U.S.,* 265 U.S. 57 (1924).
77. *Oliver* v. *U.S.,* 466 U.S. 170 (1984).
78. *California* v. *Ciraolo,* 476 U.S. 207 (1986).
79. *Dow Chemical Company* v. *U.S.,* 476 U.S. 227 (1986).
80. *U.S.* v. *Dunn,* 480 U.S. 294 (1987).
81. *Carroll* v. *U.S.,* 267 U.S. 132 (1925).
82. *California* v. *Acevedo,* 111 S. Ct. 1982 (1991).
83. *Skinner* v. *Railway Labor Executives' Association,* 489 U.S. 602 (1989).
84. *Verona School District* v. *Wayne Acton,* 1995 U.S. *LEXIS* 4275.
85. *Counselman* v. *Hitchcock,* 142 U.S. 547 (1892).
86. *Brown* v. *Mississippi,* 297 U.S. 278 (1936).
87. *Lynumn* v. *Illinois,* 372 U.S. 528 (1963).
88. 384 U.S. 436 (1966).
89. *Rhode Island* v. *Innis,* 446 U.S. 291 (1980).
90. *Arizona* v. *Fulminante,* 111 S. Ct. 2067 (1991).
91. 232 U.S. 383 (1914).
92. 367 U.S. 643 (1961).
93. *Stone* v. *Powell,* 428 U.S. 465 (1976).
94. *Johnson* v. *Zerbst,* 304 U.S. 458 (1938).
95. *Powell* v. *Alabama,* 287 U.S. 45 (1932).
96. 372 U.S. 335 (1963).
97. *Argersinger* v. *Hamlin,* 407 U.S. 25 (1972).
98. *Scott* v. *Illinois,* 440 U.S. 367 (1979).
99. *Strauder* v. *West Virginia,* 100 U.S. 303 (1880).
100. *Taylor* v. *Louisiana,* 419 U.S. 522 (1975).
101. Peremptory challenges are discretionary challenges. A lawyer representing an abortion clinic protestor, for example, could use peremptory challenges to rid the jury of pro-choice advocates. "For cause" challenges, by contrast, are based on legal reasoning and not on an educated guess about the best persons to serve on the jury. In a capital case, for example, persons morally opposed to the death penalty could be removed "for cause."
102. *Batson* v. *Kentucky,* 476 U.S. 79 (1986).
103. 114 S. Ct. 1419 (1994).
104. *Hallinger* v. *Davis,* 146 U.S. 314 (1892).
105. *O'Neil* v. *Vermont,* 144 U.S. 323 (1892).
106. See Michael Meltsner, *Cruel and Unusual: The Supreme Court and Capital Punishment* (New York: Random House, 1973).
107. 408 U.S. 238 (1972).
108. 428 U.S. 153 (1976).
109. 481 U.S. 279 (1987).
110. 111 S. Ct. 2841 (1991).
111. *Olmstead* v. *United States,* 277 U.S. 438 (1928).
112. 381 U.S. 481 (1965).
113. *Poe* v. *Ullman,* 367 U.S. 497 (1961).
114. *Eisenstadt* v. *Baird,* 410 U.S. 113 (1972).
115. 410 U.S. 113 (1973).
116. *Beal* v. *Doe,* 432 U.S. 438 (1977) and *Harris* v. *McRae,* 448 U.S. 297 (1980).
117. 492 U.S. 490 (1989).
118. 112 S. Ct. 931 (1992).
119. *Barnes* v. *Moore,* 113 S. Ct. 656 (1992).
120. *Bray* v. *Alexandria Women's Health Clinic,* 113 S. Ct. 753 (1993).

121. 111 S. Ct. 1759 (1991).
122. *Board of Education of City of Oklahoma City* v. *National Gay Task Force*, 53 U.S.L.W. 4408 (1985).
123. 478 U.S. 186 (1986).
124. Reported in David M. O'Brien, *Constitutional Law and Politics*, Vol. 1 (New York: Norton, 1991), p. 1223.
125. *National Organization for Women* v. *Scheidler*, 114 S. Ct. 798 (1994).

Chapter 5

1. By 1831, only 1,420 former slaves had returned to Liberia.
2. 60 U.S. 393 (1857).
3. See Ellen Carol DuBois, *Feminism and Suffrage* (Ithaca, New York: Cornell University Press, 1980).
4. 83 U.S. (16 Wall.) 36 (1873).
5. 83 U.S. (16 Wall.) 130 (1873).
6. 88 U.S. (21 Wall.) 162 (1875).
7. See Karen O'Connor, *Women's Organizations' Use of the Courts* (Lexington, MA: Lexington Books, 1980).
8. 109 U.S. 3 (1883).
9. 163 U.S. 537 (1896).
10. *Williams* v. *Mississippi*, 170 U.S. 213 (1898).
11. 175 U.S. 528 (1899).
12. Juan Williams, *Eyes on the Prize: America's Civil Rights Years, 1954–1965* (New York: Penguin, 1987), p. 10.
13. 208 U.S. 412 (1908).
14. Quoted in Judith Papachristou, *Women Together* (New York: Knopf, 1976), p. 144.
15. See Eleanor Flexner, *Century of Struggle* (New York: Atheneum, 1971).
16. *Missouri* ex rel. *Gaines* v. *Canada*, 305 U.S. 337 (1938).
17. Richard Kluger, *Simple Justice* (New York: Vintage, 1975), p. 268.
18. 339 U.S. 629 (1950).
19. 339 U.S. 637 (1950).
20. 347 U.S. 483 (1954).
21. 347 U.S. at 495 (1954).
22. Quoted in Juan Williams, *Eyes on the Prize: America's Civil Rights Years, 1954–1965* (New York: Penguin Books, 1987), p. 34.
23. Nancy E. McGlen and Karen O'Connor, *Women, Politics and American Society* (New York: Prentice Hall, 1995).
24. *Brown* v. *Board of Education of Topeka II,* 349 U.S. 294 (1955).
25. Quoted in Williams, *Eyes on the Prize,* p. 37.
26. 358 U.S. 1 (1958).
27. *Browder* v. *Gayle*, 142 F. Supp. 707 (1956).
28. 379 U.S. 241 (1964).
29. Paul Brest and Sanford Levinson, *Processes of Constitutional Decision-making*, 2nd ed. (Boston: Little, Brown, 1983), pp. 471-480.
30. 402 U.S. 1 (1971).
31. *Milliken* v. *Bradley*, 418 U.S. 717 (1974).
32. *Freeman* v. *Pitts*, 112 S. Ct. 1430 (1992).
33. 401 U.S. 424 (1971).
34. Mary King, *Freedom Song* (New York: Morrow, 1987).
35. Quoted in Jo Freeman, *The Politics of Women's Liberation* (New York: Longman, 1975), p. 57.
36. 368 U.S. 57 (1960).
37. New York: Dell, 1963.
38. 410 U.S. 113 (1973).
39. Rex E. Lee, *A Lawyer Looks at the ERA* (Provo, UT: Brigham Young University Press, 1980).
40. The U.S. Constitution is silent on the effect of a state's recision of its earlier ratification while an amendment is pending.
41. See Jane J. Mansbridge, *Why We Lost the ERA* (Chicago: University of Chicago Press, 1986).
42. *Palko* v. *Connecticut*, 302 U.S. 319 (1937).
43. 404 U.S. 71 (1971).
44. 429 U.S. 190 (1976).
45. *Rostker* v. *Goldberg*, 453 U.S. 57 (1981).

46. Joyce Gelb and Marian Lief Palley, "Women and Interest Group Politics: A Case Study of the Equal Credit Opportunity Act," *American Politics Quarterly* (July 1977): 336.
47. U.S. Senate, Subcommittee on Indian Education, *Indian Education: A National Tragedy—A National Challenge*, 91st Congress, 1st Session, (1969), p. 9.
48. Rennard J. Strickland, "Native Americans," in Kermit L. Hall, ed., *The Oxford Companion to the Supreme Court of the United States* (New York: Oxford University Press, 1992), p. 557.
49. Dee Brown, *Bury My Heart at Wounded Knee* (New York: Holt, Rinehart and Winston, 1971).
50. Strickland, "Native Americans," p. 579.
51. F. Chris Garcia, *Latinos and the Political System* (Notre Dame: University of Notre Dame Press, 1988), p. 1.
52. See Karen O'Connor and Lee Epstein, "A Legal Voice for the Chicano Community: The Activities of the Mexican-American Legal Defense and Educational Fund, 1968–1982," *Social Science Quarterly* 65 (June 1984): 245–256.
53. *White* v. *Regester*, 412 U.S. 755 (1973).
54. *San Antonio Independent School District* v. *Rodriguez*, 411 U.S. 1 (1973).
55. *Edgewood Independent School District* v. *Kirby*, 777 S. W. 2d 391 (1989).
56. 478 U.S. 186 (1986).
57. Paul Quinn-Judge, "Senate OKs Tougher Version of Policy on Gays in Military," *The Boston Globe* (September 10, 1993): 6.
58. 438 U.S. 265 (1978).
59. *United Steelworkers of America* v. *Weber*, 443 U.S. 197 (1979).
60. 480 U.S. 616 (1987).
61. Ruth Marcus, "Hill Coalition Aims to Counter Court in Job Bias," *Washington Post* (February 8, 1990): A10.

Chapter 6

1. Humphrey Taylor, "Louis Harris Poll: Confidence in Leaders Down," Gannett News Service, March 6, 1994, NEXIS.
2. Richard Benedetto, "Congress Knows It's 'Show-Me Time' to Voters," *USA Today*, March 7, 1994:11A.
3. 369 U.S. 186 (1962).
4. 377 U.S. 533 (1964).
5. *Thornburg* v. *Gingles*, 478 U.S. 30 (1986). The Act was amended in 1982.
6. *Shaw* v. *Reno*, 113 S. Ct. 2816 (1993).
7. Hedrick Smith, *The Power Game* (New York: Ballantine Books, 1989), p. 97.
8. Ibid. p. 108.
9. Marjorie Randon Hershey, "The Congressional Elections," in Gerald M. Pomper et al., eds. *The Election of 1992: Reports and Interpretations* (Chatham, NJ: Chatham House, 1993), p. 159.
10. Alan I. Abramowitz, "Incumbency, Congressional Spending, and the Decline of Competition in House Elections," 53 *Journal of Politics*, (February 1991): 34–56.
11. Hershey, "The Congressional Elections," p. 166. (See n. 9.)
12. Ibid.
13. Ibid., p. 175.
14. Sue Thomas, *How Women Legislate* (New York: Oxford University Press, 1994).
15. Quoted in Stacey Edwards, "Health Act to End Discrimination in Health Issues, Mikulski Says," *States News Service* (February 27, 1991) NEXIS.
16. Clifford Krauss, "The Budget Struggle: The House; Whips Use Soft Touch to Succeed," *The New York Times* (August 7, 1993): A7.
17. Woodrow Wilson, *Congressional Government: A Study in American Government* (New York: Meridian Books, 1956, originally published in 1885), p. 79.
18. Richard L. Hall, "Participation, Abdication, and Representation in Congressional Committees," in Lawrence C. Dodd and Bruce I.

Oppenheimer, *Congress Reconsidered*, 5th ed. (Washington, DC: CQ Press, 1993), p. 162.

19. Dan Greenberg, "New House Rules: A Victory for Congressional Reform," *Heritage Foundation Reports* (January 3, 1995), NEXIS.

20. Steven S. Smith and Christopher J. Deering, *Committees in Congress*, 2nd ed. (Washington, DC: CQ Press, 1990), p. 126.

21. Quoted in "Senate 'Holds' System Developing as Sophisticated Tactic for Leverage, Delay," 1991 *Daily Reports for Executives* (August 26, 1991, No. 165): C–1.

22. Aage R. Clausen, *How Congressmen Decide: A Policy Focus* (New York: St. Martin's Press, 1973).

23. Lynn Marek, "Schroeder Hails Women's Gains," *The Plain Dealer* (December 28, 1993): 1–C.

24. "House Caucuses Reorganize as New Rules Go into Effect," *The Arizona Republic* (February 12, 1995): A22.

25. Ibid.

26. James Sterling Young, *The Washington Community, 1800–1820* (New York: Columbia University Press, 1966), pp. 98–105.

27. Donald R. Matthews and James A. Stimson, *Yeas and Neas* (Chapel Hill: University of North Carolina Press, 1975).

28. Quoted in Martin Tolchin, "19,000 Congressional Aides Discover Power but Little Glory on Capitol Hill," *The New York Times* (November 12, 1991): A–22.

29. Ann Reilly Dowd, "How To Get Things Done in Washington," *Fortune* (August 9, 1993): 60.

30. Lloyd Grove, "White House Declares War on Upstart Senator," *Atlanta Constitution* (April 6, 1993): A–15.

31. Ibid.

32. John W. Kingdon, *Congressmen's Voting Decisions*, 3rd ed. (Ann Arbor: University of Michigan Press, 1989).

33. Arthur Schlesinger, *The Imperial Presidency* (New York: Houghton Mifflin, 1973).

34. Joel D. Aberbach, *Keeping a Watchful Eye: The Politics of Congressional Oversight* (Washington, DC: The Brookings Institution, 1990).

35. Morris S. Ogul and Bert A. Rockman, "Overseeing Oversight: New Departures and Old Problems," *Legislative Studies Quarterly*, 25 (1990): 548–574.

36. Quoted in Smith and Deering, *Committees in Congress*, p. 23. (See n. 20.)

37. 462 U.S. 919 (1983).

38. *The Wall Street Journal* (April 13, 1973): 10.

Chapter 7

1. Edward S. Corwin, *The President: Office and Powers, 1787–1957*, 4th ed. (New York: New York University Press, 1957), p. 5.

2. F.N. Thorpe, ed., *American Charters, Constitutions, Etc.*, VIII (Washington, 1909), pp. 3816–3817.

3. Quoted in Corwin, *The President*, p. 11.

4. Winston Solberg, *The Federal Convention and the Formation of the Union of the American States* (Indianapolis: Bobbs-Merrill, 1958), p. 235.

5. Alfred Steinberg, *The First Ten: The Founding Presidents and Their Administrations* (New York: Doubleday, 1967), p. 59.

6. "Is the Vice Presidency Necessary?" *Atlantic* 233 (May 1974): 37.

7. Benjamin I. Page and Mark P. Petracca, *The American Presidency* (New York: McGraw-Hill, 1983), p. 268.

8. "Text of Bush's Pardon of Weinberger, 5 Others in Iran–Contra Probe," *Los Angeles Times* (December 25, 1992): A20.

9. Elizabeth Frost, ed. *The Bully Pulpit: Quotations from America's Presidents* (New York: Facts on File Publications, 1988), p. 187.

10. Quoted in Richard E. Neustadt, *Presidential Power: The Politics of Power from FDR to Carter* (New York: Wiley, 1980), p. 9.

11. Page and Petracca, *The American Presidency*, p. 40. (See n. 7.)

12. See also Terry Moe, "The Politicized Presidency" in John E. Chubb and Paul Petersen, *New Directions in American Politics* (Washington, DC: Brookings Institution, 1985).

13. Quoted in Paul F. Boller, Jr., *Presidential Anecdotes* (New York: Penguin Books, 1981), p. 78.

14. Abraham Lincoln, "Special Session Message," July 4, 1861, in *Borzoi Reader in American Politics*, Edward Keynes and David Adamany, eds. (New York: Knopf, 1973), p. 539.

15. Quoted in Page and Petracca, *The American Presidency*, p. 57. (See n. 7.)

16. Merlin Gustafson, "The President's Mail," *Presidential Studies Quarterly* 8 (1978): 36.

17. Dan Balz, "Changing the Capital, More So the Man," *The Washington Post* (January 17, 1994): A1.

18. Franklin Delano Roosevelt, Press Conference, July 23, 1937.

19. Lyndon B. Johnson, *The Vantage Point* (New York: Holt, Rinehart and Winston, 1971), p. 448.

20. David Stockman, *The Triumph of Politics* (New York: Harper and Row, 1986), p. 251.

21. Morris P. Fiorina, *Divided Government* (New York: Macmillan Publishing Co., 1992).

22. Boller, *Presidential Anecdotes,* p. 50. (See n. 13.)

23. James David Barber, *The Presidential Character: Predicting Performance in the White House*, 3rd ed. (Englewood Cliffs, NJ: Prentice Hall, 1985).

24. Gary Wills, *The Kennedy Imprisonment* (Boston: Little, Brown, 1982), p. 186.

25. George E. Reedy, *The Twilight of the Presidency* (New York: New American Library, 1970), p. 33.

26. Ibid., pp. 38–39.

27. Neustadt, *Presidential Power: The Politics of Leadership from FDR to Carter*, p. 10. (See n. 15.)

28. Neustadt, *Presidential Power,* p. 44. (See n. 10.)

29. Sam Kernell, *Going Public: New Strategies of Presidential Leadership* (Washington, DC: CQ Press, 1986).

30. Michael R. Kagay, "History Suggest Bush's Popularity Will Ebb," *The New York Times* (May 22, 1991): A10.

31. Aaron B. Wildavsky, "The Two Presidencies," *Transaction* (December, 1966): 7–14.

32. Foster committed suicide in July 1993, leaving behind a note indicating the stresses of the job led him to that action.

33. Quoted in Page and Petracca, *The American Presidency,* p. 169. (See n. 7.)

34. "Address Before a Joint Session of the Congress of the Union, January 28, 1992," *Weekly Compilation of Presidential Documents*, 28 (February 3, 1992): 175.

Chapter 8

1. Harold D. Lasswell, *Politics: Who Gets What, When, and How* (New York: McGraw-Hill, 1938).

2. In Britain, the bureaucracy is commonly referred to as the *civil service* or *Whitehall*, the name of the building in London that houses many government ministries.

3. Quoted in Robert G. Caldwell, *James A. Garfield* (Hamden, CT: Archon Books, 1965).

4. *NLRB* v. *Jones & Laughlin Steel Corp.*, 301 U.S. 1 (1937).

5. *U.S.* v. *Darby Lumber Co.* 312 U.S. 100 (1941) and *Wickward* v. *Filburn*, 317 U.S. 111 (1942).

6. "Federal News: Hatch Act," *Government Employee Relations Report* (October 11, 1993): 1317.

7. On the difficulty of counting the exact number of government agencies, see David Nachmias and David H. Rosenbloom, *Bureaucratic Government: U.S.A.* (New York: St. Martin's Press, 1980).

8. The classic work on regulatory commissions is Marver Bernstein, *Regulating Business by Independent Commission* (Princeton, NJ: Princeton University Press, 1955).

9. *Humphrey's Executor* v. *U.S.*, 295 U.S. 602 (1935).

10. Arthur Schlesinger, Jr., *A Thousand Days* (Greenwich, CT: Fawcett Books, 1967), p. 377.

11. Andrew Rosenthal, "White House Retreats on Ruling That Curbs Minority Scholarships," *The New York Times* (December 18, 1990): A1.

12. Irene Murphy, *Public Policy on the Status of Women* (Lexington, MA: Lexington Books, 1974).

13. Peter Woll, *American Bureaucracy,* 2nd ed. (New York: Norton, 1977), p. 244.

14. James G. March and Johan P. Olson, "Organizing Political Life: What Administrative Reorganization Tells Us About Government," *American Political Science Review* 77 (June 1983): 281–296.

15. Benjamin I. Page and Mark P. Petracca, *The American Presidency* (New York: McGraw-Hill, 1983), p. 224.

16. According to Greek legend, Damocles was a courtier and constant flatterer of Dionysus, King of Syracuse. Damocles coveted the happiness and glory of kings until Dionysus gave a banquet in his honor. Damocles enjoyed the banquet immensely until he looked up and saw a sword over his head, hung by a single thread. The sword was meant to teach him of the constant danger faced by the kings he envied.

17. For more on iron triangles, see Randall Ripley and Grace Franklin, *Congress, Bureaucracy and Public Policy*, 4th ed. (Homewood, IL: Dorsey Press, 1984).

18. "Issue Networks and the Executive Establishment," in Anthony King, ed., *The New American Political System* (Washington, DC: American Enterprise Institute, 1978), pp. 87–124.

19. Martin Shapiro, "The Presidency and the Federal Courts," in Arnold Meltsner, ed. *Politics and the Oval Office*, (San Francisco: Institute for Contemporary Studies, 1981), Chapter 8.

20. See Joyce Gelb and Marian Lief Palley, *Women and Public Policies* (Princeton, NJ: Princeton University Press, 1982), Chapter 5.

21. Thomas V. DiBacco, "Veep Gore Reinventing Government—Again!" *USA Today* (September 9, 1993): 13A.

22. John Erlichman, "Government Reform: Will Al Gore's Package of Changes Succeed Where Others Failed? Washington's 'Iron Triangles'," *Atlanta Journal and Constitution* (September 16, 1993): A15.

23. Gerald R. Ford, *A Time to Heal: The Autobiography of Gerald R. Ford* (New York: Harper and Row, 1979), p. 272.

Chapter 9

1. Bernard Schwartz, *The Law in America,* (New York: American Heritage Publishing Co., 1974), p. 48.

2. Julius Goebel Jr., *History of the Supreme Court of the United States*, Vol. 1: *Antecedents and Beginnings to 1801* (New York: Macmillan, 1971), p. 206.

3. Quoted in Ibid., p. 280.

4. Schwartz, *The Law in America,* p. 11.

5. 2 Dall. 419 (1793).

6. 3 Dall. 171 (1796).

7. 5 U.S. 137 (1803).

8. David W. Neubauer, *Judicial Process: Law, Courts and Politics* (Pacific Grove, CA: Brooks/Cole, 1991), p. 57.

9. John R. Vile and Mario Perez-Reilly, "The U.S. Constitution and Judicial Qualifications: A Curious Omission," *Judicature* (December/January 1991): 198–202.

10. Quoted in Nina Totenberg, "Will Judges Be Chosen Rationally?" *Judicature* (August/September 1976): 93.

11. Sheldon Goldman, "The Bush Imprint on the Federal Judiciary: Carrying on a Tradition," *Judicature* (April/May 1991): 297.

12. Elliot E. Slotnick, "Federal Appellate Judge Selection During the Carter Administration: Recruitment Changes and Unanswered Questions," *Justice System Journal* 6 (Fall 1981): 293–304.

13. Quoted in Judge Irving R. Kaufman, "Charting a Judicial Pedigree," *The New York Times* (January 24, 1981): 23.

14. Quoted in Lawrence Baum, *The Supreme Court,* 3rd. ed. (Washington: CQ Press, 1989), p. 108.

15. But see Sue Davis, *Justice Rehnquist and the Conservative Judicial Philosophy* (Princeton, NJ: Princeton University Press, 1989).

16. Clarence Thomas is considered Catholic here, although he currently attends an Episcopalian church, having been barred from Catholic sacraments because of his remarriage.

17. See Bruce Allen Murphy, *The Brandeis/Frankfurter Connection* (New York: Oxford University Press, 1982).

18. Phil Rosenthal, "Why Not Wapner?" *The San Diego Union-Tribune* (March 25, 1993): F-5.

19. Marcia Coyle, "How Americans View High Court," *The National Law Journal* (February 26, 1990): 1.

20. Stephen L. Wasby, *The Supreme Court in the Federal Judicial System,* 4th ed. (Chicago: Nelson-Hall, 1988), p. 194.

21. Ibid.

22. Neubauer, *Judicial Process,* p. 370. (See n. 8.)

23. William P. McLauchan, "The Business of the United States Supreme Court, 1971–1983: An Analysis of Supply and Demand," paper presented at the 1986 annual meeting of the Midwest Political Science Association.

24. 111 S. Ct. 596 (1991).

25. Justice Stevens chooses not to join this pool. According to one former clerk, "He wanted an independent review," but Stevens himself examines only about 20 percent of the petitions, leaving the rest to his clerks. Tony Mauro, "Ginsburg Plunges into the Cert Pool," *Legal Times* (September 6, 1993): 8.

26. See Gregory A. Caldeira and John R. Wright, "The Discuss List: Agenda Setting in the Supreme Court," *Law Society Review* 24 (1990), pp. 809-813; H.W. Perry, Jr., *Deciding to Decide: Agenda Setting in the United States Supreme Court* (Cambridge, MA: Harvard University Press, 1991), and Doris Marie Provine *Case Selection in the United States Supreme Court* (Chicago: University of Chicago Press, 1980).

27. Wasby, *The Supreme Court,* p. 199. Much of this change occurred as the result of an increase in state criminal cases, of which nearly 100 percent concerned constitutional questions.

28. "Retired Chief Justice Warren Attacks . . . Freund Study Group's Composition and Proposal," *American Bar Association Journal* 59 (July, 1973): 728.

29. Kathleen Werdegar, "The Solicitor General and Administrative Due Process," *George Washington Law Review* (1967–1968): 482.

30. Rebecca Mae Salokar, *The Solicitor General: The Politics of Law* (Philadelphia: Temple University Press, 1992), p. 3.

31. Quoted in Elder Witt, *A Different Justice: Reagan and the Supreme Court* (Washington, DC: CQ Press, 1986), p. 133.

32. Lawrence Baum, *The Supreme Court,* 4th ed. (Washington, DC: CQ Press, 1992), p. 106.

33. Richard C. Cortner, *The Supreme Court and Civil Liberties* (Palo Alto, CA: Mayfield, 1975), p. vi.

34. Gregory A. Caldeira and John R. Wright, "*Amicus Curiae* before the Supreme Court: Who Participates, When and How Much?" *Journal of Politics* 52 (August 1990): 803.

35. 114 S. Ct. 367 (1993).

36. Quoted in Wasby, *The Supreme Court,* p. 229. (See n. 20.)

37. 458 U.S. 176 (1982).

38. Milton Dickens and Ruth E. Schwartz, "Oral Argument Before the Supreme Court: Marshall v. Davis in the School Segregation Cases," *Quarterly Journal of Speech* 57 (February 1971): 39.

39. Reported in Anthony Lewis, "The Justices' Supreme Job," *The New York Times Magazine* (June 11, 1961): 31.

40. 478 U.S. 186 (1986).

41. "Justices' Files Show Struggle Over Georgia Sodomy Case," *The Atlanta Journal and Constitution* (May 25, 1993): A-9. The Marshall papers also reveal politics at the *certiorari* stage.

42. 418 U.S. 683 (1974).

43. Bob Woodward and Scott Armstrong, *The Brethren* (New York: Simon and Schuster, 1979), pp. 65, 288–347.

44. 492 U.S. 490 (1989).

45. C. Neal Tate, "Personal Attribute Model of the Voting Behavior of U.S. Supreme Court Justices: Liberalism in Civil Liberties and Economic Decisions, 1946–1978," *American Political Science Review* 75 (June 1981): 355–367.

46. See, for example, Jeffrey A. Segal, "Predicting Supreme Court Cases Probabilistically: The Search and Seizure Cases, 1962–1981," *American Political Science Review* 78 (September 1978): 891–900, where he argues that the facts of the case are a critical determinant in Supreme Court voting.

47. According to role theory, which posits that individual justices act differently in different cases primarily due to differing expectations about what is proper, helps explain how the justices vote. James L. Gibson, "Discriminant Functions, Role Orientations and Judicial Behavior: Theoretical and Methodological Linkages," *Journal of Politics* 39 (November 1977): 984–1007.

48. Stanley C. Brubaker, "Reconsidering Dworkin's Case for Judicial Activism," *The Journal of Politics* 46 (1984): 504.

49. Donald L. Horowitz, *The Courts and Social Policy* (Washington, DC: Brookings Institution, 1977), p. 538.

50. Edwin Meese III, in *The Great Debate: Interpreting Our Written Constitution* (Washington, DC: The Federalist Society, 1986), p. 2.

51. William J. Brennan Jr., in *The Great Debate: Interpreting Our Written Constitution* (Washington, DC: The Federalist Society, 1986), p. 18.

52. *Webster* v. *Reproductive Health Services*, 492 U.S. at 518 (1989).

53. 112 S. Ct. 2791 (1992).

54. William H. Rehnquist, "Constitutional Law and Public Opinion," paper presented at Suffolk University School of Law, Boston, April 10, 1986, pp. 40–41.

55. 323 U.S. 214 (1944).

56. 343 U.S. 579 (1952).

57. 462 U.S. 919 (1983).

58. See *Colegrove* v. *Green*, 328 U.S. 549 (1946), for example.

59. *Baker* v. *Carr*, 369 U.S. 186 (1962).

60. Charles Johnson and Bradley C. Canon, *Judicial Policies' Implementation and Impact* (Washington, DC: CQ Press, 1984), Chapter 1.

61. 377 U.S. 533 (1964).

62. *Ex parte McCardle*, 74 U.S. 506 (1869).

Chapter 10

1. Allan M. Winkler, "Public Opinion," in Jack Greene, ed., *The Encyclopedia of American Political History* (New York: Charles Scribner's Sons, 1988), p. 1038.

2. *Public Opinion Quarterly* 29 (Winter 1965–66): 547.

3. Winkler, *Public Opinion,* p. 1035.

4. Ibid.

5. *Literary Digest* 122 (22 August 1936): 3.

6. *Literary Digest* 125 (14 November 1936): 1.

7. Richard Dawson et al. *Political Socialization,* 2nd ed. (Boston: Little, Brown, 1977), p. 33.

8. F. Christopher Arterton, "The Impact of Watergate on Children's Attitudes Toward Political Authority," *Political Science Quarterly* 89 (June 1974): 273.

9. Alejandro Portest and Rafael Mozo, "The Political Adaptation Process of Cubans and Other Ethnic Minorities in the United States: A Preliminary Analysis," in F. Chris Garcia, ed. *Latinos and the Political System,* (Notre Dame, IN: University of Notre Dame Press, 1988), p. 161.

10. John A. Garcia and Carlos H. Arce, "Political Orientations and Behaviors of Chicanos: Trying to Make Sense Out of Attitudes and Participation," in Ibid., pp. 125–151.

11. Pamela Johnson Conover and Virginia Sapiro, "Gender, Feminist Consciousness, and War," *American Journal of Political Science* 37 (November 1993): 1079–1099.

12. Lloyd Free and Hadley Cantril, *The Political Belief of Americans* (New York: Simon & Schuster, 1968).

13. Philip E. Converse, "The Nature of Belief Systems in Mass Publics," in David E. Apter, ed., *Ideology and Discontent* (New York: Free Press, 1964), pp. 206–221.

14. "Geography: A Lost Generation," *Nation* (August 8, 1988): 19.

15. Lee Sigelman and Ernest Yanarella, "Public Information on Public Issues," *Social Science Quarterly* 67 (June 1986): 404.

16. Doris Graber, *Mass Media and American Politics,* 2nd ed. (Washington, DC: CQ Press, 1984), p. 157.

17. John E. Mueller, *War, Presidents and Public Opinion* (New York: Wiley, 1973), p. 69.

18. Ibid.

19. Roderick P. Hart, *The Sound of Leadership: Presidential Communication in the Modern Age* (Chicago: University of Chicago Press, 1987).

20. Quoted in Eric Pace, "George H. Gallup Is Dead at 82," *The New York Times* (July 28, 1984): A–1.

21. Walter Shapiro, "Breakthrough in Virginia," *Time* (November 20, 1989): 54.

22. Michael W. Traugott, "The Polls in 1992: Views of Two Critics; A General Good Showing, But Much Work Needs to Be Done," *The Public Perspective,* 4 (November/December 1992): 14–16.

23. Benjamin Ginsburg, "How Polls Transform Public Opinion," in Michael Margolis and Gary A. Mauser, eds., *Manipulating Public Opinion* (Pacific Grove, CA: Brooks/Cole, 1989), p. 273.

24. See, for example, Benjamin Page and Robert Shapiro, "Effects of Public Opinion on Policy" *American Political Science Review* 57 (March 1983): 175–190.

25. Quoted in Pace, "George Gallup." (See n. 20.)

26. Herbert Asher, *Polling and the Public: What Every Citizen Should Know* (Washington, DC: CQ Press, 1988), p. 109.

27. Benjamin Ginsburg, *The Captive Public* (New York: Basic Books), 1986, chapter 4.

28. Ibid.

Chapter 11

1. E. E. Schattschneider, *Party Government* (New York: Holt, Rinehart and Winston, 1942), p. 1. This book stands as one of the most eloquent arguments for a strong political party system ever penned.

2. For more information on this topic, see Larry J. Sabato, *The Party's Just Begun: Shaping Political Parties for America's Future* (Glenview, IL: Scott, Foresman/Little, Brown, 1988).

3. The National Republican (one forerunner of the Whig Party) and the Anti-Masonic Parties each had held more limited conventions in 1831.

4. By contrast, Great Britain did not develop truly national, broad-based parties until the 1870s.

5. Voter turnout in presidential elections from 1876 to 1900 ranged from 75 to 82 percent of the potential (male) electorate, compared with 50 to 55 percent in contemporary elections. See *Historical Statistics of the United States: Colonial Times to 1970,* Part 2, Series Y–27–28 (Washington, DC: Government Printing Office, 1975), based on unpublished data prepared by Walter Dean Burnham.

6. Frank J. Sorauf, *Party Politics in America,* 5th ed. (Boston: Little, Brown, 1984), p. 22.

7. Schattschneider, *Party Government,* p. 48. (See n. 1.)

8. As quoted in Ken Bode, "Hero or Demagogue?" *The New Republic* 195 (March 3, 1986): 28.

9. Gerald M. Pomper with Susan Lederman, *Elections in America,* 2nd ed. (New York: Longman, 1980), pp. 145–150, 167–173.

10. See David E. Price, *Bringing Back the Parties* (Washington, DC: CQ Press, 1984), pp. 284–288.

11. See, for example, Sarah McCally Morehouse, "Legislatures and Political Parties," *State Government* 59:1 (1976): 23.

12. Pomper with Lederman, *Elections in America,* p. 150. (See n. 9.)

13. Walter Dean Burnham, *Critical Elections and the Mainsprings of American Politics* (New York: Norton, 1970), pp. 132–133.

14. See V. O. Key Jr., *American State Politics: An Introduction* (New York: Knopf, 1956).

15. See V. O. Key Jr., *Southern Politics in State and Nation* (New York: Knopf, 1949).

16. See Bibby et al., "Parties in State Politics," in Virginia Gray, Herbert Jacob, and Kenneth Vines, eds., *Politics in the American States,* 4th ed. (Boston: Little, Brown, 1983), Table 3.3, p. 66; also see Larry J. Sabato, *Goodbye to Good-Time Charlie: The American Governorship Transformed,* 2nd ed. (Washington, DC: CQ Press, 1983), pp. 116–138.

17. Sorauf, *Party Politics in America,* p. 51. (See n. 6.)

18. Such cases are few, but a deterrent nonetheless. Several U.S. senators were expelled from the Republican Caucus in 1925 for having supported the Progressive candidate for president the previous year. In 1965, two Southern House Democrats lost all their committee seniority because of their 1964 endorsement of GOP presidential nominee Barry Goldwater, as did another Southerner in 1968 for his backing of George Wallace's third-party candidacy. In early 1983 the House Democratic Caucus removed Texas Representative Phil Gramm from his Budget Committee seat because of his "disloyalty" in working more closely with Republican committee members than with his own party leaders. (Gramm resigned his seat in Congress, changed parties, and was reelected as a Republican. He then used the controversy to propel himself into the U.S. Senate in 1984.)

19. See Julius Turner with Edward V. Schneier Jr., *Party and Constituency: Pressures on Congress* (Baltimore: John Hopkins University Press, 1970), pp. 33–39.

20. Joseph A. Schlesinger, "The New American Political Party," *American Political Science Review* 79 (1985): 1168.

21. Sara Brandes Crook and John R. Hibbing, "Congressional Reform and Party Discipline: The Effects of Change in the Seniority System on Party Loyalty in the U.S. House of Representatives," *British Journal of Political Science* 15 (April 1985): 207–226.

22. Rhodes Cook, "Reagan Nurtures His Adopted Party to Strength," *Congressional Quarterly Weekly* 43 (September 28, 1985): 1927–1930.

23. George C. Edwards III, *Presidential Influence in Congress* (New York: Freeman, 1980); and Herbert M. Kritzer and Robert B. Eubank, "Presidential Coattails Revisited: Partisanship and Incumbency Effects," *American Journal of Political Science* 23 (1979): 615–626.

24. Lyn Ragsdale, "The Fiction of Congressional Elections as Presidential Events," *American Politics Quarterly* 8 (1980): 375–398; and Thomas E. Mann and Raymond E. Wolfinger, "Candidates and Parties in Congressional Elections," *American Political Science Review* 74 (1980): 617–632.

25. See Sidney Ulmer, "The Political Party Variable on the Michigan Supreme Court," *Journal of Public Law* 11 (1962): 352–362; Stuart Nagel, "Political Party Affiliation and Judges' Decisions," *American Political Science Review* 55 (1961): 843–850; David W. Adamany, "The Party Variable in Judges' Voting: Conceptual Notes and a Case Study," *American Political Science Review* 63 (1969): 57–73; Sheldon Goldman, "Voting Behavior on the United States Courts of Appeals, 1961–1964," *American Political Science Review* 60 (1966): 374–383; and Robert A. Carp and C. K. Rowland, *Policymaking and Politics in the Federal District Courts* (Knoxville: University of Tennessee Press, 1983).

26. Morehouse, "Legislatures and Political Parties," pp. 19–24. (See n. 11.)

27. Senator George J. Mitchell (D.-Me.), as quoted in *The Washington Post* (February 9, 1986): A–14.

28. As quoted in a speech to the RNC by the Associated Press, January 24, 1987, and in *The Washington Post* (same date): A–3.

29. See Steven E. Finkel and Howard A. Scarrow, "Party Identification and Party Enrollment: The Difference and the Consequence," *Journal of Politics* 47 (May 1985): 620–642.

30. The presidential election of 1960 may be an extreme case, but John F. Kennedy's massive support among Catholics and Nixon's less substantial but still impressive backing by Protestants demonstrates the polarization that religion could once produce. See Philip E. Converse, "Religion and Politics: The 1960 Election," in Angus Campbell et al., *Elections and the Political Order* (New York: Wiley, 1966), pp. 96–124.

31. This idea is discussed in more detail in Sabato, *The Party's Just Begun,* pp. 179–183, 197–198. The poll results mentioned in this section are taken from the survey conducted for that study of parties. (See n. 2.)

32. See, for example, Jack Dennis, "Public Support for the American Party System," in William J. Crotty, ed., *Paths to Political Reform* (Lexington, MA: D. C. Heath, 1980), p. 43.

Chapter 12

1. On the subject of party realignment, see Walter Dean Burnham, *Critical Elections and the Mainsprings of American Politics* (New York: Norton, 1970); Kristi Andersen, *The Creation of a Democratic Majority* (Chicago: University of Chicago Press, 1979); and John R. Petrocik, "Realignment: New Party Coalitions and the Nationalization of the South," *Journal of Politics* 49 (May 1987): 347–375.

2. Barbara Farah and Helmut Norpoth, "Trends in Partisan Realignment, 1976–1986: A Decade of Waiting," paper prepared for delivery at the annual meeting of the American Political Science Association, Washington, DC, August 27–31, 1986.

3. Morris P. Fiorina, *Retrospective Voting in American National Elections* (New Haven, CT: Yale University Press, 1981); and Charles H. Franklin and John E. Jackson, "The Dynamics of Party Identification," *American Political Science Review* 77 (1983): 957–973.

4. See, for example, V. O. Key Jr., "A Theory of Critical Elections," *Journal of Politics* 17 (February 1955): 3–18.

5. The less dynamic term "creeping realignment" is also sometimes used by scholars and journalists.

6. See Paul Allen Beck, "The Dealignment Era in America," in Russell J. Dalton et al., *Electoral Change in Advanced Industrial Democracies: Realignment or Dealignment?* (Princeton, NJ: Princeton University Press, 1984), p. 264. See also Philip M. Williams, "Party Realignment in the United States and Britain," *British Journal of Political Science* 15 (January 1985): 97–115.

7. The Kennedy–Johnson years (1961–1969) and the Nixon–Ford years (1969–1977) are each considered an eight-year unit for our purposes here.

8. Cited in Everett Carll Ladd Jr., "On Mandates, Realignments, and the 1984 Presidential Election," *Political Science Quarterly* 100 (Spring 1985): 23.

9. Thomas E. Mann and Raymond E. Wolfinger, "Candidates and Parties in Congressional Elections," *American Political Science Review* 74 (September 1980): 617–632; Albert D. Cover, "One Good Term Deserves Another: The Advantage of Incumbency in Congressional Elections," *American Journal of Political Science* 21 (August 1977): 535; and Gary C. Jacobson, *The Politics of Congressional Elections,* 2nd ed. (Boston: Little, Brown, 1987), p. 86.

Chapter 13

1. See Alan Ehrenhalt, *The United States of Ambition* (New York: Random House, 1990).

2. See Larry J. Sabato, ed., *Campaigns and Elections: A Reader in Modern American Politics* (Glenview, IL: Scott, Foresman, 1989), pp. 3–4.

3. From a 1987 cartoon by Tom Toles, copyrighted by the *Buffalo News.*

4. Data provided by the Federal Election Commission.

5. See Howard Penniman, "U.S. Elections: Really a Bargain?" *Public Opinion* (June/July 1984): 51.

Chapter 14

1. See Dom Bonafede, "First Amendment on Trial," *National Journal* 23 (July 20, 1991): 1833.
2. For more on this topic, see Larry J. Sabato, *Feeding Frenzy* (New York: The Free Press, 1991).
3. See Mitchell Stephens, *A History of News: From the Drum to the Satellite* (New York: Viking, 1989).
4. Charles Press and Kenneth VerBurg, *American Politicians and Journalists* (Glenview, IL: Scott, Foresman, 1988), pp. 8–10.
5. See Merrill D. Peterson, *Thomas Jefferson and the New Nation* (New York: Oxford University Press, 1970), pp. 185–187.
6. For a delightful rendition of this episode, see Shelley Ross, *Fall from Grace* (New York: Ballantine, 1988), Chapter 12.
7. The name strictly derived from printing the comic strip "Yellow Kid" in color.
8. Doris A. Graber, *Mass Media and American Politics,* 3rd ed. (Washington, DC: CQ Press, 1989), p. 12.
9. See Thomas C. Leonard, *The Power of the Press: The Birth of American Political Reporting* (New York: Oxford University Press, 1986), Chapter 7.
10. Richard L. Rubin, *Press, Party, and Presidency* (New York: Norton, 1981), pp. 38–39.
11. Stephen Bates, *If No News, Send Rumors* (New York: St. Martin's Press, 1989), p. 185.
12. Barbara Matusow, "Washington's Journalism Establishment," *The Washingtonian* 23 (February 1989): 94–101, 265–270.
13. See Eleanor Randolph, "Extra! Extra! Who Cares?" *The Washington Post* (April 1, 1990): C1, 4.
14. Sunday newspapers are exceptions to the trend. More than one hundred new Sunday papers were created in the decade of the 1980s, and Sunday circulation as a whole has increased 25 percent since 1970.
15. Harold W. Stanley and Richard G. Niemi, *Vital Statistics on American Politics* (Washington, DC: CQ Press, 1988), Table 2-8, p. 58.
16. See Evans Witt, "Here, There, and Everywhere: Where Americans Get Their News," *Public Opinion* 6 (August/September 1983): 45–48; June O. Yum and Kathleen E. Kendall, "Sources of Political Information in a Presidential Primary Campaign," *Journalism Quarterly* 65 (Spring 1988): 148–151, 177.
17. This was the fundamental conclusion of Shanto Iyengar and Donald R. Kinder, *News That Matters* (Chicago: University of Chicago Press, 1987).
18. American Society of Newspaper Editors, *The Changing Face of the Newsroom* (Washington: ASNE, May 1989), p. 29.
19. See Tom Wolfe, *The New Journalism* (New York: Harper & Row, 1973), especially pp. 9–32.
20. The first and best in White's series was *The Making of the President 1960* (New York: Atheneum, 1961). See also Joe McGinniss, *The Selling of the President 1968* (New York: Trident, 1969).
21. See James David Barber, *The Presidential Character* (Englewood Cliffs, NJ: Prentice Hall, 1972), p. 445.
22. 376 U.S. 254 (1964). See also Steven Pressman, "Libel Law: Finding the Right Balance," *Editorial Research Reports* 2 (August 18, 1989): 462–471.
23. *Curtis Publishing Co.* v. *Butts,* 388 U.S. 130 (1967); *Associated Press* v. *Walker,* 388 U.S. 130 (1967).
24. American Society of Newspaper Editors, "The Changing Face," p. 33; William Schneider and I. A. Lewis, "Views on the News," *Public Opinion* 8 (August/September 1985): 6–11, 58–59; and S. Robert Lichter, Stanley Rothman, and Linda S. Lichter, *The Media Elite* (Bethesda, MD: Adler & Adler, 1986).
25. See Dom Bonafede, "Crossing Over," *National Journal* 21 (January 14, 1989): 102; Richard Harwood, "Tainted Journalists," *Washington Post* (December 4, 1988): L6; Charles Trueheart, "Trading Places: The Insiders Debate," *The Washington Post* (January 4, 1989): D1, 19; and Kirk Victor, "Slanted Views," *National Journal* 20 (June 4, 1988): 1512.
26. "*Roe* v. *Webster,*" *Media Monitor* 3 (October 1989): 1–6. See also David Shaw, "Abortion and the Media" (four-part series), *Los Angeles Times* (July 1, 1990): A1, 50–51; (July 2, 1990): A1, 20; (July 3, 1990): A1, 22–23; (July 4, 1990): A1, 28–29.
27. The importance of the agenda-setting function is discussed throughout Iyengar and Kinder, *News That Matters,* especially pp. 4, 33. (See n. 17.)
28. David Whitman, "Who's Who Among the Homeless," *The New Republic* 199 (June 6, 1988): 18–20.
29. See Mark Hertsgaard, *On Bended Knee: The Press and the Reagan Presidency* (New York: Farrar, Straus & Giroux, 1988).
30. 408 U.S. 665 (1972).
31. 403 U.S. 713 (1971).
32. House of Commons, Defense Committee, *The Handling of the Press and Public Information during the Falklands Conflict* (London: Her Majesty's Stationery Office, 1982), p. x.
33. For further reading, see Jeffrey B. Abramson, F. Christopher Arterton, and Gary R. Orren, *The Electronic Commonwealth: The Impact of Media Technologies on Democratic Politics* (New York: Basic Books, 1988).

Chapter 15

1. Samuel Eliot Morrison and Henry Steel Commager, *The Growth of the American Republic* (New York: Oxford University Press, 1930), p. 163.
2. Alexis de Tocqueville, *Democracy in America,* Vol. 1, trans. Phillips Bradley (New York: Knopf, Vintage Books, 1945; orig. published 1835), p. 191.
3. Ibid.
4. Mark P. Petracca, "The Rediscovery of Interest Group Politics," in Mark Petracca, ed. *The Politics of Interests* (Boulder, CO: Westview Press, 1992), p. 5.
5. Clive Thomas and Ronald J. Hrebenar, "Changing Patterns of Interest Group Activity: A Regional Perspective," in Ibid., p. 4.
6. Graham Wilson, *Interest Groups in the United States* (New York: Oxford University Press, 1981), p. 4.
7. David B. Truman, *The Governmental Process: Political Interests and Public Opinion* (New York: Knopf, 1951), p. 33.
8. Robert H. Salisbury, "Interest Groups," in Fred I. Greenstein and Nelson W. Polsby, eds. *Handbook of Political Science,* Vol. 4 (Reading, MA: Addison-Wesley, 1975), p. 175.
9. V. O. Key Jr. *Politics, Parties, and Pressure Groups* (New York: T. J. Crowell, 1942), p. 23.
10. Robert H. Salisbury, "An Exchange Theory of Interest Groups," *Midwest Journal of Political Science,* 13 (1969): 1–32.
11. Jeffrey Berry, *Lobbying for the People: The Political Behavior of Public Interest Groups* (Princeton, NJ: Princeton University Press, 1977), p. 7.
12. "Will Ruling on S.A.T. Affect College Admissions?" *New York Times* (February 8, 1989): B–10.
13. Salisbury, "An Exchange Theory of Interest Groups," pp. 1–32. (See n. 10.)
14. Jack L. Walker, "The Origins and Maintenance of Interest Groups in America," 77 *American Political Science Review* (June 1983): 390–406.
15. Truman, *The Governmental Process,* chap. 16. (See n. 7.)
16. Quoted in Grant McConnell, "Lobbies and Pressure Groups," in Jack Greene, ed. *Encyclopedia of American Political History,* Vol. 2 (New York: Macmillan, 1984), p. 768.
17. Lee Epstein, *Conservatives in Court* (Knoxville: University of Tennessee Press, 1985).
18. Kay Lehman Schlozman and John T. Tierney, *Organized Interests and American Democracy* (New York: Harper and Row, 1986).
19. Peter Stienfels, "Moral Majority to Dissolve; Says Mission Accomplished," *The New York Times* (June 12, 1989): A–14.
20. Karen O'Connor and Bryant Scott McFall, "Conservative Interest Group Litigation in the Reagan Era and Beyond," in Mark P. Pe-

tracca, ed. *The Politics of Interests* (Boulder, CO: Westview Press, 1992), pp. 263–281.

21. David Mahood, *Interest Groups Participation in America: A New Intensity* (Englewood Cliffs, NJ: Prentice-Hall, 1990), p. 23.

22. Quoted in Ronald J. Hrebenar and Ruth K. Scott, *Interest Group Politics in America,* 2nd ed. (Englewood Cliffs, NJ: Prentice-Hall, 1990), p. 263.

23. Michael Wines, "For New Lobbyists, It's What They Know," *New York Times* (November 3, 1993): B-14.

24. Quoted in Schlozman and Tierney, *Organized Interests,* p. 85. (See n. 18.)

25. Quoted in Norman J. Ornstein and Shirley Elder, *Interest Groups, Lobbying and Policy Making* (Washington, DC: CQ Press, 1978), p. 77.

26. Thomas Cronin, *The State of the Presidency* (Boston: Little, Brown, 1975), p. 123.

27. Ibid.

28. Quoted in Hrebenar and Scott, *Interest Group Politics,* p. 216. (See n. 22.)

29. Some political scientists speak of iron rectangles, reflecting the growing importance of a fourth party, the courts, in the lobbying process.

30. Richard C. Cortner, "Strategies and Tactics of Litigation in Constitutional Cases," *Journal of Public Law* 17 (1968): 287.

31. Joel Brinkley, "Cultivating the Grass Roots to Reap Legislative Benefits," *The New York Times* (November 1, 1993): A–1.

32. Ibid.

33. Glenn R. Simpson, "Study: PAC Spending Jumps 18% in 1992," *Roll Call* (June 3, 1993).

34. E. E. Schattschneider, *The Semi-Sovereign People* (New York: Holt, Rinehart and Winston, 1960), p. 35.

35. Truman, *The Governmental Process,* p. 511. (See n. 7.)

36. Mancur Olson, Jr. *The Logic of Collective Action: Public Goods and the Theory of Groups* (Cambridge, MA: Harvard University Press, 1965).

37. Walker, "The Origins and Maintenance of Interest Groups," pp. 390–406. (See n. 14.)

38. Ibid.

39. 112 S. Ct. 2791 (1992).

40. Schattschneider, *The Semi-Sovereign People,* p. 35. (See n. 34.)

Policy Portfolio

1. James E. Anderson, *Public Policymaking: An Introduction,* 2nd ed. (Boston, Houghton Mifflin, 1994), p. 5. This discussion draws on Anderson's study.

2. Roger W. Cobb and Charles D. Elder, *Participation in American Politics: The Dynamics of Agenda-Building,* 2nd ed. (Baltimore: Johns Hopkins University Press, 1983), Chapter 5.

3. Ibid., p. 85.

4. This discussion draws on Anne Schneider and Helen Ingram, "Behavioral Assumptions of Policy Tools," *Journal of Politics,* 52 (May 1990): 510–529.

5. *Zobrest* v. *Catalina Foothills School District,* 113 S. Ct. 2462 (1993).

6. *Board of Education of Kiryas Joel Village School District* v. *Grumet,* 114 S. Ct. 2481 (1994).

7. John J. Harrigan, *Policy and Politics in States and Communities,* 3rd ed. (Glenview, IL: Scott, Foresman, 1988), pp. 300–301.

8. See Randy Shilts, *And the Band Played On* (New York: St. Martin's Press, 1987).

9. *Statistical Abstract of the United States,* 1993, p. 92; and *New York Times* (January 5, 1993): 1.

10. Henry J. Aaron, *Serious and Unstable Condition: Financing America's Health Care* (Washington, DC: Brookings Institution, 1991), Chapter 2.

11. Lawrence R. Jacobs, Robert Y. Shapiro, and Eli C. Schulman, "Medical Care in the United States: An Update," *Public Opinion Quarterly,* 57 (Fall 1993): 394–427. This article contains data from a large number of opinion polls.

12. The following discussion draws on James E. Anderson, David W. Brady, Charles S. Bullock III, and Joseph Stewart Jr., *Public Policy and Politics in America,* 2nd ed. (Monterey, CA: Brooks/Cole, 1984), Chapter 2.

13. *Time* (March 7, 1994): 42.

14. William Greider, *Secrets of the Temple: How the Federal Reserve Runs the Country* (New York: Simon & Schuster, 1987), Chapter 10.

15. Anderson et al., *Public Policy,* pp. 38–40. (See n. 12.)

16. *Annual Report of the Council of Economic Advisers, 1993* (Washington, DC: Government Printing Office, 1993), p. 108.

17. Ibid., p. 109.

18. This discussion of budgeting draws on Anderson, *Public Policymaking,* Chapter 5. (See n. 1.)

19. Donald F. Kettl, *Deficit Politics: Public Budgeting in Its Institutional and Historical Context* (New York: Macmillan, 1992), pp. 140–141.

20. *Congressional Quarterly Weekly Report* (August 7, 1993): 2122–2129.

21. John Cranford, *Budgeting for America,* 2nd ed. (Washington, DC: CQ Press, 1989), pp. 197–198.

22. Paul E. Peterson, "The New Politics of Deficits," in John E. Chubb and Paul E. Peterson, eds., *The New Direction in American Politics* (Washington, DC: Brookings Institution, 1985), Chapter 13.

23. Robert Eisner and Paul J. Peiper, "A New View of the Federal Debt and Budget Deficits," *American Economic Review,* 74 (March 1994): 23.

24. This discussion is based on *Budget of the United States, Fiscal Year 1995: Analytical Perspectives* (Washington, DC: Government Printing Office, 1994), pp. 423–424.

CASE GLOSSARY

Abrams **v.** *United States,* 250 U.S. 616 (1919): Federal Espionage Act, which banned distribution of leaflets critical of the government, did not violate the First Amendment. (Chapter 4)

Baker **v.** *Carr,* 369 U.S. 186 (1962): Equitable apportionment of voters among legislative districts is not a political question; instead it is a constitutional question involving the Fourteenth Amendment's equal protection clause. (Chapter 6)

Barron **v.** *Baltimore,* 7 Pet. (32 U.S.) 243 (1833): The federal Bill of Rights limits only the action of the national government and not those of the states. (Chapter 4)

Batson **v.** *Kentucky,* 476 U.S. 79 (1986): The equal protection clause prohibits prosecutors from using peremptory challenges to remove African Americans from juries. (Chapter 5)

Board of Education **v.** *Mergens,* 110 S. Ct. 2356, (1990): A school board's refusal to allow a high-school religious group to meet during a weekly activity period violates the Equal Access Act of 1984. (Chapter 4)

Board of Education of Hendrick Hudson School District **v.** *Rowley,* 458 U.S. 176 (1982): Public schools must provide assistance to deaf school children. (Chapter 9)

Bolling **v.** *Sharpe,* 347 U.S. 497 (1954): The due process clause of the Fourteenth Amendment forbids discrimination in public schools by the federal government. (Chapter 5)

Bowers **v.** *Hardwick,* 478 U.S. 186 (1986): Georgia's anti-sodomy law does not violate a gay man's privacy rights. (Chapters 4, 5, 9)

Brandenburg **v.** *Ohio,* 385 U.S. 444 (1969): Advocacy of illegal action can be punished only if "such advocacy is directed at inciting or producing imminent lawless action and is likely to incite or produce such actions." (Chapter 4)

Bradwell **v.** *Illinois,* 16 Wall. (83 U.S.) 130 (1873): A woman's right to practice law was not a privilege of citizenship protected by the Fourteenth Amendment. (Chapter 5)

Branzburg **v.** *Hayes,* 408 U.S. 665 (1972): The press is not protected by the First Amendment from divulging sources necessary for government investigation. (Chapters 4, 14)

Briggs **v.** *Elliott,* (1952): See *Brown* v. *Board of Education of Topeka.* (Chapter 5)

Brown **v.** *Board of Education of Topeka,* 347 U.S. 483 (1954): The Court reversed its approval of the separate but equal doctrine first enunciated in *Plessy* and ruled that separate but equal in education violates the equal protection clause of the Fourteenth Amendment. (Chapters 3, 4, 5, 9)

Brown **v.** *Board of Education of Topeka* II, 349 U.S. 294 (1955): The decision in *Brown I* was to be carried out with all deliberate speed and oversight of implementation was placed in the hands of local federal district court judges. (Chapter 5)

Buckley **v.** *Valeo,* 424 U.S. 1 (1976): The First Amendment prohibits congressional legislation limiting the amount of money candidates can spend from their families' personal resources. (Chapter 13)

Cantwell **v.** *Connecticut,* 310 U.S. 296 (1940): The First Amendment allows for an absolute freedom to believe and a more restricted freedom to act. (Chapter 4)

Chaplinsky **v.** *New Hampshire,* 315 U.S. 568 (1942): "Fighting words" are not protected by the First Amendment because "such expressions are no essential part of any exposition of ideas . . ." (Chapter 4)

Chisholm **v.** *Georgia,* 2 U.S. 419 (1793): The Supreme Court has jurisdiction to review disputes involving citizens of one state against another state. (Chapter 9)

Civil Rights Cases, 109 U.S. 3 (1883): Congress could prohibit only governmental but not private acts of discrimination. (Chapter 5)

Cooper **v.** *Aaron,* 358 U.S. 1 (1958): Delay in the implementation of integration plans in the interest of avoiding unrest violates the rights of African-American students. (Chapter 5)

Craig **v.** *Boren,* 429 U.S. 190 (1976): The Court fashioned a new intermediate standard of review by which to evaluate claims of sex discrimination. The challenged law did not serve an important governmental purpose nor was it substantially related to achievement of those objectives. Therefore it violated the Fourteenth Amendment's equal protection clause. (Chapter 5)

Cumming **v.** *County Board of Education,* 175 U.S. 528 (1899): Taxpaying African-American parents challenged the practice of using their tax dollars to support a "whites only" high school. The Court upheld this disparate treatment. (Chapter 5)

Davis v. Prince Edward County, (1954): See *Brown* v. *Board of Education of Topeka.* (Chapter 5)

Debs v. United States, 249 U.S. 211 (1919): The conviction of socialist and anti-war activist Debs was upheld because his speech had the natural tendency of obstructing war recruitment. (Chapter 4)

Dred Scott v. Sandford, 19 How. 393 (1857): The Court ruled that slaves were not citizens of the United States, therefore they had no standing to sue in federal court. The 1820 Missouri Compromise was also ruled invalid because Congress did not have the authority to outlaw slavery in states or territories because slaves were property protected by the Constitution. (Chapters 3, 5)

Edwards v. Aguillard, 482 U.S. 578 (1987): A Louisiana statute requiring that creationism be taught as balance to evolution violated the establishment clause of the First Amendment. (Chapter 4)

Engle v. Vitale, 370 U.S. 241 (1962): Recitation of nondenominational prayers in public schools violates the establishment clause. (Chapter 4)

Everson v. Board of Education of Ewing Township, 330 U.S. 1 (1947): Reimbursing parents for the transportation costs for students of Catholic schools did not violate the establishment clause because it was not furtherance of religion but instead a subsidy to parents. (Chapter 4)

Ex Parte McCardle, 74 U.S. 506 (1869): McCardle, a civilian newspaper editor, was jailed by a military court during Reconstruction. He argued that he was being held unlawfully. Congress removed the Courts jurisdiction over these kinds of cases forcing the Court to concede that it had no authority to hear McCardle's appeal. (Chapter 8)

Furman v. Georgia, 408 U.S. 238 (1972): The arbitrary nature of the death penalty violates Eighth and Fourteenth Amendment provisions against cruel and unusual punishment. (Chapter 4)

Garcia v. San Antonio Metropolitan Transport Authority, 469 U.S. 528 (1985): Reversed *National League of Cities* and held that Congress had authority under the commerce clause to set minimum wage and maximum hour laws for state workers. (Chapter 3)

Gebhart v. Belton: See *Brown* v. *Board of Education of Topeka.* (Chapter 5)

Gibbons v. Ogden, 22 U.S. 1 (1824): Marshall Court broadly interpreted Congress's authority under the commerce clause to include the right to regulate navigation. (Chapter 3)

Gideon v. Wainwright, 372 U.S. 335 (1963): Counsel must be provided to indigents in all felony cases. (Chapter 4)

Gitlow v. New York, 268 U.S. 652 (1925): Although Gitlow's conviction was upheld, the Court found that speech is one of

the fundamental rights applied to the states through the due process clause of the Fourteenth Amendment. (Chapter 4)

Gregg v. Georgia, 428 U.S. 153 (1976): Georgia's rewritten death penalty sentence guidelines upheld as constitutional. (Chapter 4)

Griggs v. Duke Power Company, 401 U.S. 424 (1971): The use of non-job related tests that excluded African-American workers from certain positions violates the Civil Rights Act of 1964. (Chapter 5)

Griswold v. Connecticut, 381 U.S. 479 (1965): A Connecticut statute making it illegal to disseminate contraceptive devices or information was found to violate a married couple's right to privacy as guaranteed by the First, Third, Fourth, Fifth, and Fourteenth Amendments. (Chapter 4)

Grove City College v. Bell, 465 U.S. 555 (1984): Title IX of the Education Amendments of 1972 prohibits gender discrimination on the part of colleges and universities receiving federal funds. However, only those programs directly receiving the funds needed to be nondiscriminatory. (Chapter 5)

Harris v. Forklift Systems, 114 S.Ct 367 (1982): Plaintiffs need not show proof of severe psychological damage to prove that illegal sexual harassment occurred. (Chapter 9)

Heart of Atlanta Motel v. United States, 379 U.S. 619 (1964): The Civil Rights Act of 1964, barring discrimination in public accommodations, was held constitutional when the Court found that Congress was within its right to regulate interstate commerce. (Chapter 5)

Hoyt v. Florida, 368 U.S. 57 (1961): The exclusion of women from juries did not violate the equal protection clause of the Fourteenth Amendment. (Chapter 5)

Hylton v. United States, 3 Dall. (3 U.S.) 171 (1796): Excise tax on carriages not a direct tax; therefore constitutional. (Chapter 9)

Immigration and Naturalization Service v. Chadha, 462 U.S. 919 (1983): Legislative veto ruled unconstitutional. (Chapters 6, 9)

J.E.B. v. Alabama, 1994 U.S. LEXIS 3421 (1994): Alabama's use of peremptory challenges to exclude men from the jury for a paternity case was unconstitutional. (Chapter 4)

Johnson v. Santa Clara Transportation Agency, 480 U.S. 616 (1987): For the first time, the Court ruled that a public employer could use a voluntary plan to promote women even if there was no judicial finding of prior discrimination. (Chapter 5)

Keyes v. School District No. 1, Denver, Colorado, 413 U.S. 189 (1973): School district's maintenance of segregated schools through racially gerrymandered school attendance zones was ruled unconstitutional. (Chapter 5)

Korematsu v. United States, 323 U.S. 649 (1944): Internment of Japanese-American citizens held constitutional during World War II. (Chapter 9)

Lee **v.** *Weisman,* 112 S. Ct. 2649 (1992): A public middle-school's practice of prayer at graduation was ruled unconstitutional as a violation of the establishment clause. (Chapter 4)

Lemon **v.** *Kurtzman,* 403 U.S. 602 (1971): The Court devised "the Lemon test" to measure the constitutionality of state laws that appear to further a religion. Such practices are constitutional if they have a secular purpose; neither advance nor inhibit religion; and don't foster excessive governmental entanglement with religion. (Chapter 4)

Lynch **v.** *Donnelly,* 465 U.S. 668 (1984): A city's inclusion of a creche as part of its holiday display in a private park does not violate the establishment clause. (Chapter 4)

Mapp **v.** *Ohio,* 367 U.S. 643 (1961): Evidence obtained in violation of the Fourth Amendment's prohibition of unreasonable searches and seizures cannot be used as evidence at trial. The exclusionary rule applies to the states through the Fourteenth Amendment. (Chapter 4)

Marbury **v.** *Madison,* 1 Cranch (5 U.S.) 137 (1803): The Court first asserted the power of judicial review in finding that a congressional statute extending the Court's original jurisdiction was unconstitutional. (Chapters 2, 9)

McCleskey **v.** *Kemp,* 481 U.S. 279 (1987): Even if the death penalty was imposed in a racially discriminatory manner, it did not violate the equal protection clause of the Fourteenth Amendment. (Chapter 4)

McCleskey **v.** *Zant,* 111 S.Ct. 1454 (1991) Although the use of conversations with another prisoner as evidence violated McCleskey's right to counsel, the Court ruled that this challenge should have been made earlier in proceedings. Thus, McCleskey's conviction was upheld. (Chapter 4)

McCulloch **v.** *Maryland,* 4 Wheat. 316 (1819) Congress's authority under the commerce clause gives it the power to create a bank. (Chapters 3, 6, 9)

McLaurin **v.** *Oklahoma State Regents for Higher Education,* 339 U.S. 637 (1950): Segregation in graduate education was a violation of the Fourteenth Amendment's equal protection clause. (Chapter 5)

Miller **v.** *California,* 413 U.S. 15 (1973): The Court set out a new test for obscenity. It must first ask "whether the work depicts or describes in a patently offensive way, sexual conduct specifically defined by law." It then must ask "whether the work, as a whole, lacks serious literary, artistic, political or scientific value." (Chapter 4)

Minor **v.** *Happersett,* 88 U.S. 162 (1875): Women were not enfranchised by the privileges and immunities clause of the Fourteenth Amendment. Voting is not a privilege of citizenship. (Chapter 5)

Miranda **v.** *Arizona,* 384 U.S. 436 (1966): The Fifth Amendment requires that persons arrested for a crime must be advised of their right to remain silent and to have counsel present. (Chapter 4)

Missouri **v.** *Holland,* 252 U.S. 416 (1920): National law and treaties are supreme over state law. (Chapter 3)

Muller **v.** *Oregon,* 208 U.S. 412 (1908): Oregon's ten-hour-a-day maximum hour law for women upheld as constitutional. (Chapter 5)

National League of Cities **v.** *Usery,* 426 U.S. 833 (1976): Congress overstepped its authority under the commerce clause when it included state workers under the Fair Labor Standards Act. (Chapter 3)

Near **v.** *Minnesota,* 283 U.S. 697 (1931): The first case in which the Court overturned a conviction ruling that the state had violated freedom of the press under the First Amendment. (Chapter 4)

Nebraska Press Association **v.** *Stuart,* 427 U.S. 539 (1976): Any attempts by the government to prevent expressions carry a heavy presumption against their constitutionality. Thus, a trial court's "gag order" barring the press from reporting the details of a crime was unconstitutional. The press's right to cover the trial outweighed the defendant's right to a fair trial. (Chapter 4)

New York Times Co. **v.** *Sullivan,* 376 U.S. 254 (1964) "Actual malice" must be proved to support a finding of libel against a public figure. (Chapters 4, 14)

New York Times Co. **v.** *United States,* 403 U.S. 713 (1971): *The New York Times* printed classified documents known as "The Pentagon Papers" regarding the war in Vietnam. After the first installment in the series, the government moved to restrain publication. The Court found that this kind of prior restraint was in violation of the First Amendment. (Chapters 4, 14)

Oregon **v.** *Smith,* 294 U.S. 872 (1990): An Oregon law banning the use of peyote was challenged by Native Americans who used the drug as part of a religious observance. The Court ruled that the law does not violate the free exercise clause because peyote is a dangerous drug. (Chapter 4)

Palko **v.** *Connecticut,* 302 U.S. 319 (1937): Established the principle that only rights fundamental to our notions of ordered liberty were to be applied to the states via the Fourteenth Amendment's due process clause. (See *selective incorporation* in Glossary.) (Chapter 4)

Planned Parenthood of Southeastern Pennsylvania **v.** *Casey,* 112 S. Ct. 931 (1992): Pennsylvania's wide array of abortion restrictions including a 24-hour waiting period and parental consent notifications were held constitutional so long as they do not place an undue burden on women seeking abortions. (Chapters 3, 4, 9, 15)

Plessy **v.** *Ferguson,* 163 U.S. 537 (1896): Plessy challenged a Louisiana statute requiring that railroads provide separate accommodations for blacks and whites. The Court found that separate but equal accommodations did not violate the equal protection clause of the Fourteenth Amendment. (Chapters 2, 3, 5, 9)

Red Lion Broadcasting Company, Inc. v. FCC, 395 U.S. 367 (1969): The fairness doctrine allows the government to regulate use of the public air waves. Federal Communication Commission regulations, therefore, do not violate the First Amendment. (Chapter 14)

Reed v. Reed, 404 U.S. 71 (1971): For the first time, the Court found that unreasonable gender discrimination violated the equal protection clause of the Fourteenth Amendment. (Chapter 5)

Regents of the University of California v. Bakke, 438 U.S. 265 (1978): The Court found quotas unconstitutional but noted, however, that race may be taken into account along with other admission factors. (Chapter 5)

Regina v. Hicklin, L.R. 2 Q.B. 360 (1868): English tradition holding that, in order to be obscene, material must be shown to deprave and corrupt those into whose hands it might fall. (Chapter 4)

Reynolds v. Sims, 377 U.S. 533 (1964): Congressional and state legislative districts must have "substantially equal" populations, in essence guaranteeing "one man, one vote." (Chapters 6, 9)

Roe v. Wade, 410 U.S. 113 (1973): The Court found that a woman's right to an abortion (in consultation with her physician) was protected by the right to privacy found in the penumbras of several amendments. (Chapters 3, 4, 5, 9, 15)

Roth v. United States, 354 U.S. 476 (1957): To be considered obscene, material must be utterly without redeeming social importance. The *Roth* test asks "whether to the average person, applying contemporary community standards, the dominant theme of the material taken as a whole appeals to the prurient interests." (Chapter 4)

Rust v. Sullivan, 111 S.Ct. 1759 (1991): Prohibiting medical personnel from dispensing abortion information at health clinics receiving federal funding upheld as constitutional. (Chapter 4)

Schenck v. United States, 249 U.S. 47 (1919): Schenck, a Socialist, was convicted of mailing anti-war leaflets encouraging eligible men to avoid the draft. The Court upheld Schenck's conviction finding that Schenck's speech presented a "clear and present" danger to the United States's ability to carry on the war effort successfully. (Chapter 4)

The Slaughterhouse Cases, 83 U.S. 36 (1873): A butcher's association charged Louisiana's granting of a monopoly for the running of slaughterhouses deprived their members of their livelihood in violation of the Fourteenth Amendment. The Court found that the Fourteenth Amendment's privileges and immunities clause applied only to national and not state citizenship. Thus, the states had the right to create a monopoly. (Chapters 3, 5)

Smith v. Allright, 321 U.S. 649 (1944): White primaries violate the Fifteenth Amendment. (Chapter 12)

Stromberg v. California, 283 U.S. 359 (1931): For the first time, the Court ruled that symbolic speech was entitled to protection under the First Amendment. (Chapter 4)

Swann v. Charlotte-Mecklenburg School District, 402 U.S. 1 (1971): Federal courts could order busing as an appropriate remedy to end segregated education. (Chapter 5)

Sweatt v. Painter, 339 U.S. 629 (1950): Creation of a separate law school for African Americans did not meet the mandates of the Fourteenth Amendment's equal protection clause because the facilities were not equal. (Chapter 5)

Texas v. Johnson, 491 U.S. 397 (1989): Burning the U.S. flag during the Republican National Convention was symbolic political speech protected by the First Amendment. (Chapter 4)

Tinker v. Des Moines Independent Community School District, 393 U.S. 503 (1969): Students' symbolic speech—wearing black arm bands to protest the Vietnam War—was entitled to First Amendment protection. (Chapter 4)

United States v. Nixon, 418 U.S. 683 (1974): There is no constitutional absolute executive privilege that would allow a president to refuse to comply with a court order to produce information needed in a criminal trial. (Chapters 7, 9)

U.S. v. Seeger, 380 U.S. 163 (1965): The Court invalidated the denial of conscientious objector deferments to members of "nontraditional" religions, finding that the men's belief in a supreme being put their religion on a par with others, thus deserving the same constitutional protections. (Chapter 4)

Wallace v. Jaffree, 472 U.S. 38 (1985): An Alabama law requiring a minute of silence for meditation or voluntary prayer was found to not serve a secular purpose and therefore violated the constitutionally required separation of church and state. (Chapter 4)

Webster v. Reproductive Health Services, 492 U.S. 490 (1989): The Court upheld state-required fetal viability tests in the second trimester and upheld portions of the state law prohibiting abortions to be performed in state hospitals or by state-funded doctors or nurses. (Chapters 3, 4, 9)

Weeks v. United States, 232 U.S. 383 (1914): The Court first articulated the exclusionary rule, which bars the use of illegally obtained evidence in trial. (Chapter 4)

Wisconsin v. Yoder, 406 U.S. 205 (1972): A Wisconsin law requiring school attendance until the age of eighteen violated the free exercise clause because it interfered with the Amish's practice of their religion. (Chapter 4)

Youngstown Steel & Tube Company v. Sawyer, 343 U.S. 579 (1952): President Truman lacked executive power to seize the nation's steel mills. (Chapter 9)

GLOSSARY

absolutist approach: The belief that the First Amendment's wording "Congress shall make no law" must be construed to bar any government regulation of First Amendment freedoms. (Chapter 4)

accomodationist approach: A belief that holds that in recognition of religious diversity in the United States, some accommodation for religious differences should be allowed by the government. (Chapter 4)

actual representation: A system by which legislators represent only those voters who elect them. (Chapter 6)

administrative adjudication: A quasi-judicial process in which a bureaucratic agency settles disputes between two parties in a manner similar to the way courts resolve disputes. (Chapter 8)

administrative discretion: The ability of the bureaucracy to make choices concerning the best way to implement congressional intentions. (Chapter 8)

affiliates: Local television stations that carry the programming of a national network. (Chapter 14)

affirmative action: Policies designed to give special attention or compensatory treatment to members of a previously disadvantaged group. (Chapter 5)

agenda: A set of problems to which policy makers believe they should be attentive. (Policy Portfolio)

agenda setting: The constant process of forming the list of issues to be addressed by government. (Policy Portfolio)

Americans with Disabilities Act: 1990 law making it illegal for employers to discriminate against persons with physical or mental disabilities. It also guarantees access to all public facilities and requires modifications to make existing facilities available. (Chapters 5, 6)

amicus curiae: "Friend of the court"; a third party to a lawsuit who files a legal brief for the purpose of raising additional points of view in an attempt to influence a court's decision. (Chapters 9, 15)

Anti-Federalists: Those who favored strong state governments and a weak national government; opposed the ratification of the U.S. Constitution. (Chapters 2, 4, 7)

appellate courts: Name given to courts of appeal and supreme courts that hear and review cases that already have been decided in lower courts. (Chapter 9)

appellate jurisdiction: A court's authority to hear appeals from other courts in the state or federal system. (Chapter 9)

apportionment: The determination and assignment of representation in a legislature based on population. (Chapters 5, 6)

appropriations: The earmarking of funds by Congress in particular pieces of legislation for particular programs, agencies and so forth. (Chapters 6)

aristocracy: A system of government in which control is based on rule of the highest. (Chapter 1)

Articles of Confederation: The basic framework of the new U.S. government approved by the Second Continental Congress in 1777. Used to govern the United States during the Revolutionary War, the Articles provided for a Congress with very limited authority. (Chapters 2, 6)

articles of impeachment: Precise charges against a president, vice president, or other "civil officers" that are approved by the House of Representatives as a first step to that individual's removal from office. (Chapter 7)

bad tendency test: Engaging in speech that has a tendency to induce illegal behavior or to create a danger; speech that is not protected by the First Amendment. (Chapter 4)

Balanced Budget Amendment: A proposal to require that Congress annually adopt a budget in which revenues at least equal expenditures. (Chapter 6)

bicameral legislature: A legislature divided into two houses; the U.S. Congress and every U.S. state legislature are bicameral (except Nebraska, which is unicameral). (Chapters 2, 6)

bill: A proposed law. (Chapter 6)

bill of attainder: A law declaring an act illegal without a judicial trial. (Chapter 3)

Bill of Rights: The first ten amendments to the U.S. Constitution guaranteeing specific rights and liberties; ratified in 1791. (Chapters 2, 4)

Black Codes: Laws passed by Southern states following the Civil War to deny most legal rights to newly freed slaves. (Chapter 5)

blanket primary: A primary in which voters may cast ballots in either party's primary (but not both) on an office-by-office basis. (Chapter 12)

block grants: Broad grants with few strings given to states by the federal government for specified activities, such as secondary education or health services. (Chapter 3)

Brady Bill: Law passed in 1993 requiring a national five-day waiting period for purchase of handguns. (Chapters 1, 3, 4)

Brandeis brief: A legal brief that relies heavily on sociological and other forms of nonlegal data, such as statistics, instead of legal precedent. (Chapter 5)

brief: The collected legal written arguments in a case filed with a court by a party prior to a hearing or trial. (Chapter 9)

bureaucracy: A set of complex hierarchical departments, agencies, commissions, and their staffs, that exist to help the president carry out his constitutionally mandated charge to enforce the laws of the nation. (Chapter 8)

bureaucratic theory: The belief that all governmental and all nongovernmental institutions are, in effect, controlled by an all-powerful bureaucracy. (Chapter 1)

bureaucrats: Career government employees who work for federal, state, or local governments. (Chapter 8)

Cabinet: The secretaries of major departments of the federal government, the Attorney General, the vice president, and the U.S. Ambassador to the United Nations. All Cabinet members are appointed by the president and confirmed by the Senate. (Chapters 7, 8)

calendar: Congressional schedule. (Chapter 6)

candidate debates: Forums in which political candidates face each other to discuss their platforms, records, and character. (Chapter 13)

capitalism: The economic system that favors private control of business and minimal governmental regulation of private industry. (Chapters 1)

categorical grants: Grants for which Congress appropriates funds for a specific purpose. (Chapter 3)

caucus: Formal or informal groupings of members of Congress by political party, interest, region, or class, and/or other distinctions. (Chapter 6)

checks and balances: A governmental structure that gives each of the three branches of government some degree of oversight and control over the actions of the others. (Chapter 2)

circuit court of appeals (court of appeals): The intermediate appellate courts in the federal system; were established in 1789 to hear appeals from federal district courts. (Chapter 9)

civil law: Noncriminal law, such as the law of property, commercial law, or family law. (Chapter 9)

civil liberties: The personal rights and freedoms that the federal government cannot abridge by law, constitution, or judicial interpretation. (Chapter 4)

civil rights: The political and social right to be free from arbitrary infringement by the government or any individual. (Chapters 4, 5)

Civil Rights Act of 1964: Legislation passed by Congress to outlaw segregation in public facilities and racial discrimination in employment, education, and voting; created the Equal Employment Opportunity Commission. (Chapter 5, 6)

Civil Rights Cases: Five separate cases involving the convictions of private individuals found to have violated the Civil Rights Act of 1875. The Supreme Court ruled that Congress lacked the authority to prohibit private discrimination in public accommodations.

civil service: A federal bureaucracy with appointments made on the basis of competitive examinations rather than political influence. (Chapter 11)

civil service laws: These acts removed the staffing of the bureaucracy from political parties and created a professional bureaucracy filled through competition. (Chapters 11, 12)

Civil Service Reform Act of 1883: See *Pendleton Act.* (Chapter 8)

civil service system: The system created by civil service laws by which many appointments to the federal bureaucracy are made. (Chapter 8)

Civil War Amendments: Name given to the Thirteenth, Fourteenth, and Fifteenth Amendments to the Constitution, which were concerned with the rights of newly freed slaves. (Chapter 5)

class-action lawsuit: A legal action in which a small number of individuals can sue on behalf of themselves *and* the class of all other citizens who are similarly situated. (Chapter 9)

clear and present danger test: Used by the Supreme Court in an attempt to draw a line between protected and unprotected speech. As the test is applied, the Court looks to see if there is an imminent danger that illegal action would occur in response to the contested speech. (Chapter 4)

clientele agencies: Executive departments that are directed by law to foster and promote the interests of a specific segment or group in the U.S. population (such as the Department of Education). (Chapter 8)

closed primary: A primary election in which only a party's registered voters are eligible to vote. (Chapter 12)

cloture: Senate rule that allows the vote of sixty Senators to cut off a filibuster. (Chapter 6)

coalition: A group of interests or organizations that join forces for the purpose of electing public officials. (Chapter 11)

Coercive (or Intolerable) Acts: A series of five acts passed by Parliament in 1774 to punish the American colonists for the Boston Tea Party. (Chapter 2)

collective good: Something of value that cannot be withheld from a noninterest group member, e.g., a tax write off, a good feeling. (Chapter 15)

commander-in-chief: The constitutional power of the president over all combined U.S. armed forces. (Chapter 7)

commerce clause: Article I, Section 8 of the Constitution allows Congress to "regulate Commerce with foreign Nations, and among the several States, and with the Indian Tribes." (Chapters 2, 3)

Committees of Correspondence: Organizations originated by Samuel Adams in each of the American colonies to keep colonists abreast of developments with the British; served as powerful molders of public opinion against the British. (Chapter 2)

common law: Judge-made law based on adherence to precedents; law common to the realm in the British empire. (Chapter 2)

Common Sense: Pamphlet written by Thomas Paine calling for independence from Great Britain. (Chapter 2)

communism: A political philosophy posited by Karl Marx in which he argued that government was simply a manifestation of underlying economic forces and could be understood according to types of economic production. (Chapters 1, 4)

concurrent powers: Powers shared by the national and state governments. (Chapter 3)

concurring opinions: Opinions written by judges who agree with the outcome of the case but do not agree with the legal rationale for the opinion. (Chapter 9)

confederation: Type of government in which the national government derives its powers from the states; a league of independent states. (Chapter 2)

conference committee: Joint committee created to iron out differences between Senate and House versions of a specific piece of legislation. (Chapter 6)

Connecticut Compromise: Proposal for a bicameral legislature made by Connecticut during the Philadelphia Convention at which the U.S. Constitution was drafted. (Chapter 2)

conservatives: Those thought to believe that a government is best that governs least and that big government can only infringe on individual, personal, and economic rights. (Chapters 1, 5, 10)

constituency: The individuals who reside in an area from which a representative is elected. (Chapter 6)

constitution: Set of written laws and principles that set out a framework for governing. (Chapter 2)

constitutional courts: Courts established by Article III of the Constitution or by congressional action authorized by the Constitution. (Chapter 9)

contemporary community standards: In obscenity cases, the Supreme Court allows local communities to determine what they consider to be obscene. (Chapter 4)

content regulation: Governmental attempts to regulate the electronic media. (Chapter 14)

Contract with America: Republican 10-point plan to reform government. (Chapter 6)

contrast ads: Political campaign advertisements that compare the records of the candidates, favoring the ad's sponsor. (Chapter 13)

cooperative federalism: A term used to characterize the relationship between the national and state governments that began with the New Deal. (Chapter 3)

Council of Economic Advisors (CEA): An agency created in 1946 as part of the Executive Office of the President; consists of three economic experts appointed by the president subject to Senate confirmation plus a small staff evenly divided between support personnel and professional economists. (Chapter 7)

covenant: In biblical terms, an agreement, or bargain, between God and his people. In a governmental sense, a formal agreement sworn to a new government to abide by its terms. The Mayflower Compact was a covenant. (Chapter 1)

criminal law: The branch of law dealing with crimes and their punishments. (Chapter 9)

critical elections: An election that signals a party realignment through voter polarization around new issues. (Chapter 12)

Declaration of Independence: Document drafted by Thomas Jefferson in 1776 that proclaimed the right of the American colonies to separate from Great Britain. (Chapter 2)

Declaration of Rights and Resolves: Call issued by the First Continental Congress for colonial rights of petition and assembly, trial by peers, freedom from a standing army, and the selection of representative assemblies to levy taxes. (Chapter 2)

Declaration of Sentiments: 1848 statement that described widespread discrimination against women in society. (Chapter 5)

deep background: Information gathered for news stories that must be completely unsourced. (Chapter 14)

de facto **discrimination:** Racial discrimination that results from practice (such as housing patterns or other social factors) rather than law. (Chapter 5)

deficit: The amount spent by the government that exceeds what is taken in. (Chapter 7)

de jure **discrimination:** Racial discrimination that is a direct result of law or official policy. (Chapter 5)

democracy: A system of government that gives power to the people, whether directly or through their elected representatives. (Chapter 1)

direct democracy: A system of government in which members of the polity meet to discuss all policy decisions and then agree to abide by majority rule. (Chapter 1)

direct incitement test: The advocacy of illegal action is protected by the First Amendment unless imminent action is intended and likely to occur. (Chapter 4)

direct mailer: A professional who supervises a political campaign's direct-mail fund-raising strategies. (Chapter 13)

direct primary: The selection of party candidates through the ballots of qualified voters rather than at party nomination conventions. (Chapter 11)

discharge petitions: Petitions that give a majority of the House of Representatives the authority to bring an issue to the floor in the face of committee inaction. (Chapter 6)

discount rate: The rate of interest at which member banks can borrow money from their regional Federal Reserve Bank. (Policy Portfolio)

"discuss list": A list of cases taken from the U.S. Supreme Court "cert. pool" that are to be discussed by the Justices; only about 30 percent of submitted petitions make it to this list. (Chapter 9)

dissenting opinions: Opinions written by judges who disagree with the opinion of the majority. (Chapter 9)

district courts: The federal court of original jurisdiction, where most federal cases begin. (Chapter 9)

disturbance theory: The theory offered by political scientist David Truman that posits that interest groups form in part to counteract the efforts of other groups. (Chapter 15)

divided government: The situation that exists when the Congress and president come from different political parties. This often makes enactment of policies difficult and had been blamed for gridlock in Washington, DC. (Chapters 2, 6, 7)

divine right of kings: The belief that monarchs were given the right to govern directly from God. (Chapters 1, 2)

double jeopardy: Trying an individual in court more than once for the same crime; prohibited by the U.S. Constitution. (Chapter 4)

dual federalism: The belief that having separate and equally powerful levels of government is the best arrangement. (Chapter 3)

dualist theory: The theory claiming that there has always been an underlying binary party nature to U.S. politics. (Chapter 11)

due process clause: Clause contained in the Fifth and Fourteenth Amendments. Over the years, it has been construed to guarantee to individuals a variety of rights ranging from economic liberty to criminal procedural rights to protection from arbitrary governmental action. (Chapter 4)

due process rights: Procedural guarantees provided by the Fourth, Fifth, Sixth and Eighth Amendments for those accused of crimes.

economic interest groups: Groups with the primary purpose of promoting the financial interests of their members. (Chapter 15)

economic stability: A situation in which there is economic growth, rising national income, high employment, and steadiness in the general level of prices.

elastic clause: See *necessary and proper clause.* (Chapter 3)

electoral college: The body of presidential electors from each state who cast their ballots in their respective state capitals for the president and vice president of the United States. (Chapters 2, 11)

electorate: Those citizens eligible to vote. (Chapter 12)

electors: Members of the electoral college chosen by methods determined in each state. (Chapters 2, 12)

electronic media: The newest form of broadcast media including television, radio, and cable. (Chapter 14)

elite theory: The view that a small group of people actually makes most of the important decisions. C. Wright Mills argued that important policies were set by three loose coalitions of groups—the military, corporate leaders, and a small set of government officials. He termed the "power elite." (Chapter 1)

Emancipation Proclamation: Proclamation issued by President Abraham Lincoln that provided that all slaves in states still in active rebellion against the United States would automatically be freed on January 1, 1863. (Chapter 5)

Enlightenment: A movement that occurred in Western Europe in the 1700s that espoused human reason, science, and religious toleration. (Chapter 1)

enumerated powers: Seventeen specific powers granted to Congress under Article I, Section 8 of the U.S. Constitution; these powers include taxation, coinage of money, regulation of commerce, and the authority to provide for a national defense. (Chapters 2, 3)

Equal Employment Opportunity Commission: Federal agency created to enforce provisions of the Civil Rights Act of 1964. (Chapters 5, 9)

equal protection clause: Section of the Fourteenth Amendment that guarantees that all citizens receive "equal protection under the laws"; has been used to bar discrimination against African Americans, women, and other groups. (Chapter 5)

equal time rule: The rule that requires broadcast stations to sell campaign air time equally to all candidates if they choose to sell it to any. (Chapter 14)

establishment clause: The first clause in the First Amendment that prohibits the national government from establishing a national religion. (Chapter 4)

exclusionary rule: Judicially created rule that prohibits police from using illegally seized evidence at trial. (Chapter 4)

executive agreement: A secret and highly sensitive arrangement with a foreign nation entered into by the president that does not require the "advise and consent" of Congress. (Chapter 7)

Executive Office of the President: Establishment created in 1939 to help the president oversee the bureaucracy. (Chapters 7, 8)

executive orders: Presidential directives to an agency that provide the basis for carrying out laws or for establishing new policies. (Chapter 8)

executive power: The authority to execute or carry out the laws of the nation; a power vested in the chief executive by Article II of the Constitution. (Chapters 2, 7)

executive privilege: The belief that, at the president's discretion, communications between him and his aides can be kept confidential from Congress and the courts. (Chapter 7)

exit polls: Polls conducted at selected polling places on election day. (Chapter 10)

ex post facto law: Law passed after the fact, thereby making previously legal activity illegal and subject to current penalty; prohibited by the U.S. Constitution. (Chapters 3, 4)

extradite: To return criminals to states where they have been convicted or are to stand trial. (Chapter 3)

faction: Group of individuals with shared traits or common interests. (Chapters 2, 15)

fairness doctrine: Rule in effect from 1949 to 1985 requiring broadcasters to cover events adequately and to present contrasting views on important public issues. (Chapter 14)

Farewell Address: George Washington's last public statement as president, in which he discussed the dangers of divisive party politics and warned strongly against foreign entanglements. (Chapter 7)

Federal Employees Political Activities Act: 1993 liberalization of Hatch Act. Federal employees are now allowed to run for office in nonpartisan elections and to contribute money to campaigns in partisan elections. (Chapter 8)

federalism: The philosophy that describes the governmental system created by the Framers. See also *federal system.* (Chapter 3)

The Federalist Papers: A series of eighty-five political papers written by John Jay, Alexander Hamilton, and James Madison in support of ratification of the U.S. Constitution. (Chapter 2)

Federalists: Those who favored a stronger national government and supported the proposed U.S. Constitution; later became the first U.S. political party. (Chapters 2, 3, 4, 7)

Federal Register: A daily publication of the federal government that contains all proposed and final regulations of all federal agencies. (Chapter 8)

federal system: Plan of government created by the U.S. Constitution in which power is divided between the national government and the state governments and in which independent states are bound together under one national government. (Chapters 2, 3)

Fifteenth Amendment: Last of the three Civil War Amendments; prohibited states from discriminating against potential voters because of race or previous condition of servitude. (Chapter 5)

fighting words: Words intended to incite or cause injury to those at whom they are addressed; not protected by the First Amendment. (Chapter 4)

filibusters: A formal way of halting action on a bill by means of long speeches or unlimited debate in the Senate. (Chapter 6)

First Continental Congress: Meeting held in Philadelphia from September 5 to October 26, 1774, in which fifty-six delegates (from every colony except Georgia) adopted a resolution that opposed the Coercive Acts. (Chapter 2)

Fourteenth Amendment: Second of the three Civil War Amendments; guaranteed equal protection and due process of laws to all U.S. citizens. (Chapter 5)

franchise: The right to vote. (Chapter 5)

free exercise clause: The second clause of the First Amendment. It prohibits the U.S. government from interfering with a citizen's right to practice his or her religion. (Chapter 4)

free market economy: The production and exchange of goods and services without interference from the government. (Chapter 1)

free media: Coverage of a candidate's campaign by the news media. (Chapter 13)

free-rider problem: A problem that occurs when those who don't join or work for the benefit of the group still reap the rewards of the group's activity. (Chapter 15)

"freedom of choice" plans: Plans enacted by Southern states in the aftermath of *Brown* v. *Board of Education* to allow parents to send their children to the school of their choice and not to the school closest to their home (especially if it had black children enrolled). (Chapter 5)

freedom rides: Bands of college students and other civil rights activists traveled throughout the South by bus in an effort to force bus stations and other public facilities to desegregate. (Chapter 5)

freedmen: Name given to slaves who obtained freedom either individually (before the Emancipation Proclamation) or collectively (upon the Emancipation Proclamation and the end of the Civil War). (Chapter 5)

full faith and credit clause: Clause in the U.S. Constitution that requires that judicial decrees and contracts made in one state will be binding and enforceable in another. (Chapter 3)

gender gap: The difference between the partisan choices of women and men in the aggregate. (Chapter 11)

general election campaign: That part of a political campaign following a primary election, aimed at winning a general election. (Chapter 13)

general elections: Elections in which voters decide which candidates will actually fill elective public offices. (Chapter 12)

gerrymandering: The legislative process through which the majority party in each statehouse tries to assure that the maximum number of representatives from its political party can be elected to Congress through the redrawing of legislative districts. (Chapter 6)

get-out-the-vote: A push at the end of a political campaign to encourage supporters to go to the polls. (Chapter 13)

government: The institutions and procedures by which a given nation or other territory and its people are ruled. (Chapter 1)

governmental agenda: The changing list of issues to which governments believe they should address themselves. (Policy Portfolio)

governmental party: The office holders and candidates who run under a political party's banner. (Chapter 11)

government corporations: Businesses set up and created by Congress that perform functions that could be provided by private businesses (such as the U.S. Postal Service). (Chapter 8)

Gramm-Rudman-Hollings Act: The Balanced Budget and Emergency Deficit Control Act of 1985 that was designed to reduce the budget deficit by 1991. (Policy Portfolio)

grandfather clauses: Statutes that allowed only those whose grandfather's had voted before Reconstruction to vote unless they passed a wealth or literacy test. (Chapter 5)

grand jury: The body of persons selected to serve as an investigatory body of court; they decide whether or not to indict individuals whose cases are brought before them. (Chapter 9)

grants-in-aid: Programs funded by Congress that provide money to state and local governments to accomplish goals desired by the national government. (Chapter 3)

Great Compromise: A decision made during the Philadelphia Convention to give each state the same number of representatives in the Senate regardless of size; representation in the House was determined by population. (Chapter 2)

Great Depression: The severe recessionary period following the stock market crash of 1929. (Chapters 1, 3, 7)

"Great Society": President Lyndon B. Johnson's plan to end poverty and discrimination in the United States through a variety of innovative programs. (Chapters 3, 5, 7)

gross domestic product: The total market value of all goods and services produced in a country during a year. (Policy Portfolio)

Gulf of Tonkin Resolution: An agreement that originally authorized a massive commitment of U.S. forces to support a series of anti-communist, although not democratic, governments in South Vietnam. (Chapter 7)

habeas corpus: A court order demanding that individuals in official custody (usually jail or prison) be brought to court and shown the reasons for their detention. According to the U.S. Constitution, *habeas corpus* can be suspended only in times of rebellion or invasion. (Chapters 4, 7)

Hatch Act: Enacted by Congress in 1939 to prohibit civil servants from taking activist roles in partisan campaigns. This act prohibited federal employees from making political contributions, working for a particular party, or campaigning for a particular candidate. (Chapter 8)

holds: A tactic by which a senator asks to be informed before a particular bill is brought to the floor. (Chapter 6)

ideology: The combined doctrines, assertions, and intentions of a social or political group that justify its behavior; a consistent pattern of opinion on political issues that stems from basic underlying beliefs or a set of beliefs. (Chapters 1, 9, 11, 15)

impeachment: The power delegated to the House of Representatives in the Constitution to charge the president, vice president, or other "civil officers," including federal judges, with "Treason, Bribery, or other high Crimes and Misdemeanors." This is the first step in the constitutional process of removing such government officials from office. (Chapters 1, 2, 6, 7)

implementation: The process by which a law or policy is put into operation by the bureaucracy. (Chapter 8)

implied power: A power derived from an enumerated power and the necessary and proper clause. These powers are not stated specifically but are considered to be reasonably implied through the exercise of delegated powers. (Chapter 3)

impoundment: Refusal of the president to spend funds for programs that have been appropriated (authorized) by Congress. (Chapter 6)

incorporation doctrine: Principle in which the Supreme Court has held that most, but not all, of the specific guarantees in the Bill of Rights limit states and local governments by making those guarantees applicable to the states through the due process clause of the Fourteenth Amendment. (Chapter 4)

incumbency: The condition of already holding elected office. (Chapter 12)

incumbency factor: The fact that being in office helps a person stay in office because of a variety of benefits from free publicity to, in the case of Congress, free mailing, which go with the position. (Chapter 6)

independent agencies: Governmental units that closely resemble Cabinet departments but have narrower areas of responsibility (such as the Central Intelligence Agency). (Chapter 8)

indictment: A formal accusation decided upon by a grand jury. (Chapter 9)

indirect (representative) democracy: A system of government that gives citizens the opportunity to vote for representatives who will work on their behalf. (Chapter 1)

inflation: A rise in the general price levels of an economy. (Policy Portfolio)

in forma pauperis: Literally, "in the form of a pauper"; a way for an indigent or poor person to appeal a case to the U.S. Supreme Court. (Chapter 9)

inherent power: Power of the president that can be derived from inferences in the Constitution. (Chapter 7)

initiative: A method by which state and local voters can propose laws or constitutional amendments. Generally, special interest groups draft the initiatives and then circulate them on petitions. (Chapter 10)

institutional agenda: The problems to which legislators or other public officials feel obliged to devote active and serious attention. (Policy Portfolio)

interest group liberalism: All organized interests get something from government, thereby having an impact on how political decisions are made. (Chapter 1)

interest groups: Organized groups that try to influence public policy. (Chapters 14, 15)

interest group theory: The belief posited by David Truman that interest groups—not elites, sets of elites, or bureaucrats—control the governmental process. (Chapters 1, 15)

intergovernmental lobby: The pressure group or groups that are created when state and local governments hire lobbyists to lobby the national government. (Chapter 3)

iron triangles: The relatively stable relationships and patterns of interaction that occur among an agency, interest groups, and congressional committees or subcommittees. (Chapter 8)

issue networks: A term used to describe the loose and informal set of relationships that exist among a large number of actors who work in broad policy areas. (Chapter 8)

issue-oriented politics: Politics that focus on specific issues rather than on party, candidate, or other loyalties. (Chapter 11)

Jay Treaty: Negotiated by John Jay, this treaty helped settle disputes between Britain and the United States over the boundaries of the new nation, debts incurred during the Revolutionary War, and commerce between the two nations. (Chapter 7)

Jim Crow laws: Laws enacted by Southern states that discriminated against blacks by requiring segregation in public schools and public facilities, including railroads, restaurants, and theaters. (Chapter 5)

joint committees: Committees formed with members from both houses of Congress, generally to coordinate investigations or special studies. (Chapter 6)

judicial review: The authority of a court to review the acts of the legislature, the executive, or states to determine their constitutionality; enunciated by Chief Justice John Marshall in *Marbury* v. *Madison* (1803). (Chapters 1, 2, 3, 9)

Judiciary Act of 1789: Established the basic three-tiered structure of the federal court system. (Chapter 9)

laissez-faire: A French term literally meaning "to let do, to leave alone." It is a hands-off governmental policy based on the belief that governmental regulation of the economy is wrong. (Chapters 1, 3, 8)

League of Nations: Created after World War I at the insistence of President Woodrow Wilson, this precursor of the United Nations was the first global organization of nation-states dedicated to preserving peace. (Chapters 6, 7)

legislative courts: Courts established by Congress for specialized purposes, such as the Court of Military Appeals. (Chapter 9)

legislative powers: The authority of Congress to make laws as enumerated in the Constitution. (Chapter 6)

legislative veto: A procedure by which one or both houses of Congress can disallow an act of an executive agency by a simple majority vote. (Chapter 6)

libel: False statements or statements tending to call someone's reputation into disrepute. (Chapter 4)

liberals: Those considered to favor extensive governmental involvement in the economy and the provision of social services and to take an activist role in protecting the rights of women, the elderly, minorities, and the environment. (Chapters 1, 5, 10)

libertarians: Those who stress that government should not involve itself in the plight of the people or attempt to remedy any social ills. (Chapter 1)

line-item veto: The power to veto specific provisions of a bill without vetoing the bill in its entirety. (Chapters 6, 7)

lobbying: The activities of groups and organizations that seek to influence legislation and persuade political leaders to support the group's position. (Chapter 15)

lobbyist: Interest group representative who seeks through political persuasion to influence legislation that will benefit his or her organization. (Chapters 14, 15)

logrolling: Congressional vote trading on bills. (Chapter 6)

Magna Carta: A charter of government signed by King John in 1215, guaranteeing the British people certain liberties, including landowner and tenant rights, the right to a trial by jury, and some measure of religious freedom. (Chapter 2)

majority leader: The elected leader of the party controlling the most seats in the U.S. House of Representatives or the Senate; is second in authority to the Speaker of the House and in the Senate is regarded as its most powerful member. (Chapter 6)

majority party: The political party in each house of Congress with the most members. (Chapter 6)

majority rule: The central premise of a direct democracy in which only policies that collectively garner the support of a majority of voters will be made into law. (Chapter 1)

mandate: A command, indicated by an electorate's votes, for the elected officials to carry out their platforms. (Chapter 12)

mandates: National laws that direct states or local governments to comply with federal rules or regulations (such as clean air or water standards) under threat of civil or criminal penalties or as a condition of receipt of any federal grants. (Chapter 3)

margin of error: See *sampling error.* (Chapter 10)

matching funds: Donations to presidential campaigns from the federal government that are determined by the amount of private funds a qualifying candidate raises. (Chapter 13)

Mayflower Compact: A covenant signed by the Pilgrims aboard the *Mayflower* on November 21, 1620, to ensure an orderly form of government upon their landing in the New World. (Chapter 1)

means-tested programs: Programs intended to assist those whose incomes fall below a designated level. (Policy Portfolio)

media campaign: That part of a political campaign waged in the broadcast and print media. (Chapter 13)

media consultant: A professional who produces political candidates' television, radio, and print advertisements. (Chapter 13)

media effects: The influence of news sources on public opinion. (Chapter 14)

Medicaid: An expansion of Medicare, this program subsidizes medical care for the poor. (Chapter 3, Policy Portfolio)

Medicare: The federal program established in the Johnson administration that provides medical care to elderly Social Security recipients. (Policy Portfolio)

Mercantilism: An economic theory popular from the sixteenth through the eighteenth centuries premised on the belief that a nation's wealth was measured by the amount of gold and silver in its treasury. This belief justified maintenance of strict import/export controls, with exports being favored over imports. (Chapter 2)

merit system: The system by which federal civil service jobs are classified into grades or levels to which appointments are made on the basis of performance on competitive examinations. (Chapter 8)

midterm convention: A national party convention held in nonpresidential congressional election years, for the purposes of rallying the party and adopting new policies. (Chapter 11)

militia: Colonial practice whereby white, male residents were deputized to keep law and order in lieu of a police force or army (Chapters 2, 4)

minority leader: The elected leader of the party with the second highest number of elected representatives in either the House or the Senate. (Chapter 6)

minority party: Party with the second most members in either house of Congress. (Chapter 6)

Miranda rights: Statements that must be made by the police informing a suspect of his or her constitutional rights protected by the Fifth Amendment, including the right to an attorney provided by the court if the suspect cannot afford one. (Chapter 4)

miscegenation laws: Laws passed by most Southern states in the post-Civil War period prohibiting blacks and whites from marrying each other. (Chapter 5)

Missouri Compromise of 1820: A compromise that attempted to maintain a balance in the Senate between slave and free states; Missouri was admitted as a slave state and Maine as a free state. (Chapter 5)

monarchy: A form of government in which power is vested in hereditary kings and queens. (Chapter 1)

monetary policy: A form of government regulation in which the nation's money supply and interest rates are controlled. (Policy Portfolio)

money: A system of exchange for goods and services that includes currency, coins, and bank deposits. (Policy Portfolio)

monopoly: The control by a single corporation or company of a particular field or enterprise; the absence of competition in a particular market. (Chapter 3)

Montgomery bus boycott: The first wide-scale nonviolent protest against discrimination in the South; blacks refused to take buses as a protest of the segregation that existed in Montgomery's public accommodations. (Chapter 5)

muckraking: A form of newspaper publishing, in vogue in the early twentieth century, concerned with reforming government and business conduct. (Chapter 14)

multi-issue groups: Groups that are concerned with more than just a single issue (e.g., the AFL-CIO). (Chapters 14, 15)

multistage sampling: See *stratified sampling.* (Chapter 10)

national convention: A party conclave (meeting) held in the presidential election year for the purposes of nominating a presidential and vice-presidential ticket and adopting a platform. (Chapter 11)

national party platforms: A statement of the general and specific philosophy and policy goals of a political party, usually promulgated at the national convention. (Chapter 11)

National Security Acts of 1947 and 1949: These acts consolidated the army, the navy, and the new air force into one department under civilian leadership. (Policy Portfolio)

National Security Council: Created by the National Security Acts of 1947 and 1949, this council advises the president on foreign and military affairs. (Chapter 7)

nation-state: Nation-states are based on the idea that one government should have sole authority over a well-defined territory. (Policy Portfolio)

natural law: A doctrine that society should be governed by certain ethical principles that are part of nature and, as such, can be understood by reason. (Chapter 1)

necessary and proper clause: A name given to the clause found in the final paragraph of Article I, Section 8 of the U.S. Constitution giving Congress the authority to pass all laws "necessary and proper" to carry out the enumerated powers specified in the Constitution; the "elastic" clause. (Chapters 1, 2, 3)

negative ads: Advertising on behalf of a candidate that attacks the opponent's platform or character. (Chapter 13)

network: An association of broadcast stations (radio or television) that shares programming through a financial arrangement. (Chapter 14)

New Deal: The name given to the program of "Relief, Recovery, Reform" begun by President Franklin D. Roosevelt in 1933 designed to bring the United States out of the Great Depression. (Chapter 3)

New Federalism: Term first coined by President Ronald Reagan to describe his administration's emphasis on the return of power to the states; later characterized by the significant reduction in federal aid to the states. (Chapter 3)

New Jersey Plan: A framework for the Constitution proposed by a group of small states. Its key features included a one-house legislature with one vote for each state, a multiperson "executive," the establishment of the acts of Congress as the "supreme law" of the land, and judiciary with limited power. (Chapter 2)

nomination campaign: That part of a political campaign aimed at winning a primary election. (Chapter 13)

nonprobability sampling: Unrepresentative sampling for surveys such as straw polls; this method often produces unreliable results. (Chapter 10)

North American Free Trade Agreement (NAFTA): A treaty between Canada, Mexico, and the United States to reduce tariff and other mutual trade barriers. (Chapters 6, 7)

nullification doctrine: The claimed right of a state to nullify, or reject, a federal law. (Chapters 3, 7)

off-the-record: Information gathered for a news story that cannot be used at all. (Chapter 14)

off-year elections: Elections that take place in the middle of a presidential term. (Chapter 12)

oligarchy: A form of government in which the right to participate is always conditioned on the possession of wealth or property. (Chapter 1)

on background: A term for when sources are not included in a news story. (Chapter 14)

one-partyism: A political system in which one party dominates and wins virtually all contests. (Chapter 11)

on-the-record: Information gathered for a news story that can be used and cited. (Chapter 14)

open market operations: The buying and selling of government securities by the Federal Reserve Bank in the securities market. (Policy Portfolio)

open primary: A primary in which party members, independents, and sometimes members of the other party are allowed to vote. (Chapter 12)

organizational campaign: That part of a political campaign involved in fund raising, literature distribution, and all other activities not directly involving the candidate. (Chapter 13)

organizational party: The workers and activists who staff the party's formal organization. (Chapter 11)

original jurisdiction: The jurisdiction of courts that hear a case first, usually in trial. Courts determine the facts of a case under their original jurisdiction. (Chapter 9)

oversight: Congress's ability to question members of the executive agencies to see whether they are enforcing and interpreting the laws passed by Congress as the members intended. (Chapters 6, 8)

paid media: Political advertisements purchased for a candidate's campaign. (Chapter 13)

pardon: The restoration of all rights and privileges of citizenship to a specific individual convicted of a crime.

pardoning power: The constitutional authority of the president to restore all rights and privileges of citizenship, usually given to specific individuals for crimes for which they have been convicted. (Chapter 7)

party caucus: A formal gathering of all party members. (Chapter 6)

party conference: Name given to the Republican and Democratic congressional party meetings at which party leaders and committee assignments are named; held at the beginning of each session in each chamber. (Chapter 6)

party identification: A citizen's personal affinity for a political party, usually expressed by his or her tendency to vote for the candidates of that party. (Chapter 11)

party-in-the-electorate: The voters who consider themselves to be allied or associated with the party. (Chapter 11)

party mobile office: Units that travel around the country in order to publicize the party, assist residents with governmental problems, and serve as a party field base. (Chapter 11)

party ombudsman: A party representative in the community who attempts to help citizens with their problems. (Chapter 11)

party realignments: A shifting of party coalition groupings in the electorate that remains in place for several elections. (Chapter 12)

party unity vote: A vote in the legislature in which a member votes with his or her party on issues that divide a majority of Democrats from a majority of Republicans. (Chapter 11)

party vote: A vote in the legislature in which a majority of Democrats and Republicans vote on opposite sides. (Chapters 6, 11)

patronage: Jobs, grants, or other special favors that are given as rewards to friends and political allies for their support. (Chapters 7, 8)

patrons: Individuals who often finance interest groups. (Chapter 15)

Pendleton Act: Reform measure that created the Civil Service Commission to administer a partial merit system. It classified the federal service by grades to which appointments were made based on the results of a competitive examination. It made it illegal for political appointees to be required to contribute to a particular political party. (Chapter 8)

personal campaign: That part of a political campaign concerned with presenting the candidate's public image. (Chapter 13)

personal liberty: A key characteristic of U.S. democracy. Initially meaning freedom from governmental interference, today it includes demands for freedom to engage in a variety of practices free from governmental discrimination. (Chapter 1)

plaintiff: The individual or organization that originally brings a lawsuit to court. (Chapter 9)

pluralist theory: Theory of government in which resources are scattered so widely in our diverse democracy that no single elite group can ever have a monopoly over any substantial area of policy. (Chapter 1)

pocket veto: If Congress adjourns during the ten days the president has to consider a bill passed by both Houses of Congress without the president's signature, it is considered vetoed. (Chapter 6)

policy adoption: The approval of a policy proposal by the people with the requisite authority, such as a legislature.

policy evaluation: The process of determining whether a course of action is achieving its intended goals. (Policy Portfolio)

policy formulation: The crafting of appropriate and acceptable proposed courses of action to ameliorate or resolve public problems. (Policy Portfolio)

policy implementation: The process of carrying out public policy through governmental agencies and the courts. (Policy Portfolio)

political action committees: Federally mandated, officially registered fund-raising committees that represent interest groups in the political process. (Chapters 13, 15)

political consultants: Professionals who manage campaigns and political advertisements for political candidates. (Chapter 11)

political equality: Government practice in which all individuals have the opportunity to participate equally in governmental affairs. (Chapter 1)

political ideology: An individual's coherent set of values and beliefs about the purpose and scope of government. (Chapter 10)

"politically correct speech" movement: Movement that developed in the late 1980s to limit free speech by banning language thought to be inappropriate or harmful. (Chapter 4)

political machine: An organization affiliated with a political party that often controlled a majority of the votes in a locality, and thus won most public offices. (Chapter 11)

political party: A group of office holders, candidates, activists, and voters who identify with a group label and seek to elect to public office individuals who run under that label. (Chapters 6, 11)

political socialization: The process through which an individual acquires particular political orientations; the learning process by which people acquire their political beliefs and values. (Chapter 10)

politics: The process by which policy decisions are made. (Chapters 1, 3)

polls: voting booth; See also *public opinion polls* (Chapter 10)

pollster: A professional who takes public opinion surveys that guide political campaigns. (Chapter 13)

poll tax: Method used by Southern states after the Civil War to exclude blacks from voting by imposing taxes or the payment of fees before a citizen could vote; outlawed in national elections by the Twenty-fourth Amendment in 1964 and in state elections by the Supreme Court in 1966. (Chapter 5)

popular consent: The idea that governments must draw their powers from the consent of the governed. (Chapter 1)

popular sovereignty: The right of the majority to govern themselves. (Chapter 1)

pork barrel: Legislation that allows representatives to "bring home the bacon" to their districts in the form of public works programs, military bases, or other programs designed to benefit their districts directly. (Chapter 6)

positive ads: Advertising on behalf of a candidate that stresses the candidate's qualifications, family and issue positions without reference to the opponent. (Chapter 13)

precedents: Prior judicial decisions that serve as rules for settling subsequent cases of a similar nature. (Chapter 9)

preemption: A concept derived from the Constitution's supremacy clause that allows the national government to override or preempt state or local actions in certain areas. (Chapter 3)

presidential character: According to political scientist James David Barber, the patterns of behavior exhibited by presidents based on their energy level and the degree of enjoyment they find in their job. (Chapter 7)

presidential style: A president's ability to get things done; determined by factors such as his character and approach to office, the perception of others of his ability to lead, and his ability to mobilize public opinion to support his actions. (Chapter 7)

Presidential Succession Act of 1947: Clarifies who replaces the president in case of a vacancy in the vice presidency (or in case of his inability to serve); by law, first the Speaker of the House of Representatives, then the president pro tempore of the Senate, and then the Secretaries of State, Treasury, Defense, and the other Cabinet heads in order of their departments creation. (Chapter 7)

primary elections: Elections in which voters decide which of the candidates within a party will represent the party in the general election. (Chapter 12)

print press: The traditional form of mass media, comprising newspapers, magazines, and journals. (Chapter 14)

prior restraint: Judicial doctrine stating that the government cannot prohibit speech or publication before the fact. (Chapter 4)

privacy: The right to be let alone; a judicially created doctrine encompassing an individual's decision to use birth control or secure an abortion. (Chapters 3, 4)

pro bono: Legal work done for no charge. (Chapter 9)

Progressive Era: Period between 1889 and 1920 that was characterized by concern with reform of political, economic, and social systems in the United States. (Chapter 5)

proportional representation: The practice of awarding legislative seats in proportion to the number of votes received. (Chapter 11)

public funds: Donations from general tax revenues to the campaigns of qualifying presidential candidates. (Chapter 13)

public-interest group: A group that seeks a collective good that will not selectively and materially benefit the members of the organization. (Chapter 15)

public opinion: What the public thinks about a particular issue or set of issues at any point in time. (Chapter 10)

public opinion polls: Interviews or surveys with a sample of citizens that are used to estimate public opinion of the entire population. (Chapter 10)

public policy: A purposive course of action followed by government in dealing with some problem or matter of concern. (Policy Portfolio)

quasi-judicial process: Process in which a bureaucratic agency settles disputes between two parties in a manner similar to the way courts resolve disputes. (Chapter 8)

quasi-legislative process: Bureaucratic rule making. The process allows bureaucrats to act as lawmakers when they make rules or draft regulations to implement various congressional statutes. (Chapter 8)

quorum: The minimum number of members of any deliberative body that must be present before official business can be conducted. (Chapter 6)

quota sample: A type of nonprobability sample in which pollsters draw their sample based on known statistics. (Chapter 10)

Radical Republicans: Division of the Republican Party that was critical of Abraham Lincoln for his handling of the Civil War, and tried to impeach Andrew Johnson for his conciliatory approach to the South after the war. They also used Reconstruction to punish Southern states. (Chapter 5)

random sampling: A method of selection that gives each potential voter or adult the same chance of being selected. (Chapter 10)

recall: A procedure for demanding the ouster of elected public officials prior to the end of their term. (Chapter 10)

recession: A short-term decline in the economy that occurs as investment sags, production falls off, and unemployment increases. (Policy Portfolio)

redistricting: The redrawing of congressional districts to reflect increases or decreases in seats allotted to the states as well as population shifts within a state. (Chapters 6, 12)

red tape: The nickname given to the confusing web of federal rules and regulations that often cause delays in the execution of policy. (Chapter 8)

referendum: The practice of putting pieces of legislation proposed by the state legislature before the voters for their approval or disapproval. (Chapter 10)

Reformation: A movement in the sixteenth century in which various doctrines and practices of the Roman Catholic Church were rejected. It led to the establishment of Protestantism. (Chapter 1)

regional primaries: A proposed system in which the country would be divided into five or six geographic areas and all states in each region would hold their presidential primary elections on the same day. (Chapter 12)

regulations: Rules that govern the operation of all government programs and have the force of law. (Chapter 8)

regulatory commission: An agency created by Congress that is generally concerned with a specific aspect of the economy. (Chapter 8)

representative democracy: See *indirect (representative) democracy.* (Chapter 1)

republic: A government rooted in the consent of the governed. A representative or indirect democracy. (Chapter 1)

reserve requirements: Governmental requirement that a portion of member banks' deposits must be retained to back loans made. (Policy Portfolio)

retrospective judgment: A voter's evaluation of the performance of the party in power. (Chapter 12)

revenue sharing: Method of redistributing federal monies back to the states with "no strings attached"; favored by President Richard M. Nixon. (Chapter 3)

right-of-rebuttal rule: A Federal Communications Commission regulation that people attacked on a radio or television broadcast be offered the opportunity to respond. (Chapter 6)

rule: Given by the House Rules Committee to legislation being reported to the floor for consideration; it contains the date the bill will come up for debate, the time that will be allotted for discussion, and often even specifications concerning what kinds of amendments can be offered. (Chapter 6)

rule making: The administrative process that results in rules and regulations. (Chapter 8)

Rule of Four: At least four justices of the Supreme Court must vote to consider a case before it can be heard. (Chapter 9)

runoff primary: A second primary election between the two candidates receiving the greatest number of votes in the first primary. (Chapter 12)

sample: A relatively small number of individuals chosen in a survey who are interviewed for the purpose of estimating the opinions of the entire population. (Chapter 10)

sampling error: A measure of the accuracy of a public opinion poll. (Chapter 10)

Second Continental Congress: Meeting that convened in Philadelphia on May 10, 1775, in which it was decided that an army should be raised to defend the colonies; George Washington of Virginia was named commander-in-chief. (Chapter 2)

secular realignment: The gradual rearrangement of party coalitions, based more on demographic shifts than on shocks to the political system. (Chapter 12)

seditious (speech): Speech that advocates the violent overthrow of the government; not protected by the First Amendment. (Chapter 4)

select committees: Temporary committees appointed for specific purposes with fairly limited mandates, generally to conduct special investigations or studies and to report back to the chamber that established them. (Chapter 6)

selective incorporation: A judicial doctrine whereby most but not all of the protections found in the Bill of Rights are made applicable to the states via the Fourteenth Amendment. (Chapter 4)

senatorial courtesy: A practice by which senators can have near veto power over laws or appointments that affect their state in a specific way. (Chapters 6, 9)

seniority: The method by which the person of the majority party with the longest continuous service on a particular committee was automatically made chair. (Chapter 6)

separation of powers: A way of dividing power among the three branches of government in which members of the House of Representatives, members of the Senate, the president, and the federal courts are selected by and responsible to different constituencies; initially offered by the French political philosopher Montesquieu. (Chapter 2)

Shays's Rebellion: A rebellion led by Daniel Shays, an army veteran, during the summer of 1786 in which an army of 1,500 disgruntled and angry farmers marched to Springfield, Massachusetts and forcibly restrained the state court from foreclosing on their farms. (Chapter 2)

single-issue groups: Groups that are concerned with only one issue. (Chapter 15)

slander: Untrue spoken statements that defame the character of a person. (Chapter 4)

"smart money": Campaign contributions to the candidate or political party expected to win in an election year. (Chapter 11)

social contract theory: The belief that people are free and equal by God-given right and that this in turn requires that all men give their consent to be governed; espoused by John Locke and influential in the writing of the Declaration of Independence. (Chapters 1, 2)

socialism: A political system in which the working class owns and controls all means of production and distribution. (Chapters 1, 4)

social welfare policy: Governmental programs designed to enhance an individual's quality of life. (Policy Portfolio)

Solicitor General: The fourth-ranking member of the Justice Department; responsible for handling all appeals on behalf of the U.S. government to the Supreme Court. (Chapter 9)

Sons of Liberty: A radical organization of colonists created in 1765 to express opposition to the Stamp Act. (Chapter 2)

sovereign: Independent or self-governing. (Chapter 3)

Speaker of the House: The only officer of the House of Representatives specifically mentioned in the Constitution; elected at the beginning of each new Congress by the entire House; traditionally a member of the majority party. (Chapter 6)

special-interest caucuses: Groups that allow congressional members from either party to cross party lines to band together with their colleagues who have a common interest. (Chapter 6)

split-ticket voting: The practice of voting for the candidate of one party for president and another for Congress. (Chapters 1, 2, 12)

spoils system: The firing of public-office holders of a defeated political party and their replacement with loyalists of the newly elected party. (Chapters 8, 11)

spot ads: Television advertising on behalf of a candidate that is broadcast in sixty-, thirty-, or ten-second durations. (Chapter 13)

Stamp Act Congress: Meeting of representatives of nine of the thirteen colonies held in New York City in 1765 during which representatives drafted a document to send to the king listing how their rights had been violated. (Chapter 2)

Stamp Act of 1765: A direct tax requiring the purchase of stamps as a tax to be affixed to all documents, including newspapers, magazines, and commercial papers. (Chapter 2)

standing: Over the years this has come to mean that a person bringing a lawsuit must have a strong interest and personal stake in the outcome of the case. (Chapter 9)

standing committees: The committees to which proposed bills are referred for consideration. (Chapter 6)

stare decisis: In court rulings, a reliance on past decisions or precedents to formulate decisions in new cases. (Chapter 9)

statute: A law. (Chapter 6)

stratified sampling: A variation of random sampling; census data are used to divide a country into four sampling regions. Sets of counties and standard metropolitan statistical areas are then randomly selected in proportion to the total national population. (Chapter 10)

straw polls: Unscientific surveys used to gauge public opinion on a variety of issues and policies. (Chapter 10)

strict constructionist: An approach to constitutional interpretation that emphasizes the Framers' initial intentions. (Chapter 9)

strict scrutiny: A heightened standard of review used by the Supreme Court to determine the constitutional validity of a challenged practice. (Chapter 5)

suffrage: The right to vote. (Chapters 1, 2, 5)

suffrage movement: Term used to refer to the drive for women's right to vote that took place in the United States from 1890 to 1920. (Chapters 1, 5)

Sugar Act of 1764: Act passed by the British Parliament to help raise revenues to pay for the French and Indian War; taxes were placed on sugar, wine, coffee, and other products commonly exported to the colonies. (Chapter 2)

sunset laws: Laws that provide that agencies or programs are automatically abolished after a fixed period of years unless Congress extends their life. (Chapter 8)

sunshine laws: After passage by Congress in 1976, sunshine laws require that about 50 multi-headed federal agencies hold their meetings in sessions open to the public. (Chapters 6, 8)

superdelegates: Delegate slots to the Democratic Party's national convention that are reserved for elected party officials. (Chapter 12)

supremacy clause: Portion of Article IV of the U.S. Constitution that mandates that national law is supreme to (i.e., supersedes) all other laws passed by the states or by any other subdivision of government. (Chapters 2, 3)

suspect classifications: Categories or classes such as race that trigger the highest standard of scrutiny from the Supreme Court. (Chapter 5)

symbolic speech: Symbols, signs, and other methods of expression generally also considered to be protected by the First Amendment. (Chapter 4)

systemic agenda: All public issues that are viewed as requiring governmental attention; a discussion agenda. (Policy Portfolio)

term limits: Legislation designating that state and/or federal elected legislators can serve only a specified number of years. (Chapter 6)

test cases: Cases brought by interest groups as a part of a planned strategy eventually to win their point before the U.S. Supreme Court. (Chapter 5)

third-partyism: The tendency of third parties to arise with some regularity in a nominally two-party system. (Chapter 11)

Thirteenth Amendment: First of the three Civil War Amendments; specifically banned slavery in the United States. (Chapter 5)

Three-Fifths Compromise: Agreement reached at the Constitutional Convention stipulating that each slave was to be counted as three-fifths of a person for purposes of determining population for representation in the U.S. House of Representatives. (Chapter 2)

ticket split: To vote for candidates of different parties for various offices in the same election. (Chapter 11)

Title IX: Federal statute prohibiting sex discrimination in educational institutions receiving federal funds. (Chapters 5, 8)

Title VII: Section of the Civil Rights Act of 1964 that prohibits employers from discriminating against employees for a variety of reasons, including race, sex, age, or national origin. (In 1978 the Act was amended to prohibit discrimination based on pregnancy.) (Chapter 5)

totalitarianism: A system of government in which unlimited powers are retained by elite rulers. (Chapter 1)

Townshend Acts: Acts passed by the British Parliament in 1767 imposing duties on a wide variety of goods imported by the colonists, at least in part to demonstrate to the colonists Britain's continued right to tax them. (Chapter 2)

tracking polls: Continuous surveys that enable a campaign to chart its daily rise or fall. (Chapter 11)

trade associations: Groups that represent specific industries. (Chapter 15)

treaty: A formal agreement between nations setting forth rights and responsibilities of each. All U.S. treaties must be approved by a two-thirds vote of the Senate. (Chapter 7)

Treaty of Versailles: See *Versailles Peace Treaty.* (Chapters 6, 7)

trusts: Business combinations that lead to monopolistic practices. (Chapter 3)

two presidencies: A theory postulated by Aaron Wildavsky that there are two presidencies; in one, a president is a strong leader in foreign affairs, and in the other he is a weak one in the realm of domestic affairs. (Chapter 7)

uncommitted delegates: Delegates to a party convention whose support prior to the convention is not pledged to a particular candidate. (Chapter 12)

unicameral: One-house legislature, as in the state of Nebraska. (Chapter 6)

unitary government: Term applied to systems in which all power resides in the central or national government as opposed to regional (subnational) governments. (Chapter 3)

unit rule: A traditional party practice under which the majority of a state delegation can force the minority to vote for its candidate. (Chapter 12)

Versailles Peace Treaty: Treaty ending World War I and establishing the League of Nations. (Chapters 6, 7)

veto: A constitutional power of the president to send a bill back to Congress with reasons for rejecting it. A two-thirds vote in each house can override a presidential veto. (Chapters 2, 7)

Virginia Plan: The first general plan for the Constitution whose key points were a bicameral legislature, an executive chosen by the legislature, and a judiciary also named by the legislature. (Chapter 2)

virtual representation: System of government in which elected representatives are considered to represent the entire nation and not only their home district. (Chapter 6)

voter canvass: The process by which a campaign gets in touch with individual voters, either by door-to-door solicitation or by telephone. (Chapter 13)

Voting Rights Act of 1965: Suspended the use of literacy tests and authorized the federal government to monitor all elections in areas where discrimination was found to be practiced or where less than 50 percent of the voting age population was registered to vote in the 1964 election. (Chapters 5, 12)

War Powers Act: Passed by Congress in 1973, the president was limited in his deployment of troops overseas to a sixty-day period in peacetime (which could be extended for an extra thirty days to permit withdrawal) unless Congress explicitly gave its approval for a longer period. (Chapters 6, 7, Policy Portfolio)

Watergate: Term used to describe the events and scandal resulting from a break-in at the Democratic National Committee headquarters in 1972 (at the Watergate office complex in Washington, DC) and the subsequent cover-up of White House involvement, which led to the eventual resignation of President Richard M. Nixon under the threat of impeachment. (Chapters 1, 7)

white primary: A primary in which nonwhite voters are systematically denied participation (no longer practiced). (Chapter 12)

wire service: An electronic delivery of news gathered by the news services' correspondents and sent to all member news media organizations. (Chapter 14)

writ of *certiorari*: A formal document issued from the Supreme Court to a lower federal or state court that calls up a case. Four of the Court's nine justices must agree to accept the case before it is granted *certiorari*. (Chapter 9)

"Year of the Woman": Name given to denote the extraordinary number of women who ran for and won elected positions at all governmental levels in the 1992 elections. (Chapter 6)

yellow journalism: A form of newspaper publishing in vogue in the late nineteenth century that featured pictures, comics, color, and sensationalized, oversimplified news coverage. (Chapter 14)